UMI ANNUAL COMMENTARY

PRECEPTS FOR LIVING®

MISSION STATEMENT

*W*e are called
of God to create, produce, and distribute
quality Christian education products;
to deliver exemplary customer service;
and to provide quality Christian
educational services, which will empower
God's people, especially within the Black
community, to evangelize, disciple,
and equip people for serving Christ,
His kingdom, and church.

Urban Ministries, Inc.
The African American Christian Publishing
& Communications Co.

UMI ANNUAL SUNDAY SCHOOL LESSON COMMENTARY
PRECEPTS FOR LIVING® 2010–2011
INTERNATIONAL SUNDAY SCHOOL LESSONS
VOLUME 13
UMI (URBAN MINISTRIES, INC.)

Melvin Banks Sr., Litt.D., Founder and Chairman

C. Jeffrey Wright, J.D., CEO

Terence Chatmon, President

All art: Copyright © 2010 by UMI.

Bible art: Fred Carter

Unless otherwise indicated, all Scripture references are taken from the authorized King James Version of the Bible.

Scripture quotations marked NIV are taken from the HOLY BIBLE, NEW INTERNATIONAL VERSION®. Copyright © 1973, 1978, 1984 Biblica. Used by permission of Zondervan. All rights reserved.

Scripture quotations marked NLT are taken from the Holy Bible, New Living Translation, copyright © 1996. Used by permission of Tyndale House Publishers, Inc., Wheaton, Illinois 60189. All rights reserved.

Scripture taken from the NEW AMERICAN STANDARD BIBLE®, Copyright © 1960, 1962, 1963, 1968, 1971, 1972, 1973, 1975, 1977, 1995 by The Lockman Foundation. Used by permission.

Scripture taken from the New King James Version. Copyright © 1982 by Thomas Nelson Inc. Used by permission. All rights reserved.

Revised Standard Version of the Bible, copyright 1952 [2nd edition, 1971] by the Division of Christian Education of the National Council of the Churches of Christ in the United States of America. Used by permission. All rights reserved.

New Revised Standard Version Bible, copyright 1989, Division of Christian Education of the National Council of the Churches of Christ in the United States of America. Used by permission. All rights reserved.

Scripture quotations are from The Holy Bible, English Standard Version® (ESV®), copyright © 2001 by Crossway, a publishing ministry of Good News Publishers. Used by permission. All rights reserved.

Scripture quotations marked (TLB) are taken from *The Living Bible, 715800037417* copyright © 1971. Used by permission of Tyndale House Publishers, Inc., Wheaton, IL 60189. All rights reserved.

Copyright © 2010 by UMI.

All rights reserved. No part of this publication may be reproduced, stored in a retrieval system, or transmitted in any form or by any means—electronic, mechanical, photocopy, recording, or otherwise—without the prior permission of the copyright owners. Lessons and/or readings based on the *International Sunday School Lessons. The International Bible Lessons for Christian Teaching.* Copyright © 2007 by the Committee on the Uniform Series. Used by permission. Supplementary Lesson Development. Copyright © 2010 by UMI. Printed in the USA.

All proper names mentioned in this publication are fictional unless otherwise indicated. Item No.: 1-2011.

ISBN-13: 978-1-60352-930-3. ISBN-10: 1-60352-930-6. Publishers: UMI (Urban Ministries, Inc.), Chicago, IL 60643.

To place an order, call us at 1-800-860-8642 or visit our website at www.urbanministries.com.

CONTRIBUTORS

Editor
Vincent Bacote, Ph.D.

Vice President of Editorial
Cheryl P. Clemetson, Ph.D.

Developmental Editor
Evangeline Carey, M.A.

Senior Copy Editor
Eric Pazdziora, B.Mus.

Assistant Copy Editor
Kyle Waalen, M.S.

Cover Design & Layout
Trinidad D. Zavala, B.A.

Bible Illustrations
Fred Carter

Contributing Writers
Essays/In Focus Stories
Melvin Banks Sr., Litt.D.
Evangeline Carey, M.A.
Aja Carr, Th.M.
Rukeia Draw, Ph.D.
Whitney M. DuPreé, B.S.
Rabbi Yechiel Eckstein
Jamal-Dominique Hopkins, Ph.D.
Rosa Sailes, Ed.D.
Harold Dean Trulear, Ph.D.

Bible Study Guide Writers
Allyson D. Nelson Abrams, Ph.D.
J. Ayodeji Adewuya, Ph.D.
Evangeline Carey, M.A.
Jimmie Wilkerson-Chaplin, M.B.A.
Jean Garrison, M.A.
Charlesetta Watson-Holmes, M.Div.
Judith St.Clair Hull, Ph.D.
Jennifer King, M.A.
Angela Lampkin, M.S.
Vanessa Lovelace, Ph.D.
LaTonya Mason, M.A.
Beverly Moore, M.S.
Eric Pazdziora, B.Mus.
Amy Rognlie, B.A.
Frederick Thomas, B.S.
Ruth Unaegbu, M.A.
Kim Varner
Kyle Waalen, M.S.
Faith Waters, M.Div.
Karen F. Williams, D.Min.

More Light on the Text
J. Ayodeji Adewuya, Ph.D.
Evangeline Carey, M.A.
Moussa Coulibaly, Ph.D.
Clay Daniel, M.Div.
Angelo Hill, Ph.D.
Kevin Hrebik, D.Min.
Judith St.Clair Hull, Ph.D.
F. Morkeh, Ph.D.
Nathan Munn, M.Div.
Anthony Myles, M.Div.
James Rawdon, D.Min.
Reuben Unaegbu, Ph.D.

Dear Precepts Customer,

It is our privilege to present the 2010–2011 *Precepts For Living*®. As you grow your knowledge and experience of God's Word through these lessons, we believe that you will find this resource to be indispensable to your study of God's revelations to us.

Precepts For Living® comes to you in three versions: the Personal Study Guide (the workbook), the CD-ROM version of Precepts, and a Large Print edition. You will also notice that the biblical text for each lesson continues to include the New Living Translation in addition to the King James Version, which is a great way to illumine your understanding of the text through side by side comparison.

Precepts For Living® is designed to be a witness through our learning and sharing more of the Bible. Our intent is to help facilitate innovative ways to pursue a deeper understanding and practice of God's Word. One of the ways we are doing this is by continuing to make more of our lessons highlight the larger framework of God's work in salvation as a key part of understanding each biblical passage. We believe it is important to help you understand not only the particulars of the text, but also the broad sweep of God's revelations to us as well. This panoramic approach enhances our ability to witness to others about the saving power of Jesus Christ.

This year we explore the following themes: God, Hope, Worship, and Community. Each year of Bible study offers great potential for deepening your Christian walk.

We want to continually refine *Precepts For Living*® as we strive to meet our customers' needs. We are always looking for ways to enhance your study of the Bible, and your comments and feedback are vital in helping us. We encourage you to help us. If you have questions or suggestions, please e-mail us at precepts@urbanministries.com or mail your comments to UMI, *Precepts For Living*®, PO Box 436987, Chicago, IL 60643-6987.

May God draw you closer to the fullness of life with Him through this book.

The Peace of Christ be with you,

Vincent E. Bacote, Ph.D.

Vincent E. Bacote, Ph.D.
Editor

Uncovering the Benefits of Precepts

It is a great privilege to participate in Christian education and play a significant role in the spiritual formation of fellow Christians in our churches. *Precepts for Living*® is a resource that is designed to help you lead others toward greater knowledge and practice of following Jesus Christ. To that end, I would like to help you take advantage of the resources provided to you in this year's commentary.

From the standpoint of your vocation as a teacher, it is very important to be aware of the great responsibility that goes along with your position. James 3:1 reminds us that we have such a great opportunity in front of us that we run the risk of greater judgment if we are derelict in our duties. This is a strong word to us that helps us understand the great influence that we have when we help our students learn about God's Word.

To be a teacher means that we are participating in one of the church's greatest tasks, one that the ancient church called "catechesis." While this word is often associated with particular denominations and with a form of teaching that relies upon a systematic question and answer format, the central meaning of the word is "teaching," and it carries with it the idea of teaching the entirety of the faith to Christians. While many Sunday School teachers might not be familiar with this word, the truth is that every time any of us helps others learn about God's Word and ways, we are participating in this great task of the church, which has been with us from the beginning. Our participation in catechesis is central to the life of the church, and at times this function of the church gets lost in the midst of other concerns. As a teacher, you have an opportunity to energize and/or revitalize this aspect of your church's ministry. Are you up for the challenge?

What is the goal when you are using *Precepts for Living*® to open up the riches of the Bible to your students? It is more than merely the acquisition of "spiritual data." Certainly we want our students to grow in knowledge, but the knowledge we seek to pass on is not merely Bible facts, but a larger sense of knowledge where the information and doctrine conveyed is oriented toward a faithful life of discipleship. The People, Places, and Times; Background; In Depth; and More Light on the Text sections are there to help you with providing insight and understanding of the text. But, the lesson is about more than simply compiling information. In each lesson, you will also see that we have In Focus stories and the sections Lesson in Our Society and Make It Happen. These sections are there to serve as catalysts for bringing the biblical text to our life situations.

It is very important that we as teachers pass on knowledge that will enable our students to deepen their devotion to God in an "upward" focus and help them to be able to better embody that devotion in a way that makes their lives a living witness to the world. In each lesson, our goal should be one of helping our students become better at being living examples of the Scriptures, because their lives may be the only Bible some people ever read.

In order to best take advantage of this commentary, you will find it beneficial to utilize the essays which highlight notable African-Americans and quarterly themes, and they also help you to become a better teacher by providing insight on enhancing the classroom experience and ways to convey the lesson across a range of learning styles. We believe that this commentary is a great tool which can help the church form fully devoted followers of Christ, and we invite you to take advantage of the variety of resources provided here. May God be glorified as you play your part in this great task of the church!

Creative Teaching

• **Energizing the Class.** If the class does not seem as enthusiastic or energy is low, after you open with prayer, have everyone stretch to the sky or outward. Then tell the class to shake off the low energy, and open up their hands to receive the love of God that is right there. You can always have a 30-second meet and greet time. This usually helps to wake people up so that you can begin class on a higher energy level.

• **Two Teachers in One Class—Bring Out the Best in Both.** Taking turns works in some classes, but in others it creates tension and favorites. Encourage teachers to study together, and then divide the segments of the lesson. Perhaps one will teach the introduction while the other teaches a section of the text. Encourage them to also become a true team with each contributing throughout the lesson.

• **Remember.** Everyone cannot read or write on the same level. Use different teaching techniques and styles when teaching. How you learn affects how you teach, so be open and willing to learn and teach through various mediums.

• **Avoid Study in Isolation.** People often "get it" when they are involved with more than talking about the lesson. Why not allow the class to see the connections themselves. Try using a chart to have adult students work in pairs or groups to compare and contrast Bible persons such as David and Solomon or Ruth and Orpah, Naomi's daughters-in-law. To help the students get started, suggest specific categories for comparisons such as lifestyles, families, or public ministry. As class members search the Scriptures, they will learn and remember much more than if you had told them about either person.

• **Group Studies.** Have the class form groups, and have each group read the Scripture lesson and a section of the Background for the text. Have each group create a two-minute skit about the Scripture to share with the class. Encourage the groups to use their imaginations and energy. You may want to have at least one "leader" in a group if you have more than two or three reserved persons in your class.

• **Volunteers.** Many classes begin with reading the lesson. When class members have studied, this activity is more "bringing minds" together than about the actual lesson. Still some classes can benefit from dramatic and creative reading of Bible passages at any point in the lesson. When the passage under study lends itself, assign parts to volunteers. This need not be formal—standing up isn't even critical. This strategy works best in passages that have a story such as the conversation between Moses and his father-in-law, Jethro, or Paul confronting the merchants in Thessalonica. Assign one person to each speaking character in the Bible text. Feel free to be creative with giving the class roles as "the crowd." Make sure to assign a narrator who will read the non-speaking parts. It is fun, it is fast, and it makes for memorable Bible reading.

• **Alternatives.** Select one or two persons from the class to read the Scripture lesson with enthusiasm and drama. Ask a few persons to develop a newspaper or magazine headline with a brief story that explains the headlines. Have another group write the headlines and a story that will be used in a cell phone video. (Let the class know that they should bring their cell phones—with video recording—so that most people can share in this activity. Presently, there is technology available for cell phone videos.)

• **Materials.** You may want to have large sheets of paper, markers, glue or tape, newspapers, and magazines available on a weekly basis for the various activities.

• **Additional Methods.** Write the theme on a large poster board or sheet of paper, and ask each person to write a word or draw a picture that best describes the theme. Read the themes aloud, and discuss any of the pictures before you begin your class discussion or activities. If you have a very large class or time is limited, only select a few words and/or pictures for discussion. The discussion can be led by you, or you can invite the class to have a brief dialogue with you.

• **Websites.** Log on to our website: www.urban-ministries.com. E-mail us at precepts@urban-ministries.com, and send us some of your favorite Teaching Tips for ages 18 and over that you want to share with others. If yours is selected, we will post them under our Teaching Tips sections for Precepts. If you have ice breaker activities, please indicate this as well. Your submissions should be no longer than 125 words.

• **Closing.** At the end of the lesson, give your class the assignment of looking for scenes from films or television, advertisements, or parts of songs that either demonstrate the coming week's In Focus story, Lesson in Our Society section, or Make It Happen section. Encourage them to be creative and to come up with an explanation of how their contribution helps make the truth of the lesson come to life.

• **Prayer.** Have a Prayer Request Board for persons to write their prayer requests on each Sunday. You may want to make this a weekly activity.

Have someone read the prayer request and let the class decide which prayer requests they will pray for during the week. One Sunday School teacher has his class write their prayer requests on sheets of paper and place them in the middle of the floor once a year. He then shares with the class that he will write them all down in a prayer journal that he keeps and prays over them at least once a week. Be creative and create your own prayer journal or prayer tradition(s) within your class.

Possible Questions Related to the Heritage Profiles:

1. Why are some people chosen over others to be recognized for their achievements?

2. When reading the Heritage Profiles, what contemporary person comes to mind? A family member or friend can be a part of your decision.

3. Have you ever been recognized for a special achievement? How did you feel, and who have you lifted up to receive a special award in your church, community, or family? Why?

4. List three things that you believe are important that someone else knows.

5. What similarities do you see between the historical figure and your life? If there are none, share some ways that the person's life may have impacted your life and for future generations.

6. List three characteristics that stand out about the Heritage Profiles that you think are either positive or negative. List three characteristics about your life that you believe are either positive or negative. Compare the lists and write a short paragraph about the similarities and/or differences.

Remember that creative teaching can maximize your students' learning experience.

TABLE OF CONTENTS

2010–2014 Scope and Sequence—Cycle Spread

	FALL	WINTER	SPRING	SUMMER
YEAR ONE 2010–11	GOD **The Inescapable God** Exodus Psalms 8, 19, 46, 47, 63, 66, 90, 91, 139	HOPE **Assuring Hope** Isaiah Matthew Mark	WORSHIP **We Worship God** Matthew Mark 1, 2 Timothy Philippians 2 Jude Revelation	COMMUNITY **God Instructs the People of God** Joshua Judges Ruth
YEAR TWO 2011–12	TRADITION **Tradition and Wisdom** Proverbs Psalms 16, 25, 111, 119 Ecclesiastes Song of Solomon Esther	FAITH **God Establishes a Faithful People** Genesis Exodus Luke Galatians	CREATION **God's Creative Word** John	JUSTICE **God Calls for Justice** Exodus Leviticus Deuteronomy 1, 2 Samuel 1, 2 Kings 2 Chronicles Psalm 146 Isaiah Jeremiah Ezekiel
YEAR THREE 2012–13	FAITH **A Living Faith** Psalm 46 1 Corinthians 13:1–13 Hebrews Acts	GOD: JESUS CHRIST **Jesus Is Lord** Ephesians Philippians Colossians	HOPE **Beyond the Present Time** Daniel Luke Acts 1, 2 Peter 1, 2 Thessalonians	WORSHIP **God's People Worship** Isaiah Ezra Nehemiah
YEAR FOUR 2013–14	CREATION **First Things** Genesis Exodus Psalm 104	JUSTICE **Jesus and the Just Reign of God** Luke James	TRADITION **Jesus' Fulfillment of Scripture** Zechariah Malachi Deuteronomy Matthew	COMMUNITY **The People of God Set Priorities** Haggai 1, 2 Corinthians

Come Let Us "Kiss the King"

(Putting Down Deep Roots in the Inescapable God)

by Evangeline Carey

"But the root of the righteous shall not be moved" (from Proverbs 12:3).

This past summer while finishing up my Master of Arts in Biblical Studies, I was blessed to take a course in Psalms. I learned so much about the Psalms and how most of them are paying homage to Almighty God or as one professor deemed it, "Kissing the King." One aspect of "Kissing the King" is recognizing and obeying God's voice. It is about following His commands; praising a compassionate, merciful God with our lives; and letting our roots go down deep in Him because His reputation is at stake in us. Therefore, we must walk the walk of a believer as well as talk the talk. (Be a doer of His Word [James 1:23].) "Kissing the King" is letting God use us to rescue the perishing, to engage in brokenness, and to enter the broken places in our world and bring the light of Jesus Christ, in order to engage in our culture, to engage in our community, and to engage in our world. Finally, "Kissing the King" is being devoted and loyal to One who loved us so much that He sent His one and only Son to die a horrendous death on the Cross so that we might have eternal life (see John 3:16).

As we explore the themes of "God—The Inescapable God" and "Hope—Assuring Hope" for September and December 2010 and "Worship—We Worship God" and "Community—God Instructs the People of God" for March and June 2011, we want you to consider your own relationship with Almighty God (how far your spiritual roots go down into the good soil of God's Word... [Matthew 13:23]). We want you to consider how you have responded to the Good News of salvation...how you have put down roots in our Lord and Savior, Jesus Christ, and worshipped Him with your all. Our cover, therefore, should remind you that we worship a Holy (set apart from sin) God who tells us in His inerrant Word, "Ye shall be holy: for I the LORD your God am holy" (from Leviticus 19:2) and "God is a Spirit: and they that worship him must worship him in spirit and in truth" (John 4:24). Therefore, our roots must go down deep in God's righteousness—in God's holiness. We must connect with the Master. In essence, God is calling for us, who are "believers," to not only feel humbled and thankful that He speaks to and calls us, but to also worship Him because He is worthy to be praised.

In the Hebrew, the word "praise" is HALA-Land means "boast, glory, to flash forth light." Therefore, we as believers (whose roots go down deep in the Lord) should go and flash forth the light of God in the dark places of our world! The word "worship" in Hebrew is *proskuneo*, and it means "in the New Testament by kneeling or prostration to do homage (to one) or make obeisance, whether in order to express respect or to make supplication."

When we reflect on God's forgiveness, love, mercy, and faithfulness to us,

When we reflect on God's majesty and the human dignity He has bestowed on us,

When we watch God's sustaining roles in the universe and appreciate how He gave us stewardship over the work of His hand,

When we reflect on the fact that God gave us His Laws to support His creation so that there would be order in our lives,

When we think of how God has provided us refuge in trying times,

When we think of Sovereign God's rule over all the earth...

We should praise and worship Him for His awesome leadership. We should be inspired to let our roots go down deep in Him—dig deep into His Word and lift up holy hands to Him and say,

"Thank You!" God is indeed the "Inescapable God," and He is worthy of our praise and worship at all times.

We should:
Praise and worship Him
For sharing our pain,
For listening to us
Again and again!
We should:
Praise and worship Him
For loving us still,
Even when we fail
To do His will!

Appreciate our cover, let your roots go down deep in Him, lift up holy hands, and "Kiss our King"—give praises to our Lord and Savior! Praise and worship God because He is our Sustainer, Refuge, Hope, Solid Rock, and Savior. Praise Him because He is God. "Let everything that hath breath praise the LORD. Praise ye the LORD" (Psalm 150:6).

Source:
Strong, J. *The Exhaustive Concordance of the Bible* (electronic ed.). Woodside Bible
   Fellowship: Ontario, 1996.

Evangeline Carey is the Developmental Editor for Precepts For Living®, has been an Adult Sunday School Teacher for more than 25 years, and holds a Master of Arts in Biblical Studies from Moody Bible Institute, Chicago, IL.

The Inescapable God

The study this quarter focuses on the nature of God as the first person of the Trinity (Father). Its three units look at Old Testament texts from the Exodus narrative and from the poetry of Psalms.

UNIT 1 • GOD REVEALS

These lessons trace God's emerging relationship with Israel. The first three lessons approach the theme through the biblical stories of Moses: God calls Moses, God discloses the terms of the covenant, and the people lose faith in Moses' leadership (and God's). In Lesson 4, God forgives Israel and they vow to keep their covenant promises.

Lesson 1: September 5, 2010
God's Revelation to Moses
Exodus 3:1–6, 13–15

God gained Moses' attention with the supernatural burning bush and spoke to him. Then God went on to establish His identity by instructing Moses to tell the Israelites that "I Am—the God of Abraham, Isaac, and Jacob" who had sent Moses to them.

Lesson 2: September 12, 2010
God's Law as a Covenantal Agreement
Exodus 20:1–11

God gives the Children of Israel the first four of the Ten Commandments that deal with humanity's relationship with God.

Lesson 3: September 19, 2010
God versus "gods"
Exodus 32:1–10

Frustrated and impatient by Moses' absence, the Israelites convince Aaron to create a god they can see. Aaron complies and makes a golden calf. This angers God, who is ready to destroy the nation.

Lesson 4: September 26, 2010
God Promises an Awesome Thing
Exodus 34:1, 4–10

God reveals His loving, merciful, and faithful nature to Moses. Such self-revelation caused Moses to worship God and seek forgiveness for his people.

UNIT 2 • GOD SUSTAINS

Each of the five lessons in this unit focuses on psalms that sing of God's majesty, sovereignty, and steadfast love.

Lesson 5: October 3, 2010
God's Majesty and Human Dignity
Psalm 8

God is sovereign and sustains humankind and creation. He has given us dominion (stewardship) over the works of His hand.

Lesson 6: October 10, 2010
God's Law Sustains
Psalm 19:7–14

The psalmist praises God and His Law. When we pay attention to God's Laws, they alert us to danger, and when we obey them, they provide us with rewards.

Lesson 7: October 17, 2010
God Provides Refuge
Psalm 46:1–7

The psalmist declares that God is ever-present in times of trouble, providing strength, refuge, and peace.

Lesson 8: October 24, 2010
God's Rule Over the Nations
Psalm 47

God is the Sovereign King; all are invited to praise Him and acknowledge His kingship.

Lesson 9: October 31, 2010
God's Presence Comforts and Assures
Psalm 63

The psalmist, David, expresses dependence on God and a deep yearning for God's presence.

UNIT 3 • GOD PROTECTS

These four lessons focus on psalms that extol the attributes of God, who is good, everlasting, secure, and omnipresent.

Lesson 10: November 7, 2010
God Is Awesome
Psalm 66:1–12

The psalmist offers a hymn of praise to God and notes God's great deed of turning the sea into dry land as a reminder that God is dependable to help us when we are in need.

Lesson 11: November 14, 2010
God Is Forever
Psalm 90:1–12

The psalmist acknowledges God's greatness and human frailty, recognizing the need for wisdom in light of life's brevity and God's wrath.

Lesson 12: November 21, 2010
God Delivers and Protects
Psalm 91:1–6, 9–16

God is a shelter and a refuge in the midst of our fears. We are to love and trust Him and place our faith in His ability to protect us.

Lesson 13: November 28, 2010
God Is All-Knowing
Psalm 139:1–6, 13–16, 23–24

The psalmist, David, praises the all-knowing, all-seeing, ever-present God, who knows everything about him and us, including the number of hairs on our heads (Matthew 10:30). David recognizes and appreciates that even though God knows everything about us—including our failures—He still accepts and loves us. He is our Creator, who is worthy to be praised.

The Inescapable God

by Melvin E. Banks Sr., Litt.D.

When Billy Conn was about to fight Joe Louis in 1946, Conn boasted that he would win by punching Joe Louis and then running away from him. When a reporter asked Joe Louis about Bill Conn's strategy, Louis said, "Yeah, he can run, but he can't hide."

What Joe Louis said about Billy Conn can apply when it comes to our dealing with God—we can run, but we cannot really hide or escape from God. Why can we not get away from God?

God is inescapable. As our Creator, He brought us into existence and supplies every single breath we take. God protects us from danger, and He sustains us with food and nourishment from day to day—God alone does all this. The apostle Paul asserted this as he spoke on Mars Hill (Acts 17:25). Paul said that God made the world and everything in it. He is Lord of heaven and earth. He gives to all *life, breath, and all things*" (Acts 17:25, NLT, emphasis added). Since God created us, sustains us, and determines our destiny, how in the world could we ever escape from God?

In reality, people who have their heads screwed on right do not want to escape from God. Rather, they rejoice in God and in these great attributes of God:

God is present everywhere. There is no place inside or outside the universe where God is absent! David reminds us of this when he writes (in Psalm 139:7–10, NKJV), "Where can I go from Your Spirit? Or where can I flee from Your presence? If I ascend into heaven, You are there; If I make my bed in hell, behold, You are there. If I take the wings of the morning, And dwell in the uttermost parts of the sea, Even there Your hand shall lead me, and Your right hand shall hold me."

David delighted in knowing that he could never get away from God's presence. Just as a child who feels secure when he or she knows that his or her parents are present, we can feel secure knowing that we are always in God's presence. And it is refreshing to realize that God is not in *our* presence; rather, we are in God's presence because God is everywhere all the time.

God possesses full knowledge of everything everywhere. The prophet Isaiah asked these revealing questions concerning God: "With whom did He take counsel, and who instructed Him... Who taught Him knowledge, And showed Him the way of understanding?" (from Isaiah 40:14, NKJV). The obvious answer to each of these questions is no one.

David appreciated how God's knowledge applied to him personally. He wrote, "You have searched me and known me. You know my sitting down and my rising up; You understand my thought afar off. You comprehend my path and my lying down, And are acquainted with all my ways" (Psalm 139:1–2, NKJV).

When God revealed Himself to Moses with the burning bush, God said to Moses, "I have certainly seen the oppression of my people in Egypt. I

3

have heard their cries of distress because of their harsh slave drivers. Yes, I am aware of their suffering" (Exodus 3:7, NLT). Even though God had waited some 400 years before He acted to deliver the people, He was thoroughly aware of their condition. In the same way, God is fully aware of everything that happens to us. We can relax more easily when we know and accept that God knows our situation.

God is perfect in wisdom. Isaiah asked two other questions: "Who has measured the waters in the hollow of his hand, Measured heaven with a span And calculated the dust of the earth in a measure? [Who has] weighed the mountains in scales and the hills in a balance?" (Isaiah 40:12, NKJV). Such wisdom demonstrated in the intricate manner in which the universe has been created could only be done by a God who is perfect in wisdom.

The apostle Paul weighed in on God's wisdom by exulting, "Oh, the depth of the riches both of the wisdom and knowledge of God! How unsearchable are His judgments and His ways past finding out!" (Romans 11:33, NKJV). The existence and perfect nature of God's wisdom led James to advise, "If any of you lacks wisdom, let him ask of God, who gives to all liberally and without reproach, and it will be given to him" (James 1:5, NKJV). God cannot make a mistake. This is a truth we remember when we are passing through circumstances that seem hard to understand.

God is eternal. God existed from eternity past and will exist forever. Moses declared God's eternality this way: "In the beginning, God..." (from Genesis 1:1). Moses repeated that declaration in the psalm he penned: "from everlasting to everlasting, you are God" (from Psalm 90:2); likewise, the apostle John declared, "In the beginning was the Word, and the Word was with God, and the Word was God" (John 1:1).

God is the source of all truth. Not only is God truth and the source of all truth, any *purported* truth must be measured or evaluated by the truth God has revealed in His Word. Moreover, God re-

mains faithful to the truth. We can count on God to remain faithful to what He has promised—both now and into eternity. When you stop to think about it, all that God has promised us into eternity is predicated on His faithfulness.

The unchanging nature of truth as revealed by God has profound implications for the moral values which are under attack in our day. Quite apart from certain cultural traditions, habits which may conceivably change from time to time, God has revealed unchanging moral values which do not change. For example, the Ten Commandments reveal that it is always right to give God priority in our affections and practices and to honor our parents. It is always wrong in any age to steal, commit adultery, etc.

God possesses all power. Nothing is beyond God's ability do what God chooses to do. Once more, God speaks through Isaiah to say concerning the myriads of stars and planets, "Lift up your eyes on high, And see who has created these things, Who brings out their host by number; He calls them all by name, By the greatness of His might And the strength of His power" (from Isaiah 40:26, NKJV). God has the absolute right and power to do anything God chooses to do.

God is love. All genuine love originates with Him, and what we call love must be measured by Him (1 John 4:16). Love gives for the benefit of others. God has given us the perfect demonstration of love by becoming human as we are. God sacrificed Himself when His Son died as our Sin-bearer so that we could be reconciled to His favor.

Since it is impossible to escape God, right thinking people don't even try. Rather, they aim to...

Know God more clearly: They spend time with God alone exploring the truth God has revealed in His Word. They participate in church activities where the Word of God is honored and taught.

Love God more dearly: They express love to God in prayer and by cultivating a love relationship with God.

Obey God more nearly: They seek God's will and God's guidance in the decisions they make and in the things they do. They long to please Him in all they do. They aim to please God so much that they spend time cultivating their relationship with Him. They look for opportunities to represent God in their families, their church, their communities, in the education of their children and youth, and in the larger community. They want to please God in all they do.

And there is plenty to do, both in America and around the world. Bishop Charles E. Blake Sr., Presiding Senior Bishop of the Church Of God In Christ, spoke recently at a Morehouse College Baccalaureate Service. Among many significant things he said was:

"We need to promote broad-scale African American awareness of the plight of our brothers and sisters in Africa. We need to motivate African Americans to pursue a post civil rights movement response, with new paradigms and approaches to an African disaster of epic proportions. We need to investigate, not a temporary response, but rather, a new pan-African vision for mobilizing a comprehensive response to the AIDS pandemic. Almost everywhere you find people of African descent, they are the poorest, most malnourished, unemployed, uneducated, most oppressed people, and in every nation they exist at the bottom of all social strata. This is a direct and indirect result of slavery, colonialism, racism, and discrimination. But this is not the time to obsess about that; we must take charge of our own destiny. For many reasons, it is long since time for us to now assume a global pan-African mentality."

Since our accountability to God is inescapable, we should take seriously what we do for God's Son, Jesus Christ, and His kingdom.

Sources:
Blake, Bishop Charles. "Commencement Address at Morehouse College, Atlanta, GA, June 2009." monograph, n.d.
Buswell, James Oliver. *Zondervan Pictorial Bible Dictionary.* Merrill C. Tenney, gen. ed. Grand Rapids, MI: Zondervan Publishing House, 1963. 316–67.
"Joe Louis." *Oxford Dictionary of Modern Quotations.* 3rd ed. Edited by Elizabeth Knowles. Oxford, UK: Oxford University Press, 2007. 203.

Melvin E. Banks Sr., Litt.D., is the Founder and Visionary of Urban Ministries, Inc.

Christian Education in Action

Religious Education: The Contributions of African American Women

by Cheryl P. Clemetson, Ph.D.

The preserving, teaching, reshaping, and creating within Christian education for African American women are all witnessed from historical, social, and spiritual perspectives. The lives and the work of African American women in the field of Christian education are very much affected and connected to the political and religious milieu of their times. The contribution of African American women is more than educating persons about the Bible. As we shall see, it includes learning about the religious journey of God's people from the past, its contemporary application, and future manifestations of God's Word in the lives of His people.

I believe that Christian education is the very fiber of the church. Christian education serves as the vehicle that leads people to discover or rediscover the truth about themselves, God, and the world around them. Such discovery is found in all aspects of the church. The aesthetics of the church, the foods we serve, the Bible classes we teach, the preached Word, and the Sunday School lessons we share are all pieces of the fabric that Christian education weaves together. African American women often have had to knit the pieces together with very little or weak thread.

Before slavery to contemporary times, African American women have served in the forefront of religious education. Through preaching, teaching, writing, lecturing, and just plain living, African American women have provided a powerful part of the cornerstone for struggling to keep God's Word alive.

Historically, religious education in the church has involved not only studying Scriptures and moral values, but also basic academic skills such as reading, writing, and mathematics. For example, a child could learn to identify numbers and sequential ordering of numbers as she or he discovered how to locate chapter 10 and verse 1, 2, and 3 of a particular book. Adults and children also develop oratorical skills through plays and other public speaking opportunities in church. Socially, religious education provides a forum to discuss the issues that have plagued our people and our society. Unlocking the Scriptures for ways to support and make God's Word a living reality has been the fight for many African American women. Spiritually, religious education provides the conduit by which women, men, and youth learn to develop a personal and collective relationship with God, Christ, and the Holy Spirit. This can be accomplished through a variety of ways, including Bible lessons, arts and crafts, drama, and other vehicles to create a means of illuminating God's Word in our souls and throughout our lives.

Religious education for people of color must always go beyond the traditional ways of proclaiming God's Word because of the historical, social, and spiritual dynamics that impact and shape our lives. Therefore, there must be a myriad of vari ous personalities, styles, and a passion for God's Word to help pass on a new legacy of Christian education within our community and the world. We need persons such as Harriet Tubman and Sojourner Truth, who were not educated at the Harvard or Howard Universities of their time, yet still had fire and determination to end the injustice of slavery and abuses relating to women of color. Their strong, eternal belief in God allowed them to demonstrate what God can do through us if we are willing vessels. Tubman and Truth have contributed to Christian education by showing us that God's Word is not to bind us to a life of injustice.

The work of such persons as Amanda Smith, "evangelist and missionary"; Mary McLeod Bethune, educator and social activist; Nannie Helen Burroughs, educator, social activist, religious educator, and humanitarian; and Julia Cooper, "feminist, educator, and writer" provided spiritual, social, and educational leadership for many. They preached the Gospel, lectured, and wrote for racial equality and the suffrage movement for Black women in particular. Institutions of higher learning, such as the Bethune College (now known as Bethune-Cookman College in Daytona, Florida) were started by Mary McLeoud Bethune with $1.50. Nannie Helen Burroughs founded the now known Nannie Helen Burroughs School in Washington, DC, for women and girls. Later it became a co-ed elementary and middle school. Each of these women used the resources that were available to them to share knowledge and encourage others to fight for justice.

When we look at the contributions of African American women today in the field of Christian education, the legacy of having the social, spiritual, and historical dimensions of Christian educators is still significant. We still have persons like Dorothy Height, a living legend for justice and equality of women and all humanity. We need our Sunday School teachers and religious education directors to reflect the images of doctors, lawyers, custodians, bakers, and computer programmers so that our children and our adults are exposed to various occupations and teaching experiences. There are more educational materials being written and illustrated by African American women. Dr. Delores Carpenter, professor of Christian Education at Howard Divinity School, is an educator, pastor, writer, and lecturer. Her contributions to Christian education include lessons and writings for children and adults. She is imaginative and insightful in her writings and preaching. Dr. Carpenter also addresses the issues of women. She emphasizes the importance of women in the church and the ministry. Dr. Carpenter is a role model for girls and women. Her talents and gifts in the ministry as an activist, leader, teacher, and mother are genuine and uplifting.

If Christian education is to continue addressing God's Word in a way that is relevant and enlightening to others, then African American women must work in the political, social, and spiritual facets that shape and affect our lives as a people and as women of God. Consequently, we need to hear and see the voices of Representative Maxine Waters and Representative Eleanor Holmes Norton as they address political and social issues. This will help us to illustrate the prophet Amos' words to "let justice roll on like a river," as we compare Amos' times to today (Amos 5:24, NIV). We need to hear the clarion and pastoral voice of Dr. Vashti McKenzie as her words from the Lord give direction and guidance.

In addition to our famous or better known persons, we should never forget the unsung "sheroes," such as our grandmothers, mothers, aunts, Sunday School teachers, and church mothers, who were tough and loving babysitters who helped us to learn to say grace and to hold our hands to pray, and the African American nuns who helped us understand what it means to "reverence the Lord." Please do not forget the importance of the neighborhood watch mom before "Neighborhood Watch" became a nationally known community event. She helped us better understand what the omnipresence of God means because the neighborhood watch mom always seemed to be watching you. We must remember our schoolteachers and principals who made us have a moment of silence to acknowledge and respect God in our cultures and who emphasized prayer. Keep this quiet because the law said that we could not, but we did.

The contributions of African American women to Christian education are found in the stories and lessons that we write and share, the music that we teach and sing, the preaching that we preach on Sundays, and our involvement in voter registration, voting, and running for public office. Our contributions are found in our ability to tell the same story about the birth, life, death, and resurrection of Jesus Christ. Our contributions are reflected in being able to accept the role of Sunday School teacher, even when we know God has called us to preach. Yet, the church may still say, "God does not operate that way."

To paraphrase Maya Angelou, "we still keep rising" and contributing to Christian education in the church and in the community. The contributions of African American women to Christian education include more inclusive language and illustrations. There are more women entering and completing seminary training in pastoral ministry and religious education. This means that the roles of women in the church are being stretched to new depths. The political and social changes and issues concerning women and girls are being lifted closer to the forefront. Issues concerning women and girls in the work of Christ that have either been overlooked or not emphasized are opening new avenues of understanding the ministry of Christ. As the Lord continues to pour out His spirit upon "all flesh" (Joel 2:28) and as we receive this outpouring, change happens. The wheels of progress often turn slowly, but there are changes that demonstrate through women the power of God. Therefore, we will continue to benefit from the excellence of African American women in the field of Christian education.

Sources:
Angelou, Maya. *Maya Angelou: Poems.* "And Still I Rise." New York: Bantam Books, 1971. 154.
Richardson, Marilyn. *Black Women and Religion—A Bibliography.* Boston: G. K. Hall & Co., 1980. 66–67.

Cheryl P. Clemetson, Ph.D., is the Vice President of Editorial at Urban Ministries, Inc.

God's Power Is Awesome

by Evangeline Carey

God's power is awesome!
He used it to create His world,
To make humans in His own image,
And to give Him stewardship—authority
Over all His creatures.

God's power is awesome!
He speaks and the floodwaters overflow.
He speaks again and they recede.
His voice splits the 120-foot cedars of Lebanon,
And the world quakes at His command!

God's power is awesome!
He used it to heal diseases like leprosy,
To cast out demons and send them into a herd of pigs,
To make the paralyzed walk, the dumb talk,
And to restore the sight of a blind beggar.

God's power is awesome!
He used it to heal all who touched Him
Even a desperate woman,
Who had a 12-year ongoing battle
With a life-threatening blood disease.

God's power is awesome!
He used it to feed 5,000
With five loaves and two fish,
Then feed 4,000 more
With seven loaves and a few little fish.

God's power is awesome!
He used it to let Peter walk on water
And to transfigure
The long-awaited Messiah on a mountain
Before Peter, James, and John.

God's power is awesome!
He used it to get the Good News of His salvation
To a hated people—the Samaritans
Through a woman known to be living in sin,
Thus, breaking established customs and laws.

Oh, God's power is awesome!
He used it
To raise Jesus Christ from the dead
And bring everlasting life to those who believe
On Him and what He did on the Cross at dark Calvary.

God's power is awesome!
He used it to build His church
To propel His Gospel from Jerusalem,
To Judea, Samaria,
And the uttermost parts of the earth.

God's power is awesome!
And we can use it today to help us
With our daily concerns and problems,
To push away the despair and fear,
To gain divine strength for life's journey.

God's power is awesome!
Thank God that it is the same power
That controls creations,
That heals the sick,
That raises the dead in sin,
That builds His church,
And is there for us in our times of need.

Oh, how I praise the Inescapable God for His awesome power!

Cornel West, Ph.D.

Cornel West is one of the United States' most distinguished intellects and authors. He is most noted for his commitment to the African American community as a civil rights activist, pastor, and philosopher. He currently serves as a professor at the Ivy League institution Princeton University, where he teaches in the Center for African American Studies and the religion department. He is a messenger of hope because of his urgency in promoting education and political enlightenment in the Black community.

West was born in Tulsa, Oklahoma, on June 2, 1953, and grew up in Sacramento, California. As a young man, he participated in many civil rights protests and demonstrations. West also took a leadership role in organizing protests demanding African American studies classes at his high school, where he served as class president. At the young age of 17, West enrolled at Harvard University and graduated in three years, magna cum laude. In 1980, he earned his Ph.D. in philosophy from Princeton. He went on to teach as an assistant professor at Union Theological Seminary, and he later attended Yale Divinity School in 1985. West's civil rights activism extended beyond the United States when he organized a protest at Yale in support of the South African apartheid victims, which resulted in his arrest. Following his arrest, he taught at Haverford College, Harvard University's Divinity School, and Princeton University.

West has received more than 20 honorary degrees and the American Book Award. He also has served as honorary chair of the Democratic Socialists of America and co-chair of the Network of Spiritual Progressives and the Tikkun Community. He is one of the world's most sought after speakers and honorary chair members. His published works include *Black Theology and Marxist Thought* (1979), *Democracy Matters* (2004), and *Hope on a Tightrope* (2008). He will continue to influence the Black community and urge us to recognize its roots and rise up from deep-rooted oppression.

Sources:

"Cornel West." Finding Dulcinea, Librarian of the Internet. New York, NY: Dulcinea Media, Inc. http://www.findingdulcinea.com/features/profiles/w/cornel-west.html (accessed July 15, 2009).

"Cornel West." Pragmatism Cybrary. International Pragmatism Society. Amherst, NY: Center for Inquiry Transnational. http://www.pragmatism.org/library/west/ (accessed July 15, 2009).

Teaching Tips

1. Words You Should Know

A. Midian (Exodus 3:1) *Midyan* (Heb.)—Land and people associated with an ancient tribe; (Midianites) believed to have been descended from Abraham.

B. Holy (v. 5) *qodesh* (Heb.)—Anything consecrated and set aside for sacred use.

2. Teacher Preparation

Unifying Principle—No Excuses. We all have experienced the surprise of someone whose voice we do not recognize calling our name. When Moses heard God's voice, he responded by saying, "Here I am."

A. Before class, study the entire lesson.

B. Engage three students who will practice reading the Focal Verses as a dramatization and assign roles for the narrator, Moses, and the Lord.

3. Open the Lesson

A. Open your class with prayer, keeping the Aim for Change in mind.

B. Ask class members to name a dramatic and impressive request that they recall being made of them, such as marriage proposals, job offers, etc. Explain that today's lesson involves God's request of Moses.

C. Tie the In Focus story in with the discussion of God's revelation to humanity, including Moses.

4. Present the Scriptures

A. Have the prepared volunteers present their dramatization of the Focal Verses.

B. Read The People, Places, and Times; Background; At-A-Glance outline; In Depth; Search the Scriptures; and More Light on the Text.

5. Explore the Meaning

A. Use the Discuss the Meaning and Lesson in Our Society sections to help lead a discussion on the methods God uses today to get our undivided attention.

B. Also use both sections to help your students know how to apply the lessons Moses learned in His encounter with God to their own lives.

6. Next Steps for Application

A. Have students respond to the Follow the Spirit and Remember Your Thoughts sections.

B. Close with prayer.

Worship Guide

For the Superintendent or Teacher
Theme: God's Revelation to Moses
Theme Song: "Even Me"
Devotional Reading: Luke 20:34–40
Prayer

God's Revelation to Moses

Bible Background • EXODUS 3
Printed Text • EXODUS 3:1–6, 13–15 | Devotional Reading • LUKE 20:34–40

Aim for Change

By the end of the lesson, we will: REVIEW God's call to Moses from the burning bush; FEEL humbled and thankful that God speaks to us and calls us; and COMMIT to recognizing and obeying God's voice.

In Focus

When Jay and Reba had to go to court with their 15-year-old son, they were almost nervous wrecks. Their son, Drey, had been arrested with some other boy at his school who had started a fight just outside of the school building. Jay and Reba were leaders in their church and had raised their son in the church as well. In fact, he had been in church all of his life. They could not understand how and why he would fall in with some troublemakers at school, who were constantly in and out of skirmishes.

Jay and Reba had gone into prayer and asked others at their church to also pray over the situation. In addition, they asked God to soften Drey's heart so that he would learn from the situation and draw from the Christian principles he had been taught all of his life.

God was with them in the courtroom, and because Drey did not have a record, he was given mercy.

Just as Jay, Reba, and Drey learned another attribute of God, He revealed to them that He is indeed the merciful Living God and is the ultimate Lawyer in a courtroom. Moses learned in today's lesson that not only is this God holy (set apart from sin), but He is the God of Abraham, Isaac, and Jacob, who were Moses' ancestors. He revealed Himself to Moses as the One who delivers His people.

Keep in Mind

"Moreover he said, I am the God of thy father, the God of Abraham, the God of Isaac, and the God of Jacob. And Moses hid his face; for he was afraid to look upon God" (Exodus 3:6).

"Moreover he said, I am the God of thy father, the God of
Abraham, the God of Isaac, and the God of Jacob. And Moses hid
his face; for he was afraid to look upon God"
(Exodus 3:6).

Focal Verses

KJV **Exodus 3:1** Now Moses kept the flock of Jethro his father-in-law, the priest of Midian: and he led the flock to the backside of the desert, and came to the mountain of God, even to Horeb.

2 And the angel of the LORD appeared unto him in a flame of fire out of the midst of a bush: and he looked, and, behold, the bush burned with fire, and the bush was not consumed.

3 And Moses said, I will now turn aside, and see this great sight, why the bush is not burnt.

4 And when the LORD saw that he turned aside to see, God called unto him out of the midst of the bush, and said, Moses, Moses. And he said, Here am I.

5 And he said, Draw not nigh hither: put off thy shoes from off thy feet, for the place whereon thou standest is holy ground.

6 Moreover he said, I am the God of thy father, the God of Abraham, the God of Isaac, and the God of Jacob. And Moses hid his face; for he was afraid to look upon God.

3:13 And Moses said unto God, Behold, when I come unto the children of Israel, and shall say unto them, The God of your fathers hath sent me unto you; and they shall say to me, What is his name? what shall I say unto them?

14 And God said unto Moses, I AM THAT I AM: and he said, Thus shalt thou say unto the children of Israel, I AM hath sent me unto you.

15 And God said moreover unto Moses, Thus shalt thou say unto the children of Israel, the LORD God of your fathers, the God of Abraham, the God of Isaac, and the God of Jacob, hath sent me unto you: this is my name for ever, and this is my memorial unto all generations.

NLT **Exodus 3:1** One day Moses was tending the flock of his father-in-law, Jethro, the priest of Midian. He led the flock far into the wilderness and came to Sinai, the mountain of God.

2 There the angel of the LORD appeared to him in a blazing fire from the middle of a bush. Moses stared in amazement. Though the bush was engulfed in flames, it didn't burn up.

3 "This is amazing," Moses said to himself. "Why isn't that bush burning up? I must go see it."

4 When the LORD saw Moses coming to take a closer look, God called to him from the middle of the bush, "Moses! Moses!" "Here I am!" Moses replied.

5 "Do not come any closer," the LORD warned. "Take off your sandals, for you are standing on holy ground.

6 I am the God of your father—the God of Abraham, the God of Isaac, and the God of Jacob." When Moses heard this, he covered his face because he was afraid to look at God.

3:13 But Moses protested, "If I go to the people of Israel and tell them, 'The God of your ancestors has sent me to you,' they will ask me, 'What is his name?' Then what should I tell them?"

14 God replied to Moses, "I AM WHO I AM. Say this to the people of Israel: I AM has sent me to you."

15 God also said to Moses, "Say this to the people of Israel: Yahweh, the God of your ancestors—the God of Abraham, the God of Isaac, and the God of Jacob—has sent me to you. This is my eternal name, my name to remember for all generations."

The People, Places, and Times

Israelites. The Israelites were the descendants of Jacob, whose name was changed when he wrestled with God (Genesis 32:28). They were composed of people from the 12 sons or grandsons of Jacob. His descendants are variously called "the House of Jacob," "the Children of Israel," "the people of Israel," or "the Israelites."

Moses. He was born in a time threatened by war. The large increase in the number of his people concerned the Pharaoh, who was worried that they might help Egypt's enemies. When the Pharaoh ordered all newborn Hebrew boys to be killed, Moses' Hebrew mother, Jochebed, hid him and he ended up being adopted into the Egyptian royal family (Exodus 2:1–9). After killing an Egyptian slave-master, Moses fled across the Red Sea to Midian on the slopes of Mount Horeb where he tended the flocks of Jethro, a priest of Midian.

Background

In the first book of his history, Genesis, Moses preserved and transmitted the records of God's people, focusing on individual families. Now, as we come to this second book featuring him, Exodus, we learn how the people grow from one family to that of a great nation. The beginning of this book shows us how God formed Israel for Himself, and both accounts were meant to bring forth His praises. In Genesis, we have the creation of the world in history; here in Exodus, we read about the symbolic redemption of the world. The Greek translators, in calling this book "Exodus from Egypt" were basing the phrase on their word *exodos* (**EX-od-os**), which means "taking the road out and exiting." Indeed, the forming of Israel into a people was a departure from the past, a new creation.

In today's lesson, we see the contrast between Moses' royal life as an Egyptian prince and his ordinary life as a Midianite shepherd, doing the lowly job of caring for sheep. Even though as a prince he had servants who did much for him, in his new life, he most likely had to do everything for himself. However, all was not lost, because God was training him to lead other sheep—the sheep of God's pastures—the Israelites, God's chosen people.

At-A-Glance

1. Moses Prepares for God
(Exodus 3:1–3)

2. Moses Responds to God's Call
(vv. 4–5)

3. Moses Appreciates the Awesomeness
of God (v. 6)

4. Moses Receives Specific Instructions from
God (vv. 13–15)

In Depth

1. Moses Prepares for God (Exodus 3:1–3)

Many times it is not until we are away from everyone who has held our attention, away from our hectic, busy, overworked schedules and lifestyles, and away from the cares of this world that we are able to move into a place of quietness and solitude that facilitates us to surrender ourselves to the Lord. In this place of quietness, we are able to give God our undivided attention. In this place of quietness, all other voices are removed. This place of quietness enables a spirit of searching and seeking God's face. This is where we find Moses at the beginning of this lesson. As it so happened, Moses was deep in the wilderness, tending his father-in-law's sheep near Mount Sinai, the mountain of God (v. 1). God got Moses away from the hustles and bustles of life so that He could speak to Moses, instruct him, and give Moses his calling. In this place where God allowed Moses to go, away from the busyness of each day, God begins to purge Moses and remove the hindrances that prevented what God ordained for him. This is where God would give His revelation and instructions that Moses was to follow from that day forth.

2. Moses Responds to God's Call (vv. 4–5)

As Moses turned to see why the bush was not burning up, God moved forward with His plan. The Lord appeared to Moses in a burning bush that was not consumed. It was a miracle that God used as His medium of revelation to Moses. Fire is a symbol of God's consuming, powerful presence. God issued the call to Moses upon his inspection of this unusual sight. When the Lord spoke Moses' name to Moses from the burning bush, he responded by saying, "Here am I."

Then in verse 5, God made Moses aware that he was in the presence of a holy God—One who is totally and completely without sin. In other words, where Moses stood was holy. He needed to keep a respectful distance and remove his sandals because the ground was sacred, consecrated because God's presence is holy.

3. Moses Appreciates the Awesomeness of God (v. 6)

God took the time to speak and reveal that He is the same God of Moses' forefathers. Once Moses understood this revelation, he hid his face. And through God's revelation of the promise of Abraham, Moses understood the mighty presence that he was not to look upon. After God makes it clear to us who He is and that we are in His presence, we then realize how unworthy we are to even stand before Him.

4. Moses Receives Specific Instructions from God (vv. 13–15)

Whenever God gives us an assignment, we must be sure to obey His instructions and not try to do it our way. God sent Moses with a message for the Children of Israel: The God of their ancestors sent Moses and this God is called "I AM THAT I AM" (v. 14). The phrase "I AM" is connected with a form of the verb "to be," and it expresses God's character and essence. God disclosed Himself in this manner to Moses to demonstrate His ability and power. "I AM" was not a new God to the Children of Israel, for He was the same God of Abraham, Isaac, and Jacob. This name discloses that God is able to be in any situation that He sends His people into. The same God was now sending Moses to them. God's name was linked with other men of God who had a relationship with the one true God. It was to be a memorial, used throughout all generations.

Today, when God gives us instructions on things to say or things to do, we must be sure to obey the instructions fully. We must do this so that God's purpose and plan might be accomplished. There is an assurance from

Him that He will be with us and He is able to do anything but fail.

Search the Scriptures

1. Whose flock was Moses tending when he came to Mount Horeb (Exodus 3:1)?

2. In what natural way did God appear to Moses on Mount Horeb (v. 2)?

3. Why did Moses hide his face (v. 6)?

Discuss the Meaning

1. Do you think Moses would have been attentive to God if a bush wasn't burning without being consumed? How might the outcome have been different if God simply called Moses' name (Exodus 3:2–4)?

2. Why did God have to tell Moses to take his sandals off? When we come into God's presence, are we expected to remove anything (v. 5)?

Lesson in Our Society

Sometimes before we will surrender to God or submit to His command, He has to do something drastic to get our attention. A bush that is burning without being consumed is only a small revelation of God's power to do anything He pleases in His world. It is drastic enough to get any viewer or bystander's attention. Just as God used an undeniably supernatural revelation with Moses, He does the same with us. And once we see these signs, which we know that only an Almighty God can give, God then has our attention. Once God has our undivided attention, He is then able to speak and thus we listen. However, we don't want to just listen; we need to respond in obedience to God's voice.

Make It Happen

This week, ask God to reveal His purpose for you on your journey. Make this a consistent prayer request. Look for signs that God may be giving you to get your attention.

Follow the Spirit

What God wants me to do:

_____

_____

_____

_____

Remember Your Thoughts

Special insights I have learned:

_____

_____

_____

_____

More Light on the Text

Exodus 3:1–6, 13–15

1 Now Moses kept the flock of Jethro his father-in-law, the priest of Midian: and he led the flock to the backside of the desert, and came to the mountain of God, even to Horeb.

Up to this point in Exodus, the reader has seen the life of Moses divided up into 40–year periods. Moses passes his first 40 years in Egypt, during which time God has miraculously delivered the infant Moses through the faithfulness of his mother and the kindness of Pharaoh's daughter (2:1–10). The next 40 years take place in the region of Midian, where Moses flees after killing an Egyptian he sees beating one of his fellow Hebrews, comes to stay with a priest named Jethro, marries one of Jethro's daughters, Zipporah, and has a son with her, named Gershom (2:11–22). Acts 7:30 tells us that the period in Midian lasted 40 years. Now Moses is about to embark on his third 40–year journey, and despite Moses' pleas of un-worthiness, Exodus 2 makes it clear that God has prepared him for this moment by giving Moses opportunities to help the oppressed (Exodus 2:11–12, 16–17).

In this phase of Moses' life, we are told that he now tends the flock of his father-in-law, Jethro. This is not an unimportant detail, for it shows us God's further preparation of Moses for the shepherding task that lies ahead of him: leading the people of Israel out of slavery and into their inheritance. In addition, this piece of background information prepares the reader for a story in which God is dramatically the center of attention.

2 And the angel of the LORD appeared unto him in a flame of fire out of the midst of a bush: and he looked, and, behold, the bush burned with fire, and the bush was not consumed.

The same word for "looked upon" in 2:25 is now used for the word here translated as "appeared"—God's merciful concern for His people moves Him to action. Here we are told that it was "the angel of Yahweh" (for when-ever "the LORD" [in capital letters] appears in the Old Testament it is a reference to "Yah-weh," the covenantal, intimate name of God) appeared to Moses; in verse 4 we see also a reference to "God" Himself. How should the reader deal with this information? Was it God's angel who appeared to Moses, or God Himself? The Old Testament often connects the two so closely that it becomes difficult

to separate or distinguish them. (See Gen-esis 16:7–13; Numbers 22:22–25; Zechariah 3:1–6.) For this reason, many interpreters throughout the history of the church have believed the "angel" (or "messenger," for the Hebrew word) can mean either the pre-incarnate Son of God or the second Person of the Trinity (Jesus Christ). The NIV Appli-cation Commentary has a helpful note here: "The notion of the close relationship in the Old Testament between the Messenger/an-gel of the Lord and Yahweh himself is some-thing that is fully manifested in the person of Christ, who is both one with the Father yet distinct from him as the second person of the Trinity. This is not to say, however that the angel of the Lord is a preincarnate manifestation of Christ. Rather, the angel of the Lord foreshadows Christ in the same way that Moses, the priesthood, or the sacrificial system do" (Enns, 96).

The Lord's appearance in the Scriptures is often represented with fire, to call to mind His all-consuming power. The phrase "of fire" in the Hebrew is *'es* (**aysh**), which means "a fire, flames, supernatural fire."

This fire, of course, is unlike the Bible's other flaming theophanies. (A "theophany" is an appearance of God in some form recog-nizable to human beings.) In this case, the fire interacts with a "bush" (probably a small thornbush of the acacia variety which is na-tive to that area) in a way that compels Moses to investigate.

3 And Moses said, I will now turn aside, and see this great sight, why the bush is not burnt.

This verse serves as a transition between verses 2 and 4. In a passage where the focus is clearly on the person and character of God, the man Moses serves mostly to high-light God's holiness (set apart from sin) and graciousness in His dealings with people. In case there was any doubt in the reader's mind after the description of the burning bush in verse 2, Moses now reacts with the kind of curiosity that indicates the presence of the miracle; like the reader, he wonders "why the bush is not burnt." The Lord now has Moses' attention, to say the least.

4 And when the LORD saw that he turned aside to see, God called unto him out of the midst of the bush, and said, Moses, Moses. And he said, Here am I.

The verse begins with perhaps an unexpected introduction: "And when the LORD saw..." The almost human ways in which God acts in this passage, set alongside the powerful theophany in the form of fire, highlights both the transcendence (God is wholly other, different from our world, the all-sufficient God) and the immanence (nearness) of Yahweh, both of which the Israelites would soon encounter repeatedly throughout their journey out of Egypt and to the Promised Land. God shows Moses both His power and His intention to be intimately involved with His people. The reader should not ignore the sublime scene of Almighty God, who "is a consuming fire" (Hebrews 12:29), appearing mercifully to Moses, His chosen mouthpiece and leader.

The author of Exodus then tells us in 3:4 that God "called" to Moses; "called" is of course no small word. In the Hebrew, "called" is qara' (**kaw-RAW**) which means "be summoned, be named." This is the beginning of Moses' true ministry for which God has prepared him throughout the events of his life and the fulfillment of his destiny. Despite Moses' stubborn and unbelieving response to God's call (see Exodus 4:1–13), it is the call that prevails.

5 And he said, Draw not nigh hither: put off thy shoes from off thy feet, for the place whereon thou standest is holy ground.

The mood of the scene changes here, as God (the "he" at the beginning of verse 5) demonstrates once again His transcendence and awesome power. Because of the warning tone of God's command, it appears that Moses' curiosity led him too close to the burning manifestation of God's presence. Moses is now shown more fully what is taking place before him. Like any ancient person in the East, he would have known immediately what it meant to remove his shoes: putting aside the dusty reminders of one's earthliness out of respect for another, greater existence. Such an action took place not only upon entry to a person's house (as is still commonly done today), but also upon entry to the house of a deity (there were many worshiped in those days). In Hebrew, the word "holy" (qodesh, **KO-desh**), means "sacredness, separateness." This command is the beginning of Moses' fear and trembling, seen more clearly in the next verse, for God has shown by this command the otherworldly and awe-inspiring nature of the scene before Moses. But it also points to the magnitude of God's mercy. He sees to it that Moses will not be consumed by His glory, but rather admonishes Moses in a way that brings him into this holy and gracious encounter.

6 Moreover he said, I am the God of thy father, the God of Abraham, the God of Isaac, and the God of Jacob. And Moses hid his face; for he was afraid to look upon God.

God's warning to Moses is really just a prologue to the more crucial revelation: the identification of this Holy Other who has arrested the shepherd's attention. The word for God in this Hebrew text is *'elohiym* (**el-o-HEEM**), which means "the God," connoting that this is the one true God. The true God announces His identity first as "the God of thy father." Many commentators note that this phrase would have been understood by the Hebrews hearing the words of Exodus as more or less the same as "the God of thy fathers." Indeed, some later manuscripts of this verse have added the "s" on the end of "father." In this light, the phrase points to the more specific way in which God will describe Himself: "the God of Abraham, the God of Isaac, and the God of Jacob." But as the *IVP Bible Background Old Testament Commentary* also points out, "God's identification of himself with the 'God of your father' suggests that the concept of patron deity may still provide the most accurate understanding of how the Israelites thought about Yahweh" (Walton et al.).

Though we know from God's own mouth that "I am the LORD, I change not" (Malachi 3:6), the covenant people's understanding of who their God was and is did seem to grow and evolve over time, as God revealed Himself to them in increasing measure. In connecting Himself to the patriarchs Abraham, Isaac, and Jacob, God now reveals to Moses exactly whom he is dealing with in this encounter.

3:13 And Moses said unto God, Behold, when I come unto the children of Israel, and shall say unto them, The God of your fathers hath sent me unto you; and they shall say to me, What is his name? what shall I say unto them?

In verses 7–12, God has revealed to Moses an announcement that may have been more shocking than even the fact that God had appeared to him in the first place: God will rescue the Israelites from their slavery in Egypt, and Moses will be the instrument of that deliverance! Moses' initial response, in verse 11, is understandable: "Who am I [that I should do such a thing]?" Moses' question in this verse is complex. On the one hand, it is true that the Egyptians, among whom the Israelites had lived for generations, worshiped many gods, and called them by various names. Each name pointed directly to the way in which each god was understood. For example, the name of Ammon, one of the Egyptian gods, means "the concealed god" (Spence and Exell, 57). Moses may have been anticipating that the Israelites would adopt that framework as they sought to understand what was taking place, and would want a corresponding name that would explain the nature of the God who would deliver them.

But the text itself points us to a more important reason for Moses' question. Moses' incredulous response in verse 11 and his continuing efforts to escape his calling (all the way through 4:13), show what his real concern is. It is not so much the identity of this God that he is questioning, but rather the authority that he, himself, will have when he takes to the Israelites what will no doubt seem like a crazy proclamation.

14 And God said unto Moses, I AM THAT I AM: and he said, Thus shalt thou say unto the children of Israel, I AM hath sent me unto you.

God's resounding response to Moses (it is fitting that the King James Version puts the words in capital letters) echoes throughout history. For one thing, the very name "Yahweh" comes from these words; in the Hebrew, the words translated "I am that I am" are *'ehyeh 'aser 'ehyeh* (**eh-hyeh ah-sher eh-hyeh**). It contains as its first and last word the basic consonants YHWH, which, when given vowels later in the history of the nation, yields "Yahweh" (a name so holy that observant Jews even to this day do not pronounce it). Further, the phrase itself is a puzzle that has fascinated interpreters from the very beginning. It can be translated "I am that am," "I will be what I will be," or "I am the one who is," among many other possible translations.

The exact wording of the phrase, when translated, is less important than how we understand the phrase as a whole. Taken in context, God seems to be giving Moses a sort of non-answer, or at least not the answer he is looking for. While Moses wants a specific name to which he can refer for his authority (and also, perhaps, a way to put God in a box of sorts and make Him less fearful), God simply says, "I am the One who is."

15 And God said moreover unto Moses, Thus shalt thou say unto the children of Israel, the LORD God of your fathers, the God of Abraham, the God of Isaac, and the God of Jacob, hath sent me unto you: this is my name for ever, and this is my memorial unto all generations.

Once again, God's interaction with Moses includes not only terrifying holiness but also merciful condescension. In verse 15, He does answer Moses' question more specifically, albeit by more or less repeating what He had said in verse 6. He reminds Moses of the "name" that matters for him and for the Israelites: Yahweh is the same God who showed covenantal kindness to Abraham, to Isaac, and to Jacob, and the same God who will fulfill His covenantal promises. Now the Lord explicitly states, "God of your fathers," connecting Himself directly with those who have come before, even as He combines that title with the new name (that is not really a name) "Yahweh." So we could say that the fullest answer to Moses' question, "What is his name?"

(v. 13) is, "The LORD [Yahweh] God of your fathers, the God of Abraham, the God of Isaac, and the God of Jacob" (v. 15).

Say It Correctly

Gershom. GUHR-shahm.
Pharaoh. FEHR-o.
Sinai. SI-ni, also si-nee-i.
Zipporah. zip-o-ra.

Daily Bible Readings

M: A God of the Living
Luke 20:34–40

T: God Has Spoken
Numbers 23:18–26

W: Waiting for God to Speak
Psalm 62:5–12

T: God Speaks Through the Son
John 3:31–36

F: God Knows Our Suffering
Exodus 3:7–12

S: God Will Relieve Our Misery
Exodus 3:16–22

S: God Speaks and Reveals
Exodus 3:1–6, 13–15

Teaching Tips

September 12
Bible Study Guide 2

1. Words You Should Know

A. Covenant (Exodus 19:5) *b@riyth* (Heb.)—An agreement; a covenant with God based on God's character, strength, and grace.

B. Graven image (Exodus 20:4) *pecel* (Heb.)—An idol or likeness cut from stone, wood, or metal and then worshiped as a god.

2. Teacher Preparation

Unifying Principle—Who's the Boss? People look for guidance from someone or something they can trust. In the Ten Commandments, God laid out unimpeachable instructions for building a trusting relationship with God.

A. Early in the week, read the In Depth and More Light on the Text sections.

B. Also read all the surrouding text.

3. Open the Lesson

A. Pray based on the Aim for Change and Keep in Mind verse.

B. After opening with prayer, ask class members to identify laws that dominate our lives, such as laws regarding stop signs, criminal acts, etc. Then ask why we obey these laws.

C. Have a volunteer tell the In Focus story, and then engage in a discussion of how it relates to today's text.

4. Present the Scriptures

A. Have the class read aloud the Focal Verses.

B. Use a review of The People, Places, and Times; Background; At-A-Glance; In Depth; Search the Scriptures questions; and More Light on the Text to help present the lesson.

5. Explore the Meaning

A. Use the Discuss the Meaning questions and Lesson in Our Society to help students know how to apply the truth to their lives.

B. Allow students to share their answers.

6. Next Steps for Application

A. Have class members read the Make It Happen section.

B. In the Follow the Spirit section, challenge students to create a description of a lifestyle "that pleases God at all times."

C. Close with prayer, asking for God's strength and encouragement as class members seek to please God.

Worship Guide

For the Superintendent or Teacher
Theme: God's Law as a Covenantal Agreement
Theme Song: "Let Us Worship Him"
Devotional Reading: John 1:14–18
Prayer

God's Law as a Covenantal Agreement

Bible Background • EXODUS 20
Printed Text • EXODUS 20:1–11 | Devotional Reading • JOHN 1:14–18

Aim for Change

By the end of the lesson, we will: KNOW that the Ten Commandments are God's instructions to believers; DESIRE to follow God's commands; and DEVELOP ways of living that reflect godly obedience.

 **In Focus**

Cheryl was very excited and yet had some trepidation as well when it was time to take her son to get his learner's permit. She knew that he had come of age, and she celebrated that fact. But she also realized that there were many problems and pitfalls that a teenage driver, especially a young Black male, could encounter in our often unjust society. She also recognized and appreciated that like all drivers, in order to be safe and so that others could be safe as well, he had to learn to obey the rules of the road. Therefore, Cheryl had serious discussions with her son about some of the challenges that he might encounter as a driver under the age of 25. In addition, she made sure that her son studied the drivers' manual diligently.

When she felt that he was ready, they drove to their local department of motor vehicles. For added support, Cheryl also asked some of her coworkers to remember her son in prayer.

Like the rules that we have to follow when we drive a car, God also gives us rules to protect us. In today's lesson, God gave the Children of Israel His Law (the Ten Commandments) as a covenantal agreement. This agreement was binding.

Keep in Mind

"I am the LORD thy God, which have brought thee out of the land of Egypt, out of the house of bondage. Thou shalt have no other gods before me" (Exodus 20:2–3).

"I am the LORD thy God, which have brought thee out of the land of Egypt, out of the house of bondage. Thou shalt have no other gods before me" (Exodus 20:2–3).

Focal Verses

KJV **Exodus 20:1** And God spake all these words, saying,

2 I am the LORD thy God, which have brought thee out of the land of Egypt, out of the house of bondage.

3 Thou shalt have no other gods before me.

4 Thou shalt not make unto thee any graven image, or any likeness of any thing that is in heaven above, or that is in the earth beneath, or that is in the water under the earth:

5 Thou shalt not bow down thyself to them, nor serve them: for I the LORD thy God am a jealous God, visiting the iniquity of the fathers upon the children unto the third and fourth generation of them that hate me;

6 And shewing mercy unto thousands of them that love me, and keep my commandments.

7 Thou shalt not take the name of the LORD thy God in vain; for the LORD will not hold him guiltless that taketh his name in vain.

8 Remember the sabbath day, to keep it holy.

9 Six days shalt thou labour, and do all thy work:

10 But the seventh day is the sabbath of the LORD thy God: in it thou shalt not do any work, thou, nor thy son, nor thy daughter, thy manservant, nor thy maidservant, nor thy cattle, nor thy stranger that is within thy gates:

11 For in six days the LORD made heaven and earth, the sea, and all that in them is, and rested the seventh day: wherefore the LORD blessed the sabbath day, and hallowed it.

NLT **Exodus 20:1** Then God gave the people all these instructions:

2 "I am the LORD your God, who rescued you from the land of Egypt, the place of your slavery.

3 "You must not have any other god but me.

4 "You must not make for yourself an idol of any kind or an image of anything in the heavens or on the earth or in the sea.

5 You must not bow down to them or worship them, for I, the LORD your God, am a jealous God who will not tolerate your affection for any other gods. I lay the sins of the parents upon their children; the entire family is affected—even children in the third and fourth generations of those who reject me.

6 But I lavish unfailing love for a thousand generations on those who love me and obey my commands.

7 "You must not misuse the name of the LORD your God. The LORD will not let you go unpunished if you misuse his name.

8 "Remember to observe the Sabbath day by keeping it holy.

9 You have six days each week for your ordinary work,

10 but the seventh day is a Sabbath day of rest dedicated to the LORD your God. On that day no one in your household may do any work. This includes you, your sons and daughters, your male and female servants, your livestock, and any foreigners living among you.

11 For in six days the LORD made the heavens, the earth, the sea, and everything in them; but on the seventh day he rested. That is why the LORD blessed the Sabbath day and set it apart as holy."

The People, Places, and Times

Jethro. This Midianite priest became a crucial person in Moses' time line. He welcomed Moses into his home at a time when Moses really needed help because he was fleeing from the Egyptian king. Jethro's daughter Zipporah became Moses' wife, and, while tending Jethro's sheep, Moses encountered God and learned about his destiny as leader of God's people. Though not an Israelite, Jethro became a worshiper of the true God. In Exodus 18, the chapter just before the account of Moses' experience with God that resulted in the Ten Commandments, Jethro visited him. After Moses told Jethro all that God had done for him and the people of Israel, Jethro proclaimed, "Now I know that the LORD is greater than all gods" (18:11).

The Times. Egyptian dynastic history dates back to 4000 B.C., when the kingdoms of upper and lower Egypt, already highly sophisticated, were united. Egypt's golden age coincided with the 18th and 19th Dynasties (sixteenth to thirteenth centuries B.C.), during which the empire was established. The book of Exodus was probably written between 1450–1410 B.C. Some scholars prefer a later date.

Background

The Law (the Ten Commandments) is "(1) A law of God's making and (2) a law of God's own speaking. God has many ways of speaking to the children of men (Job 33:14); he never spoke, at any time, on any occasion, as he spoke the Ten Commandments. This law God had given to man before (it was written in his heart by nature); but sin had so defaced that writing that it was necessary, in this manner, to revive the knowledge of it" (*NIV Matthew Henry Commentary in One Volume*, 97).

The Ten Commandments is also called the Mosaic Law because God gave these commands to Moses on Mount Sinai, His "holy mountain or hill," to present to the Children of Israel. They were to live by this Law.

At-A-Glance

1. God Reminds the Israelites of Past Blessings (Exodus 20:1–2)

2. God Gives the Israelites His Law (vv. 3–11)

In Depth

1. God Reminds the Israelites of Past Blessings (Exodus 20:1–2)

The Children of Israel had come out of the land of Egypt and were now in the wilderness of Sinai. In chapter 19, we read that the Lord had told Moses to be ready because He would come down upon Mount Sinai in the sight of the people. Moses and the people prepared by sanctifying themselves (consecrating, setting themselves apart) and washing their clothes. They only came to the foot of the mountain, because God set boundaries that the people could not cross. Here we see God speaking to the people, after Moses went down from the mountain to the people. God ties the promise of deliverance of His people from Egypt with His name. The Lord is now proclaiming His name again, now that the deliverance is reality for the Children of Israel. God reminds the Israelites of past blessings, of His deliverance of them from slavery in Egypt.

All that the Lord is and does is embodied in His affirmation and proclamation of His name. When we consider the capacity in which God has moved in our lives and in others' lives, we are assured of His power. As a result, our faith in Him is renewed and our hope is revived. We must continue to remember what God has done in our lives and associate His marvelous works with His name. We, too, must remember past blessings and be grateful. These past blessings should cause us to worship the compassionate, merciful God, who is worthy.

2. God Gives the Israelites His Law (vv. 3–11)

Clearly, throughout the existence of this world, God has demonstrated that He is a jealous God and that we are to have no other gods before Him. This is the first commandment and the phrase "before me" (or, "no other gods but me," NIV) may seem difficult to grasp. It is best translated as "You shall not prefer other gods to me." Whichever way we embrace it, the meaning should still be understood that there is only one true God. The God that we serve is the only true God, and He is "a jealous God" who expects fidelity to the covenant made with His people.

Anything that occupies all our attention and receives our total devotion is considered a god in our lives. If something takes us away from spending time with the God of heaven, who created us, that is considered a god in our lives. There is no other god that can do what the God of heaven can do. Therefore, we must be careful not to elevate anything else above our God. If we do not keep them in their proper place and give them their proper status, even our children, education, jobs, homes, cars, etc., can become gods in our lives. We should worship God the Creator and never the things created.

In verse 8, God commanded His people to have a time set aside to pay homage to Him (worship Him) and totally dedicate themselves to Him. The word "Sabbath" is derived from the Hebrew verb *shabbath,* which means "to rest or cease from work." The command was to set aside each seventh day as belonging to the Lord. The Sabbath in essence was another sign of honoring the covenant which God had with His people.

Search the Scriptures

1. How does God refer to the land of Egypt (Exodus 20:2)?

2. In what way does God describe His feelings toward persons who bow down to carved images and other gods (v. 5)?

3. What type of love does God show to those who love Him (v. 6)?

Discuss the Meaning

1. Was there a need for God to remind the people about Egypt? How might the people, as well as Moses, have responded if God did not bring this to their remembrance (Exodus 20:2)?

2. What makes God jealous? How might the people have responded differently to God saying not to have any other gods before Him (vv. 3–5)?

Lesson in Our Society

Clearly, God has the power to bring us out of the things that have us bound. We need to realize that God is omnipotent (all-powerful) and He can do anything but fail. So when the challenges of life knock at our door, we need to remember the God that we serve. When we are faced with obstacles and mountains that seem too high to climb, we also need to remember the God that we serve. We need to consider His track record and know that He still has a lot more that He can do in our lives. However, if we want God's blessings to continue to shower down upon us, we need to make sure that we are obedient to His Word. We should not constantly challenge Him as the Israelites, His chosen people, did.

Make It Happen

This week, ask God to help you to follow His commands, His statutes, His Word. Pray that God will aid you in successfully living in a way that reflects the commands that He has given. Remember that our lifestyles are also a direct witness to a lost and dying world. We talk the talk of a Christian, but can we walk the walk?

Follow the Spirit

What God wants me to do:

_____

_____

_____

_____

Remember Your Thoughts

Special insights I have learned:

_____

_____

_____

_____

More Light on the Text

Exodus 20:1–11

1 And God spake all these words, saying,

This week's passage recounts one of the most climactic moments of the Old Testament: God giving the Ten Commandments to Moses for him to pass along to the Children of Israel. Another word for "Ten Commandments" is "Decalogue," which comes from the Greek *deka logos* (**DEK-ah LOG-os**), or "ten words," as they are called later in the Old Testament (see Exodus 34:28, where the words translated "Ten Commandments" literally mean "ten words").

"God spake all these words." We must not ignore the importance of God speaking. The alert Bible reader will connect this passage to Genesis chapter 1, where God first speaks into history. We see there that God's speech is not like ours; it does not simply describe what is already there. On the contrary, when God speaks, things come to be, things that were not there before! In the same way, when God speaks here, we might well describe it as an "act of re-creation" (Enns, 411) in which God is forming not only the worlds themselves but also His people after His image and character. So the words that come after demonstrate not just the "thou shalts" and "thou shalt nots" to be observed by God's people, but also the very nature of God Himself, out of whose perfect holiness and justice these heaven-sent commands come forth.

2 I am the LORD thy God, which have brought thee out of the land of Egypt, out of the house of bondage.

How do we know that the Ten Commandments are more than arbitrary do's and don'ts? This verse demonstrates the twofold foundation on which the Decalogue is built: God and His grace. First we see the majestic self-revelation of God, as Yahweh ("the LORD"), who revealed Himself by this name to Moses and showed His kindness to the Israelite forefathers, all the way back to Abraham (see last week's lesson). The declaration "I am the LORD thy God" shows the innate authority God possesses. It is enough to declare His identity as the reason that Israel is bound to His commands. (Think of a parent saying to a child, "I am your father," or "I am your mother"—this usually speaks for itself!) But God also demonstrates His kindness to His people in that He does not stop at the simple declaration, "I am your God." Though His character and authority are reason enough for Israel to obey, He brings forth another reason: *I have redeemed you*; I have brought you out of slavery.

The phrase "have brought" in Hebrew is *yatsa'* (**yaw-TSAW**), which means "to cause to go or come out." As though Israel needed reminding, God points back to the recent events of the Exodus. There's no doubt that the people would have thought back to the plagues on the Egyptians, to the Passover miracle, and to their stunning deliverance through the Red Sea. Even before the last of these events takes place, God prepares the people to remember the greatness of His power and of His kindness toward them: "And it shall be when thy son asketh thee in time to come, saying, What is this? that thou shalt say unto him, By strength of hand the LORD brought us out from Egypt, from the house of bondage" (Exodus 13:14). Here we see the pattern God establishes for His people: first, He acts to save them in His mercy; second, they remember the greatness of what He has done; and third, they respond by honoring Him with their obedience.

3 Thou shalt have no other gods before me.

This first command, though just eight short words in the King James Version, conveys powerfully the heart of biblical religion from beginning to end. In an age that already managed to develop an innumerable number of "gods" to worship (not unlike the age in which Christ lived, or our own age), Yahweh ensures that the Israelites will make no mistake about the call to monotheistic, wholehearted devotion to their Lord.

4 Thou shalt not make unto thee any graven image, or any likeness of any thing that is in heaven above, or that is in the earth beneath, or that is in the water under the earth:

The phrase "graven image" translates the Hebrew word *pecel* (**PEH-sel**), meaning "carved image" or "idol." The second commandment is closely tied to the first. Though most cultures today no longer make actual physical idols that receive worshipful adoration, this kind of literal idol-making was common in the day of Moses. (Again, the golden calf incident will show us just how common it was!) So Yahweh addresses specifically what it looks like not to have any other gods before (besides) Him. Knowing the waywardness of the Israelites' hearts and the frequency of idol-making among their neighbors, Israel's God reveals that to make an image ("graven" means "engraved" or "made out of physical things") is to violate the heart of the first commandment. To worship images is, by definition, to have other gods beyond the Lord. Whether the object of the image is "in heaven above" (either the sky or heaven itself) or somewhere on or under the earth, such worship turns upside down the proper and beautiful relationship between Creator and creature. The Bible calls this worship *idolatry*. But the prohibition found in verse 4 does not apply only to worshiping images of things that are *not* God; it also clearly includes the worship or veneration of images *of* God. The telling phrase here is "in heaven above." Though this phrase can sometimes refer simply to the sky, usually in that case it uses the plural "heavens."

5 Thou shalt not bow down thyself to them, nor serve them: for I the LORD thy God am a jealous God, visiting the iniquity of the fathers upon the children unto the third and fourth generation of them that hate me;

God repeats the command against worshiping idols or other gods but now answers the "why" question that may have been lingering in the minds of the hearers. "I...am a jealous God" may not be the answer that a generation bent on pleasing itself might want to hear, but it is the answer nevertheless. As noted above, God's jealousy is perfect and appropriate, like a husband's intense desire that his wife's body be his and his alone. Yahweh, by His covenant and powerful acts of salvation, has claimed Israel for Himself. For them to take any other master is not just ungrateful, but deeply offensive and detestable. "For the LORD thy God is a consuming fire, even a jealous God" (Deuteronomy 4:24). When the mountain quaked with smoke and fire as God delivered the Decalogue, the Israelites could hardly have had any doubt about that!

The word "visiting" in the Hebrew is *paqad* (**paw-KAD**), which means "appoint, assign," or "punish." The noun "iniquity" is *avon* (Heb. `avown, **aw-VONE**), which means "sin, depravity, fault." The latter part of Exodus 20:5 might trouble us. Is it fair, after all, to punish children or grandchildren for the sins of their parents or grandparents? Many interpreters of this verse have pointed out that God may have been speaking about the consequences of sin; certainly a grievous sin committed by one generation can reverberate harmfully into the next generation and the one beyond it. This may explain the verse in part, but we do not do the idea justice if we do not remember that God gives this pronouncement as part of His *covenant.* God's covenants are always made with corporate bodies (like Israel, or the church), not simply individuals. And so it is important for us to acknowledge that the sins of God's people affect each other, even other generations, not just in a natural sense but also in a covenantal sense.

6 And shewing mercy unto thousands of them that love me, and keep my commandments.

However severe God's justice might seem, such justice is completely miniscule when compared to His mercy (see James 2:13). If justice lasts a few generations, then mercy lasts for thousands and thousands! Exodus 20:6, like verse 5, deals with the covenant. The word translated "mercy" is, in the Hebrew *checed* (**KHEH-sed**), the word typically used in the Old Testament to describe God's particular love to His covenant people. Likewise, the phrase "those who love me and obey my commands" (NLT) is covenant language; it speaks to those who are called to keep up their end of the deal, in response to God's overwhelming mercy and grace. So the reference does not mean that God's mercy only comes to people when they are loving God and keeping His commandments; rather, His mercy comes at all times to those found in His covenant. Their love and commandment-keeping flow out of this mercy.

7 Thou shalt not take the name of the LORD thy God in vain; for the LORD will not hold him guiltless that taketh his name in vain.

This commandment is probably the one about which the church has had the most confusion. Part of the confusion comes from the importance God places on His name—something not as familiar to modern society as it was to the ancients. As *The NIV Application Commentary* puts it, "What's in a name? Plenty. The name of God, the tetragrammaton (Hebrew name for God) YHWH, is *God's* name. It is the name whose significance was patiently explained to Moses in chapters 3–4. It is the name whose very mention connected the Exodus community to the patriarchs. It is God's salvation name (3:15; 6:6; 15:3), and as such must be treated with the highest respect" (Enns, 417). With this in mind and considering the focus of the first two commandments, we can see that God is primarily concerned about how the Israelites used the holy name of Yahweh. The phrase "in vain" in Hebrew is *shav'* (**shawv**), which means "falsely, lying," or "worthlessness." God's name, then, should never be used in spells or incantations, for example, as other nations would use their gods' names. If the name was used in a vow, then that vow should be very carefully kept.

But the third commandment, like all the others, says more than it appears to at first, as Jesus makes clear in His treatment of the commandments about murder and adultery in Matthew 5:21–22, 27–32. It concerns not just the mouth but also the *heart*. As such, this commandment forbids both speaking and believing things about God that are untrue or unworthy of Him.

8 Remember the sabbath day, to keep it holy.

The fourth commandment brings to a close what is often called the "first table" of the Ten Commandments—the ones that deal particularly with the people's relationship to God, rather than to each other. As such, the fourth commandment goes with the other three; the honor and worship of God are the paramount concern for those who would keep the Sabbath holy. The first way to honor God concerning the Sabbath is to "remember." The word "remember" in Hebrew (*zakar*, **zaw-KAR**) means "be mindful, recall," or "call to mind." Throughout the Bible, remembering is never just something done with the mind, but rather an act of worship, and something that prompts the people to thankful obedience. Israel is a remembering people, and remembrance of their deliverance in the Exodus continues

to shape the lives of Jews even to this day. God's people are called to "remember" the Sabbath. In Hebrew, *shabbath* (**shab-BAWTH**) means "ceasing from work." The Sabbath, then, should be observed in the way verses 9–10 demonstrate for a particular reason: "to keep it holy." The phrase "to keep it holy" in Hebrew is *qadash* (**kaw-DASH**), which means "keep sacred" or "honor as sacred." As verse 11 will demonstrate, the Sabbath is a holy day because God has made it so. God's people have the awesome duty of preserving the day's holiness!

9 Six days shalt thou labour, and do all thy work:

We see God's mercy in the explanation of the Sabbath command: though the chief issue is God's honor and glory, the people's Sabbath rest is certainly also for their blessing (for a New Testament picture of this blessing, see Hebrews 4:1–11). The Bible always assumes that God's people will work hard. The word "labour" in Hebrew (*`abad*, **aw-BAD**) means "to work, serve." Whether gathering manna (food) or doing more modern tasks, the pattern of six days' work is an ancient one. It is the gracious gift of rest, finding peace with God, that stands as the central point of God's command. The six days of work will culminate with feasting, celebration, and worship, even as God's rest followed His work of creating the world (v. 11).

10 But the seventh day is the sabbath of the LORD thy God: in it thou shalt not do any work, thou, nor thy son, nor thy daughter, thy manservant, nor thy maidservant, nor thy cattle, nor thy stranger that is within thy gates:

God's Sabbath command, when spelled out in detail, shows itself to be a *covenantal* command. The hallowing of the seventh day is not simply a matter of respecting oneself, but of revering the solemn commitment of one's entire household. The Lord calls on the covenantal heads of the families to see to it that He is honored by their conduct on this day of days. Even animals are included in this matter! Certainly it is true that animals need a day of rest just as much as human beings, and in this sense God is gracious also to His creation.

11 For in six days the LORD made heaven and earth, the sea, and all that in them is, and rested the seventh day: wherefore the LORD blessed the sabbath day, and hallowed it.

The third commandment contains not only the "what" of the command but the "why": "for the LORD will not hold him guiltless that taketh his name in vain" (20:7). The second commandment, likewise, contains its own reasons for why God forbids graven images: "for I the LORD thy God am a jealous God" (20:5). We might even say that the first commandment has its own reason for being, as explained in the verse before it: "I am the LORD thy God, which have brought thee out of the land of Egypt, out of the house of bondage" (20:2). Likewise, the Lord graciously grounds the Sabbath command for His people on the foundation of His own character and work. "The LORD blessed the sabbath day, and hallowed it" (20:11). The word "hallowed" is a synonym for the Hebrew *qadash* (**kaw-DASH**), and here it means "consecrated, dedicated, or set apart." Surely anything that Almighty God has consecrated, dedicated, or set apart should also be consecrated, dedicated, and set apart by those who are called by His name!

Say It Correctly

Decalogue. DEK-uh-log.
Hallowed. ha-lod, HA-lo-wed.
Sabbath. SAB-uhth.

Daily Bible Readings

M: Your Law Is My Delight
Psalm 119:73–77

T: The Tablet of Your Heart
Proverbs 7:1–5

W: The Law with Grace and Truth
John 1:14–18

T: Righteousness That Comes from Faith
Romans 10:5–13

F: Justified Through Faith
Galatians 2:15–21

S: God's Claims on Our Relationships
Exodus 20:12–21

S: God's Claims on Us
Exodus 20:1–11

Teaching Tips

1. Words You Should Know

A. Play (Exodus 32:6) *tsachaq* (Heb.)—Revelry, implies immoral sexual activity.

B. Corrupted (v. 7) *shachath* (Heb.)—Spoiled, ruined, destroyed.

2. Teacher Preparation

Unifying Principle—Keeping Faith. The commitments of our time and energy demonstrate where our devotion lies. The story of the golden calf illustrates that God—and God alone—deserves our complete devotion and loyalty.

A. Prepare by reading, studying, and meditating on the entire lesson.

B. If you have it, use the *Precepts For Living*® CD to locate places mentioned in The People, Places, and Times. Be prepared to share this information with the class.

3. Open the Lesson

A. Open by praying based on the Aim for Change.

B. Connect the In Focus story with today's discussion.

4. Present the Scriptures

A. Lead a discussion of the two items listed under The People, Places, and Times.

B. Show the video of the "graven image" scene from the 1956 film *The Ten Commandments*.

C. Have the class read the Focal Verses and use the The People, Places, and Times; Background; At-A-Glance; In Depth; Search the Scriptures questions; and More Light on the Text to help clarify meaning.

5. Explore the Meaning

A. After fully exploring the Scripture meanings, ask if patience played a role in the disobedience of Aaron and the Israelites.

B. Follow this with a discussion of the first question under Discuss the Meaning.

C. Have the class read Lesson in Our Society and respond to the article in *USA Today* and the closing questions.

6. Next Steps for Application

A. Ask each person to use the Make It Happen section of the lesson as a springboard into their personal devotion this week.

B. Close with prayer, asking God for strength for each class member and for the church-at-large.

Worship Guide

For the Superintendent or Teacher
Theme: God versus "gods"
Theme Song: "Amazing Grace"
Devotional Reading: John 5:39–47
Prayer

God versus "gods"

Bible Background • EXODUS 32
Printed Text • EXODUS 32:1–10 | Devotional Reading • JOHN 5:39–47

Aim for Change

By the end of the lesson, we will: TELL why God wanted Israel's complete devotion and loyalty; REFLECT on our own devotion and loyalty to God; and REAFFIRM our devotion and loyalty to God.

In Focus

Shaé, a 33-year-old committed Christian, was a talented singer and songwriter who desired to record her own CD. When her cousin, Greg, also a dedicated Christian, began working for the Christian music industry, he encouraged her to make a demo recording that he could pass on to label executives. She did, and within three months Shaé had a recording contract.

Despite this great opportunity, one thing bothered Shaé about the contract. The recording company wanted her to write several songs as crossover music that could be played on secular radio stations and at clubs. Shaé felt that she would be compromising her faith by singing and producing songs that were secular.

Shaé was unsure. *I don't want to compromise my faith,* she thought. When it was time for Shaé to sign the contract, she was still uncertain. She prayed silently: Lord, I do not want to miss out on this opportunity to be a witness for You.

Do you think Shaé was compromising her faith by signing the contract? Our lesson deals with serving the true and living God versus "gods"—false gods.

Keep in Mind

"They have turned aside quickly out of the way which I commanded them: they have made them a molten calf, and have worshipped it, and have sacrificed thereunto, and said, These be thy gods, O Israel, which have brought thee up out of the land of Egypt" (Exodus 32:8).

"They have turned aside quickly out of the way which I commanded them: they have made them a molten calf, and have worshipped it, and have sacrificed thereunto, and said, These be thy gods, O Israel, which have brought thee up out of the land of Egypt" (Exodus 32:8).

Focal Verses

KJV **Exodus 32:1** And when the people saw that Moses delayed to come down out of the mount, the people gathered themselves together unto Aaron, and said unto him, Up, make us gods, which shall go before us; for as for this Moses, the man that brought us up out of the land of Egypt, we wot not what is become of him.

2 And Aaron said unto them, Break off the golden earrings, which are in the ears of your wives, of your sons, and of your daughters, and bring them unto me.

3 And all the people brake off the golden earrings which were in their ears, and brought them unto Aaron.

4 And he received them at their hand, and fashioned it with a graving tool, after he had made it a molten calf: and they said, These be thy gods, O Israel, which brought thee up out of the land of Egypt.

5 And when Aaron saw it, he built an altar before it; and Aaron made proclamation, and said, Tomorrow is a feast to the LORD.

6 And they rose up early on the morrow, and offered burnt offerings, and brought peace offerings; and the people sat down to eat and to drink, and rose up to play.

7 And the LORD said unto Moses, Go, get thee down; for thy people, which thou broughtest out of the land of Egypt, have corrupted themselves:

8 They have turned aside quickly out of the way which I commanded them: they have made them a molten calf, and have worshipped it, and have sacrificed thereunto, and said, These be thy gods, O Israel, which have brought thee up out of the land of Egypt.

9 And the LORD said unto Moses, I have seen this people, and, behold, it is a stiffnecked people:

10 Now therefore let me alone, that my wrath may wax hot against them, and that I may consume them: and I will make of thee a great nation.

NLT **Exodus 32:1** When the people saw how long it was taking Moses to come back down the mountain, they gathered around Aaron. "Come on," they said, "make us some gods who can lead us. We don't know what happened to this fellow Moses, who brought us here from the land of Egypt."

2 So Aaron said, "Take the gold rings from the ears of your wives and sons and daughters, and bring them to me."

3 All the people took the gold rings from their ears and brought them to Aaron.

4 Then Aaron took the gold, melted it down, and molded it into the shape of a calf. When the people saw it, they exclaimed, "O Israel, these are the gods who brought you out of the land of Egypt!"

5 Aaron saw how excited the people were, so he built an altar in front of the calf. Then he announced, "Tomorrow will be a festival to the LORD!"

6 The people got up early the next morning to sacrifice burnt offerings and peace offerings. After this, they celebrated with feasting and drinking, and they indulged in pagan revelry.

7 The LORD told Moses, "Quick! Go down the mountain! Your people whom you brought from the land of Egypt have corrupted themselves.

8 How quickly they have turned away from the way I commanded them to live! They have melted down gold and made a calf, and they have bowed down and sacrificed to it. They are saying, 'These are your gods, O Israel, who brought you out of the land of Egypt.'"

9 Then the LORD said, "I have seen how stubborn and rebellious these people are.

10 Now leave me alone so my fierce anger can blaze against them, and I will destroy them. Then I will make you, Moses, into a great nation."

The People, Places, and Times

Aaron. He was the older brother of Moses (Exodus 7:7) and the son of Amram and Jochebed. According to Exodus 7:1, Aaron acted in the role of one of the early prophets. As a prophet, he did not foretell future events (as many of the Old Testaments prophets did). Rather, he served as a mouthpiece for Moses. Because Moses had a speech impediment and was afraid to speak to the pharoah, God used Aaron instead of Moses to speak God's words (Exodus 4:15–16).

Sinai. This name contains three different meanings: (1) the peninsula south of the Wilderness of Paran, (2) the Wilderness of Sinai, and (3) the mountain itself, Mount Sinai, also called Mount Horeb. The wilderness region, arid and with rough terrain, was where the Israelites camped for about a year. The distance from the Israelites' initial flight from the Red Sea to this mountain was approximately 150 miles. A record of all the events that occurred at this location is in Exodus 22–40; Leviticus; and Numbers 1–11.

Background

The setting of today's lesson is the wilderness at Mount Sinai, where the Israelites (God's chosen people) are encamped. In the six chapters prior to Exodus 32, God gives Moses instructions for setting up a physical dwelling place for God, the tabernacle referred to as the "Tent of Meeting." These detailed instructions provided exact dimensions, specifications, number, and exact objects that should form and be contained in the tabernacle. During this time, Moses has been on Mount Sinai for 40 days, and the Israelites have become impatient with waiting on him. The Israelites' last response to Moses, prior to the 40–day wait, is in chapter 24, where they agreed to follow the civil and religious laws (book of the covenant). At that time, the people responded: "All that the LORD hath said will we do, and be obedient" (Exodus 24:7).

At-A-Glance

1. The Quick Fix (Exodus 32:1)

2. The Golden Silence and Golden Calf (vv. 2–4)

3. The Living God and "gods" in Worship (vv. 5–6)

4. The Speedy Intervention (vv. 7–10)

In Depth

1. The Quick Fix (Exodus 32:1)

The Children of Israel grew impatient in the Sinai region. Forty days before, Moses went up Mount Sinai and had not returned. He was their spiritual leader, the voice of God for the people, their spiritual commander-in-chief, who led the people from point A to point B at God's command. Now this great captain was missing in action, and they had no idea what had happened to him. Nevertheless, the people still needed spiritual leadership. Perhaps, in Moses' absence, they felt vulnerable, powerless, and directionless, realizing that their enemies the Amorites, Hittites, and the Canaanites (to name a few) were still real threats. So the people gathered and devised a solution. They requested that Aaron make them tangible leaders—gods to lead them.

The Children of Israel wanted to be fully covered, so they did not request one god; they asked that Aaron would make for them some "gods." Although they were out of Egypt, this did not deter them from worshiping gods as the Egyptians did. God had taken them out of the land of Egypt , but the culture of Egypt was still in them.

2. The Golden Silence and Golden Calf (vv. 2–4)

In verses 2–4, Aaron appears to use the old adage "silence is golden" as his defense. He readily succumbed to the Israelites' request for gods and said nothing to the people about the covenant they had made with God earlier. He was silent. His silence turned to gold in the literal sense as he initiated the fashioning of the golden calf.

The text does not mention any resistance on Aaron's part, so he appears in this passage as a spiritually feeble leader. Not only was he a weak leader, but Aaron's acquiescence to the group also went contrary to the Lord's leadership order that was stated to Moses: "You shall speak to [Aaron] and put words in his mouth...[Aaron] will speak to the people for you, and it will be as if he were your mouth and as if you were God to him" (Exodus 4:15–16, NIV). According to this passage, Moses was to act as an intermediary and relay God's message to Aaron. Aaron would then proclaim to the Israelites (and anyone else) the word that Moses received from God. Contrarily, in this passage, the Israelites usurped God's authority and told Aaron what to do. The Israelites' "perverse reflection" was the result of their lack of complete devotion to the one true God.

3. The Living God and "gods" in Worship (vv. 5–6)

The Children of Israel had a new god, the golden calf. Aaron set the stage for worship of this idol by creating an altar for it. Then, he proclaimed a day of worship and feasting. Both the burnt offering and the peace offering were ways of offering thanksgiving and reverencing God. *The Jewish Encyclopedia* states that for the Israelites, the burnt offering is "honorific and devotional, implying homage to Yahweh and a complete surrender to His service" (675). Interestingly, Aaron proclaimed this worship as *supposedly* "a feast to the LORD" (v. 5). So, were the Israelites worshiping both the calf and the Lord at this altar? Or were they simply giving a nonchalant, mental assent to the Lord, but worshiping the calf? Just as the correlative conjunctions "both" and "and" depend on each other in a sentence structure, the Israelites felt they needed both the Lord and the calf. They seemed to think very little of this syncretistic and corrupt worship.

The tabernacle represented God's presence with and among the Israelites and was a movable tent so they could travel from place to place. It was to be the Lord's ordained physical and tangible representation of His presence. But the people settled for a calf and their impatience took them deeper and deeper into sin. However, God knew the destructiveness of disobedience, so He commanded the Israelites' complete devotion and faithfulness.

4. The Speedy Intervention (vv. 7–10)

As swiftly as the Israelites demanded gods and received their golden calf, God with similar haste insisted that Moses descend the mountain. Verses 7–10 provided two interventions for Israel's departure from true worship. First, God sent Moses to stop the group from even further corruption. God knew that Moses would act expediently on God's behalf. Second, God intended to destroy this rebellious people. His mind was made up, and the Lord did not want Moses to intercede. Consequently, God told Moses, "Let me alone, that my wrath may wax hot against them" (v. 10). The biblical narrative in this lesson concluded with a cliffhanger that could produce questions similar to old radio dramas: *What will become of the Israelites? Will Yahweh kill them all? Will Moses intercede for these stiffnecked people? Stay tuned next week to hear the dramatic conclusion of the Sinai Journey.* Actually, Exodus 32:11–35 contains the dramatic conclusion. Although Israel's sin did include fatal consequences—the death of 3,000 (vv. 19–28)—God's mercy also intervened. The text further states that Moses interceded on the Israelites' behalf so that God did not destroy them all (vv. 11–14).

Search the Scriptures

1. What motivated the Israelites to insist that Aaron make gods for them (Exodus 32:1)?

2. What was God's remedy for Israel's corruption (vv. 9–10)?

Discuss the Meaning

1. In what ways can our being impatient lead us into sin?

2. Moses frequently offered intercession to God on behalf of the Israelites' sin. Do you think God uses intercessors today to stop or delay God's wrath in certain situations?

Lesson in Our Society

"God versus 'gods'" is a timely topic in today's society, as so many persons, things, and issues—family; jobs or employment searches; technology such as e-mail, cell phones, smartphones; fears caused by escalating crime and violence—compete for our time and attention.

Make It Happen

As you studied today's lesson, were there any scriptural verses or passages that spoke to your devotion to God? Each of us is at a different place on the pathway to complete devotion to God. Where do you think you are on the path? Do you feel that you are totally committed, partially committed, or not committed at all? Since none of us is perfect, we should always be striving toward a closer relationship with God. Spend time in prayer and devotion this week asking God to show you areas of your life that are not fully devoted to Him. As God reveals to you this area or areas of growth, find supporting Scriptures that you can meditate on to keep you focused.

Follow the Spirit

What God wants me to do:

_____

_____

_____

_____

Remember Your Thoughts

Special insights I have learned:

_____

_____

_____

_____

More Light on the Text
Exodus 32:1–10

1 And when the people saw that Moses delayed to come down out of the mount, the people gathered themselves together unto Aaron, and said unto him, Up, make us gods, which shall go before us; for as for this Moses, the man that brought us up out of the land of Egypt, we wot not what is become of him.

Chapters 25 through 31 of Exodus focused on God's instructions for building the Tent of Meeting, a special, mobile tabernacle. This tabernacle was to be the place of God's dwelling with the Israelites in the desert. Though they could not bear the weight of His full glory (see 20:19), in a very real sense His presence would be among them in the Tent of Meeting. The elaborate and detailed instructions God reveals through Moses give the Israelites an opportunity for obedience according to the covenant (see last week's lesson), but such instructions also create a series of symbols through which God will demonstrate His glory to the Israelites. The bottom line is that, as anticipated by the second commandment (20:4), Yahweh and Yahweh alone will determine where and how He will be worshiped.

After the Lord gives Moses all these instructions, along with the Ten Commandments and many laws that expand upon them (chapters 20–24), we are told very briefly, "And [God] gave unto Moses, when he had made an end of communing with him upon mount Sinai, two tables of testimony, tables of stone, written with the finger of God" (31:18). So this ends, it would seem, the establishment of God's holy covenant with the Israelites. We might expect a confirming, covenantal response from the people, like the one found in 19:8: "All that the LORD hath spoken we will do."

But instead, with their leader absent, the people turn to the second-in-command, with evil desires in mind. They "gathered themselves together unto Aaron" (32:1). The Hebrew word translated "gathered... together" is *qahal* (**kaw-HAL**) which means "to assemble." It can also mean "against Aaron," with probable hostile consequences. They seem to be rebuking him as weak or passive; there's a curtness in the imperative wording, as they command him, "Up, make us gods." In Hebrew, "up" is *quwm* (**koom**), meaning "arise, stand, rise up." In other words, "What are you waiting for? Do as we say!" Their command to make them "gods, which shall go before us," is shocking for its lack of reverence and covenantal memory.

The people go on to refer to their leader as "this Moses," with a clearly disrespectful and dismissive attitude. At the same time, however, they refer to him as "the man that brought us up out of the land of Egypt," inappropriately giving Moses the credit for the deliverance instead of Yahweh.

2 And Aaron said unto them, Break off the golden earrings, which are in the ears of your wives, of your sons, and of your daughters, and bring them unto me.

It appears that Aaron gives in very quickly to the Israelites' demands. Though we might speculate about the threatening nature of these troublemakers, or probe Aaron's own doubts about his brother's leadership, the fact of his own complicity in the idolatry is impossible to avoid. The details of his request, however, do bring to mind what he may have been thinking about, at least as a rationalization. In requesting that gold be used for the making of the "gods," Aaron may have had in mind the recently given instructions for the tabernacle, which stipulated that much of its interior be lined with gold (see, for example, Exodus 30:1–5). Further, this gold was to come from the offerings of the people; such offerings always supplied the necessary materials for Israel's sacred gathering places. The Lord's mandates combined with Aaron's instructions concerning the gold earrings, suggest that Aaron at least had details like these in mind—and that at some level he may have thought he was honoring God by using precious materials in the making of the calf. Such a connection hardly excuses Aaron, but it does show how he, like many when tempted to doubt God and disobey Him, could have found ways to rationalize the rebellion in his own mind.

3 And all the people brake off the golden earrings which were in their ears, and brought them unto Aaron.

Like Aaron, the people appear willing to go along with the rebellion without much of a fuss. Adding offense to their idolatry is the fact that these gold earrings were likely obtained when they plundered the Egyptians before the Exodus (Exodus 12:35–36). This opportunity to get expensive items was a gracious gift of God, completely unnecessary but provided out of His sheer, extravagant generosity. Now the people were using their freely gotten gold to fashion an idol, which they knew He detested.

4 And he received them at their hand, and fashioned it with a graving tool, after he had made it a molten calf: and they said, These be thy gods, O Israel, which brought thee up out of the land of Egypt.

What exactly Aaron "fashioned" is not entirely clear. The word "fashioned" in Hebrew is *tsuwr* (**tsoor**), which means "to form." It may have been a calf made entirely of gold and "a graving tool" was used to decorate the surface; alternatively, the

structure of the idol may have been made of wood, plated in gold on the outside using the engraving tool. More important is the significance of the calf itself. The word "calf" is probably not the best translation of the Hebrew word *egel* (**ay-GHELL**); the word refers most specifically to "a young bull in his first strength ... the word can describe a three-year-old animal" (Cole, 214). In ancient Near Eastern religion, "it was thought that calves or bulls functioned as pedestals for the gods seated or standing over them" (Enns, 569).

5 And when Aaron saw it, he built an altar before it; and Aaron made proclamation, and said, Tomorrow is a feast to the LORD.

We now see even more fully how the Israelites had sunk into syncretism (the mixing together of various religions; what might, in our day, be informally called "cafeteria religion"). Aaron, who by now is clearly more than just an unwilling participant, responds to the creation of the calf by building an altar of sacrifice in front of it; this means that worship will now take place with the calf at the center of the event. At the same time, Aaron proclaims that a "feast to Yahweh" will take place after the people's worship. This pattern follows the pattern that Israel would repeat throughout its history—sacred worship followed by joyous festivals—but in this case, both the worship (as we see here) and the feasting (as we see in verse 6) are hopelessly corrupted and perverted forms of what God has in mind for Israel.

6 And they rose up early on the morrow, and offered burnt offerings, and brought peace offerings; and the people sat down to eat and to drink, and rose up to play.

The scene that unfolds before us now is a sad parody of the holy events in Exodus 24. There we see that Moses "wrote all the words of the LORD, and rose up early in the morning, and builded an altar under the hill, and twelve pillars, according to the twelve tribes of Israel" (24:4). God had initiated His covenant and was so gracious in giving the people His words; Moses responded in worship, representing the entire 12 tribes of Israel before God. But here, in chapter 32, the people "rose up early" with something different on their minds; though they indeed worshiped, it was neither the one true God they were worshiping, nor the way in which He had called them to adore His holiness.

For the Israelites, the cycle of sin has brought them to a terrible place of judgment. Beginning with impatience before God that led ultimately to unbelief in His promises, they acted to secure a divine blessing in a way God had expressly forbidden.

7 And the LORD said unto Moses, Go, get thee down; for thy people, which thou broughtest out of the land of Egypt, have corrupted themselves:

The scene now shifts to the top of the mountain, where Moses stands in Yahweh's holy presence. Though the people have acted as though the Lord does not see their rebellion and impurity, the author now shows us how omniscient (all-knowing) Yahweh is; He has not missed the idolatrous wanderings of His people at the foot of Sinai. In fact, God now speaks concerning the Israelites in a way that must have been chilling for Moses to hear: He calls them not "My people" but "thy people." We see here foreshadowing of what is about to take place: God is about to disown Israel! Further, Yahweh says with some irony that "thou [Moses] broughtest [them] out of the land of Egypt." In speaking this way, the Lord is sarcastically adopting the people's viewpoint; they have stopped seeing Yahweh in His holiness as the One who has delivered them, so Yahweh momentarily

takes their point of view, even though its falseness is obvious. Finally, we learn that the moral guilt of Israel is now realized: they "have corrupted themselves" in God's eyes. The phrase "have corrupted" is, in Hebrew, *shachath* (**shaw-KHATH**), which means "spoiled, ruined, destroyed." If there were any doubt that Israel's trampling of the second and third commandments, while profaning God's worship with sexual impurity, will go unnoticed or unpunished by their holy God, that doubt can exist no longer.

8 They have turned aside quickly out of the way which I commanded them: they have made them a molten calf, and have worshipped it, and have sacrificed thereunto, and said, These be thy gods, O Israel, which have brought thee up out of the land of Egypt.

Since Moses, unlike the Lord, has not been omnisciently watching the proceedings at the foot of Mount Horeb, God shows Him what is taking place there. God reveals each part of the ugly situation, particularly the idolatry that has taken place. The "rising up to play" is not mentioned, suggesting that Israel's idolatry is at the heart of what enrages Yahweh; their sexual impurity is merely an outcome, and a symptom, of their rebellion. God's piece-by-piece recounting of the scene taking place below is heart-rending; for both the unknowing Moses and the knowing reader, horror and grief are now aroused.

9 And the LORD said unto Moses, I have seen this people, and, behold, it is a stiffnecked people:

God now summarizes the reason for Israel's impending doom with a word that will become commonplace in His description of the Israelites throughout the Old Testament: "stiffnecked." In the Hebrew, "stiffnecked" is *qasheh* (**kaw-SHEH**), which means "obstinate and difficult." This word choice is based in agriculture, "a farmer's metaphor of an ox or a horse that will not respond to the rope when tugged" (Cole, 216). We can see why such a word-picture would be used for Israel; from the time Moses first comes to them in Exodus 4, it is as though the people have to be dragged unwillingly to their own salvation.

10 Now therefore let me alone, that my wrath may wax hot against them, and that I may consume them: and I will make of thee a great nation.

God has already declared that the people are no longer His but Moses' (v. 7). We now see the consequence of this appraisal. To understand what is taking place here, we must keep in mind where God's loyalties lie. First, God has made promises to the patriarchs Abraham, Isaac, and Jacob (Genesis 12:1–3, then repeated throughout the book of Genesis); nothing will keep Him from fulfilling those promises. Second, His loyalty is to Moses, whom He has appointed as shepherd of the people. In this light and given Israel's hideous rebellion, God's response is consistent with His character and promise; He will be faithful to His promises to the patriarchs and His loyalty to Moses. As the people have decisively broken their covenant, God owes them nothing. Thus His command, "Let me alone, that my wrath might wax hot." In the Hebrew, "wrath" (*'aph, af*) means "extreme anger." It appears that it is time for Moses the mediator to step aside, so that God might confront the people directly. As we know from Exodus 20:18–19, this will be their worst fear realized.

But there is another aspect of this account that we must consider before the close of the lesson: Moses as shepherd of Israel, appointed by God. In Exodus 32:11–13, Moses pleads with God to spare the people, reminding God of His promise to the patriarchs. Moses

also shows his awareness of the likelihood that the Egyptians and others who, upon hearing of the Israelites' destruction, will say that God was unable to bring them into the land He promised.

Say It Correctly

Amram. AM-ram.
Jochebed. JOK-uh-bed.
Yahweh. YAH-veh, -vay.

Daily Bible Readings

M: Warnings Against Idolatry
1 Corinthians 10:1–11

T: Flee from Idol Worship
1 Corinthians 10:14–21

W: Idols—The Work of Human Hands
Psalm 135:13–18

T: Keep Yourselves from Idols
1 John 5:13–21

F: Confronting Idolatry
Exodus 32:15–24

S: The Consequence of Idolatry
Exodus 32:30–35

S: The Infidelity of Idolatry
Exodus 32:1–10

Teaching Tips

SEPT 26th

1. Words You Should Know

A. Hew (Exodus 34:1, 4) *pacal* (Heb.)—To carve stones, to chisel.

B. Marvels (v. 10) *pala* (Heb.)— Extraordinary and wonderful things or events; miracles.

2. Teacher Preparation

Unifying Principle—Steadfast Love. People have different ideas about how their behavior affects relationships. In the face of Israel's unfaithfulness, God revealed to Moses that God is steadfast, forgiving, and faithful.

A. Carefully read the entire lesson for the week.

B. Include the Daily Bible Readings in your study.

C. Spend time meditating on the power behind God's promises in this text.

3. Open the Lesson

A. Open with prayer, based on the Aim for Change.

B. Allow volunteers to share their devotional experiences from last week.

C. Have the class read and respond to the In Focus story, tying it in to today's discussion.

4. Present the Scriptures

A. Play the recorded Focal Verses from the *UMI Sunday School Lesson CD*, or read the Focal Verses in both the KJV and NLT translations.

B. Then use The People, Places, and Times; Background; At-A-Glance; In Depth; Search the Scriptures questions; and More Light on the Text to help clarify meaning.

5. Explore the Meaning

A. Using the Discuss the Meaning and Lesson in Our Society sections, explore the meaning of the text for life today.

B. Stress that even when we are unfaithful to God, He is forgiving and faithful to us as He was to the Israelites.

6. Next Steps for Application

A. Ask, "How can we remain committed to serve, obey, and follow God?"

B. Have your students write an answer under the Follow the Spirit section.

C. Close with prayer.

Worship Guide

For the Superintendent or Teacher
Theme: God Promises an Awesome Thing
Theme Song: "I Am Thine O Lord"
Devotional Reading: Acts 3:19–26
Prayer

God Promises an Awesome Thing

Bible Background • EXODUS 34:1–10
Printed Text • EXODUS 34:1, 4–10 | Devotional Reading • ACTS 3:19–26

Aim for Change

By the end of the lesson, we will: LIST God's attributes as revealed to Moses; REFLECT on God's love, mercy and faithfulness; and PRAISE God for His love, mercy, and faithfulness.

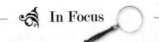 In Focus

Sierra and Julius had a mutual love for God and encouraged one another. When Sierra and Julius were married, like all couples, they had ups and downs in their marriage. Yet they purchased a home and had two children. Sierra was faithfully committed to her husband, Julius. When Julius's company downsized, he was laid off after 12 years as a sales manager. Sierra continued to work, care for the children, and encourage Julius that God had something wonderful for him and their family.

Each day, Julius seemed more hesitant to attend church and Bible study with the family. He seemed more withdrawn. Sierra didn't complain; she continued to praise God for His provisions. One Friday afternoon, Sierra was paying the bills. As she opened the mail, Sierra said, "Thank You, God, for Your provisions!"

Julius asked, "What is it?"

As she gave Julius the letter, Sierra said, "Our tax refund was adjusted…."

Before Sierra could finish, Julius said, "We're probably receiving less."

Sierra quickly responded, "No, there is an increase. Because He loves us, God is faithful to provide."

Let today's lesson help you to consider God's continual blessings in the midst of the world's unfaithfulness.

Keep in Mind

"And the LORD passed by before him, and proclaimed, The LORD, The LORD God, merciful and gracious, longsuffering, and abundant in goodness and truth" (Exodus 34:6).

"And the LORD passed by before him, and proclaimed, The LORD, The LORD God, merciful and gracious, longsuffering, and abundant in goodness and truth" (Exodus 34:6).

Focal Verses

KJV **Exodus 34:1** And the LORD said unto Moses, Hew thee two tables of stone like unto the first: and I will write upon these tables the words that were in the first tables, which thou brakest.

34:4 And he hewed two tables of stone like unto the first; and Moses rose up early in the morning, and went up unto mount Sinai, as the Lord had commanded him, and took in his hand the tables of stone.

5 And the LORD descended in the cloud, and stood with him there, and proclaimed the name of the LORD.

6 And the LORD passed by before him, and proclaimed, The LORD, The LORD God, merciful and gracious, longsuffering, and abundant in goodness and truth,

7 Keeping mercy for thousands, forgiving iniquity and transgression and sin, and that will by no means clear the guilty; visiting the iniquity of the fathers upon the children, and upon the children's children, unto the third and to the fourth generation.

8 And Moses made haste, and bowed his head toward the earth, and worshipped.

9 And he said, If now I have found grace in thy sight, O LORD, let my LORD, I pray thee, go among us; for it is a stiffnecked people; and pardon our iniquity and our sin, and take us for thine inheritance.

10 And he said, Behold, I make a covenant: before all thy people I will do marvels, such as have not been done in all the earth, nor in any nation: and all the people among which thou art shall see the work of the LORD: for it is a terrible thing that I will do with thee.

NLT **Exodus 34:1** Then the LORD told Moses, "Chisel out two stone tablets like the first ones. I will write on them the same words that were on the tablets you smashed."

34:4 So Moses chiseled out two tablets of stone like the first ones. Early in the morning he climbed Mount Sinai as the LORD had commanded him, and he carried the two stone tablets in his hands.

5 Then the LORD came down in a cloud and stood there with him; and he called out his own name, Yahweh.

6 The LORD passed in front of Moses, calling out, "Yahweh! The LORD! The God of compassion and mercy! I am slow to anger and filled with unfailing love and faithfulness.

7 I lavish unfailing love to a thousand generations. I forgive iniquity, rebellion, and sin. But I do not excuse the guilty. I lay the sins of the parents upon their children and grandchildren; the entire family is affected—even children in the third and fourth generations."

8 Moses immediately threw himself to the ground and worshiped.

9 And he said, "O Lord, if it is true that I have found favor with you, then please travel with us. Yes, this is a stubborn and rebellious people, but please forgive our iniquity and our sins. Claim us as your own special possession."

10 The LORD replied, "Listen, I am making a covenant with you in the presence of all your people. I will perform miracles that have never been performed anywhere in all the earth or in any nation. And all the people around you will see the power of the LORD—the awesome power I will display for you."

The People, Places, and Times

Mount Sinai. This is the highest mountain in Egypt. At 2,285 meters high, it is located in the south central part of Sinai Peninsula. God made many revelations of Himself and for the Israelites at Mount Sinai. There, He also gave the Ten Commandments to Moses. The entire peninsula, 150 miles long, is located in the northwestern end of Saudi Arabia and is in the shape of an inverted base. Mount Sinai refers to the mountain peak where God revealed Himself to Moses. Sinai has been referred to as the "mountain of God" (Exodus 3:1) and "mount of the LORD" (Numbers 10:33).

Stone Tablets. The stone tablets, which are inscribed with the Ten Commandments, give insight into the nature of God. There were two sets of stone tablets. In anger, Moses destroyed the first set, which God inscribed, when Moses saw the Israelites worshiping a golden calf. He cut the second set, which was rewritten by God. The tablets, which were stored in the Ark of the Covenant, were rounded off rectangles.

Background

For 400 years, the Israelites were slaves in Egypt, where they were oppressed and cruelly treated. God heard their prayers for deliverance. He sent Moses, a shepherd, to deliver the Israelites and reveal mighty miracles. God revealed His power through 10 calamities or plagues that He inflicted on Egypt. As an act of God, about two million Israelites escaped from Egypt and began the Exodus through the Sinai wilderness in 1446 B.C. In one last attempt, Pharaoh tried to bring the Israelites back to Egypt, but God parted the Red Sea and rescued the Israelites.

In the wilderness, the Israelites complained about the bitter water. Moses prayed to God, and God made the water sweet. God promised to meet the Israelites' needs, but He stipulated that the people must obey Him. After traveling through the wilderness, the Israelites arrived at Mount Sinai. Through His servant, Moses, God gave His people the Law and direction on worshiping at the Tabernacle. God made a covenant with the Israelites and revealed the Law to lead the Israelites to live holy and responsibly. He also gave Moses specific instructions to build a tabernacle, the Tent of Meeting that would be their special place for worship.

At-A-Glance

1. God Instructs Moses (Exodus 34:1)

2. Moses Carries Out God's Instructions on Mount Sinai (v. 4)

3. God's Love and Graciousness (vv. 5–7)

4. Moses Worships God for Who He Is (vv. 8–9)

5. God Renews the Covenant (v. 10)

In Depth

1. God Instructs Moses (Exodus 34:1)

God spoke with Moses and instructed him to cut two new tablets of stone. Previously, God had provided the two tablets and written upon them; but Moses broke them when he was angered by the Israelites' idol worship (32:19). However, this did not deter Sovereign God (He is in control of His universe) from His plan to write the Ten Commandments and give them to His people. Even though the people failed to be obedient, while Moses received instruction from God on Mount Sinai, God was still merciful. He started again and provided instructions for the Israelites to live righteously.

God wanted the Israelites to be a holy nation. So He gave them instructions to obey Him. He did so through the Ten Commandments, which taught them how to live for God both morally and spiritually.

2. Moses Carries Out God's Instructions on Mount Sinai (v. 4)

Moses obeyed God's instructions and cut two more stone tablets. In verses 2–3, God also gave him specific directives that included what time of day to come to Mount Sinai, and he was not to bring anyone with him nor could anyone be seen near the mountain. In addition, neither flocks nor herds could graze in front of the mountain. (Only Moses was allowed to come before God on holy ground; see 34:3.)

Early the next morning Moses obediently went to Mount Sinai as God commanded. He carried the two stone tablets, which were probably made of slate. Although he had chiseled the stones, God would inscribe His handiwork on the tablets.

3. God's Love and Graciousness (vv. 5–7)

In chapter 33 of Exodus, Moses requested to see the glory of God—the presence of God. but Moses was too finite (limited) to see the manifest glory of God. If anyone saw God, they would not live. God, however, came up with a plan. He promised to allow Moses to see Him when God had passed ("from behind," 33:23, NLT). After Moses climbed Mount Sinai, God met him. In 34:5, Moses saw God descend "in the cloud." The cloud that God descended in may have been the same pillar of cloud that led the Israelites by day when they escaped Egypt (13:21). The day before indirectly seeing God, as Moses "entered into the tabernacle, the cloudy pillar descended...and the LORD talked with

Moses" (33:9). Thus, the pillar of a cloud was a visible sign that God was present.

As God passed by, He declared His character and the meaning of the name "Yahweh." God made Himself known by His name, which revealed that God is steadfast, loving, and forgiving. In Hebrew, the word "passed" (*'abar*, **aw-BAR**) is translated "crossed over." In a way that Moses would never forget, God revealed His glory or character, which is gracious, merciful, and long-suffering.

The attributes of God include the benevolent and overwhelming graciousness of God. Because God's character reveals a loyal love, God is good. He consistently cares about humankind. God revealed to Moses that He is truth; therefore, He is faithful and constant. In the book of Numbers, when he prayed for the rebellious people, Moses recorded the attributes or character of God (Numbers 14:18–19). Moses relied on God's love, patience, forgiveness, and mercy when he prayed for the people. In today's lesson, God revealed His glory or character: compassion, constancy, and consistent love. In the midst of Israel's unfaithfulness, God still revealed His love.

The Israelites sinned when they worshiped the golden calf, but because of God's love and mercy, He offered them forgiveness. God willingly offered forgiveness for the sins and transgressions of the Israelites and all people. However, Numbers 14:18 (NLT) declares, "The LORD is slow to anger and filled with unfailing love, forgiving every kind of sin and rebellion. But he does not excuse the guilty. He lays the sins of the parents upon their children; the entire family is affected—even children in the third and fourth generations." Yet, He shows His mercy toward everyone. God's divine grace offers consistent forgiveness to sinners whenever they ask with a repentant heart. Because God is merciful, He offers forgiveness for offenses, transgressions, and sinfulness. When we accept Jesus Christ, we can be confident that our sins will be forgiven.

4. Moses Worships God for Who He Is (vv. 8–9)

Moses was impressed by God's proclamation of His glory. His revelation of His glory to Moses sufficiently answered Moses' request. In response, Moses bowed in humble respect, love, and adoration for God. He honored the name of God and worshiped Him. Moses was thankful for God's goodness and submitted to God's will.

Believers belong to God's family. Therefore, we too should praise God for His goodness, love, and mercy. If we consider the goodness of God, our response should be overflowing praise and thankfulness for God's loving-kindness, forgiveness, and faithful love and mercy.

Moses continued to pray for the Israelites as he asked God to "go among us" (Exodus 34:9). He interceded for the people and asked God to pardon their sins. Moses remembered God's promises and desired that God reverse His judgment to remove Himself from the Israelites' presence (33:1–3). Moses desired that God forgive their sins and His presence remain with His people. God responded to Moses' request.

If God were to remove Himself from our presence, we would be forever lost—eternally separated from the Holy (set apart from sin) God—forever dead. However, like Moses, we can humbly pray to God and trust that God's goodness, love, and mercy are everlasting. When we truly desire God's presence, we will go to Him with a broken and contrite heart. Not only will we experience His presence, but also His glory (His splendor, His grandeur).

5. God Renews the Covenant (v. 10)

Moses interceded for the people and God responded; God restored His covenant with Israel. He promised that the Israelites would experience great things, "marvels, such as have not been done in all the earth, nor in any nation." The covenant blessings from God would be incredible—an awesome God can do incredible things. Because the Israelites remained faithful, God would deliver them from their enemies and any inhabitants in the land of Canaan would be destroyed for the benefit of Israel. Thus through obedience to God, the Israelites would be blessed.

Search the Scriptures

1. What happened to the first set of stone tablets that contained the Ten Commandments (Exodus 32:19)?

2. What did God require Moses to do before he met Him on Mount Sinai (34:1)?

3. What does it mean when God "passed by before" Moses (v. 6)?

Discuss the Meaning

1. Why was Moses unable to gaze upon the glory of God?

2. How is God's glory revealed to believers today?

3. How can sin affect generations in a family "unto the third and to the fourth generation" (Exodus 34:7)?

Lesson in Our Society

Today, the consequences of sin, rebellion, and transgressions against God's commands are not considered by many people in the world. The glory and majesty of God's goodness, love, and mercy are not recognized or praised. Many people have personal agendas that do not include obedience or faithfulness to God. An example of this flawed behavior occurs when some people achieve financial success and their faithfulness to God diminishes.

As believers, God requires His children to faithfully serve Him and with the help of the Holy Spirit, withstand the sinfulness that exists in the world.

Make It Happen

Focus on the attributes of God and His glory. Pray that He will become real in your life. Realize that God's presence dwells within our hearts through the Holy Spirit. Then, pray for God to lead, guide, and direct you to remain committed to serve, obey, and follow Him. If you transgress against God, seek God's forgiveness with a repentant heart.

Follow the Spirit

What God wants me to do:

_____

_____

_____

_____

Remember Your Thoughts

Special insights I have learned:

_____

_____

_____

_____

More Light on the Text

Exodus 34:1, 4–10

1 And the LORD said unto Moses, Hew thee two tables of stone like unto the first: and I will write upon these tables the words that were in the first tables, which thou brakest.

Moses already had been with God on Mount Sinai once, during which God personally inscribed His commandments onto two stone tablets ("tables" in KJV, 31:18). When Moses came down the mountain to deliver God's Laws to the people, however, he found them engaging in idol worship, and understandably, "Moses' anger waxed hot" (32:19). The real problem was not so much the actual worship of the golden calf, as egregious as that was, but the fact that the Israelites had just agreed to God's covenant, that He would be their God and they would be His people, His "peculiar treasure" (19:3–8). No one had forced them to agree to the covenant; rather, they readily agreed. After all, they had just witnessed God's miraculous deliverance from the hands of the Egyptians, as well as His ongoing guidance and provision in the wilderness. Even though the Israelites had persistently grumbled and complained, He still delivered them; took care of their every need (manna and water), and even some of their wants (quail); and guided them day and night with pillars of cloud and fire, bringing them to a place of freedom and safety.

34:4 And he hewed two tables of stone like unto the first; and Moses rose up early in the morning, and went up unto mount Sinai, as the LORD had commanded him, and took in his hand the two tables of stone.

Through Moses, who has become the official mediator for the Israelites (a prefiguring of Christ), God is going to give the Israelites another chance. The Lord has commanded Moses to chisel out another two tablets. God knows it is important for Israel always to have in their possession an inscribed set of tablets containing His Laws—which soon would be housed in the Ark of the Covenant (1 Kings 8:9; Hebrews 9:4). After giving instructions to clear the base of the mountain (Exodus 34:2–3), Moses obediently ascends Mount Sinai a second time (see 19:20). Where would Israel be without their faithful mediator—indeed, where would the church be without our faithful Mediator, Jesus Christ?

5 And the LORD descended in the cloud, and stood with him there, and proclaimed the name of the LORD.

God descends upon Sinai for the second time in a cloud, which most scholars believe was the *Shekinah* glory, the same "thick cloud" that had enveloped Moses during the first trip up the mountain, and which also had been accompanied by thunder and lightning, as well as a piercingly loud trumpet (19:16). While the Hebrew for "cloud" in its normal use is `anan (**aw-NAWN**), what distinguishes this use from other, similar instances is that it represents God's presence, as in some form of the phrase "cloud of the LORD" (40:38), "glory of the LORD" (16:10), or other such direct associations with God's presence. This was the same *Shekinah* cloud (or *Shekinah* glory) that had guided the Israelites by day during their exodus from Egypt (13:21–22); the same cloud that had descended on Moses and the Tent of Meeting (33:9–10); and the same "pillar of cloud" that was to descend on the newly built tabernacle (40:34–35), and of which both the Old and New Testaments spoke frequently.

6 And the LORD passed by before him, and proclaimed, The LORD, The LORD God, merciful and gracious, longsuffering, and abundant in goodness and truth,

An interesting and instructional method to extract core meanings from passages in Scripture is to examine the verbs and verb phrases. The verbs in Exodus 34:4–9 reveal an interesting comparison between the actions of Moses and the actions of God. Indeed, with a little imagination, the essence of the entire story can be read with only the following 10 verbs, alternating between actors:

GOD	MOSES
Commanded	Chiseled
Descended	Ascended
Stood	Bowed
Passed	Called
Proclaimed	Prayed

One of the Hebrew words used in verse 6 is exceptionally significant for many reasons. KJV's "goodness" comes from the Hebrew *checed* (**KHEH-sed**). *Checed* is translated variously as "lovingkindness" (NASB), "love" (NIV), "goodness" (NKJV), "unfailing love" (NLT), "steadfast love" (ESV), and other synonyms. *Checed* also is essential theologically, being applicable throughout Scripture, as attested by its extremely prolific usage throughout the Old Testament—approximately 250 uses in all its variations.

It is specifically because God's heart is "abundant" with *checed* and because His nature is *checed* that He is in the process here of renewing His covenant with Israel. God had the choice to either condemn or forgive His people for their shameful rebellion after He had just performed so many miracles for them. That He chose to forgive them proved both His faithfulness and His goodness, His *checed*.

7 Keeping mercy for thousands, forgiving iniquity and transgression and sin, and that will by no means clear the guilty; visiting the iniquity of the fathers upon the children, and upon the children's children, unto the third and to the fourth generation.

Comparing translations is often helpful. In this case, comparing with the ESV, God's divine grace and mercy—being "slow to anger, and abounding in steadfast love [*checed*] and faithfulness, keeping steadfast love [*checed*] for thousands, forgiving iniquity and transgression and sin" (vv. 6–7, ESV)—are balanced by His divinely just belief in the covenant He made with the Children of Israel, because He does not "clear the guilty; visiting the iniquity of the fathers on the children and the children's children, to the third and the fourth generation" (v. 7).

Many preachers and teachers have struggled with the meaning and implications of verse 7. Many are familiar with the tragic repetition of children of alcoholics, for example, becoming alcoholics themselves, or abused children becoming abusers, too. An intervention by Christ is the only hope to break the chains of generational sins and the long-term effects of those sins.

8 And Moses made haste, and bowed his head toward the earth, and worshipped. 9 And he said, If now I have found grace in thy sight, O Lord, let my Lord, I pray thee, go among us; for it is a stiffnecked people; and pardon our iniquity and our sin, and take us for thine inheritance.

All those who remember their first revelation of God's love surely remember their response, which was worship, or returned love. How could Moses have responded otherwise during an actual theophany, an in-person meeting with the living God?

On the subject of Israel's sin, Moses' prayer in verse 9 uses all three of the main Hebrew words for disobedience to God in the Old Testament—"stiffnecked" or wicked (*qasheh*, **kaw-SHEH**), "iniquity" or rebellion (*avon*, **aw-VONE**), and "sin" (*chatta'ah*, **khat-taw-AW**). In Ronald Youngblood's words, "'*Wickedness*' is literally the 'bending' or 'twisting' of God's will and purpose, '*rebellion*' is open revolt against God's commands, and '*sin*' (by far the most common term) is 'missing the mark,' or goal, that God has set for us" (emphasis added, 134). It is this level of egregiousness to which Moses confesses and pleads on behalf of Israel, the three-synonym description of which underlines just how far from true worship they had fallen. In juxtaposition, the passage also illustrates how great was God's forgiveness, demonstrating fully His worthiness for their true worship. God's "abundant...goodness" (34:6) or *checed* was diametrically opposite the Israelites' "steadfast rebellion," and proved beyond question His self-description of being compassionate, gracious, slow to anger, and abounding in *checed* and faithfulness.

10 And he said, Behold, I make a covenant: before all thy people I will do marvels, such as have not been done in all the earth, nor in any nation: and all the people among which thou art shall see the work of the LORD: for it is a terrible thing that I will do with thee.

While God's response to Moses' prayer technically is an official relaunching of the recently broken covenant, essentially He reiterates the prior agreed-upon covenant, which also had been accompanied by a great display of God's power. In Hebrew, "covenant" is *b@riyth* (**ber-EETH**), which means "a promise" or "agreement," which is deeply felt and to be strictly honored.

Say It Correctly

Mount Horeb. 'ho˙r-ˌeb.
Pentateuch. 'pen-tə-ˌtük, -ˌtyük.
Shekinah. shuh-KI-nuh.

Daily Bible Readings

M: God's Mercy
Psalm 57:1–5

T: God's Faithfulness
Lamentations 3:22–26

W: God's Forgiveness
Psalm 103:1–5

T: God's Justice
Psalm 103:6–10

F: God's Compassion
Psalm 103:11–16

S: God's Steadfast Love
Psalm 103:17–22

S: God's Inheritance
Exodus 34:1, 4–10

Notes

55

Teaching Tips

1. Words You Should Know

A. Ordained (Psalm 8:2–3) *yacad* (Heb.)—Established and founded by God.

B. Strength (v. 2) *'oz* (Heb.)—Boldness and power.

2. Teacher Preparation

Unifying Principle—Caring for Creation. Psalm 8 declares that the sovereign God sustains creation, but God expects humans to share responsibility for the care of all living things.

A. Study the entire lesson, including the Daily Bible Readings.

B. Gather interesting photographs of human beings as well as nature and galactic scenes.

C. Secure a recording of a worshipful song, such as "Great Is Thy Faithfulness."

3. Open the Lesson

A. As the class gathers, play the recording of "Great Is Thy Faithfulness" and display the photos. Encourage meditation as class members view the photos.

B. After ample time, use the Aim for Change and Keep in Mind verse in a prayer.

C. Have a volunteer read the In Focus story, and use it to segue into today's theme and discussion.

4. Present the Scriptures

A. Have the class read Psalm 8 silently as one member with an expressive voice reads the text aloud.

B. Use The People, Places, and Times; Background; At-A-Glance; In Depth; Search the Scriptures questions; and More Light on the Text to help clarify meaning.

5. Explore the Meaning

A. Use the Discuss the Meaning and Lesson in Our Society sections to help lead a discussion on how we can better praise, worship, and honor God by being good stewards of His creation.

B. Also use both sections to help your students learn how to take time each day to praise God.

6. Next Steps for Application

A. Have the class read Make It Happen and discuss the suggestions listed for making a difference in the community.

B. Brainstorm additional suggestions and write them under Follow the Spirit and Remember Your Thoughts.

C. Close with prayer, worshiping God for His majesty and faithfulness.

Worship Guide

For the Superintendent or Teacher
Theme: God's Majesty and Human Dignity
Theme Song: "Great Is Thy Faithfulness"
Devotional Reading: Genesis 1:26–31
Prayer

God's Majesty and Human Dignity

Bible Background • PSALM 8
Printed Text • PSALM 8 | Devotional Reading • GENESIS 1:26–31

—— Aim for Change ——

By the end of the lesson, we will: TELL how God is sovereign and sustains humankind and creation; EXPRESS appreciation for God's sustaining roles; and COMMIT to stewardship over the work of God's hand.

OCT 3rd

In Focus

After a seven-mile run through the park, Stephanie said, "Don't forget the Community Awareness seminar today! My friend, Dr. Edwards, is the organizer for the fifth year in a row. We plant trees and meet organizers in the community who promote the Community Earth Project. I still help out with several projects on recycling and conserving energy. It's a great initiative to care for God's creation. I hope we can join a project together!"

After a few seconds, Aisha said, "I believe that God knows exactly what He wants to do with His earth. He hasn't needed me this far, so I think God can handle it."

When Aisha and Stephanie arrived, Dr. Edwards greeted them. Stephanie introduced Aisha to Dr. Edwards.

"It's a pleasure to meet you, Aisha," Dr. Edwards said. "I hope we can use your project management skills as we organize the various grant cycles and writers. We don't want to miss an opportunity to apply and receive a community grant."

Aisha listened as Dr. Edwards listed the federal, state, and local companies that funded their project to care for the earth.

In today's lesson, Psalm 8 praises God for His majesty and sustaining power in all the earth and invites us to do the same.

—— Keep in Mind ——

"Thou madest him to have dominion over the works of thy hands; thou hast put all things under his feet" (Psalm 8:6).

"Thou madest him to have dominion over the works of thy hands; thou hast put all things under his feet" (Psalm 8:6).

Focal Verses

KJV **Psalm 8:1** O LORD our Lord, how excellent is thy name in all the earth! who hast set thy glory above the heavens.

2 Out of the mouth of babes and sucklings hast thou ordained strength because of thine enemies, that thou mightest still the enemy and the avenger.

3 When I consider thy heavens, the work of thy fingers, the moon and the stars, which thou hast ordained;

4 What is man, that thou art mindful of him? and the son of man, that thou visitest him?

5 For thou hast made him a little lower than the angels, and hast crowned him with glory and honour.

6 Thou madest him to have dominion over the works of thy hands; thou hast put all things under his feet:

7 All sheep and oxen, yea, and the beasts of the field;

8 The fowl of the air, and the fish of the sea, and whatsoever passeth through the paths of the seas.

9 O LORD our Lord, how excellent is thy name in all the earth!

NLT **Psalm 8:1** O LORD, our Lord, your majestic name fills the earth! Your glory is higher than the heavens.

2 You have taught children and infants to tell of your strength, silencing your enemies and all who oppose you.

3 When I look at the night sky and see the work of your fingers—the moon and the stars you set in place—

4 what are mere mortals that you should think about them, human beings that you should care for them?

5 Yet you made them only a little lower than God and crowned them with glory and honor.

6 You gave them charge of everything you made, putting all things under their authority—

7 the flocks and the herds and all the wild animals,

8 the birds in the sky, the fish in the sea, and everything that swims the ocean currents.

9 O LORD, our Lord, your majestic name fills the earth!

The People, Places, and Times

David. The name "David" means "favorite" or "beloved." David was born in Jerusalem and was the son of Jesse. David had several wives who included Michal, Ahinoam, Bathsheba, and Abigal. He fathered four sons, Absalom, Amnon, Solomon, Adonijah, and one daughter, Tamar. David was the ancestor of Jesus and the greatest human king of Israel, who ruled from 1005 to 965 B.C. God described David as "a man after His [God's] own heart" (1 Samuel 13:14). However, he was not perfect; he sinned greatly many times and genuinely repented to God. Even though David was a liar, adulterer, murderer, and betrayer, on the positive side, he was a musician, singer, and composer of poems. As king, David was the first to unite Judah and Israel. He wrote Psalm 8, the focus of today's lesson, a psalm of praise that reveals a view of God as Creator—His hand in nature and the responsibility of humanity. In essence, this psalm reveals David's love for God's creation.

Creation. Creation is the universe, the world, and everything in the earth. It points to God's existence and helps us to have faith. Without faith in God, we do not believe that God exists and created the universe. His creation is valuable because it is a reflection of God's love.

Gittith. This musical instrument resembles a Spanish guitar that, in ancient times, provided a musical tune or tempo during a ceremony or festival. Psalm 8 was to be sung to the tune or tempo of the gittith. The tempo may have been a popular marching tempo used in the land of Gath.

Background

The Psalms provide poetry for the worship and praise and confession of God. David, the greatest king of Israel, wrote 73 psalms. Other writers of the psalms and the number of psalms they wrote include: Asaph (12), sons of Korah (9), Solomon (2), Herman (1), Ethan (1), and Moses (1). The writers of 51 psalms are unknown. The psalms are also a collection of songs and prayers for heartfelt worship and the expression of the soul. The writers of the psalms pour their emotions into their confessions and reflections of God's love and friendship.

The book of Psalms is divided into five sections called "books." Psalms 1–41 is the first book. Therefore, Psalm 8 is contained in the first book. David is credited with writing 37 of the 41 psalms. In the first book, the name most frequently used for God is "LORD" or "Yahweh."

Psalm 8 is a worship psalm that praises God. King David wrote the psalm for "the chief Musician" ("the director of music," NIV; or "choir director," NLT) to play upon the "Gittith," a musical instrument associated with Gath, a Philistine city. The term "Gittith" may speak to a rhythm or song that followed the work of the grape treaders in the wine press. Psalm 8 also describes the artistry of God's creative hand in the universe. David writes that "thou [God] has made him [man] a little lower than the angels" (Psalm 8:5). This verse points to Jesus Christ, who offers humanity restoration through faith.

At-A-Glance

1. The Glory of God (Psalm 8:1–2)

2. The Revelation of God (vv. 3–5)

3. The Role of Stewardship (vv. 6–8)

4. God Is Worthy of Praise (v. 9)

In Depth

1. The Glory of God (Psalm 8:1–2)

King David recognizes the glory of God that is seen throughout the heavens and earth. He sees and extols that God is excellent and amazing in the entire universe. David writes, "O LORD, our Lord" to praise and exalt God, who sits above the universe. God is most high and sovereign (in control of His universe and never out of control) over all. As God's children, we should praise God for His glory that is beyond expression and human comprehension. David addresses God as "LORD," which stands in for "YHWH" in Hebrew. The Hebrew language does not use vowels. The word "YHWH" was considered too holy to pronounce; therefore, David and others used "Adonai" or "LORD."

The psalmist describes God by His name and His glory. When God spoke to Moses, He told Moses, "I AM THAT I AM" (Exodus 3:14). God is the one and only God. Because God is eternal, the promises God made with the fathers over 400 years ago would be completed through Moses.

David expresses that the name of God reveals God's attributes and the person of God to everyone. When believers acknowledge God, we believe He is Lord and He is our Lord. We recognize that God is the Creator, who made us, provides for us, and cares for us. God is magnificent because He is the Creator and Provider of everything. Psalm 8 expresses the sovereignty of God that is completely awe-inspiring because God is the Creator of all things. God's power, glory, and presence are awesomely expressed through all things that are living. When we look at God's creation, we see the display of God's glory, which is who He is. God reveals Himself to human beings to prompt worship, adoration, and praise.

In verse 2, David reveals that humans cannot express the praise of God because His majesty is beyond expression. Our praise of God sounds like the babbling of "children and infants" (NLT), who cannot speak intelligibly but reveal God's love and power, because God created them (Psalm 8:2). Nevertheless, when humankind praises God, the enemy is silenced. At the same time, believers must praise and trust God like children. When believers have childlike faith, we can completely depend on God and remove any self-sufficient tendencies. Just as a baby completely depends on someone to care for him or her, believers must completely depend upon God to sustain and provide.

2. The Revelation of God (vv. 3–5)

David expresses that God's fingers created the universe. The vastness of God is evident when compared to the minuteness of the universe. Like David, believers should be in awe of the wonders and splendor of nature and praise God. Because David refers to aspects of God's creation that are seen at night (e.g., moon and stars), he may have recognized the greatness of God as he walked after dark.

David meditated, worshiped, and reflected upon the greatness of God. He realized that all creation pointed to God, the Creator. While David reflects, he asks God why He has consideration for humans, who are weak and sinful. God not only considers, but cares for humans. Just as the universe is small when compared to the Creator, likewise, humanity is much smaller and less significant, yet God's love sustains His children.

The author of Hebrews reiterates verses 4–5. In Hebrews 2, believers are reminded that God sent Jesus Christ to die for the world's sins and offer eternal life to humanity that believes by faith. The author of Hebrews reveals how Jesus is the ultimate example of a "son of man" (Hebrews 2:6), who has been given the authority to rule over creation and who will ultimately reign over everything on the Last Day when everyone will see Him crowned with glory.

3. The Role of Stewardship (vv. 6–8)

David emphasizes humankind's purpose, the role of stewardship. God created humans to have dominion over creation, and humanity is responsible to care for creation wisely. God's Word tells us that He created us in His likeness to "have dominion over the fish of the sea...the fowl of the air... over every living thing that moveth upon the earth" (Genesis 1:28). This means that God has ultimate dominion over Creation, but He has instructed us to have authority over and responsibility for the environment and creatures that inhabit the earth. But we must not be careless. In fact, God desires that people care for both the earth and creatures with love and compassion.

Humanity has a unique relationship with creation. God has created us to be His representative to rule over creation. We have a unique command from God, which separates us from the rest of creation. God gives this divine instruction to accomplish and fulfill His purpose through us. Humanity is purposed by God to have dominion over God's works, which means not only environmental concerns, but also everything related to the flourishing of creation, from politics to education to art.

4. God Is Worthy of Praise (v. 9)

After David explains that humanity has dominion over the environment, he again praises the divine name of God, the Sovereign Lord. David admires the divine greatness and glory of God, which is revealed through God's goodness to us. God's love is even revealed in the very creation of humanity. The close of Psalm 8 reminds believers that God is in control and God created us to praise Him, who is holy, sovereign, and worthy to be praised. David calls upon us in this psalm to reflect and meditate on the glory of God.

Search the Scriptures

1. How does David express the greatness of God when He writes, "O LORD our Lord" (Psalm 8:1)?

2. Why does the praise of God quiet the enemy (v. 2)?

Discuss the Meaning

1. Why does childlike faith allow believers to be more open to praise, worship, and honor God?

2. How can believers obey God's instruction to have dominion over creation and fulfill God's purpose?

Lesson in Our Society

In today's society, people are focused on selfish agendas and self-serving motives. Few people acknowledge or praise God until they need or want something. These individuals do not praise God because He is God, but for His provisions and blessings. However, the psalmist praised God because He is all-powerful, great, holy, and majestic—for who God is, not just because He answered a prayer or need. He praised God because God's wonders of nature are majestic and God's name is excellent. Remember to take time each day to praise God.

Make It Happen

Pray for God's instruction to lead His children to be responsible and care for God's creation. Pray for God to help you to take time to focus on God's creation and praise Him. Then thank God that you are created in His image with a God-given purpose. Remember that you are valuable and important to Him.

Follow the Spirit

What God wants me to do:

_____

_____

_____

_____

Remember Your Thoughts

Special insights I have learned:

_____

_____

_____

_____

More Light on the Text

Psalm 8

Introduction:

From start to finish, this "creation" psalm praises God, and is the first "praise" psalm in the Hebrew Psalter (hymnal). Even though it does not follow the traditional form of a praise psalm, with an invitation to praise and reasons to praise, it does have a typical inclusion. This means that the first words and the last words are the same, forming bookends or an envelope around the content. One writer described the psalm as the first "non-lament" psalm in Book One, Psalms 1–41 (Walford, 67). Another called it an "articulation of creation

faith" (Brueggemann, 36). Brueggemann also called Psalm 8 a "hymn of creation praise" and a "song of creation," (28) and Frank E. Gaebelein called it a "masterful composition" (1991). In essence, all agree, and putting them together, the picture becomes abundantly clear: "An articulate hymn of creation praise and masterful song of creation faith."

1 O LORD our Lord, how excellent is thy name in all the earth! who hast set thy glory above the heavens.

The word "LORD" is *Y@hovah* (**yeh-ho-VAH**) in Hebrew, more commonly spelled *Yahweh* (many scholars simply use the Hebrew spelling with consonants only, *YHWH*), which is God's name. The second word for God in verse 1 is *'adonay* (**ad-o-NOY**) in Hebrew, which means "lord, king, or ruler," and can refer to God or man. Because of the psalm's context of creation, the opening salutation can be interpreted, "O Creator, our King!" or "O God, our Ruler!" *Expositor's Bible Commentary* worded it, "The Redeemer-King of Israel is the Creator" (110).

"Excellent" comes from the Hebrew word *'addiyr* (**ad-DEER**), which means "mighty," "great one," or "majestic" (ESV, NASB, NIV). While it can refer to waters, trees, nations, gods, or even servants, in this context, it clearly references a royal attribute. John Goldingay reminds us that this is not an aloof recognition: "The response then is not merely wonder or admiration, but deferent submission" (155). The glorious King Yahweh has generously showered the earth with His own glory, and in turn all creation gives abundant evidence to the glory of His name.

It is noteworthy to point out that only God's people are fully aware of His glory, and can genuinely ascribe the glory of creation to His name. Those whose minds are blinded by sin cannot see or know God, or even recognize whose glory surrounds them for their entire lives—yet they will be held accountable for not making the connection (Romans 1:20). Many superlatives could have been chosen, and all would be applicable, yet none would fully capture the inexpressible glory of God. His glory for now is only fully appreciated by the heavenly creatures, but soon the redeemed will see it firsthand for eternity, and all present suffering will be forgotten in an instant (2 Corinthians 4:17; 1 Peter 5:10).

2 Out of the mouth of babes and sucklings hast thou ordained strength because of thine enemies, that thou mightest still the enemy and the avenger.

While here "babes and sucklings" ("babes and nursing infants," NKJV; "children and infants," NIV) are imbued with strength from the Creator, Matthew 21:15–16 references the same phrase "babes and sucklings" in the similar context of them emitting perfect praise. Jesus exhorts that those who do not come to God as little children will never enter His kingdom (Mark 10:15). Thus, in the mouths of infants and children are found not only perfect praise, but also perfect faith, which effectively stops the enemy in his tracks. As one might expect, various uses of the phrase are found in the Old Testament, as if underlining that God is fully aware of humankind's vulnerability and inherent weakness, since after all, every human once was a nursing infant. Several members of the animal kingdom are able to survive on their own after birth or hatching, but no human infant could survive without being cared for and protected. Regardless of how weak and vulnerable, God is all the strength any child or adult needs.

The word "ordained" (Heb. *yacad*, **ya-SAD**) means "to found, fix, appoint," or "establish,"

as in "ordaining" a foundation, such as during the act of creation (see Job 38:4; Psalm 24:2; 102:25; 104:5, 8; and Isaiah 48:13). *Yacad* also is used throughout the Old Testament to refer to the physical foundation of the temple at Jerusalem (1 Kings 5:17; Ezra 3:10; Psalm 78:69; see also Numbers 24:23 regarding life itself being given only by God). What God establishes, no enemy can overcome. This is eloquently described in the classic verse, Isaiah 28:16: "I lay in Zion for a foundation a stone, a tried stone, a precious corner stone, a sure foundation." By the same token, the inverse also is true—not only is God the One who establishes the foundations of creation, life, and salvation, but of equal importance is the fact that "other foundation can no man lay than that is laid, which is Jesus Christ" (1 Corinthians 3:11).

3 When I consider thy heavens, the work of thy fingers, the moon and the stars, which thou hast ordained;

Here the speaker changes voices, from second person plural to first person singular. The language of God's fingers at work in creation lends itself to the image of a personal relationship with a very personally involved, hands-on type of God—not at all a distant, impersonal force or intelligence that indiscriminately issues power or change. In sharp contrast to someone who would leave God out of the equation, the psalmist recognizes God's handiwork in every corner of creation. The first of two primary arenas of creation—heaven and earth (Job 38:33; Psalm 89:11)—are in view; this includes all celestial bodies, each of which has an appointed place over which humankind has no control and no authority (Isaiah 40:26). The psalmist says, "The heaven, even the heavens, are the LORD's: but the earth hath he given to the children of men" (Psalm 115:16).

4 What is man, that thou art mindful of him? and the son of man, that thou visitest him?

This verse, which is found nearly verbatim in Job 7:17 and Psalm 144:3, is an example of parallelism, a poetic device found throughout Old Testament poetry. The rhetorical question is framed in two parts, much like a proverb, in which one line redefines and reinforces the other. "Man" (Heb. *'enowsh*, **en-OSHE**) is paired in meaning with "son of man" (from two Hebrew words, *ben 'adam*, **bane aw-DAM**), although the latter has a literal translation in English of "ruddy-skinned people; Nazarites." The word "mindful" (Heb. *paqad*, **paw-KAD**) is paired with "visitest" (Heb. *zakar*, **zaw-KAR**), which also means "called to mind," or "kept in mind." In other words, *mortal man* is paired with *human being*, and God's *thinking* is paired with God's *actions*. Verse 4 does not seek an answer to the two-part rhetorical question, but rather is a continuation of the wonder begun in verse 3. Even as the psalmist ponders how insignificant he is, compared to the vastness of the universe and the incomprehensible glory of God, at the same time he realizes that God chose to care for humans and even to place them at the center of all creation. On one hand, there is the all-powerful Creator, and on the other hand, there is flawed, finite (limited), mortal humanity.

5 For thou hast made him a little lower than the angels, and hast crowned him with glory and honour. 6 Thou madest him to have dominion over the works of thy hands; thou hast put all things under his feet:

For reasons not entirely known, the incredible truth is that not only is God "mindful" of humanity and not only does He "attend" to us, He also crowns us with "glory

and honour" (Heb. *kabowd*, **kaw-BODE**, *hadar*, **ha-DAR**). These verses are strongly reminiscent of the creation story in Genesis (1:1–2:3). Also, *kabowd* is the same Hebrew word used for the *Shekinah* glory, which Moses witnessed on Mount Sinai and which filled the Tabernacle (Exodus 24:16, 40:34). Additionally, glory and honor are God's attributes, to which dozens of Scriptures attest (e.g., Psalm 96:6, 104:1, 145:5; Isaiah 2:19), yet here they also become attributes of humankind. We are the crowning glory of God's creation, the highest of all creatures, except the angels.

While humanity is not divine, we are just short of divine. As many say, "we all carry the spark of the divine." Similarly, Goldingay refers to German theologian Werner H. Schmidt, whose views on Psalm 8 position humankind, commissioned by God, between Him and the rest of the world (159). All of this endorses and reinforces the original Creation account in which we are made "in the image of God" and "in the likeness of God" (Genesis 1:26–27; 5:1; 9:6). Even though our present glory has been corrupted, it still has not been obliterated. Even the Fall was not enough to completely erase God's glory from humankind. Not only that, but we will once again be perfect, as we once were (1 Corinthians 13:10; 15:53; 1 John 3:2).

God did not intend for us to be idle on earth; He created us for a purpose—to have "dominion" (Heb. *mashal*, **maw-SHAL**) over creation, where all things have been placed under our authority. Nancy deClaissé-Walford observes, "Thus we see God engaging humanity in a kind of partnership in the care of creation" (69). First, we are endowed with attributes normally assigned exclusively to God, and then we are given what normally would be divine authority to have dominion over any part of God's creation.

7 All sheep and oxen, yea, and the beasts of the field; 8 The fowl of the air, and the fish of the sea, and whatsoever passeth through the paths of the seas.

From such verses as these should spring many sermons on our responsibility over creation, and all that proper stewardship of the planet entails. While some would heap guilt endlessly on all humankind's many failings, a more realistic (and biblical) view is to take up the yoke that is not a burden (Matthew 11:30), and gladly shoulder what has been given to us to responsibly bear. Even so, all of creation, along with all of humankind, groans for its deliverance (Romans 8:22). An interesting perspective of Psalm 8:7–8 is that none of the animals are able to govern the others: fish are unable to teach cattle, cattle are unable to school fish, and birds are unable to do more than pester both, at best, occasionally snatching a fish from the surface or picking meat from a carcass. Oxen have four legs but no fingers; apes can walk upright and have fingers but no real ingenuity, at least not enough to rule the planet, in spite of Hollywood's most creative projections. Only humankind is given the ability both to enter and rule over all domains and all creatures on the planet; only human animals are made in the image of God. They alone are the recipient of the sacrificial, atoning blood of the Lamb.

9 O LORD our Lord, how excellent is thy name in all the earth!

The inclusion repeats the first part of verse 1, and thus encapsulates the psalm with the repeated words of praise. The return to a focus on God takes the focus off of self, as if anticipating how even mentioning our position as a steward on earth might tempt some to leave the emphasis there, rather than returning to a position of praise of the Creator, and implied trust and confidence in His sustaining power, His sovereign direction and guidance, and His ultimate unveiling of His purposes and direction for each of our lives. In Brueggemann's words, "Human power is always bounded and surrounded by divine praise" (37).

Say It Correctly

Abigail. AB-ih-gayl.
Absalom. AB-suh-luhm.
Adonijah. ad-oh-NI-juh.
Amnon. AM-non; AM-nuhn.
Gittith. GIT-ith; GIH-tith.
Tamar. TAY-mahr.

Daily Bible Readings

M: A Faithful Creator
1 Peter 4:12–19

T: The Creator of the Earth
Isaiah 45:9–13

W: God Rules Over All
1 Chronicles 29:10–16

T: Remember Your Creator
Ecclesiastes 12:1–8

F: All God's Works Give Thanks
Psalm 145:8–13

S: God's Image in Humanity
Genesis 1:26–31

S: God's Majesty in All the Earth
Psalm 8

Teaching Tips

1. Words You Should Know

A. Law (Psalm 19:7) *Torah* (Heb.)—God's commandments.

B. Faults (v. 12) *chet'* (Heb.)—Crimes, sins.

C. Dominion (v. 13) *mashal* (Heb.)—To rule or reign.

2. Teacher Preparation

Unifying Principle—Seeking Wisdom. Psalm 19 affirms that God's perfect Law protects and sustains creation.

A. Prayerfully read the entire lesson, including the Daily Bible Readings, which shed particular light on Psalm 19.

B. Create a four-column sheet for use in class. Label columns: "The Law," "Is," "Does What," and "Why."

C. Prepare a flip chart and marker to record class responses.

3. Open the Lesson

A. Open with prayer, using the Aim for Change and Keep in Mind verse.

B. Have class members raise their hands to agree or disagree with the statement, "Even today, we must keep God's Law." Record the responses on the flip chart. Discuss.

C. After reading the In Focus story, discuss one of the most important tenets of life that Eric (at first) and Elijah did not understand.

D. Use the story to segue into today's lesson.

4. Present the Scriptures

A. Have volunteers read the Focal Verses.

B. Use The People, Places, and Times; Background; At-A-Glance; In Depth; Search the Scriptures questions; and More Light on the Text to help clarify the meaning.

5. Explore the Meaning

A. Using the Discuss the Meaning and Lesson in Our Society sections, explore the meaning of the text for life today.

B. Stress that we as believers should reflect on our attitudes toward keeping God's Laws, and also give Him thanks for the Laws that He gave to help lead and guide us.

6. Next Steps for Application

A. Read and discuss the Make It Happen section.

B. Then ask, "How can temporary rewards and accolades in the world lead us away from a life with God?"

C. Have your students write an answer under the Follow the Spirit section and continue under Remember Your Thoughts, if they need more space.

D. Close with prayer.

Worship Guide

For the Superintendent or Teacher
Theme: God's Law Sustains
Theme Song: "Thank You, Lord"
Devotional Reading: 1 Chronicles 22:7–13
Prayer

OCT
10th

God's Law Sustains

Bible Background • PSALM 19
Printed Text • PSALM 19:7–14 | Devotional Reading • 1 CHRONICLES 22:7–13

———— Aim for Change ————

By the end of the lesson, we will: EXPLAIN how God's Laws sustain His creation; REFLECT on our attitudes toward keeping God's Laws; and GIVE thanks to God for His Laws.

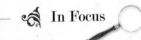
In Focus

Eric and Elijah had constant academic and athletic successes. After working as summer interns while in college, they were offered lucrative employment with several companies. However, neither Eric nor Elijah had a consistent relationship with God. Although they were both raised in Christian families, they were more focused on worldly accolades, instead of a life with God.

One Friday after work, Eric said, "Elijah, I have tickets for a two-day men's conference. My director thought I would enjoy it. Let's grab something quick for dinner and go to the conference."

Elijah said, "I pass...maybe tomorrow night. I'm watching the NBA playoffs tonight. You know I can't miss the Lakers!"

On Monday morning before work, Eric and Elijah went to the gym. As they worked out, Eric said, "The conference was amazing! I was encouraged and inspired by the men who professed their love for God. The message was, 'Where Is Your Reward?' I gave my life to God. I realized that I left God out of my life."

God's Law sustains, but Eric (at first) and Elijah did not understand this important tenet of life. What had Eric and Elijah missed when they did not have a relationship with God?

———— Keep in Mind ————

"The law of the LORD is perfect, converting the soul: the testimony of the LORD is sure, making wise the simple. The statutes of the LORD are right, rejoicing the heart: the commandment of the LORD is pure, enlightening the eyes" (Psalm 19:7–8).

"The law of the LORD is perfect, converting the soul: the testimony of the LORD is sure, making wise the simple. The statutes of the LORD are right, rejoicing the heart: the commandment of the LORD is pure, enlightening the eyes" (Psalm 19:7–8).

Focal Verses

KJV **Psalm 19:7** The law of the LORD is perfect, converting the soul: the testimony of the LORD is sure, making wise the simple.

8 The statutes of the LORD are right, rejoicing the heart: the commandment of the LORD is pure, enlightening the eyes.

9 The fear of the LORD is clean, enduring for ever: the judgments of the LORD are true and righteous altogether.

10 More to be desired are they than gold, yea, than much fine gold: sweeter also than honey and the honeycomb.

11 Moreover by them is thy servant warned: and in keeping of them there is great reward.

12 Who can understand his errors? cleanse thou me from secret faults.

13 Keep back thy servant also from presumptuous sins; let them not have dominion over me: then shall I be upright, and I shall be innocent from the great transgression.

14 Let the words of my mouth, and the meditation of my heart, be acceptable in thy sight, O LORD, my strength, and my redeemer.

NLT **Psalm 19:7** The instructions of the LORD are perfect, reviving the soul. The decrees of the LORD are trustworthy, making wise the simple.

8 The commandments of the LORD are right, bringing joy to the heart.

9 Reverence for the LORD is pure, lasting forever. The laws of the LORD are true; each one is fair.

10 They are more desirable than gold, even the finest gold. They are sweeter than honey, even honey dripping from the comb.

11 They are a warning to your servant, a great reward for those who obey them.

12 How can I know all the sins lurking in my heart? Cleanse me from these hidden faults.

13 Keep your servant from deliberate sins! Don't let them control me. Then I will be free of guilt and innocent of great sin.

14 May the words of my mouth and the meditation of my heart be pleasing to you, O LORD, my rock and my redeemer.

The People, Places, and Times

The Law. Written by Moses, the *Torah*, which means "instrument" or "direction," is the first five books of the Old Testament. It is also known as the "Pentateuch" and is called the "Mosaic" Law or "Divine" Law. The first five books of the Old Testament, as well as the Old Testament as a whole, reveal the entire set of legal and religious instructions that God gave, through Moses, for God's people. Terms that are synonymous for the "Law" include commandments, ordinances, statutes, legal regulations, authoritative instructions, and teachings. The Law presents God's knowledge in order to provide divine instruction that governs and defines human affairs.

Obedience to the Law expressed the Israelites' covenant relationship with God. As part of the covenant, they were to obey God and God would bless and care for His people. Obedience to the Law requires a commitment to God.

Septuagint. The Septuagint, which means "seventy," is the ancient Greek translation of the Hebrew Old Testament by 70 Jewish scholars. The translation, which is one of the oldest Hebrew to Greek translations, occurred between 3 B.C. and 1 B.C. in Alexandria.

The Ten Commandments. The Ten Commandments, or Decalogue, is a list of God's instructions and Laws for right living given to Moses at Sinai, God's holy mountain. Obedience to the Ten Commandments leads to future blessings, while disobedience leads to God's judgment. The first four statements of the Ten Commandments protect the rights of the covenant Lord, while the last six commandments protect the rights of the covenant community. God is concerned about our relationship to Him as well as our relationship to each other.

Psalm. The term "psalm" is a Hebrew title that means "praise." The Greek word "*psalmoi*" means "songs," and suggests the idea of "songs of praise" or "praise songs." There are 150 psalms in the book of Psalms. David is credited with writing 70 psalms. At least 14 of the 70 psalms are connected with specific events in David's life and reveal David's relationship with God.

Background

The book of Psalms is a collection of songs and prayers expressed through 150 individual psalms. The book of Psalms covers a 1,000–year period, from around 1440 B.C. (the time of Moses) until the postexilic period, particularly that of Babylonian captivity (586 B.C.). The majority of the psalms were written during the time of David and Solomon (David's son), which was 1010 B.C. to 930 B.C.

Psalm 19, which was written by King David, celebrates the world of God and the Word of God. David believed that God was faithful and forgiving. Even though he had a heart for God, he still sinned. Scholars believe that not long after he wrote Psalm 19, David committed adultery with Bathsheba (see 2 Samuel 10–11); arranged the murder of Uriah, Bathsheba's husband; disobeyed God and took a census of the people; and did not deal with His children's sins. But when David sinned, he confessed from the heart and genuinely repented.

At-A-Glance

1. The Law of God (Psalm 19:7–9)

2. Appreciation of God's Law (vv. 10–11)

3. God's Law Reveals Humankind's Sin (vv. 12–13)

4. God's Law Lights Humankind's Path (v. 14)

In Depth

1. The Law of God (Psalm 19:7–9)

God's Law provides God's will for His children to live obediently, holy, and righteous before Him. The believer's duty to God and what we can expect from Him are expressed in God's inerrant Word. David uses the following words to describe the Word of God (emphasis added): "*law*" (v. 7), "*testimony*" (v. 7), "*statutes*" (v. 8), "*commandment*" (v. 8), "*fear of the LORD*" (v. 9), and "*judgments*" (v. 9). When David describes the Word of God, he acknowledges through repetition that the authority and excellence of the Word come from the Creator. The Word is a testimony or statement of authenticity from the Creator of the universe. Because it is divine instruction for God's people, David refers to God's Word as "the commandment" (v. 8). When God's Word lives within their hearts, believers will follow God's Word with reverence and fear. As believers revere God, the Word directs us so we can please God. Finally, the Law of God is called His "judgments"; they are the standards by which all people will be judged by God and sentenced.

Then David evaluates the Word of God and describes the Word as *perfect, sure, right, pure, clean, true,* and *righteous* (vv. 7–9, emphasis added). The Word of God is perfect because it is free from corruption, filled with goodness to obey God, and results in eternal happiness. The Word completely and perfectly expresses God's divine will for His people. David describes the Word of God as "trustworthy" and "right" (vv. 7–8, NIV) because it does not mislead anyone; instead, it provides the truth. The Word of God is pure because there are no errors or misinformation in God's instructions. On behalf of the Lord, the apostle John wrote that believers "are clean through the word which I [Jesus] have spoken" (John 15:3).

Through true discipleship, because sin is removed with God's Word, the heart is purified. Then as believers pray, obey, and follow God, the Word will make us clean. Consequently, the Word of God is indeed true and righteous; it guides believers to learn the truth.

In Psalm 19:7–9, David also expresses the results of God's Word when God's children hear and believe. Because God's Word is the truth, it (1) converts the soul, (2) makes wisdom possible, (3) brings joy to the heart, (4) enlightens the eyes, (5) endures forever, and (6) is righteous altogether. When a person accepts God's Word, a change begins within the heart. The Word cleanses the soul, reveals sin, and brings humankind back to God. In addition, through the power of the Holy Spirit, Christians have a new heart and spirit to live and follow God's Word.

Further blessings that come with internalizing and obeying God's Word include a desire to share God's love, which is revealed through Jesus Christ, with the world. God's Word reveals our sin and misery, so we humbly allow God's Word to direct our path and in obedience to the "Great Commission" (Matthew 28:19–20). Also, there is the desire that God directs the paths of others who do not know Him.

2. Appreciation of God's Law (vv. 10–11)

David writes that God's Word is more precious than any wealth the world can offer. It is purer and more precious than pure gold. The grace (unmerited favor) that the Word of God reveals is eternal; it is a gift. We cannot do works to earn it, and the temporary pleasures of the world cannot compare to its value. Through the Word of God, believers can receive joy, wisdom, freedom from sin, and eternal life. Therefore, the benefits of God's Word are eternal and exceed any pleasure or delight the world can offer.

David reminds believers who receive God's Word, by faith, that the Word is "sweeter also than honey and the honeycomb" (Psalm 19:10). The temporary satisfaction of honey cannot compare to the spiritual victory, new life, and eternal reward believers receive by faith. As the psalmist wrote, God's Word is pure, holy, just, and good; it is the foundation for lasting hope. Like David, we should appreciate God's Word more than the pleasures of the world; indeed, nothing is more substantial and satisfying.

God's Word also gives believers instruction for their responsibility and duty and warns the believers of dangers to avoid. When we as believers humble ourselves before God and receive God's Word, we will be guided by the Word.

3. God's Law Reveals Humankind's Sin (vv. 12–13)

A sin is anything that does not please God, a transgression of God's Law; it is a deviation from following God's Word and His way. David recognized his own imperfections and desired to be delivered from "secret *faults*" or sins that were hidden from humans, but never from an omnipresent (all-present) and omniscient (all-knowing) God (Psalm 19:12). Because no sin is hidden from God, David did not specify the details of his sins. He made a general plea that God forgive his sins. No one is perfect; therefore, we also must plead to God for mercy. All believers have two kinds of sin: committed sins that they know of, and sins of omission—sins that they may not remember committing (e.g., wrong thoughts). However, like David, we must pray and ask for cleansing and forgiveness of any and all sins.

In Psalm 51, David cried out to God for mercy, forgiveness, and cleansing. David wrote, "Have mercy upon me, O God,...blot out my transgressions" (v. 1). Then after David committed adultery with Bathsheba and murdered her husband, Uriah, he was truly sorry—he had heartfelt sorrow and not just sorrow for being caught. As a result, God was merciful and forgave him. Like David, we must repent for our sins. We need to know that we not only sin against others, but we also sin against a loving, merciful, and compassionate God.

In the Scripture passage for today, David prays that God would keep him from purposeful or "willful sin" against God's Word (Psalm 19:13, NIV). He did not want purposeful sin to have control over his life. If we allow "willful" sin and malice to control our lives, we are not following God's Word.

4. God's Law Lights Humankind's Path (v. 14)

The psalmist concludes the celebration of God's creation and His Word by praying for God's divine acceptance of his thoughts. David knew and appreciated that God is so powerful that God even knows our thoughts. Therefore, David prays that his meditation would be acceptable before God. Because David repented from secret and willful sin, he prays that his life, words, and actions would please God.

David makes his supplication to his "Redeemer" (God), who offers freedom from the bondage of sin (Psalm 19:14, NIV). He recognizes that God is his "Rock"—the Unchanging God, the Solid Foundation—therefore, God is his Source of strength and power (v. 14). Like David, believers are strengthened when we trust and depend upon God and His Word.

Search the Scriptures

1. What are six words that David used to describe the Law of God (Psalm 19:7–9)?

2. What six evaluations does David present for the Law of God (vv. 7–9)?

Discuss the Meaning

1. How does the Word of God make "wise the simple" and provide guidance for the believers?

2. What does the Word of God provide for the righteous and for the unrighteous?

Lesson in Our Society

Throughout society, "secret" and "willful" sins continue to plague human lives. Because they view it as large or small, people dismiss sin. However, all sin, regardless of the extent that humankind categorizes it, displeases God. The world does not have a heart to please God. Because we live in the world, we must continue to follow the standards of God's Word to be acceptable before Him. Do not allow the world to guide your heart and spirit. Instead, study and apply God's Word to obey and please Him.

Make It Happen

As believers study God's Word and apply it to our lives, we grow in wisdom. Therefore, we should be doers of God's Word and not just hearers (James 1:22). When we trust God and give Him honor and reverence within our lives, our actions and words will grow in wisdom. Do you belong to and regularly attend a Bible study group? If not, join a group that allows you to grow as a believer. Encourage your friends and family members to join as well so they, too, can learn to apply God's Word to their lives.

Follow the Spirit

What God wants me to do:

_____

_____

_____

_____

Remember Your Thoughts

Special insights I have learned:

_____

_____

_____

_____

More Light on the Text

Psalm 19:7–14

Introduction:

In addition to Psalm 8 in last week's lesson, Psalm 19 is another "Creation" psalm, which echoes the beginning of Psalm 8, speaking of the glory of God in the heavens and how all of creation magnifies God's name and handiwork. Along with many others, C. S. Lewis had nothing but praise for Psalm 19: "I take this to be the greatest poem in the Psalter and one of the greatest lyrics in the world" (63). What is new with Psalm 19 is the introduction of *Torah* (the Law) instead of the uninterrupted praise of Psalm 8. In fact, many categorize Psalm 19 as a "Torah psalm." As with all the many psalm types (such as wisdom, royal, thanksgiving, lament, etc.), the original authors had nothing to do with the much later (nineteenth century) categorizing of their work, but wrote to express their faith, their experiences, and their relationship with God. The fact that the subjects of creation and Torah are combined (some have suggested the parts were once separate psalms) should not end with a debate about form, but should begin a celebration of the *works* of God (creation, natural revelation) and the *words* of God (Torah, special revelation).

7 The law of the LORD is perfect, converting the soul: the testimony of the LORD is sure, making wise the simple. 8 The statutes of the LORD are right, rejoicing the heart: the commandment of the LORD is pure, enlightening the eyes.

Starting with the first six verses of Psalm 19, the psalm writer does not address anyone in particular (unlike, for example, Psalm 8 and others where the writer opens with an invocation to God), and the same general, open speech continues until verse 11 when God finally is addressed. One writer divided this psalm into three parts based on the speaker—the cosmos speaks (vv. 1–6); God speaks (vv. 7–11); and the psalmist speaks (vv. 12–14) or as another puts it, "words about God, via words of God, and words to God" (Goldingay, 299). This week's lesson focuses on the Torah part of this psalm (vv. 7–11), and the penitence of the psalmist (vv. 12–14). Just as creation reveals, in Paul's words, God's "eternal power and divine nature" (Romans 1:20), so the Torah also glorifies God. Just as the splendor of the cosmos declares the splendor of the Creator of the cosmos (Psalm 19:1–2), so the glory of the Torah declares the glory of the author of the Torah (v. 7).

According to John Goldingay, the Law (Heb. *towrah*, **to-RA**) can refer to *the* Torah (Psalm 1:2), but also to prophets and thinkers, oral or written teaching, and could refer to God's acts with Israel (290–91). The scholar makes it clear, however, that the context

of Psalm 19:7–8 "embraces the concrete instructions in their specificity as well as the whole in its unity (teaching, declaration [in Hebrew, this translates as ʿēdût or *eduwth*, **ay-DOOTH**])."

9 The fear of the LORD is clean, enduring for ever: the judgments of the LORD are true and righteous altogether.

Scholars agree that "fear of the LORD" (Heb. *yir'ah*, **yir-AW**), really means God's Torah teaches what it means to have a proper, pure, or clean fear of the Lord, which also means awe, reverence, or respect. There is a vast difference between a healthy, essentially positive awe of God and an unhealthy terror of God. This is a point of Christian language with which believers should be cautious in their use with unbelievers. Often such "Christianese" is quickly and easily misunderstood. Since the Hebrew word *yir'ah* means "reverence" or "awe," this is the language that one should use whenever one is outside of a clear Christian context or understanding. Anyone can understand reverence, even an unrepentant sinner; few among the many unsaved in the world, however, will properly understand that fear really means reverence.

10 More to be desired are they than gold, yea, than much fine gold: sweeter also than honey and the honeycomb.

The verse still refers to God's judgments or decisions, which are good, right, and true in every way, but even more than that they are precious and valuable, like gold. As though even gold is not sufficient to describe them, fine gold puts a sharper point on it. In today's language, this would read ".999% pure gold." If even fine gold somehow was insufficient, however, honey, the universal standard for sweetness, is applied—and even that is further qualified with honey fresh from the honeycomb. These rich metaphors attempt to express the reality that in God's decisions we find perfect value and perfect delight (see Proverbs 3:14; 8:19; 16:16; 25:11).

11 Moreover by them is thy servant warned: and in keeping of them there is great reward.

"If only I could take back those words, or that day, or that action," lament so many who find themselves facing the painful consequences of their unwise decisions. "If only," could be edited to say, "If only I had obeyed God's perfect Torah; if only I had taken His wise counsel to heart, and followed His ways of truth and integrity." For those with ears to hear and eyes to see (Matthew 11:15), let them be forewarned by the foolishness of others, and, in order to avoid the same disastrous consequences, let them not make all the same mistakes. Rather, let them take heed, and in humility learn wisdom and uprightness and integrity—for in doing these things many rewards will ensue, not the least of which is the pure delight of God's joy and His peace filling their souls (Isaiah 26:3; Philippians 4:7). Moreover, obeying His Word will help to avoid disaster and loss, and will help retain all that might otherwise have been lost, with the expectation of increase as these persons continue to walk in wisdom and soundness of judgment (Proverbs 11:18; 24:14; 1 Timothy 5:18; 2 John 1:8). An additional, unwritten caution is that obedience precludes God's just chastisement of wrongdoing and unrighteous conduct.

12 Who can understand his errors? cleanse thou me from secret faults.

In one sense, verses 12–14 are another sudden transition in which the psalmist abruptly changes gears again, this time to express a series of pleas or payers. In another sense, the prayers can be seen as a natural reaction to the preceding verses' description

of all the good things that result from a proper response to God's instructions for life. Actually, this view was introduced in verse 11's warning, which was the start of the psalmist's realization that he will not, in fact, be able to obey perfectly. The truth is that life is not that neat and tidy, and sin-prone humans have an ongoing tendency (to borrow a bowling term) to become gutter balls. We run off the train tracks, we cross the double yellow line, we miss the target, and we come up short, over and over again. Thus the psalmist David prays for protection, even from "secret" flaws. One meaning for such "cleansing," says Goldingay, is "to acquit" (Heb. *nāqâ*, **na-KA**); the secret flaw is not yet a full-blown wrongdoing, which would require forgiveness (as some translations such as NIV have it) or pardon, but secret, hidden, potential sins that require acquittal.

13 Keep back thy servant also from presumptuous sins; let them not have dominion over me: then shall I be upright, and I shall be innocent from the great transgression.

Continuing his prayer, David asks for protection from his own "presumptuous" (Heb. *zed*, **zade**), meaning "arrogant," "proud," "insolent," or "willful" sins. He also asks God to protect him from those who do not hesitate to sin, those who are "presumptuous" or willful (see other examples in Psalm 86:14; 119:69; and their punishment in Isaiah 13:11; Malachi 4:1). The text here can be read as a plea for God's help from sin and other sinners.

14 Let the words of my mouth, and the meditation of my heart, be acceptable in thy sight, O LORD, my strength, and my redeemer.

This is a classic, familiar passage, well-worn from believers' frequent, fond use. The words are in focus because most sinful acts start as sinful words, especially when there are plots involved to do wrong, or to harm others (such as the willful, who are actively planning against Christians). Adultery, for example, is usually preceded by a great many words, each increasing in sinful intent—likewise, other sins follow the same pattern. Instead, however, if the psalmist has pure meditations, and if his mouth is filled only with acceptable words, which he is not ashamed to speak in God's presence, then he prays he will not end up committing sins, doing wrong, and making unwise choices that will carry disastrous consequences, causing death, destruction, and regret. There is a clear connection between one's words and one's thoughts, which are not always congruent, but God will only accept words that come from a pure heart.

"Strength" is an interesting word (Heb. *tsuwr*, **tsur**), which means "rock," "cliff," or "boulder." It is the same word used of the place in the side of the mountain where God hid Moses as He passed by (Exodus 33:22), and the origin of the famous lyrics, "Rock of Ages, cleft for me, let me hide myself in thee" (see also Psalms 62:6; 94:22; 144:1). On one hand, we resist the evil from outside, from the willful, which would pressure us into sin; on the other hand, we stand firm against our own self-will from the inside, which would lead us astray. The psalmist is asking God to intervene, just as families of addicts lovingly, but strongly, intervene when one of their own is in trouble. In this sense, God is the Father figure who intervenes when one of His own is in danger of wandering down a wrong road.

Say It Correctly

Septuagint. SEP-too-uh-jint.
Torah. TOR-uh.

Daily Bible Readings

M: The Testimony of Creation
Psalm 19:1–6

T: An Everlasting Covenant
Psalm 105:1–11

W: The Law as Revelation
Deuteronomy 29:25–29

T: The Law as Obedient Love
Deuteronomy 30:1–10

F: The Law as Witness
Deuteronomy 31:19–26

S: The Law as Covenant
Jeremiah 31:31–37

S: The Testimony of the Law
Psalm 19:7–14

Teaching Tips

1. Words You Should Know

A. Refuge (Psalm 46:1) *machaceh* (Heb.)—Place of shelter.

B. Tabernacles (v. 4) *mishkan* (Heb.)—Literally means "dwelling places" and was the name of the portable temple constructed by Moses and the people of Israel.

C. Hosts (v. 7) *tsaba'* (Heb.)—Those which go forth; armies.

2. Teacher Preparation

Unifying Principle—Seeking Refuge. The psalmist tells us that God is our refuge and strength, a tested help in times of trouble.

A. Pray for your class.

B. Prayerfully read the entire lesson.

C. Be prepared to give a biblical definition of "refuge" (see More Light on the Text).

D. Be prepared to discuss what it means to "need" refuge. Share a testimony.

E. Use the song "Rock of Ages" in your discussion.

3. Open the Lesson

A. Open with prayer, incorporating the Aim for Change.

B. Write the word "refuge" on the board and then explain the definition.

C. From your hymnal, have a volunteer read the words of the song, "Rock of Ages."

D. Have another volunteer explain what the words mean to him or her.

E. Then use the In Focus story to segue into today's lesson.

4. Present the Scriptures

A. Have volunteers read the Focal Verses.

B. Use The People, Places, and Times; Background; At-A-Glance; In Depth; Search the Scriptures questions; and More Light on the Text to further help clarify meaning.

5. Explore the Meaning

A. Have volunteers give answers to the Discuss the Meaning section.

B. Conclude with a discussion of the Lesson in Our Society and Make It Happen sections.

6. Next Steps for Application

A. Summarize discussion points.

B. Close with prayer.

Worship Guide

For the Superintendent or Teacher
Theme: God Provides Refuge
Theme Song: "Rock of Ages"
Devotional Reading: Hebrews 6:13–20
Prayer

God Provides Refuge

Bible Background • PSALM 46:1–7
Printed Text • PSALM 46:1–7 | Devotional Reading • HEBREWS 6:13–20

—— Aim for Change ——

By the end of the lesson, we will: IDENTIFY ways that God is a present help in times of trouble; FEEL COMFORTED in knowing that God provides refuge in times of trouble; and SHARE experiences where God has provided refuge in trying times.

In Focus

It was the worst time in Kim's life. Her dad had just died of cancer, and she had moved her mom into her home with her family so they could care for her. Her mom was very sweet, but she needed so much care. Kim was glad her husband and her daughter were so helpful.

OCT 17th

Kim was completing her doctorate, which meant she was gathering data for the all-important dissertation. On top of that, her stay-at-home job had suddenly become one in which she had to drive 36 miles each way into another state every day. But the worst thing of all was her boss. Every time he called a meeting, he seemed to delight in making Kim cry in front of all her coworkers.

Every morning, as Kim opened her Bible, she would cry out to the Lord and ask Him to take her home. Things were that bad. She knew that suicide was not an option for a Christian, but this time in her life was unbearable. It was only by the grace of God that she held on.

Have you experienced God as your refuge and strength in a time of great trouble? Often you cannot feel His presence at the time, but looking back over the experience, you can see how He sustained you.

—— Keep in Mind ——

"God is our refuge and strength, a very present help in trouble" (Psalm 46:1).

"God is our refuge and strength, a very present help in trouble"
(Psalm 46:1).

Focal Verses

KJV **Psalm 46:1** God is our refuge and strength, a very present help in trouble.

2 Therefore will not we fear, though the earth be removed, and though the mountains be carried into the midst of the sea;

3 Though the waters thereof roar and be troubled, though the mountains shake with the swelling thereof. Selah.

4 There is a river, the streams whereof shall make glad the city of God, the holy place of the tabernacles of the most High.

5 God is in the midst of her; she shall not be moved: God shall help her, and that right early.

6 The heathen raged, the kingdoms were moved: he uttered his voice, the earth melted.

7 The LORD of hosts is with us; the God of Jacob is our refuge. Selah.

NLT **Psalm 46:1** God is our refuge and strength, always ready to help in times of trouble.

2 So we will not fear when earthquakes come and the mountains crumble into the sea.

3 Let the oceans roar and foam. Let the mountains tremble as the waters surge!

4 A river brings joy to the city of our God, the sacred home of the Most High.

5 God dwells in that city; it cannot be destroyed. From the very break of day, God will protect it.

6 The nations are in chaos, and their kingdoms crumble! God's voice thunders, and the earth melts!

7 The LORD of Heaven's Armies is here among us; the God of Israel is our fortress.

The People, Places, and Times

King David, the Musician. Although we do not have the musical notes for the psalms, they were written to be sung. Many of the psalms were written by or for King David, and thus we can see his ear for the rhythm of Hebrew poetry. We also learn from Scripture that David organized the Levites into choirs. Levi had three sons: Gershon, Kohath, and Merari. From each of these three clans, David organized a choir. The title of today's psalm tells us that it was composed to be sung by the choir selected from the sons of Korah, who were descended from the Kohath clan.

The Choir Director. The superscription to this psalm also directs it to the music director. This could mean that the director was supposed to add this psalm to the collection of music for the worship services. Or it may mean that this part was to be sung or spoken by him as the congregation responded with "Amen," "Praise the Lord," or "Hallelujah." The call-and-response type of worship music

Background

There is very little in Scripture to help us understand the background of this particular psalm. Several psalms are ascribed to the family guild of Korah: Psalms 42–49; 84; 85; and 87. Today's psalm is included in that group. This does not mean that the psalm was composed by a committee, but that each one was probably the work of an individual in the group.

During the reign of King Hezekiah, there was much religious reform and organization. It was also a time to bring together various sources of history to compile written records under the inspiration of the Lord, which became part of our Bible. Many psalms are believed to have been compiled, edited, and composed in this era. Psalm 46 may have been written during Hezekiah's reign to celebrate the great victory of God's people over Sennacherib, but that

is only a conjecture. The wonderful story of Hezekiah's prayer and the victory of the Lord are recorded in 2 Kings 18:17–19:36.

At-A-Glance

1. God's Protection in the Worst of Times (Psalm 46:1–3)

2. God Provides a River of Blessings in His City (vv. 4–5)

3. God Is Our Fortress (vv. 6–7)

In Depth

1. God's Protection in the Worst of Times (Psalm 46:1–3)

God has never promised us that life would be easy. The writer of this psalm tells us that we do not need to fear even if the earth itself falls into the sea. Verses 2 and 3 speak of things that would be like a nightmare to the Israelites. The Israelites were not accomplished sailors. Even when King Solomon sent ships on sailing expeditions from the Gulf of Aqaba down the eastern coast of Africa, it was in ships provided by and manned by King Hiram of Tyre (1 Kings 9:26–28). Time spent at sea held the potential for great uncertainty.

The people also had reason to be afraid of earthquakes. Earthquakes are common in Israel. If you have lived through even a minor earthquake, you know the unsettling feeling of having the earth move under your feet. A major earthquake is devastating. Both Amos and Zechariah mention an earthquake during the reign of King Uzziah (Amos 1:1; Zechariah 14:5). But even if we have not experienced an earthquake or even if we enjoy sailing and going on cruises, the descriptions in Psalm 46:2–3 are very frightening. Verse 2 portrays the entire earth—all of the dry land—shaken up and tossed into the midst of the sea or ocean. Verse 3 goes on with the description. An enormous storm on the sea is roaring with waves pitching everything to and fro. The mountains, which are usually pictured as enormous hunks of stability, are shaking.

This psalm is written in the plural; it is written from the perspective of not just an individual, but the whole nation of Israel. The entire existence of Israel may be in jeopardy. So what happens in such a time of great turmoil and danger? We back up to verse 1 and see that in spite of all these troubles, God is our refuge and strength. He is always there with us to help us in times of trouble. He may not take us out of our difficulties, but He is there with us, protecting us and helping us.

Verse 2 says that this has a great effect upon us. In spite of all the problems that we may be in the midst of, we have no need to fear. Our courage is not based upon our own ability to find solutions to our problems, but our courage is based upon the character of God. He is the Creator and Sustainer of our universe and all the universes beyond. Surely, our God has the strength to help us in all our troubles.

2. God Provides a River of Blessings in His City (vv. 4–5)

Most of the great cities of ancient times had rivers. Even most modern cities were built on the banks of a river or a sea. But Jerusalem, the city of God, had no river. Instead, Jerusalem had the river of God, a metaphor for God's blessings continually flowing to His people. The Middle East has much wilderness and desert, so people understand the importance of water. Without water, nothing will grow, and without crops, the people will starve.

Most people today throw around the word "blessings" without any real understanding of the biblical meaning of the word. When God blesses us, He gives us inner peace and joy which are not dependent upon our outward circumstances. The peace comes from our relationship with Him. We are not saddled down with sin and guilt because He has forgiven us, washed us clean through the death of Jesus on the Cross, and has given us the power to live godly lives.

This river in the city of God is mentioned several times in Scripture. Ezekiel had a vision of a new temple in Jerusalem with a river flowing from it (Ezekiel 47:1). Revelation describes the New Jerusalem with a river flowing from the throne of God (Revelation 22:1). The New Jerusalem will have no temple because God Himself will be there.

Jesus offered the Samaritan woman everlasting water, water that would be gushing up inside into eternal life (John 4:13–15). Later, Jesus invited people to come to Him and drink of that living water, which is the Holy Spirit. So when we receive Jesus, we have God Himself living within us. God's presence in us brings us this true inner gladness. The circumstances of our lives do not make us dried up and bitter; we are continually being moisturized by the Holy Spirit.

In Psalm 46:5, we read about God helping us early in the day. At dawn, the enemies of Israel were most likely to attack. Perhaps they had been sneaking up during the night. They were ready to begin the war as soon as the sun came up. But in Psalm 121:4, we read that "he that keepeth Israel shall neither slumber nor sleep." And elsewhere we read that God gives His loved ones sleep (Psalm 127:2). Psalm 46:5 tells us that we can rest at night because God is right there with us; problems may be brewing, but God is taking care of things for us as we sleep soundly on our pillows. We don't need to lie awake worrying about the "what ifs."

3. God Is Our Fortress (vv. 6–7)

Verse 6 describes a world in turmoil, not unlike today. We may often feel helpless to do anything about wars, corruption, the economy, and the things going on in other parts of the world. But no matter how world leaders may rant and rave, God is so powerful that if He even speaks, His voice can melt the earth. World leaders may think they are in charge, but in reality our Lord is in charge.

Verse 7 is the chorus; it's repeated in verse 11. Imagine the soloist or the choir singing verses 1 through 6; the congregation sings verse 7. Then the soloist or choir takes up singing verses 8 through 10 and everyone joins together singing the chorus again in verse 11.

"The LORD of hosts" has also been translated as "The LORD of Heaven's Armies" (NLT). The Lord Almighty is with us, and He can call all of His angels to fight for us.

Finally, the verse returns to the main theme of our psalm: God is our refuge. A refuge is a place to hide, a place to be safe. Verse 5 tells us that God will help us early in the morning. This is a good time to open our Bibles and pray—when we first wake up. We can hide out in quietness with our Lord before the busyness of the day enters our lives.

Search the Scriptures

1. What can we expect God to do for us when we are in the midst of trouble (Psalm 46:1)?

2. What sort of natural disasters does the psalmist say we need not fear (vv. 2–3)?

Discuss the Meaning

1. God promises to help us and be with us in times of trouble. Why doesn't He just remove us from our problems? Why does He allow us to go through times of suffering?

2. The psalmist sings of a river whose streams make the city of God glad. For those of us who have received the Lord Jesus as Savior, we no longer have to go to the temple in Jerusalem to be in His presence. Jesus has come into our hearts, and His living water is within us. How does this water give us gladness?

Lesson in Our Society

Today's psalm talks about natural disasters and nations at war—things that are often in the news today. Some people are afraid to read the news or watch it on TV because it is so unsettling. A better approach is to be in prayer as we read our papers or watch the news. As we read about devastating tsunamis or other tragedies, we can pray that Christians will be involved in relief work and that this disaster will cause people to turn to Christ.

Make It Happen

Spend some time discussing times of great trouble in your lives and how the Lord helped you. Share prayer requests for current problems. Pray for class members who are in the midst of troubles right now.

Follow the Spirit

What God wants me to do:

_____

_____

_____

_____

Remember Your Thoughts

Special insights I have learned:

_____

_____

_____

_____

More Light on the Text

Psalm 46:1–7

1 God is our refuge and strength, a very present help in trouble.

The psalm begins with a simple but profound proposition about God. God is the all-powerful Creator who called the universe into existence with mere words and continues to hold it together by the word of His power. He is the just and righteous Judge to whom all of us must give account for every thought, word, and deed. He is invisible to human eyes, but is more real than anything in His Creation. He is transcendent, which means that He is beyond our ability to understand. This is the God (Heb. *'elohiym*, **el-o-HEEM**) whom the psalmist claims as our refuge. *El* (**el**), the Hebrew word for "god" or "mighty one," was a word used by many Semitic languages. However, only Hebrew uses *elohiym*—the plural form—to refer to the one God who is the only true God, the one who is over all others. God is over all people, but He is the refuge of a select group. "Our" reminds us that only the people of God find Him to be a refuge. The enemies of God have good reason to shrink from Him in terror (Psalm 21:8; 68:1).

The psalmist uses three terms to express God's protective care of His people. "Refuge" (Heb. *machaceh*, **makh-as-EH**) means a place of shelter. It is used in the Old Testament literally to refer to a shelter from threatening weather or figuratively to refer to a source of confidence such as a god or a military ally. "Strength" (Heb. *'oz*, **oze**) may mean that the Lord is our source of strength or that He is a strong refuge. Of course, both are absolutely true. "Help" (Heb. *'ezrah*, **ez-RAW**) is a common Old Testament word. Military assistance was a common type of help the people of Israel received from God. "A very present help in trouble" is a loose translation of the Hebrew—which reads something like "in distress, [He] is very much

to be found." In other words, troubled times are when the Lord frequently shows up and provides assistance to His people. He is present when we need Him most urgently.

2 Therefore will not we fear, though the earth be removed, and though the mountains be carried into the midst of the sea; 3 Though the waters thereof roar and be troubled, though the mountains shake with the swelling thereof. Selah.

Because of who God is for His people, the psalmist says with confidence that we have nothing to fear, even if the world falls apart. These verses create a graphic picture of the undoing of creation. "Be removed" (Heb. *muwr*, **moor**) is a Hebrew word meaning "change." Other English versions such as NIV translate it as "give way." "Be carried" (Heb. *mowt*, **mote**) literally means "totter." The mountains—which to us are such symbols of strength and permanence—are shaken loose from their foundations and become no more stable than a piece of butter on a warm plate. They end up in the midst (literally "heart") of the oceans. The waters of the oceans are an aggressive destructive force—they "roar" and are "troubled" (literally "foam," NLT).

4 There is a river, the streams whereof shall make glad the city of God, the holy place of the tabernacles of the most High.

The scene now shifts from the chaotic unraveling of creation to a place where all is well. Ironically, the picture starts with water—but of a very different sort than the raging oceans. This river is a river of living water, an unending source of life and joy. This river of life imagery appears throughout the Old and New Testaments and speaks of God's sustaining and renewing grace. A river first appears in the pages of Scripture to water the Garden of Eden (Genesis 2:10). The psalmist speaks of the Lord's gentle and gracious provision as His leading of His sheep "beside the still waters" (Psalm 23:2). In Psalm 36:8, the Lord blesses His people by offering them drink from His river of delights. In Isaiah 8:6, the Lord's grace is compared to the gentle waters of Shiloah. Then in Zechariah 14:8, we are promised that on the Day of the Lord, living waters will flow out of Jerusalem.

The Old Testament image of the river of life climaxes in Ezekiel 47. In Ezekiel's vision of the temple, he sees a river flowing out from under the temple. The river gets progressively deeper the farther Ezekiel follows it, and he sees trees growing on both banks. He also learns that the river flows into the Arabah—an arid area—where it turns salt water into fresh. In this water, all the creatures of the sea thrive and become plentiful. The trees that grow along the river's banks provide food and their leaves are used for healing.

The river of life and living water imagery continues in the New Testament. Jesus Himself claimed to be the source of living water (John 4:14). All who believe in Him will themselves be springs of living water (John 7:38). But the most powerful water image comes at the end of the New Testament in Revelation 22:1–3. A prominent feature of the heavenly Jerusalem is a river flowing out from under God's throne.

In Psalm 46:4, the word "tabernacles" (Heb. *mishkan*, **mish-KAWN**) literally means "dwelling places" and was the name of the portable temple constructed by Moses and the people of Israel after the Exodus. In the Old Testament system of worship, God's presence was manifested through the temple worship. God did sometimes reveal Himself in other ways at other locations, but the normal way for ordinary God-fearing people to experience communion with God was by traveling to the temple and participating in the temple rituals.

In Psalm 46:4, the phrase "most High" (Heb. *'elyown*, **el-YONE**) is derived from a Hebrew verb that means "to go up." This descriptive name portrays Jehovah as the one who is exalted above all the nations and above all other gods.

5 God is in the midst of her; she shall not be moved: God shall help her, and that right early.

The river of verse 4 is not a symbol of joy that springs from blissful ignorance. The people of the city of God dwell in genuine safety and security because God's presence guarantees that evil cannot overtake them. "In the midst of her" simply means that God is actually within the city limits—He is near to His people and shares the same space that they occupy. Acting as their refuge, He does not look on from a distance; He comes close to His people.

"Moved" (*mowt*, **mote**) is the same Hebrew word used in verse 2 to describe the mountains being carried into the sea. In contrast to the chaos happening outside the city walls, the city is completely stable. It does not totter, slip, or hang on by a thread. It is firmly established and well-defended.

"Right early" is translated "at the break of dawn" by most English translations. The break of day was the customary time for an attack against a city to begin, so this phrase makes the point that God defends His people in their hour of need.

6 The heathen raged, the kingdoms were moved: he uttered his voice, the earth melted.

The psalmist changes the scene once more. We now go back outside the city of God to observe the chaos and God's response to it. The word "heathen" (Heb. *gowy*, **GO-ee**) literally means "nations" and is used in the Old Testament to refer to the Gentiles—all those who are not a part of the people of God. "Raged" (Heb. *hamah*, **haw-MAW**) has a variety of meanings that all involve making some kind of noise: murmur, be in uproar, moan, roar. "Were moved" is the same Hebrew word (*mowt*, **mote**) used in verse 2 to describe the mountains falling into the sea and in verse 5 to say that the city of God will not be moved.

7 The LORD of hosts is with us; the God of Jacob is our refuge. Selah.

"The LORD of hosts" is a name for God that reflects His power and His faithfulness to fight for His people. In the Old Testament, this name for God first appears in 1 Samuel 1:3 and is used frequently (along with other variations such as "God of hosts") in the historical books, psalms, and prophetic books. In Psalm 46:7, the word "hosts" (Heb. *tsaba'*, **tsaw-BAW**) means "those which go forth; armies." The English transliteration of the plural form of this Hebrew word is "Sabaoth," or "Almighty," a term that appears in the New Testament in Romans 9:29 and James 5:4.

"LORD" in Psalm 46:7 is the name Jehovah (alternately Yahweh), the name which He identified Himself to Moses in Exodus 3:15 as the name by which He is to be remembered forever. Although the precise meaning of this name is not certain, it is a play on the Hebrew verb "to be." Yahweh's own explanation of His name in Exodus 3 as well as study of the word itself has led scholars to understand it to mean "I am," "He is," or some variation such as "I will be."

"With us" (Psalm 46:7) reminds us that the Lord is omnipresent (everywhere all the time), so He is our refuge and is never absent in our hour of need.

In Psalm 46:7, the word "refuge" (Heb. *misgab*, **mis-GAWB**) means "stronghold" or "fortress"—a place to which we can run when the enemy threatens and be secure. Yahweh delights to protect and defend His people.

Say It Correctly

Ezekiel. ee-ZEE-kyl, -kee-el.
Hezekiah. heh-zuh-KY-uh.
Kohath. KOH-hath.
Levite. LEE-vite.
Merari. muh-RAIR-i.

Daily Bible Readings

M: Our Strong Yet Gentle God
Isaiah 40:6–11

T: Our Faithful God
Deuteronomy 7:7–11

W: Our Comforting God
2 Corinthians 1:3–7

T: Our Rescuing God
2 Corinthians 1:8–11

F: God Before and After Us
Isaiah 52:7–12

S: God's Provision for the Needy
Psalm 68:4–10

S: God's Help in Times of Trouble
Psalm 46:1–7

Teaching Tips

1. Words You Should Know

A. Terrible (Psalm 47:2) *yare'* (Heb.)—A form of the verb "to fear," it describes the awe-inspiring effect that the Lord has on people.

B. Excellency (v. 4) *ga'own* (Heb.)—It refers to a right and proper joy in God's good gift of the Promised Land.

2. Teacher Preparation

Unifying Principle—Good Leaders. The psalmist describes how people joyfully respond to God's sustaining leadership.

A. Pray a prayer of thanksgiving for God's rule over the nations.

B. Prayerfully study the entire lesson.

C. Study the word "sovereign" in a Bible dictionary, and be prepared to discuss the fact that God is sovereign (in control of His universe and never out of control).

3. Open the Lesson

A. Open with prayer, thanking God for His sovereignty.

B. Then introduce the Words You Should Know for today's study.

C. Use the In Focus story to segue into today's theme and discussion.

D. Ask: "Who is ruling over the nations? How do you know that He is the Supreme Ruler?" Discuss.

4. Present the Scriptures

A. Have volunteers read the Focal Verses.

B. Use The People, Places, and Times; Background; At-A-Glance; In Depth; Search the Scriptures questions; and More Light on the Text to further help clarify meaning.

5. Explore the Meaning

A. Use the Discuss the Meaning and Lesson in Our Society sections to explore the meaning of the text for life today, stressing still who is ruling over the nations.

B. Allow the class to give their own input.

6. Next Steps for Application

A. Examine the salient points in the Make It Happen section.

B. Finally, summarize the attributes of God—a good leader.

C. Close with prayer.

Worship Guide

For the Superintendent or Teacher
Theme: God's Rule Over the Nations
Theme Song: "All Hail the Power"
Devotional Reading: Jeremiah 10:6–10
Prayer

God's Rule Over the Nations

Bible Background • PSALM 47
Printed Text • PSALM 47 | Devotional Reading • JEREMIAH 10:6–10

Aim for Change

By the end of the lesson, we will: IDENTIFY reasons to praise God's rule over all the earth; BE FILLED with joy that God rules over all the earth; and PRAISE God for His sustaining leadership.

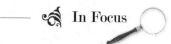 In Focus

For many years, Beatrice was an enthusiastic fan of several Black leaders who she considered to be good leaders. She even joined a number of organizations that heralded an excellent leadership staff.

But by the time Barack Obama was running for president, Beatrice was somewhat ambivalent. Although she voted for him, she felt that racism was too deeply entrenched in this country for a Black man ever to be voted in as president. Then the evening of election day came. Beatrice was standing with the crowds, tears streaming down her face as Barack Obama, the president-elect, gave his victory speech.

OCT 24th

The U.S. is the only superpower in today's world, and this superpower is led by an African American man. At times it does seem almost unbelievable. But President Obama is probably facing bigger problems than any recent American president has ever faced. We cannot expect him to do what only God can do. We need to uphold our president in prayer every day and be reminded that it is God who rules over the nations—America included.

Keep in Mind

"Sing praises to God, sing praises: sing praises unto our King, sing praises. For God is the King of all the earth: sing ye praises with understanding"
(Psalm 47:6–7).

Focal Verses

KJV **Psalm 47:1** O clap your hands, all ye people; shout unto God with the voice of triumph.

2 For the LORD most high is terrible; he is a great King over all the earth.

3 He shall subdue the people under us, and the nations under our feet.

4 He shall choose our inheritance for us, the excellency of Jacob whom he loved. Selah.

5 God is gone up with a shout, the LORD with the sound of a trumpet.

6 Sing praises to God, sing praises: sing praises unto our King, sing praises.

7 For God is the King of all the earth: sing ye praises with understanding.

8 God reigneth over the heathen: God sitteth upon the throne of his holiness.

9 The princes of the people are gathered together, even the people of the God of Abraham: for the shields of the earth belong unto God: he is greatly exalted.

NLT **Psalm 47:1** Come, everyone! Clap your hands! Shout to God with joyful praise!

2 For the LORD Most High is awesome. He is the great King of all the earth.

3 He subdues the nations before us, putting our enemies beneath our feet.

4 He chose the Promised Land as our inheritance, the proud possession of Jacob's descendants, whom he loves. Selah.

5 God has ascended with a mighty shout. The LORD has ascended with trumpets blaring.

6 Sing praises to God, sing praises; sing praises to our King, sing praises!

7 For God is the King over all the earth. Praise him with a psalm.

8 God reigns above the nations, sitting on his holy throne.

9 The rulers of the world have gathered together with the people of the God of Abraham. For all the kings of the earth belong to God. He is highly honored everywhere.

The People, Places, and Times

Kings. From the earliest days of written history in the Ancient Near East, people were mostly organized under kings. The first monarchies arose from city–states. Rural living did not need the rules, regulations, and organization that cities required, so monarchies first began in urban areas.

Israel was slower in adopting a monarchy, because it began as a group of mostly rural clans. But from as early as Genesis 17:6, God promised Abram that he would become the father of kings, and so it was assumed that Israel would be ruled by kings. The major problem that Israel had, when they first asked Samuel for a king like all the other nations, was that they were breaking off the covenant relationship with God as their King (1 Samuel 8:4–8). They did not trust Him to lead them and protect them, and they desired leaders just like the nations around them.

Christ, the King. When God chose David to be the king of Israel, the people had a charismatic leader, a great military man, and a man after God's own heart (1 Samuel 16:12–13; 2 Samuel 5:1–5; Acts 13:22). And it was through the line of David that our Lord and Savior, Christ our King came. The Old Testament made it very clear that this King would be called "Wonderful, Counsellor, The mighty God, The everlasting Father, The Prince of Peace" (Isaiah 9:6). Jesus Christ fulfilled the Old Testament prophecies of God as King.

Jesus announced that with His coming, His kingship began (Luke 17:21). At this time, He is King in the hearts of those who follow Him. He is also ruling over the physical world, which He created and sustains (John 1:3). But in the future, everyone everywhere will see Jesus as the King and all things will come under His rule (Revelation 11:15).

Background

When the Israelites settled in the Promised Land, they were surrounded by idol-worshiping nations and living among people who had numerous gods. The Gentile nations thought of their gods as ruling over the areas in which they lived. This idea often filled the hearts of the Israelites, and they began worshiping the gods they found in their land. The Canaanites had gods of fertility (Baal and Asherah) that the Israelites thought would help them in their farming. The people worshiped the gods of fertility in many decadent ways, such as in religious prostitution.

The Moabites, who were descendants of Lot and lived just to the southeast of Israel, worshiped Chemosh, a god who demanded child sacrifice. We even read that King Ahaz, a descendant of King David, burned his own children as sacrifices to foreign gods (2 Chronicles 28:1–3). Molech, the god of the Ammonites, was also worshiped with human sacrifice. No wonder God detested these religions!

At-A-Glance

1. God Is King Over All the Earth (Psalm 47:1–4)

2. God Has Ascended (vv. 5–6)

3. God Is Reigning Over All the Earth (vv. 7–9)

In Depth

1. God Is King Over All the Earth (Psalm 47:1–4)

This psalm presents the coronation of our God, the King over all. No wonder everyone everywhere is commanded to clap! This psalm was composed during the period when Israel had kings, but always needed to be reminded that the Almighty God was their King.

The sons of Korah (temple assistants) wrote Psalm 47 for a Jewish religious festival, probably for the Feast of Tabernacles, in which Jews fashioned structures of branches and lived in them for one week, once a year, to commemorate the 40 years they lived in tents in the wilderness. First Kings 8:2 reveals that when the temple was inaugurated, Solomon led the people in celebrating the Feast of Tabernacles. According to *Oxford Universal Dictionary,* a "tabernacle" is a temporary dwelling place made of canvas, branches, or boards. It is a hut, a tent, or a booth. During the wilderness years, God dwelt with His people in a tent called the Tabernacle.

Perhaps Solomon was reminding the people that when they lived in tents in the wilderness, so did their God. But now that they lived in the Promised Land in houses of mud, brick, and stone, the temple was to be a permanent facility for His presence. And as Solomon dedicated the brand new temple to the Lord, He saw God symbolically living in the temple. However, as the King of all nations, God is enthroned in heaven above. We read these words in Solomon's prayer of dedication for the temple: "Behold, the heaven and heaven of heavens cannot contain thee" (1 Kings 8:27). Even Solomon's beautiful temple was not the throne of God; heaven itself is not big enough to contain Him.

All of God's people worship the Lord Most High, who is the King over all the nations; but Psalm 47:3–4 reminds us that He chose the Jews specifically. God was the one who empowered them to subdue the nations in Canaan and around them. He gave them an inheritance, that is, the Promised Land. And He took great pride in them and loved them.

But when we look back at verse 1, we see the anticipation of the evangelization of every nation, which is happening right now. Imagine the day when we will all be praising our God together!

2. God Has Ascended (vv. 5–6)

Verses 5 and 6 are the center of this psalm, which was composed as a liturgical procession. When Solomon dedicated the temple, the Ark of the Covenant was solemnly carried on the proscribed poles to bring it to the temple. The ark symbolized God's throne and the temple as His heavenly palace, so it is not hard to imagine that this psalm was used or composed for this occasion. Other processions portrayed in the book of Psalms are meant to be sung as the pilgrims made their way toward the temple in Jerusalem to celebrate the special festivals.

However, many Christians today like to read Psalm 47 on Ascension Sunday, the day that commemorates the day that Christ ascended from earth back to heaven. Angels sang songs of praise when our Savior came to earth as a baby. Surely the whole heavenly host welcomed Him back with shouts of joy, sounds of trumpets, and songs of heavenly praise.

In verse 6, we are commanded four times to sing praises to our King. This is more than the enthusiastic, raucous praise of verse 1. This is the more formal singing of praise. Now we are commanded to make beautiful music to our King.

3. God Is Reigning Over All the Earth (vv. 7–9)

These verses portray the grand finale of history. God is now sitting upon His throne, King over all the earth. Once more we are commanded to sing praises to Him.

This is a missionary psalm. It views the day when God's plan for all people is finally accomplished. God is the King over all the earth. This reminds us of Isaiah 52:7, NIV, which commissions us as missionaries, "How beautiful on the mountains are the feet of those who bring good news, . . .who proclaim salvation, who say to Zion, 'Your God reigns!'" We have an important part in the installation of our God as King over all the earth. Our job is to bring the Good News of salvation to people all over the earth.

Psalm 46:10 tells us that God will be exalted among people all over the earth. The book of Revelation speaks over and over again about the Lord Jesus sitting upon the throne. Angels encircle His throne and sing, "Worthy is the Lamb, who was slain, to receive power and wealth and wisdom and strength and honor and glory and praise!" (5:12).

Search the Scriptures

1. Name some audible ways of praising God, our King (Psalm 47:1, 6–7).

2. Name some reasons for praising God (vv. 2–4, 7–9).

Discuss the Meaning

1. In what ways is God the King over all the earth now?

2. In what ways is His reign in the future?

Lesson in Our Society

When we look around, it's plain to see that Satan still has control over our world today. As believers, we are the ambassadors for the kingdom of God. We represent the interests of our King. Discuss some of the things that God cares about and how we can lobby for His kingdom and do our part to reflect God's kingdom in our society.

Make It Happen

Today, God wants to be King of our lives. What are some areas of your life that you need to more fully turn over to Him?

Follow the Spirit

What God wants me to do:

_____

_____

_____

_____

Remember Your Thoughts

Special insights I have learned:

_____

_____

_____

_____

More Light on the Text

Psalm 47

1 O clap your hands, all ye people; shout unto God with the voice of triumph.

The psalmist begins by calling all the people of God to worship with clapping and shouts of triumph. The Hebrew word for "people" ('*am*, **ahm**) is not the word for "nations" (*gowy*, **GO-ee**), which is normally used to refer to people outside the Jewish nation (Gentiles), but instead carries a more general meaning in this context.

However, the theme of this verse is parallel to the theme of other verses in the Psalms which call all the earth to worship the Lord as King. Consider Psalm 117:1: "O praise the LORD, all ye nations: praise him, all ye people." Psalm 67:3 reads, "Let the people praise thee, O God; let all the people praise thee." And Psalm 86:9 foretells a time when all peoples will unite in praise to the one true God: "All nations whom thou hast made shall come and worship before thee, O Lord; and shall glorify thy name." There is a sense in which the call to worship is a call to separate ourselves from the world and devote ourselves to God and His glory. However, there is also a real sense in which the people of God are called to worship in order to lead the non-believing peoples of the world to worship. Jesus taught that the Father is actively seeking true worshipers from every nation, who will worship in spirit and truth (John 4:23). God-honoring worship is one way that the people of God display the worship that God is seeking.

Hand clapping in Old Testament times was sometimes a derisive gesture (see Lamentations 2:15 and Nahum 3:19), but in Psalm 47, the clapping is an expression of joy. In 2 Kings 11:12, the people clapped in celebration of Joash's installation as king.

In Psalm 47:1, the invitation to shout recalls the celebration David led when he brought the Ark of the Covenant back to Jerusalem in 2 Samuel 6:1–19. This event was marked with extraordinary amounts of sacrifice and dancing to the Lord. Of course, 2 Samuel 6:15 notes that shouting and trumpets were also a part of this joyous event. At this event, David danced with such abandon that his wife Michal derided him for making a fool of himself in front of the people (v. 20). The people of God also celebrated with shouting in Ezra 3:11–13 when the foundation of Zerubbabel's temple was built.

2 For the LORD most high is terrible; he is a great King over all the earth.

In verses 2–4, the psalmist gives reasons for the call to clap and shout. The first reason is that the Lord is "terrible" (Heb. *yare'*, **yaw-RAY**). *Yare'* is a form of the verb "to fear," and it describes the effect that the God has on people. His enemies shudder before Him in absolute terror. His people stand before Him in reverent awe. Other English versions use words such as "awe-inspiring, awesome, glorious, to be feared."

The name of God used here emphasizes the greatness and glory that provokes fear. "Most high" (Heb. *'elyown*, **el-YONE**) describes the Lord as the one who outranks all other rulers and authorities.

3 He shall subdue the people under us, and the nations under our feet.

From the time of Abel (Genesis 4), the people of God have faced opposition from those who are in rebellion against the Lord. The promise of God has always been that He will fight for His people and subdue our enemies. In fact, apart from His efforts on our behalf, the fight would be hopeless.

Believers in Jesus must remember that although we are surrounded by people who do not share our allegiance to Christ, unbelievers are not our true enemies. Our ultimate enemies are sin, death, and Satan. And the Scriptures clearly teach that the Lord's subduing of the nations is uniquely and finally fulfilled in the resurrection of Jesus from the dead. Psalm 2:8–9 hints at this when it predicts the consummation of God's reign over all the earth.

4 He shall choose our inheritance for us, the excellency of Jacob whom he loved. Selah.

If verse 2 directed our attention to God's nature and verse 3 to His certain victory, verse 4 calls us to recognize His generosity. "Inheritance" (Heb. *nachalah,* **nakh-al-AW**) is used frequently in the Old Testament to refer to Canaan—the Promised Land which the Lord promised to Abraham and his descendants forever. An inheritance is a permanent possession and cannot be taken or lost, either voluntarily or involuntarily. In fact, the law of the Jubilee required that land in Canaan not be sold permanently, but return to the family to which it was allotted in the days of Joshua every 50 years (the Year of Jubilee, Leviticus 25:8–17). This was a perpetual testimony to God's eternal promise.

"Excellency" (Heb. *ga'own,* **gaw-OHN**) is translated "pride" or "glory" by other English translations such as NLT and NIV. In other contexts, it refers to the sin of pride (overestimating one's own worth). Here, however, it refers to a right and proper joy in God's good gift of the Promised Land.

5 God is gone up with a shout, the LORD with the sound of a trumpet.

This verse reminds the reader of 2 Samuel 6:15, in which David and the people of Israel bring the Ark of the Covenant into Jerusalem with shouting and the blowing of trumpets. In fact, the psalmist has used key words from 2 Samuel 6:15 in this text to link the passages. "Shout" (Heb. *t@ruw`ah,* **ter-oo-AW**) can refer to shouts of joy or victory, or shouts of fear and alarm. The word is used to mention shouts at the coronation of a king (1 Samuel 10:24), and in battle (Joshua 6:10). In Psalm 47:5, the phrase "sound of a trumpet" is literally "voice of the ram's horn"

in the Hebrew text. The *showphar* (**sho-FAR**), or "ram's horn," was used in celebration as well as in signaling armies or large groups of people in civil assembly. It was a blast of the *showphar* that signaled the people to approach Mount Sinai to receive the Ten Commandments (Exodus 19:16).

The Ark of the Covenant served as the "seat" for God's presence in the tabernacle and the later temple. Thus, the Lord is referred to as the one who is enthroned between or above the cherubim (1 Samuel 4:4; 2 Kings 19:15).

6 Sing praises to God, sing praises: sing praises unto our King, sing praises. 7 For God is the King of all the earth: sing ye praises with understanding.

The psalm begins its final, climactic section with a rousing call to the people of God to join together in loud and passionate worship. The repetition of "sing praises" raises the intensity of the psalm's message, but without losing any focus on the truth. The description of God also builds in intensity, progressing from God, to King, to King of all the earth.

"Sing" (Heb. *zamar,* **zaw-MAR**) may mean either "sing" or "make music." The precise meaning of "with understanding" (Heb. *maskil* or *maskiyl,* **mas-KEEL**) is uncertain. Some English versions translate this "with a psalm" (NLT, RSV) or "a psalm" (NIV), at least partly because *maskil* is used as a title for some 13 psalms (for example: 32, 42). Even though we don't know its precise meaning, *maskil* is derived from a Hebrew word meaning "wisdom, understanding." So we can be certain that the psalmist is not calling his hearers to a type of worship that is based exclusively on human-generated emotion. Worship that honors God is marked by a passionate, sincere, thoughtful response to the truth of who He is and the great things He has done for us.

8 God reigneth over the heathen: God sitteth upon the throne of his holiness.

The Lord is not only the King of His people. He is King over all the earth, even over those who do not acknowledge Him as God. God tells us, "That unto me every knee shall bow, every tongue shall swear" (Isaiah 45:23). The word for "heathen" in Psalm 47:8 is the Hebrew word *gowy* (**GO-ee**), which literally means "nations," but is used frequently in the Old Testament to refer to the Gentiles.

9 The princes of the people are gathered together, even the people of the God of Abraham: for the shields of the earth belong unto God: he is greatly exalted.

The final verse of the psalm points out another reason why God's reign is cause for rejoicing. It is only right and proper for the Creator and Owner of the universe to be on the universe's throne. After all, He is the greatest, the highest; therefore He should reign. "Princes" (Heb. *nadiyb*, **naw-DEEB**) are people of exalted social position such as nobles or overlords. The "shields of the earth" may be a reference to the princes of the people. They are both the protectors and the representatives of all the peoples of the earth, so the Lord's rule over the "shields" expresses both His power over even the greatest human rulers and the universal reach of His reign.

Say It Correctly

Asherah. ASH-uh-ruh.
Baal. BAY-uhl.
Canaanite. KAY-nuh-night.
Chemosh. KEE-mosh.

Daily Bible Readings

M: There Is None Like God
Jeremiah 10:6–10

T: The Lord Is King
Psalm 97

W: The Lord Rules Over All
2 Chronicles 20:5–12

T: The Lord Delivers
Psalm 3

F: The Lord Keeps Safe
Deuteronomy 33:26–29

S: The Lord Loves Justice
Psalm 99

S: The Lord Is Worthy of Praise
Psalm 47

Teaching Tips

1. Words You Should Know

A. God (Psalm 63:1) *'elohiym* (Heb.)—The (true) God, Lord.

B. Power (v. 2) *'oz* (Heb.)—Boldness, might, strength, especially God's.

C. Glory (v. 2) *kabowd* (Heb.)—Splendor, unparalleled honor, dignity, or distinction.

2. Teacher Preparation

Unifying Principle—Filling Our Emptiness. King David rejoices in the comfort and confidence he found in God's presence.

A. Pray that God will use this lesson to meet your students' mental, physical, and spiritual needs.

B. Prayerfully study the entire lesson.

C. Prepare to give a testimony on what it means to feel empty and how God met your need.

3. Open the Lesson

A. Pray based on the Aim for Change.

B. Introduce the Words You Should Know for today's study.

C. Have a volunteer share with the class what it feels like mentally and emotionally to function on empty.

D. Give your testimony.

E. Using the In Focus story, discuss what spending time in God's presence does in building a close relationship with Him.

4. Present the Scriptures

A. Have volunteers read the Focal Verses.

B. Use The People, Places, and Times; Background; At-A-Glance; In Depth; Search the Scriptures questions; and More Light on the Text to clarify meaning.

5. Explore the Meaning

A. Explore the Discuss the Meaning, Lesson in Our Society, and Make It Happen sections.

B. Stress principles from the lesson to help students see how to apply the truth to their daily lives.

6. Next Steps for Application

A. Use the Follow the Spirit and Remember Your Thoughts sections to jot down points to ponder during the week.

B. End with prayer.

OCT
31st

Worship Guide

For the Superintendent or Teacher
Theme: God's Presence Comforts
and Assures
Theme Song: "Does Jesus Care"
Devotional Reading: Psalm 3:1–6
Prayer

God's Presence Comforts and Assures

Bible Background • PSALM 63
Printed Text • PSALM 63 | Devotional Reading • PSALM 3:1–6

—————— Aim for Change ——————

By the end of the lesson, we will: EXPLAIN how David yearned for God's presence; FEEL COMFORTED by God's presence in our lives; and REJOICE in the comfort and confidence found in God's presence.

 In Focus

Charles had a long commute on the train every morning and evening, so he always took along his Bible and his Sunday School lesson. When he was done with his reading, he would lie back in the seat, shut his eyes, and pray. This time with the Lord was the best time of his day.

One morning, Ronny, one of his neighbors, got on the train. "Hey, Charles! I decided to start taking the train, too. With gas prices up, it's the only sensible thing to do." Then Ronny sat down with Charles, and they talked the whole way in to work.

Charles enjoyed talking with Ronny, but after a week of sitting with his neighbor, he realized he was missing his time alone with the Lord. He longed for the opportunity to commune with God. He resolved to do something about it.

If you have a close relationship with the Lord, you will miss it when it is interrupted. What are some of the things that can interrupt that relationship? What do you think Charles can do to get back on track with time alone with God? Remember that God and only God can fill our emptiness; therefore, we must spend time with Him.

—————— Keep in Mind ——————

"O God, thou art my God; early will I seek thee: my soul thirsteth for thee, my flesh longeth for thee in a dry and thirsty land, where no water is"
(Psalm 63:1).

Focal Verses

KJV **Psalm 63:1** O God, thou art my God; early will I seek thee: my soul thirsteth for thee, my flesh longeth for thee in a dry and thirsty land, where no water is;

2 To see thy power and thy glory, so as I have seen thee in the sanctuary.

3 Because thy lovingkindness is better than life, my lips shall praise thee.

4 Thus will I bless thee while I live: I will lift up my hands in thy name.

5 My soul shall be satisfied as with marrow and fatness; and my mouth shall praise thee with joyful lips:

6 When I remember thee upon my bed, and meditate on thee in the night watches.

7 Because thou hast been my help, therefore in the shadow of thy wings will I rejoice.

8 My soul followeth hard after thee: thy right hand upholdeth me.

9 But those that seek my soul, to destroy it, shall go into the lower parts of the earth.

10 They shall fall by the sword: they shall be a portion for foxes.

11 But the king shall rejoice in God; every one that sweareth by him shall glory: but the mouth of them that speak lies shall be stopped.

NLT **Psalm 63:1** O God, you are my God; I earnestly search for you. My soul thirsts for you; my whole body longs for you in this parched and weary land where there is no water.

2 I have seen you in your sanctuary and gazed upon your power and glory.

3 Your unfailing love is better than life itself; how I praise you!

4 I will praise you as long as I live, lifting up my hands to you in prayer.

5 You satisfy me more than the richest feast. I will praise you with songs of joy.

6 I lie awake thinking of you, meditating on you through the night.

7 Because you are my helper, I sing for joy in the shadow of your wings.

8 I cling to you; your strong right hand holds me securely.

9 But those plotting to destroy me will come to ruin. They will go down into the depths of the earth.

10 They will die by the sword and become the food of jackals.

11 But the king will rejoice in God. All who trust in him will praise him, while liars will be silenced.

The People, Places, and Times

The Wilderness of Judah. The Wilderness of Judah was an area of land that was northwest of the Dead Sea. Its western tip was the city of Jerusalem. En-Gedi, located on the shore about 35 miles from Jerusalem, was the place where David hid with his followers when King Saul was pursuing him (1 Samuel 23:29), as well as when Absalom attempted to take the kingdom (2 Samuel 15:1–23).

Background

This psalm was probably written when King David was fleeing from his son, Absalom. We deduce this because David refers to himself as "king" in verse 11. Other times when he escaped to the wilderness were when he was not yet the official king and he would run away from King Saul. David was a mighty warrior, a charismatic king, and a man after God's own heart, but his personal life was a mess. He would definitely not have won an award for father of the year. So Absalom, his son with the long beautiful hair, had stolen the hearts of the people right out from under King David. (Read 2 Samuel 15–17.) A takeover was imminent; his life was in danger, so David hastily fled the city of Jerusalem. He went down into the Kidron Valley just to the east of the city and then to the Wilderness of Judah. Many people who were still loyal to David fled with him, and the Levites came along carrying the Ark of the Covenant. At this time the Levites set down the Ark, and Abiathar the priest offered sacrifices to God until all the people of Jerusalem had safely joined David and his band of loyal followers.

At-A-Glance

1. David Longs for God (Psalm 63:1)

2. David Reflects on Time with God (vv. 2–5)

3. David Meditates on God During the Night (vv. 6–8)

4. David's Enemies Will Get What They Deserve (vv. 9–10)

5. David Rejoices in God (v. 11)

In Depth

1. David Longs for God (Psalm 63:1)

Not only does David know there is a holy, majestic God over all, he also claims this God as his own. When he wakes up in the morning, he intensely desires to meet with the Lord. The word in the KJV is "early," but this word also implies earnestness, so other translations use "earnestly" instead (see NIV and NLT). The idea is that we so desire to have time with our Lord that we can hardly wait to get out of our beds in the morning to open our Bibles and listen to Him.

But David is not lying down in a nice, warm bed; he is out in the wilderness. He has been running for his life, he is exhausted, and he is so hot and thirsty that he is almost delirious with the thought of a drink of cold water. But he is singing of a far greater thirst and that is for God. His whole being is thirsting after the Lord.

2. David Reflects on Time with God (vv. 2–5)

How would you feel if you were somehow incapacitated and could not go to church?

How would you feel if you were living in a country where Christian churches were rare or were not allowed? David did not know how long he would be out in the wilderness and unable to go to the sanctuary to worship, but he was longing to be back in the sanctuary worshiping the Lord. Of course, God's presence goes with us, but it is especially important for the times when we are out in "the wilderness" that we should be able to look back on glorious times of worship with other believers.

David remembers special times in the sanctuary when he was able to really see God's power and glory. He longs to see God's might and awesome splendor again; these thoughts sustain him in the wilderness. We, too, will go through times when we cannot see or feel God, but if we have had true experiences of the holiness of the Lord, we will be able to persevere through the hard times.

3. David Meditates on God During the Night (vv. 6–8)

This psalm begins with waking up early in the morning to worship the Lord; now it moves into mediating on God as we lie in our beds at night. Perhaps David is having trouble sleeping. Maybe this is when he composed this psalm. But this is a great example to us. When we are having trouble sleeping, we can utilize the time in praising God.

As David praised God, he began thinking of all the times in the past when God had helped him. When we are thinking of difficulties we have gone through, we should also think of the things that God taught us as we went through these times. As David thought of God's blessings to him, he began singing in the shadow of God's wings. Imagine David in the hot, unrelenting sun of the Judean wilderness; suddenly, a shadow moves over him to protect him.

4. David's Enemies Will Get What They Deserve (vv. 9–10)

David had very complex and ambiguous feelings toward his son Absalom, because Absalom had murdered Amnon, Absalom's stepbrother. Absalom had stolen David's throne, but David still cared for him because he was his son. In 2 Samuel 18:5, David commanded his generals to be gentle with him. But Joab disobeyed the king and plunged his sword into Absalom's heart. Then Joab's armor-bearers all surrounded him and struck Absalom—a sure overkill. After this, they threw Absalom's body into a pit and made a pile of rocks over him (18:14–17). In Psalm 63:9–10, David does not say he wants to kill his son and his followers; he merely predicts what will happen to them. Those who are not following the Lord will reap eternal punishment and sometimes they will receive punishment while still on this earth. It is important to remember that the writers of our Bible were speaking with God's voice, so David's enemies were God's enemies in a real sense. What David's enemies had plotted for him, they received instead.

5. David Rejoices in God (v. 11)

After David's warning about the end of his enemies, he returns to praising God. Everyone who swears allegiance to God will praise Him, too. But those who live by falsehood shall come to final condemnation. Revelation 21:8 says that all liars will be cast into the lake of fire. The benefits of a life of deception are not worth the final price. How much better to follow after God and praise Him with both our words and deeds!

Search the Scriptures

1. What did the psalmist want to do first thing in the morning (Psalm 63:1)?

2. Where had David seen God's power and glory (v. 2)?

Discuss the Meaning

1. According to today's study, David hungered and thirsted after God from the moment he woke in the morning until he lie awake in bed at night. Why don't we feel the same way?

2. How can we increase our hunger for God?

Lesson in Our Society

Our society today has much that distracts us from focusing on God throughout the day. Online pornography is perhaps one of the biggest hindrances to staying in a right relationship with God. How can we cleanse it from our own lives? How can we help those who are already addicted?

Make It Happen

One of the best ways to increase our desire for God is to spend more time with Him. Share ideas on how to spend that time. How can you get more out of Bible reading? How can you develop the habit of meeting with God every morning? Talk about ideas such as writing a sentence or two in response to your morning Bible reading, keeping a prayer diary, etc.

Follow the Spirit

What God wants me to do:

_____

_____

_____

_____

Remember Your Thoughts

Special insights I have learned:

_____

_____

_____

_____

More Light on the Text
Psalm 63

1 O God, thou art my God; early will I seek thee: my soul thirsteth for thee, my flesh longeth for thee in a dry and thirsty land, where no water is;

The title of the psalm tells us that David is the author and that it was written in the wilderness of Judah. There are two times in his life that potentially led to his proclamations: his flight from Saul (1 Samuel 23–24) and his flight from his son Absalom (2 Samuel 15). The words of Psalm 63, especially the author's referral to himself as "king" (v. 11), fit best with the story of David's flight from Absalom. But the description of the area in which it was written best aligns with the record of his flight from Saul. Thankfully, the resolution of this issue is not necessary for us to fully appreciate this psalm. We can identify with David at both points in his life—on the run from enemies, feeling that friends are few and far between, running low on essential supplies such as food and water, feeling hurt and betrayed, and wondering if and when the Lord is going to make good on His promises to us.

David's way of dealing with his painful ordeal is to declare that God and God alone is the only source of satisfaction. He is the only One who can fill our emptiness.

"Early will I seek" translates the Hebrew verb *shachar* (**shaw-KHAR**), which means "to seek or search early or diligently." The picture here is of a man on a mission. He doesn't just want to find God. He needs God desperately and he knows it. He craves God's presence the way he craves water while running in the desert.

2 To see thy power and thy glory, so as I have seen thee in the sanctuary.

Having identified God as the mainstay of his life, David reflects on previous experiences of God's presence. He remembers and longs for God's power and glory. The "power" (Heb. *`oz*, **oze**) of God is His might or strength which He shows in His acts of deliverance. There is a literal sense in which it is impossible to see God's power, but David is speaking figuratively. He has seen God's power in the stories of the Old Testament: the birth of Isaac, the Exodus from Egypt, and Joshua's conquest of Canaan, to name a few. He has also seen God's power in his own life, perhaps most notably when he defeated Goliath, causing the more powerful Philistine army to flee in terror before the Israelite army (1 Samuel 17). The "glory" (Heb. *kabowd*, **kaw-BODE**) of God refers to His honor, fame, and reputation. It also refers to the majesty, brightness, and splendor of His presence. David recalls his experience of God's power and glory in the "sanctuary" (Heb. *qodesh*, **KO-desh**), a word which means "holy" when used as an adjective. The "holy place" of which David speaks is the tabernacle, the portable temple built under Moses' leadership after the Exodus from Egypt. Exodus 40:34–38 describes how, once it was set up, God's presence descended in a cloud on the Tent of Meeting. Consequently, Moses was not able to enter the tabernacle because of the glory of the Lord. It is possible that David had observed the same display

of God's glory. A more likely explanation, however, is that David saw God's power and glory in his mind's eye during worship. He heard the word of God proclaimed and reflected on God's mighty acts to deliver the people of Israel. He did not attend worship simply for the sake of going through the rituals; David saw the ceremonial acts and the words of Scripture as a revelation of God, whom he longed to know. So he savored the times he had in worship and reflected back on them when he was not able to be present in Jerusalem.

3 Because thy lovingkindness is better than life, my lips shall praise thee.

"Lovingkindness" is an attempt to create an English word for the Hebrew *checed* (**KHEH-sed**). In other passages where it is used, the King James Version translates it "mercy" or "goodness." Other English translations use terms such as "steadfast love," "faithful love," and "unfailing love." Used over 200 times in the Old Testament, *checed* is more than just love, kindness, or mercy. It is God's steadfast kindness to His people no matter the circumstances. When we have sinned and need forgiveness, we can count on His *checed*. When we are oppressed and afflicted, we know that God will defend us because of His *checed*. When we are in the dark night of despair, God is faithful to comfort and sustain us because of His *checed*.

This is why David can say that the Lord's lovingkindness is better than life.

4 Thus will I bless thee while I live: I will lift up my hands in thy name.

The psalmist responds to the steadfast love of God with blessing and praise. To "bless" (Heb. *barak*, **baw-RAK**) the Lord is to simply speak well of Him. Blessing that honors God will focus on His attributes (qualities, characteristics) and His acts. Psalm 145 is a

103

good example, starting with the passionate declaration, "I will bless thy name for ever and ever." The verses that follow describe God's love, mercy, righteousness, and compassion, as well as His mighty acts to save His people.

Lifting hands in prayer and worship is a symbolic act that recognizes God's greatness. Other Scriptures show hands being lifted in a variety of moods. Solomon lifted his hands in a prayer of gratitude and honor when he dedicated the temple (1 Kings 8:22). In Psalm 28:2, David describes lifting his hands in a plea for God's help. Then in Psalm 119:48, the psalmist speaks of lifting hands in respect and love for God's commandments. In addition, Habakkuk 3:10 tells us that the ocean figuratively lifts its hands on high, perhaps in surrender or submission to its Creator.

5 My soul shall be satisfied as with marrow and fatness; and my mouth shall praise thee with joyful lips:

The tone of the psalm changes slightly here as David turns from rejoicing in God's steadfast love to finding his satisfaction in God. Verses 5–8 give us insight into the mindset that motivated David to pursue God wholeheartedly.

He saw communion with God as a great joy that surpasses all the other pleasures this life has to offer. "Soul" (Heb. *nephesh*, **NEH-fesh**) here refers not to the immaterial part of the human being (what leaves the body when death occurs), but to the whole being—the self. "Satisfied" (Heb. *saba`*, **saw-BAH**) means "to be full or to have enough." All that God is for His people—a constant companion, protector, friend, comfort, guide, deliverer, provider (to name a few)—means that when we are experiencing true communion with Him, we will not long for the sinful pleasures the world offers.

6 When I remember thee upon my bed, and meditate on thee in the night watches.

David's thoughts of God at night reveal that his satisfaction in God is not a temporary obsession. He is not simply riding an emotional high for as long as it lasts. No, his highest goal in life is to be satisfied in God, so that is where his thoughts turn when the day is done. What we truly live for is revealed in our secret thoughts—especially when there are no other demands on us and our mind can turn wherever it wants. David's thought patterns reflect a conviction that nothing else can satisfy the deepest desires of his heart except for a relationship with God.

7 Because thou hast been my help, therefore in the shadow of thy wings will I rejoice.

Satisfaction in God requires a right relationship with Him. David describes God as "my help," meaning not that God is his genie in a bottle, but that everything he has accomplished has only come to pass because of God's power.

8 My soul followeth hard after thee: thy right hand upholdeth me.

"Followeth hard after" is literally "clung to" (*dabaq*, **daw-BAK**) in the Hebrew. The expression means "to pursue with determination." We see an example of this determined pursuit of God in Jacob the night he wrestled with God. In Genesis 32:26, Jacob refuses to let go of the angel, saying, "I will not let thee go, except thou bless me." God honored Jacob's attitude by saying that he had prevailed—not meaning that he had overpowered God, but that he had gotten the divine blessing for which he longed. If we are to experience David's satisfaction in God, we must pursue God with more than casual, occasional effort. We must make our relationship with God our first priority and be willing to sacrifice less important things.

9 But those that seek my soul, to destroy it, shall go into the lower parts of the earth. 10 They shall fall by the sword: they shall be a portion for foxes.

A new theme emerges in the final three verses: the psalmist is confident that he will experience God's salvation. This salvation is expressed in two ways: the downfall of his enemies and his final vindication.

"Soul" (Heb. *nephesh*, **NEH-fesh**) is the same Hebrew word used in verses 1 and 5 as a poetic expression for "self." Here it refers to the psalmist's life. As noted above, David wrote this psalm at a time when he was literally running for his life. But he is confident that his enemies will have an unhappy end. The "lower parts of the earth" is a figurative expression for the place of the dead, also referred to as "the pit" or *Sheol* in the Old Testament. See Ezekiel 26:20 where "the low parts of the earth" and "the Pit" are used in parallel and both contrast with "the land of the living."

Verse 10 adds stark detail to the imagery of the death of the psalmist's enemies. It will be violent—a fitting end for those who seek to do violence to the Lord's king. They will also rest in ignominy: "a portion for foxes." Some English translations render the Hebrew *shuw`al* (**shoo-AWL**) as "jackals" instead of "foxes," since the word could refer to either animal and jackals are scavengers. In Middle Eastern culture, one's dignified burial was of paramount importance.

11 But the king shall rejoice in God; every one that sweareth by him shall glory: but the mouth of them that speak lies shall be stopped.

In contrast to his enemies, who will mourn their own demise, David envisions himself celebrating God's deliverance. Those who swear by God (take oaths in His name) are true worshipers of God. The Lord commanded the people of Israel to worship Him alone and take their oaths in His name (Deuteronomy 6:13). This was to be a way they expressed faith that He is the one true God, who will judge righteously between liars and truth tellers.

Say It Correctly

Abiathar. uh-BI-uh-thahr.
Zadok. ZAY-dok.

Daily Bible Readings

M: Hiding from God's Presence
Genesis 3:1–8

T: Fleeing from God's Presence
Jonah 1:1–10

W: Trembling at God's Presence
Psalm 114

T: Coming into God's Presence
Psalm 100

F: Refreshing at God's Presence
Acts 3:17–26

S: Praising in God's Presence
2 Samuel 22:2–7

S: Dwelling in God's Presence
Psalm 63

Teaching Tips

1. Words You Should Know

A. Make a joyful noise (Psalm 66:1) *ruwa`* (Heb.)—A command that literally means "shout."

B. Glorious (v. 2) *kabowd* (Heb.)—Literally, "weighty" or "heavy" with adoration.

C. Proved (v. 10) *bachan* (Heb.)— Examined, tested, tried.

D. Tried (v. 10) *tsaraph* (Heb.)—Smelted or refined, purified.

2. Teacher Preparation

Unifying Principle—Wholly Dependable. We can sing to the Lord because God's great power holds our lives in God's hand and keeps our feet from slipping.

A. Read the entire lesson.

B. Prepare a PowerPoint presentation of beautiful nature scenes of water, foliage, animals, and humankind. Alternately, collect pictures from magazines of beautiful nature scenes to share with the class.

C. Obtain a recording of the song "Awesome God."

3. Open the Lesson

A. Open with prayer using the Aim for Change, and thank God for His dependability.

B. View the PowerPoint presentation while the CD is playing "Awesome God."

C. Discuss how God's creations testify to His awesomeness and power.

D. Use the In Focus story to segue into our theme that our God is an awesome God and He alone is powerful enough to ease our every pain, heartache, and burden.

4. Present the Scriptures

A. Read the Focal Verses.

B. Use The People, Places, and Times; Background; At-A-Glance; In Depth; Search the Scriptures questions; and More Light on the Text to clarify the meaning.

5. Explore the Meaning

A. Explore the Discuss the Meaning, Lesson in Society, and Make It Happen sections.

B. Tie them in with today's discussions.

6. Next Steps for Application

A. Share how we can render honor and praises to God for all He has done.

B. Close with prayer.

Worship Guide

For the Superintendent or Teacher
Theme: God Is Awesome
Theme Song: "Awesome God"
Devotional Reading: Psalm 40:1–5
Prayer

God Is Awesome

Bible Background • PSALM 66
Printed Text • PSALM 66:1–12 | Devotional Reading • PSALM 40:1–5

—————————— Aim for Change ——————————

By the end of the lesson, we will: DISCUSS God's dependability; FEEL confidence in God's ability to save and deliver; and PRAISE God for His dependability.

———————— 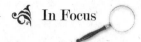 In Focus ————————

Horatio Spafford was a successful Chicago lawyer. He had a wife named Anna and five children (four daughters and a son) whom he adored. Early in 1871, his only son died suddenly. That same year during the Great Chicago Fire, Spafford lost his vast real estate holdings and his life savings. Then in November 1873, he planned a cruise to Europe with his wife and four daughters. At the last minute, a business matter came up, so he arranged for his wife and daughters to sail on ahead, and he promised to join them in a few days. Tragedy struck again. The ship his family was sailing aboard was struck by another ship, and it sank. Spafford's four daughters died along with 240 others, but his wife, Anna, was among the survivors who were rescued.

When Horatio Spafford made the trip to meet his grieving wife, he sailed near the place where his four daughters had drowned. There, in the midst of his sorrow, he wrote the words to a song that has brought hope and consolation to millions: "It Is Well with My Soul."

NOV 7th

Psalm 66 is a song of thanksgiving. As we study this lesson, let us keep in mind that just as Spafford found out, God—and God alone—is powerful enough to ease our every pain, heartache, and burden.

———————— Keep in Mind ————————

"Come and see the works of God: he is terrible in his
doing toward the children of men"
(Psalm 66:5).

"Come and see the works of God: he is terrible in his doing
toward the children of men" (Psalm 66:5).

Focal Verses

KJV **Psalm 66:1** Make a joyful noise unto God, all ye lands:

2 Sing forth the honour of his name: make his praise glorious.

3 Say unto God, How terrible art thou in thy works! through the greatness of thy power shall thine enemies submit themselves unto thee.

4 All the earth shall worship thee, and shall sing unto thee; they shall sing to thy name. Selah.

5 Come and see the works of God: he is terrible in his doing toward the children of men.

6 He turned the sea into dry land: they went through the flood on foot: there did we rejoice in him.

7 He ruleth by his power for ever; his eyes behold the nations: let not the rebellious exalt themselves. Selah.

8 O bless our God, ye people, and make the voice of his praise to be heard:

9 Which holdeth our soul in life, and suffereth not our feet to be moved.

10 For thou, O God, hast proved us: thou hast tried us, as silver is tried.

11 Thou broughtest us into the net; thou laidst affliction upon our loins.

12 Thou hast caused men to ride over our heads; we went through fire and through water: but thou broughtest us out into a wealthy place.

NLT **Psalm 66:1** Shout joyful praises to God, all the earth!

2 Sing about the glory of his name! Tell the world how glorious he is.

3 Say to God, "How awesome are your deeds! Your enemies cringe before your mighty power.

4 Everything on earth will worship you; they will sing your praises, shouting your name in glorious songs."

5 Come and see what our God has done, what awesome miracles he performs for people!

6 He made a dry path through the Red Sea, and his people went across on foot. There we rejoiced in him.

7 For by his great power he rules forever. He watches every movement of the nations; let no rebel rise in defiance.

8 Let the whole world bless our God and loudly sing his praises.

9 Our lives are in his hands, and he keeps our feet from stumbling.

10 You have tested us, O God; you have purified us like silver.

11 You captured us in your net and laid the burden of slavery on our backs.

12 Then you put a leader over us. We went through fire and flood, but you brought us to a place of great abundance.

The People, Places, and Times

Selah. This Hebrew expression (**SEH-lah**) is found almost exclusively in the book of Psalms. There it is used some 73 times. It also appears in Habakkuk 3:3, 9, and 13. The meaning of the word is widely debated by biblical scholars. On one hand, many feel that it is a technical term for music or recitation. Some believe that "Selah" denotes a pause or a suspension in singing of the psalm or recitation, and the insertion of an instrumental musical interlude. The Greek Septuagint renders the word *dia'psalma,* meaning "a musical interlude." The psalms were sung and sometimes accompanied by instruments. In Psalm 9:16, "Selah" is paired with the Hebrew word *Higgaion* or *Higgayown* (**hig-gaw-YONE**), indicating an association with a harp or some other soft musical instrument.

Background

The psalms or *mizmôr* (Heb. **miz-MORE**) were an integral part of ancient Israel's formal worship service. They were prayers set to music and sung by the worshipers. The psalms provided the Israelites with an opportunity for an intimate and honest conversation with their God. The breadth and range of human experience and emotions are contained in Psalms. In them, we see God's people approach their Creator with fervent appeals and exuberant praise. The emotional experiences expressed in the psalms are both raw and reverent. It should not be surprising to us that the book of Psalms, more than any other section of the Old Testament, remains so widely used in present-day worship. Psalm 23 for instance, is often used to teach children Bible memorization.

The words of many hymns that we sing are actually based on wording found in the Psalms. Similarities in structural patterns allow psalms to be categorized and divided into various genres or types. These genres include hymns or songs of praise; laments; wisdom psalms; royal or kingship psalms; and psalms of blessings and cursing (where the Israelites cursed their enemies and petitioned God to deliver them from their enemies), remembrance, and thanksgiving. Psalm 66 is generally classified as a psalm of thanksgiving. This type of psalm is a response to God having answered the psalmist's plea for His help.

At-A-Glance

1. The Call for Universal Praise
(Psalm 66:1–4)

2. Thanksgiving for God's Power
(vv. 5–7)

3. Testimony of God's Protection
(vv. 8–12)

In Depth

1. The Call for Universal Praise (Psalm 66:1–4)

While David is credited with authorship of nearly half of the 150 psalms, it is believed that there were more than a dozen composers of psalms. These other authors include King Solomon, King Hezekiah, Asaph the Levite, the sons of Korah (a family of singers charged with leading the singing in Israel), and court musicians Heman and Ethan. Psalm 90 is attributed to Moses. David's name is not ascribed to Psalm 66; rather, the subscription is simply to "the director of music." This anonymous identification occurs in 54 other psalms.

Psalm 66 opens with a call to glorify God. Note that this call is not limited to the author or even to the people of God (Israel); the psalm's author insists that the call is for "all the earth" (66:1, NLT). All the nations of the earth are to join in a collective calling out to God; they are to pay homage to Him. This vocal cry is a part of deliberate worship of God.

Verse 2 calls for the people to follow their shout with singing. This praise to God will extend beyond the borders of Israel and will be heard throughout the earth (from all nations and tongues).

In verse 3, the people are directed to address God directly: "Say unto God..." It is here that the reason for this communal praise is made clearer. The nations of the world are paying homage to the awesome nature of the Lord God and His mighty works. In this passage, the word "terrible" is better rendered "awesome." So then, "How terrible art thou in thy works!" refers to a fearful reverence that is inspired by God's workings.

The emphasis on the collective praising of God's name is demonstrated through the repetition of the call to worship in verse 4. The word "Selah" appears at the end of this verse. Here, the author is instructing the choir director to have the music stopped so that the celebrants may enter into a brief meditation and thoughtfully consider what they have just sung.

2. Thanksgiving for God's Power (vv. 5–7)

Another key feature of the thanksgiving psalms genre is thanking God for answered prayer. Expressions of gratitude for God's mercy or blessings are a frequent feature of psalms, and they are frequently seen in other Old Testament texts. David prayed a prayer of thanksgiving after God made a covenant

promise with him (2 Samuel 7:18–29). King Solomon led the people in a thanksgiving prayer at the dedication of the Temple (1 Kings 8:23, 27–30). Prayers of thanksgiving are also prevalent in the New Testament. Paul often thanked God for the spiritual vibrancy of the people to whom he wrote primarily (Romans 1:8; 2 Corinthians 8:11–16; 1 Thessalonians 1:2–3). Christians today live with the assurance that we are under the watchful care of a God who is concerned with our every need.

The psalmist now turns his attention to the works of God done "toward the children of man" (Psalm 66:5) or, in other words, on man's behalf. Specifically, God has intervened on Israel's behalf. The psalmist's reference to "what God has done" in verse 5 is describing an earlier period in Israel's history. When the Children of Israel were suffering under harsh Egyptian bondage, they had "cried out" to God for deliverance (Exodus 3:7, 9). The psalmist now recounts how God parted the Red Sea and allowed the Children of Israel to cross on dry land to escape Pharaoh's army. God also made the River Jordan dry in front of the Children of Israel as they crossed into the Promised Land (Joshua 3). Both of these occurrences were national events and highly significant to the Jews. They were both occasions for thankfulness to God for His dependability.

The focus now abruptly shifts from divine works directed toward Israel to recognition of the omnipresence (everywhere present) of the Creator. The psalmist declares, "His eyes behold the nations" (Psalm 66:7). The psalmist's reassurance of the omnipotence (all-powerfulness) and omnipresence of God extend beyond Israel's borders. Once again, the psalmist inserts "Selah," indicating that this is a fitting place for silence and for the worshipers to contemplate that they, and indeed, all the inhabitants of the earth are under God's watchful protection.

3. Testimony of God's Protection (vv. 8–12)

The universal call for praise that we saw earlier is again repeated. This time the people are urged to "bless our God" (v. 8). It is significant that the psalmist calls for the people to bless God. In general, "bless" is a special word that means God will make good things happen to people. In the Old Testament when God blessed people, we often see them having healthy babies or an increase in their crops or livestock. Here we see the people being called upon to bless God. This means that they are being called on to glorify God. The psalmist is confident that he is praising God who answers prayer. Because he is bearing witness that those prayers have reached and touched the very heart of God in the past, there is no question that his cries reach God.

The psalmist now talks in Psalm 66:10 about being "tried," and he uses the metaphor of silver refining to make his point clear. A refiner's fire is so hot that it causes any metal being heated to separate from the dross that is inside of it. This dross is the waste and impure materials contained in metal in its raw state. As the silver gets hotter, these impurities rise to the surface and form a scum-like coating. The silversmith is now able to skim it off, and remove these impurities. The more dross is removed during this process, the finer the grade of silver that will remain. The finer the silver, the more valuable it becomes to the refiner. The refiner's role in this process is crucial, and he is ever present; the refiner monitors the heat of the fire and removes the impurities. He is assured that the silver is pure when he can see his reflection in it.

In this way, our faith becomes more precious to the Lord as the impurities in our lives are removed. Our faith can only grow as we claim the promises of God's Word and look to Him for comfort and strength through the trials that He allows to come into our lives.

Search the Scriptures

Fill in the blanks.

1. "Make a _____ noise unto God, all ye lands" (Psalms 66:1).

2. "All the earth shall _____ thee, and shall sing unto thee; they shall sing to thy name. Selah" (v. 4).

Discuss the Meaning

1. Consider verse 10 when the psalmist says, "Thou, O God, hast proved us." When have you felt you were being tested by God or overwhelmed by hardship?

2. We sometimes communicate more with God during times of emotional turmoil and during periods of intense joy. How has God used these times to strengthen your relationship with Him?

Lesson in Our Society

God has freely given humankind so many things. He gives us physical life and all of the things necessary to sustain that life (e.g., food, water, shelter, and the very air that we breathe). Through the sacrifice of His only Son, our Lord Jesus, the Christ, God has provided us with a rich spiritual life and the promise of life ever after. Our response to such lovingkindness should be, "Thanks be unto God for his unspeakable gift" (2 Corinthians 9:15). Because of this, Christians, like the psalmists, ought to praise and thank God at all times.

Make It Happen

This week, examine your commitment to wholly depending on God by asking yourself the following questions at the end of each day: "How often did I thank God today? How many people did I tell about my thankfulness?" Did the things I said today reflect that God is in control of my life?" Don't worry if your end-of-the-day report is not terrific. After your morning prayers, stand in front of the mirror and say, "Lord, I thank You for the opportunity to get it right today. Lord, help me trust in You. Father, give me a mind like Jesus Christ so that I can let You reign and rule in my life. Amen."

Follow the Spirit

What God wants me to do:

_____

_____

_____

_____

Remember Your Thoughts

Special insights I have learned:

_____

_____

_____

_____

More Light on the Text

Psalm 66:1–12

1 Make a joyful noise unto God, all ye lands: 2 Sing forth the honour of his name: make his praise glorious.

The first four verses open the psalm by calling the entire earth to worship God. "Make a joyful noise" (Heb. *ruwa`*, **roo-AH**) is a command that literally means "shout." *Ruwa* may refer to a variety of different shouts, but the translators of most English versions render it "shout for joy" or "shout with joy" (NIV, NLT) because the context is clearly one of worship and celebration.

"All ye lands" is literally "all the earth" in Hebrew (*'erets,* **EH-rets**). As Creator of the entire world, the Lord deserves to receive praise from people everywhere. The praise that is offered to God should reflect the truth of who He is. The "honour" (Heb. *kabowd,* **kaw-BODE**) of His name is translated "glory" in most English versions. "Glorious" (verse 2) is the same word in the Hebrew text. *Kabowd* literally means "weighty, heavy." When used of a person, it means "impressive, honorable, worthy of respect."

3 Say unto God, How terrible art thou in thy works! through the greatness of thy power shall thine enemies submit themselves unto thee.

"Terrible" (Heb. *yare',* **yaw-RAY**) literally means "to be feared." Other English versions translate it "awesome" (e.g., NLT and NIV). A sober contemplation of all that God has done should create a healthy respect for Him in us and give pause to anyone who is hostile to God. He called the universe into existence, creating everything that exists with the power of His Word. He holds the power of life and death in His hand. No one should think that he or she can prevail against the Lord of the universe.

113

The verb in Psalm 66:3 translated "submit" (Heb. *kachásh*, **kaw-KHASH**) often means "to deceive." For this reason, some English translations render this phrase "give feigned obedience." However, another meaning the word carries is "to grow lean." The verb is sometimes used to mean "cower or cringe in fear" and this translation is preferred (see RSV and NIV; see also Deuteronomy 33:29; Psalm 81:15). The enemies of God will be cut down to size when they face His holy judgment. Christ's death and resurrection means that He has defeated all of His and our enemies (see Colossians 2:15). Those who align themselves with the enemies of the Cross will share in their defeat.

4 All the earth shall worship thee, and shall sing unto thee; they shall sing to thy name. Selah.

"Worship" (Heb. *shachah*, **shaw-KHAW**) means "bow down deeply, show obeisance." Worship is central to the purpose for which God created humankind, and God has ordained that we must worship Him. There is a sense in which all the earth already does worship—there are worshipers of the true God all over the world from an incredible variety of ethnic and linguistic groups.

However, the worship of the whole earth is not yet what it will be one day. Isaiah 45:23 foretells a day in which "every knee shall bow." Philippians 2:10 applies this prediction to Christ—He will receive the praises of all people. Clearly, some of those who worship on that last day will do so willingly and gladly because they have embraced Christ's lordship. Others, however, will do so because they can no longer resist Him. Psalm 2:9 paints a graphic picture: "Thou shalt break (or rule) them with a rod of iron."

In Psalm 66:4, the repetition of the word "sing" (Heb. *zamar*, **zaw-MAR**) makes it clear that this worship of God will be a genuinely joyful time for the people of God. Isaiah 2:2–4 describes this joyful day: all of God's people will gather in Zion, and peace and justice will reign.

5 Come and see the works of God: he is terrible in his doing toward the children of men.

"Come and see" invites the audience in; the psalmist is serving as our tour guide. He will point out the items of significance to us and help us understand them.

We see first a characterization of God as "terrible" (Heb. *yare'*, **yaw-RAY**) in His works. This is the same word used in verse 3 which literally means "fearsome" or "awe-inspiring." Verse 3 called us to confess the awesome, fear-inspiring nature of God's works. Now we are to consider them by examining them closely in our mind's eye.

The precise meaning of the phrase "toward the children of men" is unclear. Some English translations use the same approach as the Septuagint (the ancient Greek translation of the Old Testament) and take the preposition "toward" to mean "on behalf of; for." The phrase may also emphasize that God's greatness overwhelms anything that human beings can do or comprehend, expressing a thought similar to that of Romans 11:34: "For who hath known the mind of the Lord?"

6 He turned the sea into dry land: they went through the flood on foot: there did we rejoice in him.

In Exodus 14:21–22, the Lord sent a strong wind that pushed back the waters of the Red Sea, creating a stretch of dry land with walls of water on both sides. The people of Israel passed through, and the pursuing Egyptians followed them. But the Lord caused the Egyptian chariots to bog down in the middle of the Red Sea, and the Egyptians realized that the Lord was fighting for Israel. They wanted to run, but it was too late. Before they could escape, the Red Sea returned to its place, wiping out the entire chariot force of the Egyptian army.

In the psalm we are studying this week, the word "flood" is literally "river" (*nahar*, **naw-HAWR**) in the Hebrew, so it may be a reference to another story in which Israel passed through a body of water: the parting of the Jordan River in Joshua 3, which enabled the Israelites to cross over. However, *nahar* may refer to bodies of water other than rivers (see Jonah 2:3), so the exclusive reference is not certain.

"There did we rejoice" (Psalm 66:6) is actually a command in the Hebrew. Some English translations and the Septuagint interpret it as a command for the reader: "come, let us rejoice" (NIV).

7 He ruleth by his power for ever; his eyes behold the nations: let not the rebellious exalt themselves. Selah.

"His eyes" is an example of anthropomorphism (a figure of speech in which human characteristics are attributed to a nonhuman—in this instance, God). We know that, being a spirit, the Lord does not literally have eyes. However, He is fully aware of all that is happening. Nothing is hidden from Him. The people of God can live in confidence because He is always watching. To the righteous, the eyes of the Lord are a source of comfort and assurance. Second Chronicles 16:9 tells us that He watches in order to support those who fear Him. But to the wicked, the eyes of the Lord are menacing reminders of certain judgment.

The word "rebellious" as used in Psalm 66:7 is a form of the Hebrew verb *carar* (**saw-RAR**), which means both "to be stubborn" and "to be rebellious." The rebellious are those who refuse to listen and resist those who are in authority over them. "Exalt" (Heb. *ruwm*, **room**) means "to raise up." The rebellious are being warned not to think too highly of themselves. They will be humbled when they stand before the Lord. Though they are proud now, they will one day regret their attitude and actions.

8 O bless our God, ye people, and make the voice of his praise to be heard:

The theme of the psalm now shifts to praising God for His faithfulness to His people. Although the people of Israel have been the direct beneficiaries of His goodness, the invitation to bless the Lord goes out to all peoples (see Deuteronomy 32:43). Most English versions translate "people" (Heb. `am, **ahm**) as "peoples." The New Living Translation goes even further: "Let the whole world bless our God."

9 Which holdeth our soul in life, and suffereth not our feet to be moved.

Verses 9–12 give three reasons for all peoples to lift their voices in praise to God. We see in verse 9 that God has preserved His people. "Holdeth our soul in life" simply means that He has kept us alive. "Suffereth not our feet to be moved" means that He has not permitted our feet to slip. Psalm 121:3 is a parallel passage: "He will not suffer thy foot to be moved: he that keepeth thee will not slumber."

These passages remind us that the righteous are distinguished by their willingness to entrust themselves fully to God's care.

10 For thou, O God, hast proved us: thou hast tried us, as silver is tried.

Verses 10 and 11 provide the second reason to praise God. The Lord, who preserves His people, is also the Lord who tests and tries us. "Proved" (Heb. *bachan*, **baw-KHAN**) means "examined, tested, tried." Here it is used in parallel with "tried" (Heb. *tsaraph*, **tsaw-RAF**), a word that means "smelted," or "refined." Refining is a metallurgical process of removing impurity (dross) from metals. Refiners use heat to melt ore and may add substances that help to promote the separation of elements.

God's use of "heat" (trial) to purify, prove, and strengthen His people is a common theme in the Scriptures.

11 Thou broughtest us into the net; thou laidst affliction upon our loins. 12 Thou hast caused men to ride over our heads; we went through fire and through water: but thou broughtest us out into a wealthy place.

The psalmist uses several graphic word pictures to depict the Lord's purifying work. "Net" (Heb. *matsuwd*, **maw-TSOOD**) here is a "cage, hunting implement, snare," or "trap." The traps are the devices that the wicked—Satan and his allies—use in their attempts to snare the people of God. "Affliction" (Heb. *muw`aqah*, **moo-aw-KAW**) means "compression, distress, pressure." Some other English versions translate it "oppressive burden" or "crushing burden." "Men to ride over our heads" is simply a word picture of being dominated and humiliated by an oppressor.

The Lord's servant is distinguished by his or her reliance on God to deliver him or her from the enemy's cruel traps and torture (Psalm 31:4). However, sometimes the Lord's purifying work is accomplished through the work of His enemies. For a time it may appear as though the evil one has triumphed over God's kingdom when a Christian experiences pain, trouble, or loss. Because he or she knows that the Lord is sovereign and will work all things to the good (Romans 8:28), the psalmist can praise the Lord for these travails.

Say It Correctly

Asaph. AY-saf.
Selah. SEE-luh, -lah.
Zacharias. zak-uh-RI-uh.

Daily Bible Readings

M: Deliver Us This Day!
Judges 10:10–16

T: Direct Your Heart to the Lord
1 Samuel 7:3–13

W: The Lord Will Save Me
1 Samuel 17:31–37

T: God Gives a New Song
Psalm 40:1–5

F: God Hears My Prayer
Psalm 66:13–20

S: God Rules Over the Nations
Psalm 22:19–28

S: God Rules Forever
Psalm 66:1–12

Teaching Tips

1. Words You Should Know

A. Lord (Psalm 90:1) *Adonay* (Heb.)—
Another way of saying "my lord" or "God."

B. Dwelling place (v. 1) *ma'ownah*
(Heb.)—A location that is a person's refuge,
home.

C. Hearts (v. 12) *lebab* (Heb.)—The
place, figuratively, where our emotions and
passions exist.

D. Unto wisdom (v. 12) *chokmah* (Heb.)—
The ability to be prudent and ethical.

2. Teacher Preparation

Unifying Principle—Life Is Short. Psalm
90 reminds us that though life is fleeting,
with God's eternal presence, we can live
wisely.

A. Study the complete lesson.

B. Be prepared to list on the board how
God makes life worthwhile.

C. Study the statistics in the In Focus
presentation and prepare to discuss.

3. Open the Lesson

A. Open with prayer, using the Aim for
Change.

B. Start your list on the board and ask the
class to help you complete it. Discuss.

C. Link the statistical data from the In
Focus presentation and the list to Psalm
90:1–12.

4. Present the Scriptures

A. Have a volunteer read Psalm 90:1–12.

B. Use The People, Places, and Times;
Background; At-A-Glance; In Depth; Search
the Scriptures questions; and More Light on
the Text to clarify the meaning.

5. Explore the Meaning

A. Explore the meaning of the text for life
today with the Discuss the Meaning, Lesson
in Our Society, and Make It Happen sections.

B. Allow input from your students.

6. Next Steps for Application

A. Summarize with a discussion on how
we can live out our days wisely (i.e., act as
though we know our days are numbered).

B. Close with prayer.

Worship Guide

For the Superintendent or Teacher
Theme: God Is Forever
Theme Song: "Lead Me, Guide Me"
Devotional Reading: 1 Timothy 1:12–17
Prayer

God Is Forever

Bible Background • PSALM 90
Printed Text • PSALM 90:1–12 | Devotional Reading • 1 TIMOTHY 1:12–17

———— Aim for Change ————

By the end of the lesson, we will: LIST ways that God makes life worthwhile; ACKNOWLEDGE God's greatness and the frailties of humanity; and ASK God to help us live out our days wisely.

————  In Focus ————

Each year, the United States Department of Labor's Bureau of Labor Statistics prepares its American Time Use Survey (ATUS). This report details the average amount of time per day that Americans spend working, doing household chores, caring for their children, and participating in educational activities. The survey also reports how much time is spent engaging in leisurely activities. The results from the 2008 ATUS were fascinating. There are 168 hours in each week. On average, we will spend about 56 of those hours sleeping, about 24 hours eating and attending to our personal hygiene, and about 50 hours working or traveling to work. This only leaves us with about 35 hours a week or 5 hours per day of "discretionary" time. Sadly, the study indicated that mothers working outside the home spent an average of 11 minutes a day on weekdays, and 30 minutes a day on weekends with their children. The picture was even worse for fathers. The men only spend an average of eight minutes a day on weekdays and 14 minutes a day on weekends in different activities with their children.

In Psalm 90, Moses reminds us that the number of our days is short and that time is a precious commodity that we dare not squander.

———— Keep in Mind ————

"Before the mountains were brought forth, or ever thou hadst formed the earth and the world, even from everlasting to everlasting, thou art God"
(Psalm 90:2).

"Before the mountains were brought forth, or ever thou hadst formed the earth and the world, even from everlasting to everlasting, thou art God" (Psalm 90:2).

Focal Verses

KJV **Psalm 90:1** LORD, thou hast been our dwelling place in all generations.

2 Before the mountains were brought forth, or ever thou hadst formed the earth and the world, even from everlasting to everlasting, thou art God.

3 Thou turnest man to destruction; and sayest, Return, ye children of men.

4 For a thousand years in thy sight are but as yesterday when it is past, and as a watch in the night.

5 Thou carriest them away as with a flood; they are as a sleep: in the morning they are like grass which groweth up.

6 In the morning it flourisheth, and groweth up; in the evening it is cut down, and withereth.

7 For we are consumed by thine anger, and by thy wrath are we troubled.

8 Thou hast set our iniquities before thee, our secret sins in the light of thy countenance.

9 For all our days are passed away in thy wrath: we spend our years as a tale that is told.

10 The days of our years are threescore years and ten; and if by reason of strength they be fourscore years, yet is their strength labour and sorrow; for it is soon cut off, and we fly away.

11 Who knoweth the power of thine anger? even according to thy fear, so is thy wrath.

12 So teach us to number our days, that we may apply our hearts unto wisdom.

NLT **Psalm 90:1** Lord, through all the generations you have been our home!

2 Before the mountains were born, before you gave birth to the earth and the world, from beginning to end, you are God.

3 You turn people back to dust, saying, "Return to dust, you mortals!"

4 For you, a thousand years are as a passing day, as brief as a few night hours.

5 You sweep people away like dreams that disappear. They are like grass that springs up in the morning.

6 In the morning it blooms and flourishes, but by evening it is dry and withered.

7 We wither beneath your anger; we are overwhelmed by your fury.

8 You spread out our sins before you—our secret sins—and you see them all.

9 We live our lives beneath your wrath, ending our years with a groan.

10 Seventy years are given to us! Some even live to eighty. But even the best years are filled with pain and trouble; soon they disappear, and we fly away.

11 Who can comprehend the power of your anger? Your wrath is as awesome as the fear you deserve.

12 Teach us to realize the brevity of life, so that we may grow in wisdom.

The People, Places, and Times

The Book of the Psalms. The book of Psalms, also called The Psalter, is actually divided into five sections or books: 1–41; 42–72; 73–89; 90–106; 107–150. Each of these five sections ends with a doxology, a formal ascription or assigning of praise to God. Psalm 150 is itself a doxology to the entire collection of psalms. The psalms are not arranged in chronological order, although within the five books they are often grouped together according to shared themes, purpose, author, or collector.

Background

The information in the superscription or title of Psalm 90 credits Moses as the author. This would make Psalm 90 one of the oldest psalms. Moses lived during the time the Children of Israel lived under Egyptian captivity and during the period of their exodus from Egypt. This was the great salvation story of the Old Testament, and Jews referred back to it often, much like we refer back to the death and resurrection of Jesus as a turning point in our Christian history.

While it is not clear exactly when Moses wrote Psalm 90, it is widely speculated that it was written during the final 40 years of his life. By this time, Moses had witnessed the Israelites' hasty departure from Egypt, he had seen the Red Sea parted to allow them to cross over and escape the Egyptian army, he had seen his people fed with bread from heaven, and he had stood on the border that would lead them into the Promised Land. Sadly, the faithlessness and disobedience of the Israelites caused them to have to wander in the desert another 40 years. Anyone over the age of 40 died in the desert and never entered into the land God had promised to His people. Moses, too, sinned, and even

though he was the leader, he never crossed over into the Promised Land.

During his years of leadership, Moses experienced and witnessed the entire gamut of human emotions. He had seen his people crying out to God for His mercy, and he had watched as they willfully sinned against the same God who had answered their prayers and delivered them.

At-A-Glance

1. Remember That God Is Eternal
(Psalm 90:1–2)

2. Remember That Humans Are Temporal
(vv. 3–6)

3. Remember That Humans Are Sinful
(vv. 7–12)

In Depth

1. Remember That God Is Eternal (Psalm 90:1–2)

The first two verses of the psalm are a praise statement, and they appear to be Moses addressing God: "LORD, thou hast been our dwellingplace in all generations" (v. 1). The expression "dwellingplace" is generally used in the Bible to describe a remote place of safety for wild animals like lions to go for safety and rest, rather than a human home. As they wandered through the desert, the Israelites surely saw such shelters, and perhaps even envied the animals for them. In their nomadic state, they could see that even wild beasts had a place to stay. Without a place to call their home, Moses rightly recognizes that God is their only source of rest and protection. This fact is further strengthened by the knowledge that God has offered that security "in all generations."

Moses proceeds to describe the eternal nature of God. He declares that even something that appeared as ageless and immovable as the mountains was in fact created by the hands of God. God had always been present. This mirrors the apostle Peter's admonition, "Do not forget this one thing... With the Lord a day is like a thousand years, and a thousand years are like a day" (2 Peter 3:8, NIV). Moses acknowledges that God is not bound by physical laws of time.

2. Remember That Humans Are Temporal (vv. 3–6)

While Moses is clearly confident in his belief that God provided a "dwelling place" for the Israelites (v. 1, NLT, NIV), his long association with them made Moses aware that they were a people who could be ungrateful and hard-hearted. He seems to anticipate that this provision of a "dwellingplace" from God was not enough to compel the Israelites to trust God completely.

Moses begins by addressing humankind's temporal nature. People, Moses points out, are *not* immortal; rather, they are finite, and will not live forever. Moses says that the people will return to the earth. When he uses the word "destruction" (v. 3), Moses is actually speaking of human beings dying and returning to dust. We want to pause here and remember that our mortality is founded in our sin. God created humans from the dust of the earth, and because of the original humankind's (Adam's) sin, we were condemned to return to dust.

In verse 4, Moses compares the transitory nature of humans with the eternal nature of God. He insists that, to God, a thousand years is like "yesterday" or like a "watch in the night" (v. 4). Because we have not experienced that length of time, a thousand

years is incomprehensible to us. However, the totality of God's existence (forever) makes a thousand years seem insignificant.

In verses 5 and 6, Moses uses examples to demonstrate how insignificant the lifetime of a person is when compared to the eternity of God. First, he says that we are like an object gliding "along the tides of time on a racing river" (v. 5, LB). Within a few seconds, time has carried us downstream out of sight and memory. Secondly, Moses compares humans to a dream. As soon as the sleeping person awakens, the dream has vanished, forgotten. Finally, he compares people to newly growing grass. In the morning it is green and growing, yet after a long day of heat, it dries out, withers, and is cut down.

3. Remember That Humans Are Sinful (vv. 7–12)

Until this point, Moses' discussion about human life has been general. We want to remember that although what he is discussing in this psalm applies to our present-day lives, when he penned Psalm 90, he was writing about the Israelites (God's Chosen People) that he was leading. Moses now becomes very specific about what is happening in their lives. Moses declares that it is the sinful life of the people that causes their lives to be short. God has "set" or placed humankind's sins or "iniquities" before Him (v. 8). Even "secret sins," Moses warns, are seen by God.

Theologian Dr. Lewis Sperry Chafer once quipped, "Your sin may be a secret here on earth, but it's an open scandal in heaven." God is everywhere. He sees and hears what we say, do, and think. There is no sin we can hide from Him.

Moses implores God to "teach" us how to "number our days" (v. 12). In Hebrew, this expression means "to allot" or "apportion." This word emphasizes the value of each day. Moses knows that only God can direct us on how to redeem this valuable commodity to reach the desired result of gaining "a heart of wisdom" (NIV).

Search the Scriptures
Fill in the blanks.

1. "LORD, thou hast been our _____ _____ place in all generations" (Psalm 90:1).

2. "Thou turnest man to destruction; and sayest, Return, ye _____ of _____" (v. 3).

Discuss the Meaning
1. The psalmist declares that God has been "our dwelling place." What does this mean for our own relationships with God?

2. Verses 7–11 vividly describe God's anger and judgment. How do we reconcile this depiction of God with the Bible's portrayal of His fatherly love toward us?

Lesson in Our Society
Why should we care that God is our dwelling place? God oversees all of history—past, present, and the future. Our understanding is limited, so we have no idea how history is unfolding. But because we do know that God knows what is going on, this is not a cause for worry or concern. He has it under control. We do not always understand why God allows terrible things to happen in history, but we can be sure that He knows what is best for us and what is best for the world.

Make It Happen
Psalm 90 makes it clear that God is fully aware of our sin. Those "secret" sins that others may not know about, or sins that we have rationalized, are fully exposed before an all-knowing God. Not only are our lives shortened by sin, but these sins can also bring unnecessary pain and sadness to ourselves and sometimes to those we care about. This week, ask the Lord to help you address any unconfessed sin in your life so that you might draw closer to Him and to His will.

Follow the Spirit
What God wants me to do:

_____

_____

_____

_____

Remember Your Thoughts
Special insights I have learned:

_____

_____

_____

_____

More Light on the Text
Psalm 90:1–12

1 LORD, thou hast been our dwelling place in all generations. 2 Before the mountains were brought forth, or ever thou hadst formed the earth and the world, even from everlasting to everlasting, thou art God.

This portion of Scripture opens with the author extolling and establishing the pre-existent, eternal, and everlasting nature of the Almighty God; the psalmist confirmed this by the use of the words, "Before the..." The name of the Lord used in this context came from the Hebrew word *Adonay* (**ad-o-NOY**), which means "my lord, lord" and stresses the glory, majesty, and power of the great Yahweh who has supreme authority and jurisdiction over the whole earth and all its contents.

Moses emphasized that the Lord ruled in the past, reigns now, and will continue to exercise supremacy over every creature in every corner of the earth and in the lives of all humanity, especially His redeemed children. The psalmist established that God is not only there for His people, but He also "hast been our dwelling place," which in Hebrew is *ma`ownah* (**meh-o-NAW**) and means "refuge, habitation." In other words, moment after moment, and generation after generation, forever and ever, God has been Moses' refuge from life's storms!

3 Thou turnest man to destruction; and sayest, Return, ye children of men. 4 For a thousand years in thy sight are but as yesterday when it is past, and as a watch in the night.

God's perfect will is to bring all His people back to Himself to experience divine love and grace in line with His established, ultimate purpose. The Lord intends to heal, restore, redeem, and transform His people from sin and waywardness. The Fall in Eden surely had its impact on the nature of humankind and the environment in which we make our living. However, God's original plans and purposes are infallible.

A "thousand years in [God's] sight" (90:4), according to biblical interpretation, is like just a day before the Lord. The metaphoric use of a thousand years in the text adequately demonstrates God's everlasting patience and long-suffering nature to forgive and accept His people whenever they truly repent and change their wicked ways as they respond to God's invitation to reposition themselves in His original purpose.

5 Thou carriest them away as with a flood; they are as a sleep: in the morning they are like grass which groweth up. 6 In the morning it flourisheth, and groweth up; in the evening it is cut down, and withereth.

It is a biblical fact that humankind, without the abiding presence of God working in their personal and community lives, is worthless. In verse 5, there is a strong suggestion regarding the transience of human beings. That is, without God, the mere human life is on a journey toward decay and depreciation as the moments and times hurry by. God's eternal plan for living forever in His presence, specifically a life in full obedience to His revealed will, cannot be undermined by any spiritual or natural forces.

7 For we are consumed by thine anger, and by thy wrath we are troubled. 8 Thou hast set our iniquities before thee, our secret sins in the light of thy countenance. 9 For all our days are passed away in thy wrath; we spend our years as a tale that is told.

When we fail to live a life of obedience and do not completely depend on God's prescribed will for our lives for successful living, we are in danger of facing His wrath to be vented on us because of His nature of justice and holiness. In the text, the Hebrew word for "consumed" (*kalah,* **kaw-LAW**), which means "to be spent, used up, destroyed." The word "wrath" in Hebrew is *chemah* (**khay-MAW**), which means "burning anger, rage." God is portrayed here as the consuming fire whose indignation consumes and swallows anything that contradicts His holy nature and divine essence. If we want God to be our place of refuge in times of trouble or persecution, we must fully entrust our lives and everything to Him, and pattern our lives in accordance to His perfect will and Word for us (John 15:1–8).

10 The days of our years are threescore years and ten; and if by reason of strength they be fourscore years, yet is their strength labour and sorrow; for it is soon cut off, and we fly away. **11** Who knoweth the power of thine anger? even according to thy fear, so is thy wrath. **12** So teach us to number our days, that we may apply our hearts unto wisdom.

In a general sense, the psalmist continues to remind us of our human frailty and weaknesses because of the original sin and its resultant expressions or practices of evil through our actions or deeds. Consequently, our longevity on earth is limited to a certain time frame: "The days of our years are..." Moses reminds us that one day our lives will be over on earth because natural death will "soon cut off" our existence on earth in our mortal bodies. Yet it is important to know that God has put His people on earth in particular geographic locations for a specific purpose (Acts 17:24–29). It is therefore incumbent on all the children of God to use wisely all the opportunities, resources, and talents which the Lord has endowed us with.

Dwelling in the Lord for our salvation, security, peace, and long life not only takes into account our human limitations, but it also focuses on God's divine umbrella or canopy covering our lives. Because we have completely surrendered everything unto Him without any reservation, we can expect Him to cover and protect us.

In the Hebrew, the word "hearts" is *lebab* (**lay-BAWB**), which means "the seat of emotions and passion." Therefore, from generation to generation, as God's children apply themselves to true "wisdom" (Heb. *chokmah*, **khok-MAW**), which means "prudence, an understanding of ethics," we will enjoy His glorious presence of protection.

Say It Correctly

Adonay. a-DOH-ni, a-doh-NIGH.
Omnipotent. om-NIP-uh-tent.
Omniscient. ahm-NIH-shunt.
Omnipresent. ahm-nih-PREHZ uhnt.
Shalom. shah-LOHM.

Daily Bible Readings

M: The King of the Ages
1 Timothy 1:12–17

T: Stand Up and Bless the Lord
Nehemiah 9:1–5

W: God's Eternal Purpose
Ephesians 3:7–13

T: God's Eternal Power
Romans 1:18–24

F: An Eternal Weight of Glory
2 Corinthians 4:13–18

S: All Our Days
Psalm 90:13–17

S: From Everlasting to Everlasting
Psalm 90:1–12

Teaching Tips

1. Words You Should Know

A. Dwelleth (Psalm 91:1) *yashab* (Heb.)—Inhabits, lives in, stays with.

B. In the secret (v. 1) *cether* (Heb.)—Covering, for the purpose of protection.

C. Pestilence (v. 3) *deber* (Heb.)—A plague; an extremely contagious disease of epidemic.

2. Teacher Preparation

Unifying Principle—Where Is My Security Blanket? Psalm 91 tells us that if we trust in God, God will rescue and honor us.

A. Study and meditate on the complete lesson.

B. Use various Bible commentaries that explain the link between Psalms 90 and 91. Be prepared to discuss that link.

C. Prepare to also share a testimony of how God protected you in a time of trouble or a trial.

3. Open the Lesson

A. Open with prayer, using the Aim for Change.

B. Discuss the In Focus story in light of Psalm 91, and ask, "Does God always deliver the way that we expect? Why? Why not?"

C. Share your testimony and allow a few students to do the same.

4. Present the Scriptures

A. Have a volunteer dramatically read Psalm 91.

B. Share the information you researched on the link between Psalms 90 and 91.

C. Then use The People, Places, and Times; Background; At-A-Glance; In Depth; Search the Scriptures questions; and More Light on the Text to clarify meaning.

5. Explore the Meaning

A. Use the Discuss the Meaning, Lesson in Our Society, and Make It Happen sections for further discussion.

B. Allow students to give input.

6. Next Steps for Application

A. Remind the class that they can use the Follow the Spirit and Remember Your Thoughts sections to write points that they would like to meditate on during the week.

B. Close with prayer.

Worship Guide

For the Superintendent or Teacher
Theme: God Delivers and Protects
Theme Song: "He Hideth My Soul"
Devotional Reading: Isaiah 52:7–12
Prayer

God Delivers and Protects

Bible Background • PSALM 91
Printed Text • PSALM 91:1–6, 9–16 | Devotional Reading • ISAIAH 52:7–12

Aim for Change

By the end of the lesson, we will: EXPLAIN how God is a shelter and refuge in the midst of fears; FEEL confidence in God's ability to protect us; and DECLARE faith in God's ability to protect us.

In Focus

Kristine tried to adjust her eyes to the darkness that surrounded her. Through the dust, she could make out forms nearby—bodies. The last thing she remembered was that she and about six ladies from the Women's Ministry had been in the Fellowship Hall packing groceries for the needy. Then she remembered hearing a low, rumbling noise. It was an earthquake.

Kristine recalled screaming out for everyone to get under the tables. Something must have struck her, because after that, everything went black. She wasn't sure how long she had been unconscious, but she did know she needed to get the other ladies and herself out of the building. Then she sniffed. There was a disturbingly familiar smell in the room. It was the odor of escaping gas. Kristine closed her eyes and began to pray. "Lord", she prayed, "protect us. Thank You for being our refuge, a very present help in our time of trouble." God kept them safe.

Psalm 91 reassures us that God hears the call of those who trust in Him and He is our refuge and our protection. Even if He chooses to take us home to be with Him, He still protects our soul from eternal damnation. We are under God's divine covering of salvation.

Keep in Mind

NOV 21st

"Because he hath set his love upon me, therefore will I deliver him: I will set him on high, because he hath known my name"
(Psalm 91:14).

Focal Verses

KJV **Psalm 91:1** He that dwelleth in the secret place of the most High shall abide under the shadow of the Almighty.

2 I will say of the LORD, He is my refuge and my fortress: my God; in him will I trust.

3 Surely he shall deliver thee from the snare of the fowler, and from the noisome pestilence.

4 He shall cover thee with his feathers, and under his wings shalt thou trust: his truth shall be thy shield and buckler.

5 Thou shalt not be afraid for the terror by night; nor for the arrow that flieth by day;

6 Nor for the pestilence that walketh in darkness; nor for the destruction that wasteth at noonday.

91:9 Because thou hast made the LORD, which is my refuge, even the most High, thy habitation;

10 There shall no evil befall thee, neither shall any plague come nigh thy dwelling.

11 For he shall give his angels charge over thee, to keep thee in all thy ways.

12 They shall bear thee up in their hands, lest thou dash thy foot against a stone.

13 Thou shalt tread upon the lion and adder: the young lion and the dragon shalt thou trample under thy feet.

14 Because he hath set his love upon me, therefore will I deliver him: I will set him on high, because he hath known my name.

15 He shall call upon me, and I will answer him: I will be with him in trouble; I will deliver him, and honour him.

16 With long life will I satisfy him, and show him my salvation.

NLT **Psalm 91:1** Those who live in the shelter of the Most High will find rest in the shadow of the Almighty.

2 This I declare about the LORD; He alone is my refuge, my place of safety; he is my God, and I trust him.

3 For he will rescue you from every trap and protect you from deadly disease.

4 He will cover you with his feathers. He will shelter you with his wings. His faithful promises are your armor and protection.

5 Do not be afraid of the terrors of the night, nor the arrow that flies in the day.

6 Do not dread the disease that stalks in darkness, nor the disaster that strikes at midday.

91:9 If you make the LORD your refuge, if you make the Most High your shelter,

10 no evil will conquer you; no plague will come near your home.

11 For he will order his angels to protect you wherever you go.

12 They will hold you up with their hands so you won't even hurt your foot on a stone.

13 You will trample upon lions and cobras; you will crush fierce lions and serpents under your feet!

14 The LORD says, "I will rescue those who love me. I will protect those who trust in my name.

15 When they call on me, I will answer; I will be with them in trouble. I will rescue and honor them.

16 I will reward them with a long life and give them my salvation."

The People, Places, and Times

Poetic Imagery in Psalms. Imagery is present throughout the Bible; however, it is most prevalent in the poetic sections of Scripture. It includes a wide variety of literary devices, including three that we encounter quite frequently in Psalms: simile, metaphor, and personification.

With simile, the psalmist helps us see some truth by explicitly comparing it to something else, using the words "like" or "as." An example of simile is found in the opening verse of Psalm 42. Here, the simile compares a thirsty deer looking for water with the psalmist's own search for satisfaction in the Lord.

Conversely, a metaphor makes more direct comparisons. These comparisons are made without the use of the words "like" or "as." For instance, in Psalm 23, we read: "The LORD is my shepherd; I shall not want." Here, the comparison of the Lord to a shepherd is made directly.

Personification is the technique of ascribing human qualities to something that is non-human. We are seeing personification when we read, "Why was it, O sea, that you fled, O Jordan, that you turned back" (Psalm 114:5, NIV).

Background

Because Psalm 91 has no superscription or title, we cannot, with any certainty, determine the writer or its date of composition. Scholars are equally divided about the authorship. Some ascribe it to David, and yet others strongly believe that Moses is the most likely author. Many of the latter are following the Jewish tradition, which holds if the author of a psalm is not explicitly identified in the superscription, then the reader should go back to the nearest psalm that is identified and assume a connection of authorship. In this case, the nearest psalm to return to is Psalm 90, which is clearly ascribed to Moses.

Another textual clue indicating Moses as the author lies in Psalm 91:14: "he hath set his love upon me." We find a variation of that phrase, "The LORD did not set his love upon you, nor choose you, because ye were more in number than any people; for ye were the fewest of all people," in only one other place in the Bible: Deuteronomy 7:7. Because this is in one of the five books of Moses, some hold it as evidence that Moses is the most probable writer of Psalm 91.

At-A-Glance

1. Proof and Province of the Protector
(Psalm 91:1–2)

2. The Character of God's Protection
(vv. 3–6)

3. Testimony of God's Protection
(vv. 9–10)

4. Instruments of God's Protection
(vv. 11–13)

5. God's Promise of Protection
(vv. 14–16)

In Depth

1. Proof and Province of the Protector (Psalm 91:1–2)

One of the most fascinating features of this particular psalm is that, in its opening verses, it identifies God by three different names. Each of these names reveals to the reader an aspect of God's divine nature. First, the psalmist identifies God as "most High." Here we see that God is above all hardship, difficulties, and dangers. Secondly, we're told God is "Almighty," meaning that no one and nothing is powerful enough to overcome God. Finally, the psalmist identifies God as "the LORD." LORD or Yahweh is God's covenant name. When Moses addressed God in the form of a burning bush, this is how God identified Himself—"I Am That I Am." By identifying His name this way, we should see that God was assuring Moses, "I am, " and that "I am with you." All three of these names emphasize deity and the unlimited strength and power of God.

The "secret place" the writer refers to is that place where God dwelt. As the Children of Israel traveled from Egypt to the Promised Land, they spent some time at Sinai and lived in an encampment which had a specific design. It was surrounded by three tribes on each of its sides. The encampment was enclosed with a six-foot fence fashioned of cloth and wooden poles. On one side of the encampment was an entrance into the outer court. When someone entered this way, the first thing they saw was the brazen altar. This was where worshipers would bring their sacrifices to the priests. The priests would then prepare and place it on the altar. The first thing ancient worshipers approaching God encountered was their sin and the need to sacrifice in atonement (payment for sin).

Further inside of the encampment's outer court was a laver. This was a large, water-filled bowl on a base. The laver was used for cleansing by the priests. Behind the laver was yet another structure constructed of skins stretched over poles. Inside of this structure, and behind a special curtain, was the "holy place." To the left were the golden candlesticks. To the right was the table of showbread, and directly in front was the altar that burned with incense. Just beyond the incense was the veil and cubicle that was known as the holiest of holies. The Ark of the Covenant was kept here. This was a most sacred area, and the place where the ancient Israelites believed God dwelt. An ordinary Israelite could never enter this place, and even the priests were only allowed to enter once a year.

Notice in Psalm 91's opening verses that the psalmist has been speaking in the third person, using the impersonal pronoun "he." In this way we can understand that what he is saying is directed toward anyone seeking wisdom about the protection God offers. Now we see that the psalmist is actually depicting someone looking for God in the "secret place" where He abides. The psalmist speaks of taking his search to that sacred inner chamber where God dwells. Here and here alone the worshiper may enjoy fellowship with God.

2. The Character of God's Protection (vv. 3–6)

The psalmist goes on to explore the theme of God as the ultimate source of protection. He uses symbolic figures of speech to present images of God's toughness and tenderness. First he implies that danger, both natural and human-made, abound. Danger can be swift and can entrap and ensnare us suddenly.

God's power of protection is presented in poetic imagery. We are presented with the image of a mother bird safely tucking her young in the safety and protection of her wing. There, they remain securely guarded. We are invited to imagine God tenderly sheltering and caring for us. In sharp contrast to this is the imagery of "shield" or "armor" (v. 4). For those He protects, God is gentle and tender. For the attacker, or those who pose a threat to His beloved, however, God is a strong opponent who cannot be defeated.

The psalmist asserts that God's "truth," or the words and promises that He has given to us, are our protection, but the writer does not in any way minimize the dangers we face. Then verses 5–6 offer assurance that no matter what the threat is, God is able to protect us. Whether the attacks come from "arrow[s]...by day" (men) or from "pestilence [illness or natural disaster] that walketh" at night, we need only remain close to the heart or the will of God. Because our God gives us 24-hour protection, neither seen or unseen threats can catch Him unaware.

3. Testimony of God's Protection (vv. 9–10)

In these verses, the psalmist offers assurance that sin will not go unpunished. The wicked will have to endure the wrath of God, but this wrath will not fall on those who trust in Him. The protection of those who abide "under the shadow of the Almighty" should erase any unwarranted fears the believer may harbor. With God as our shield, we need not have to fear the opposition. With God as our refuge, we cannot fall. This assurance is made repeatedly in the New Testament, including the reminder, "What then shall we say to these things? If God be for us, who can be against us? He that spared not his own Son, but delivered him up for us all, how shall he not with him also freely give us all things?" (Romans 8:31–32).

4. Instruments of God's Protection (vv. 11–13)

The psalmist offers further comfort by reminding us that God's means of protection are more powerful than Satan's means of opposition. God, the psalmist asserts, will employ His angels to protect and guard us "in all thy ways" (v. 11). In other words, nothing is too small to escape the loving and watchful eye of God. This angelic care will include protection from even minimal danger like striking our feet against a stone, where God will deploy the angels to "bear" or carry us up in their hands so no harm will come to us (v. 12). This promise of protection is stated in a figure of speech to emphasize the extent of God's care. His protection is intended to put away unhealthy fears and to prevent us from falling. However, this does not mean that we will not stumble.

5. God's Promise of Protection (vv. 14–16)

Here we have the final word on our protection. The narration now switches from third person to first person: God is talking directly to us. It is only fitting that His word should be the last word. God Himself promises to "deliver" those who are in great danger (v. 14). We could interpret this to mean that God will spare us from a dangerous circumstance, or that He may bring us safely through the danger.

Perhaps even more importantly, God promises the one who knows His name that He will "honour him" (v. 15). This means that not only will God deliver us, but He will do it in a way that preserves our dignity and His glory. For example, God's deliverance of Israel from the Egyptian army at the Red Sea was glorious. In verses 14–16, God promises that if we trust Him, He will deliver us and honor us.

The promise of God's protection is conditional. It is for those who are personally related to Him: "Because he hath set his love upon me, therefore will I deliver him" (v. 14).

Search the Scriptures

Fill in the blanks.

1. "He that _____ in the secret place of the most High shall abide under the _____ of the Almighty" (Psalm 91:1).

2. "He shall _____ thee with his feathers, and under his wings shalt thou trust: his _____ shall be thy shield and buckler" (v. 4).

Discuss the Meaning

1. How has the way you pray in times of trouble and distress changed over the years?

2. Have you gone or are you going through a trial that has caused you to doubt God? Explain.

Lesson in Our Society

Because Christians have experienced the forgiveness of their sins in Jesus Christ, we can experience the safety and security promised to us in Psalm 91 by abiding "in the shelter of the Most High" (v. 1, RSV). We must take God's provision of protection seriously. While Psalm 90 demonstrated a healthy fear of God, Psalm 91 presents a fear of failing and being trampled by opposition. This latter fear can keep us, if left unchecked, from obeying His Word and serving the Lord.

Make It Happen

What events are occurring in your life that are making you fearful? God is waiting for you to call on Him and ask for His help in this area of your life. Spend some time this week allowing Psalm 91 to minister to you. Make a commitment to read this psalm each night.

Follow the Spirit

What God wants me to do:

_____

_____

_____

_____

Remember Your Thoughts

Special insights I have learned:

_____

_____

_____

_____

More Light on the Text

Psalm 91:1–6, 9–16

1 He that dwelleth in the secret place of the most High shall abide under the shadow of the Almighty.

The Hebrew word for "dwelleth" is *yashab* (**yaw-SHAB**), and it means "inhabits" or "remains." In this text, *yashab* describes the importance of remaining "in the secret place." (The Hebrew word for "in the secret" is *cether*, **SAY-ther,** which means "covering" or "protection.") The phrase "of God's protection" conveys the idea of returning into God's abode, staying constantly in His presence, getting completely acquainted or connected with Him, and resting permanently in Him. The "secret place" is a refuge, a place of safety and a covering from all forms of destructive elements that seek to attack or destroy the children of God, and to prevent us from experiencing the fullness of God's blessings and peace and His divine providence.

The word translated "Almighty" here is in Hebrew *shadday* (**shad-DAH-ee**). It represents an ancient title of God's protective character, and it was greatly feared by the enemies of God's people.

2 I will say of the LORD, He is my refuge and my fortress: my God; in him will I trust.

The writer moves the audience into an entirely new realm, from theology and doctrine into realistic and personal experiences of faith. God's children must completely focus and surrender their entire lives and resources to Almighty God.

3 Surely he shall deliver thee from the snare of the fowler, and from the noisome pestilence. 4 He shall cover thee with his feathers, and under his wings shalt thou trust; his truth shall be thy shield and buckler.

The psalmist deliberately established a connection between natural and physical occurrences and their corresponding spiritual and demonic elements. For instance, on the one hand, words such as "snare of the fowler" in Hebrew is *yaquwsh* (**yaw-KOOSH**), meaning "trapper" or "bait-layer" for game or fish. This phrase seems to imply human-made threats with intent to spiritually invoke forces to cause supernatural havoc in people's lives, rather than mere natural disasters. The word "pestilence" in Hebrew is *deber* (**DEH-ber**), which means "plague" or "disease." *Deber* has its origins from the Hebrew word *middeber*, which suggests a treacherous plot and heartbreaking slander or accusation. This part of Psalm 91 conveys how supernatural and evil forces can work against people and their communities to bring about death and destruction.

5 Thou shalt not be afraid for the terror by night; nor for the arrow that flieth by day; 6 Nor for the pestilence that walketh in darkness, nor for the destruction that wasteth at noonday.

Fear is an enemy with the power to create torment and disruptive behavior. Fear has the power to neutralize a person's deep faith and absolute trust in the power and wisdom of God (compare 2 Timothy 1:7; 1 John 4:18). When the children of God believe in the faithfulness of God and the unchanging power of His promise to protect, lead, and provide for them, it lays a very good foundation for exercising absolute confidence in His ability to provide for their well-being and salvation. When a child of God dwells in His secret place, there is no reason to be frozen because of the "terror [that comes] by night" and "the arrow that flieth by day" (v. 5).

The Hebrew word *qeteb* (**KEH-teb**) translated as "destruction" in the text refers to pestilential epidemics geared to cut off our godly objectives or dreams from becoming reality. The Lord is ever ready, in His love and power, to defend and protect us from challenges which the enemy has designed to destroy our initiatives or efforts as we desire to make progress according to God's plan for our lives.

91:9 Because thou hast made the LORD, which is my refuge, even the most High, thy habitation; 10 There shall no evil befall thee, neither shall any plague come nigh thy dwelling. 11 For he shall give his angels charge over thee, to keep thee in all thy ways. 12 They shall bear thee up in their hands, lest thou dash thy foot against a stone.

The concept of divine protection in this discussion is built on the premise that the people of God must be dependent and obedient to the basic conditions or principles laid down in the Word of God in order to enjoy the fullness of God's blessings of protection, deliverance, and security. In other words, God's children must make the Lord their *refuge* and *habitation*. In the Hebrew, the word "refuge" (*machaceh*, **makh-as-EH**) means "shelter from rain or storm, from danger." Therefore, the Lord has delegated His angels and given us the power of the Holy Spirit to build a solid spiritual wall of defense around His people to keep them from destruction.

13 Thou shalt tread upon the lion and adder: the young lion and the dragon shalt thou trample under thy feet. 14 Because he hath set his love upon me, therefore will I deliver him: I will set him on high, because he hath known my name. 15 He shall call upon me, and I will answer him: I will be with him in trouble; I will deliver him, and honour him. 16 With long life will I satisfy him, and show him my salvation.

The image of a lion is used in the Scriptures to represent Jesus Christ, the Lion of the tribe of Judah, because of His kingship and conquering power (Revelation 5:1–5). A lion is also used to refer to the devil: destructive, seeking to attack the people of God (1 Peter 5:8–9). In this particular context in the Psalm, the writer used "lion" to represent Satan and Israel's predatory enemies, as well as the actual possibility of facing such a dangerous creature. The psalmist also employed the image of the "serpent" or "adder" to symbolize actual and potential dangers posed by satanic and physical enemies of the people of God (Genesis 3:1–15; Mark 16:15–18).

The image of the "dragon" describes how the enemy works to destroy God's children. The dragon has been used in the Scriptures to portray how the wicked arm of the enemy, Satan, has been stretched out for the destruction and annihilation of the lives and resources of the people of God (Revelation 12:1–17).

Say It Correctly

Atonement. uh-TOHN-muhnt.
Deuteronomy. doo-tuh-RON-uh-mee.
Laver. LAY-vuhr.
Yahweh. YAH-veh, -vay.

Daily Bible Readings

M: Call Upon the Lord
Psalm 18:1–6

T: A Refuge for the Poor
Psalm 14

W: A Refuge for the Needy
Isaiah 25:1–5

T: A Refuge for the Children
Proverbs 14:22–27

F: A Refuge for the Future
Jeremiah 16:14–21

S: God Is My Fortress
Psalm 59:1–10

S: Those Who Love the Lord
Psalm 91:1–6, 9–16

Teaching Tips

1. Words You Should Know

A. Known (Psalm 139:1) *yada`* (Heb.)—Have knowledge of, are wise about, have revealed.

B. Path (v. 3) *'orach* (Heb.)—Connotes an ongoing process of taking dynamic steps toward an expected end.

C. Reins (v. 13) *kilyah* (Heb.)—Literally means the kidneys, the inner parts.

2. Teacher Preparation

Unifying Principle—Comforting Awareness. The psalmist proclaims that God knows us better than we know ourselves.

A. Study all the sections of the lesson.

B. Use various Bible commentaries that will help you better understand Psalm 139, noting which of the five books this psalm appears in and its meaning.

C. Be prepared to discuss in detail.

3. Open the Lesson

A. Open with praying the Aim for Change.

B. Write on the board "Our God is all-knowing." Discuss.

C. Now, discuss the link between a holy God and having a clean heart.

D. For further discussion, use the In Focus story.

4. Present the Scriptures

A. Have three volunteers dramatically read the Focal Verses: verses 1–6, 13–16, and 23–24.

B. Share the information you researched in the commentaries on Psalm 139.

C. Use The People, Places, and Times; Background; At-A-Glance; In Depth; Search the Scriptures questions; and More Light on the Text to clarify meaning.

5. Explore the Meaning

A. From the Discuss the Meaning and Lesson in Our Society sections, challenge your students to think about who they really are—their "real" selves.

B. Allow volunteers to share.

6. Next Steps for Application

A. From the Make It Happen section, challenge your students to commit portions of Psalm 139 to memory and completely trust our Creator.

B. Close with prayer.

Worship Guide

For the Superintendent or Teacher
Theme: God Is All-Knowing
Theme Song: "It Took a Miracle"
Devotional Reading: 1 John 3:18–24
Prayer

NOV
28th

God Is All-Knowing

Bible Background • PSALM 139
Printed Text • PSALM 139:1–6, 13–16, 23–24 | Devotional Reading • 1 JOHN 3:18–24

—— Aim for Change ——

By the end of the lesson, we will: CITE how much and how well God knows us; REFLECT on the all-knowing God and our relationship; and INVITE the Lord to create a clean heart within each of us.

 In Focus

When Valerie entered her kitchen, her husband was hanging up the telephone. He collapsed into a chair laughing. She asked, "What's so funny?"

Brian told her that he had just been talking with their son's kindergarten teacher. "The teacher told me that Junior came to class and regaled them with stories about his daddy. The teacher told me that Junior said his daddy knew everything—even secret stuff!" Junior had told his classmates that his daddy knew that Junior had hidden a stash of uneaten Brussels sprouts in the recycling container in their garage.

Valerie laughed too. She and Brian had ferreted out the Brussels sprouts because of the pungent odor that filled the garage for a week. Junior had also told the class that his daddy had taken him to work on a Saturday, and when they played Hide-and-Seek in the big office, his daddy found him each and every time. Brian told Valerie that he had simply turned on the office surveillance cameras and then watched their son as he hid in the various offices.

Psalm 139 teaches us that God is omnipresent (all-present or present everywhere), omniscient (all-knowing), and omnipotent (all-powerful). Nothing can escape His divine presence or knowledge.

—— Keep in Mind ——

"For there is not a word in my tongue, but, lo, O LORD, thou knowest it altogether" (Psalm 139:4).

"For there is not a word in my tongue, but, lo, O LORD, thou knowest it altogether" (Psalm 139:4).

Focal Verses

KJV **Psalm 139:1** O LORD, thou hast searched me, and known me.

2 Thou knowest my downsitting and mine uprising, thou understandest my thought afar off.

3 Thou compassest my path and my lying down, and art acquainted with all my ways.

4 For there is not a word in my tongue, but, lo, O LORD, thou knowest it altogether.

5 Thou hast beset me behind and before, and laid thine hand upon me.

6 Such knowledge is too wonderful for me; it is high, I cannot attain unto it.

139:13 For thou hast possessed my reins: thou hast covered me in my mother's womb.

14 I will praise thee; for I am fearfully and wonderfully made: marvellous are thy works; and that my soul knoweth right well.

15 My substance was not hid from thee, when I was made in secret, and curiously wrought in the lowest parts of the earth.

16 Thine eyes did see my substance, yet being unperfect; and in thy book all my members were written, which in continuance were fashioned, when as yet there was none of them.

139:23 Search me, O God, and know my heart: try me, and know my thoughts:

24 And see if there be any wicked way in me, and lead me in the way everlasting.

NLT **Psalm 139:1** O LORD, you have examined my heart and know everything about me.

2 You know when I sit down or stand up. You know my thoughts even when I'm far away.

3 You see me when I travel and when I rest at home. You know everything I do.

4 You know what I am going to say even before I say it, LORD.

5 You go before me and follow me. You place your hand of blessing on my head.

6 Such knowledge is too wonderful for me, too great for me to understand!

139:13 You made all the delicate, inner parts of my body and knit me together in my mother's womb.

14 Thank you for making me so wonderfully complex! Your workmanship is marvelous—how well I know it.

15 You watched me as I was being formed in utter seclusion, as I was woven together in the dark of the womb.

16 You saw me before I was born. Every day of my life was recorded in your book. Every moment was laid out before a single day had passed.

139:23 Search me, O God, and know my heart; test me and know my anxious thoughts.

24 Point out anything in me that offends you, and lead me along the path of everlasting life.

The People, Places, and Times

Psalms and the Davidic Monarchy. The book of Psalms represents the perfect manifestation of Hebrew poetry. It contains 150 individual works composed at different times over six centuries. The full range of the Jewish religious experience is expressed throughout this book. The writers of the psalms respond to the various changes in Israel's history which affected their relationship with God. An outstanding feature of the psalms is their emphasis on the monarchy of King David and his heirs. In fact, a connection with the house of David is exhibited by the writers of the psalms and the men who later edited them.

The "royal" psalms, one of the many genres of psalms, are primarily concerned with the reign of David as the vehicle of blessing for the people of Israel. Psalm 110 assures the king that his enemies will be defeated, gives the king priestly status, and makes clear a link between David and Jesus.

The "pre-exile" psalm writers celebrated the close relationship between God and His chosen rulers. Still other psalms were composed long after the Davidic dynasty was overthrown in 587 B.C.E. (Before the Common Era—also known as B.C.). These writers continued to express hope in the Davidic Covenant, which assured the appointment of a descendant of David to lead the people.

Background

Today one often hears of people having an identity crisis, or a midlife crisis. These expressions refer to people in search of answers to the question, "Who am I, really?" It should not be surprising to us that this question is asked so frequently. The prevailing notion is that we are a part of a vast universe. Psalm 139 presents us with a man who is seriously thinking about himself and his relationship to an all-knowing, ever present, all-powerful Creator.

At-A-Glance

1. The Unfathomable Knowledge of God
(Psalm 139:1–2)

2. The Inescapable Presence of God
(vv. 3–6)

3. The Unattainable Power of God
(vv. 13–16)

4. The Perfect Justice and Mercy of God
(vv. 23–24)

In Depth

1. The Unfathomable Knowledge of God (Psalm 139:1–2)

The psalm opens with David's declaration of God's divine omnipresence. David rejoices in the fact that the Lord has intimate knowledge of our thoughts and our actions. His declaration is fueled by a repetition of verbs that define the word "know" (NIV, emphasis added): *"You have searched"* (v. 1); *"you perceive"* (v. 2); *"you discern"* and *"are familiar"* (v. 3); and *"you know it completely"* (v. 4). These phrases make it clear that there is no part of David's (or, by extension, our) character that is hidden from God, who has exhaustive knowledge of David's very soul.

Because we are human, we perceive through our senses of sight, hearing, touch, taste, and smell. There are limits to what our senses let us perceive and understand. For instance, scientists have discovered that our sense of taste is altered if we are blindfolded and asked to taste something. God's senses are not limited in any way. His Spirit "searcheth all things"(1 Corinthians 2:10). The exhaustive knowledge God has concerning each of us is echoed further in the New Testament. God is so aware of us that He has numbered the hairs on our heads (Luke 12:7). God knows our prayers before we pray them (Matthew 6:8). God hears every whispered word, and one day He will shout them from the housetops (Luke 12:3).

The phrase in Psalm 139:3, "My downsitting and mine uprising," denotes God's awareness of our actions and our conduct. God also is aware of our strengths and our weaknesses. We can rest in the knowledge that He is aware of every frustration in our lives. The temptations we battle daily are known to Him; our dreams and aspirations are no secret to Him.

2. The Inescapable Presence of God (vv. 3–6)

When David acknowledges, "Thou compassest my path" (v. 3), he is saying that God is in control. It is not fate, not chance or happenstance that charts the path ahead for us; it is He—the true and living God. It is God who tells us when to stop and rest. He gives us time for spiritual refreshment to pause from the stress and weariness of this life. Consequently, we should be careful to listen when the Lord tells us to slow down and rest. These are times for us to meditate and rest in Him, and He will reward our obedience with spiritual renewal.

The next verses reveal that God is fully aware of our motivations and actions. Even when it is unclear to us why we say and do the things we say and do, God knows because He has planned our days, guided our ways, and protected our path.

3. The Unattainable Power of God (vv. 13–16)

David has praised God's omniscience (all-knowing) and omnipresence (all-present). He now turns his attention to the power of God in the creation of man and woman, and begins praising God's omnipotence (all-powerfulness). Before human conception, David declares that God is forming and fashioning us. David evokes a sense of artistry as he relates that he is "fearfully and wonderfully made" (v. 14). Every aspect of our being is hewn by the mighty hand of God who has carefully and lovingly molded each one of us. Phrases such as "curiously wrought" (v. 15) cause us to picture God skillfully and lovingly molding us, His most precious creations.

4. The Perfect Justice and Mercy of God (vv. 23–24)

Scripture warns us, "The heart is deceitful above all things... Who can know it?" (Jeremiah 17:9). And yet we now see David imploring, "Search me, O God, and know my heart: try me, and know my thoughts" (Psalm 139:23). In response, we ask ourselves: "What kind of a heart do I have?" Hopefully, our hearts are patient and willing to be instructed by God. When David asks God to "search" him, he is aligning himself with God. He is distancing himself from the "men of blood" (v. 19, RSV) whom he refers to earlier, who take the name of God in vain. As David has, we must also have willing hearts. We must be willing to serve God, not just based on commands, but willing to enter into a genuine love relationship with Him. We can only pray that God searches our hearts if we are willing to forsake our evil and selfish ways and try to live clean before Him.

Search the Scriptures

Fill in the blanks.

1. "O LORD, thou hast _____ me, and _____ me" (v. 1).

2. "Such _____ is too wonderful for me; it is high, I cannot attain unto it" (v. 6).

3. "I will praise thee; for I am _____ and wonderfully made: marvellous are thy works; and that my _____ knoweth right well" (v. 14).

Discuss the Meaning

1. Read Psalm 139:13–15. What, to you, is the most amazing thing about the body that God has created for you?

2. As we grow and mature in our relationship with the Lord, we become more Christlike and we also become more aware of our sin. Explain why our hatred of sin should grow as we mature in our relationship with the Lord.

Lesson in Our Society

This lesson raises a very important question for Christians: Exactly what does it mean to be so completely *known* by God? Many of us spend a great deal of time and energy hiding ourselves from other people. We are so afraid that people won't accept the "real" us. So it may be a terrifying thought to some to know that because God is all-knowing, we have nowhere to hide. Well, here's the wonderful news: Yes, God knows absolutely everything about each one of us— everything! And in His infinite wisdom, He loves us just the way we are! Like the most loving of parents, He continues to call us into a loving relationship with Him.

Make It Happen

We live in a world where nothing and no one can be trusted. We are encouraged not to trust anything we cannot see, taste, touch, hear, or smell. Yet we are designed to trust our Creator. This week, make a sincere effort to trust God completely in everything that you do and in all decisions that you make.

Follow the Spirit

What God wants me to do:

_____

_____

_____

_____

Remember Your Thoughts

Special insights I have learned:

_____

_____

_____

_____

More Light on the Text

Psalm 139:1–6, 13–16, 23–24

1 O LORD, thou hast searched me, and known me.

King David, the writer of this psalm, focused on God's all-knowing, all-seeing, and all-powerful attributes and characteristics with respect to his own life, and in particular, his strengths, weaknesses, successes, and failures. David, a man after God's own heart, wanted to please God, who is holy (set apart from sin). But in his desire to please God by submitting to His ultimate authority because of His involvement in the everyday experiences of His people, David was driven to appreciate the fact that God knows everything about him, even his secret sins. David acknowledged that the Lord has carefully examined his heart and mind and is familiar with every minute detail of his story—his daily life experiences (compare Proverbs 25:3; Romans 8:26–28).

In Psalm 139:1, the phrase "known me" in Hebrew is (*yada`*, **yaw-DAH**), which means "to have knowledge," "be wise," "be revealed." The text connotes a twofold idea of God's omniscience to bring about His justice and glory into the lives of His people and to judge them whenever they sin against Him.

2 Thou knowest my downsitting and mine uprising, thou understandeth my thought afar off. 3 Thou compassest my path and my lying down, and art acquainted with all my ways. 4 For there is not a word in my tongue, but, lo, O LORD, thou knowest it altogether.

The psalmist writes, "Thou knowest my downsitting and mine uprising" (v. 2). The Lord knows our *"uprising"*—active involvement and constant engagement in our daily life issues—and our *"downsitting"*— when we are inactive and withdrawn from our responsibilities and roles (emphasis added). In the next part of this verse, a key word used in the original Hebrew text is *rea`* (**RAY-ah**). In English, *rea`* means "thought," one's deep intentions, hidden rationale, and original motivations. In other words, it suggests that even before David (and we) thought about anything, the Lord has *always* foreknown and foreseen every detail—how it started, developed, and later manifested (compare John 1:47–50; Luke 22:33–34, 57–59). The psalmist goes on to explain that the Lord has engulfed his paths in life

(Psalm 139:3). The Hebrew word used here for "my path" is *'orach* (**O-rakh**). It denotes a process in a person's life journey, daily experiences, and a continuous pilgrimage in life. In other words, "my path" suggests an ongoing process of taking steps toward an expected end. David also noted that even in times of his "lying down," which implies the moments when a person becomes stagnant or inactive, God still sees and knows all. Even then, God's divine presence does not desert His people. Believers have the Lord's presence constantly surrounding or enfolding them in every circumstance and dilemma in which they find themselves. It is very comforting and reassuring to know that the Lord is always there with you when you formulate your initial ideas and take your first steps, and later progressively nurture them through daily life experiences.

In addition, the writer went on to declare, "Thou [God] ...art acquainted with all my ways" (v. 3). It is reassuring to understand that the Lord monitors, follows, and accustoms Himself *with us* in our specific routines, experiences, and developmental processes as we make our decisions, nurture our dreams, and act on our aspirations throughout our daily life struggles.

5 Thou hast beset me behind and before, and laid thine hand upon me. 6 Such knowledge is too wonderful for me; it is high, I cannot attain unto it.

David affirms God's encompassing power and presence in his life. Surely, the Almighty God is the Source, Sustainer, and Terminator of all things, both physical and spiritual, seen and unseen. He fills every part of the earth with His glorious presence and communicates His purpose through general and specific revelations. The Scripture teaches that the Lord is aware of every little thing on earth, the worlds of flora and fauna, and other realms. Not a strand of our hair can be plucked without the Lord's knowledge, and no bird ever falls on the ground without His knowledge (Matthew 10:29–31). God is ever-present in the affairs of people, especially in the midst of His children.

In recognition of this, the psalmist writes, "Such knowledge is too wonderful for me" (Psalm 139:6). The phrase "too wonderful" in Hebrew is *pil'iy* (**pil-EE**), which means "incomprehensible" or "extraordinary." "Such knowledge," literally "the knowledge of you" as rendered in some ancient documents, communicates the awesomeness and depth of God's knowledge. David was clearly expressing his limited understanding of the complexities of God's wisdom and knowledge as He is involved in the affairs of human beings (compare Romans 11:33–36). After a very deep reflection on these matters, the psalmist concluded that such an unlimited depth of God's divine knowledge is absolutely beyond his grasp because of his human limitations.

139:13 For thou hast possessed my reins; thou has covered me in my mother's womb. 14 I will praise thee; for I am fearfully and wonderfully made; marvellous are thy works; and that my soul knoweth right well.

God has the ability to see through every issue, event, and circumstance that is hidden in the uttermost darkness of the earth, as well as those that are exposed to broad daylight. The Hebrew word *kilyah* (**kil-YAW**) rendered in this text as "my reins" literally means "my kidneys" or "inward parts." The statement "possessed my reins" in the verse expresses God's ability to master and completely comprehend, without any reservation, the deep, secret thoughts and intentions of the innermost parts of the psalmist and us.

The writer continued to document the Lord's personal investment of time, resources, and will in him and us. He shows how God was able to conceptualize, initiate, and develop the process which resulted in bringing him into life. Oh, how wonderful! This transports us into a realm of appreciating and adoring the Almighty, the Creator of heaven and earth. The Lord is the weaver of the essence of life and destiny.

The writer uses two words—"fearfully" (Heb. *yare'*, **yaw-RAY**) and "wonderfully" (Heb. *palah*, **paw-LAW**)—to describe and put value on how God made us. There seems to be a natural progression along this line of reasoning, in which invaluable credit was ascribed to the Lord's unlimited power to see and understand clearly every hidden or latent element of the complexities of human life.

The psalmist's use of the word "soul" (Heb. *nephesh*, **NEH-fesh**) to explain how God sees through the intricate and hidden parts of humankind shows that the Lord has absolute power and right to be in charge or control of a person's holistic life. It is exciting to know that before we were conceived in our mothers' wombs, God knew us, and He has a definite agenda for us in His ultimate purpose (see Galatians 1:15–17; Jeremiah 1:4–7).

15 My substance was not hid from thee, when I was made in secret, and curiously wrought in the lowest parts of the earth. 16 Thine eyes did see my substance, yet being unperfect; and in thy book all my members were written, which in continuance were fashioned, when as yet there was none of them.

The words "my substance" in verse 15, translated from the Hebrew word *'otsem* (**O-tsem**), has its etymology rooted in the concept of a person's fundamental genetic material. Some Bible scholars claim that the psalmist's wording merely uses certain mythological word pictures that portrayed people as creatures from the soil of the earth in Eden. Yet most scholars agree that the literal meaning is the most accurate interpretation: God initiates the existence of the human embryo. This is not to say that Psalm 139 reflects modern science centuries ahead, but that the psalm expresses the basic idea about the elemental component in the womb that develops into a fully formed person. More accurately, from the framework of the text, the psalmist must be understood as saying that the source, origin, and the very essence of his life was from God, who created him for His divine purpose (Jeremiah 1:5).

139:23 Search me, O God, and know my heart; try me, and know my thoughts: 24 And see if there be any wicked way in me, and lead me in the way everlasting.

Finally, David asks God to thoroughly search his heart and thoughts, his entire being, and point out to him his shortcomings, failures, and sins. The psalmist acknowledges himself as a human being who was born with a sinful nature and has also been living in a fallen world system, continually exposed to temptations and besetting sinful orientations. There is also an indication of the various tests and trials that we all go through in our day-to-day engagements, which sometimes prompt us to lean toward shortcuts on destructive pathways (see also Psalm 51:1–19; Proverbs 14:12; Romans 3:23; 1 Corinthians 10:1–14; James 1:12–15). The call from the writer for the Lord to know his heart is a very important step in the life of every child of God. As we make efforts through the power of the Holy Spirit to live sanctified lives in our spiritual walk with the Almighty, we must constantly open our minds and hearts to the presence of His Spirit to perform "spiritual surgery" on us on a daily basis. The word "heart" in Psalm 139:23 (Heb. *lebab*, **lay-BAWB**) denotes our central and inward being, the most intricate, deepest, innermost part of our being. It is a call asking the Lord to cleanse or purge the psalmist from any form of sin or wickedness in order to be set apart from things that displease God.

Say It Correctly

Babylonian. bab-uh-LO-nee-uhn.
Bathsheba. bath-SHEE-buh.
Chronicles. KRON-ih-kuhlz.
Jeremiah. jer-uh-MY-uh.
Nathan. NAY-thuhn.
Uriah. yoo-RI-uh.

Daily Bible Readings

M: God Sees and Knows All
Matthew 6:1–8

T: God Keeps Watch Over All
Proverbs 15:1–7

W: God Knows Our Ways
Job 23:8–13

T: The Expanse of God's Presence
Psalm 139:7–12

F: The Expanse of God's Understanding
Psalm 147:1–6

S: The Expanse of God's Knowledge
Psalm 139:17–21

S: The Intimacy of God's Knowledge
Psalm 139:1–6, 13–16, 23–24

Lesson 1, September 5

Baltes, A. J., ed., Biblespeech.com. http://www.biblespeech.com (accessed September 23, 2009).

Barker, Kenneth L., and John R. Kohlenberger. *Zondervan NIV Bible Commentary*, Vol. 1. Grand Rapids, MI: Zondervan, 1999. 67–69.

Church, Leslie F., ed. *NIV Matthew Henry Commentary in One Volume*. Grand Rapids, MI: Zondervan, 1992. 75.

Cole, R. Alan. *Exodus: An Introduction & Commentary*. Downers Grove, IL: Tyndale House, 1973. 66.

"Egypt: History, Geography, Government, and Culture." Infoplease.com. http://www.infoplease.com/ipa/A0107484. html (accessed May 2, 2009).

Enns, Peter. *The NIV Application Commentary: Exodus*. Grand Rapids, MI: Zondervan, 2000. 96, 411, 417.

Fairchild, Mary. "Introduction to the Books of the Bible— Exodus." About.com Christianity. http://christianity.about. com/oldtestamentbooks/qt/exodusintro.htm (accessed May 1, 2009).

Life Application Study Bible. Wheaton, IL: Tyndale House, 1996. 98–99.

Spence, H. D. M., and Joseph S. Exell, eds. *Genesis and Exodus*. Vol. 1 of *The Pulpit Commentary*. McLean, VA: McDonald, 1988–2009. 57.

Walton, John H., Victor H. Matthews, and Mark W. Chavalas. "Comment on Exodus 3:6." In *IVP Bible Background Old Testament Commentary*. electronic ed. Seattle, WA: BibleSoft, 2000.

Lesson 2, September 12

Baltes, A. J., ed., Biblespeech.com. http://www.biblespeech.com (accessed September 23, 2009).

Barker, Kenneth L., and John R. Kohlenberger. *Zondervan NIV Bible Commentary*, Vol. 1. Grand Rapids, MI: Zondervan, 1999. 67–69.

Church, Leslie F., ed. *NIV Matthew Henry Commentary in One Volume*. Grand Rapids, MI: Zondervan, 1992. 97.

Cole, R. Alan. *Exodus: An Introduction & Commentary*. Downers Grove, IL: Tyndale House, 1973. 153.

"Egypt: History, Geography, Government, and Culture." Infoplease.com. http://www.infoplease.com/ipa/A0107484. html (accessed May 2, 2009).

Enns, Peter. *The NIV Application Commentary: Exodus*. Grand Rapids, MI: Zondervan, 2000. 411, 417.

Fairchild, Mary. "Introduction to the Books of the Bible— Exodus." About.com Christianity. http://christianity.about. com/oldtestamentbooks/qt/exodusintro.htm (accessed May 1, 2009).

Life Application Study Bible (New Living Translation). 2ⁿᵈ ed. Carol Stream, IL: Tyndale House, 2007. 125.

Merriam-Webster Online Dictionary. Merriam-Webster, Inc. http://www.merriam-webster.com (accessed September 16, 2009).

Lesson 3, September 19

Alexander, Pat, org. ed. "Deities in Ancient Egypt." In *The Lion Encyclopedia of the Bible*. rev. ed. Pleasantville, NY: The Reader's Digest Association, 1987. 262.

Baltes, A. J., ed., Biblespeech.com. http://www.biblespeech.com (accessed September 23, 2009).

Cole, R. Alan. *Exodus: An Introduction and Commentary*. Downers Grove, IL: Tyndale House, 1973. 214, 216.

Easton, Matthew George. "Sinai." In *Easton's Bible Dictionary*. 1897. StudyLight.org. http://www.studylight.org/dic/ebd/view.cgi?number=T3442 (accessed on May 1, 2009).

Enns, Peter. *The NIV Application Commentary: Exodus*. Grand Rapids, MI: Zondervan, 2000. 569, 571.

Tenney, Merrill C., ed. *Zondervan's Pictorial Bible Dictionary*. Grand Rapids, MI: Zondervan, 1967. 797.

Lesson 4, September 26

Archaeological Study Bible (New International Version). Grand Rapids, MI: Zondervan, 2005. 84–85.

Baltes, A. J., ed., Biblespeech.com. http://www.biblespeech.com (accessed September 23, 2009).

Brand, Chad, Charles Draper, and Archie England, eds. *Holman Illustrated Bible Dictionary*. Nashville, TN: Holman Bible Publishers, 2003. 1151–54.

Enns, Peter. *NIV Application Commentary: Exodus*. Grand Rapids, MI: Zondervan, 2000.

Fretheim, Terence E. "Exodus." *Interpretation, A Bible Commentary for Teaching and Preaching*. Louisville, KY: John Knox Press, 1991.

Gaebelein, Frank E., gen. ed. *The Expositor's Bible Commentary*, Vol. 2. Grand Rapids, MI: Zondervan, 1991.

Life Application Study Bible. Wheaton, IL: Tyndale House, 2002. 103–7, 164–66.

Merriam-Webster Online Dictionary. Merriam-Webster, Inc. http://www.merriam-webster.com (accessed September 16, 2009).

Paschall, H. Franklin, and Herschel H. Hobbs, eds. *The Teacher's Bible Commentary*. Nashville, TN: Broadman and Holman, 1972. 53–54, 77–78.

Youngblood, Ronald F. *Exodus: Everyman's Bible Commentary*. Chicago, IL: Moody, 1983. 134.

Lesson 5, October 3

Baltes, A. J., ed., Biblespeech.com. http://www.biblespeech.com (accessed September 23, 2009).

Bible.Crosswalk.com. Old Testament Hebrew Lexicons. http://Bible.crosswalk.com/Lexicons/Hebrew/ (accessed August 17, 2009).

Biblios.com. Glassport, PA: Online Parallel Bible Project. http://biblios.com (accessed May 4, 2009).

Brand, Chad, Charles Draper, and Archie England, gen. eds. *Holman Illustrated Bible Dictionary*. Nashville, TN: Holman Bible Publishers, 2003. 1342–44.

Brueggemann, Walter. *The Message of the Psalms: A Theological Commentary.* Minneapolis, MN: Augsburg, 1984.

deClaissé-Walford, Nancy L. *Introduction to the Psalms: A Song from Ancient Israel.* St. Louis, MO: Chalice, 2004.

Gaebelein, Frank E., gen. ed. *The Expositor's Bible Commentary, Volume 5: Psalms–Song of Songs.* Grand Rapids, MI: Zondervan, 1991.

Goldingay, John. *Psalms, Volume 1: Psalms 1–41.* Tremper Longman III, ed. Grand Rapids, MI: Baker Academic, 2006.

Henry, Matthew. "Commentary on Psalm 8." In *Matthew Henry's Complete Commentary on the Whole Bible.* electroniced. http://bible. crosswalk.com/Commentaries/MatthewHenryComplete/ mhc-com.cgi?book=ps&chapter=008. 1706 (accessed August 19, 2009).

IVP Bible Background Commentary (Old Testament), The. Downers Grove, IL: InterVarsity Press, 2000. 517.

Lewis, C. S. *Reflections on the Psalms.* New York: Harvest/HBJ, 1958.

Life Application Study Bible. Wheaton, IL: Tyndale House, 2002. 2–3, 949–51, 957–58.

Paschall, H. Franklin, ed. *The Teacher's Bible Commentary.* Nashville, TN: Broadman and Holman Publishers, 1972. 291, 301.

Lesson 6, October 10

Baltes, A. J., ed., Biblespeech.com. http://www.biblespeech.com (accessed September 23, 2009).

Biblos.com. Glassport, PA: Online Parallel Bible Project. http://biblios.com (accessed May 4, 2009).

Brand, Chad, Charles Draper, and Archie England, gen. eds. *Holman Illustrated Bible Dictionary.* Nashville, TN: Holman Bible Publishers, 2003. 1342–44.

Brueggemann, Walter. *An Introduction to the Old Testament: The Canon and Christian Imagination.* Louisville, KY: Westminster, 2003.

Gaebelein, Frank E., gen. ed. *The Expositor's Bible Commentary, Volume 5, Psalms–Song of Songs.* Grand Rapids, MI: Zondervan, 1991.

Goldingay, John. *Psalms, Volume 1: Psalms 1–41.* Tremper Longman III, ed. Grand Rapids, MI: Baker Academic, 2006.

Lewis, C. S. *Reflections on the Psalms.* New York: Harvest/HBJ, 1958.

Life Application Study Bible. Wheaton, IL: Tyndale House, 2002. 511, 949, 967–68, 1056, 1840.

Merriam-Webster Online Dictionary. Merriam-Webster, Inc. http://www.merriam-webster.com (accessed September 16, 2009).

Nelson's New Illustrated Bible Commentary. Nashville, TN: Thomas Nelson Publishers, 1999. 644–47, 661.

Paschall, H. Franklin, ed. *The Teacher's Bible Commentary.* Nashville, TN: Broadman and Holman Publishers, 1972. 291, 301.

Sittser, Gerald L. *Water from a Deep Well: Christian Spirituality from Early Martyrs to Modern Missionaries.* Downers Grove, IL: InterVarsity Press, 2007.

Lesson 7, October 17

Baltes, A. J., ed., Biblespeech.com. http://www.biblespeech.com (accessed September 23, 2009).

Kidner, Derek. *Psalms 1–72: An Introduction and Commentary on Books I and II of the Psalms.* Downers Grove, IL: InterVarsity Press, 1973.

Life Application Study Bible (New Living Translation). 2ⁿᵈ ed. Wheaton, IL: Tyndale House, 2004. 892.

Logan, Phil. "Earthquake." In *Holman Illustrated Bible Dictionary.* Chad Brand, Charles Draper, and Archie England, gen. eds. Nashville, TN: Holman Bible Publishing, 2003. 450.

Merriam-Webster Online Dictionary. Merriam-Webster, Inc. http://www.merriam-webster.com (accessed September 16, 2009).

NIV Study Bible, The. Grand Rapids, MI: Zondervan, 1995. 782, 820, 825–26.

Strong, James. *Strong's New Exhaustive Numbers and Concordance with Expanded Greek-Hebrew Dictionary.* Seattle, WA: Biblesoft, and International Bible Translators, 1994. 2003.

Wyngaarden, Martin J. "Psalms." In *The International Standard Bible Encyclopedia,* Vol. 4. Grand Rapids, MI: Eerdmans, 1960. 2491.

Lesson 8, October 24

Baltes, A. J., ed., Biblespeech.com. http://www.biblespeech.com (accessed September 23, 2009).

Browning, Daniel C., Jr., and E. Ray Clendenen. "Pagan Gods." In *Holman Illustrated Bible Dictionary.* Chad Brand, Charles Draper, and Archie England, gen. eds. Nashville, TN: Holman Bible Publishers, 2003. 663–66.

Dockery, David S. "Christ as King." In *Holman Illustrated Bible Dictionary.* Chad Brand, Charles Draper, and Archie England, gen. eds. Nashville, TN: Holman Bible Publishers, 2003. 984–85.

ESV Study Bible, The. Wheaton, IL: Crossway Bibles, 2008.

Halpern, Baruch. "Kingship and Monarchy." In *The Oxford Companion to the Bible.* New York: Oxford University Press, 1993. 413–16.

Kidner, Derek. *Psalms 1–72: An Introduction and Commentary on Books I and II of the Psalms.* Downers Grove, IL: InterVarsity Press, 1973.

Logan, Phil, and E. Ray Clendenen. "King, Kingship." In *Holman Illustrated Bible Dictionary.* Chad Brand, Charles Draper, and Archie England, gen. eds. Nashville, TN: Holman Bible Publishers, 2003. 985–87.

NET Bible, The. Version 1.0 (accessed in BibleWorks 7.0). Richardson, TX: Biblical Studies Foundation, 2005.

NIV Study Bible, The. Grand Rapids, MI: Zondervan, 1995. 343.

Strong, James. *New Exhaustive Strong's Numbers and Concordance with Expanded Greek-Hebrew Dictionary.* Seattle, WA: Biblesoft, and International Bible Translators, 1994. 2003.

Lesson 9, October 31

Baltes, A. J., ed., Biblespeech.com. http://www.biblespeech.com (accessed September 23, 2009).

Beitzel, Barry J. *The Moody Atlas of Bible Lands.* Chicago: Moody Press, 1985. Map 51.

Drinkard, Joel F. "En-Gedi." In *Holman Illustrated Bible Dictionary.* Chad Brand, Charles Draper, and Archie England, gen. eds. Nashville, TN: Holman Bible Publishers, 2003. 487–89.

ESV Study Bible, The. Wheaton, IL: Crossway Bibles, 2008.

Kidner, Derek. *Psalms 1–72: An Introduction and Commentary on Books I and II of the Psalms.* Downers Grove, IL: InterVarsity Press, 1973.

Matheney, M. Pierce. "Wilderness." In *Holman Illustrated Bible Dictionary.* Chad Brand, Charles Draper, and Archie England, gen. eds. Nashville, TN: Holman Bible Publishers, 2003. 1672–73.

NET Bible, The. Version 1.0 (accessed in BibleWorks 7.0). Richardson, TX: Biblical Studies Foundation, 2005.

NIV Study Bible, The. Grand Rapids, MI: Zondervan, 1995. 442–45.

Spurgeon, Charles H. *The Treasury of David,* Vol. 3. Grand Rapids, MI: Zondervan, 1957. 69.

Strong, James. *Strong's New Exhaustive Numbers and Concordance with Expanded Greek-Hebrew Dictionary.* Seattle, WA: Biblesoft, and International Bible Translators, 1994. 2003.

Lesson 10, November 7

Baltes, A. J., ed., Biblespeech.com. http://www.biblespeech.com (accessed September 23, 2009).

Easton, Matthew George. "Selah." In *Easton's Bible Dictionary.* Gresham, OR: Bible History Online. http://www.Bible-history.com/eastons/S/Selah/ (accessed May 26, 2009).

Elwell, Walter A., ed. *Baker Theological Dictionary of the Bible.* Grand Rapids, MI: Baker Books, 1996. 653–658.

ESV Study Bible, The. Wheaton, IL: Crossway Bibles, 2008.

Kidner, Derek. *Psalms 1–72: An Introduction and Commentary on Books I and II of the Psalms.* Downers Grove, IL: InterVarsity Press, 1973.

NET Bible, The. Version 1.0. (accessed in BibleWorks 7.0). Richardson, TX: Biblical Studies Foundation, 2005.

Lesson 11, November 14

Holy Bible (New King James Version), The. Nashville, TN: Nelson, 1982.

"Old Testament Hebrew Lexicon." Online Bible Study Tools. http://www.Biblestudytools.com/Lexicons/Hebrew/ (accessed August 14, 2009).

Lesson 12, November 21

Baltes, A. J., ed., Biblespeech.com. http://www.biblespeech.com (accessed September 23, 2009).

Complete Concordance to the Bible: New King James Version. Nashville, TN: Nelson, 1983.

Holy Bible (New King James Version), The. Nashville, TN: Nelson, 1982.

Longman III, Tremper. *How to Read the Psalms.* Downers Grove, IL: InterVarsity Press, 1988. 111–16.

"Old Testament Hebrew Lexicon." Online Bible Study Tools. http://www.bible.crosswalk.com/Lexicons/Hebrew (accessed August 12, 2009).

Lesson 13, November 28

Baltes, A. J., ed., Biblespeech.com. http://www.biblespeech.com (accessed September 23, 2009).

Complete Concordance to the Bible: New King James Version. Nashville, TN: Nelson, 1983.

Elwell, Walter A., ed. *Baker Theological Dictionary of the Bible.* Grand Rapids, MI: Baker Books, 1996. 653–58.

Harris, Stephen L. *The Old Testament: An Introduction to the Hebrew Bible.* New York, NY: McGraw-Hill, 2002. 287, 292.

Holy Bible (New King James Version), The. Nashville, TN: Nelson, 1982.

Assuring Hope

The study this quarter focuses on the promises of hope found in the words of the prophet Isaiah and the hope found in Christ, the Suffering Servant. The first two units look at texts from Isaiah to study the prophet's message as told to Israel. We look at Isaiah's message of comfort and hope in the context of Israel's destruction and subsequent captivity in Babylon. The final unit looks at the fulfillment of Isaiah's prophecy as it unfolds through Christ. The texts for Unit III come from Mark's gospel.

UNIT 1 • COMFORT FOR GOD'S PEOPLE

"Comfort for God's People" draws on selected texts from Isaiah 40–44 with the exception of the Christmas week lesson. The Christmas lesson focuses on Isaiah's words concerning Jesus' birth (Isaiah 9:1–7 and 11:1–9).

Lesson 1: December 5, 2010
The Highway for God
Isaiah 40:1–5, 25–26, 29–31

God commands Isaiah to speak words of comfort to the people of Jerusalem. He tells them that obstacles will be removed to give them hope. Isaiah encourages Israel to wait on the Lord and to be patient; God will strengthen them and fulfill His promises.

Lesson 2: December 12, 2010
I Am Your God
Isaiah 41:8–10, 17–20

God chose Israel so they would serve Him. He established His presence with them and desired to have a relationship to help them prosper, achieve victory, and know that He is God.

Lesson 3: December 19, 2010
The Mission of the Servant
Isaiah 9:7; 11:1–8

God promised to raise a ruler from the lineage of David and that this kingdom would never end. Jesus, the Messiah, is the fulfillment of this promise.

Lesson 4: December 26, 2010
I Will Be with You
Isaiah 43:1–7, 11–12

God professes His love for Israel and His commitment to them. He called, redeemed, protected, and saved them.

UNIT 2 • A FUTURE FOR GOD'S PEOPLE

These five lessons present a study of selected texts from Isaiah 45–53. They proclaim God's message of the coming salvation for Israel.

Lesson 5: January 2, 2011
I Am Your Redeemer
Isaiah 44:21–26

God created Israel and promised not to forsake His chosen people. He freed them and forgave them of their sins.

Lesson 6: January 9, 2011
Turn to Me and Be Saved
Isaiah 45:18–24a

God is distinguished from all other gods. He is the Creator, Savior, and Truth-speaker. He keeps His promises, and people proclaim that He is the source of all righteousness and strength.

Lesson 7: January 16, 2011
Reassurance for God's People
Isaiah 48:14–19, 21–22

God is a teacher and a guide. Peace and righteousness are promised to those who obey His words.

Lesson 8: January 23, 2011
The Servant's Mission in the World
Isaiah 49:1–6

God chose His Servant to redeem His people. The Lord honored the Servant and strengthened Him. God also said that the future Redeemer will do more than restore Israel; He will enlighten Gentiles and bring the salvation of God to the whole earth.

Lesson 9: January 30, 2011
Healed by His Bruises
Isaiah 53:4–6, 10–12

The Servant (Jesus Christ) will sacrifice Himself for the sake of Israel. His suffering will be exchanged for their salvation.

UNIT 3 • JESUS, THE PROMISED SERVANT-LEADER

These four lessons openly explain Jesus' teaching on the nature of messiahship.

Lesson 10: February 6, 2011
Jesus Is the Messiah
Mark 8:27–9:1

Jesus asks His disciples about what His reputation was publicly and who He was to them personally. After, He foretells of His death. Peter tries to correct Jesus, but Jesus rebukes Satan. Jesus then tells of the requirements expected of those who will follow Him.

Lesson 11: February 13, 2011
This Is My Beloved
Mark 9:2–13

Jesus takes Peter, James, and John to the top of a mountain and is transfigured (changed to another form) before them. Moses and Elijah appear, and God's voice from heaven proclaims Jesus as the Messiah. Jesus warns the disciples not to tell others about their experience until His resurrection, but they are confused.

Lesson 12: February 20, 2011
Jesus Came to Serve
Mark 10:35–45

The Sons of Zebedee wanted seats of honor in the new kingdom (where Christ would reign forever and ever), but Jesus pointed out their ignorance. He teaches His disciples that service is the requirement for greatness.

Lesson 13: February 27, 2011
Coming of the Son of Man
Mark 13:14–27

On the Mount of Olives, Jesus tells His disciples the future. He warns them of how terrible the end will be and how He will return with great power.

Hope: The Assurance of Hope
(A Closer Look Within Matthew's and Mark's Gospels)

by Jamal-Dominique Hopkins, Ph.D.

The notion of hope is a major theme expressed throughout the Bible. This overarching theme is uniquely captured in the New Testament, most notably in the Gospels according to Matthew and Mark. During the first half of the first century C. E. ("common era," also called A.D.), the message of Jesus was heard throughout the land of Israel.

As the message of Jesus spread, hope and the assurance of hope for redemption resonated with many people who had known poverty, suffered oppression socially or physically, and dwelled under foreign rule and domination to the Roman Empire. While many people under the influence of legal and religious magistrates desired a social-political liberation from Rome, others embraced an otherworldly notion of victory, redemption, and sovereignty from the coming kingdom of God. This was the hope and assurance of hope proclaimed by Jesus and later by the disciples and apostles (see Matthew 12:28; Mark 4:11; Acts 1:3).

The Gospel message of Jesus as Savior and long-awaited Redeemer of humanity was orally passed down from a generation of eyewitnesses. As time progressed, the anticipation of Jesus' immediate return somewhat waned. As a newer generation tarried for the Lord, some were inspired to literarily record the message and accounts of Jesus. As suggested by the author of Luke, these accounts were written for successive generations: "Since many have undertaken to set down an orderly account of the events that have been fulfilled among us, just as they were handed on to us by those from the beginning were eyewitnesses and servants of the word, I too decided, after investigating everything carefully from the very first, to write an orderly account for you, most excellent Theophilus, so that you may know the truth concerning the things about which you have been instructed" (Luke 1:1–4, NKJV).

The Gospel accounts of Jesus largely followed the epistolary (letter) writings of Paul and others who, too, were inspired by oral accounts.[1]

Hope and the assurance of hope as spelled out in the Gospels of Matthew and Mark make explicit reference to Hebrew Bible prophecies. The notion of hope is particularly told through the story of Jesus, the promised and long-awaited Messiah of Israel and humanity. As captured in the explicit summation of Matthew's retelling of Isaiah, as depicted through the life and ministry of Jesus, the people of God wait in anticipation of God's redemption promise: "This was to fulfill what had been spoken through the prophet Isaiah: 'Here is my servant, whom I have chosen, my beloved, with whom my soul is well pleased. I will put my Spirit upon him, and he will proclaim justice to the Gentiles. He will not wrangle or cry aloud, nor will anyone hear his voice in the streets. He will not break a bruised reed or quench a smoldering wick until he brings justice to victory. And in his name the Gentiles will hope'" (Matthew 12:17–21, NRSV).

Beginning in the Gospel of Matthew, the genealogy of Jesus is linked back to the promise recorded in the Pentateuch (the five books of the Law)[2], from Abraham (to whom the promise was given by way of the covenant [the agreement] between God and His chosen people, the Israelites)[3] to David, the beloved king of Israel, and from David to Joseph and Mary. Jesus is directly linked as the promise.

The Gospels according to Matthew and Mark tell the story of the promised redemption of humanity back to a sovereign God. The story is told through birth, life, ministry, death, and resurrection of the promised One as prophesied throughout the literary history of the Hebrew Bible. Both Matthew and Mark highlight some of these prophecies:

• The birth account of Jesus in Matthew 1:18–23 notes the fulfillment of Isaiah 7:14; here Jesus is noted as God. "Look, the virgin shall conceive and bear a son, and they shall name him Emmanuel," which means, "God is with us."

• The account of John the Baptist proclaiming the coming of Jesus as Lord in Matthew 3:1–12 and Mark 1:2–8, which gives a retelling of Isaiah 40:3 and Malachi 3:1. "This is the one of whom the prophet Isaiah spoke when he said, 'The voice of one crying out in the wilderness: "Prepare the way of the Lord, make his paths straight."'"

• The account of Jesus as Lord and King over Israel entering Jerusalem on a donkey in Matthew 21:1–10 and Mark 11:1–10, which notes the fulfillment and retelling of Isaiah 62:11 and Zechariah 9:9.

• The account of Jesus cleansing the temple (His house) in Matthew 21:12–13, wherein Isaiah 56:7 and Jeremiah 7:11 is restated.

• Jesus declaring Himself as the Messiah in front of the high priest and others who arrested Him in Matthew 26:57–66 and Mark 14:53–62.

• The declaration of Jesus' divinity by the centurion and those with them at the Crucifixion in Matthew 27:45–54 and Mark 15:33–39.

• The resurrection and ascension of Jesus in Matthew 28:1–20 and Mark 16.

The theme of hope has been studied in theology, namely under the rubric of Christian eschatology. Eschatology is the discipline which is concerned with last things and is especially concerned with the end of days, which also presupposes the ushering in of a new age. Eschatology (a study of the end time) is concerned with hope and is one of the major themes throughout the Bible beginning with Genesis after the fall of humanity. From Genesis through the New Testament Gospels, the eschatological hope of redemption is anticipated in light of God's covenant promise, first illustrated between Yahweh and Abraham in Genesis 15 and 17. This covenant is renewed with the Hebrew Patriarchs—the descendants of Abraham (see Exodus 2:24 and 6:3–4)—and passed down through Israel's kings and prophets.

Hope and the assurance of hope are visibly illustrated throughout the Gospels of Matthew and Mark. From the visitation of the wise men in Matthew 2:1–12 up to today, hope and the assurance of hope are expressed through our biblical witness.

Footnotes:
[1] The earliest New Testament writings are 1 Thessalonians and Galatians. This notion follows the evidence of extant manuscripts, which assume a similar chronological composition.

[2] Pentateuch means the first five books of the Hebrew Bible (Genesis, Exodus, Leviticus, Numbers, and Deuteronomy).

[3] See Genesis 15:1–21.

Jamal-Dominique Hopkins, Ph.D., is the Assistant Professor of New Testament at the Interdenominational Theological Center in Atlanta, Georgia.

Looking for Hope in All the Right Places

by Rosa M. Sailes, Ed.D

I have just heard a news bulletin announcing the suicide of a businessman who headed the largest financial institution in this country. His quiet, very upscale neighborhood is shocked at his death. His family is devastated. The political insiders (of whom he was one) are no doubt wondering if they, too, would have succumbed to the devastating loss of billions that will now mark his legacy. I cannot berate the man. I will not stomp on his grave with platitudes of rich young rulers and the eye of a needle, but I will ask—where was hope?

His parents had the best intentions for him. They sent him to the finest schools; his career ladder only headed in one direction. I'm sure that from the beginning his family beamed at the offspring who was raised to be successful. His wife married him knowing that, in addition to her personal accomplishments, she had married well. His children no doubt admired him, and his business associates wanted to ride his coattails to the bank. Each person had hope—hope in this man and his ability, his position, his perceived power, his bank account, and his connections. They had hope in their relationship with him and in his relationship with others. But where was the man's hope?

Hebrews 11 tells us that hope must be anchored in something. Hope is an active verb that looks anxiously to a particular outcome. For some of us, our hope is anchored in the success and health of our children. For others, hope equates to the sufficiency of our income now and in the future. There are those for whom hope rests in intangibles—love, joy, peace, freedom, justice. College students place hope in a future where they can capitalize on the years they have invested in education. Grandparents often find themselves hanging their hopes on children who they pray will be caregivers to them, the same children to whom they once gave loving care. Hope truly has a desire.

The desire of hope is best realized by faith. Faith is the substance of the intangible object of our desire. Our Old Testament study this quarter takes us into "the Gospel" of hope as preached by Isaiah. Through Isaiah's words, God's people were comforted. In the midst of exile and sorrow, Isaiah spoke of the coming salvation of God— a salvation that was for the captives and for the generations after them. Their fears could be cast aside and their strength could be realized because hope spoke a future without despair. God, who had formed them and made them His own, had not forgotten them. The proof was in the faith to which they clung with the assurance that only hope could give.

Isaiah spoke hope to those who felt a loss of hope. Isaiah spoke words of exaltation and gave a vision of hope. His words quickened the faith the nation needed at their lowest point. His preaching painted the picture of a future for God's people even in the midst of their sorrow. Through Isaiah's message, they found faith to believe the God who had proven Himself to them even before their Red Sea experience.

Isaiah spoke to a nation of captives about God's promise, but we are living on this side of Calvary. We have seen what Isaiah's generation hoped for, and yet we appear to have no hope. As African Americans we are, traditionally, a people of hope. We have had to be. But now we are seeing a generation that seems to have lost hope. With a death rate soaring for teens in urban areas such as Chicago, Los Angeles, and Detroit, hope has come to have a short life expectancy. With a heightening jobless rate that is fueled by injustice and devastated by greed, it is no surprise that so many of our African American young adults see no future and senior citizens find their dreams of retirement dashed on the rocks of recession.

In the midst of such trials, we must keep faith in the fact that hope took on flesh. Two thousand years ago, Jesus spoke to the disenfranchised, the hurting, and the discounted. His birth, death, and resurrection were the hope that Isaiah had preached. His message was the word of comfort that God had encouraged from Isaiah's lips.

We must keep the faith and keep hope alive because almost 400 years ago, Jesus' words fit another group of disenfranchised, hurting, and discounted people, a people stolen from a native land, placed in shackles, and made to believe that their entire lives and the lives of their children would forever be without hope. For those people, nobody seemed to care, nobody seemed to hear, and nobody seemed to want to deliver.

Those disenfranchised slaves found a way to express their hope and to wait for their change to come. They started a tradition that remains in African American churches today, a tradition called "Watch Night." It was the way they waited for the New Year, waited for the voice of Jesus to set them free as He had those people on that mountainside in His time and those who had been devas-tated by war and captivity in the days of Isaiah.

Watch Night became an expression of hope played out for decades—hoping the change was going to come, hoping that God's light would spring anew and the nightmare of enslavement would end. Those slaves had much to fear, yet they found hope and held on looking for God to open a new way, to light another direction for them, to make clear a path of escape so that they could move forward in the visions and dreams God had placed in their hearts.

On Watch Night those slaves watched and prayed, but each had a different vision of freedom. They each had a different urgency of hope. One wanted to find his mother. Another longed to find her children. Another sought enough to eat or wear. Another's heart cried for the freedom to go unfettered to a new life.

Those slaves identified with the disenfranchised listeners who heard the words of Jesus and the captives who hailed Isaiah's cry. Our foreparents, though they were slaves in bondage, realized that Jesus knew the fears and doubts that they carried. They heard the words of Jesus and they knew the release that resonated in their souls. They had hope on the eve of a New Year and hope in the dawn of a new day.

But Jesus not only spoke to those people on the mountainsides and valleys of Jerusalem. He not only spoke to slaves in small clusters throughout this country who were hovering and praying and watching for freedom to come. He also speaks to us. Like children who find themselves in the midst of anticipation waiting for their opportunity to let fly the dreams they have pent inside, it is time for a new generation to recognize the words of hope and take hold of the faith so many have held before.

As we end 2010, where are you looking for hope? After all, you know what you're hoping for. Like those who heard Isaiah's sermons or listened to the voice of Jesus during His earthly ministry, we each define our hope in different ways. Perhaps God has spoken an urgency into your life, reminding you again of the gifts He has given you, a promise that He made to you, or a promise unfulfilled that you made to Him. Like those who cried for freedom from the tyranny of Babylon or who envisioned Watch Night as a means of expressing their hope in God, we must enter Watch Night 2010 by not being burdened by the struggles of the old year, but invigorated by the hope of a new day.

We have the same assurance as those on the mountain and those who were delivered from chains. It doesn't matter what you've been through; it matters that Jesus has declared you to be a light. It doesn't matter that you shed a tear; it matters that Jesus has chosen you as His own. You may feel despondent, but Jesus has declared that your effort will make a difference in the world.

The words of Isaiah and the sacrifice of Jesus ring forth even now, telling us to turn our sights to the only place we can find hope—in God Almighty, the Great I Am. We must look for hope in Jehovah-Jireh, the God who provides. We must anchor our faith in Jesus Christ, who is the "author and finisher of our faith." Jesus Christ is, for each person who has called upon His name, our comfort in our present, our confidence of our future, and the Messiah we long to see.

_____

Rosa M. Sailes, Ed.D., is the Director of Editorial Leadership Resources at Urban Ministries, Inc.

Assuring Hope

by Rukeia Draw, Ph.D.

Surely the title of this essay brings to mind a vintage hymn written by Fanny J. Crosby:

"Blessed assurance, Jesus is mine! O what a foretaste of glory divine!

Heir of salvation, purchase of God, born of His Spirit, washed in His blood.

This is my story, this is my song, praising my Savior all the day long."

This song reminds us of that blessed assurance—that blessed hope that is found in God's inerrant Word. In fact, the Bible tells us, "Wherefore thou art no more a servant, but a son; and if a son, then an heir of God through Christ" (Galatians 4:7). Oh, what assuring hope we have in our Lord and Savior, Jesus Christ! The song also has the capacity to flood a person with all types of fond memories. For me, I think of the A.M.E. church where I learned this song in the suburbs of Chicago, Illinois. I'm ashamed to say—although I certainly can't be the only one in this postmodern era—I was almost 30 years of age before I was introduced to a hymnal in the midst of a traditional church liturgy. Only later did I realize that this is also the song my grandmother hums as she cooks every day. What a powerful song! It really has the ability to evoke strong emotions, like songs such as "Amazing Grace" or "Precious Lord" that are tied to some distant memories. Sure, it stirs up memories, but does it also inspire hope in you? It should!

Most would agree that faith is the foundation of Christianity. After all, how many times have you heard or read, "But without faith it is impossible to please him: for he that cometh to God must believe that he is, and that he is a rewarder of them that diligently seek him" (Hebrews 11:6)? Consider for a moment that faith and hope are two sides of the same coin. According to Eaton's Bible Dictionary, "hope is an essential and fundamental element of Christian life, so essential indeed, that, like faith and love, it can itself designate the essence of Christianity (1 Peter 3:15; Hebrews 10:23). In it, the whole glory of the Christian vocation is centered (Ephesians 1:18; 4:4)" (Easton, 1897). Hope is an expectation regarding things that are unseen and unknown that we want or desire to happen (Romans 8:24–25; Hebrews 11:1, 7). In addition, we have the assurance from God's Word that He (God) that promised is faithful to deliver on His promises. Because God is truth and righteousness, we can count on His Word—we can stand on His promises.

In this quarter, you will read about God's declarations through Isaiah concerning the people of God and a promise to comfort and save them through the sacrifices of a Suffering Servant. That assurance is declaring, promising, and comforting. Isaiah's messages were meant to inspire confidence and to energize the people of God toward the alternative reality he was speaking of. According to Walter Brueggeman in *The*

Prophetic Imagination, "a prophet is to criticize the dominant consciousness and energize communities by a promise toward which the community is encouraged to move." Isaiah, in his role as a major prophet, is trying to get the people of God to envision a way of being and existing that is different from their status quo among the prosperous Babylonians. It is hard because the people of God are fat and full. They don't see that they have needs, especially spiritually. But Isaiah is trying to stir up some anticipation that things could actually be better than they already are. He gives them a vision of what is to come, encourages them to move toward it, and because he knows that moving toward the intangible and unknown is scarier sometimes than staying in a bad situation, he assures them of God's greatness above all other things and God's willingness to strengthen and comfort in the midst of transition.

How does an assuring hope apply to believers? It boils down to the source of our confidence and hope. Many people are optimistic and positive thinkers. Thanks to the most recent wave of popular televangelists, people can "name it and claim it"—whatever it is—with all the gusto of a seasoned believer, even though naming it and claiming it have often brought frustration and disappointment to many. The prophet Isaiah makes it crystal clear that God wants the credit for His own handiwork and does not desire to share credit (or His glory) with idols of any kind—not our loved ones, other gods, brilliant doctors, or intelligent scientists. Isaiah's message is that there is One coming to put our hope in, a hope that can be confident and assured. In God's salvific work, through Jesus Christ, is found the fulfillment of the Old Testament promises and hope (Matthew 12:15–21). The salvation promised is available through this Suffering Servant, God's one and only Son, who came to die for the sins of humanity so that we might have eternal life. So once you have taken hold of that hope and received the promised salvation, is that it? No, the Messiah will return again. He is coming this second time not as a Suffering Servant, but as the Righteous Judge. Will you be ready to meet Him? Does the fact that He is coming back again inspire assuring hope within you?

Sources:

Brueggeman, Walter. *The Prophetic Imagination,* rev. ed. Minneapolis, MN: Augsburg Fortress, 2001.

Holy Bible (NIV). Grand Rapids, MI: Zondervan, 2001.

M.G. Easton M.A., D.D., *Illustrated Bible Dictionary,* 3rd ed., published by Thomas Nelson, 1897. World Wide Web Version. http://www.ccel.org/e/easton/ebd/ebd3.html (accessed August 30, 2009).

New National Baptist Hymnal 21st Century Edition, The. Nashville, TN: Mega Corporation dba Triad Publications, 1977. 249.

Rukeia Draw, Ph.D., is an extension educator with a land grant university in the Midwest. She works in youth development and manages a community center. She is a member of Triumph Church in Detroit, Michigan.

Stephen Biko

Stephen Biko was born on December 18, 1946, and later became one of the highest noted South African anti-apartheid activists. Early in his academic career, at the University of Natal, he demonstrated his interests in social and racial diversity. As a member of the multiracial National Union of South African Students he gained further insight in racial issues and founded his own organization geared toward Indian and Colored students, the South African Students' Organization (SASO). SASO eventually led to the Black Consciousness Movement where Biko spread the message of hope to the victims of the apartheid in South Africa and coined the phrase "Black is beautiful." During these crucial times, Biko was impressed by another leading figure in the Black Consciousness Movement, Ntsiki Mashalaba. After marrying, they had two children together.

In 1972, Biko became the honorary president of the Black People's Convention. In 1973, as he grew in prominence, the South African government saw him as more of a threat and banned him. Biko was not allowed to make public speeches, and he was restricted from certain locations. However, Biko did not let this stop his heroic efforts. He returned to the Eastern Cape, where he was born, and started several grassroots organizations, including the Zimele Trust Fund, and a community clinic. His goal was for these organizations to be self-reliant.

With the help of the sprouting organizations and the Black Consciousness Movement spreading like wildfire, Biko organized protests. On June 16, 1976, thousands of Black students marched out of school to the Orlando Stadium in protest against having to learn through Afrikaans in school. This protest was supported and organized by the Black Consciousness Movement. It was intended to be a peaceful protest, but it erupted in violence by the police. Following the intense violence of the protest, Biko became an even larger target of the South African government. On August 21, 1977, the police arrested Biko under the Terrorism Act No. 83 of 1967. Shortly after his arrival to prison, he died from what the police claimed was a result of a hunger strike. However, later evidence proved that he died of head-related injuries, most likely caused by police brutality.

Biko's commitment to being a messenger of hope extended posthumously. His death sparked awareness on a global level. With over 10,000 people in attendance at Biko's funeral, including important ambassadors and diplomats from countries all over the world, a sobering need for justice swept the world. In 2004, Biko was voted 13th in the SABC3's Great South Africans.

Sources:
http://www.answers.com/topic/steve-biko
http://www.sahistory.org.za/pages/people/bios/biko-s.htm

Teaching Tips

1. Words You Should Know

A. Comfort (Isaiah 40:1) *nacham* (Heb.)— To be sorry for, or console someone, or oneself, to repent, to regret, to offer comfort, or be comforted.

B. Straight (v. 3) *yashar* (Heb.)—To be right, straight, level, upright, just, to be lawful, and to be smooth.

2. Teacher Preparation

Unifying Principle—Receiving Comfort and Strength. In spite of weakness, trouble, and impediments, people search for a better life. The prophet Isaiah promises the people that God, with whom no one can compare, will fulfill their hopes.

A. Before class, pray that God will help you connect with your students through the lesson.

B. Study the entire lesson.

C. Be prepared to discuss "How to Wait and How Not to Wait on the Lord."

3. Open the Lesson

A. Open your class with prayer, keeping the Aim for Change in mind.

B. After prayer, begin the class with a discussion on one or two current events that seem to cause most people grief.

C. Allow students to discuss life situations or issues of their own that have caused them great stress.

D. Ask the question, "How can believers maintain hope when there seems to be no hope?" Discuss.

E. Tie in the In Focus story with the discussion.

4. Present the Scriptures

A. Have volunteers read the Focal Verses.

B. To clarify the Focal Verses, use The People, Place, and Times; Background; At-A-Glance outline; In Depth; Search the Scriptures; and More Light on the Text.

5. Explore the Meaning

A. Lead a discussion of the Discuss the Meaning section.

B. Summarize the Lesson in Our Society and Make It Happen sections.

6. Next Steps for Application

A. Have class members respond to the Follow the Spirit and Remember Your Thoughts sections.

B. Close with prayer.

Worship Guide

For the Superintendent or Teacher
Theme: The Highway for God
Theme Song: "My Hope Is
Built on Nothing Less"
Devotional Reading: Ephesians 2:11–22
Prayer

The Highway for God

Bible Background • ISAIAH 40
Printed Text • ISAIAH 40:1–5, 25–26, 29–31 | Devotional Reading • EPHESIANS 2:11–22

Aim for Change

By the end of the lesson, we will: UNDERSTAND God's promise of hope and care to the Israelites and to us; RECOGNIZE that we can hope in God; and LIST ways we can wait patiently on the Lord in times of need.

In Focus

As Valerie boarded the train, she felt optimistic about the next phase in her life. She had always loved living in the big city, and after college she couldn't wait to return to the same neighborhood in which she was born and raised. Her life's passion was helping troubled teens in her community turn their lives around, and six years ago, God blessed her with the opportunity to work in full-time ministry with them. Valerie thought she was set for life. But then the ministry lost its building and most of its funding, and it had to let go most of its employees, including Valerie. Just when she thought things couldn't get any worse, her health began to fail. The mounting hospital bills plunged her into so much debt she could no longer pay her mortgage. She lost her home. So now, Valerie was on a train headed to her uncle's place in a small town.

"How could you be so happy about losing everything and having to leave here?" her friend asked the day before.

"I cannot tell a lie. I had to remember all the rough spots God has gotten me through. I believe He will get me through this one."

Valerie knew that her only hope was in God. Just as He had taken care of her before, He would again.

Keep in Mind

"He giveth power to the faint; and to them that have no might he increaseth strength" (Isaiah 40:29).

"He giveth power to the faint; and to them that have no might he
increaseth strength" (Isaiah 40:29).

Focal Verses

KJV Isaiah 40:1 Comfort ye, comfort ye my people, saith your God.

2 Speak ye comfortably to Jerusalem, and cry unto her, that her warfare is accomplished, that her iniquity is pardoned: for she hath received of the LORD's hand double for all her sins.

3 The voice of him that crieth in the wilderness, Prepare ye the way of the LORD, make straight in the desert a highway for our God.

4 Every valley shall be exalted, and every mountain and hill shall be made low: and the crooked shall be made straight, and the rough places plain:

5 And the glory of the LORD shall be revealed, and all flesh shall see it together: for the mouth of the LORD hath spoken it.

40:25 To whom then will ye liken me, or shall I be equal? saith the Holy One.

26 Lift up your eyes on high, and behold who hath created these things, that bringeth out their host by number: he calleth them all by names by the greatness of his might, for that he is strong in power; not one faileth.

40:29 He giveth power to the faint; and to them that have no might he increaseth strength.

30 Even the youths shall faint and be weary, and the young men shall utterly fall:

31 But they that wait upon the LORD shall renew their strength; they shall mount up with wings as eagles; they shall run, and not be weary; and they shall walk, and not faint.

NLT Isaiah 40:1 "Comfort, comfort my people," says your God.

2 "Speak tenderly to Jerusalem. Tell her that her sad days are gone and her sins are pardoned. Yes, the LORD has punished her twice over for all her sins."

3 Listen! It's the voice of someone shouting, "Clear the way through the wilderness for the LORD! Make a straight highway through the wasteland for our God!

4 Fill in the valleys, and level the mountains and hills. Straighten the curves, and smooth out the rough places.

5 Then the glory of the LORD will be revealed, and all people will see it together. The LORD has spoken!"

40:25 "To whom will you compare me? Who is my equal?" asks the Holy One.

26 Look up into the heavens. Who created all the stars? He brings them out like an army, one after another, calling each by its name. Because of his great power and incomparable strength, not a single one is missing.

40:29 He gives power to the weak and strength to the powerless.

30 Even youths will become weak and tired, and young men will fall in exhaustion.

31 But those who trust in the LORD will find new strength. They will soar high on wings like eagles. They will run and not grow weary. They will walk and not faint.

The People, Places, and Times

The Prophet Isaiah. Eagles are very powerful birds of prey and have extremely keen eyesight that allows them to see clearly at great distances. With a wingspan that can be as long as nine feet in some types, eagles can soar so high, it seems they are flying close to the sun. Although eagles can be heavy, weighing up to 14 pounds, they are very swift birds.

The prophet Isaiah is often called the "Eagle-Eye" prophet because just as an eagle's eyesight can span great distances, Isaiah's prophecies span great distances of time. His actual ministry lasted from 740 B.C. to 700 B.C. in the southern kingdom of Judah in the city of Jerusalem. He ministered during the reigns of Kings Uzziah, Jotham, Ahaz, and Hezekiah. His prophecies concerning the destruction of the land and the Temple, the Babylonian captivity, and the return of the Remnant to Judah were fulfilled starting in 586 B.C., a little over 100 years after his death (696 B.C.). Isaiah is also called the Messianic Prophet because he foretold, in great detail, the coming of the Messiah.

Background

In the chapter preceding today's text, we find that King Hezekiah, who had been ill, was visited by a group from Babylon, sent to bestow upon him a gift and best wishes for recovery. Hezekiah took the group on a tour of his palace and kingdom, even showing them the treasures in the storehouses. Isaiah informed the king that the Lord said there would come a time when Babylon would seize all of Hezekiah's treasures and take some of his descendants into captivity. This of course would not be the fate of the king's family only. Because all of Judah was guilty of idol worship, God warned the people through His prophet that a period of exile awaited all of them and that destruction of the land and temple was imminent. However, in the midst of the warnings, God promised that He would still be a source of hope for His people.

At-A-Glance

1. An Offer of Comfort
(Isaiah 40:1–2)

2. Prepare the Way for the Comforter to Come
(vv. 3–5)

3. None Are Equal to the Coming Comforter
(vv. 25–26)

4. God Is the Comforter
(vv. 29–31)

In Depth

1. An Offer of Comfort (Isaiah 40:1–2)

The audience for Isaiah's prophecies could perhaps be dissected into five groups: (1) Jews who lived in Judah during his ministry; (2) Jews who approximately 100 years after Isaiah's death would find themselves living in exile in Babylon; (3) those living during Jesus' earthly ministry; (4) believers from the last 2000 years; and (5) those who will be present when Christ returns and will witness His millennial reign. Though it has meaning for any era of believers, the command, "Comfort ye, comfort ye" in verse 1 of today's text was initially directed to the second audience, those who would be in captivity. To understand why they would need comfort, we have to understand what the land of

Judah, particularly the city of Jerusalem and the temple, meant to these people.

Jerusalem was the city God chose for Himself (1 Kings 11:32). Within the city was the temple which God chose His Spirit to dwell in (1 Kings 8:11–13). The temple was the center of the Jewish belief system. It was the symbol of their identity as God's chosen people. Because of sin, they would be in exile for 70 years, away from the temple.

Although Isaiah penned these words more than 100 years before the captivity, they were in present tense. This means that while the people of Judah were still in the midst of their sin with punishment pending, God had already set the stage for the deliverance of His people. Those who would be in captivity could lift up their heads for hope that had already been planned for their future (Jeremiah 29:11).

2. Prepare the Way for the Comforter to Come (vv. 3–5)

"The voice of him that crieth..." (v. 3) has been interpreted in two ways. Matthew Henry wrote that Isaiah was referring to prophets who would be living in captivity along with their fellow Jews. (*Matthew Henry's Commentary, Vol. IV,* electronic database) These prophets would call for their people to prepare for God's deliverance. Isaiah was also prophesying about John the Baptist, who had the role to prepare the people for the Gospel of Christ through the preaching of repentance. "The voice of one crying in the wilderness, Prepare ye the way of the Lord, make his paths straight. John did baptize in the wilderness, and preach the baptism of repentance for the remission of sins" (Mark 1:3–4). In either case, Isaiah was saying now that God had extended mercy, the recipients of that mercy needed to actively respond. He likened this response to building a highway.

The painstaking work of building a highway is a metaphor for how one should prepare for God's promises. Isaiah wrote, "Make straight in the desert a highway for our God" (Isaiah 40:3). The word "straight," *yashar,* means "to be level, be smooth." When one builds a highway, you must level off the rough, uneven terrain so that the surface is smooth or straight enough for passage. *Yashar* also means "to be right, upright, just, or lawful." From this definition of the word, "straight" could refer to one's character or behavior.

3. None Are Equal to the Coming Comforter (vv. 25–26)

In the verses not included in today's lesson text, Isaiah set out to reassure the captives of God's promise. He first reiterated the surety of God's word in verse 8: "The grass withereth, the flower fadeth: but the word of our God shall stand for ever." He then wrote of more promises of God (vv. 9–11). From verse 12 to 24, Isaiah posed a series of rhetorical questions that point to the uniqueness of God. These questions build up to verse 25 where God Himself asked, "To whom will you compare me? Who is my equal?" (NLT). Of course there is no one equal to God, but instead of a direct response, Isaiah gave an example of God's power. He said to consider the stars. The practice of consulting the stars to foretell the future began in ancient times and was popular among the pagans living around the Jews (Isaiah 47:9, 12–13). Stars were considered great beings, but in all their so-called greatness, they were still subject to the call of God.

4. God Is the Comforter (vv. 29–31)

It can be challenging for people who have limited minds and perspectives to believe that God has the power to deliver them from what seems to be a bleak situation. It is especially hard to maintain hope when the situation persists for a long time. The Babylonian exile would last for 70 years. Jews who were babies when taken into exile or were born in Babylon only knew life in captivity. With every passing year, those who might have been older children, teens, or young adults when taken into exile would have understandably been resigned to believing they would die in captivity because they watched their parents and grandparents die in those conditions. If God had promised to restore them to their land, how could they sustain themselves until that time came? All hope would have seemed to be gone even though words of comfort and reassurance had been extended. If they only had their own strength to rely upon, there really would not have been hope for the captives, but Isaiah wrote that God would empower them. He promised to strengthen the weakest among them.

The Hebrew word for "wait" (*qavah*) also means "to expect and to hope." They were to wait with full expectancy that God would accomplish all He promised and that hope was on the horizon, no matter how bleak the situation.

Search the Scriptures

1. Why was comfort to be spoken to the people of Jerusalem (Isaiah 40:2)?

2. How were God's people to prepare a way for Him (vv. 3–4)?

Discuss the Meaning

1. What does it mean to wait on God with expectancy?

2. How can we prepare a way for God while waiting for His promises to come to fruition?

3. Can you think of concrete ways God renews our strength daily?

Lesson in Our Society

Most Christians, when asked, would probably say that they have hope in God. Having hope is easy when everything in our lives is the way we like them. However, when trouble comes, it is much more challenging to maintain that hope. When the trouble persists for a long period of time, we may feel that God has forsaken us, but He has not. It is in those times that we must trust God the most and know that His promise to take care of us will not fail.

Make It Happen

Make a list of situations that seem hopeless in your life. Also make a list of what you did in those situations that did not reflect patience while waiting. Make a third list of how you will wait on God in each situation. As a means of reminding yourself to be hopeful, refer to these lists in your daily devotion and at those times when you are feeling discouraged.

Follow the Spirit

What God wants me to do:

_____

_____

_____

_____

Remember Your Thoughts

Special insights I have learned:

_____

_____

_____

_____

More Light on the Text

Isaiah 40:1–5, 25–26, 29–31

1 Comfort ye, comfort ye my people, saith your God.

Isaiah begins this chapter with words of comfort to the people of Israel who have suffered the discipline of exile in Babylon. Of course, the prophecy is about the future and looks to the coming exile and the coming salvation of God from that exile. God speaks comfort to His people in the midst of the hardship in the form of exile in Babylon. The Hebrew word *nachmu* (**NAKH-moo**) literally means "to cause to breathe again." It is God breathing new life into His people. This word of comfort does not concern a one time event. The word "comfort" is *nacham* (**naw-KHAM**) in Hebrew. It is an ongoing word of hope and comfort which God is going to repeatedly speak to His people through His prophets.

2 Speak ye comfortably to Jerusalem, and cry unto her, that her warfare is accomplished, that her iniquity is pardoned: for she hath received of the LORD's hand double for all her sins.

God reinforces this word of "comfort" again in verse 2 when He calls the prophet to speak "comfortably," literally "to the heart of" Jerusalem. The message is hope in the midst of despair. And the hope is contained in the proclamation that God's discipline has come to an end. God has forgiven His people for her sins and is ready in place of His anger to show compassion to His people. Not that the discipline was in any way unloving; as Proverbs 3:11–12 says, "My son, do not despise the LORD's discipline and do not resent his rebuke, because the LORD disciplines those he loves, as a father the son he delights in" (NIV).

That Jerusalem is said to have received "double" (Heb. *kephel*, **KEH-fel**), which means "twice as much" for her sins is in no way suggesting that the punishment has been excessive. Israel has not received more than her sins deserved. The ultimate punishment for sin is death. Rather Israel's hardship is being viewed from the perspective of God's compassion. It is the love of a Father who will not remain angry long and who is ready now to show compassion where there has been discipline. Kiel and Delitzsch write in their commentary, "The turning-point [*sic*] from wrath to love has arrived. The wrath has gone forth in double measure. With what intensity, therefore, will the love break forth, which has been so long restrained!" (140–141).

3 The voice of him that crieth in the wilderness, Prepare ye the way of the LORD, make straight in the desert a highway for our God. 4 Every valley shall be exalted, and every mountain and hill shall be made low: and the crooked shall be made straight, and the rough places plain:

What does God's compassion and love for His people look like? As though He answers this question, God gives the prophet a vision of a herald crying out in the wilderness. The message he gives is that the Lord Himself will visit His people in their despair. None other than God Himself is coming! And what the herald calls the people to do is to "prepare" the way (Heb. *panah*, **paw-NAW**), which means "clear the way" for the Lord's arrival. As one would clear the way for the coming of the king to ensure that there were no impediments to his coming, so the people are called to clear the way for the Lord's coming. And the descriptions here of making "straight" (Heb. *yashar,* **yaw-SHAR**) a highway in the desert by leveling hills and mountains, making the crooked straight, and the rough places plain are all imagery that speaks to repentance (a turning away from sin and turning to God for salvation). This is in fact what John the Baptist, the fulfillment of Isaiah's voice in the wilderness, calls the people to do as they come to him in anticipation of this coming one of whom John has been speaking—the Lord Jesus Christ. So the people are to anticipate God's coming and repent of their sins, the very sins for which they had gone into exile to begin with.

5 And the glory of the LORD shall be revealed, and all flesh shall see it together: for the mouth of the LORD hath spoken it.

The coming of the Lord in salvation is God's revelation of His "glory" (Heb. *kabowd, kabod,* **kaw-BODE**), which means "abundance, riches, honor" to His creation. It is not just Israel that will see this glory, but "all flesh" (everyone). God will come in salvation and will come in such a way that He will make this salvation visible to all. Of course, God has come and has revealed His glory. He has come in the person of Jesus Christ, who is "the exact representation" of God's nature (Hebrews 1:3, NIV) and the fulfillment of this coming salvation that God promised His people. But the certainty that the people of Israel could have as they looked forward to this event is bound up in God's own Word, which never fails. How will Israel know that they will come to see and experience this salvation? Isaiah tells us, "...the mouth of

the LORD hath spoken it" (Isaiah 40:5). It will happen. It has happened in and through Jesus Christ.

40:25 To whom then will ye liken me, or shall I be equal? saith the Holy One.

One of Israel's repeated temptations was around the issue of idolatry. Verse 25 is connected with verses 18–20 where God addresses much the same question. Can God really be compared with the idols? Can He really be compared to wood and stone? Idols are the inventions of human beings. They are not real and have no power. And Israel's sin in this area was nothing less than the sin of robbing God, at least in their lives, of His rightful place as God. Yet against the false gods of the nations, God declares Himself as "the Holy One" (Heb. *qadowsh, qadosh,* **kaw-DOSHE**), which means "set apart" or "sacred." And the people whom God has made holy by setting them apart should treat their God with the same love by sanctifying Him in their own lives, individually and corporately. Of course, the reality is that there is no one to whom God can be compared.

26 Lift up your eyes on high, and behold who hath created these things, that bringeth out their host by number: he calleth them all by names by the greatness of his might, for that he is strong in power; not one faileth.

Isaiah brings the point of the incomparability of God home by focusing on God as Creator—the One who "created" (Heb. *bara',* **baw-RAW**), which means "shaped, fashioned." He invites his readers to behold the heavens with their mass of stars. He then reminds them that all of these are created, numbered, named and sustained by God, who is strong in power. He is not like the gods of the nations who have no power because they are not gods to begin with.

40:29 He giveth power to the faint; and to them that have no might he increaseth strength. 30 Even the youths shall faint and be weary, and the young men shall utterly fall:

After emphasizing the greatness of God's power against the powerlessness of the idols, Isaiah now gives Israel more good news. Not only does their God possess power, He is also the God who gives "power" (Heb. *koach*, **KO-akh**), which means "strength, might." Such news must have come as a powerful message of hope to a people whose strength was likely waning as they endured the pain of exile. What is more, the power God gives is not like the natural power of youth which inevitably fades. Even youthful vigor wears out eventually.

31 But they that wait upon the LORD shall renew their strength; they shall mount up with wings as eagles; they shall run, and not be weary; and they shall walk, and not faint.

Isaiah concludes by telling the people that their hope to find renewal of strength as they look to God's salvation is bound up in their waiting upon the Lord. The word "wait" (Heb. *qavah*, **kaw-VAW**) means "look for, hope, expect." Thus, those whose faith is in God will find their strength renewed. Isaiah's imagery demonstrates the nature of this strength. It is strength that enables God's people to fly, run, or walk according to what the circumstances require. Whatever strength God's people need, God will provide it as they put their trust in Him.

Say It Correctly

Babylon. BAB-uh-luhn, -lon'.
Hezekiah. hez'-ih-KI -uh. hez'-uh-KI-uh.
Isaiah. I-ZA-uh.
Jerusalem. juh-ROO-suh-luhm.
Jotham. JOH-thuhm.
Judah. joo-DEE-uh.
Uzziah. uhz-ZI-uh, uh-ZI-uh.

Daily Bible Readings

M: God's Glory Revealed
Deuteronomy 5:22–27

T: God's Glory Declared
1 Chronicles 16:28–34

W: God's Glory Praised
2 Chronicles 5:11–14

T: God's Glory Beseeched
Psalm 79:5–10

F: God's Glory Above the Nations
Isaiah 40:12–17

S: God's Glory Above the Earth
Isaiah 40:18–24

S: God's Coming Glory
Isaiah 40:1–5, 25–26, 29–31

Teaching Tips

1. Words You Should Know

A. Servant (Isaiah 41:8) *'ebed* (Heb.)—Slaves, subjects, worshipers (of God).

B. Chosen (vv. 8–9) *bachar* (Heb.)—Selected, elected.

C. Needy (v. 17) *'ebyown* (Heb.)—In want, chiefly poor, subject to oppression and abuse.

2. Teacher Preparation

Unifying Principle—Not Forsaken. People take comfort in knowing that someone is capable of helping them in times of need. Isaiah declared that God alone creates, controls, and redeems.

A. Pray for you and your students. Ask God to reveal those areas in your lives in which you all need to have confidence in Almighty God.

B. Study the entire lesson.

3. Open the Lesson

A. Open your class with prayer, keeping the Aim for Change in mind.

B. Then engage the class in a discussion on why it is hard for some people to ask for help.

C. Have the class discuss ways that asking for help can be beneficial.

D. As the class goes through the lesson, ask them to ponder the question, "Why do we sometimes *not* ask God for help?"

E. Have three volunteers role-play the parts of Uncle Max, Valerie, and the Narrator in today's In Focus story. Engage in discussion.

4. Present the Scriptures

A. Have volunteers read the Focal Verses.

B. To clarify the Focal Verses, use The People, Places, and Times; Background; At-A-Glance outline; In Depth, Search the Scriptures; and More Light on the Text.

5. Explore the Meaning

A. Lead a discussion of the Discuss the Meaning section.

B. Summarize the Lesson in Our Society and Make It Happen sections.

6. Next Steps for Application

A. Write points to ponder under Follow the Spirit and Remember Your Thoughts.

B. Reflect on these areas during the week.

C. Close with prayer.

Worship Guide

For the Superintendent or Teacher
Theme: I Am Your God
Theme Song: "Leaning on the Everlasting Arms"
Devotional Reading: 1 John 4:13–19
Prayer

I Am Your God

Bible Background • ISAIAH 41:14–2:9
Printed Text • ISAIAH 41:8–10, 17–20 | Devotional Reading • 1 JOHN 4:13–19

───── Aim for Change ─────

By the end of the lesson, we will: REALIZE that God desires to have a relationship with us; FEEL confident in our times of need; and TESTIFY to the magnitude of God's power and promises.

───── 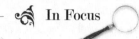 In Focus ─────

"How much did you say it would cost?" Max asked.

"It's going to be at least $20,000 to get an entire new roof," replied the contractor.

"Do I need a new roof? Why not just repair it?"

"That latest storm did a lot of damage, and it looks like all the old repairs were shoddy at best. There's no way around it. You're going to need that new roof."

"OK, well, I'll have to contact you to tell you when you can start the work."

"What's wrong, Unc?" Valerie sat down beside her Uncle Max.

"Where am I going to get the money for the roof? I'm retired and on a fixed income. I can't just take $20,000 out of my savings."

"I know you're not worried. Remember all the things God got us through this past year. He's going to take care of this, too."

"You're right, Valerie. God worked things out before, and I trust He will again."

"That's more like it, Uncle Max. Let's go to the home improvement outlet and start looking at shingle colors."

Valerie and Uncle Max had gone through some hard times, but they were not going to be discouraged. They knew that their only hope was in God, and just as He took care of them before, He would again.

───── Keep in Mind ─────

"Fear thou not; for I am with thee: be not dismayed; for I am thy God: I will strengthen thee; yea, I will help thee; yea, I will uphold thee with the right hand of my righteousness" (Isaiah 41:10).

Focal Verses

KJV **Isaiah 41:8** But thou, Israel, art my servant, Jacob whom I have chosen, the seed of Abraham my friend.

9 Thou whom I have taken from the ends of the earth, and called thee from the chief men thereof, and said unto thee, Thou art my servant; I have chosen thee, and not cast thee away.

10 Fear thou not; for I am with thee: be not dismayed; for I am thy God: I will strengthen thee; yea, I will help thee; yea, I will uphold thee with the right hand of my righteousness.

41:17 When the poor and needy seek water, and there is none, and their tongue faileth for thirst, I the LORD will hear them, I the God of Israel will not forsake them.

18 I will open rivers in high places, and fountains in the midst of the valleys: I will make the wilderness a pool of water, and the dry land springs of water.

19 I will plant in the wilderness the cedar, the shittah tree, and the myrtle, and the oil tree; I will set in the desert the fir tree, and the pine, and the box tree together:

20 That they may see, and know, and consider, and understand together, that the hand of the LORD hath done this, and the Holy One of Israel hath created it.

NLT **Isaiah 41:8** "But as for you, Israel my servant, Jacob my chosen one, descended from Abraham my friend,

9 I have called you back from the ends of the earth, saying, 'You are my servant.' For I have chosen you and will not throw you away.

10 Don't be afraid, for I am with you. Don't be discouraged, for I am your God. I will strengthen you and help you. I will hold you up with my victorious hand.

41:17 "When the poor and needy search for water and there is none, and their tongues are parched from thirst, then I, the LORD, will answer them. I, the God of Israel, will never abandon them.

18 I will open up rivers for them on the high plateaus. I will give them fountains of water in the valleys. I will fill the desert with pools of water. Rivers fed by springs will flow across the parched ground.

19 I will plant trees in the barren desert— cedar, acacia, myrtle, olive, cypress, fir, and pine.

20 I am doing this so all who see this miracle will understand what it means—that it is the LORD who has done this, the Holy One who created it.

The People, Places, and Times

The Cedar. It was known as the king of the trees in the Bible lands. The cedars were most often referred to as "the glory of Lebanon" (Isaiah 35:2; 60:13). Also known as the cedars of Lebanon, they had reddish-brown trunks that could grow as much as 40 feet around. The trees also grew very tall (Isaiah 2:13) and had plenty of branches to make shade (Ezekiel 31:3). Much of the temple, Solomon's palace, and public buildings in Jerusalem was made from cedar. The box tree, considered a species of the cedar, also grows in Lebanon and has a hard, durable wood.

The Shittah Tree. It is translated the "acacia" (Heb. *shittah,* **shit-TAW**) and consists of two species, one of which grows in the Sinai desert, where the Israelites wandered for 40 years. This tree has very hard wood that insects cannot destroy. It is "luxuriant in dry places" (Unger, 1326).

The Myrtle. This is an evergreen shrub with edible berries. It grows near Bethlehem, Hebron, the valleys of modern-day Jerusalem, and throughout central Palestine.

The Oil Tree. It is sometimes translated as "olive" tree; although the two have a physical resemblance, they are different. The oil tree grows in the mountains of Palestine and has wood hard enough to make "carved images" (WebBible, 5).

The Fir and Pine Trees. These are both translated "cypress." They grow in the mountains of Lebanon. The fir's wood was used for making musical instruments, ceilings, and decks of ships. The cypress has dark leaves and fragrant wood, and it is used as a funeral tree, a tree planted as a memorial or a sympathy gift.

Background

The Israelites would continually engage in the vicious cycle of unfaithfulness. First, they would be in right relationship with God. Then, they would start to turn away from Him, committing many sins, particularly idol worship. The Lord would send a prophet to warn the people to turn from their wicked ways or face judgment. For a time, they would repent and be in right relationship with God again. However, they would start sinning again, especially whenever they were under a king who did not do right in the eyes of God. This cycle eventually culminated in the northern kingdom (Israel) being taken into captivity in Assyria and the southern kingdom (Judah) being taken into captivity in Babylon. The Lord, however, always promised He would save a remnant of the faithful for Himself and return them to Jerusalem to the temple to worship. The remnant is referred to in Scripture as early as Deuteronomy. "And the LORD shall scatter you among the nations, and ye shall be left few in number among the heathen, whither the LORD shall lead you. But if from thence thou shalt seek the LORD thy God, thou shalt find him, if thou seek him with all thy heart and with all thy soul. When thou art in tribulation, and all these things are come upon thee, even in the latter days, if thou turn to the LORD thy God, and shalt be obedient unto his voice; (For the LORD thy God is a merciful God;) he will not forsake thee, neither destroy thee, nor forget the covenant of thy fathers which he sware unto them" (Deuteronomy 4:27, 29–31).

At-A-Glance

1. Because of the Lord, Fear Not
   (Isaiah 41:8–10)

2. The Lord Will Help (vv. 17–19)

3. The Lord Has Done This (v. 20)

In Depth

1. Because of the Lord, Fear Not (Isaiah 41:8–10)

Although Isaiah wrote prophecy from the perspective of his own time, he also wrote from the perspective of a future generation of faithful Israelites, who would find themselves living in exile in Babylon. Chapter 41 is for the comfort of this remnant. In verses 1–7, not in today's lesson text, God, through Isaiah, invites the gods of the idol worshipers to trial to see whose power and strength will prevail (v. 1). God presents His case. He "raised up the righteous man from the east" and has given victory over many nations (v. 2). This Gentile ruler, a man anointed by God, is King Cyrus, of whom the Scripture says in Isaiah 45:1, "whose right hand I [God] have holden, to subdue nations before him" (*Life Application Study Bible*, 1097). Cyrus would make a way for the remnant to return to Jerusalem to rebuild the city and the temple. Upon seeing the mighty hand of God at work, the idol worshipers, the heathens, trembling with fear, would get their idols ready to see if their gods could display the same level of power (41:7). These heathens are the people of Babylon, Israel's captors, who God would destroy (Isaiah 46).

In verse 8, focus changes from the description of the idol worshipers to the description of the Israelites. The word "but"

denotes that the following message is the polar opposite of the preceding one. The first difference is the words used to describe the idol worshipers and the Israelites. For the idol worshipers, the words "islands" and "isles" are used (Isaiah 41:1, 5). If we look at "island" figuratively, we see that the heathens with their idols are separated from God by their sin. They are not in a relationship with God. When referring to the Israelites, "my servant" is used (v. 8). A servant, a bondsman, or slave is of course subject to his master. Among the Hebrew people, a slave would serve six years and then be freed in the seventh year (Exodus 21:2). But if that slave chose to remain a servant out of love for his master, he could be in service for life (Exodus 21:5–6). With this in mind, let's look at the use of "servant" in today's text. When God calls Israel "my servant," it is not meant to suggest forced servitude; rather, its intended meaning is willing, loving worship and service, characteristic of a covenant relationship with God.

After being purged of their sin, God's people would be brought back by God from all the ends of the earth, where they had been scattered (Ezekiel 36:23–24). God would bring these faithful people back to their land and to Himself because, as He told them in Isaiah 41:9, "Thou art my servant." He reminds them that He had chosen them, not abandoned them or cast them away. As stated in *Vine's Complete Expository Dictionary*, "Being 'chosen' by God brings people into an intimate relationship with Him" (34).

Another difference between the idol worshipers and the Israelites is seen in Isaiah 41:10, which reveals the purpose for God's words in the previous verses. He has reminded Israel, "Thou art my servant; I have chosen thee, and not cast thee away," so they would not fear as the heathens do

(v. 9). They should indeed be afraid because they have chosen to worship idols, placing themselves in opposition to God. But the faithful Israelites, the remnant, do not have to fear because God is with them—He alone is their God.

2. The Lord Will Help (vv. 17–19)

In verses 11–16, God further explains why the Israelites should not fear. When the time for the end of their captivity would come, God would remove all obstacles in the way of their returning home. He would swiftly remove all their enemies. Therefore, they need not fear, for God the Redeemer would help them (v. 14).

In verse 17, God's promises continue. If taken literally, this verse could refer to a time "When the captives, either in Babylon or in their return, are in distress for want of water or shelter, God will take care of them..." (Henry). The case of the poor and needy, however, can also be figurative for any dire situation. The Hebrew word for "poor" (`aniy, **aw-NEE**) means "to be depressed in mind and circumstances." "Needy" in the Hebrew is 'ebyown (**eb-YONE**) and means "destitute, subject to oppression and abuse." The "poor and needy" refers to those in a state of mental depression with the added trouble of being socially and materially disenfranchised. The need for water represents being deprived of the fulfillment of the most basic needs and being deprived of the ability to obtain resources for oneself. From a spiritual perspective, the "poor and needy" would be those captives thirsty for the chance to worship God in their land. In our time, the "poor and needy" are the spiritually depraved; they are lost. Whatever the case may be, just when it seems the thirst will never cease and there is no glimmer of hope, the Lord will hear. "To hear" (v. 17)

simply means to apprehend sound; if our ears function correctly, we all have the ability to hear. However, when God hears, we can assume that He will respond with action.

When the captives were in the midst of their journey home, God would help them. When any of His people are depressed and disenfranchised, God will not forsake them. When Israel thirsted for worship again, God would purge them of their sin and bring them back home. When God saw that the lost had no chance for salvation, God sent His Son Jesus Christ as the propitiation ("appeasing or atonement") for our sins (Romans 3:25; Hebrews 2:17; 1 John 2:2; 4:10; Enns, 110). Isn't it wonderful that we who are in relationship with God have the privilege of Him helping us in our times of need?

Isaiah 41:18–19 shows to what lengths God would go to care for the needs of His servant, Israel. In the literal sense, God's causing these various water sources to spring up in dry barren land can refer to His replenishing the land that would have lain barren during the years of Israel's captivity (Isaiah 30:23–25). However, the references to water also illustrate the divine grace God grants His people in their times of need. It is important to note the excess of water. In one moment, there was no water, and in the next, there were four sources of water. This signifies God's ability and desire to more than meet the needs of His people (Ephesians 3:20). It shows that He is indeed their God.

We should also consider the locations of the bodies of water. These are places where the existence of water can be impossible, but this is a testament of God's power. He can take what seems hopeless and impossible and make it probable.

Verse 19 reiterates this same sentiment abut God. In the dry, barren desert, He makes the trees grow. Trees, which bring shade and protection from the heat, are symbolic of God's comfort when we are in dire straits.

3. The Lord Has Done This (v. 20)

Verse 20 is the crux of why God does what He does. "That they may see, and know, and consider, and understand together..." These four verbs are really variations of each other. "See" means "to behold, consider, discern, perceive." "Know" means "to ascertain by seeing, have understanding, to acknowledge." "Consider" means "to determine, make out." "Understand" means "to consider, have wisdom." The use of these four words together has the connotation of knowing and understanding, without a shadow or an inkling of doubt, that the Lord, by His mighty hand, would deliver the Israelites. God wanted His people to acknowledge His power and care for them. He refers to Himself as the "Holy One of Israel," emphasizing His relationship with them. God makes it clear that He would have comforted them because He was in relationship with them and loved them. We, too, can be assured that God desires to comfort all of us who are in relationship with Him. He will spare nothing for our sakes (Romans 8:32).

Search the Scriptures

1. How does one define "a servant of God" (Isaiah 41:8–9)?

2. Why were the Israelites told not to be afraid (v. 10)?

Discuss the Meaning

1. What does it mean to be called "a servant of God"?

2. How does being in a relationship with God benefit you in times of need?

3. What are ways that you can acknowledge God's power at work in your life?

Lesson in Our Society

We often say, "I believe in God," but sometimes when we find ourselves in great need of help, we don't act like we believe. We allow ourselves to become so fearful, we either forget to call out to God or resolve within ourselves that there is no way He can help us. *Newsflash!* God, the God of all things, has the power to help us in any situation. He desires to have a relationship with us and, therefore, desires to meet our every need. In fact, one of the benefits of being in relationship with God, other than the gift of eternal salvation, is having all confidence that we can depend on Him.

Make It Happen

As Christians, we should encourage each other to have confidence in God. We gain confidence by remembering how He helped us in the past. Make a list of how God has helped you. Choose at least three people and ask them to share with you some examples of times God helped them. With their permission, make a list of what each one tells you. You should also share your list with them. Ask God to help you recognize those areas in your life in which you need to have more confidence in Him.

Follow the Spirit

What God wants me to do:

_____

_____

_____

_____

Remember Your Thoughts

Special insights I have learned:

_____

_____

_____

_____

More Light on the Text

Isaiah 41:8–10, 17–20

8 But thou, Israel, art my servant, Jacob whom I have chosen, the seed of Abraham my friend.

Isaiah starts this section of chapter 41 with a reminder of the intimate relationship into which God has entered with the people of Israel. There is nothing but the deepest of affection communicated here from God to His people. Israel is His "servant" (Heb. `ebed, **EH-bed**), which means they are worshipers or subjects. They are His chosen people, the seed of Abraham—God's friend. Whereas those who put their trust in idols can only expect judgment, God's people are reminded here of the affection God has for them and the blessing of the relationship that God has entered into with them.

9 Thou whom I have taken from the ends of the earth, and called thee from the chief men thereof, and said unto thee, Thou art my servant; I have chosen thee, and not cast thee away.

Keil and Delitzsch in their commentary tell us that the relationship between God and His people had both an objective and subjective element: "On the one hand, Israel is the servant of Jehovah by virtue of a divine act; and this act, viz. [namely] its election and call, was an act of pure grace, and was not to be traced…to any superior excellence

or merit on the part of Israel….On the other hand, Israel was the servant of Jehovah, inasmuch as it acted out what Jehovah had made it, partly in reverential worship of this God, and partly in active obedience" (162–163). Indeed, Israel was not chosen because of who she was, but because of God's own grace. God "called" (Heb. *qara'*, **kaw-RAW**)—which means "commissioned, appointed, endowed"—her from among the chief nations of the earth. As nations go, Israel was rather insignificant. And yet she was chosen to worship God and carry out God's kingdom agenda of pursuing justice, mercy, and compassion in the world. This is what it means to be the servants of Jehovah.

10 Fear thou not; for I am with thee: be not dismayed; for I am thy God: I will strengthen thee; yea, I will help thee; yea, I will uphold thee with the right hand of my righteousness.

Israel is not to fear or be dismayed because of the relationship she has with the Lord. God will not be idle in regards to her. The phrase "I will strengthen" (Heb. *'amats*, **aw-MATS**), meaning "secure, make firm, make strong," is better understood as "to lay firm hold of" (Keil and Delitzsch, 163). God is saying He has laid firm hold of His people, Israel. He has attached His people to Himself, which guarantees that God will aide and uphold her in His purposes for her as His people. He will uphold her with His right hand of "righteousness" (Heb. *tsedeq*, **TSEH-dek**), which means "justness, rightness."

It is important to note two things about this particular righteousness. First, this righteousness is God's righteousness. It is God's justness and rightness, which He also works as a gift in His people. Secondly, this righteousness will uphold Israel in the face of her enemies. It is God's righteousness which He works in His people as a gift that will put to shame and confound Israel's enemies.

41:17 When the poor and needy seek water, and there is none, and their tongue faileth for thirst, I the LORD will hear them, I the God of Israel will not forsake them.

Isaiah now describes to the people what God's upholding His people in righteousness looks like as God comes to the aide of His people. God's righteousness is such that when He gives support to His people, the poor and needy will be raised up. God will not forsake them, but will hear their cry and come to their assistance.

18 I will open rivers in high places, and fountains in the midst of the valleys: I will make the wilderness a pool of water, and the dry land springs of water. 19 I will plant in the wilderness the cedar, the shittah tree, and the myrtle, and the oil tree; I will set in the desert the fir tree, and the pine, and the box tree together:

Isaiah continues the description of what God's coming in righteousness to aid His people looks like. It is a beautiful picture of God causing water to flow and plants and trees to grow in what was once a wilderness. God, who creates out of nothing, turns what was once a desert into a garden. The people of God, who may have felt forsaken as they considered their circumstances, are now shown this glorious depiction of God's coming consolation.

20 That they may see, and know, and consider, and understand together, that the hand of the LORD hath done this, and the Holy One of Israel hath created it.

To underline the certainty of God's coming consolation for His people, God speaks through the prophet Isaiah to declare that it is His own "hand"—which in Hebrew is *yad* (**yawd**), meaning "strength, power"— that has accomplished their deliverance and provisions. It is through no work of persons,

nor of the idols, but through God's hands' crafting that will bring about this salvation. God's own hand will bring it to pass. This is meant to give great hope to the people of God in the midst of their despair. It is meant to draw their hearts to greater faith in Jehovah, who has delivered before and now promises to deliver again.

Say It Correctly

Deuteronomy. doo'-tuh-RON-uh-mee.
Ezekiel. i-ˈzē-kyəl, -kē-əl.
Lebanon. LEB-uh-nuhn.
Shittah. ˈshi-tə.
Solomon. SOL-uh-muhn.

Daily Bible Readings

M: A God of Love
1 John 4:13–19

T: A God of Grace and Mercy
2 Chronicles 30:6–9

W: A God Ready to Forgive
Nehemiah 9:16–21

T: A God of Hope
Psalm 71:1–6

F: The Lord, First and Last
Isaiah 41:1–7

S: Do Not Fear
Isaiah 41:11–16

S: The Lord's Promise to Protect
Isaiah 41:8–10, 17–20

Teaching Tips

1. Words You Should Know

A. Peace (Isaiah 9:7) *shalowm, shalom* (Heb.)—Wholeness, quietness, contentment, health, prosperity.

B. Rod (11:1) *choter* (Heb.)—A branch or twig.

C. Knowledge (v. 2) *da`ath* (Heb.)—The presence of discernment, understanding, wisdom.

2. Teacher Preparation

Unifying Principle—Hope for Good Leadership. Jesus is the Leader conceived of the Holy Spirit and born from the line of Jesse and David.

A. Pray earnestly for God's guidance in studying and presenting the lesson.

B. Study the entire lesson.

C. Prepare to write three columns on the board: (1) "Attributes of a Servant"; (2) "Attributes of a 'Good' Leader"; and (3) "Attributes of a 'Poor' Leader."

3. Open the Lesson

A. Open with prayer, using the Aim for Change.

B. After prayer, put the three headings on the board: (1) "Attributes of a Servant"; (2) "Attributes of a 'Good' Leader"; and (3) "Attributes of a 'Poor' Leader."

C. Allow your class to help you make the three lists. Discuss.

D. Use the In Focus story to further clarify the attributes of a servant—a good leader.

4. Present the Scriptures

A. Have volunteers read the Focal Verses.

B. To clarify the Focal Verses, form groups and have them list and present two salient points from The People, Places, and Times; Background; and At-A-Glance outline.

5. Explore the Meaning

A. Lead a discussion of Discuss the Meaning and Search the Scriptures.

B. Summarize the Lesson in Our Society and Make It Happen sections.

6. Next Steps for Application

A. Challenge students to write under Follow the Spirit and Remember Your Thoughts what it means to be a disciple of Christ. Have them think and pray on these things during the week.

B. Close with prayer.

Worship Guide

For the Superintendent or Teacher
Theme: The Mission of the Servant
Theme Song: "My Tribute"
Devotional Reading: John 4:19–26
Prayer

The Mission of the Servant

Bible Background • ISAIAH 9:1–7; 11:1–9; MATTHEW 1:18–25
Printed Text • ISAIAH 9:7; 11:1–8 | Devotional Reading • JOHN 4:19–26

Aim for Change

By the end of the lesson, we will: REALIZE that Jesus is the fulfillment of God's promise in Isaiah's prophecy; DESIRE for Jesus to be the Lord of our lives; and PRAISE God for sending His Son, Jesus, to the earth.

 In Focus

Johnny spent hours in the garage polishing his new car. He had worked long hours in the summer to save money to purchase his beautiful used Audi. His younger brother, Karl, admired the car very much. However, Johnny firmly and persistently warned Karl not to touch or drive his car.

One evening, the garage door was left unlocked and someone stole Johnny's Audi. Although Karl insisted that he had nothing to do with the missing car, Johnny relentlessly accused his brother of stealing it. A police report was filed, and two weeks later the car was confiscated. The thief who actually stole the Audi was arrested and put in police custody. Johnny realized he had accused Karl unfairly and apologized. Karl's feelings were hurt; nonetheless, he forgave his brother.

Human beings have a tendency to judge too quickly, and our hasty conclusions hurt other people. Could Johnny have handled this situation without accusing his brother of stealing? In this lesson we will learn that God is the only fair assessor of human behavior. His calculations are never wrong, and He is just in His distribution of rewards and punishment. He fulfills our hope for "good" leadership.

Keep in Mind

"And righteousness shall be the girdle of his loins, and faithfulness the girdle of his reins" (Isaiah 11:5).

"And righteousness shall be the girdle of his loins, and
faithfulness the girdle of his reins" (Isaiah 11:5).

Focal Verses

KJV **Isaiah 9:7** Of the increase of his government and peace there shall be no end, upon the throne of David, and upon his kingdom, to order it, and to establish it with judgment and with justice from henceforth even for ever. The zeal of the LORD of hosts will perform this.

11:1 And there shall come forth a rod out of the stem of Jesse, and a Branch shall grow out of his roots:

2 And the spirit of the LORD shall rest upon him, the spirit of wisdom and understanding, the spirit of counsel and might, the spirit of knowledge and of the fear of the LORD;

3 And shall make him of quick understanding in the fear of the LORD: and he shall not judge after the sight of his eyes, neither reprove after the hearing of his ears:

4 But with righteousness shall he judge the poor, and reprove with equity for the meek of the earth: and he shall smite the earth with the rod of his mouth, and with the breath of his lips shall he slay the wicked.

5 And righteousness shall be the girdle of his loins, and faithfulness the girdle of his reins.

6 The wolf also shall dwell with the lamb, and the leopard shall lie down with the kid; and the calf and the young lion and the fatling together; and a little child shall lead them.

7 And the cow and the bear shall feed; their young ones shall lie down together: and the lion shall eat straw like the ox.

8 And the sucking child shall play on the hole of the asp, and the weaned child shall put his hand on the cockatrice' den.

NLT **Isaiah 9:7** His government and its peace will never end. He will rule with fairness and justice from the throne of his ancestor David for all eternity. The passionate commitment of the LORD of Heaven's Armies will make this happen!

11:1 Out of the stump of David's family will grow a shoot—yes, a new Branch bearing fruit from the old root.

2 And the Spirit of the LORD will rest on him—the Spirit of wisdom and understanding, the Spirit of counsel and might, the Spirit of knowledge and fear of the LORD.

3 He will delight in obeying the LORD. He will not judge by appearance nor make a decision based on hearsay.

4 He will give justice to the poor and make fair decisions for the exploited. The earth will shake at the force of his word, and one breath from his mouth will destroy the wicked.

5 He will wear righteousness like a belt and truth like an undergarment.

6 In that day the wolf and the lamb will live together; the leopard will lie down with the baby goat. The calf and the yearling will be safe with the lion, and a little child will lead them all.

7 The cow will graze near the bear. The cub and the calf will lie down together. The lion will eat hay like a cow.

8 The baby will play safely near the hole of a cobra. Yes, a little child will put its hand in a nest of deadly snakes without harm.

The People, Places, and Times

David. He is called a man after God's own heart and considered Israel's greatest king. Second Samuel and 1 Chronicles are two Old Testament books devoted to David's reign. Nearly half of the Bible's psalms are ascribed to David, and his power and influence are glorified throughout Old Testament history. In the New Testament, he is described as predecessor to Jesus Christ and in the lineage of the Messiah. Throughout the New Testament, the Gospel writers refer to Jesus as the "son of David" (meaning that Jesus would come through that ancestry). God's covenant with David promised that an eternal King would come from David's family. The Bible tells us that Jesus came from David's descendants; nevertheless, the Gospels also clearly teach that Jesus Christ is the Son of the Living God.

Jesse. He is the father of David and an ancestor of Jesus Christ. The "root of Jesse" is a figure of speech used by the prophet Isaiah to convey the hope of a Savior coming from David's family tree.

Background

In previous chapters of Isaiah, we read that the Israelites suffered under God's punishment for their rejection of God's righteous will for their lives. God used Isaiah as a tool to warn the Israelites of the dire consequences of their disobedience. Isaiah was permanently changed when he was called as a prophet for God. Because the Lord had warned him that the people would not listen, he knew that speaking as a mouthpiece for the Lord would not grant him great success. The omniscient (all-knowing) Lord knew a remnant would obey His word, so Isaiah was charged to speak and write his message in spite of Israel's defiance. The Children of Israel were contrasted with a tree that had to be cut and humbled through trials and tribulations. This was done to ensure that a new tree could grow from an old stump. From the old stub would come the Messiah, the Savior of the universe.

At-A-Glance

1. The Faithful Reign of God
(Isaiah 9:7; 11:1–2)

2. The Compassionate Reign of God (11:3)

3. The Righteous Reign of God (vv. 4–5)

4. The Peaceful Reign of God (vv. 6–8)

In Depth

1. The Faithful Reign of God (Isaiah 9:7; 11:1–2)

Throughout world history, we have seen great dynasties rise and fall. Isaiah reminds us that there is no dynasty or government that compares to the majesty of Christ Jesus. His dynasty, the kingdom of God, is an everlasting dominance, superior to any and all human regimes (Isaiah 9:7).

Assyria is Israel's enemy, and by the power of God is cut down, defeated, and never to rise to supremacy again. The old generation of Israelites, the royal line of David, would also experience a "cutting down" whereby God left only a remnant to serve Him. From this residue would sprout a fruitful branch, and out of that branch will come the True Vine—the Lord Jesus Christ, Ruler of all humankind and the Author and Finisher of our faith. The remnant represents the people of God who stayed obedient to His Word. There is nothing humankind can do to thwart the plan of God. Nathan had prophesied that a descendant from David would rule forever (2 Samuel 7:16). His government would be greater than any that had existed or were to come. The fulfillment of God's Word would manifest through those who trust in His faithfulness (Isaiah 11:1).

To hear that relief is finally on its way after years of oppressive control surely made the Israelites feel better. The reigning King would not rule with human understanding, but with the superior wisdom that comes from God. His judgments would be motivated by reverential fear of the Father in heaven. His discernment would be rooted in love and not favoritism. He would be incapable of bribery with material possessions or persuaded by flattering tongues. He would be a wise judge, seeking fairness for all people. This King is like no other king that ever existed; His compassion and love for humankind extends beyond the human imagination. This prophetic illustration describes the superior authority of Jesus Christ. Jesus is God's promise, the fulfillment of prophecy to the people of Israel.

2. The Compassionate Reign of God (Isaiah 11:3)

God sees through eyes of love, compassion, and justice. Unlike humanity, the Lord does not judge according to our status or position in life. His vision pierces through the superficial facades and images some of us "showboat" in front of others. He sees through the shields we use to cover our shame, insecurities, and inadequacies. The Lord sees past our faults and focuses on our potential. He judges the motives and contents of the heart. He can separate the soul and spirit by the cutting edge of His Word so that all our secrets are exposed. God sees our potential when everyone else is concentrating on our shortfalls.

In addition, through our petitions and prayers, God hears our hearts. We may not speak eloquently or possess a vocabulary of scholarly distinction, yet our Heavenly Father hears the moans and groans of a sincere and contrite heart.

3. The Righteous Reign of God (vv. 4–5)

Isaiah's prophecy reminds us of a great hope—one that rests in the ruling powers of a just God. God's judgment will not favor the rich and despise the poor. The righteous rule of God will uphold fair treatment of people. So often we face discrimination or unfair treatment by others solely based on our socioeconomic, racial, or political status. Unfortunately, the poor in our society suffer from inadequate health care, housing, and legal representation. They are most often the victims of crime. In a society that idolizes success and fosters a love-hate relationship with the elite, the plight of the poor gains little or no attention at all. Due to their lack of economic clout, income, or education, the poor are sometimes viewed with contempt. Here in this passage of Scripture, the voice of Isaiah reminds the people of the Lord's faithfulness to the needy, downtrodden, and afflicted in society. The Lord has not forgotten His promise to them. Isaiah's message is one of hope in the midst of despair, and faith in the middle of fear and confusion. God would not only keep His word, but also lift the burden of unrighteous rule off the shoulders of the poor (v. 4).

This promise came at a time during great trials and tribulation. Judah had become dishonest, disobedient, and full of idolatry. The nation had turned its back on God and lusted after the foreign and hostile entities that infiltrated her territories. The nation needed a revival from God, one that would restore righteous and just order to a corrupt environment. The country had turned from what the forefathers had taught them—to be kindhearted to the poor and needy and not to abuse or oppress the marginalized and less fortunate.

4. The Peaceful Reign of God (vv. 6–8)

The prophet Isaiah points to a future time, perhaps during Christ's second coming, where peace will not only reign among humankind, but also in the animal kingdom. No longer will the lamb be afraid of the wolf or the calf be afraid of the lion. Carnivorous appetites will end. Predator and prey will feast on grass and straw. Poisonous snakes will not harm little children. Isaiah's prophecy reminds the Children of Israel, despite their hardship, suffering, and disobedience, that the Lord is still faithful. He has not forgotten His promise made to their ancestors. He sent His only begotten Son, Jesus Christ, as the answer to this pledge.

Search the Scriptures

1. "The spirit of the _____ shall rest upon him" (Isaiah 11:2).

2. How will the poor be judged (v. 4)?

3. How will the wolf and lamb dwell together (v. 6)?

Discuss the Meaning

1. How should Christians treat others less fortunate?

2. Why is it important for us to remember that God is faithful in keeping His promises?

3. How does it make you feel to know that one day there will be total peace on earth?

Lesson in Our Society

To be disciples of Christ is becoming more and more unpopular in our society. Christians are ridiculed for standing and supporting the values of God's Word. Too often we as children of God buckle under or give in to the pressure of societal demands. We cannot compromise what we believe. The Lord did not compromise or neglect His promise to us. Knowing that God made tremendous sacrifices on our behalf, how can we renege on our service to God?

Make It Happen

It is unrealistic to try to meet every need in our church, family, or community, but there are some things we can do to support a particular cause. For example, we can volunteer our time in a food pantry, deliver home-cooked meals to the sick and shut-in, donate or buy clothes for needy families, or offer to babysit the child of a single parent when he or she is out seeking employment. Pray and ask the Lord to reveal a particular need in your church, family, and community.

Follow the Spirit

What God wants me to do:

_____

_____

_____

_____

Remember Your Thoughts

Special insights I have learned:

_____

_____

_____

_____

More Light on the Text
Isaiah 9:7; 11:1–8

9:7 Of the increase of his government and peace there shall be no end, upon the throne of David, and upon his kingdom, to order it, and to establish it with judgment and with justice from henceforth even for ever. The zeal of the LORD of hosts will perform this.

Verse 7 of chapter 9 focuses on the nature of the coming Messianic kingdom. His kingdom is to be one of "peace" (Heb. *shalowm, shalom,* **shaw-LOME**), which means "quietness, contentment, health, prosperity," and is to be a kingdom without end. In keeping with God's promise to David, the Messiah will sit on David's throne, which is a way of saying He will rule on the human side as a descendant of David. Yet He is not just a man; He is the God-Man and thus His rule and reign will have no end. The foundations of His kingdom will be "justice" (Heb. *tsâdaqah,* **tsed-aw-KAW**), which means "a righteousness in government." Over against the cruel, oppressive, and destructive kingdoms of men and women, His Kingdom will be characterized by justice and righteousness.

11:1 And there shall come forth a rod out of the stem of Jesse, and a Branch shall grow out of his roots:

The word "rod" in Hebrew is *choter* (**KHO-ter**), and it means "branch, twig." The Hebrew word for "stem" is *geza`* (**GEH-zah**), and it means "the trunk of a tree." The house of David, because of its repeated rebellion against God, had been reduced to a remnant, a twig. The great powers around the house of David were like tall trees. However, God in His righteous judgment will cut them down (Isaiah 10:33–34). Yet with Israel, He has left a branch out of which Isaiah prophecies that a shoot, a twig will spring forth. And it will not remain a shoot or a twig. It will blossom and it will bear fruit. Its beginning will be that of humility and lowliness, but it will be exalted. Of course, the shoot is the coming Messiah—Jesus.

2 And the spirit of the LORD shall rest upon him, the spirit of wisdom and understanding, the spirit of counsel and might, the spirit of knowledge and of the fear of the LORD;

In Isaiah 11:2, Isaiah prophecies of the Spirit resting upon Him and then gives the nature of the Spirit's empowerment. This King will not be like the kings of the earth or the ungodly kings of Israel. He will be characterized by "wisdom" (Heb. *chôkmah,* **khok-MAW**), which means "skill, prudence, ethics"; "understanding" (Heb. *biynah,* **bee-NAW**), which means "knowledge, wisdom, discernment"; "counsel" (Heb. *`etsah,* **ay-TSAW**), which means "advice, purpose"; "might" (Heb. *gâbuwrah,* **gheb-oo-RAW**), which means "mastery, strength, force"; "knowledge" (Heb. *da`ath,* **DAH-ath**), which means "discernment, understanding, wisdom"; and "the fear of the Lord" (Heb. *yir'ah,* **yir-AW**), which means "respect, reverence."

3 And shall make him of quick understanding in the fear of the LORD: and he shall not judge after the sight of his eyes, neither reprove after the hearing of his ears:

It only makes sense that the Messiah, who is endowed with the Spirit, will delight in that which the writer of Proverbs says is "the beginning of wisdom"—"the fear (reverence) of the LORD" (Proverbs 9:10). It is the disposition which makes the glory of God primary. Because of this fear or reverence, the Messiah will not "judge" (Heb. *shaphat,* **shaw-FAT**)—which means "govern, vindicate, punish"—unjustly, which is the point of the second half of Isaiah 11:3.

4 But with righteousness shall he judge the poor, and reprove with equity for the meek of the earth: and he shall smite the earth with the rod of his mouth, and with the breath of his lips shall he slay the wicked.

What will be at the heart of the Messiah's rule, Jesus' rule? At the heart of His kingdom will be nothing less than "righteousness" (Heb. *tsedeq*, **TSEH-dek**), meaning "justice, rightness"—righteousness exercised on behalf of the needy and poor of the earth. Whereas the surrounding nations and even God's own people at times treated the poor of the earth with injustice and oppression, the Messiah's kingdom was prophesied to be one that would defend the cause of the most vulnerable.

5 And righteousness shall be the girdle of his loins, and faithfulness the girdle of his reins.

For emphasis, Isaiah uses this metaphor of the belt and sash to speak of righteousness as characteristic of the Messiah's kingdom. He wants the people of God to know that the righteousness that God has promised to work in them and through them in the earth will be accomplished. No matter what they see around them or even within their own ranks, God will bring about this kingdom of righteousness and "faithfulness" (Heb. *'emuwnah*, or *'emunah*, **em-oo-NAW**), which means "fidelity, steadfastness, steadiness," that He has promised.

6 The wolf also shall dwell with the lamb, and the leopard shall lie down with the kid; and the calf and the young lion and the fatling together; and a little child shall lead them. 7 And the cow and the bear shall feed; their young ones shall lie down together: and the lion shall eat straw like the ox.

The next verses paint a picture of what the kingdom will look like when it comes. He uses the hostility in the animal kingdom to show the depth of the peace this kingdom will usher in. Predator and prey will lie down together, and a little child will lead them. Of course, this is not just about animals getting along, but a picture of the redemption that God is bringing to the whole of creation. In Jesus, everything is being redeemed and reconciled. People from every tongue, tribe, nation, and language will stand before the Lord, and the hostilities that once separated them will be no more.

8 And the sucking child shall play on the hole of the asp, and the weaned child shall put his hand on the cockatrice' den.

This verse further conveys the fully reconciled creation in which there is peace, wholeness, and complete harmony among all creatures. As the New Living Translation puts it, "Yes, a little child will put its hand in a nest of deadly snakes without harm." Even that which would bring death no longer can, because in the Messiah's kingdom, there is no death. Jesus' kingdom is one of life—life as God intended it to be from the very beginning of creation. Hallelujah for the Lord Jesus, whose sacrifice has accomplished it all and guarantees its final fulfillment!

Say It Correctly

Cockatrice. KAH-kuh-truhs, -tris'.
Isaiah. i -ZAY-uh, -yuh.
Israelites. 'iz-rē-ə-ˌlīt.
Jesse. JES-ee.
Judah. 'jü-də.
Omniscient. om-NISH-uhnt,
ahm-NIH-shuhnt.

Daily Bible Readings

M: The God of Peace
Romans 15:25–33

T: The Gospel of Peace
Ephesians 6:13–17

W: Peace with God
Romans 5:1–5

T: Peace Given to You
John 14:25–31

F: A Child Is Born
Isaiah 9:1–6

S: His Mission—Our Mission
Matthew 28:16–20

S: The Prince of Peace
Isaiah 9:7; 11:1–8

Notes

_____

_____

_____

_____

_____

Teaching Tips

1. Words You Should Know

A. Redeemed (Isaiah 43:1) *ga'al* (Heb.)—Atoned for, ransomed, purchased.

B. Saviour (v. 3, 11) *yasha`* (Heb.)—Defender, rescuer, deliverer.

C. Precious (v. 4) *yaqar* (Heb.)—Highly valued, prized, esteemed.

2. Teacher Preparation

Unifying Principle—Whom Shall I Follow? How are people to know whom to follow? In Isaiah 43, God promises deliverance even greater than the Exodus.

A. Pray and seek the Holy Spirit's help in presenting this lesson.

B. Study each section.

C. Be prepared to talk about some current events that show people needing other people and people desperately needing God.

3. Open the Lesson

A. Open with prayer, keeping the Aim for Change in mind.

B. After prayer, begin the class with your current events presentation.

C. Ask the question, "Have you ever really needed God to come into your dire situation?" Discuss.

D. Summarize the In Focus story, and discuss how the Lord is committed to loving us and how His love offers reliable protection, just as it did for the Israelites.

4. Present the Scriptures

A. Have volunteers read the Focal Verses.

B. To clarify the Focal Verses, use The People, Places, and Times; Background; At-A-Glance outline; In Depth; Search the Scriptures; and More Light on the Text.

C. Highlight the overall theme: "I (God) Will Be with You."

5. Explore the Meaning

A. Summarize the Discuss the Meaning section.

B. Summarize the Lesson in Our Society and Make It Happen sections.

C. Discuss the Search the Scriptures section.

6. Next Steps for Application

A. List under Follow the Spirit and Remember Your Thoughts some ways to keep from having a "Spiritual blowout."

B. Close with prayer, having each student silently pray over his or her list.

Worship Guide

For the Superintendent or Teacher
Theme: I Will Be with You
Theme Song: "I Come to the Garden"
Devotional Reading: Isaiah 63:7–14
Prayer

I Will Be with You

Bible Background • ISAIAH 43
Printed Text • ISAIAH 43:1–7, 11–12 | Devotional Reading • ISAIAH 63:7–14

Aim for Change

By the end of the lesson, we will: EXPLAIN how God was committed to Israel, His Chosen People; REALIZE that God is committed to us, too; and PRAISE God for His love, redemption, and protection.

 In Focus

Dana is tired when she gets home from work. All she wants to do is take a hot shower and go to bed. Unfortunately, Dana's apartment complex has a problem with water pressure. She never knows what to expect when she takes a shower. At first, the water flows as a steady stream, and then suddenly it stops or tapers off to annoying drips. The temperature shifts from hot to extreme cold. The fluctuation in the water pressure makes taking a shower uncomfortable and unpredictable.

Life can offer the same inconsistencies. Some days we are on top of the world; then suddenly, we can hit rock bottom. Life is full of erratic, unexpected twists and turns, and if we are not careful, the pressures of life can overwhelm us.

During the turbulent storms of life, the Lord promises to be with us. He is our Protector and Provider. How do you handle pressure? Do you try to handle it alone or do you remember that God promises to never forsake us? The Lord is committed to loving us, and His love offers a shower of reliable protection just as it did for His Chosen People, Israel.

Keep in Mind

"When thou passest through the waters, I will be with thee; and through the rivers, they shall not overflow thee: when thou walkest through the fire, thou shalt not be burned; neither shall the flame kindle upon thee" (Isaiah 43:2).

Focal Verses

KJV Isaiah 43:1 But now thus saith the LORD that created thee, O Jacob, and he that formed thee, O Israel, Fear not: for I have redeemed thee, I have called thee by thy name; thou art mine.

2 When thou passest through the waters, I will be with thee; and through the rivers, they shall not overflow thee: when thou walkest through the fire, thou shalt not be burned; neither shall the flame kindle upon thee.

3 For I am the LORD thy God, the Holy One of Israel, thy Saviour: I gave Egypt for thy ransom, Ethiopia and Seba for thee.

4 Since thou wast precious in my sight, thou hast been honourable, and I have loved thee: therefore will I give men for thee, and people for thy life.

5 Fear not: for I am with thee: I will bring thy seed from the east, and gather thee from the west;

6 I will say to the north, Give up; and to the south, Keep not back: bring my sons from far, and my daughters from the ends of the earth;

7 Even every one that is called by my name: for I have created him for my glory, I have formed him; yea, I have made him.

43:11 I, even I, am the LORD; and beside me there is no saviour.

12 I have declared, and have saved, and I have shewed, when there was no strange god among you: therefore ye are my witnesses, saith the LORD, that I am God.

NLT Isaiah 43:1 But now, O Jacob, listen to the LORD who created you. O Israel, the one who formed you says, "Do not be afraid, for I have ransomed you. I have called you by name; you are mine.

2 When you go through deep waters, I will be with you. When you go through rivers of difficulty, you will not drown. When you walk through the fire of oppression, you will not be burned up; the flames will not consume you.

3 For I am the LORD, your God, the Holy One of Israel, your Savior. I gave Egypt as a ransom for your freedom; I gave Ethiopia and Seba in your place.

4 Others were given in exchange for you. I traded their lives for yours because you are precious to me. You are honored, and I love you.

5 "Do not be afraid, for I am with you. I will gather you and your children from east to west.

6 I will say to the north and south, 'Bring my sons and daughters back to Israel from the distant corners of the earth.

7 Bring all who claim me as their God, for I have made them for my glory. It was I who created them.'"

43:11 I, yes, I, am the LORD, and there is not other Savior.

12 First I predicted your rescue, then I saved you and proclaimed it to the world. No foreign god has ever done this. You are witnesses that I am the only God," says the LORD.

The People, Places, and Times

Egypt. This is the ancient nation along the Nile River which held Israelites captive for 400 years before being rescued by the power of God through Moses. Before the time of Abraham, Egypt flourished as a successful, civilized culture for several centuries. It was the home of Abraham when he fled there to escape the famine (Genesis 12:10). Joseph, Abraham's great-grandson, was sold into slavery in Egypt and rose to a position of power. Through Joseph's intercession, Jacob and the rest of the Hebrew patriarchs living in Palestine resided in the eastern delta region of Goshen. The Jews eventually became slaves to the Egyptians. In due course, God's mercy liberated the Israelites. In fact, the Egyptians became prey to the mighty hand of God; they suffered the terrible consequences of Pharaoh's hardened heart and endured the devastating effects of 10 plagues. For 40 years, the Israelites wandered in the Egyptian Sinai where they received the Mosaic Law, specifications for building the tabernacle, and instructions for cleric and sacrificial systems. In the New Testament, Egypt became the location which served as the refuge for Joseph, Mary, and Baby Jesus as they fled to escape the murderous attempts by Herod.

Background

Sins of omission are less easily identified and numbered than sins of commission. In the presence of Almighty God, both are considered transgressions. The prophet Isaiah was called to confront a disobedient and rebellious people: God's Chosen People, the Israelites. This generation lacked the basic skills to recognize the presence of a Holy God. They did not comprehend the depth of God's compassion. The lack of these rudimentary abilities was evident in their shallow worship and religious distortion. The blatant perversion, attraction to idolatry, and repugnant practices were serious offenses to God, which had to be dealt with.

At-A-Glance

1. We Are Called God's Creation (Isaiah 43:1)

2. We Live Under God's Protection (v. 2)

3. We Live by God's Compassion (v. 3)

4. We Praise God's Redemption (vv. 4–7)

5. We Yield to God's Command (vv. 11–12)

In Depth

1. We Are Called God's Creation (Isaiah 43:1)

Our Creator is an amazing, wonderful God. In the book of Genesis, we witness God making something out of nothing. He created a universe out of a disordered nonexistence. He called Jacob and Israel— some scholars describe this as one of God's greatest acts of creation and compare it to the first celestial act. Creation is an unrelenting act of God that exists throughout the ages. History reflects the constant challenges to the Creator's divine rule. Yet because of God's mercy and compassionate attributes, He still calls people, those whom He deemed the beneficiaries of His divine grace. God reiterates that Israel's plight, past, present, and future are known to Him, for the Lord knows their names! In spite of their disobedience, God has chosen to redeem His people. It is a wonderful, almost unexplainable joy to know that despite our unlovable ways, God still cares for us! We belong to Him! He knows us by name.

2. We Live Under God's Protection (v. 2)

After years of captivity and suffering, the prophet finally speaks of God's deliverance and protection. He declares the Lord will go with the Israelites through the "waters" and "fire" of life.

We can only imagine how the words "fire" and "waters" echoed in the ears of the Israelites. The message probably summoned memories of the past. We can only picture how the Jews toiled with visions of the Egyptian Exodus, remembering how the Red Sea opened its mouth and swallowed the massive Egyptian army. No doubt their minds raced over stories of fire, recalling the tragedy of Sodom and Gomorrah (Genesis 18:1–19:13), the annihilation of a city by the fiery wrath of God. Or, could the prophet's words insinuate the forthcoming of another catastrophic flood, one that covered the earth while only Noah and his family survived? What kind of troubled waters or blazing trials would the people have to endure? One thing they did understand was that fire and water were instruments God used against a rebellious people.

Likewise, the same questions are asked by Christians in regard to their everyday walk with Jesus. How do we respond to the call to walk through turbulent times? God has not created a fireless or water-free environment. Our battles may not be identical to the Israelites, yet many of us face situations in our lives that are equally life-threatening. The Word of God reminded the Jews that in order to pass safely through the storms of life, they must remain aware of the presence of God. Similarly, we cannot survive life's rough currents and unexpected twists and turns unless Jesus is our anchor.

3. We Live by God's Compassion (v. 3)

God sacrificed other nations for the sake of returning the Jews back to their homeland. We are precious in the sight of God. His love for us is continuously demonstrated in His desire to bring us back to a rightful fellowship with Him. Sometimes we forget about the sacrifices God makes on our behalf. The sacrifice Christ made on the Cross was out of sheer unconditional love.

As human beings, we have a tendency to complain and become frustrated in our Christian walk. Life demands so much from us that oftentimes we want to throw in the towel. Yet, when we read God's Word, as Isaiah reminded the Israelites we should be reminded of how much God willingly, relentlessly, and consistently pours into our lives. Even when we ask the Lord to give us more, He goes beyond what we can ever think, dream, or imagine! He gives us what we need and so much more! (See Ephesians 3:20.)

4. We Praise God's Redemption (vv. 4–7)

It is amazing how God sees beyond our faults to our needs. The Jews were living a lifestyle contrary to the purpose of God, yet the Lord still saw them as valuable and worth saving. Regardless of all the betrayal and heartache the Lord experienced with the Jews, He kept loving and forgiving them. God is still the same faithful God. The Lord could have easily left the Israelites and us in our wretched state, but because He sees us as precious jewels, He saved us! It is not because we are worthy of His redemption, but because of His loving grace (see Ephesians 2:1–10). When something is precious, it is considered priceless, valuable, and prized! What a beautiful reality to know God sees us as valuable and worthy vessels.

The Jews were God's chosen people. As believers in Christ Jesus, we are also the chosen children of God. The prophet reminds the Israelites that God is going to do a new thing in their lives. He is going to retrieve all His sons and daughters from every nation, country, and tribe to the very ends of the earth. This is also a reminder to us that God knows who belongs to Him. He will not allow us to wander too far out of His reach. We are made in the image of God, and we are created to give Him glory (Genesis 1:26). Therefore, we should always follow His lead, His commands, and His edicts.

5. We Yield to God's Command (vv. 11–12)

God refuses to share His place in our hearts with anyone else. He is God on the throne, and He is second to none. This was a part of His covenant with Israel, and it is a part of His covenant with all believers. Oftentimes we are unaware of erected idols in our hearts. Sometimes we can be overly committed to our careers, advancements, educational pursuits, families, relationships, or financial gains—all can become idols in our lives. God is a jealous God (Exodus 20:5). The Lord commands our affection and attention, just as He did the Israelites. The greatest witness to others is not what we say or don't say, but how we live out what we believe in the good and bad times. God wants us to be more than mere listeners of His Word; He wants us to practice living what we teach and preach! Just as He called the Israelites to a higher standard, He is calling us as well.

Search the Scriptures

1. What was God's promise to the Israelites as they passed through the waters and rivers (Isaiah 43:2)?

2. How does the Lord view the Israelites (v. 4)?

3. What image are we created in and whose glory do we honor (v. 7)?

4. Why does the Lord require the people to be a witness for Him (v. 12)?

Discuss the Meaning

1. How are situations in your life similar to that of the Israelites?

2. Discuss how your life has been or can be a witness to others who don't know Jesus.

Lesson in Our Society

After a flat tire or blowout, we oftentimes use the manufacturer's spare tire to replace the damaged tire. This spare is convenient, but it has limitations. The manufacturer warns that a temporary tire should be replaced immediately with a regular size tire. The spare tire is limited in its capacity to drive long distances and maintain adequate air pressure. If it is not replaced soon, we could experience another blowout or flat tire. Many Christians are riding on "temporary tires." We rely on temporary fixes instead of permanent solutions to ease our pain. Sometimes we begin to resort to the things that brought us comfort before we got saved. We may become restless and hopeless. Folks cannot understand why we look or feel out of sync, but it is because we are out of balance. We need realignment with Jesus!

Make It Happen

Pray that God will help you remain faithful and committed to Him regardless of your circumstances. Share with the class a situation where you felt you depended on everything and everyone else except God. Share a testimony of how God got you through a difficult time. How did it affect your trust and faith in the Lord?

Follow the Spirit

What God wants me to do:

_____

_____

_____

_____

Remember Your Thoughts

Special insights I have learned:

_____

_____

_____

_____

More Light on the Text

Isaiah 43:1–7, 11–12

1 But now thus saith the LORD that created thee, O Jacob, and he that formed thee, O Israel, Fear not: for I have redeemed thee, I have called thee by thy name; thou art mine.

Isaiah begins this chapter with words of encouragement from the Lord to the people of Israel, who are facing exile in Babylon. God speaks to His people through the prophet to encourage them not to fear the difficult trial of exile in Babylon. The people are reminded even before this, however, that it is God, their Creator, the One who formed them, who is speaking to them. The words are meant to be an assurance that God is in control of their lives, not the rulers of Babylon. What is more, God tells them it is He who has "redeemed" (Heb. *ga'al*, **gaw-AL**) them. "Redeemed" means God has

"ransomed" or "purchased" the Israelites— He has "called [them] by name" (Heb. *liy*, **li**, which literally means "to me"). Ultimately because they belong to the Lord, the people of Israel are not to fear; they are His. And, of course, this is meant to remind them that God has entered into a covenant relationship with them. He has bound Himself to them as He promised Abraham that He would be his God and would be God to his descendants.

2 When thou passest through the waters, I will be with thee; and through the rivers, they shall not overflow thee: when thou walkest through the fire, thou shalt not be burned; neither shall the flame kindle upon thee.

The reality that Israel belongs to the Lord is meant to encourage and strengthen them as they face the trial of exile. They as a people will not be destroyed by this trial. God's purposes for them will be fulfilled. So whatever the trial, they will not be destroyed. The imagery of water and fire is meant to bring home the reality of the trial they are facing. However, God wants them to know that they are safe because He will be with them in the very midst of the trial.

3 For I am the LORD thy God, the Holy One of Israel, thy Saviour: I gave Egypt for thy ransom, Ethiopia and Seba for thee.

Again God reinforces His relationship to His people as their God, their "Holy One" (Heb. *qadowsh*, *qadosh*, **kaw-DOSHE**), which means "set apart, sacred," their "Saviour" (Heb. *yasha`*, **yaw-SHAH**), which means "defender, rescuer, deliverer." All of these titles emphasize the unique relationship that God has with His people. They are His and He is theirs. Therefore, to reinforce this point, He reminds them of His past actions on their behalf to deliver them. The reference here of giving up Egypt and

Ethiopia is likely a reference to the Assyrian threat. While Egypt and Ethiopia were defeated by the Assyrians, Israel was spared. God defeated Sennacherib's army and saved His people from certain destruction. Thus, Israel is to take confidence in the fact that God is her God and Savior, the Holy One who defends her cause. We, too, while going through trials and tribulations, can look back on what God has brought us through in the past. This should encourage us in the Lord.

4 Since thou wast precious in my sight, thou hast been honourable, and I have loved thee: therefore will I give men for thee, and people for thy life.

God reinforces His reason for saving His people, the Israelites. It is not because of who they are but because of whose they are—whom they belong to—God Himself. It is because they are "precious" (Heb. *yaqar,* **yaw-KAR**), meaning "prized, esteemed" in His sight—because of His love for them—that God saves them. The word "honourable" in Hebrew (*kabad, kabed,* **kaw-BAD**) means "to be weighty, to be glorious," and it does not mean that the people of Israel always acted in an honorable way. Indeed, they were facing exile because of their repeated rebellion. The word literally means "glorified." The idea is that God has raised Israel to a place of honor in His sight.

5 Fear not: for I am with thee: I will bring thy seed from the east, and gather thee from the west; 6 I will say to the north, Give up; and to the south, Keep not back: bring my sons from far, and my daughters from the ends of the earth;

Again God calls the people not to "fear" (Heb. *yare',* **yaw-RAY**), which means "to be afraid, terrified," because He is with them. And this time, the proof that He is with them

is this promise that He will re-gather His people. He will bring them back from all the places to which they have been scattered. In other words, troubles won't last always. They will not always be in the "fiery furnace." From the east, west, north and south, God will one day gather His people and bring them back to the land from which they have been taken; they will come back to the Promised Land, the land of Israel. The promise, of course, is a future promise, one that finds its fulfillment ultimately in the new heavens and the new earth when believers will be gathered together before the Lord their God.

7 Even every one that is called by my name: for I have created him for my glory, I have formed him; yea, I have made him.

God now makes clear that those who will be gathered are those who are called by His name. The point is twofold. First, not everyone who is a part of the nation of Israel really belongs to Him. Within the visible community of faith, there are wheat and tares. There are in the community of faith those who believe and those who really do not. Only those who are called by His name—believers—those who belong to Him can claim God's promises. Secondly, in the broader sense, everyone despite race, class, etc., who is called by His name will enjoy God's promises. This is one of the great blessings of Christianity. No one who calls on the name of the Lord is excluded. God is the Creator of all. Every person on the face of the earth is formed in His image and after His likeness, and anyone who calls on Him can be saved and enjoy the blessings of a relationship with the Lord.

43:11 I, even I, am the LORD; and beside me there is no saviour.

God now declares through the prophet that there is no other Savior besides Himself. Of course, the point here is to discourage the people of Israel from seeking salvation through some other means, which Israel was prone to do. God wants her to know that He alone saves. He alone is her Deliverer. He alone is her Redeemer. There is no salvation in human alliances or idols, but in God alone.

12 I have declared, and have saved, and I have shewed, when there was no strange god among you: therefore ye are my witnesses, saith the LORD, that I am God.

God concludes by calling the people as His witnesses that He alone is Savior. Even before Israel thought to turn to idols, God had shown Himself to be the God who saves. They had seen it in the lives of the patriarchs and in God's deliverance from Egypt. God has proven Himself to be the only true and living God. All Israel had to do was remember what God has done and she would have no cause to fear because the true and living God was her God. Is the true and living God your God as well?

Say It Correctly

Babylon. BAB-uh-luhn, -lon'.
Egypt. 'ē-jipt.
Genesis. JEN-uh-sis.
Goshen. GOH-shuhn.
Pharaoh. FAIR-oh, FAR-oh.

Daily Bible Readings

M: Remember God's Mercy
Isaiah 63:7–14

T: Chosen by God
Isaiah 43:8–10

W: God Forgets Our Sins
Isaiah 43:22–28

T: Obey and Find Mercy
Jeremiah 42:7–17

F: The Lord Is with You
Haggai 1:7–15

S: God with Us
Matthew 1:18–25

S: No Other Savior
Isaiah 43:1–7, 11–12

195

Teaching Tips

1. Words You Should Know

A. Formed (Isaiah 44:21, 24) *yatsar* (Heb.)—Fashioned, framed, created.

B. Transgressions (v. 22) *pesha`* (Heb.)—Sins, rebellion.

C. Diviners (v. 25) *qacam* (Heb.)—Soothsayers, false prophets of Israel.

2. Teacher Preparation

Unifying Principle—Experiencing Redemption. How can we know that something can be rebuilt out of destruction? Isaiah 44 speaks comfort and hope that God will not forget Israel and will redeem all things.

A. Pray that God will bring redemption to needy students in your class.

B. Prayerfully study and meditate on the Daily Bible Readings for the week, the Focal Verses, and the surrounding sections.

C. Prepare a bag of mixed candies with three different kinds of candy bars.

3. Open the Lesson

A. Open with prayer, keeping the Aim for Change in mind.

B. Explain Jesus Christ's role as our Redeemer and why He should be recognized as such.

C. Connect the In Focus story to today's theme.

4. Present the Scriptures

A. Have volunteers read the Focal Verses.

B. After selecting a candy bar from your bag, the students are to form groups based on the candy bar they have selected and choose a spokesperson.

C. Assign The People, Places, and Times to one group, Background to another, etc.

D. After each group meets, discuss their findings with the class.

E. Using the At-A-Glance outline, In Depth, and More Light on the Text, clarify the Focal Verses.

5. Explore the Meaning

A. Have a volunteer lead a discussion of the Discuss the Meaning section.

B. Summarize the Lesson in Our Society and Make It Happen sections.

6. Next Steps for Application

A. Reemphasize Jesus Christ as our Redeemer.

B. In prayer, praise God for His love, redemption, and protection.

Worship Guide

For the Superintendent or Teacher
Theme: I Am Your Redeemer
Theme Song: "I Know that My
Redeemer Liveth"
Devotional Reading: Psalm 106:40–48
Prayer

I Am Your Redeemer

Bible Background • ISAIAH 44
Printed Text • ISAIAH 44:21–26 | Devotional Reading • PSALM 106:40–48

Aim for Change

By the end of the lesson, we will: REVIEW God's redemption of Israel; REFLECT on God's redemptive power in our lives; and ASK God to help us to be faithful and true to Him.

JAN 2nd

In Focus

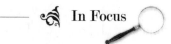

Tara serves the church by singing in the church choir. Lately, she has been distracted by Doug, an attractive new neighbor. Doug's views and decisions conflict with her ideas. He likes to go out to parties and drink, while she prefers spending time with family and friends. Doug is charming and persuasive and attends church with Tara on Sunday. He uses his charm to entice Tara to skip choir rehearsal and attend parties with him on Saturdays. The choir depends on Tara's spectacular voice on Sunday. When Tara yields to Doug's relentless pressure, she comes to church tired, so she hasn't been performing at her best on Sundays. Tara is torn between her affection for Doug and her devotion to serving the Lord. How can Tara resolve this tension without compromising her service to the Lord? How can she ask God to help her to be faithful?

Just as God is calling Tara in today's lesson, God is calling His chosen people—Israel—back to Himself and calling them to be faithful. He reminds them that it is He who has redeemed or saved them.

Keep in Mind

"I have blotted out, as a thick cloud, thy transgressions, and, as a cloud, thy sins: return unto me; for I have redeemed thee" (Isaiah 44:22).

Focal Verses

KJV **Isaiah 44:21** Remember these, O Jacob and Israel; for thou art my servant: I have formed thee; thou art my servant: O Israel, thou shalt not be forgotten of me.

22 I have blotted out, as a thick cloud, thy transgressions, and, as a cloud, thy sins: return unto me; for I have redeemed thee.

23 Sing, O ye heavens; for the LORD hath done it: shout, ye lower parts of the earth: break forth into singing, ye mountains, O forest, and every tree therein: for the LORD hath redeemed Jacob, and glorified himself in Israel.

24 Thus saith the LORD, thy redeemer, and he that formed thee from the womb, I am the LORD that maketh all things; that stretcheth forth the heavens alone; that spreadeth abroad the earth by myself;

25 That frustrateth the tokens of the liars, and maketh diviners mad; that turneth wise men backward, and maketh their knowledge foolish;

26 That confirmeth the word of his servant, and performeth the counsel of his messengers; that saith to Jerusalem, Thou shalt be inhabited; and to the cities of Judah, Ye shall be built, and I will raise up the decayed places thereof:

NLT **Isaiah 44:21** "Pay attention, O Jacob, for you are my servant, O Israel. I, the LORD, made you, and I will not forget you.

22 I have swept away your sins like a cloud. I have scattered your offenses like the morning mist. Oh, return to me, for I have paid the price to set you free."

23 Sing, O heavens, for the LORD has done this wondrous thing. Shout for joy, O depths of the earth! Break into song, O mountains and forests and every tree! For the LORD has redeemed Jacob and is glorified in Israel.

24 This is what the LORD says—your Redeemer and Creator: I am the LORD, who made all things. I alone stretched out the heavens. Who was with me when I made the earth?

25 I expose the false prophets as liars and make fools of fortune-tellers. I cause the wise to give bad advice, this proving them to be fools.

26 But I carry out the predictions of my prophets! By them I say to Jerusalem, 'People will live here again,' and to the towns of Judah, 'You will be rebuilt; I will restore all your ruins!'"

The People, Places, and Times

Redeemer. To redeem something is to purchase property which has been forfeited because of indebtedness or buy back a person who had been sold into slavery. God acts as a redeemer when He acts to bring about reconciliation between His people and Himself. This concept illustrates the perfect and complete work of Christ who bought us back from sin and death through His sacrificial death on the Cross.

Diviners. This term is associated with foretelling the future or determining the unknown through executing acts of magic or reading signs. Divination is an abomination to God and is condemned in Deuteronomy (18:10). Diviners or soothsayers claim to reveal secrets and interpret dreams.

Judah. It refers to the nation of Judah or the southern kingdom which is largely composed of the tribes of Benjamin and Judah. The disloyal 10 tribes of the northern region maintained the name of Israel. After a succession of kings, the nation succumbed to pagan idolatry. Rehoboam, son of Solomon, was the first king of Judah. God used Isaiah and Jeremiah as mouthpieces to turn Israel's heart back to the Lord. However, the people had developed rebellious and hardened hearts toward God's words. Eventually, Judah was taken into exile and overthrown by Babylonian leadership. Around 530 B.C., a remnant of Israelites returned to Jerusalem to rebuild the city (see Jeremiah 11:1).

Background

Chapter 44 deals primarily with acts of idolatry which is the worship of anything other than God, our Creator. We are called to serve God, and Isaiah reminded the Israelites of this purpose. We are the Lord's servants, and Isaiah reemphasizes this relationship to the people of God. Throughout the Old Testament, the Jews are reprimanded for worshiping other gods. Despite their defiance, the Lord gives them a promise of restoration. He reiterates His love and allegiance to them; He promises to remove the blemish of transgressions and redeem them. Today, the Lord still requires that we serve Him and abandon the notion of serving other masters. Whom and what we serve becomes our master; we are slaves to whatever we give our minds and hearts to. God requires our complete allegiance because He loves and cherishes us. He knows what we need. No humanmade god can give us what we require. False prophets, teachers, or diviners do not have the capacity to speak truth over our lives. Only the Word of God—the words given to us from our Creator—can instruct us on how we should live.

At-A-Glance

1. The Redeeming Power of God (Isaiah 44:21–22)

2. The Rejoicing Power of God (v. 23)

3. The Creative Power of God (v. 24)

4. The Distinctive Power of God (vv. 25–26)

In Depth

1. The Redeeming Power of God (Isaiah 44:21–22)

There are certain facts that all believers should hold as true. They include: (1) We are God's servants—we belong to Him and should serve no other god but our Lord. (2) The Lord's commandments are not burdensome. Jesus promises His children that His yoke is easy and His burden is light (Matthew 11:28–30). (3) When we serve the Lord, He will provide the love, grace, mercy, and strength we need to carry out His will. Serving God is an act of humility. It is a privilege to serve the One who is responsible for our existence. (4) Our God is a Creative Lord—He made us! He redeems and loves us. There is no humanmade idol that can create, save, or love us. The depth of God's love is found in His Son Jesus Christ. (5) Our Savior's atoning death on the Cross saved us from eternal damnation. Christ made the ultimate sacrifice—He died for us!

It may be easy for many of us to turn up our noses at the Israelites' foolishness and declare we would never put any wooden sculpture before God. However, idolatry does not always mean we are worshiping a tangible object. Much of what we unknowingly worship involves intangible things. For example, if career advancement is the essence of our self-image, our jobs can become an object of worship. When acquiring a degree is more important than spending quality time with Jesus, educational development can spur idolatry. It can also occur while serving in ministry. We can perform awesome works all in the name of Jesus, while secretly craving the admirable self-exalting applause from our peers, family, friends, and acquaintances. Seeking career and educational accomplishments, establishing goals, and serving in ministry are all commendable qualities to possess. The danger occurs when things we seek become "mini-gods" (our source) and consciously or unconsciously we depend on them more than God.

2. The Rejoicing Power of God (v. 23)

When we are called into the sheepfold of faith, God undergirds us with His redemptive power. Isaiah tells the people of God that the Lord has redeemed Jacob and is gloried in Israel. After so many years of despair and disconnection from God, the Lord encourages a time of celebration, for He decided to forgive and restore a nation. If God can restore a whole nation, just imagine what He can do for an individual! We must recognize His redeeming powers in our personal lives. When God redeems, He sets free what was once enslaved and in bondage. When we become aware of our freedom in Christ, we can celebrate and rejoice. When we understand that God freed us from the shackles of living unfruitful and unproductive lives, we can shout victoriously about the goodness of our Lord! Our voices can testify to how far God has brought us. We may not be where we want to be in life, but we are not where we used to be! We are saved and blood-washed in Jesus! It is a matter of choosing to be liberated or set free from sin.

Two thousand years ago, Jesus made a choice to set us free. He chose to go to Calvary and die on a cross. He made the choice before any of us were born. Now, after we have been given the opportunity to come to the saving knowledge of Christ, we can choose to live victoriously or live defeated lives.

3. The Creative Power of God (v. 24)

The words of Isaiah remind us how incredible God is. God is not only the Creator of humankind but also the Creator of the entire earth, universe, and heavens. Our human minds cannot grasp the depth of God's creative ability. Yet, we often forget to give Him thanks for all that He has done. Humankind tends to take credit for all the wonderful things we enjoy on earth such as scientific discoveries, nature's beauty, and the earth's resources. But the Lord created nature so we can enjoy the parks, beaches, and oceans. God created the herbs, minerals, metals, and resources that scientists use to develop breakthroughs in medicine and other fields. God created humankind with the ability to produce all that we see and enjoy in the world. None of the things we enjoy on earth would be possible without the Lord.

4. The Distinctive Power of God (vv. 25–26)

False teaching and prophecy existed in the Old and New Testament, and they are alive and well among today's teachers and preachers. Heresy is oftentimes mixed with some truth, making it difficult for some believers to discern the difference. These verses in Isaiah speak of false prophets who claim to have a message from God. Their teaching is contradictory to God's mandates. Nevertheless, God's Word prevails; His truth puts to shame the heretics' teaching and reveals their hearts' content—foolishness, lies, self-righteousness, and anger! We must be very careful to discern the truth and identify false teaching. The only way to capture this skill is to rightfully handle the truth of God's Word (see 2 Timothy 2:15). We cannot distinguish truth if we do not know the truth. We cannot recognize the voice of God if we are not familiar with the sound, pitch, and tone of the Lord's voice! Sometimes His voice is a mere whisper. Can you hear Him among the noise, above the roar of the crowd? Can you identify His sound in the midst of confusion? It is imperative that we develop keenness and sensitivity to God's voice, for Jesus said, "My sheep know My voice!" (see John 10:3).

God's Word is also "living and active" (Hebrews 4:12, NIV). His Word accomplishes its goal; it never returns to the Lord void of its fulfillment (Isaiah 55:11).

Search the Scriptures

1. What did God blot out in the lives of the Israelites (Isaiah 44:22)?

2. Why were the heavens and lower parts of the earth required to sing praises to God (v. 23)?

3. What is the response of liars and diviners to the actions of God (v. 25)?

Discuss the Meaning

Scripture clearly says that before we were born, God had formed us in the womb. How does knowing that God formed you change your perspective on the Lord? How can you use this reality to strengthen your knowledge of His redemptive power in your life?

Lesson in Our Society

The superstar status of celebrities in our society has created idolatry in the hearts of many. These icons are seen as "gods," and fans revere the very ground they walk on. In some cases the untimely death of a famous person sends shock waves of disbelief; some distraught fans suffer chronic depression and even attempt and succeed at committing suicide. Although we all may adore a favorite celebrity, we must not deify him or her. Celebrities are humans, like us, and are products of God's creation. We can admire and respect the gifts and talents the Lord has given them, but we should never place them on pedestals of worship.

Make It Happen

Ask God to reveal your heart to you. Are you faithful in serving and worshiping Him? Write down what He tells you. Ask the Lord to help you eradicate anything in your heart that has more power and influence over your life. Remember, developing a faithful lifestyle to Jesus takes time, practice, and commitment. Share your experience with the class next week.

Follow the Spirit

What God wants me to do:

_____

_____

_____

_____

Remember Your Thoughts

Special insights I have learned:

_____

_____

_____

_____

More Light on the Text

Isaiah 44:21–26

21 Remember these, O Jacob and Israel; for thou art my servant: I have formed thee; thou art my servant: O Israel, thou shalt not be forgotten of me.

God's first reminder to every member of His chosen people was "for thou art my servant." Jacob was the grasping, conniving, shrewd, clever father of 12 sons, who became the patriarchs of the 12 tribes of Israel. Because he was born gripping his twin brother Esau's heel, his original name literally meant "(one who is) grasping the heel" (Genesis 25:26, NIV). His name came to have the figurative meaning of one who overreaches or one who deceives. He symbolizes humanity in all our sinful selfishness.

After Jacob wrestled with God all night at Peniel on the Jabbok River, God renamed him "Israel." His new name means "(one who) struggled with God" (Genesis 32:28, NIV). By addressing both Jacob and Israel, God was speaking to His people in their weak and sinful humanity and was focusing as well on people for whom He had commissioned Jacob to pursue His highest purposes (Jeremiah 29:12–13).

Isaiah 44:21 ends by restating the Israelites' role as His people: "Thou art my servant: O Israel, thou shalt not be forgotten of me." God repeatedly stated His refusal to give up on His plans for His people.

In between declaring Israel's responsibility to serve God's purposes, God said, "I have formed thee" (Isaiah 44:21). The Hebrew word for "formed" is *yatsar* (**yaw-TSAR**), which described the process a potter or a wood carver went through to shape a bowl or a piece of furniture. God's involvement in the lives of His people was a long process.

22 I have blotted out, as a thick cloud, thy transgressions, and as a cloud, thy sins; for I have redeemed thee.

Hosea 13:3 uses the same word as Isaiah used here for "cloud" (Heb. *anan,* **aw-NAWN**). "Therefore they shall be as the morning cloud, and as the early dew that passeth away, as the chaff that is driven with the whirlwind out of the floor, and as the smoke out of the chimney." Clearly "cloud" represents something filmy, passing, and of no great weight. The New Living Translation words the second phrase of Isaiah 44:22 as, "I have scattered your offenses like the morning mist."

This is a perfect example of the loving and forgiving grace of God, perfectly expressed in Jesus' willing death on the Cross. As 1 John 4:10 assures believers, "Herein is love, not that we love God, but that he loved us." Thus, "blotted out" referred to "an erasing of something written, canceled debt or obliterating memories from the mind." Rather than their sins held over their heads as a constant threat, God said they were gone like smoke on a windy day or like dew that disappears as soon as the sun rises.

God did not tell the exiled Jews "I will redeem you." Instead, He contends, "I have redeemed you." This is one of five times in the second section of Isaiah that emphasizes the past tense, that their future deliverance from captivity was a completed act (Isaiah 43:1; 44:22, 23; 48:20; 52:9). God took the initiative and set them free to return to Jerusalem. "Redeemed"

(Heb. *ga'al,* **gaw-AL**), refers to paying off a debt in order to prevent someone from losing ownership of something.

23 Sing, O ye heavens; for the LORD hath done it: shout, ye lower parts of the earth: break forth into singing, ye mountains, O forest, and every tree therein: for the LORD hath redeemed Jacob, and glorified himself in Israel.

This verse is an Old Testament parallel to Paul's statement in 2 Corinthians 5:17. The New International Version translates that verse, "Therefore, if anyone is in Christ, he is a new creation; the old has gone, the new has come!" Isaiah proclaims that for any of the captive exiles, who accepted the freedom God would make available to them, the world would become a brand-new place.

To return to Jerusalem it would take nearly 750 miles by traveling back up the Tigris-Euphrates River Valley to the Syrian Desert, and then down through the Lebanon Mountains and the hill countries of Galilee, Samaria, and Judah to Jerusalem. In the midst of this verse, Isaiah reminds them, "The LORD hath done it" (44:23). Their liberty would not be something they brought about themselves.

Isaiah reminds them how it came to pass: "for the LORD hath redeemed Jacob, and glorified himself in Israel" (v. 23). It was all God's doing. Here again he mentions Jacob and Israel. The contrast is obvious. God helped Jacob when he had cheated, or at least tricked, his brother Esau and lied to, or at the least misled, his father, Isaac. Yet God in His grace appeared to Jacob as Jacob fled for his life and worked for years in a place distant from his home and his people. Then God led Jacob to a place where he became a new and different person—Israel. God "glorified" (Heb. *pa'ar,* **paw-AR**) Himself through Jacob who, in spite of his many flaws, fears, and repeated failures,

became Israel. The nation of Israel had been carried off into oblivion, but God continued to work in the lives of those willing to return to Him and His purposes. The word "glorify" is translated "to gleam" or "to beautify." When people are willing to change the direction of their lives—turn back to God and trust His plan for their lives—God is able to do beautiful things as He shines through their lives.

24 Thus saith the LORD, thy redeemer, and he that formed thee from the womb, I am the LORD that maketh all things; that stretcheth forth the heavens alone; that spreadeth abroad the earth by myself;

Like a caring and responsible next of kin, God steps in to rescue His people when they were helpless to deliver themselves. This makes one of 13 times following Israel's deliverance that Isaiah called God "Redeemer," as he laid out God's plans for God's people.

In addition to calling Himself the Israelites' "Redeemer," God reminds them that He was their Maker. Here Isaiah used a form of the same word as in verse 21, a word that portrays someone who works with his hands, such as a potter. Again the suggestion is that God has been involved across the years in making them into what they were. This verse reminds us that God is involved in the lives of His people from the day each of us is born, even when we are in the womb.

25 That frustrateth the tokens of the liars, and maketh the diviners mad; that turneth wise men backward, and maketh their knowledge foolish;

The Babylonian Empire was obsessed with occult practices, which were used to explain causes of events or to predict the future. In this verse, Isaiah lists two: the liars and the diviners, who were considered to be "wise" men by themselves and others, but not by God. The

King James Version translates the first group as "liars" (Heb. *bad*, **BAD**), referring to false prophets. Literally the term meant "empty talkers." These supposed prophets would predict future events or causes of natural events such as earthquakes, storms, or other disasters which they said indicated coming events. When the events did not occur, God revealed their claims to be simply self-serving, empty talk.

The second group Isaiah mentions are "diviners" (Heb. *qacam*, **kaw-SAM**), which referred to "magicians," "astrologers" or "people claiming supernatural insights." A popular type of diviners examined sheep livers as a source for their predictions. Daniel 2:2 records that the Babylonian King Nebuchadnezzar "summoned the magicians, enchanters, sorcerers and astrologers" (NIV).

26 That confirmeth the word of his servant, and performeth the counsel of his messengers; that saith to Jerusalem, Thou shalt be inhabited and to the cities of Judah, Ye shall be built, and I will raise up the decayed places thereof:

In the Bible, the proof of prophecy is whether it comes true (Deuteronomy 18:22). The prophets of Assyria, Babylon, Persia, Greece, and Rome all made glowing predictions about the futures of their kingdoms. Today, all of these kingdoms exist as relics in museums and ruins that world travelers go to see—the coliseum in Rome, the Parthenon in Athens, and the pyramids of Egypt. Nowhere in ancient pagan records of magic, occult, or supernatural practices is there any mention found of the defeat or destruction of these empires.

Isaiah and other biblical prophets prophesied first the defeat and deportation of the northern kingdom of Israel and later the captivity, exile, and liberation of the southern kingdom of Judah. The fanciful predictions of Babylonian and Persian religions have proved to be foolish. The diviners' prophesies turned completely backward from all they predicted. Yet over 2,000 years, the Jewish people still exist. The fullness of God's will has been perfectly revealed in His Son Jesus Christ.

Say It Correctly

Corinthians. kuh-RIN(T)-thee-uhnz.
Ezra. EHZ-ruh.
Idolatry. idol-a-trē.
Isaiah. i -ZAY-uh, -yuh.
Israel. IZ-ree-uhl.
Judah. ˈjü-də.
Leviticus. lih-VIT-ih-kuhs.
Samaria. suh-MAIR-ee-uh.

Daily Bible Readings

M: My Redeemer Lives!
Job 19:23–27

T: Know That I Am with You
Genesis 28:10–17

W: Do Not Fear
Isaiah 44:1–5

T: God's Steadfast Love
Psalm 106:40–48

F: Redeemed to Be Heirs
Galatians 4:1–7

S: Assured of the Future
Isaiah 44:6–8

S: Rejoice in Redemption
Isaiah 44:21–26

Teaching Tips

1. Words You Should Know

A. Established (Isaiah 45:18) *kuwn* (Heb.)—Set up, done, accomplished, made.

B. Righteousness (vv. 19, 23, 24) *tsedeq* (Heb.)—Justness, rightness; referred to the right way to live as opposed to a lifestyle that treats others unfairly or unjustly.

C. Graven Image (v. 20) *pecel* (Heb.)— "Carved image, idol."

2. Teacher Preparation

Unifying Principle—Hope for the Future. God's mighty acts since the beginning of time present hope for the future while showing that no one else can demonstrate such ability.

A. Pray for the students in your class, asking God to open their eyes so they may see wondrous things from His Law (Psalm 119:18).

B. Study the entire lesson.

3. Open the Lesson

A. Open with prayer, keeping the Aim for Change in mind.

B. After prayer, introduce the class to the Words You Should Know section.

C. Connect the In Focus story to today's theme and remind the students that God wants us to truly know who He is and make Him the Lord of our lives.

4. Present the Scriptures

A. Have volunteers read the Focal Verses.

B. Explain their relevance to today's AIM for Change.

C. Clarify the Focal Verses by using The People, Places, and Times; Background; the At-A-Glance outline; In Depth; Search the Scriptures; and More Light on the Text.

5. Explore the Meaning

A. Have volunteers lead a discussion of the Discuss the Meaning, Lesson in Our Society, and Make It Happen sections.

B. Connect these sections to the Aim for Change.

6. Next Steps for Application

A. Under the Follow the Spirit and Remember Your Thoughts sections, have students share the seriousness of looking to God to be saved.

B. Challenge them to reflect on what they have written throughout the week.

C. Close with prayer.

Worship Guide

For the Superintendent or Teacher
Theme: Turn to Me and Be Saved
Theme Song: "Trust and Obey"
Devotional Reading: Exodus 15:11–18
Prayer

Turn to Me and Be Saved

Bible Background • ISAIAH 45
Printed Text • ISAIAH 45:18–24a | Devotional Reading • EXODUS 15:11–18

———————————— Aim for Change ————————————

By the end of the lesson, we will: IDENTIFY how we can turn to God and be saved; APPRECIATE that God is the source of all; and CONTEMPLATE ways to turn from false gods to the true and living God.

 In Focus

On June 25, 2009, Michael Jackson, the King of Pop, died at age 50. Every TV and radio station in the nation broadcasted this news; foreign language-speaking stations also flashed his picture and reported on his demise. Without a doubt, Michael was truly a legend in his own time; young and old knew something about him. The news of his death stunned people because he passed away suddenly at such an early age.

There were people who idolized Michael Jackson. They were no different from others who put other celebrities, including sports figures, on high pedestals from which many of them fall due to personal indiscretions. We are to put no one on the level of Almighty God. As of June 25, 2009, Michael's time here on earth was no more. It was time for Him to meet the true and living God. One day, we all will have to do the same.

The Bible warns us that those who carry about idols of wood and who pray to gods that cannot save us are ignorant. However, the true and living God tells us that there is no other God besides Himself. In today's lesson, we are forced to recognize who God is. Who or what are your idols?

———————————— Keep in Mind ————————————

"Look unto me, and be ye saved, all the ends of the earth: for I am God, and there is none else" (Isaiah 45:22).

Focal Verses

KJV Isaiah 45:18 For thus saith the LORD that created the heavens; God himself that formed the earth and made it; he hath established it, he created it not in vain, he formed it to be inhabited: I am the LORD; and there is none else.

19 I have not spoken in secret, in a dark place of the earth: I said not unto the seed of Jacob, Seek ye me in vain: I the LORD speak righteousness, I declare things that are right.

20 Assemble yourselves and come; draw near together, ye that are escaped of the nations: they have no knowledge that set up the wood of their graven image, and pray unto a god that cannot save.

21 Tell ye, and bring them near; yea, let them take counsel together: who hath declared this from ancient time? who hath told it from that time? have not I the LORD? and there is no God else beside me; a just God and a Saviour; there is none beside me.

22 Look unto me, and be ye saved, all the ends of the earth: for I am God, and there is none else.

23 I have sworn by myself, the word is gone out of my mouth in righteousness, and shall not return, That unto me every knee shall bow, every tongue shall swear.

24a Surely, shall one say, in the LORD have I righteousness and strength:

NLT Isaiah 45:18 For the LORD is God, and he created the heavens and earth and put everything in place. He made the world to be lived in, not to be a place of empty chaos. "I am the LORD," he says, "and there is no other.

19 I publicly proclaim bold promises. I do not whisper obscurities in some dark corner. I would not have told the people of Israel to seek me if I could not be found. I, the LORD, speak only what is true and declare only what is right.

20 "Gather together and come, you fugitives from surrounding nations. What fools they are who carry around their wooden idols and pray to gods that cannot save!

21 Consult together, argue your case. Get together and decide what to say. Who made these things known so long ago? What idol ever told you they would happen? Was it not I, the LORD? For there is no other God but me, a righteous God and Savior. There is none but me.

22 Let all the world look to me for salvation! For I am God; there is no other.

23 I have sworn by my own name; I have spoken the truth, and I will never go back on my word: Every knee will bend to me, and every tongue will confess allegiance to me."

24a The people will declare, "The LORD is the source of all my righteousness and strength."

The People, Places, and Times

Cyrus. He was the third king of Anshan and was known as Cyrus the Great. He assumed the throne about 550 B.C. According to the best histories, Cyrus was reared by a shepherd after his grandfather, Astyages, king of Media, ordered that he be killed. Apparently, Astyages had dreamed that Cyrus would one day succeed him as king before the reigning monarch's death. The officer charged with the execution instead carried the boy into the hills to the shepherds.

Babylon. Babylon was a city-state in southern Mesopotamia during Old Testament times, which eventually became a large empire that absorbed the nation of Judah and destroyed Jerusalem.

Isaiah. His name means "Yahweh saves." He was a prophet active in Judah about 740 to 701 B.C. Isaiah's ministry spanned the period from his call in a vision (about 740 B.C.) until the last years of Hezekiah (716–687 B.C.) or the early years of Manasseh (687–642 B.C.). The prophet lived during the reigns of the Judean Kings Uzziah, Jotham, Ahaz, Hezekiah, and perhaps the first years of Manasseh. He was contemporary with the last four kings of Israel: Menahem, Pekahiah, Pekah, and Hosea. The tragic fall of Samaria to the Assyrian King Sargon II in 722 B.C. occurred during his ministry.

Background

Isaiah chapters 44 and 45 are a forecast of Israel's return from captivity under Cyrus, with special emphasis on God's unique power to predict the future. Isaiah predicts or even tells the future that God's power will work through Cyrus, who was a pagan king of Persia who reigned from 538–529 B.C. He permitted the Jews to return to Jerusalem and issued a decree authorizing the rebuilding of the Temple (2 Chronicles 36:22–23;

Ezra 1:1–4). God's power will motivate King Cyrus to set Israel free from the captivity of Babylonian. Isaiah gave this prophecy more than 150 years before it would actually take place. This was done even before Cyrus was born. Yet Isaiah calls him by name and predicts that he would rebuild the Temple, which in Isaiah's day had not yet fallen. Because of God's omniscience (all-knowing or eternal knowledge) and omnipotence (or infinite power), He was able to give these facts to Isaiah.

At-A-Glance

1. I Am the Lord (Isaiah 45:18–19)

2. There Is No Other God but Me (Isaiah (vv. 20–21)

3. Look to Me and Be Saved (vv. 22–24a)

In Depth

1. I Am the Lord (Isaiah 45:18–19)

In Isaiah 41, the Almighty God is challenging the false idols to do what only He can do. He says, "Bring in your idols to tell us what is going to happen. Tell us what the former things were, so that we may consider them and know their final outcome. Or declare to us the things to come. Tell us what the future holds, so we may know that you are gods. Do something, whether good or bad, so that we will be dismayed and filled with fear" (Isaiah 41:22–23, NIV). However, none of those false gods took up God's challenge. To tell the truth, they couldn't. They dared not accept a challenge from the true and living God to be like He is. There is truly none like Him.

Isaiah goes on to tell what God says: "I am the LORD; and there is none else" (Isaiah

45:18). He is the Lord, and He is the only Lord. He is not equal to anyone. He alone is God. He doesn't get voted in or voted out. It is He who is God! There is no comparison or question as to God being God.

2. There Is No Other God but Me (vv. 20–21)

It is God's desire to save people so that they will not have to endure the coming judgment. Therefore, God makes this threefold appeal to all people of all nations. God petitions the people to turn from their idols, from their humanmade material objects. These objects have no life, nor can they give life. We can make idols out of anything and even anyone. In fact, idols can be considered anything we put in place of God or give more place to in our lives than God. There is nothing these idols can do for their worshipers; they cannot talk back to their servers or even bring them comfort or joy. These idols can do nothing eternal. When we worship idols, it puts us in unprotected situations that can be hurtful. Idols don't have power or any substance that a person can hold to find the things he or she needs. So if we pray to an idol god, they cannot help us in our time of need.

We can only find what we need in the true and living God, and He is equal to none. He has proven who He is and stated who He is. He has told what He is capable of doing and tells our future before it ever happens. There is no other god or anything else that can do what God can do. He is worthy of our trust, and He is worthy of our praises. Proverbs 3:5–6 (NIV) teaches, "Trust in the LORD with all your heart and lean not on your own understanding; in all your ways acknowledge him, and he will make your paths straight." The King James Version states, "And he shall direct thy paths." He cannot direct our paths if He doesn't know what lies ahead. However, He does know what lies ahead, behind, and

even on each side of us; therefore, He is able to direct our paths with His perfect wisdom and knowledge. He is able, through His Holy Spirit, to lead and guide us into all righteousness.

3. Look to Me and Be Saved (vv. 22–24a)

God challenges His people to look to Him and be saved. There is nothing and no one else they could turn to for spiritual salvation. God alone is the sinless God, and He sent His Son to save sinful humanity. He is the only One who is able to meet their needs, no matter what the need may be. What greater need is there than to have eternal salvation?

God wants the people to understand they are to look to Him, and in verses 22–24a, He declares two parts of a three-part oath (verse 25 contains the third part of the oath). The Lord promises that there will come a time when every knee will bow and every tongue will confess to Him—the entire world will bow before Christ Jesus. Those who worship idols and those ones who do not will all confess to Him. "They will say of me," promises God, "'In the LORD alone are righteousness and strength.'" We have a choice now to confess Jesus Christ as our Lord and Savior, but whatever you believe or don't believe, when the time is right, all will confess to God. The Bible says, "For it is written, As I live, saith the Lord, every knee shall bow to me, and every tongue shall confess to God. So then every one of us shall give account of himself to God" (Romans 14:11–12). And as Paul states, "Wherefore God also hath highly exalted him, and given him a name which is above every name: That at the name of Jesus every knee should bow, of things in heaven, and things in earth, and things under the earth; And that every tongue should confess that Jesus Christ is Lord, to the glory of God the Father" (Philippians 2:9–11).

This passage informs us that included in the *all* who will confess him are those who have raged against God (the agnostics, the atheists, etc.); they, too, will come to Him and be put to shame. Everyone who goes against the Lord and lives unrighteously or sinfully will one day face God's final judgment.

Search the Scriptures

1. Who established the earth (Isaiah 45:18)?

2. Who speaks righteousness (v. 19)?

3. What other God is there (v. 21)?

Discuss the Meaning

1. What would happen if idol worshipers prayed to their wooden gods and asked to be saved?

2. Will those who have not acknowledged God still have to bow their knees to Him in the future?

Lesson in Our Society

So often we create our own idols out of things we've worked hard to acquire, such as our jobs, cars, houses, or in some cases even in the people we've come to love greatly, such as our children and other loved ones. We may not actually take a piece of wood and carve it into an object and begin to worship it or pray to it; however, when we finally buy that nice car or house and we take a special interest in it and strive to take care of it by any means necessary, we are in danger of idol worship. We must be careful that humanmade things do not come between us and our relationship with God.

Make It Happen

As you go about your everyday life this week, ask yourself: Does my life show that I am turning to God to be saved? Will my neighbor see me in the lottery line instead of turning to God to supply my needs and fulfill my desires? Will my family watch as I put television ahead of personal time with the only God? Will I procrastinate and delay my personal study time with God by putting other things and other people before the only God? Will I bow the knee now and confess to Him right now, or will I feel like I'm being made to do it like the unbeliever?

Follow the Spirit

What God wants me to do:

_____

_____

_____

_____

Remember Your Thoughts

Special insights I have learned:

_____

_____

_____

_____

More Light on the Text

Isaiah 45:18–24a

18 For thus saith the LORD that created the heavens; God himself that formed the earth and made it; he hath established it, he created it not in vain, he formed it to be inhabited: I am the LORD; and there is none else.

In this verse, God begins with the beginning. All that exists, He created, not just the earth, but Cyrus, Cyrus's kingdom of Persia, and the kingdoms he had defeated and now ruled. But as the writer of Genesis says, God created the measureless breadth of the heavens that contained the sun that the Egyptians wrongly worshiped and the moon that the Babylonians falsely assumed was a god. He did not simply create an empty mass which He then ignored. After creation, God "formed (Heb. *yatsar*, **yaw-TSAR**) the earth." The prophet uses the same term here as when Jeremiah described watching a potter shape clay into a pot. God shaped the earth to fulfill His purposes.

In addition to giving the world its initial shape, Isaiah adds that God "made (Heb. *asah*, **aw-SAW**) it." At first glance, God may seem to be repeating Himself. The emphasis in the prophet's second description of God's creative activity was on His continued involvement with the world He created.

God's loving purpose was not temporary. As Isaiah 45:18 states, "He hath established it." "Established" (Heb. *kuwn*, **koon**) means "accomplished," or in a contemporary sense, "all done." His will was fixed unchangeably from day one. As God insisted in His final prophetic declaration before His supreme revelation of Himself in Jesus, "For I am the LORD, I change not; therefore ye sons of Jacob are not consumed" (Malachi 3:6). Thus, from the beginning, God determined not to give up on His purposes for the world He created: "he created it not in vain" (Isaiah 45:18). The phrase "in vain" (Heb. *tohuw*, **TO-hoo**) means "a waste, a worthless thing," or simply "emptiness." Yet "in vain" is close in meaning to the second verse in the Bible, used to describe the universe as God first made it: "And the earth was without *form*" (Genesis 1:2, emphasis added).

19 I have not spoken in secret, in a dark place of the earth: I have not said unto the seed of Jacob, Seek ye me in vain: I the LORD speak righteousness, I declare things that are right.

Rather than darkness, God and His Word are called light, as seen in Psalm 27:1: "The LORD is my light and my salvation" (see also Psalm 119:105; Proverbs 6:23). Later, Isaiah admonished the Israelites, "Seek ye the LORD while he may be found, call ye upon him while he is near" (55:6). Although God wanted His people to seek to know Him, He never intended to be deliberately obscure. Nor did He want finding and knowing Him to be an empty experience that felt it was all in vain. God wanted His people to experience joy, peace, and fulfillment.

"Righteousness" (Heb. *tsedeq*, **TSEH-dek**) refers to the right way to live, as opposed to a lifestyle that treats others unfairly or unjustly. A person can't claim to live a life committed to God while treating others with cruelty, injustice, or contempt. The most basic meaning of righteousness is rightness in attitude, in intention, and in practice. God's final statement describes the results of a righteous lifestyle. The way He wanted people to live reads in English like a repeat of what He just said: "I declare things that are right" (Heb. *meyshar*, **may-SHAWR**). Literally, that meant, "I declare what is smooth, level, even." God was saying, "If you want things to go smoothly, if you don't want to feel like you're always walking uphill or over rocky ground, live according to the way I'm instructing you." That didn't mean God's people never had problems. It meant that they could know God was with them and would guide them through whatever situation they faced.

20 Assemble yourselves together and come; draw near together, ye that are escaped of the nations: they have no knowledge that set up the wood of the graven image, and pray unto a god that cannot save.

In verses 1–6, the prophet began this chapter by addressing Cyrus, the conqueror. Then he switched to warning any in those nations defeated by Cyrus, "ye that are escaped from the nations" (v. 20). "Nations" translates as a word that means specifically "people who weren't Israelites." And when the plural form was used as it was here, it meant "people groups" or "nations." "Ye that are escaped" pictures fugitives who survived the attacks by Cyrus' troops and fled.

God ordered everyone to come together and present themselves to Him to hear His verdict on their thinking. This presents a picture of God's final judgment that is repeated again and again by the Old Testament prophets and the apostles of the New Testament church (Jeremiah 7:10; Nahum 1:6; Romans 14:10; Revelation 20:12).

Although God's final judgment threatened to be severe for those who ignored His will, His judgment in Isaiah 45:20 was as much a warning as it was a judgment. Rather than "set up" graven images as the King James Version says, most modern translations (NIV, NLT, RSV, NEB) use the word "carry" or "holding." It was a common practice for worshipers of pagan gods to carry their idols about, especially in New Year's observances or even into battles hoping for protection. The key word in connection with "graven image" (Heb. *pecel*, **PEH-sel**) is "wood." In last week's study of Isaiah 44, verses 13–20 referred to and ridiculed the making of and reliance on those idols, including those made of wood. God jeered at this kind of belief, stating in effect that they were nothing but "dolled-up tree trunks."

21 Tell ye, and bring them near; yea, let them take counsel together: who hath declared this from ancient time? who hath told it from that time? have not I the LORD? and there is no God else beside me; a just God and Saviour; there is none beside me.

"Tell" (Heb. *nagad*, **naw-GAD**) means "to speak clearly or loudly, to be conspicuous or to stand out." God was telling those who worshiped their pagan idols to say why they did so—justify their foolishness. "Let them take counsel together" was another way of God saying, "Talk it over and give Me your best defense for why you believe what you believe."

The God who revealed Himself in the truthfulness of His word through the prophets was obviously a God of *limitless* knowledge and *overwhelming* power. But more than that, He was also just and caring. The prophet wrote that God was "just" (Heb. *tsaddiyq*, **tsad-DEEK**), a word often rendered as "righteous." The book of Proverbs helps to clarify the prophet's emphasis here. Proverbs uses this word twice at its beginning. Both times it sandwiches "just" between "right" and "fair." God wants people to get what's "right and just and fair" (Proverbs 1:3; 2:9, NIV).

In Isaiah 45:21, the other description the prophet gave for God besides "just" was "Saviour," from a form of the Hebrew word *yasha'* (**yaw-SHAH**). Its original meaning was "to be open, free" or "safe." In the prophet's time, it described someone who delivered another from danger or liberated a person from captivity. That was exactly what God would do through Cyrus. In justice, God had been faithful to the warning He had prophesied through Isaiah and other prophets. Yet the justice of His judgment never cancelled out the centrality of His love. God could honestly claim "there is none beside me" (v. 21). He is One-of-a-kind, truly "the Holy One of Israel" (Isaiah 37:23).

22 Look unto me, and be ye saved, all the ends of the earth: for I am God, and there is none else.

What an incredible statement! What God had brought to pass for Israel, a defeated group of captives living in exile in Babylon, He offered to the whole world. But the salvation He offered went beyond freedom from captivity and exile, or from poverty and hopelessness. The salvation He offered was an individual freedom of spirit and soul as well as a social freedom where His merciful justice could grow and prevail (Micah 6:8; Amos 5:24).

23 I have sworn by myself, the word has gone out from my word in righteousness and shall not return, That unto me every knee shall bow, every tongue shall swear.

Still today whenever a person vows to tell the truth, the surety for truthfulness is based on something greater than that person alone. When the President of the United States takes his oath of office, he does so with his hand on the Bible, pledging on God's Word to faithfully fulfill his duty. However, God vowed by Himself because "there is none beside me" (v. 21).

When He mentions that "the word has gone out of my mouth," the phrase in Hebrew is similar in meaning to "turn" as was used in verse 22. This time, though, the phrase is closer in meaning to "repent" (Heb. *shuwb*, **SHOOB**), as in Jeremiah 3:14, "Turn, O backsliding children, saith the LORD." God said, in essence, that the Word and therefore the guarantee for His people was, "I will never repent—change or turn back— from My intention to save those who turn to Me in faith. Regardless of who does or doesn't turn to Me, the time will come when every person will admit, either gratefully or grudgingly, that's who I am."

24a Surely, shall one say, in the LORD have I righteousness and strength:

The first word "surely" means "without doubt." Life must have been confusing for people across the 1000-plus-mile expanse that Cyrus had conquered. The gods they had worshiped were proven to be unworthy; their bold promises and predictions were shown to be empty. For those who would gratefully turn in faith to their Creator, He promised to save them from sin and an empty life without any lasting meaning.

The prophet Isaiah assures those who look to the one God, who told the truth, that in Him they would find the right ways to live life and the strength to live it. When Jesus came, He made "the way, the truth and the life" even clearer.

Say It Correctly

Anshan. ahn-shahn.
Astyages. as-TI-uh-jeez.
Chronicles. KRON-ih-kuhlz.
Cyrus. SI-ruhs.
Damascus. duh-MAS-kuhs.
Hosea. hoh-SEE-uh, hoh-ZEE-uh.
Menahem. MEN-uh-hem.
Philistia. fə-'lis-tē-ə.
Tyre. TI-r (rhymes with "dire," "fire")

Daily Bible Readings

M: The People God Redeemed
   Exodus 15:11–18

T: Two Different Opinions
   1 Kings 18:17–29

W: Answer Me, O Lord
   1 Kings 18:30–38

T: The Prayer of Faith
   James 5:13–18

F: Building God a House
   2 Chronicles 36:15–23

S: The Lord Creates Weal and Woe
   Isaiah 45:1–8

S: A Righteous God and Savior
   Isaiah 45:18–24a

Notes

_____

_____

_____

_____

_____

SPECIAL APPEARANCE BY 21:03!

McDonald's *presents*

INSPIRATION CELEBRATION GOSPEL TOUR

Featuring

Hezekiah Walker

June 16th • 7:00 PM
Doors open at 6:00 PM

Deliverance
Evangelistic Church
Philadelphia, PA

365BLACK.com

UMI
www.urbanministries.com

i'm lovin' it®

FREE PASSES are available at this host church, many neighboring churches and other local outlets, while supplies last. To get your FREE PASSES for these shows, please visit www.365BLACK.com for more information. A FREE ADMISSION PASS is required for entry to the show. Seating is limited, first come, first seated.

FREE ADMISSION
ADMIT ONE

©2011 McDonald's

...aching Tips

January 16
Bible Study Guide 7

...Know

... 48:15) *tsalach*,
... of progress,

... *qadowsh*, *qadosh*
..., set apart from

...(Heb.)—To gain

...n

...tting the Past
...rgive sin and to

...n your class.
...meditate on the

...eans "to forgive"
...eady to generate

...of your students
...emembering the

...a definition of

C. Then ask what it feels like to *not* forgive someone of a transgression and *to not be* forgiven of a transgression against a loved one or friend.

D. Explain why it was necessary for a holy God to forgive us of our sins.

E. Now ask a volunteer to read the In Focus story aloud, and then explain its relevance to today's Aim for Change.

4. Present the Scriptures

A. Have volunteers read the Focal Verses.

B. Explain their relevance to today's Aim for Change.

C. Explain the Focal Verses by using The People, Places, and Times; Background; the At-A-Glance outline; In Depth; Search the Scriptures; and More Light on the Text.

5. Explore the Meaning

A. Have volunteers summarize and lead a discussion of the Discuss the Meaning, Lesson in Our Society and Make It Happen sections.

B. Connect these sections to the Aim for Change.

6. Next Steps for Application

A. Use the Keep in Mind verse to sum up the lesson.

B. Close with prayer.

Worship Guide

For the Superintendent or Teacher
Theme: Reassurance for God's People
Theme Song: "Serving the Lord Will Pay Off"
Devotional Reading: 1 Kings 8:33–40
Prayer

Reassurance for God's People

Bible Background • ISAIAH 48
Printed Text • ISAIAH 48:14–19, 21–22 | Devotional Reading • 1 KINGS 8:33–40

Aim for Change

By the end of the lesson, we will: EXPLAIN God's promises to forgive sin and redeem His people; CHERISH God's mercy and loving forgiveness; and PRAISE God for His mercy and loving forgiveness.

In Focus

On Wednesday, August 5, 2009, at 8:33 p.m., Bryant A. Tolliver III entered the world weighing 8 lb., 11 oz. and measuring 21 in. long. This strong, healthy newborn baby boy gave an attention-grabbing scream. His excited parents were concerned. Since Bryant was their first child, they had to admit to themselves that they did not fully know what to expect, how to act, or how best to take care of Baby Bryant. So they both sought answers from their own parents. Baby Bryant's father wanted to teach him everything he possibly could; he wanted to guide his son in the right direction.

As new parents, both the father and mother realized that in order for this baby to be safe and to learn how to act and treat himself and others, over time he was going to have to learn to be obedient. Baby Bryant's dad asked his own dad how he should teach his son to be obedient. Before the baby's grandfather could speak, the baby's grandmother chimed in and responded that they should do so by following the guidelines set forth in the Bible.

In today's lesson, we are reminded that God is the Teacher and the Guide. He will reward those who obey His Word with blessings upon blessings.

Keep in Mind

"Go ye forth of Babylon, flee ye from the Chaldeans, with a voice of singing declare ye, tell this, utter it even to the end of the earth; say ye, The LORD hath redeemed his servant Jacob" (Isaiah 48:20).

Focal Verses

KJV **Isaiah 48:14** All ye, assemble yourselves, and hear; which among them hath declared these things? The LORD hath loved him: he will do his pleasure on Babylon, and his arm shall be on the Chaldeans.

15 I, even I, have spoken; yea, I have called him: I have brought him, and he shall make his way prosperous.

16 Come ye near unto me, hear ye this; I have not spoken in secret from the beginning; from the time that it was, there am I: and now the Lord GOD, and his Spirit, hath sent me.

17 Thus saith the LORD, thy Redeemer, the Holy One of Israel; I am the LORD thy God which teacheth thee to profit, which leadeth thee by the way that thou shouldest go.

18 O that thou hadst hearkened to my commandments! then had thy peace been as a river, and thy righteousness as the waves of the sea:

19 Thy seed also had been as the sand, and the offspring of thy bowels like the gravel thereof; his name should not have been cut off nor destroyed from before me.

48:21 And they thirsted not when he led them through the deserts: he caused the waters to flow out of the rock for them: he clave the rock also, and the waters gushed out.

22 There is no peace, saith the LORD, unto the wicked.

NLT **Isaiah 48:14** Have any of your idols ever told you this? Come, all of you, and listen: The LORD has chosen Cyrus as his ally. He will use him to put an end to the empire of Babylon and to destroy the Babylonian armies.

15 "I have said it: I am calling Cyrus! I will send him on this errand and will help him succeed.

16 Come closer, and listen to this. From the beginning I have told you plainly what would happen." And now the Sovereign LORD and his Spirit have sent me with this message.

17 This is what the LORD says—your Redeemer, the Holy One of Israel: "I am the LORD your God, who teaches you what is good for you and leads you along the paths you should follow.

18 Oh, that you had listened to my commands! Then you would have had peace flowing like a gentle river and righteousness rolling over you like waves in the sea.

19 Your descendants would have been like the sands along the seashore—too many to count! There would have been no need for your destruction, or for cutting off your family name."

48:21 They were not thirsty when he led them through the desert. He divided the rock, and water gushed out for them to drink.

22 "But there is no peace for the wicked," says the LORD.

217

The People, Places, and Times

Chaldea. This term is found only in the books of Jeremiah and Ezekiel (Jeremiah 50:10; 51:24; and Ezekiel 11:24; 16:29; 23:15–16). Geographically, this land was originally the southern part of Babylonia, which included the lower Tigris and Euphrates valley. However from 605 to 562 B.C., during the reign of Nebuchadnezzar II (king of Babylonia), the term included most of Babylonia and was synonymous with the Neo-Babylonian Empire.

The Chaldeans. "These are the ancient peoples who dominated Babylonia, especially beginning with King Nebuchadnezzar's empire (605 to 562 B.C.). They were first mentioned in secular literature in the annals of the Assyrian King Ashurnasirpal II (who reigned from 884/883 to 859 B.C)" (*Nelson's New Illustrated Bible Dictionary*, 254–55).

Background

There were many idols, sorcerers, and enchanters in Babylon, yet still the Babylonians could not stand against Cyrus's mighty armies. Unfortunately, the people put their trust in the wrong god instead of the true and living God, who is sovereign (in control of His universe and never out of control). Thus, idol gods could not save them or their city. The Babylonians paid dearly for their mistake—they suffered the humiliation of being hauled away "as loot on beasts and in wagons" (303). Indeed, God controls history!

At-A-Glance

1. The Lord Speaks to the Nations
(Isaiah 48:14–17)

2. The Lord Calls for Obedience (vv. 18–22)

In Depth

1. The Lord Speaks to the Nations (Isaiah 48:14–17)

This is an open invitation for the people to reflect on what the gods had done. Had the idol gods ever once told the people to come and listen and inform them of what the Lord was going to do? Did the idol gods know and were they able to reveal that the Lord had chosen Cyrus as His own? Did the idol gods know the Lord would use Cyrus for His ally? Were the idol gods able to convey that the Lord would use Cyrus to put an end to the Babylonian empire and to destroy the Babylonian allies? God was the only One able to know ahead of time what would happen, tell what would happen, and then make it happen. There is no other God like our God! It was God's power, which is independent of any other source. Only God could raise up an individual to execute justice and judgment against Babylon. That same God would stir up Cyrus, the King of Persia, to let God's people go and allow them to return to the Promised Land of Judah.

Only God's word was needed to guarantee such a prophecy. As stated in Genesis 1:3, "And when God said, Let there be light: and there was light." He had just spoken the deliverance of His people. Once He had spoken, the event would take place when, where, and however God said.

2. The Lord Calls for Obedience (vv. 18–22)

Let's look at who God is, their Redeemer, the Holy One of Israel. In order to be holy, one would have to be set apart, distinct, and different. God is set apart from sin—He is sinless. Considering who God is—perfect, pure and righteous—He *always* does the right thing. Also considering that He is omnipotent (all-powerful), God can and

218

will fulfill any and every promise He made or makes. He would also deliver His people from their Babylonian captivity. He had to deliver because He said it, and if He said it, it would definitely come to pass.

In verses 18–19 of today's text, four blessings specifically are promised to those obeying God. The first of these blessings is peace. This correlates with what was stated in Psalm 119:165, which promises peace if we love God's commandments. This isn't just a peace without conflict, but a peace that surpasses understanding in the midst of conflict. God's peace reaches the depths of a human's soul. This brings confidence that we have God's presence and His leadership and guidance. In Isaiah 48:18, God's peace is referred to as "a river." A river continuously flows without breaks; it doesn't stop like rain. Because God's peace is continually flowing in spite of our circumstances, this brings satisfaction, fulfillment, and confidence in God's presence.

Next, Isaiah points out that obeying God will bring the blessing of righteousness to a person. Righteousness is another one of the great blessings of redemption. The more we obey God, the more we show the fruit of His Spirit. That fruit consists of "love, joy, peace, longsuffering, gentleness, goodness, faith, meekness, and temperance" (Galatians 5:22–23). The believer who is obedient is more moral and just in his dealings with other people and desires to treat others like he or she wants to be treated. This believer is more compassionate, caring, and merciful. The more we obey God, the more we want to help those who are in need. Therefore, the obedient believer is an ambassador for our God, who is our Redeemer.

There is a third advantage to the Israelites' obedience of God: population growth. Many, many children were promised to the Israelites for obeying God. This is still true for us today. As we obey God, we lead more and more souls to the Lord; consequently, we will increase the population of God's kingdom.

Fourth, obeying God assures the believer of an eternal place in God's "book of life" (see Revelation 21:27). In other words, the obedient believer is further blessed by receiving eternal life—forever and ever he or she will be with our Lord and Savior. God gives this eternal life and He doesn't take it away. Therefore, life-giving water flows from our God—eternal life. Through believing on the Lord Jesus Christ, we are saved (John 3:16).

Search the Scriptures

1. How can we receive peace and righteousness (Isaiah 48:18)?

2. Who caused the water to flow out of the rock (v. 21)?

3. Who does not receive peace (v. 22)?

Discuss the Meaning

1. The message of redemption should be carried out for how long (Isaiah 48:20)?

2. Why did the Israelites not get thirsty in the desert (v. 21)?

3. What are the consequences for not obeying God (v. 22)?

Lesson in Our Society

When speaking to someone who doesn't attend church on a regular basis, we may sometimes realize that they feel that they have done something that is unforgivable. There are times when we may find ourselves doing something we knew we shouldn't have done and are concerned whether we can go to God with our confessions. In our hearts, we feel a sense of drawing back to God, but in our minds we ask if God can really forgive us for what we have done. Even though the

219

Bible teaches that we should not intentionally sin just because we know God will forgive us, it also teaches that God will forgive us when we confess and repent.

Make It Happen

As ambassadors for our redeeming Savior, Jesus Christ, we should shout from the mountaintops God's message of redemption to all. We don't need a megaphone to exclaim this message, but we can do it in the way we daily live. Unknowingly, people watch us and how we carry out our everyday dealings with others. Therefore, we should be mindful of the way we carry ourselves and treat other people. This week, make a conscious effort to be sure God's message is spoken in the way you live and deal with others.

Follow the Spirit

What God wants me to do:

_____

_____

_____

_____

Remember Your Thoughts

Special insights I have learned:

_____

_____

_____

_____

More Light on the Text

Isaiah 48:14–19, 21–22

14 All ye, assemble yourselves, and hear: which among them hath declared these things? The LORD hath loved him: he will do His pleasure on Babylon, and his arm shall be on the Chaldeans.

Like a judge calling his or her courtroom to order, God addresses the captive Israelites as though evidence was being presented in a trial. He demands everyone's attention. For nearly 70 years, it had appeared that the Jewish exiles worshiped a weak God who had failed them. They were deported 1,000 miles from their homeland; many of their fellow citizens had been killed; and their capital city and the temple of their God had been left in ruins by the Babylonian army. God asked who foresaw this. The Israelites had dismissed it when the prophets of their God predicted it. They didn't want to believe it. They were God's chosen people, weren't they? They were guardians of His holy earthly dwelling place, the beautiful temple built to God's specifications and under His express instructions by King Solomon.

Looking back, everything that Isaiah and the other prophets had warned would happen if they refused to change how they lived had come to pass. Isaiah also foretold an eventual deliverance, but when it arrived it was from a source the Israelites would have assumed impossible—a non-Israelite, the Persian conqueror Cyrus. The prophet had mentioned him twice before the text for this week (44:28; 45:1), but leaves out his name here. He simply states, "The LORD hath loved him" (Isaiah 48:14).

The Jews would have thought that impossible, but as release from captivity and exile approached, an important new emphasis in God's revelation was God's love for all He created. That love included even worshipers of pagan gods, such as Cyrus, of whom God acknowledged, "...though thou hast not known me" (45:5). That love for all people, however deeply lost in sin and unbelief, was only fully revealed "when the fulness of time was come, God sent forth his Son, made of a woman" (Galatians 4:4).

Liberation from an unbelievable source was included in God's question, "Which among them hath declared these things?" (Isaiah 48:14) What the Israelites were completely helpless to do for themselves God was breaking into history to do for them. He was intervening in world history just as He would again when He sent Jesus as a helpless baby into a world dominated by the Roman Empire "to be the propitiation [pay the ransom] for our sins" (1 John 4:10).

As Jesus came to obediently do His Father's will—trusting His purposes—likewise the prophet assured the captive exiles that Cyrus "will do his pleasure on Babylon" (Isaiah 48:14). This is exactly what happened. After gaining control of every nation for 1,000 miles to the west, Cyrus laid siege against Babylon, which until then had controlled much of the Near East. The "arm" referred to Cyrus's strength. Babylonian records state that in 539 B.C., Cyrus's army entered Babylon—without a battle, or as is said today, without a shot being fired. "Chaldeans" (Heb. *kasday*, **kas-DAH-ee**) was an ancient term for people from the Babylonian region.

15 I, even I, have spoken; yea, I have called him: I have brought him, and shall make his way prosperous.

God begins this verse by answering His own question. Twice He repeats "I" (Heb. *aniy*, **an-EE**). His emphasis, over and over, was that no other god said it or even suggested it. As Isaiah 45:18 closes with, "For I am God and there is none else" (see also Isaiah 45:5, 6, 21). God had a purpose for Cyrus and worked in his life to fulfill that purpose. Earlier in Isaiah 45:4–5, God said of Cyrus, "For Jacob my servant's sake, and Israel mine elect, I have called thee by thy name...I have girded thee." The phrase in Isaiah 48:15 "to be called" (Heb. *qara*, **kaw-RAW**) means "to be appointed or commissioned to fulfill a task." An appointment or calling also referred to builders who selected a plank of wood to fit into a specific place. God had a will for Cyrus. Likewise, He has a will for each person's life. He works in our lives to bring that will to fulfillment. How much more satisfying and fulfilling can life be when a person chooses to trust God, to seek His will, and to commit to do it!

When God said, "I have brought him," the question is, "Where?" Since the Israelites were exiled in Babylon and God had declared in verse 14 that Cyrus would do His will there, the Revised English Bible correctly added the word "here." God brought Cyrus to confront Babylon, the greatest national power other than Persia in that part of the world. The Israelites seemed to be doomed to endless captivity as aliens in a foreign land, but God brought Cyrus to put an end to their captors' power. What Israel was helpless to do for themselves, God acted to do for them.

When God says of Cyrus, "He shall make his way prosperous," the word "prosperous" (Heb. *tsaleach*, **tsaw-LAY-akh**) didn't refer to personal profit. Rather, it meant "to move forward or succeed in one's efforts," which is how both NLT and NIV translate it.

16 Come ye near unto me, hear ye this; I have not spoken in secret from the beginning; from the time that it was, there am I: and now the LORD God, and His Spirit, hath sent me.

Again God affirms His desire for the Israelites to make the true and living God part of their lives. Although they were exiled 1,000 miles from their ravaged homeland and the rubble of its broken-down temple, He instructs them to come before Him and hear His guidance for their lives. A temple was not necessary for them to enter into God's presence. Before there was a Promised Land and before there was a temple, from the beginning of time, God said, "there am I."

As in Isaiah 45:19, He declared that He had not revealed Himself "in secret." He announced Himself and made known what was to come (Isaiah 48:3).

17 Thus saith the LORD, thy Redeemer, the Holy One of Israel; I am the LORD thy God which teacheth thee to profit, which leadeth thee by the way that thou shouldest go.

The book of Isaiah deals with a period extending over 200 years from Isaiah's call to be a prophet in 740 B.C. to King Cyrus's invasion of Babylon in 539 B.C. During those centuries, the Israelite kingdoms of southern Judah and northern Israel lived through three periods: the judgment or defeat, the punishment of exile, and deliverance from it. Throughout the book of Isaiah, from the first chapter almost to its last (Isaiah 1:4; 60:14), the prophet describes God as "the Holy One of Israel." That description of God is used more in Isaiah than in all other Old Testament books combined, more than 25 times, and ties the book together. The word "holy" (Heb. *qadosh*, **kaw-DOSHE**) means "to be exalted and thus above, apart from or separate from the usual, common or ordinary." Repeatedly, God defines Himself

and His exclusive authority (Isaiah 45:22; see also 43:11, 15).

In all those difficult, punishing times, God was teaching lessons the Israelites could profit from if they were willing to learn. Nearing the end of the exile, He told them, "Behold, I have refined thee, but not with silver; I have chosen thee in the furnace of affliction" (Isaiah 48:10). In the exile, the lesson was what not to do, what to change, and what offends God's holiness. In Israel's coming liberation, the lesson was God's enduring love in spite of the sinful unfaithfulness of their past.

When God promised to "lead" Israel, the prophet used a word meaning "to tread ahead or tread down." The image was of a trailblazer who pushed ahead, trampling the underbrush to make a path for those coming behind Him to follow. It was a fitting picture for the exiles, who would have a 1,000-mile trek back to Jerusalem when Cyrus freed them to return to Judah. The Supreme Spiritual Trailblazer is Jesus, whom the Revised Standard Version titles "the *pioneer* and perfecter of our faith" (Hebrews 12:2, emphasis added). Jesus Christ came into our world to show us the best way to live the new life God gives us when we turn from sin and self and entrust our lives to Him as Lord.

18 O that thou hadst hearkened to my commandments! then had thy peace been as a river, and thy righteousness as the waves of the sea:

Matthew 23:37 records how Jesus grieved "O Jerusalem, Jerusalem" over the city's deadly rejection of God's messengers. Here God expressed His grief that the Israelites failed to learn the benefits of living by His Law. The results would have transformed their individual lives and their nation's destiny. The tender compassion His grief revealed warned that they should live their new life after redemption from exile by new God-directed values. The difference in the past would have brought "peace" (Heb. *shalom*, **shaw-LOME**) to the whole flow of their lives. Peace meant far more than an absence of conflict or problems, but that every part of life would be blessed.

God began to reveal His loving will for humankind when Abraham wisely chose to trust Him. God declared, "...in thee shall all families of the earth be blessed" (Genesis 12:3). That fullness of life wasn't intended as a one-time thing. Instead, God's concern for His people's lives was continuous. As they trusted Him and lived by His will, their relationship would continue to bless their lives. Their "righteousness" (Heb. *tsâdaqah*, **tsed-aw-KAW**) is plural, a lifestyle, not just a single event. God promised that as they continued to trust Him, blessing would continue flooding their lives as waves steadily flood onto the seashore.

19 Thy seed also had been as the sand, and the offspring of thy bowels like the gravel thereof; his name should not have been cut off nor destroyed from before me.

God's desire was that those descended from Abraham's faith would become as numberless as grains of sand on the seashore (Genesis 22:17, 32:12). That would have been the result had the Israelites chosen to let the Law that God had given them shape their lifestyle. God grieved that that had not happened. Instead, that divine purpose had been frequently thwarted by a faked obedience to it or outright rebellion against it. The consequence was that the insult to God's justice finally smothered His love, resulting in the Exile. Instead of multiplying into countless numbers like grains of sand, many starved inside Jerusalem while

barricaded against the Babylonian army's siege. Thousands were slaughtered when its walls were breached, and the city was invaded and burnt. Many more died as they were marched as captives to exile by Nebuchadnezzar's army.

For nearly 70 years, Jerusalem and its sacred temple had existed as mere piles of burnt rubble. The surrounding territory had been ravaged by marauding bands (Lamentations 1:3; Obadiah 11). In spite of God's love for His people expressed in His grieving care in Isaiah 48:18, the reminder here was that a sad aftermath could result from choosing to exclude God from their lives. That is equally true for us today.

48:21 And they thirsted not when he led them through the deserts: he caused the waters to flow out of the rock for them: he clave the rock also, and the waters gushed out.

Liberation from exile in Babylon approached with the successful advance of Cyrus. In verse 20, God encouraged the captives to be positive and prepare to leave. As they looked toward the long journey back to Jerusalem, God reminded them of the help He had given their forefathers during their exodus wandering. As they escaped through the desert from slavery in Egypt, He had given them what they needed to survive in spite of their desperate need.

The word "deserts" (*chorbah*, **khor-BAH**) can mean "a hot, waterless region" as it does here, but not necessarily. Its basic meaning is "a wasteland, a ruin, a place of desolation." In order to get back to the Promised Land, the released captives would have to tramp through hundreds of miles of rough terrain. There would be no paved roads or sidewalks to follow. But as God emphasized in verse 17, He wanted to teach them lessons on their journey back home. Even more importantly,

He knew every step of the way ahead. He had already pointed out, "I have made the earth, and created man upon it" (Isaiah 45:12). This tells us that wherever we are in life, God knows it fully. He has been there before we arrived. If we trust Him, He will lead us through whatever we stumble into.

22 There is no peace, saith the LORD, unto the wicked.

The only Hebrew word most non-Jews know is *shalom*. It is often translated "peace" as it is here, but the word has a much fuller meaning than the absence of turmoil or conflict. *Shalom* means "wholeness, good health, or safety." David prays to be restored to health: "Lord, have mercy on me. Make me well again" (Psalm 41:10, NLT). That's why the word is often used by Jews as a greeting or a farewell.

Isaiah closes this passage by emphasizing that however well a person might appear to be doing, without God, that person's life is missing something vital. Without God, life lacks a secure foundation that only faith in God provides. Solomon said, "When the storms of life come, the wicked are whirled away, but the godly have a lasting foundation" (Proverbs 10:25, NLT; see also 1 Corinthians 3:11).

Say It Correctly

Assyria. uh-SIHR-ee-uh.
Babylon. BAB-ih-luh.
Euphrates. yoo-FRAY-teez.
Jerusalem. juh-ROO-suh-luhm.
Mesopotamia. mes'-uh-puh-TAY-mee-uh,
mes'-oh-puh-TAY-mee-uh.
Persian. PUHR-zhuhn.
Tigris. TI-gris.

Daily Bible Readings

M: God Hears Confession
1 Kings 8:33–40

T: God's Chosen Instrument
Acts 9:3–6, 10–18

W: God Will Deliver
Jeremiah 15:19–21

T: God Spoke Long Ago
Isaiah 48:1–5

F: God Discloses New Things
Isaiah 48:6–8

S: God, the First and the Last
Isaiah 48:9–13

S: God Leads the Way
Isaiah 48:14–19, 21–22

Teaching Tips

1. Words You Should Know

A. **Bowels** (Isaiah 49:1) *me`ah* (Heb.)—The place of emotions or distress or love.

B. **Servant** (vv. 3, 5, 6) *`ebed* (Heb.)—A slave, subject, worshiper.

2. Teacher Preparation

Unifying Principle—Pay It Forward. God reminds Israel of the gifts they received from Him and charges them to bring hope to the nations.

A. Pray and ask God to guide you through the lesson.

B. Read the entire text and its surrounding sections.

C. Reflect on the saying, "To whom much is given, much is required" (see Luke 12:48). Be prepared to discuss.

D. Think of this saying in relation to what God gave His chosen people, Israel, and what He called them to do for themselves and the nations.

3. Open the Lesson

A. Open with prayer, remembering the Aim for Change.

B. Discuss what it means "to be a servant of Christ."

C. Explain that Jesus was a servant-leader and He also expects His followers to be servants in helping to build His kingdom.

D. Introduce the adage "To whom much is given, much is required" and tie it in with today's discussion on Israel as a light to the nations.

E. Summarize the In Focus story, linking it to today's theme.

4. Present the Scriptures

A. Have volunteers read the Focal Verses.

B. Explain the Focal Verses by using The People, Places, and Times; Background; the At-A-Glance outline; In Depth; Search the Scriptures; and More Light on the Text.

5. Explore the Meaning

A. Emphasize the salient points in the Discuss the Meaning, Lesson in Our Society, Search the Scriptures, and Make It Happen sections.

B. Connect these sections to the Aim for Change.

6. Next Steps for Application

A. Give praises to honor God for bringing salvation to us.

B. Close with prayer.

> ## Worship Guide
>
> For the Superintendent or Teacher
> Theme: The Servant's Mission in the World
> Theme Song: "Here Am I, Send Me"
> Devotional Reading: Hebrews 10:19–25
> Prayer

JAN
23rd

The Servant's Mission in the World

Bible Background • ISAIAH 49:1–6
Printed Text • ISAIAH 49:1–6 | Devotional Reading • HEBREWS 10:19–25

Aim for Change

By the end of the lesson, we will: IDENTIFY Jesus' mission in the world as Redeemer; BE grateful for Jesus' mission; and GIVE praises to honor God for bringing salvation to us.

In Focus

Wilma Glodean Rudolph was the first American woman to win three gold medals in one Olympics. However, her achievement must have astonished many who knew her as a child. She was born in 1940, poor and Black in the segregated South. She was a sickly child, stricken with polio at the age of four. The disease left her left leg and foot impaired. Wilma's doctor said that she would never walk again. However, her parents' faith in God and their love for their daughter were greater than the illness afflicting her.

Wilma's mother and siblings nursed her leg until she regained her ability to walk without assistance. She was encouraged to run track and eventually became a track star. Many nations were witnesses to her grace and athleticism at the 1960 Olympics in Rome, Italy. That same year she was voted the United Press Athlete of the Year. Wilma was eventually inducted into the U.S. Olympics Hall of Fame.

How could Wilma's achievements inspire someone who is feeling discouraged by his or her life's circumstances? Wilma's life was a witness to the nations. In a similar way, how can we be witnesses of God's salvation through our actions?

Keep in Mind

"I will also give thee for a light to the Gentiles, that thou mayest be my salvation unto the end of the earth" (from Isaiah 49:6).

Focal Verses

KJV Isaiah 49:1 Listen, O isles, unto me; and hearken, ye people, from far; The LORD hath called me from the womb; from the bowels of my mother hath he made mention of my name.

2 And he hath made my mouth like a sharp sword; in the shadow of his hand hath he hid me, and made me a polished shaft; in his quiver hath he hid me;

3 And said unto me, Thou art my servant, O Israel, in whom I will be glorified.

4 Then I said, I have laboured in vain, I have spent my strength for nought, and in vain: yet surely my judgment is with the LORD, and my work with my God.

5 And now, saith the LORD that formed me from the womb to be his servant, to bring Jacob again to him, Though Israel be not gathered, yet shall I be glorious in the eyes of the LORD, and my God shall be my strength.

6 And he said, It is a light thing that thou shouldest be my servant to raise up the tribes of Jacob, and to restore the preserved of Israel: I will also give thee for a light to the Gentiles, that thou mayest be my salvation unto the end of the earth.

NLT Isaiah 49:1 Listen to me, all you in distant lands! Pay attention, you who are far away! The LORD called me before my birth; from within the womb he called me by name.

2 He made my words of judgment as sharp as a sword. He had hidden me in the shadow of his hand. I am like a sharp arrow in his quiver.

3 He said to me, "You are my servant, Israel, and you will bring me glory."

4 I replied, "But my work seems so useless! I have spent my strength for nothing and to no purpose. Yet I leave it all in the LORD's hand; I will trust God for my reward."

5 And now the LORD speaks—the one who formed me in my mother's womb to be his servant, who commissioned me to bring Israel back to him. The LORD has honored me, and my God has given me strength.

6 He says, "You will do more than restore the people of Israel to me. I will make you a light to the Gentiles, and you will bring my salvation to the ends of the earth."

The People, Places, and Times

Israel. This was, at first, a personal name meaning "God strives," "God rules," "God heals," or "He strives against God." God gave Jacob this name as a mark of his struggle with the divine messenger and his piety (Genesis 32:27–28). Jacob became the father of the 12 sons after whom were named "the twelve tribes of Israel." His descendants were later identified by the name Israel ("Children of Israel"). The resulting nation became the nation of Israel.

The Servant of the Lord. The phrase "the servant of the Lord" (or "My servant" or "His servant" where the pronoun refers to God) in the Bible is applied to several individuals chosen by God to lead the people, including Moses, David, and Israel as a nation in a number of instances. The writer of the gospel of Matthew attributed the title to Jesus, an allusion to the Old Testament, especially Isaiah 40–55 (see Matthew 12:18–21).

Babylon. This was a major city in ancient Mesopotamia (recognized today as modern Iraq) located on the Euphrates River. Babylon played an important role in the history of the ancient Near East during the second and first millennia B.C. It is mentioned some 200 times in the Bible, mostly in the books of Kings and Isaiah in the Old Testament and referring to the Neo-Babylonian Dynasty (founded by Nabopolassar in 626 B.C. and continued by Nebuchadnezzar his son). Babylon is also mentioned in the New Testament, symbolically and literally. In the book of Revelation, the city of Babylon symbolized every kind of evil. Babylon is famous traditionally for its Hanging Gardens, which were once one of the Seven Wonders of the ancient world.

Background

At the start of today's lesson we find that, having destroyed Judah, exiled many of the people, and leaving Judah and its capital city Jerusalem desolate, the Babylonian Empire was on the verge of collapse. King Cyrus of Persia had marched against Babylon. So formidable was he that when his army entered Babylon, they captured the city without a fight.

The deportees anticipated returning to Judah with the imminent rule by the Persians. Although some despaired and believed that God had forgotten them, despite more than 80 years in exile, many Jews managed to maintain much of their religious and cultural identity. Cyrus's defeat of Babylon was a sign to the people that God had not abandoned them and that the appointed time to return to Judah was now.

God sent His servant to announce to the nations, who had also believed that God had rejected His people and deeply despised them because of the exile, that God was about to restore His people to the land and bring salvation to the ends of the earth. His message was also meant to reassure the deportees that God had neither abandoned nor forgotten them.

At-A-Glance

1. The Commission of the Servant
   (Isaiah 49:1–3)

2. The Servant's Response (v. 4)

3. The Restoration of Israel (vv. 5–6)

In Depth

1. The Commission of the Servant (Isaiah 49:1–3)

Isaiah 49:1–6 is the second of such passages identified as the "Servant songs" (42:1–4; 49:1–6; 50:4–11; 52:13–53:12). The servant of the Lord commands the attention of the nations so that he may announce his divine commission. The divinely chosen leader proclaims to the nations that the Lord called him from before his birth and even named him at that time. However, Isaiah does not reveal his name just yet. His call is similar to the prophet Jeremiah, whom the Lord also predestined to serve even before his birth, to be a prophet to the nations (Jeremiah 1:5; compare Galatians 1:15).

Isaiah informs his audience that God made his mouth like a sharp sword, giving him words to speak which were meant to cut right to the hearts of his listeners. His mission is to deliver God's Word to the nations and to the Children of Israel in exile. Because God has promised to keep him hidden from those who might seek his destruction, he should have no fear that his words will bring him harm.

After having revealed that God had named him before his birth, previously the servant did not mention himself by name. In Isaiah 49:3 he reveals that God has called him "my servant," and explicitly reveals his name: Israel. In him God will be glorified.

2. The Servant's Response (v. 4)

The servant's response is to complain of exhaustion that prevents him from performing the task before him. He feels, like the other deportees, that his efforts to remain faithful to God during the exile have been a labor in vain. Similar to Moses before him, he protests that his shortcomings make him inadequate for such a huge responsibility (Exodus 4:10–17). He will also have the Moses-like task of leading the deportees back to Jerusalem (vv. 8–12). In the meantime, like Moses, this servant surrenders to God's will. He also acknowledges that whatever God has in store for him and whatever God has called him to do is just. God already assured him that what God has planned will surely come to pass and he shall accomplish it.

3. The Restoration of Israel (vv. 5–6)

The servant reiterates that the Lord has formed him in the womb to be His servant. There can be no misunderstanding that this is a mission with divine origins. The task at first glance is to bring Jacob back to God and gather Israel (v. 5). However, the servant is not the subject of these verses. The subject is God, and it should be understood that God will bring Jacob back to Himself and gather Israel to Himself. God is the One who will bring to fruition the work the servant has been called to reveal, the one to whom Israel belongs.

God is also the subject in verse 6. God is the One who will raise up the tribes of Jacob and restore the preserved of Israel. The "servant of the LORD" proclaims that God will place him as a light to the nations so that His salvation may reach to the end of the earth (cf. Isaiah 42:6). Israel's neighbors ordinarily used images to represent their gods. In several instances, the nations were challenged to bring forth witnesses to prove that they and their gods were more powerful than the God of Israel. Since Israelite law forbade the use of images to represent God, the nation of Israel would become God's witness to the presence and supremacy of God. By its restoration before the other nations, who had mocked Israel because they believed Israel's destruction was a sign of her abandonment by her God, Israel became a witness to God's supreme power.

Moreover, God's restoration of Israel would become the means by which God's salvation would be extended to the whole earth. The nations, which had witnessed the annihilation of Israel, would be astonished and humbled by the rescue of Israel from the Babylonian exile by the God who chose Israel as His own. It was through Israel that Jesus would come as a light shining upon the nations to lead them from the farthest corners of the earth to the salvation of God (Luke 2:32; Acts 13:47).

Search the Scriptures

1. Who is addressed by the servant whom God has called (Isaiah 49:1)?

2. By whom does the Lord declare that He will be glorified (v. 3)?

3. Who will be restored to the Lord (v. 5)?

4. Why will "the servant" be given as a light to the nations (v. 6)?

Discuss the Meaning

1. What do you think is the significance of being called before your birth?

2. Why do you think God made "the servant's" mouth like a sharp sword?

3. Why do you think "the servant" was reluctant to accept his call?

Lesson in Our Society

1. In today's society, many of us face uncertainty on a daily basis. We hope that we won't face a health crisis out of fear of insufficient insurance coverage; we fear for our children's safety on their way to and from school; we feel threatened by economic insecurity including soaring unemployment rates, bankruptcies, foreclosures, and credit card debt. However, we can have confidence in God's Word that no matter what we are experiencing, we have the hope of God's salvation.

2. Our family members, friends, neighbors, and coworkers are watching us as Christians to see how we respond to life's challenges. We can collapse in defeat or stand as witnesses to the presence and supremacy of God in the world.

Make It Happen

Pray that God will give you the courage to carry on Jesus' Great Commission to take the light of the Gospel to all nations, beginning with those closest to you (Matthew 28:19–20). Pray that you remain strong under attacks on your faith by those who would mock you for confessing that Jesus is your Lord and Savior. Also pray that God will reveal the gifts and resources you have to bring the light of the Gospel to the world. Discuss in class today what it means to be a light in the world and ways that you can practice bringing that light out of one another.

Follow the Spirit

What God wants me to do:

_____

_____

_____

_____

Remember Your Thoughts

Special insights I have learned:

_____

_____

_____

_____

_____

More Light on the Text
Isaiah 49:1–6

1 Listen, O isles, unto me; and hearken, ye people, from far; The LORD hath called me from the womb; from the bowels of my mother hath he made mention of my name.

This passage is unusual because rarely did biblical writers address Scripture to people who weren't Israelites. The book of Nahum castigates Nineveh, the capital of Assyria, for its ruthlessness, and Obadiah, the Old Testament's shortest book, criticizes Edom for taking advantage of Judah after its defeat by and exile to Babylon. With few exceptions like this verse and Micah 1:2, almost all of the Old Testament was clearly written to people descended from the 12 tribes of Israel.

But here the prophet makes his audience the "isles" (Heb. *'iy,* **ee**) and "ye people" (Heb. *le'owm,* **leh-OME**), meaning "from far." The New Living Translation combines the two terms into "all you in distant lands." "Isles" was a nautical term meaning coastlands where sailing ships could dock, but the word was also used for islands, which explains why the Revised English Bible words it, "you coasts and islands."

"Ye people" means "communities or nations." When "from far" was added, the prophet meant from far-off places. What is highly unusual is that Isaiah was speaking to people that Israelites traditionally thought of as outside of God's covenant promises. This fit God's call to Abraham through whom the tribes of Israel began with Isaac. Genesis 18:18 says, "For Abraham will certainly become a great and mighty nation, and all the nations of the earth will be blessed through him" (NLT).

God's plan from the beginning was to have a worldwide effect through His chosen people, the Israelites. His message of deliverance, however, was not just for the exiles or the people of Israel, but for all people everywhere. As Isaiah 45:22 says, "Look unto me, and be ye saved, all the ends of the earth: for I am God, and there is none else."

As soon as he identified to whom he was speaking, the prophet switched Isaiah 49:1 to talking about himself. "From the womb" was a way of saying, "Before I was born the LORD called me" (NIV). Isaiah recognized that before he was born, God was already thinking about what He wanted Isaiah to do with his life. His service as God's prophet had been part of God's determined plan. More than that, the prophet wasn't just a random cog in the wheel of God's plan.

2 And he hath made my mouth like a sharp sword; in the shadow of his hand he hath hid me, and made me a polished shaft; in his quiver hath he hid me;

The prophet compares the message God has commissioned him to deliver with two offensive weapons: a sword and an arrow. One was used up close in hand-to-hand combat, and the other was used to attack from a distance. The prophet's message could not be treated with indifference, either by those close at hand or those far off. Almost certainly the writer of Hebrews must have recalled the prophet's comparison of God's message here to the life-altering effect of a sword's slash. He wrote, "For the word of God is alive and powerful. It is sharper than the sharpest two-edged sword, cutting between soul and spirit, between joint and marrow. It exposes our innermost thoughts and desires" (Hebrews 4:12, NLT).

When the prophet compares the impact of the message God gave him to deliver to weapons, both times he adds the word "hid" (Heb. *cathar,* **saw-THAR**). That didn't mean God put Isaiah in a place to avoid use or combat. Just the opposite was true. A soldier's sword was always placed in a scabbard at his waist "in the shadow of his hand" (Isaiah 49:2). The arrow was placed "in his quiver." In both cases they were kept close at hand ready for use at the appropriate time. The term given for the arrow's "shaft" was "polished" (Heb. *barar*, **baw-RAR**), which also meant "chosen." Both meanings suggest a weapon kept ready for use. Dr. Kyle Yates wrote, "He [Isaiah] is the chief weapon in God's plan, kept for the hour of greatest need" (100).

The prophet compared his message to an arrow that could pierce a person deeply or a sword that could slash a person open. That meant that his words should not be ignored.

3 And he said unto me, Thou art my servant, O Israel, in whom I will be glorified.

An often debated question about the book of Isaiah is, who was the servant to whom God was speaking here? Was it the nation of Israel? Or was it the prophet himself? Or was it to some unknown Israelite that God had chosen and called for that special time in the revelation of Himself through His chosen people?

In Isaiah 41–53, the prophet refers a dozen times to "my servant," a term used only twice in the 40 chapters before and only once in the 13 chapters afterward. Sometimes Israel as God's chosen people were clearly identified. In other places, the description seems to be of a particular person, as in Isaiah 50:4–6 where the person's beard and back were mentioned. So who is the servant, a person or a group of persons? Paul Hanson interprets the answer this way: "The Servant is both faithful individual and obedient community in the era in which God's plans begins to unfold...." From the beginning of His covenant with Abraham, God's express intent was to create a nation that would make known, demonstrate, and lead the whole

world toward the fulfillment of His purposes. Israel as a nation and as individuals failed God and betrayed His purposes many times, as often as we still do.

The ultimate purpose for "the servant," whether as a nation or as an individual, was to reveal God's glorious greatness. The same remains true for all God's people today. As was true for the Israelites then, God commissions those who today trust and follow Him in Christ to be living witnesses to God's power to liberate from sin and take life in a new direction. What is unusual in Isaiah 49:3 was who received glory. People often boast of working for someone wealthy, powerful, or famous. Because of who their master is, they gain glory through their service. God says just the opposite here. He is "glorified" (Heb. [*pa'ar*, **paw-AR**], when people are willing to trust and follow Him in difficult circumstances. The only person who ever fulfilled God's purposes perfectly was Jesus, "who for the joy that was set before him endured the cross, despising its shame, and is set down at the right hand of the throne of God" [Hebrews 12:2]). In doing so, He confirmed forever the truth of the servant's message.

4 Then I said, I have laboured in vain, I have spent my strength for nought, and in vain; yet surely my judgment is with the LORD, and my work with my God.

In response to God's declaration of His exalted plan for him, the servant countered by evaluating all his efforts as utter failure. In response to God's assertion that His servant would reveal His glory, the New Living Translation begins this verse, "But my work all seems so useless!" After 70 powerless years of exile, the lack of belief by Israelites that they could do anything to glorify God was understandable. Even though God called him to a specific task, twice the servant judge declared himself to be a complete failure; all he had ever done seemed like a waste of breath and strength.

The Israelites' lack of belief that God could and would work out His will through them would persist for decades after the exile. A later prophet, Zechariah, recognized that their poverty and powerlessness had convinced them that God could do little or nothing among them. God inspired Zechariah to remind them how God's purposes were fulfilled: "Not by might, nor by power, but by my spirit, saith the LORD of hosts" (Zechariah 4:6).

In spite of the absence of faith in himself, God's servant determined to hold onto his faith in God's promises. In contrast with the servant's lack of faith in himself, he affirms his faith in God's Word. He claims God's promise as a reality. "Judgment" (Heb. *mishpat,* **mish-PAWT**) did not suggest condemnation or guilt. Rather, the word is often translated "justice" and referred to a person's legal rights. The New International Version words "judgment" as "what is due me." "My work" symbolizes what the servant can expect from God, his reward or recompense. Rather than trusting in his own efforts, he relies on the merciful justice of a loving God.

5 And now, saith the LORD, that formed me in the womb to be his servant, to bring Jacob again to him, Though Israel be not gathered, yet shall I be glorious in the eyes of the LORD, and my God shall be my strength.

In English, to emphasize an object, an action, or other factor in a statement, the word is printed in italics, underlining, or bold type. In Hebrew, the Old Testament did that by moving the word to the front of the statement. That is what the prophet did here with the word "now" (Heb. ʻ*attah,* **at-TAW**). He wanted the Israelites to focus on their

present and not their past sins or failures; not their defeat, exile, or captivity; and not the sorry state of Jerusalem or their destroyed temple. In verse 4, the servant had lamented at how inadequate he felt in fulfilling God's call. Now God reminded him that even before he was born, God created him with a specific purpose in mind, "to bring Jacob again to him." Two words are important here. First, "bring" (Heb. *shuwb,* **SHOOB**) means "to turn back." It is translated as "repent" in Jeremiah 26:3 and Ezekiel 14:6; 18:30. The second word to note is "again" (Isaiah 49:5). From the time of Moses and forward, God's people strayed from His will and had to be brought back (Exodus 16:2). They complained, made excuses, blamed others, lied, and took advantage of each other. The prophet/servant confirms this, stating, "This is a rebellious people, lying children, children that will not hear the law of the LORD" (Isaiah 30:9).

God's intention wasn't for Israel to merely survive their time in exile, to see them resettled in the Promised Land or even restored to the purpose they had temporarily forfeited by their gross unfaithfulness. Whether the servant was an individual member of Israel or the nation as a whole, God intended their future to be *glorious.* For those who trusted God, the prophet wanted to assure them: The future was as bright as the promises of God. By declaring "God shall be my strength," Isaiah affirmed his faith that God could make it happen.

6 And he said, it is a light thing that thou shouldst be my servant to raise up the tribes of Jacob, and to restore the preserved of Israel: I will also give thee for a light to the Gentiles, that thou mayest be my salvation unto the end of the earth.

After reminding the faithful individual or nation of His initial purpose as God's servant, God announces that He had greater plans for them. What they had started with was too "light" (Heb. *qalal*, **kaw-LAL**). It was a good place to start, but compared to God's fullest will for them, it was too slight or trifling. Their Creator, God, knew them better than they knew themselves. He understood what they were capable of, when their faith in Him was not diluted by sin or selfishness (Ephesians 4:7, 13). So He started with what they could handle, but was unwilling to stop with little plans—plans that focused only on them. He wanted more for them than reestablishing their various tribal customs or getting the ones who survived the exile back home. He declared, in essence, "You need a bigger challenge and more responsibility than that. From now on I give you a task that involves the whole world. As Creator of the whole world and as My chosen people, I commission you to be 'a light to the Gentiles.'" Thus, "Gentiles" (Heb. *gowy*, **GO-ee**) refers to the masses of people, the foreign nations.

God's greater goal was first, for the individual committed to His service and eventually, to all those who call Him Lord. He started by choosing one man who was willing to trust Him fully and through him a nation. He gave that nation the mission of a source of light for the whole world, so that all the people He had created could find the source of lasting meaning for their lives.

Say It Correctly

Ezekiel. Eh-ZEE-kee-uhl.
Galatians. guh-LAY-shuhnz.
Jehoiakim. juh-HOI-uh-kim.
Jeremiah. jer'-uh-MI-uh.
Micah. MI-cuh.
Nahum. NAY-huhm, NAY-uhm.
Nineveh. NIN-uh-vuh.
Obadiah. oh'-buh-DI-uh.
Revelation. rev'-uh-LAY-shuhn.
Shalmaneser. shal'-muh-NEE-zuhr.
Zechariah. zak'-uh-RI-uh.

Daily Bible Readings

M: The Lord Has Chosen You
Isaiah 49:7–11

T: Faithful or Unfaithful Servants
Matthew 24:45–51

W: The Greatest as Servant
Matthew 23:2–12

T: Made a Slave to All
1 Corinthians 9:19–23

F: A Testimony to the Gentiles
Matthew 10:16–24

S: Hope for the Gentiles
Matthew 12:15–21

S: A Light to the Nations
Isaiah 49:1–6

Teaching Tips

January 30
Bible Study Guide 9

1. Words You Should Know

A. Borne (Isaiah 53:4) *nasa', nacah* (Heb.)—Carried, brought forth.

B. Smitten (v. 4) *nakah* (Heb.)—Killed, slained.

C. Iniquities (vv. 5–6, 11) *`avon, `avown* (Heb.)—Perversities, depravities, guilt.

2. Teacher Preparation

Unifying Principle—Suffering for Others. Isaiah reveals that Israel's hope is secure in the Suffering Servant, who will pay a terrible price for the sake of Israel—even death.

A. Pray and ask God to meet the spiritual needs of your class.

B. Read the entire lesson.

C. Bring a hymnal to class and be prepared to share a recording of the song "Jesus Paid It All."

3. Open the Lesson

A. Softly play your recording of "Jesus Paid It All" as your class enters.

B. Open with prayer, remembering the Aim for Change.

C. Have a volunteer read the words of "Jesus Paid It All" from the hymnal. Discuss.

D. Explain what being healed by His bruises means *(healed by His suffering, death, and resurrection).*

E. Share the In Focus story, and then compare and contrast it with the punishment that Jesus took for our sins.

4. Present the Scriptures

A. Have volunteers read the Focal Verses.

B. Explain the Focal Verses using The People, Places, and Times; Background; the At-A-Glance outline; In Depth; Search the Scriptures; and More Light on the Text.

5. Explore the Scriptures

A. Emphasize the salient points in the Discuss the Meaning, Lesson in Our Society, and Make It Happen sections.

B. Connect these sections to the Aim for Change.

6. Next Steps for Application

A. Challenge your students to reflect on Jesus' sacrifice and thank Him for His wonderful salvation.

B. Have a "Call to Discipleship" and then end the class with prayer.

JAN
30th

Worship Guide

For the Superintendent or Teacher
Theme: Healed by His Bruises
Theme Song: "Jesus Paid It All"
Devotional Reading: 2 Corinthians 5:16–21
Prayer

Healed by His Bruises

Bible Background • ISAIAH 53
Printed Text • ISAIAH 53:4–6, 10–12 | Devotional Reading • 2 CORINTHIANS 5:16–21

Aim for Change

By the end of the lesson, we will: EXPLAIN how we are healed by Jesus' bruises; REFLECT on Jesus' sacrifice; and THANK God for His wonderful salvation.

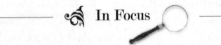

In Focus

Ed was a strong young man with rippling muscles that were developed from years of grueling field work on Master Whitman's sprawling plantation. Ed began manual labor at the age of 10, carrying buckets of water out to the field hands. The task shifted to heavier work as he got older. His workday began before the sun rose in the morning and lasted until the stars shone brightly in the sky. He ate his meals standing up when a couple of slaves would come out to the fields at high noon carrying pots, rationing out corn pone and molasses and a dipper full of water to the men and women toiling under the hot sun.

On Saturday nights, some of the slaves might gather in the "brush arbors" to sing and pray. At one such meeting, Ed had a conversion experience. Not long after, he escaped the plantation. Runaway slaves or slaves found without a pass were almost always severely punished or killed as an example to the other slaves. Just as Master Whitman was about to strike Ed's bare back with the whip, Otis, the oldest slave on the plantation, stepped forward and asked to be punished in Ed's place.

In our lesson today, we will learn how God sent His one and only Son, Jesus, to take our punishment so that we could have salvation.

Keep in Mind

"But he was wounded for our transgressions, he was bruised for our iniquities: the chastisement of our peace was upon him; and with his stripes we are healed"
(Isaiah 53:5).

"But he was wounded for our transgressions, he was bruised for our iniquities: the chastisement of our peace was upon him; and with his stripes we are healed" (Isaiah 53:5).

Focal Verses

KJV Isaiah 53:4 Surely he hath borne our griefs, and carried our sorrows: yet we did esteem him stricken, smitten of God, and afflicted.

5 But he was wounded for our transgressions, he was bruised for our iniquities: the chastisement of our peace was upon him; and with his stripes we are healed.

6 All we like sheep have gone astray; we have turned every one to his own way; and the LORD hath laid on him the iniquity of us all.

53:10 Yet it pleased the LORD to bruise him; he hath put him to grief: when thou shalt make his soul an offering for sin, he shall see his seed, he shall prolong his days, and the pleasure of the LORD shall prosper in his hand.

11 He shall see of the travail of his soul, and shall be satisfied: by his knowledge shall my righteous servant justify many; for he shall bear their iniquities.

12 Therefore will I divide him a portion with the great, and he shall divide the spoil with the strong; because he hath poured out his soul unto death: and he was numbered with the transgressors; and he bare the sin of many, and made intercession for the transgressors.

NLT Isaiah 53:4 Yet it was our weaknesses he carried; it was our sorrows that weighed him down. And we thought his troubles were a punishment from God, a punishment for his own sins!

5 But he was pierced for our rebellion, crushed for our sins. He was beaten so we could be whole. He was whipped so we could be healed.

6 All of us, like sheep, have strayed away. We have left God's paths to follow our own. Yet the LORD laid on him the sins of us all.

53:10 But it was the LORD's good plan to crush him and cause him grief. Yet when his life is made an offering for sin, he will have many descendants. He will enjoy a long life, and the LORD's good plan will prosper in his hands.

11 When he sees all that is accomplished by his anguish, he will be satisfied. And because of what he has experienced, my righteous servant will make it possible for many to be counted righteous, for he will bear all their sins.

12 I will give him the honors of a victorious soldier, because he exposed himself to death. He was counted among the rebels. He bore the sins of many and interceded for rebels.

The People, Places, and Times

Community of Exiles or "People of the Exile." This was the Judahites, including the prophet Ezekiel, deported to Babylon in three waves (597 B.C., 587 B.C., 581 B.C.) following the destruction of the state of Judah and its capital city Jerusalem by Babylonian King Nebuchadnezzar (ca. 605–539 B.C.). Among the 10,000 deportees in the first wave were political and military leaders, religious leaders, and skilled craftsmen. Babylon became an important center of Jewish religion and culture. Some Jews were allowed to own land, become Babylonian officials, and even own slaves. Nevertheless, many longed for Jerusalem and would not sing the Lord's song in Babylon (Psalm 137).

Restoration. King Cyrus of Persia defeated the Babylonian Empire in 539 B.C., permitting the deportees and their descendants to return to Jerusalem some 70 years after their exile. Cyrus gave them the resources and support to reconstruct Jerusalem and the Temple, which had been destroyed in 597 B.C. Exiled Judahite King Jehoiachin's grandson, Zerubbabel, led the first exiles back from Babylon in 538 B.C. (Ezra 2:2; Haggai 1:1).

Background

At the start of today's lesson, the community of exiles have been singing psalms of thanksgiving for their rescue by the servant of the Lord. The exiles are surprised to have been rescued by one so lowly. Servants in the Bible were often of lowly origins, many times using their status in life to argue why they were not worthy of the task to which the Lord had called them.

Isaiah 52:13–53:12 represents the fourth, last, and longest of what scholars refer to as the "Servant Songs" (42:1–4; 49:1–6; 50:4–9; 52:13–53:12). The Lord has promised in Isaiah 52:13–53:12 that the servant Israel, who has suffered greatly during the exile, will be exalted so that the nations will be astonished by Israel's recovery and restoration to prominence. These same nations, who had despised and rejected Israel, will be astonished because Israel was such an insignificant, unassuming nation from whom such a recovery would not be expected. Even kings will be amazed at the transformation of Israel from a decimated nation rejected by God to one restored to life by God.

At-A-Glance

1. The Servant Was Wounded for Our Transgressions (Isaiah 53:4–6)

2. The Servant and the Will of the Lord (vv. 10–11)

3. The Servant's Reward (v. 12)

In Depth

1. The Servant Was Wounded for Our Transgressions (Isaiah 53:4–6)

The speakers of this passage declare that the servant has borne their sins and been wounded for their transgressions. Scholars have debated who the speakers are. Some contend that the speakers represent the nations, who initially took the sufferings of Israel as a sign of God's rejection of the nation, but have come to realize that Israel's affliction was to atone for their sins. Others maintain that the speakers are the community of exiles, to whom the servant addressed the song in the first place to explain why God allowed them to be punished by being carried away to Babylon and to suffer.

Another source of debate is the identity of the servant in Isaiah 53 (see 53:11). There are those scholars who identify Israel as the servant—not the whole people of Israel but the community of exiles, whose sufferings and restoration will lead to the redemption of the whole earth. The New Testament (e.g., 1 Peter 2:24) and first century Christian traditions interpret the "servant" as referring to Jesus and especially the suffering He endured during His ministry and at His crucifixion. The speakers' acknowledgment that they had "esteem[ed] him stricken, smitten of God, and afflicted" (Isaiah 53:4) is a testament to the fact that they viewed the servant's suffering as a sign that God had abandoned His people. However, the people now realize that the servant's sufferings were to atone for their sins so that they could be made whole. The King James Version reads "peace" for "made us whole" (v. 5, RSV). The Hebrew word *shalom* means "completeness," "soundness," "welfare," or "peace." To be made whole or at peace is to be made righteous and restored to right relationship with God.

2. The Servant and the Will of the Lord (vv. 10–11)

The speakers reiterate what they have pronounced before: the suffering of the servant was part of God's divine plan in order that the sins of the many might be forgiven. The servant is punished so that others do not have to suffer for their transgressions. Yet the servant's suffering also offers an explanation for the deportees' situation in exile. They can accept that their exile is deserved punishment from God toward a greater end.

3. The Servant's Reward (v. 12)

The subject shifts from the speakers to the Lord. The Lord concludes the song by declaring that since the servant endured the pain of exile in accordance with God's will and borne the grief of the many, interceding on their behalf, he will be exalted among the great and strong. He will also see the restoration to the people of Israel, of the land that had been destroyed.

The writer of the gospel of Luke, in describing the final days of Jesus' earthly ministry, includes the words of Jesus telling the disciples that the Scripture must be fulfilled in Him. Then Jesus quotes Isaiah 53:12—"And he was numbered with the transgressors"—to foretell that He would be put to death among criminals (Luke 22:37).

Search the Scriptures

1. For what reason was the servant bruised and wounded (Isaiah 53:5)?

2. How are the people described as behaving (v. 6)?

3. Who shall bear the iniquities of the world (v. 11)?

4. God will exalt the servant among whom (v. 12)?

Discuss the Meaning

1. Why do you think that the people of Israel strayed from God?

2. Why do you think that a just God allowed His servant to take the punishment for the sins of others upon Himself?

3. Why do some people make fun of or put down others when they are at their lowest point?

Lesson in Our Society

1. In today's lesson, we find that God's servant suffers vicariously for the sins of others and makes atonement for sin. Christians accept the identity of the autonomous servant as Jesus, the promised Messiah, sent by God to die for our sins. Jesus offered Himself for our sins, suffering and dying on the Cross to make us whole in our relationship to God.

2. The idea of someone suffering in the place of others is an almost foreign notion in today's society. Many people refuse to accept responsibility for their own sins and shortcomings, and when given the opportunity, they will blame others for their offenses. How could they fathom that Jesus died for their sins so that they could have eternal life?

3. How do we make relevant today the message of Jesus' death on the Cross to atone for our sins, so that we can be brought into right relationship with God?

Make It Happen

We can be thankful to God for sending His Son to die for our sins so that we could have the gift of salvation. Additionally, we can acknowledge the sacrifice of others on our behalf. For example, some of us have parents or grandparents who sacrificed material comfort so that we could have food on the table, clothes on our backs, or get an education, to name a few advantages. Or it could be a coworker who worked overtime so that you could have some time off. Ask God to help you recognize those who have sacrificed on your behalf and write them a note of thanks.

Follow the Spirit

What God wants me to do:

_____

_____

_____

_____

Remember Your Thoughts

Special insights I have learned:

_____

_____

_____

_____

More Light on the Text

Isaiah 53:4–6, 10–12

4 Surely he hath borne our griefs, and carried our sorrows: yet we did esteem him stricken, smitten of God, and afflicted.

The prophet states emphatically the certainty of his message—the sacrificial suffering and humiliation of the Redeemer. Although the prophecy points to the future, the prophet is so certain of its fulfillment that he states it in the past—completed action. As though to eliminate any doubt or skepticism of the certainty of his proclamation, the prophet applies the Hebrew word 'aken (**aw-KANE**), translated as "surely, truly," "certainly," "nevertheless." With 'aken, the writer appears to affirm what he has been saying about the Messiah as being "the truth, nothing but the truth," that essentially, "He has borne our griefs." "Surely" is also rendered "yet" (TLB, NLT), and means that, even though He was despised and rejected, yet He was the one who has taken our grief on Him and carried our sorrows.

The phrase "he hath borne our griefs, and carried our sorrows" has the idea of one lifting a heavy load or weight off someone's shoulders or head and placing it oneself—taking over another person's weight with the purpose of giving him or her relief. Here the Messiah Himself took on the grief and sorrow that were meant for the people of Israel, and indeed all humanity, as a consequence of their sin and defiance. The word "griefs" in Hebrew is *choliy* (**khol-EE**) and is translated as "sickness" (Deuteronomy 7:15; 28:61; 1 Kings 17:17); "disease" (Exodus 15:26; 2 Chronicles 16:12; 21:18; Ecclesiastes 6:2); and "anxiety, affliction." The NIV translates "griefs" as "infirmities." This refers to physical ailment and suffering rather than spiritual illness or sin. Matthew provided an affirmation and fulfillment of this prophecy when he quoted this passage following Christ's healing ministry (Matthew 8:16–17). The phrase "he hath borne our griefs" therefore means that the Savior took them up and hauled them away—that by His divine power and authority He, in effect, lifted them up and removed them by hauling them away from the redeemed. The word translated "borne" in Isaiah 53:4 is the Hebrew *naasaa'* or *nasa'* (**naw-SAW**), also meaning "to take away," and it is essentially the same word Matthew (8:17) translated in Greek from the word *lambano* (**lam-BAN-o**).

The prophet states that the Messiah, in addition to bearing or taking away our sickness and diseases, also "carried our sorrows" as well. The word "sorrows" comes from the Hebrew *mak'ob* (**mak-OBE**) and means "pains, grief, or sadness." The word is translated in the Old Testament as "sorrow" and "sorrows" (Ecclesiastes 1:18; Isaiah 65:14; Jeremiah 30:15; 45:3; Lamentations 1:12); "grief" (Job 16:6; Psalm 69:26); "pain" (Job 33:19; Jeremiah 15:18; 51:8). Whereas *choliy* speaks of physical sickness, the word here tends to refer to the emotional pain or grief of the mind, or a mental anguish; it also speaks of the anxiety of the soul and of a troubled mind. Both seem to be related—the latter is often as a result of the former.

The act of taking another person's punishment and sufferings on oneself so that person does not have to bear it is called "substitution." This is what the Messiah did for us; it is a demonstration of His love and compassion for us.

In spite of all that the Messiah has done for us, "yet we did esteem him stricken, smitten of God, and afflicted" (Isaiah 53:4). The idea is that the people whose punishment the Messiah substituted Himself for considered His suffering as a consequence for the sins and crimes He committed, not their own. The word "esteemed" comes from the Hebrew verb *chashab* (**khaw-SHAB**), meaning "considered, counted, thought, conceived of." They considered in their minds and believed that God was meting out His justice on the Messiah by striking, smiting, and afflicting Him, but it was not for His sins that God allowed Him to be stricken, smitten, and afflicted (He was sinless). Rather, the punishment was for our sins. He took our penalty on Himself; He took our sicknesses and diseases, our sorrows and pain.

5 But he was wounded for our transgressions, he was bruised for our iniquities: the chastisement of our peace was upon him; and with his stripes we are healed.

In an effort to refute this notion and correct the misconception about the Messiah's suffering, the prophet vigorously attempts to set things straight. Rather than suffering for

His sins, the prophet states that the Messiah's suffering was as a consequence of *our* sin. He uses two synonymous verbs, "wounded" and "bruised," to describe the type of affliction He suffered, and two synonymous nouns, "transgressions" and "iniquities," to depict the sins of the people. The word rendered "wounded" is the translation of the Hebrew verb *chalal* (**khaw-LAL**), which means "bore through, pierced" (NIV), "perforated, and wounded" (TLB, NLT, RSV). This speaks to the literal, painful and physical piercing of the body; it refers to the infliction of bodily wounds rather than mere mental anguish. Here Isaiah prophesied that there would be an actual piercing or penetrating of the body (with sharp instruments) that would result in death.

Apart from being pierced on account of our transgressions, the prophet states that He was also "bruised for our iniquities" (Isaiah 53:5). The word "bruised" used here is the Hebrew word *daka'* (**daw-KAW**), which means "beat to pieces, crushed, humbled, destroyed" (see verse 10; 3:15; Psalm 72:4; 94:5). This was fulfilled by the lacerations from the scourging the Messiah received at the hands of His executioners, the cuts by the thorns on the crown that was placed on His head, and other bodily suffering inflicted on Him. All this is on account of our "iniquities" (Romans 4:25; 2 Corinthians 5:21; Hebrews 9:28; 1 Peter 3:18).

The prophet further describes the suffering the Messiah endured as "chastisement." The phrase "the chastisement of our peace was upon him" means that He was chastised so that we might have peace; He took our beating in order to secure our peace with God. The word "chastisement" is from the Hebrew *cuwr* (**soor**), which has the idea of correction or discipline (or "punishment," NIV) meted out to children by their parents (Proverbs 22:15; 23:13) with the purpose of correcting them. It also refers to the need for kings to submit to God's authority (Job 22:18), and it refers to God's discipline and correction for those He loves (Job 5:17; Hosea 5:2). Here the Redeemer took on the discipline and punishment meant for us so that we can enjoy peace with our Creator. Jesus also took this on Himself.

Furthermore, through the Messiah's suffering and humiliation, "we are healed," the prophet declares (Isaiah 53:5). The prophet described this suffering as "stripes," which is derived from the Hebrew *chabuwraah* or *chabbuwrah* (**khab-boo-RAW**). It also means "bound," or "weal" (or the black-and-blue mark itself), "blueness, bruise, hurt, or wound." It refers to a mark, print, or swelling caused by a forceful infliction or blow with an object on the skin. The word translated "healed" is derived from the Hebrew *rapha'* (**raw-FAW**), which means "to cure, heal, repair or to make whole." The word is frequently used for both physical and spiritual healing or wellness.

6 All we like sheep have gone astray; we have turned every one to his own way; and the LORD hath laid on him the iniquity of us all.

In verse 6, the prophet confesses the people's sin. He symbolically compares and describes humankind's corrupt nature as "sheep" that "have gone astray." By using the pronoun "all" and the first person plural pronoun "we," the prophet includes the whole of humanity, including himself, as sinful people who have wandered away from their Creator. Paul says all humanity has sinned and come short of God's glory (Romans 3:23; cf. 5:12). By applying the simile "sheep" to humanity, the prophet

243

depicts the helplessness of all humanity like that of sheep.

It is not just true that "we like sheep have gone astray" and wandered from God; "we have (also) turned every one to his own way," the prophet emphasizes (Isaiah 53:6). The idea here is that each person pursues his or her own interests, makes his or her own plans, and selfishly seeks to satisfy his or her own interests without any regard, neither for God nor for others' good, interests, and well-being.

Instead of meting out the punishment due to us as a consequence of our sins and wayward behavior, "the Lord," the prophet declares, "...hath laid on him the iniquity of us all" (Isaiah 53:6). The words "hath laid" translate in Hebrew as *paga`* (**paw-GAH**), which means "to lay, fall upon, cause to entreat, or make intercession." It is also translated as "to cause to fall upon, to light upon" (Exodus 5:3; 1 Samuel 22:17, 18; 1 Kings 2:29, 31). The thought here is that the Lord caused the iniquities of all humanity to fall upon Him, and He bore them away. The Messiah took the place of all humans, and suffered on their behalf for their sins; He carried their burden of sin and interceded on their behalf. Although He was sinless, He suffered as though He were a sinner.

53:10 Yet it pleased the LORD to bruise him; he hath put him to grief: when thou shalt make his soul an offering for sin, he shall see his seed, he shall prolong his days, and the pleasure of the LORD shall prosper in his hand.

The Lord's purpose for allowing the Messiah to suffer and to be crucified for humankind is to bring about redemption of the whole creation in order that His eternal plan could be fulfilled on earth. Thus it pleased the Lord to bruise Him and put Him to grief. The phrase "it pleased the LORD to bruise him" does not mean that God would take (or that He took) pleasure in afflicting Him with pain and suffering. The statement does not imply that God believed His Son deserved to be punished—Jesus, being perfect, was sinless. Rather, it means that because of His love for His rebellious creation, God willingly would allow His beloved Son, the Messiah, to suffer and be subjected to grief and pain for the remission of the sins of the world—including those who bruised Him (see Christ's prayer on the Cross, Luke 23:34). The Messiah willingly paid the penalty for the sins of the world so that the world will have eternal life (John 3:16; 10:18).

The second part of Isaiah 53:10 appears to be spoken by the prophet to God. There are a number of differences of opinions as to who was speaking at this point—the prophet or the Lord (see various translations of this passage). However, the gist of the statement here is that as a result of the Messiah's sacrificial suffering and humiliation for the world's sin, He shall see a great multitude saved, He will enjoy eternal life, and the Father's pleasure and plan will be accomplished through Him.

11 He shall see of the travail of his soul, and shall be satisfied: by his knowledge shall my righteous servant justify many; for he shall bear their iniquities.

God the Father appears to be speaking here about His Son, the Messiah. The word "travail" comes from the Hebrew `amal (**aw-MAL**), which means "labor as in childbirth, toil, trouble, worry or pain." Here it refers to the suffering and pain the Messiah would undergo. The Messiah would be "satisfied" (content or happy), not because of the pain or the trouble He would undergo, but because of the outcome and benefit of the suffering. Through His trouble and affliction, multitudes will be saved, humanity will be restored to its Creator, and salvation will be extended to Israel and to the whole world because "he shall bear their iniquities." The Father proclaims, "By his knowledge shall my righteous servant justify many." That is, through the knowledge of God's plan of salvation and by becoming acquainted with the Messiah (God's righteous Servant), many will be justified. "Knowledge" here refers to having a relationship with the Messiah. Praying for His disciples, Jesus says, "And this is life eternal, that they might know thee the only true God, and Jesus Christ, whom thou hast sent" (John 17:3).

12 Therefore will I divide him a portion with the great, and he shall divide the spoil with the strong; because he hath poured out his soul unto death: and he was numbered with the transgressors; and he bare the sin of many, and made intercession for the transgressors

Because of what He accomplished for us in obedience to the will of His Father, the Messiah is rewarded. In this verse, the Lord declares that He would "divide him a portion with the great." That means God will restore the Messiah's honor and authority. The phrase "and he shall divide the spoil with the strong" speaks about the Servant as a triumphant King sharing the spoils (reward) with His warriors after a victory (Psalm 2:8; Isaiah 52:13). Beyond speaking of God's immediate faithfulness to Israel, this seems to refer to Christ's defeat of Satan and sharing of the blessings of victory with His followers—those who are joint heirs with Him (Colossians 2:15, Romans 8:17–18).

Say It Correctly

Colossians. kuh-LOSH-uhnz, -LAH-shuhnz, also -shee-uhnz.
Ecclesiastes. eh-klee-sih-AS-teez
Haggai. HAG-i.
Jehoiachin. juh-HOI-uh-kim, jih.
Zerubbabel. zee-RUB-uh-buhl, zuh-RUHB-uh-buhl.

Daily Bible Readings

M: Reconciled Through Christ
2 Corinthians 5:16–21

T: A Sacrifice for All Time
Hebrews 10:10–18

W: Offering and Sacrifice
Ephesians 4:25–5:2

T: Grace and Righteousness
Romans 5:12–17

F: Despised and Rejected
Isaiah 52:13–53:3

S: Oppressed and Afflicted
Isaiah 53:7–9

S: Wounded and Crushed
Isaiah 53:4–6, 10–12

Teaching Tips

February 6
Bible Study Guide 10

1. Words You Should Know

A. Disciples (Mark 8:27, 33–34) *mathetes* (Gk.)—Learners, pupils.

B. Prophets (v. 28) *prophetes* (Gk.)—Men filled with the Spirit of God, uttering divinely authorized revelations from God, focused usually on humanity's need to be saved.

C. The Scribes (v. 31) *grammateus* (Gk.)—Secretaries, recorders, men skilled in the Law.

2. Teacher Preparation

Unifying Principle—A Matter of Identity. For people of faith, Jesus' words contain truth about His identity and mission to bring in the kingdom and about what He requires of His followers.

A. Pray for your class.

B. Study the entire text (including the In Depth and More Light on the Text).

C. "Who Do You Say That I Am?"—Be prepared to share some important accomplishments of several important Black figures. Have your class guess the names of the figures.

3. Open the Lesson

A. Open with prayer, remembering the Aim for Change.

B. After prayer, share the bios and have the class guess who the figures are.

C. Link the discussion to the In Focus story.

D. Then engage your class in a discussion of Jesus' identity and what this means to all humanity.

4. Present the Scriptures

A. Have volunteers read the Focal Verses.

B. Explain the Focal Verses using The People, Places, and Times; Background; the At-A-Glance outline; In Depth; Search the Scriptures; and More Light on the Text.

5. Explore the Meaning

A. Emphasize the salient points in the Discuss the Meaning, Lesson in Our Society, and Make It Happen sections.

B. Connect these sections to the Aim for Change and the Key Verse.

6. Next Steps for Application

A. Summarize today's discussion and theme.

B. Close with prayer.

Worship Guide

For the Superintendent or Teacher
Theme: Jesus Is the Messiah
Theme Song: "Jesus, the Light of the World"
Devotional Reading: Luke 3:7–18
Prayer

Jesus Is the Messiah

Bible Background • MARK 8:27–9:1
Printed Text • MARK 8:27–9:1 | Devotional Reading • LUKE 3:7–18

———————— Aim for Change ————————

By the end of the lesson, we will: EXPLAIN who Jesus really is; FEEL confident in Jesus' identity as the Messiah; and MAKE a personal profession of faith.

———— In Focus ————

In the fall of 1935, theologian, preacher, writer, and mystic Howard Thurman traveled on a pilgrimage of friendship with American students to India, Burma (Myanmar), and Ceylon (the Republic of Sri Lanka). During his visit to Ceylon and after lecturing at the campus, Thurman had the opportunity to speak with the principal of the Law College, University of Colombo. The principal, a Hindu, told Thurman he did not understand how Thurman, an African American, could be a Christian, since it was Christians who trafficked in the slavery of Africans. Even the famous Christian hymn writer John Newton, he noted, made his money from the sale of slaves to the New World.

The man went on to observe that Thurman lived in a Christian nation in which Blacks were segregated, lynched, and burned. In conclusion, he told Thurman, "I do not wish to seem rude to you. But, sir, I think you are a traitor to all the darker peoples of the earth. I am wondering what you, an intelligent man, can say in defense of your position."

Thurman could be a follower of Jesus Christ because of who Jesus is. In this week's lesson, we will explore the true identity of Jesus.

FEB 6th

———————— Keep in Mind ————————

"And he saith unto them, But whom say ye that I am? And Peter answereth and saith unto him, Thou art the Christ" (Mark 8:29).

"And he saith unto them, But whom say ye that I am? And Peter answereth and saith unto him, Thou art the Christ" (Mark 8:29).

248

Focal Verses

KJV **Mark 8:27** And Jesus went out, and his disciples, into the towns of Caesarea Philippi: and by the way he asked his disciples, saying unto them, Whom do men say that I am?

28 And they answered, John the Baptist: but some say, Elias; and others, One of the prophets.

29 And he saith unto them, But whom say ye that I am? And Peter answereth and saith unto him, Thou art the Christ.

30 And he charged them that they should tell no man of him.

31 And he began to teach them, that the Son of man must suffer many things, and be rejected of the elders, and of the chief priests, and scribes, and be killed, and after three days rise again.

32 And he spake that saying openly. And Peter took him, and began to rebuke him.

33 But when he had turned about and looked on his disciples, he rebuked Peter, saying, Get thee behind me, Satan: for thou savourest not the things that be of God, but the things that be of men.

34 And when he had called the people unto him with his disciples also, he said unto them, Whosoever will come after me, let him deny himself, and take up his cross, and follow me.

35 For whosoever will save his life shall lose it; but whosoever shall lose his life for my sake and the gospel's, the same shall save it.

36 For what shall it profit a man, if he shall gain the whole world, and lose his own soul?

37 Or what shall a man give in exchange for his soul?

38 Whosoever therefore shall be ashamed of me and of my words in this adulterous and sinful generation; of him also shall the Son of man be ashamed, when he cometh in the glory of his Father with the holy angels.

9:1 And he said unto them, Verily I say unto you, That there be some of them that stand here, which shall not taste of death, till they have seen the kingdom of God come with power.

NLT **Mark 8:27** Jesus and his disciples left Galilee and went up to the villages near Caesarea Philippi. As they were walking along, he asked them, "Who do people say I am?"

28 "Well," they replied, "some say John the Baptist, some say Elijah, and others say you are one of the other prophets."

29 Then he asked them, "But who do you say I am?" Peter replied, "You are the Messiah."

30 But Jesus warned them not to tell anyone about him.

31 Then Jesus began to tell them that the Son of Man must suffer many terrible things and be rejected by the elders, the leading priests, and the teachers of religious law. He would be killed, but three days later he would rise from the dead.

32 As he talked about this openly with his disciples, Peter took him aside and began to reprimand him for saying such things.

33 Jesus turned around and looked at his disciples, then reprimanded Peter. "Get away from me, Satan!" he said. "You are seeing things merely from a human point of view, not from God's."

34 Then, calling the crowd to join his disciples, he said, "If any of you wants to be my follower, you must turn from your selfish ways, take up your cross, and follow me.

35 If you try to hang on to your life, you will lose it. But if you give up your life for my sake and for the sake of the Good News, you will save it.

36 And what do you benefit if you gain the whole world but lose your own soul?

37 Is anything worth more than your soul?

38 If anyone is ashamed of me and my message in these adulterous and sinful days, the Son of Man will be ashamed of that person when he returns in the glory of his Father with the holy angels."

9:1 Jesus went on to say, "I tell you the truth, some standing here right now will not die before they see the Kingdom of God arrive in great power!"

The People, Places, and Times

Caesarea Philippi. It is an area also known as Caesarea Paneas, located at the southwestern foot of Mt. Hermon and strategically located between Syria and Palestine. Prior to the Hellenistic period, the name of the site is unknown. However, the Seleucid ruler Antiochus the Great called it Panion (later Paneas) in recognition of a cave and spring in the area dedicated to the nature god, Pan. Earlier cultic use in this region may be evident in the names of sites bearing the personal names of the Canaanite god, Baal, such as Baal-gad (Joshua 11:17; 12:7; 13:5) and Baal-hermon (Judges 3:3; 1 Chronicles 5:23).

Some scholars have suggested that the Transfiguration, which follows Peter's confession in each Gospel account (Matthew 17:1–8; Mark 9:2–9; Luke 9:28–36), took place in Caesarea Philippi.

Elias or Elijah. It is a personal name meaning "Yahweh is my God." He was a ninth century B.C. prophet and sojourner of Gilead in the northern kingdom (see 1 Kings 17–19, 21; and 2 Kings 1–2). Elijah is portrayed as in constant conflict with the royal house of Israel over faithfulness to Yahweh and the worship of other gods, particularly Baal. His most famous skirmish was the contest between the prophets of Yahweh and the prophets of Baal and Asherah on Mount Carmel, resulting in Yahweh being declared the one true God and Baal's prophets being executed. Elijah was carried away to heaven in a whirlwind after commissioning Elisha as his successor.

Peter. He is also known as Simon Peter, Simon, and Cephas. His personal name means "rock." Peter was the most prominent of the 12 disciples of Jesus. Peter was the son of Jona (or John) and brother of Andrew. Both he and his brother were fishermen.

Jesus renamed him Peter (Mark 3:14–16) even though his name was Simon. Before being called by Jesus, Peter and Andrew were drawn to the teachings of John the Baptist.

Peter was with Jesus at His arrest. Although he denied Jesus, Jesus later restored his place among the disciples. Peter was later an early church leader in Jerusalem and a source of tradition about Jesus for the apostle Paul.

Background

Jesus and the disciples are headed southward to Jerusalem where Jesus as the Son of man will give His life for the sins of the world. Their journey begins at the northernmost point in Caesarea Philippi, followed by other stops until they reach their final destination. Along the way, Jesus makes three passion predictions, but the disciples misunderstand what Jesus is telling them. Jesus has to further instruct them in the way of discipleship by word and deed.

At-A-Glance

1. Jesus Asks Peter an Important Question (Mark 8:27–30)

2. Jesus Foretells His Death and Resurrection (vv. 31–38)

3. Jesus Emphasizes the Imminence of the Kingdom of God (9:1)

In Depth

1. Jesus Asks Peter an Important Question (Mark 8:27–30)

The disciples, listening as Jesus speaks to them while they travel toward Caesarea Philippi, have known for some time the true identity of Jesus and His ministry: He is the Son of God, meant to bring glad tidings of salvation to many (Mark 1:1). However, it is not until Mark 8 that we read about the disciples, based on Peter's confession, recognizing who Jesus is. Initially, the disciples offered that some said Jesus was John the Baptist. King Herod, who had ordered John the Baptist beheaded, believed that Jesus was John raised from the dead (Mark 6:14). However, others said that Jesus was Elijah or a prophet like the prophets of old (v. 15). Elijah was expected to precede Christ's arrival. Therefore, the speculation by some that Jesus was Elijah demonstrated that they did not believe Jesus was the Christ.

Finally, Peter correctly answers, "Thou art the Christ," when Jesus asks the disciples who they thought He was (Mark 8:29). The title "Christ," from the Greek word for the Hebrew term "Messiah" or "anointed one," was understood by the Jews as the anointed king of the House of David who would come and deliver Israel from Roman hegemony and restore Israel to a place of world prominence. Peter likely understood Jesus as "the Christ" in this manner. The disciples frequently misunderstood Jesus' mission until after His death and resurrection.

2. Jesus Foretells His Death and Resurrection (vv. 31–38)

Jesus tried to prepare His disciples for His death and resurrection by telling them on three occasions that He was going to suffer and be put to death, but would be resurrected three days after His death (Mark 8:31; 9:31; 10:33–34). The disciples misunderstand His teaching, as evidenced by Peter's reaction of rebuking Jesus (8:32). They would misunderstand Jesus two more times.

Peter's reaction has been interpreted in several ways: he had an expectation of acquiring glory and renown through his relationship with Jesus the Christ; he had no conception of what the title "Christ" meant and was rebuking Jesus out of his love for Him; he thought he understood better than Jesus whom the Christ was to be. The Greek word for "rebuke" is also "to sternly order." Perhaps Peter was sternly ordering Jesus not to speak discouraging words to the disciples and the crowds that had assembled so as not to turn them away from following Jesus.

Jesus sternly responds by specifically identifying Peter with Satan. "Satan" in the Old Testament was not a personal name identified with an evil one, but rather meant an "adversary" or "accuser." In the New Testament, Satan is identified as those who oppose Jesus. Peter responds according to his human understanding of Jesus' teachings. He did not understand that Jesus' suffering was prophesied in Isaiah 53.

Jesus gathers the disciples along with the crowd to teach them what it really means to follow Christ, who will suffer and die. In Mark 8:34, He states in part that following Christ means taking up their crosses. The cross was a brutal means of capital punishment used by the Romans to set an example for those whom they believed undermined their power and authority. Jesus is letting them know that their end could lead to the Cross just as Jesus' would.

3. Jesus Emphasizes the Imminence of the Kingdom of God (9:1)

In the gospel of Mark, Jesus began His ministry in Galilee by preaching the imminence of the kingdom of God and encouraging His hearers to repent and believe in the Gospel (Mark 1:14–15; see also Matthew 4:23; 9:35; Luke 4:43; 8:1). The kingdom of God or kingdom of heaven in the New Testament is God's kingly rule or sovereignty. Jesus told the crowd that some of the hearers would be alive when God's kingdom became manifest. Jesus taught that, in a sense, the kingdom of God had come in His time, as evidenced by Jesus' ability to cast out the demons (Luke 11:20). The Lord's Prayer is a model of God's reign.

Search the Scriptures

1. Whom did the disciples say that Jesus was (Mark 8:28)?

2. What did Jesus begin to tell the disciples (v. 31)?

Discuss the Meaning

1. Many first century Jews expected God to send the Messiah to deliver them from their enemies. They had been under the hegemony (domination, control) of the Egyptians, Assyrians, Babylonians, Persians, Greeks, and now the Romans. The disciples expected Jesus to be the Messiah in this way. Why do you think the disciples misunderstood who the Messiah was to be?

2. Peter, along with his brother, Andrew, was the first disciple called by Jesus to follow Him. Yet his relationship with Jesus seemed rocky (pun intended). Why do you believe that Peter took Jesus aside and rebuked Him for saying that He must suffer and be rejected by the religious leaders and eventually be killed?

Lesson in Our Society

1. In today's society, many people who grew up in the church have turned their backs on "organized religion." There are others who maintain that they believe in Jesus, but refuse to identify themselves as "Christians." In both groups, several claim to believe in the principle teachings of Jesus. Even Muslims and Hindus believe that Jesus was a prophet of God or a man to be admired. Mohandas K. Gandhi, the nonviolent leader of Indian independence, was drawn to the nonviolent teachings of Jesus' Sermon on the Mount.

2. Is it enough to say that Jesus was a good man, or a prophet, or a wise teacher to be admired for His teachings and ministry? Why or why not?

Make It Happen

Spend some time this week reflecting on what it means to be a follower of Jesus the Christ. Reread Mark 8:34–38; then write down some of the ways you believe that Jesus is leading you to live according to how He would have you live. Write down what you believe are some of your challenges to submitting to His will. Pray for the strength to be a faithful follower of Jesus.

Follow the Spirit

What God wants me to do:

_____

_____

_____

_____

Remember Your Thoughts

Special insights I have learned:

_____

_____

_____

_____

More Light on the Text

Mark 8:27–9:1

27 And Jesus went out, and his disciples, into the towns of Caesarea Philippi: and by the way he asked his disciples, saying unto them, Whom do men say that I am?

As He and His disciples approach Caesarea Philippi, along the way, Jesus asks His disciples what people have been speculating about Him—His identity. What was the basis for the question? There are a few possible reasons to note here. One reason was that even though He was human, Jesus knew the hearts of all humankind; He was able to discern their inner thoughts. Nothing is hidden from Him. He also must have heard people talking about Him as He went about His work. People had been speculating about Him because of the extraordinary and miraculous works He has been doing in the region. For example, astonished by what Jesus had been doing, King Herod stated, "This is John the Baptist; he is risen from the dead, and therefore these powers are at work in him" (Mark 6:14; Matthew 14:2–3; Luke 9:7–9).

Another reason was probably that Jesus wanted to use the question to start an important discussion and revelation to His disciples of who He really was and His true mission. This will unfold further as we study this passage. Until then, the "disciples" (Gk. *mathetes*, **math-ay-TES**), meaning the "pupils,"

were still oblivious of the true identity and nature of their Master.

Jesus also asked His disciples the question, not because He was unaware of people's speculations about Him, but He wanted to give them an opportunity to express and confess their faith. Through such confession, Jesus would strengthen the disciples and reveal more of Himself to them.

28 And they answered, John the Baptist: but some say, Elias; and others, One of the prophets.

The disciples responded with various answers, repeating the same commonly held views of the people. They told Him that people identified Him with different people. Some thought that He was "John the Baptist," while others said that He was "Elias (Elijah)." Some even said that He was Jeremiah (Matthew 16:14). Yet others, the disciples stated, had speculated that He was "One of the prophets" (Mark 8:28). This assumption was based on the doctrine of some ancient sects, such as the Pharisees. The teaching of and belief in the reincarnation of the soul was common in the ancient Near East, as it is in different cultures and religions of the world today.

29 And he saith unto them, But whom say ye that I am? And Peter answereth and saith unto him, Thou art the Christ. 30 And he charged them that they should tell no man of him.

After they had stated what others thought about Him and His identity, Christ then directly asked the disciples, "But who do you say that I am?" (8:29, NKJV) Unhesitatingly and emphatically Peter declared, "Thou art the Christ." In his own account of the event Matthew adds, "the Son of the Living God" (Matthew 16:16). The word "Christ" comes from the Greek *Christos* (**khris-TOS**), which means "the anointed one" or "the Messiah" in Hebrew—"the promised One." According to Matthew's account of the event, Jesus commended Peter's answer, saying, "Blessed are you, Simon Bar-Jonah, for flesh and blood has not revealed this to you, but My Father who is in heaven" (Matthew 16:17–18, NKJV). This confession is essential in the transformation of people's lives and in developing a personal relationship with the Messiah. This confession, the acknowledgement that Jesus is the Christ, is the core tenet of the Christian belief and practice. Each individual has to answer Jesus' question, "But what about you?" (Mark 8:29, NIV).

31 And he began to teach them, that the Son of man must suffer many things, and be rejected of the elders, and of the chief priests, and scribes, and be killed, and after three days rise again.

Following Peter's confession, Jesus began to teach the disciples about His mission, which involved suffering, rejection, death, and resurrection. It is uncertain when Jesus started His teaching, probably immediately following the confession. It served as the springboard on which Jesus launched His teaching about the purpose of His earthly advent to His disciples and other followers. Up to this point, Jesus had been teaching His disciples and the public through parables. He had been showing who He was, His power, and His authority through miraculous works, but His true identity was veiled to the people. With this confession, Jesus began to unveil His true nature and the nature of His mission on earth. He began to "teach," which in Greek is *didasko* (**did-AS-ko**), meaning "to teach" or "to learn." It has the idea of a long process of instruction. That is, from that time on, Jesus began to explain to His disciples in plain language and in detail the purpose of His earthly mission and God's plan (Matthew 16:21).

The teaching here is the first of the three predictions according to Mark about the death of Christ (8:31; 9:31; 10:33–34). In Mark 8, Jesus began to prepare the disciples' minds for His future plight. With this confession, it seemed the right time for Him to reveal His real identity—the Messiah.

32 And he spake that saying openly. And Peter took him, and began to rebuke him.

The phrase "he spake that saying openly," referring to Jesus' teaching to His disciples, means that He spoke "boldly, frankly, plainly, and bluntly." He was not mincing words. No longer was He speaking in parables; He informed them exactly what was to take place. This was too much for the impulsive Peter to handle. It was unimaginable. How could the Messiah—the one to liberate His people—suffer such fate? "Peter took [Jesus], and began to rebuke him." The picture here is of an immediate and impulsive action. Here Peter probably interrupted Him and called Him aside, or took Him by the hand away from the other disciples and talked with Him. The word "rebuke" in Greek is *epitimao* (**ep-ee-tee-MAH-o**), meaning to "admonish," "forbid" or to "charge." Peter was ignorant of God's plan. So as a friend would, Peter admonished and entreated Jesus not to wish Himself such a disgraceful suffering. This rebuke amounts to a total rejection of the divine mandate for Christ. It is therefore no wonder that Jesus attributed Peter's attitude to Satan.

33 But when he had turned about and looked on his disciples, he rebuked Peter, saying, Get thee behind me, Satan: for thou savourest not the things that be of God, but the things that be of men.

Following Peter's admonition, Jesus' rejoinder was immediate and fierce: "he rebuked Peter" and called him "Satan," ordering him to go behind Him. This command suggests rejection, since standing alongside or in front would indicate contrasting attitudes such as companionship or respect. The word "Satan" means "an adversary" or "devil," "one who always opposes the divine plan." Although Jesus' reference of Peter as Satan appears to convey an angry outburst and severe rebuke, there is no proof that Jesus meant to apply this term to Peter, or that He was cursing Peter or calling him names. Rather, Jesus viewed Peter's sentiments as an opposition to divine design for Him. Therefore, in order to put an immediate stop to the discussion and not to give Satan any ground, Jesus applied the strongest terms as He had done previously, during His temptation (Matthew 4:10). Although Peter was showing a genuine concern for his Master, he was unknowingly playing into the hands of Christ's archenemy—the devil (cf. Matthew 4:8–10).

34 And when he had called the people unto him with his disciples also, he said unto them, Whosoever will come after me, let him deny himself, and take up his cross, and follow me.

Shortly after the brief dialogue with Peter, and for the first time predicting His death and resurrection, Jesus began to lay down the requirements for discipleship. Gathering people to join His disciples as He spoke to them, Jesus informed them that to follow Him would be costly. He taught, "Whosoever will come after me, let him deny himself, and take up his cross and follow me."

At this time many people were beginning to follow Him, probably hoping for some material gain, or personal recognition. By now Jesus was becoming quite popular because of His teachings and miraculous works (see John 6:22–27).

35 For whosoever will save his life shall lose it; but whosoever shall lose his life for my sake and the gospel's, the same shall save it.

Verse 35 may seem incomprehensible. How can you save your life by losing it or lose your life by saving it? This makes sense only in the realm of the divine economy. Here Jesus applies "life" in two senses: "temporal, earthly, or physical life" and "permanent or eternal life." Jesus is stating a fundamental, spiritual truth. That is, for one to have "eternal life" and enjoy life ever after, one must be willing to let go of the comforts and security of this earthly life. Being a disciple of Christ may require the loss of physical life, a loss that is quite insignificant when compared with gaining eternal life. The loss of physical life means a gain of spiritual life. Conversely, holding tight to earthly comforts and pleasures is tantamount to losing spiritual or eternal life. You will either hold to self and lose Christ or lose self and gain Christ—eternal life.

The above saying is also based on common sense, as Joel Marcus writes, as dispensed today by people and in many cultures: "[This kind of perspective]...fills the Old Testament book of Proverbs. In the seventh century B.C., the Greek lyric poet Tyrtaeus wrote, 'The man who risks his life in battle has the best chance of saving it; the one who flees to save it is the most likely to lose it.' In other words, what is most important in the heat of battle is not to lose your head (either figuratively or literally)" (860).

In the same way, Jesus says when we attempt to save our lives by avoiding persecution or holding on to worldly passions, pleasures and desires, we will eventually lose the more important life—our soul. As we shall see in the next two verses, nothing can be exchanged for the soul; nothing can replace the preservation of the soul in God's kingdom.

36 For what shall it profit a man, if he shall gain the whole world, and lose his own soul? 37 Or what shall a man give in exchange for his soul?

Employing a commercial analogy, Jesus asks a rhetorical question to stress His point. In the previous verses, Jesus points out how foolhardy it is for anyone to hold on to this temporal life because this will cause the person to lose his or her soul. In other words, Jesus says that saving one's soul is more important than gaining all the earthly comforts, pleasures, and achievements. Jesus knew this danger; He had experienced the same temptation from Satan (Matthew 4:1–10). To "gain the whole world" is a rejection of Christ; it means being ashamed of Christ, and this results in losing one's soul (v. 36). How can this possibly be worthwhile?

38 Whosoever therefore shall be ashamed of me and of my words in this adulterous and sinful generation; of him also shall the Son of man be ashamed, when he cometh in the glory of his Father with the holy angels.

Earlier, in verse 34, Jesus stated that we need to deny self, take up our crosses, and follow Him. According to human perspective, suffering (cross-bearing) is a shameful thing. Jesus states that anyone who is ashamed to identify with Him—anyone

who is more anxious about fitting into this worldly mold—is part of an "adulterous and sinful generation" and is ashamed of Him. Therefore, Christ will be ashamed of the person—that means the person will have no portion in His kingdom when He returns in glory.

9:1 And he said unto them, Verily I say unto you, That there be some of them that stand here, which shall not taste of death, till they have seen the kingdom of God come with power.

Jesus then assured the audience that there were some people in their midst who would not taste death (that is, die) until they see the kingdom of God come in power. This event appeared to be imminent, and therefore doesn't seem to refer to the final return of Christ and His kingdom. Rather, it appears that He was referring to an immediate event that was about to take place—the Transfiguration (9:2 ff.). He was probably referring to Peter, James, and John, who accompanied Him to the mountain where they witnessed a glimpse of the Resurrection and the return of the kingdom of God. This event prefigures the overpowering glory of Christ in His return (Daniel 7:13 ff.; Matthew 16:28; Mark 13:26–27).

Different people have proposed different interpretations of this prediction. These include what Jesus was referring to: (1) His transfiguration (9:2–12; Matthew 17:1–8); (2) His resurrection; (3) the coming of the Holy Spirit at the Pentecost; (4) the spread of the kingdom through the preaching of the early church; (5) the destruction of the temple and Jerusalem in A.D. 70; and (6) the Second Coming and final establishment of His kingdom. And as also indicated above, three of the disciples were eyewitnesses of the event and saw what Jesus will be like when He comes in power and glory of His kingdom. This viewpoint was also supported by Peter (2 Peter 1:16–18).

Say It Correctly

Antiochus. an-TI-uh-kuhs.
Baal. BAY-uhl.
Bethsaida. beth-SAY-uh-duh.
Caesarea Philippi. ses'-uh-ree'-uh fih-LIP-i, ses'uh-REE-uh fuh-LIP-i.
Cephas. SEE-phus.
Elijah. ih-LI –juh.
Yahweh. YAH-weh, -way.

Daily Bible Readings

M: The Messiah Promised
Jeremiah 33:14–18

T: The Messiah Expected
Luke 3:7–18

W: The Messiah Sought
Matthew 2:1–6

T: The Messiah, Are You the One?
Luke 22:66–70

F: The Messiah Disclosed
John 4:16–26

S: The Messiah Found
John 1:35–42

S: You Are the Messiah!
Mark 8:27–9:1

Notes

_____

_____

_____

_____

Teaching Tips

February 13
Bible Study Guide 11

1. Words You Should Know
A. Transfigured (Mark 9:2) *metemorfoóthee* from *metamorphoo* (Gk.)—Changed or transformed.

B. Charged (v. 9) *diastellomai* (Gk.)—Admonished, ordered, commanded.

2. Teacher Preparation
Unifying Principle—Follow the Leader. A theophany (God's voice in the cloud) dramatically identified Jesus as God's Chosen One, the One to whom they should listen.

A. Pray for your class.

B. Prayerfully study the Daily Bible Readings, Focal Verses, and the surrounding sections.

C. Be prepared to discuss Jesus' mission on earth and His role as a servant-leader.

3. Open the Lesson
A. Open with prayer, including the Aim for Change.

B. After prayer, tell why God sent His only Son, Jesus, into the world to die for humanity.

C. Discuss how Adam and Eve's disobedience in the Garden of Eden (Genesis 3) brought sin to all humanity.

D. Compare and contrast the leader in the In Focus story with Jesus as a servant-leader.

4. Present the Scriptures
A. Have volunteers read the Focal Verses.

B. Explain the Focal Verses using The People, Places, and Times; Background; the At-A-Glance outline; In Depth; Search the Scriptures; and More Light on the Text.

5. Explore the Meaning
A. Emphasize the salient points in the Discuss the Meaning, Lesson in Our Society, and Make It Happen sections.

B. Connect these sections with the Aim for Change and the Key Verse.

6. Next Steps for Application
A. Ask the question: "How can we worship Jesus as God's Son?"

B. Ask students to write their answers in the Follow the Spirit and Remember Your Thoughts sections.

C. Have a "Call to Discipleship" and then end with prayer.

Worship Guide
For the Superintendent or Teacher
Theme: This Is My Beloved
Theme Song: "Oh, It Is Jesus"
Devotional Reading: Malachi 4:1–5
Prayer

This Is My Beloved

Bible Background • MARK 9:2–13
Printed Text • MARK 9:2–13 | Devotional Reading • MALACHI 4:1–5

——————— Aim for Change ———————

By the end of the lesson, we will: RECALL the story of Jesus' transfiguration; DISCERN that Jesus is truly the Son of God; and EXPLAIN how we can worship Jesus as God's Son.

———————  In Focus ———————

Debra had just interviewed for the internship of her life! The stipend was wonderful, the company was up-and-coming, and the work environment was extraordinary. But the executive director seemed shifty. When Debra told him that she was not yet fully licensed to provide services, he still offered her a contract for a job. No matter how many times she redirected him, he tried to assure her that she could complete her internship as a paid employee. Debra knew the laws for licensing and that he was incorrect, but she considered the position anyway. With that job she could be licensed in half the time it would take with a regular internship, and her bills would be paid. Her excitement wore off when she got home and prayed, because she knew she had to turn it down. She decided that she could not work for such a deceptive person. If the leader of the company dealt underhandedly, Debra hated to imagine how he trained his employees. She prayed, and God gave her strength to decline the job offer.

Today's lesson tells us that God chose Jesus as our Leader and said, "This is my beloved Son: hear him." God knew that as Leader, Jesus would always obey the Father.

FEB 13th

——————— Keep in Mind ———————

"And there was a cloud that overshadowed them: and a voice came out of the cloud, saying, This is my beloved Son: hear him" (Mark 9:7).

"And there was a cloud that overshadowed them: and a voice came out of the cloud, saying, This is my beloved Son: hear him" (Mark 9:7).

Focal Verses

KJV Mark 9:2 And after six days Jesus taketh with him Peter, and James, and John, and leadeth them up into an high mountain apart by themselves: and he was transfigured before them.

3 And his raiment became shining, exceeding white as snow; so as no fuller on earth can white them.

4 And there appeared unto them Elias with Moses: and they were talking with Jesus.

5 And Peter answered and said to Jesus, Master, it is good for us to be here: and let us make three tabernacles; one for thee, and one for Moses, and one for Elias.

6 For he wist not what to say; for they were sore afraid.

7 And there was a cloud that overshadowed them: and a voice came out of the cloud, saying, This is my beloved Son: hear him.

8 And suddenly, when they had looked round about, they saw no man any more, save Jesus only with themselves.

9 And as they came down from the mountain, he charged them that they should tell no man what things they had seen, till the Son of man were risen from the dead.

10 And they kept that saying with themselves, questioning one with another what the rising from the dead should mean.

11 And they asked him, saying, Why say the scribes that Elias must first come?

12 And he answered and told them, Elias verily cometh first, and restoreth all things; and how it is written of the Son of man, that he must suffer many things, and be set at nought.

13 But I say unto you, That Elias is indeed come, and they have done unto him whatsoever they listed, as it is written of him.

NLT Mark 9:2 Six days later Jesus took Peter, James, and John, and led them up a high mountain to be alone. As the men watched, Jesus' appearance was transformed,

3 and his clothes became dazzling white, far whiter than any earthly bleach could ever make them.

4 Then Elijah and Moses appeared and began talking with Jesus.

5 Peter exclaimed, "Rabbi, it's wonderful for us to be here! Let's make three shelters as memorials—one for you, one for Moses, and one for Elijah."

6 He said this because he didn't really know what else to say, for they were all terrified.

7 Then a cloud overshadowed them, and a voice from the cloud said, "This is my dearly loved Son. Listen to him."

8 Suddenly, when they looked around, Moses and Elijah were gone, and they saw only Jesus with them.

9 As they went back down the mountain, he told them not to tell anyone what they had seen until the Son of Man had risen from the dead.

10 So they kept it to themselves, but they often asked each other what he meant by "rising from the dead."

11 Then they asked him, "Why do the teachers of religious law insist that Elijah must return before the Messiah comes?"

12 Jesus responded, "Elijah is indeed coming first to get everything ready. Yet why do the Scriptures say that the Son of Man must suffer greatly and be treated with utter contempt?

13 But I tell you, Elijah has already come, and they chose to abuse him, just as the Scriptures predicted."

The People, Places, and Times

A High Mountain. The name and location of the mountain where Jesus was transfigured remains a mystery. The only description Mark offered about the mountain was that it was "high" and "apart" (Mark 9:2). Scholars have proposed three mountains that could have been the place where the Lord was transformed. Mount Tabor is a popular suggestion, but has been discounted because it is not that high and it is situated in a densely populated area. It is reported that the town of Nain is on top of it. Because the "high mountain" is traditionally associated with the prophets Moses and Elijah (who were present during Christ's transfiguration), others suggest Mount Sinai. Though Mount Sinai is highly elevated, it is remote and very far from where Jesus and the disciples were in Mark 8. The best choice is Mount Hebron. It is the highest of the three mountains at an elevation of 9,230 feet, and it is close to Caesarea Philippi, where Peter had just declared Jesus as the Christ.

Peter, James, and John. Peter, James, and John were three of 12 disciples who seemed to be closer to the Lord. Not only did Peter, James, and John get to witness Jesus' transformation, but Jesus also allowed them into the room where He raised Jairus's daughter, and they were called to keep watch while He prayed at the Garden of Gethsemane. Moreover, their names are recorded first in the listing of disciples (see Matthew 10:2; Mark 3:16–17; Luke 6:14, where Andrew was included; and Acts 1:13).

Background

Just before our lesson text, Peter rightly declared Jesus as the Messiah and then was rebuked for discounting Jesus' declaration of how the messianic mission would be accomplished (Mark 8:29–30).

Jesus knew that the cost of discipleship was so great that not everyone would want to pay it, which is why He made a specific appeal, "Whosoever will" (8:34). In Mark 9:1, the verse that precedes our lesson text, Jesus told His disciples, "Verily I say unto you, That there be some of them that stand here, which shall not taste of death, till they have seen the kingdom of God come with power."

It leaves one to wonder if this is how Peter, James, and John were selected from among the Twelve to witness Jesus' transformation. Did the threesome willingly pay the costs of discipleship—did they consistently deny themselves, take up their crosses, and follow Christ? To witness something as great as the Transfiguration, the answer would have to be a resounding "yes!"

At-A-Glance

1. Led by Jesus (Mark 9:2–4)

2. Live with Jesus (vv. 5–6)

3. Listen to Jesus (vv. 7–8)

4. Leave with Jesus (vv. 9–13)

In Depth

1. Led by Jesus (Mark 9:2–4)

Six days after Jesus met with the Twelve and told them about the coming kingdom, He took three of them—Peter, James, and John—with Him to a very high mountain. There, He was transfigured before them. The word "transfigure" means "to alter the outward appearance of, or to transform." The text records that Jesus' garment became so white that its cleanliness could not have been humanly achieved. Even if the disciples had tried to discount what they witnessed as a mere occurrence, they could not deny that they saw Elijah and Moses talking to Jesus. Scholars assert that Jesus' transfiguration was an example of the coming kingdom that He'd just predicted to the disciples.

2. Live with Jesus (vv. 5–6)

The three disciples were so astounded that they counted it as a privilege to witness Jesus' transfiguration. Peter did not want to leave and thought of a way to make his stay permanent. He asked Jesus if they could build three tabernacles (shelters). Peter did not ask for the tabernacles for himself, John, and James. He suggested that there should be dwellings for Jesus, Elijah, and Moses. Peter was known for speaking without thinking, and it was obvious that his proposal was not well thought out. As soon as his mouth stopped moving, his mind processed what he had said. Then, the Scripture reported that he did not know what else to say.

3. Listen to Jesus (vv. 7–8)

Peter had been silenced, and the next voice that was heard came from an overshadowing cloud. As if it were an introduction, the voice of God presented Christ to the disciples as His beloved Son, the Chosen One to whom they should listen. When the disciples looked again, Moses and Elijah were gone, and only Jesus was left with them.

4. Leave with Jesus (vv. 9–13)

As they departed from the mountain, the disciples listened as Jesus instructed them. He asked them to keep the Transfiguration to themselves until after He had risen from the dead. The disciples did not understand what "rising from the dead" meant and questioned each other, until they were bold enough to

question Jesus. They asked Him about the teaching that Elijah should come first (see Malachi 4:5, cf. Luke 1:17). Figuratively, the teaching was about John the Baptist, who was a forerunner of Jesus in a manner that was like Elijah.

Search the Scriptures

1. How many days had passed before Jesus went up to a very high mountain (Mark 9:2)?
2. Whom did Jesus take with Him (v. 2)?
3. What happened to Jesus while He was on the mountain (vv. 2–3)?
4. With whom was He talking (v. 4)?
5. What idea did Peter propose (v. 5)?
6. What did the voice from the cloud say to the disciples (v. 7)?

Discuss the Meaning

1. Why did Jesus only take Peter, James, and John?
2. Why were the disciples so afraid that they could not speak after Peter's proposal?
3. Why did Jesus command the disciples not to tell anyone about the Transfiguration?

Lesson in Our Society

Is it true that in today's society we have become so comfortable in our relationships with Jesus that we do not revere Him? Perhaps we are so accustomed to walking with Him that we seek more highly spiritual experiences elsewhere (such as conference-hopping and church-hopping). Is that what happened with the disciples? Is that why Jesus only took three of them? Is that why Peter wanted to stay? And is that why God commanded them to do something as basic as listen to Jesus? We must conclude by asking ourselves, "Who are *we* listening to?" If it is anyone other than our Leader, Jesus, then we are in spiritual trouble.

263

Make It Happen

Assess your relationship with Jesus. Remember how excited you were when you first believed? Do you remember how much time you spent reading His Word, talking to Him, and listening to Him? It shouldn't take a transfiguration experience to excite us enough to never want to leave the Lord's presence. This week, pray that you will be transfigured and transformed so that God's Word will come to pass in your life.

Follow the Spirit

What God wants me to do:

_____

_____

_____

_____

Remember Your Thoughts

Special insights I have learned:

_____

_____

_____

_____

More Light on the Text

Mark 9:2–13

2 And after six days Jesus taketh with him Peter, and James, and John, and leadeth them up into an high mountain apart by themselves: and he was transfigured before them.

The first verse of this chapter contains Jesus' assertion that there were "some" presently standing in the audience "who will not taste death till they see the kingdom of God present with power" (NKJV). In Mark 9:2, the phrase "And after six days" refers back to that promise and the events leading to it, which include Peter's confession of Jesus as the Christ and the teachings that issued. This suggests that Jesus was referring to Peter, James, and John.

It also appears that Jesus and His disciples are still within the region of Caesarea Philippi when He takes Peter, James, and John to a high mountain to be by themselves. The name of the mountain is omitted here, as well as in both Matthew and Luke's accounts (Matthew 17:1; Luke 9:28). Popular tradition has it that Mount Tabor is the site of the Mount of Transfiguration. Some dispute the assumption given its distance from Caesarea Philippi, the vicinity of the previous scene, and its relatively low height (about 1,800 feet). Many believe that Mount Hermon, also called Mount Hebron, fits better in the context both in its proximity to Caesarea Philippi and its height (about 9,000 feet). Luke adds "to pray" in his account of this event (9:28). Peter, James, and John are generally referred to as Christ's "inner circle" of disciples. In several occasions during very crucial moments in His earthly ministry, Jesus took these three men with Him (Matthew 26:37; Mark 5:37; Luke 8:51).

As the three watched, Jesus is transfigured. The word "transfigured" is a translation of the Greek verb *metamorphoo* (met-am-or-FO-o), which means "changed, or transformed."

3 And his raiment became shining, exceeding white as snow; so as no fuller on earth can white them.

As the disciples watch, suddenly there is a dramatic and noticeable change in the appearance of their Master—Jesus. This change includes His outfit. Mark describes Christ's clothing as "shining, exceeding white as snow." Indeed, His clothes were so dazzlingly white, that they were "far whiter than any earthly bleach could ever make them" (9:3, NLT). The word "white" or "whiteness" in the Bible is usually associated with purity. David prayed, "Purge (purify) me with hyssop, and I shall be clean: wash me, and I shall be whiter than snow" (Psalm 51:7; compare with Isaiah 1:18; Lamentations 4:7; Daniel 7:9; Matthew 28:3; Revelation 1:14). This transformation signifies the glory of God revealed to humankind and is an example of "the kingdom of God come with power" (Mark 9:1).

4 And there appeared unto them Elias with Moses: and they were talking with Jesus.

As the three disciples watch this metamorphosis take place in the appearance of Jesus, they see Elijah ("Elias") and Moses standing and chatting with Jesus. The nature of their appearance, whether through vision or trance, or whether they had a brief resurrection experience, we are not told. All we know is that Peter, James, and John were able to recognize the two people that appeared as Moses and Elijah. The significance of their appearance would only be speculative at best. However, one thing is certain: in Jesus, both the Law and prophets converge. While Moses represents the Law, and Elijah represents the prophets, Jesus fulfills both the Law and prophets (Exodus 24:1; 1 Kings 19:8; Matthew 5:17).

5 And Peter answered and said to Jesus, Master, it is good for us to be here: and let us make three tabernacles; one for thee, and one for Moses, and one for Elias. 6 For he wist not what to say; for they were sore afraid.

Overwhelmed and struck with awe, and still oblivious of the true nature of Christ, Peter with his characteristic impulsiveness suggests that the mountain was a good spot for them to establish a dwelling or settlement. He proposes that three tabernacles be erected for Jesus, Moses, and Elijah. Peter is still unaware of who Jesus was at this point. Regardless of the fact the Jesus has revealed Himself as the Messiah who "must suffer great things" (Mark 8:31), Peter still perceives Jesus as similar to Moses and Elijah. Perhaps in shock and excited by what they have witnessed, Peter wants to prolong the experience. Verse 6 gives the reason for Peter's utterance and state of mind: he did not know what he was saying or how to reply. Probably, he was confused, overwhelmed, and afraid and spoke out of fear.

7 And there was a cloud that overshadowed them: and a voice came out of the cloud, saying, This is my beloved Son: hear him.

The events here appear to happen in quick succession and spontaneity. This can be deduced by the use of the conjunction "and" (Gk., *kai*, **kahee**) at the beginning of verses 2–12. Matthew's account tends to support this assumption. He writes, "While he [Peter] was still speaking, a bright cloud overshadowed them" (Matthew 17:5, NLT, RSV). Clouds often signify the presence of God, especially in the Old Testament; they can either reveal or conceal the Lord (Exodus 13:21–22; 14:19–23; 16:10). The appearance of the cloud is accompanied with an audible voice from the cloud saying, "This is my beloved Son: hear him." The two happened simultaneously. God's audible voice has been heard on several occasions in the Bible, both in the Old Testament and New Testament (Genesis 3:8; Deuteronomy 5:22–25; Matthew 3:17; John 12:28; Revelation 10:3). Here is the second time in Mark's gospel that God the Father affirmed His Son, audibly declaring that Jesus of

Nazareth is His beloved Son (see Mark 1:11; cf. Matthew 3:17). John refers to Him as the only "begotten Son" of God (John 1:14; 3:16–18; 1 John 4:9).

8 And suddenly, when they had looked round about, they saw no man any more, save Jesus only with themselves.

After the announcement from the voice, the three disciples look around and see Jesus alone with them. Moses and Elijah have suddenly departed, leaving Jesus with His disciples. They have accomplished their mission.

9 And as they came down from the mountain, he charged them that they should tell no man what things they had seen, till the Son of man were risen from the dead.

The word "charged" in Greek is *diastellomai* (dee-as-TEL-lom-ahee) which means "admonished, ordered, commanded." After this, Jesus and His disciples come down from the top of the mountain. Jesus charges His disciples not to reveal what they have witnessed, until after His resurrection. The reason Jesus banned publicity of the event is not revealed. The most likely reason would be that He wants to avoid any popularity that would induce people to make Him a political freedom fighter or deliverer (John 6:15), which is contrary to the true purpose of His mission: suffering and dying for the redemption of humankind. The aim of this revelation is to confirm that Jesus was the Messiah and has been witnessed by the three disciples. This is in fulfillment of the requirement of Jewish law, which required the testimony of at least three people to establish a truth (Deuteronomy 17:6; Hebrews 10:28). Disclosure of this event would have provoked the Jews; they would arrest Him, thereby endangering His life

before its time. At this point, the time for His passion has not yet come. In order to prevent a premature arrest and passion, He charged them not to tell anyone until after His resurrection.

10 And they kept that saying with themselves, questioning one with another what the rising from the dead should mean.

As they descend the mountain, the three disciples keep on discussing and questioning themselves about the meaning of "rising from the dead." Although Christ has explained to them in clear terms that He would suffer and die and, on the third day would rise again (Mark 2:20; 8:31), yet they could not comprehend it. They find it difficult to reconcile the promise of the manifestation of the Messiah in His glory with His ultimate humiliation. This illustrates their ignorance and their inability to take Jesus seriously and literally. In spite of all factual evidence pointing to Christ's literal death, burial, and resurrection, many people today—even in the Christian community—still find it difficult to comprehend this fact.

11 And they asked him, saying, Why say the scribes that Elias must first come?

Still perplexed, they could not understand where Elijah fit in the scheme of things. The disciples have been taught that "Elias must first come" to restore all things before the advent of the Messiah (Malachi 3:1; 4:5–6). Although they understand that through the Transfiguration Jesus is the expected Messiah, they are unaware that Elijah has already come in the person of John the Baptist (verse 13; see Matthew 11:14). Jesus has to straighten out their thinking.

12 And he answered and told them, Elias verily cometh first, and restoreth all things; and how it is written of the Son of man, that he must suffer many things, and be set at nought.

Jesus answers them, saying, "Elias verily cometh first, and restoreth all things." With this statement, Jesus does not mean Elijah is yet to come, because He tells them immediately that he had come (v. 13; Matthew 17:12). Rather, He affirms as a true doctrine the teachings of the scribes and experts that Elijah would come before the advent of the Messiah. However they err in their understanding regarding the Messiah; they fail to realize and mention the need of the suffering of both the Messiah (Isaiah 53) and Elijah (1 Kings 19:2–10).

The phrase that the Messiah will "be set at nought" in the Greek is *exoudenoo* (**ex-oo-den-O-o**), and it means that He would be "viewed as worthless" and "rejected, despised and cast out." This prophecy was strikingly fulfilled to the letter (Luke 23:11, 14–21).

13 But I say unto you, That Elias is indeed come, and they have done unto him whatsoever they listed, as it is written of him.

Jesus sets things right. He tells the disciples that Elijah has indeed come in the person of John the Baptist to set straight the crooked (Mark 1:3–5). Prophesying about the birth of John the Baptist, the angel informs John's father, Zacharias, "And he (John) shall go before him (the Messiah) in the spirit and power of Elias, to turn the hearts of the fathers to the children, and the disobedient to the wisdom of the just; to make ready a people prepared for the Lord" (Luke 1:17). So Jesus is telling the disciples that John the Baptist has come in the power and spirit of Elijah, but the people "have done unto him whatsoever they listed, as it is written of him" (Mark 9:13). The word "list" in this instance

is an old English word from the Greek *thelo* (**THEL-o**), which means "to choose, to desire, to be inclined." Here it means that the people had done to John as they pleased—by putting him to death (Matthew 14:10).

Say It Correctly

Gethsemane. geth-SEM-uh-nee.
Hermon. HUHR-muhn.
Jairus. JAY-ih-ruhs, JAY-uh-ruhs.
Malachi. MAL-uh-ki(').
Sinai. SI -ni (also -nee-i').
Tabor. TAY-buhr, TAY-bor'.
Zacharias. zak'-uh-RI -uh.

Daily Bible Readings

M: Moses, Elijah, and the Coming Day
Malachi 4:1–6

T: Moses on the Mountain
Exodus 19:1–6

W: Elijah on the Mountain
1 Kings 19:11–18

T: A Mountain of Revelation
Ezekiel 40:1–4

F: Come Up to the Mountain
Isaiah 2:1–4

S: Ponder God's Love
Psalm 48:9–14

S: Listen to My Son!
Mark 9:2–13

Teaching Tips

1. Words You Should Know

A. Glory (Mark 10:37) *doxa/dox·ah* (Gk.)—His honor, excellence, preeminence.

B. Cup (v. 38) *poterion* (Gk.)—Refers to one's lot or experience; prosperity or adversity.

C. Minister (v. 43) *diakonos* (Gk.)—A servant, an attendant; the act of serving others' needs.

2. Teacher Preparation

Unifying Principle—True Leadership. Jesus said that He came to serve, not to be served, and demonstrated that as an example to follow.

A. Prayerfully ask God to use you to enhance your students' understanding of this lesson.

B. Study the Daily Bible Readings, Focal Verses, and the surrounding sections.

C. Make a list that includes: a child, lawyer, doctor, accountant, engineer, president, and preacher. You will have your students rank them according to whom they perceive to be the greatest.

D. Look up a definition of "servant" and be prepared to share it.

3. Open the Lesson

A. Open with prayer, including the Aim for Change.

B. Write your list on the board and play the game "Who Is the Greatest?"

C. Then discuss "servant" and "servant-leader."

D. From the In Focus story, emphasize Derrick's desire to be a servant-leader.

4. Present the Scriptures

A. Have volunteers read the Focal Verses.

B. Explain the Focal Verses using The People, Places, and Times; Background; the At-A-Glance outline; In Depth; Search the Scriptures; and More Light on the Text.

5. Explore the Meaning

A. Clarify the Discuss the Meaning, Lesson in Our Society, and Make It Happen sections.

B. Connect these sections to the Aim for Change and the Key Verse.

6. Next Steps for Application

A. Summarize your discussion on servant-leadership.

B. Close with prayer.

Worship Guide

For the Superintendent or Teacher
Theme: Jesus Came to Serve
Theme Song: "Where He Leads Me"
Devotional Reading: John 13:3–16
Prayer

Jesus Came to Serve

Bible Background • MARK 10:35–45
Printed Text • MARK 10:35–45 | Devotional Reading • JOHN 13:3–16

———— Aim for Change ————

By the end of the lesson, we will: TELL how Jesus characterized true leadership; REFLECT upon the fact that great leaders serve; and IDENTIFY a way to serve others by following Jesus' example.

————  In Focus ————

Derrick was excited and scared. He had finally grown his business to the point where he could hire employees. He knew his business would grow if he had a secretary, but being responsible for someone else's wages twisted his stomach in knots. Through word-of-mouth alone, he received a dozen resumes. He interviewed them all and brought on a young female who was able to articulate his vision for his practice. He just knew it'd be easy being a boss, but he quickly realized that he had a lot to learn.

In the first few days, he struggled with training his new secretary because he hadn't completely thought out her duties and responsibilities. Then there were times that she had questions that he did not know how to answer. At first, this irritated him, and he found himself being short with her. Finally, he went to her and apologized and said, "I don't have a clue about what I'm doing, but if you'll be patient with me, I promise I'll learn how to be a good boss."

In today's lesson, Jesus emphasizes that He came to serve and not be served. As we follow in His kingdom-building initiative, we should keep this point at the forefront of our minds.

———— Keep in Mind ————

FEB 20th

"For even the Son of man came not to be ministered unto, but to minister, and to give his life a ransom for many" (Mark 10:45).

"For even the Son of man came not to be ministered unto, but to minister,
and to give his life a ransom for many" (Mark 10:45).

Focal Verses

KJV Mark 10:35 And James and John, the sons of Zebedee, come unto him, saying, Master, we would that thou shouldest do for us whatsoever we shall desire.

36 And he said unto them, What would ye that I should do for you?

37 They said unto him, Grant unto us that we may sit, one on thy right hand, and the other on thy left hand, in thy glory.

38 But Jesus said unto them, Ye know not what ye ask: can ye drink of the cup that I drink of? and be baptized with the baptism that I am baptized with?

39 And they said unto him, We can. And Jesus said unto them, Ye shall indeed drink of the cup that I drink of; and with the baptism that I am baptized withal shall ye be baptized:

40 But to sit on my right hand and on my left hand is not mine to give; but it shall be given to them for whom it is prepared.

41 And when the ten heard it, they began to be much displeased with James and John.

42 But Jesus called them to him, and saith unto them, Ye know that they which are accounted to rule over the Gentiles exercise lordship over them; and their great ones exercise authority upon them.

43 But so shall it not be among you: but whosoever will be great among you, shall be your minister:

44 And whosoever of you will be the chiefest, shall be servant of all.

45 For even the Son of man came not to be ministered unto, but to minister, and to give his life a ransom for many.

NLT Mark 10:35 Then James and John, the sons of Zebedee, came over and spoke to him. "Teacher," they said, "we want you to do us a favor."

36 "What is your request?" he asked.

37 They replied, "When you sit on your glorious throne, we want to sit in places of honor next to you, one on your right and the other on your left."

38 But Jesus said to them, "You don't know what you are asking! Are you able to drink from the bitter cup of suffering I am about to drink? Are you able to be baptized with the baptism of suffering I must be baptized with?"

39 "Oh yes," they replied, "we are able!" Then Jesus told them, "You will indeed drink from my bitter cup and be baptized with my baptism of suffering.

40 But I have no right to say who will sit on my right or my left. God has prepared those places for the ones he has chosen."

41 When the ten other disciples heard what James and John had asked, they were indignant.

42 So Jesus called them together and said, "You know that the rulers in this world lord it over their people, and officials flaunt their authority over those under them.

43 But among you it will be different. Whoever wants to be a leader among you must be your servant,

44 and whoever wants to be first among you must be the slave of everyone else.

45 For even the Son of man came not to be served but to serve others and to give his life as a ransom for many."

The People, Places, and Times

James and John. James and John were Jesus' third and fourth picks as disciples. They are brothers, and their parents' names were Zebedee and Salome. They were fishermen alongside their father when they were called to follow Jesus. Among the Twelve, James and John were one of two pairs of brothers and were a part of Jesus' inner circle. Andrew and Simon (Peter) were brothers, too, and were chosen as the first two disciples. Often, James and John were rivals of Andrew and Simon. Because of their intense and zealous personalities, Jesus nicknamed James and John as "sons of thunder."

Background

If chapters in the Bible were given titles, it would be appropriate to call Mark 10 "Relationships 101." This chapter opens with Jesus' attempt to steal away for some downtime, but when He was found by the people, He continued to teach. He put His relationship with people before His right to personal time. Then the Pharisees posed a question about the lawfulness of divorce. He answered them by teaching on the relationship between husbands and wives. Next, children were brought to Him to be blessed. It is possible that the disciples thought it was a waste of Jesus' time or an insult to Him to be bothered with children, but Jesus picked the children up in His arms, laid His hands on them, and blessed them. Then He used them in an analogy for inheriting the kingdom of God. On His way out, Jesus was stopped by a man who asked Him how he could obtain eternal life. The man asserted that he had obeyed the first requirement since his youth, that he had always observed the commandments. Jesus told the man to sell his possessions, give to the poor, and follow Him. The man walked away. Jesus then taught on the relationship between a person's heart and his or her riches and the barrier they present to entering the kingdom of heaven. Lastly, Peter tells Jesus that the disciples had given up everything to follow Him. Jesus taught that they would receive temporal blessings with persecution and eternal life. Finally, He took the Twelve with Him and strengthened their relationship together by telling them what would happen to Him.

At-A-Glance

1. Request to Be Lifted High (Mark 10:35–40)

2. Suggestion to Be Brought Low (vv. 41–45)

In Depth

1. Request to Be Lifted High (Mark 10:35–40)

Jesus nicknamed James and John as the "sons of thunder" for a good reason. They were a pair of intense and zealous brothers. Once they wanted to call down fire from heaven to destroy some Samaritans (see Luke 9:54). So, Jesus could not have been surprised when the brothers came to Him requesting special seats in heaven. In fact, Jesus had just shared with them all the impending sufferings He would endure. The other 10 disciples were probably pondering the information, while James and John saw it as an opportune time to secure their outcomes on the other side of heaven. They requested that Jesus permit one of them to sit at His right hand, and the other at the left.

As though their request was not haughty enough, the brothers assured Jesus that they could handle any responsibilities they were given. They concurred that they could drink from the cup Jesus did and that they could be baptized with the baptism He underwent. If they had known the full figurative meanings of "cup" and "baptism," it's unlikely that they would have opened their mouths. Finally, Jesus told them that the responsibility to assign seats in heaven was not His, but the Father's.

2. Suggestion to Be Brought Low (vv. 40–45)

Imagine the other disciples' fury when they heard about James and John's request. Just who did James and John think they were? While the others might have been saddened, afraid, or angry upon hearing about Jesus' coming sufferings, James and John were opportunistic. Their boldness upset the other 10 disciples. How dare the brothers try to supersede themselves over the others! What audacity they had to try and bribe the Lord of such an opportunity that any of the Twelve could have desired. The 10 disciples could also have been upset that James and John were bold enough to ask for what they wanted.

Jesus gathered them all together to teach the paradox of leadership. What a great way to squash an argument. While the disciples focused on external evidence of greatness to determine who deserved seats in heaven, Jesus taught that the greatest of them was the one who served. While many think that great leaders lord their authority over others, Jesus taught that the opposite is true. Great leaders don't make others serve them; great leaders serve others.

Search the Scriptures

1. Who were James and John (Mark 10:35)?
2. What proposal did they make to Jesus (v. 37)?
3. Whose responsibility is it to assign seats in heaven (v. 40)?

Discuss the Meaning

1. Why were the other 10 disciples angry at James and John?
2. What "cup" and "baptism" was Jesus speaking of?

Lesson in Our Society

In today's society, we have wrongly defined leadership and have given some leaders a false sense of self and security. Too often, we look for external evidence as a measure of greatness. If one is attractive, articulate, can obtain good results, and can influence people, then some say that person is a great leader. Unfortunately, we have had many deemed "great" leaders who led others astray—Jim Jones, David Koresh, Adolf Hitler, and Bernard Madoff, to name a few. What would great leaders look like if we redefined greatness by Jesus' standards?

Make It Happen

Evaluate yourself. Every person has been given a measure of greatness as we are made in God's image. What prevents you from living up to your full potential? Perhaps your perception of greatness is skewed. This week, challenge yourself to redefine greatness and know that you are not limited by your past or present circumstances and situations.

Follow the Spirit

What God wants me to do:

_____

_____

_____

_____

Remember Your Thoughts

Special insights I have learned:

_____

_____

_____

_____

More Light on the Text

Mark 10:35–45

35 And James and John, the sons of Zebedee, come unto him, saying, Master, we would that thou shouldest do for us whatsoever we shall desire.

Earlier along the way to Capernaum (9:33–37), the disciples had been arguing about "who is the greatest." Using a child as an example, Jesus admonishes the disciples not to confuse the worldly greatness or earthly ranks with the spiritual importance. Rank was an important and prominent issue in the Jewish community. Position or earthly recognition was highly contestable in their tradition. That has not changed much today in our society and, unfortunately, even within Christian circles. This continues to be a source of serious contention in the body of Christ.

It appears that, even after Jesus' admonitions, the disciples either are still unable to fully comprehend Him, or probably they're fully engrossed by their own selfish desires and refuse to heed His teachings. As a result of this, the brothers James and John, the sons of Zebedee (a contemporary nickname might be "the Zebedee boys"), go behind the others' backs to ask Jesus to promise them the best spots in His kingdom.

It is interesting to understand James and John's method. They first try to make Jesus commit to do "whatsoever" they desire or request from Him—an open-ended request that only the naïve will fall for. But not Jesus; He knows and understands the hearts and imaginations of every human.

36 And he said unto them, What would ye that I should do for you? 37 They said unto him, Grant unto us that we may sit, one on thy right hand, and the other on thy left hand, in thy glory.

Although Jesus knows what is in their minds (He knows every human being), He asks them the nature of their request: "What would ye that I should do for you?" Get specific, He seems to tell them; never mind the open-ended "whatsoever" stuff. Their demand is clear. They want Jesus to give them the two important, special positions in the kingdom. To be on the "right hand" and the "left hand" of a ruler in a kingdom implies having the next highest positions. These are seats of power, authority, and prestige, so James and John want to be part of that.

The kingdom of Christ is the same as the "Kingdom of Heaven" (Matthew 18:1–4); it is where Jesus reigns in "glory" (Gk. *doxa*, **DOX-ah**) which means in "dignity or honor." It can also be argued that James and John might have understood the coming glory and kingdom of the Messiah (see Mark 8:38–9:1; Matthew 16:27–28), and so they want to make sure that their positions are secured on the either side of Christ.

This promise, though still oblivious to the disciples, is also still futuristic and shall be consummated at the Second Coming—the *Parousia* (**par-oo-SEE-ah**)—of Christ. Probably the two brothers think that it is something imminent, without the suffering. The request further reveals, as had happened to Peter, their ignorance in fully understanding the purpose and the nature of Christ's mission on earth (Mark 8:32; Matthew 16:22). They and the other disciples could not fully comprehend the whole concept of Christ's suffering and death, although they had constantly been taught and reminded, even after Jesus had explained to them a third time in this Gospel (Mark 10:32–34; cf. 8:31–32; 9:31).

38 But Jesus said unto them, Ye know not what ye ask: can ye drink of the cup that I drink of? and be baptized with the baptism that I am baptized with?

Their lack of knowledge is evidenced in Jesus' answer, "Ye know not what ye ask," and His subsequent questions to them. Jesus firmly informs them that they do not know or understand what they are asking for. They do not understand the implications of their request and what it takes to reign with Him (see Mark 8:35; Matthew 10:37–39; Romans 8:17; 2 Timothy 2:12; Revelation 3:21). In order to clarify what their request implies, Jesus asks them two direct questions, which have the same interpretation. Using the imagery of the "cup" and of "baptism," Jesus indirectly explains to them the true significance of their aspiration and the type of suffering He is about undergo. Used here, the word "cup" (Gk. *poterion*, **pot-AY-ree-on**) is the cup of suffering (Matthew 20:22; John 18:11); cup of death (cf. Matthew 26:39, 42; Mark 14:23; Luke 22:20); an Old Testament imagery referring to punishment and judgment (Psalm 11:6; 73:10; 75:8; Jeremiah

49:12); and retribution (Jeremiah 51:7; Ezekiel 23:31–33; Habakkuk 2:16).

39 And they said unto him, We can. And Jesus said unto them, Ye shall indeed drink of the cup that I drink of; and with the baptism that I am baptized withal shall ye be baptized:

They answered Jesus affirmatively, "Oh yes, ...we are able!" (NLT) Their answer continues to expose their ignorance; it further reveals how deeply rooted their selfish ambitions are in their minds. Their answer is indeed not unique. It unveils the true human heart which is willing to do anything and go to any length to achieve worldly honor and position. Jesus' rebuttal is significant. "Yes," He seems to say, "you certainly will experience what I am trying to forewarn you about." With this statement, Jesus predicts the suffering and death of His disciples, including the two brothers. Luke records the death of James as the first Christian and apostolic martyr (Acts 12:2); John suffered persecution and was exiled on the remote island of Patmos (Revelation 1:9).

40 But to sit on my right hand and on my left hand is not mine to give; but it shall be given to them for whom it is prepared.

Jesus continues with His rebuttal to James and John's demands. He says that although they would really go through the same suffering that He is about to encounter, it is not in His hands to determine who would sit by His side. That is a special privilege reserved only for the Father. In several passages in the Bible, Jesus makes it clear that there are certain privileges which belong to the Father (Mark 13:32; Acts 1:7). He maintains that His authority is derived from the Father (Matthew 11:27; 24:36; John 14:28). God will grant those positions to the people for whom they have been prepared; it is not granted to those who can maneuver their way through. God determines who occupies those positions in His kingdom.

41 And when the ten heard it, they began to be much displeased with James and John.

When the other 10 disciples learned about the request made by James and John, they began to resent them ("...they were moved with indignation against the brethren" Matthew 20:24). The phrase "to be much displeased" is a translation of the Greek *aganakteo,* which means "to be greatly afflicted, to be moved with indignation." James and John ignited much anger and hatred from the other disciples. Their indignation and resentment seems to stem from their own selfishness and envious ambition. It appears that they aspire for the same position, but are not bold enough to voice their request. They seem to revert to the feud they had earlier (Mark 9:33–37; Matthew 18:1–5; Luke 9:46–48). How they showed their indignation is not known. But it must be so apparent that Jesus has to step in and address the situation.

42 But Jesus called them to him, and saith unto them, Ye know that they which are accounted to rule over the Gentiles exercise lordship over them; and their great ones exercise authority upon them.

Jesus calls the disciples to order. He begins to teach all of them once again about the kingdom. He draws a contrast between the power and authority exerted among human society and the power among those who are the heirs of the kingdom. He probably is referring primarily to the Romans, whose empire was characterized by the assertion of earthly power. To "exercise lordship" (dominion) has the idea of a domineering attitude. Therefore, the pagan or Gentile leaders exercise two leadership principles, Jesus says. The first is, they "lord

it over" (NKJV) or in the Greek *katakurieuo* (**kat-ak-oo-ree-YOO-o**), meaning they "lord against, control, or subjugate." They throw their weight around and make sure they are obeyed and feared. The second leadership principle for the pagans (non-believers) is that they "exercise authority" or, in the Greek *katexousiazo* (**kat-ex-oo-see-AD-zo**), which means "to have full privilege over" with the idea of control. Literally, both phrases are parallel and mean to "tyrannize and oppress." Jesus tells His disciples that that is how the Gentile leadership operates. But He quickly cautions them that such principles should not characterize those of His kingdom.

43 But so shall it not be among you: but whosoever will be great among you, shall be your minister: 44 And whosoever of you will be the chiefest, shall be servant of all.

Jesus insists that this type of pagan leadership (lordship) will not be found among His disciples—those of the kingdom. Rather, the type of leadership expected of them should be based on service—that is the mark of greatness (v. 43). Admonishing them, Jesus tells them that anyone who wants to be great must become a "servant." In Greek, the word is *diakonos* (**dee-AK-on-os**), which means "minister" or "one who carries the orders or command of another." From this word is derived the word "deacon," which is often used in our churches today. The word *diakonos* does not exclusively mean "deacon" or "minister' (KJV) in the sense of its contemporary usage in our churches, in which it has become a position of religious or political power and badge of honor. It is a position of humble service, rather than the hierarchical position we have made it.

In case the full meaning of this teaching was to be misunderstood by the disciples, Jesus repeats it in verse 44 using a stronger Greek word, *doulos* (**DOO-los**). The word is usually translated "servant" but is better rendered "slave" (1 Corinthians 9:19; 2 Corinthians 4:5; 1 Peter 1:22; 5:1–3), which accurately defines the real spirit of servitude it demands. *Doulos* means one who gives him- or herself wholly to the service and will of another. The words "minister" and "servant" refer to the lowest secular and ecclesiastical office among Christians (Mark 10:43–44).

45 For even the Son of man came not to be ministered unto, but to minister, and to give his life a ransom for many.

There is no better example for this "new" teaching in leadership than the Son of man Himself. Explaining further this new concept of leadership and power, Jesus cites Himself as the perfect example of serving others. He is the prime example of humility and servanthood (Philippians 2:3–11). Jesus informs His disciples that He came into the world not to be ministered to—that is, not to lord it over others as in pagan practices (Mark 10:42; Matthew 20:25)— but rather to serve others (cf. John 13:4–5). He offers the idea that because of His divine origin, Jesus has every power, authority, and right to be served (Mark 10:45). Instead, He humbled Himself to the point of giving up Himself as a sacrificial lamb to atone for the sins of the world. Jesus spells out His imminent passion and the purpose of His earthly advent—"to give his life a ransom for many." The word "ransom" (Gk. *lutron*, **LOO-tron**) means "to redeem from, to pay a price for a man." Long ago, "ransom" was commonly used as a purchase price to free slaves.

Paul clearly and dramatically presents the truth of Christ's teaching, exemplified by His humility, servitude, redeeming death, and His consequent exaltation to the kingdom: "Therefore God exalted him to the highest place and gave him the name that is above every name, that at the name of Jesus every knee should bow, in heaven and on earth and under the earth, and every tongue confess that Jesus Christ is Lord, to the glory of God the Father."

Say It Correctly

Capernaum. kuh-PERR-nay-uhm.
Habakkuk. huh-BAK-uhk.
Jeremiah. jer'uh-MI-uh.
Parousia. pahr-oo-SEE-uh.
Patmos. PAT-muhs.
Salome. suh-LOH-mee.
Simon. SI –muhn.
Zebedee. ZEB-uh-dee, ZEB-ih-dee.

Daily Bible Readings

M: Serving Like a Slave
Luke 15:25–32

T: Choosing the Better Part
Luke 10:38–42

W: As One Who Serves
Luke 22:24–30

T: Come, Follow Me
Mark 10:17–22

F: Serving and Following
John 12:20–26

S: An Example Set
John 13:3–16

S: Greatness Through Service
Mark 10:35–45

Teaching Tips

1. Words You Should Know

A. Abomination (Mark 13:14) *bdelugma* (Gk.)—A foul and detestable thing.

B. "Of desolation" (v. 14) *eremosis* (Gk.)—Making something deserted, uninhabitable.

C. Affliction (v. 19) *thlipsis* (Gk.)—Anguish, burdened, persecution, tribulation, and trouble.

2. Teacher Preparation

Unifying Principle—The Return! Jesus said that false messiahs and prophets would give signs, but that He would return with true power to call the people to Himself.

A. Pray for lesson clarity.

B. Prayerfully study the Daily Bible Readings, Focal Verses, and the surrounding sections.

C. Research information on "The End Times" or "Eschatology," and be prepared to share.

3. Open the Lesson

A. Open with prayer, including the Aim for Change.

B. Write the word "Eschatology" and in parenthesis put (End Times) on the board.

C. Ask, "How many of you feel that this world is all there is?"

D. Share your notes on "Eschatology" (the End Times). Discuss.

E. Tie in today's In Focus story with the discussion.

4. Present the Scriptures

A. Have volunteers read the Focal Verses.

B. Explain the Focal Verses using the At-A-Glance outline, In Depth, and More Light on the Text.

C. Connect last Sunday's lesson by stressing that God's Beloved Son, who came as a servant-leader, is coming back the second time as a judge.

D. Explain that the opportunity for salvation will be no more.

5. Explore the Meaning

A. Emphasize the salient points in the Discuss the Meaning, Lesson in Our Society, and Make It Happen sections.

B. Connect these sections to the Aim for Change and the Key Verse.

6. Next Steps for Application

A. Reemphasize the tenets of Jesus' second coming.

B. Close with prayer.

Worship Guide

For the Superintendent or Teacher
Theme: Coming of the Son of Man
Theme Song: "Lord, I Want to See Him"
Devotional Reading: Isaiah 2:5–12
Prayer

Coming of the Son of Man

Bible Background • MARK 13
Printed Text • MARK 13:14–27 | Devotional Reading • ISAIAH 2:5–12

Aim for Change

By the end of the lesson, we will: KNOW what Jesus said about end times; HOPE for the future; and DETERMINE to be ready when Jesus returns.

In Focus

The only thing Kim hated about her job was that she was required to do 20 hours of training every year. While most of the trainings were on good subjects and the trainers were knowledgeable, she found the classes to be too long and boring. But she didn't dare complain, since the classes were free. Oftentimes, to keep herself awake, she doodled on the margins of her notes or took frequent bathroom breaks. Today's session was on "Spirituality and Recovery," and the presenter did a good job of holding the audience's attention. But when he said that he was a god, as was every participant in the room, Kim knew she was in the wrong place. She told herself not to jump to conclusions and listened more intently. The next thing she knew, the presenter sought permission to heighten everyone's level of thinking by conducting group hypnosis. Kim grabbed her belongings so fast she almost tripped over her own feet. That was one class she didn't want to take credit for.

Unlike the presenter in Kim's training class, who was a false god, Jesus, the true and living God, is coming back again, and He and His church will reign forever and ever in His kingdom.

Keep in Mind

"And then shall they see the Son of man coming in the clouds with great power and glory" (Mark 13:26).

FEB
27th

Focal Verses

KJV Mark 13:14 But when ye shall see the abomination of desolation, spoken of by Daniel the prophet, standing where it ought not, (let him that readeth understand,) then let them that be in Judaea flee to the mountains:

15 And let him that is on the housetop not go down into the house, neither enter therein, to take any thing out of his house:

16 And let him that is in the field not turn back again for to take up his garment.

17 But woe to them that are with child, and to them that give suck in those days!

18 And pray ye that your flight be not in the winter.

19 For in those days shall be affliction, such as was not from the beginning of the creation which God created unto this time, neither shall be.

20 And except that the Lord had shortened those days, no flesh should be saved: but for the elect's sake, which he hath chosen, he hath shortened the days.

21 And then if any man shall say to you, Lo, here is Christ; or, lo, he is there; believe him not:

22 For false Christs and false prophets shall rise, and shall show signs and wonders, to seduce, if it were possible, even the elect.

23 But take ye heed: behold, I have foretold you all things.

24 But in those days, after that tribulation, the sun shall be darkened, and the moon shall not give her light,

25 And the stars of heaven shall fall, and the powers that are in heaven shall be shaken.

26 And then shall they see the Son of man coming in the clouds with great power and glory.

27 And then shall he send his angels, and shall gather together his elect from the four winds, from the uttermost part of the earth to the uttermost part of heaven.

NLT Mark 13:14 "The day is coming when you will see the sacrilegious object that causes desecration standing where he should not be." (Reader, pay attention!) "Then those in Judea must flee to the hills.

15 A person out on the deck of a roof must not go down into the house to pack.

16 A person out in the field must not return even to get a coat.

17 How terrible it will be for pregnant women and for nursing mothers in those days.

18 And pray that your flight will not be in winter.

19 For there will be greater anguish in those days than at any time since God created the world. And it will never be so great again.

20 In fact, unless the Lord shortens that time of calamity, not a single person will survive. But for the sake of his chosen ones he has shortened those days.

21 "Then if anyone tells you, 'Look, here is the Messiah,' or 'There he is,' don't believe it.

22 For false messiahs and false prophets will rise up and perform signs and wonders so as to deceive, if possible, even God's chosen ones.

23 Watch out! I have warned you about this ahead of time!

24 "At that time, after the anguish of those days, the sun will be darkened, the moon will give no light,

25 the stars will fall from the sky, and the powers in the heavens will be shaken.

26 Then everyone will see the Son of Man coming on the clouds with great power and glory.

27 And he will send out his angels to gather his chosen ones from all over the world—from the farthest ends of the earth and heaven."

The People, Places, and Times

Daniel the Prophet. Daniel was the fourth of the "major prophets." His name means "judgment of God." Not much is known or recorded about his early life. He was from a noble family as he was carried into captivity by the Babylonian king who sought servants from families of nobility. He and other teenaged boys like him, who were articulate, smart, handsome, and quick to learn, were taken captive to work in the Babylonian royal courts. The boys were taught the Babylonian language and culture, but Daniel refused to defile himself and abstained from eating the king's royal foods.

Daniel is known for interpreting King Nebuchadnezzar's dreams, being promoted over the province of Babylon, being thrown into the lion's den, being rescued by God, and foretelling the end times in the Old Testament.

Background

While the disciples wanted Jesus to direct His attention to the great stones of a magnificent building, Jesus' mind was fastened on something else. He told them that not one stone from that building would stand on the day of desolation. It was not Jesus' desire for them to be ignorant of things to come, so He patiently answered their questions. They asked everything except the actual date of occurrence of the things to come. Jesus did not discourage them because He wanted them to be confident and prepared. Most who hear of the end times are afraid and full of dread.

To prepare the disciples, Jesus taught them that they should pay attention. He warned that people would come to deceive them and would succeed at deceiving many. He told them that they should not be afraid when they hear of wars or rumors of wars.

He foretold of earthquakes, famines, and other troubles and reported that these were the beginning of great sorrow. He spoke of family members being turned against each other. He taught that the disciples would be hated, dragged to courts, humiliated, and persecuted, but that they would fulfill the promise of proclaiming the Gospel everywhere.

At-A-Glance

1. Signs of the Times (Mark 13:14–23)

2. Time of the Son (vv. 24–27)

In Depth

1. Signs of the Times (Mark 13:14–23)

The "abomination of desolation" that Daniel predicted was the Roman armies descending against Judea and besieging Jerusalem. The army stood where it "did not belong" in and around the holy city. Jesus offered instructions on what to do on that day. He instructed the people to flee from Judea and not to waste time trying to gather belongings. He asked that pity be felt for mothers of young children or pregnant women, as they would not be able to move as fast as others and the former might contemplate leaving their children behind. The conditions would be inconvenient and uncomfortable enough that He urged them to pray that the desolation would not come in winter, with no time to grab shoes or coat, or with the potential of facing strong winds or blinding snow. He warned that no affliction has been as the desolation will be.

At such a time as Jesus warned about, why would false prophets arise? People will be so desperate for relief that they will be easily led away by the performance of miracles. Not only will they have to save their lives, but also their souls.

2. Time of the Son (vv. 24–27)

These verses emphasize Christ's second return and His judging of the world. After the Tribulation that He foretold, He prepared His disciples to expect His return. He told them that when neither the sun, moon, nor stars refuse to give light—when the earth will be covered in darkness—out of the clouds will come Jesus with great power and glory. And, His angels will go forth to gather His elected people (His church) unto Himself.

Search the Scriptures

1. What warnings did Jesus give about the Tribulation (Mark 13:14–18)?
2. What other affliction can be compared to that of the desolation (v. 19)?
3. Why will false prophets arise (v. 22)?
4. How will Jesus return (v. 26)?
5. What will His angels do (v. 27)?

Discuss the Meaning

1. Why would the Tribulation be harder for mothers of young children and pregnant women?
2. Why do you think the sun, moon, and stars will not give off light?

Lesson in Our Society

Many of us have heard about Christ's return since we were knee-high. When we first heard of His second coming, we expected it. At the slightest noise, we looked up at the sky expecting that the clouds would part. But since much time has passed and Christ has not yet returned, many of us live as though He may never return. Do you still hold that same reverential fear that Christ will return any day? Or are you so afraid that you try not to think about it?

Make It Happen

To renew your expectation of Christ's return, compare the list of signs in Mark 13 with present-day occurrences. Is it safe to say that they are one and the same? Will you heed the instructions given in the lesson text so that you will be ready when Christ returns? What steps will you take?

Follow the Spirit

What God wants me to do:

_____

_____

_____

_____

Remember Your Thoughts

Special insights I have learned:

_____

_____

_____

_____

More Light on the Text

Mark 13:14–27

14 But when ye shall see the abomination of desolation, spoken of by Daniel the prophet, standing where it ought not, (let him that readeth understand,) then let them that be in Judaea flee to the mountains:

This and the following verses are a continuation of Christ's discourse with the disciples on the Mount of Olives near the temple (v. 3). Probably still focusing on the temple, Jesus speaks about the events that will be fulfilled in the future. Jesus cautions and instructs the disciples on what to do as the events of the time unfold. That period will be signaled by "the abomination of desolation… standing where it ought not." A closely similar phrase is also found in the book of Daniel (9:27; 11:31; 12:11). This prophecy refers to the destruction and desecration of the temple. In Greek the word "abomination" is *bdelugma* (**BDEL-oog-mah**), meaning "a horrid, foul thing."

Historically, it is believed that Daniel's prophecy was partially fulfilled in about 168 B.C. when Antiochus IV Epiphanes banned Jewish religious practices and desecrated the temple by erecting an altar to his god, Zeus, where the altar to Jehovah was, offering burnt offerings and swine on it. It is believed that these actions led to the Maccabean revolt (1 Maccabees 1:45–59; 6:7). Here Jesus indicates that further fulfillment of this prophecy would be realized. History confirms it and it is attested by the Jewish historian, Josephus, that this prophecy took place when some Jewish Zealots desecrated the temple followed by the temple's total destruction by the Romans under General Titus in A.D. 70. This was accompanied by the total destruction of Jerusalem.

Jesus warns that when this sign appears (the temple's desecration and destruction), "let him that readeth understand"—that is, those who read Daniel's prophecy should pay attention or decipher the words. The faithful people residing in Judea should flee to the mountains. It has been told that some Christians, who lived in Jerusalem during the burning of the temple and destruction of the city in A.D. 70, fled to nearby mountainous areas.

15 And let him that is on the housetop not go down into the house, neither enter therein, to take any thing out of his house: 16 And let him that is in the field not turn back again for to take up his garment.

Jesus also cautions that when these things will occur, those "on the housetop" should not attempt to go into their houses to retrieve their belongings. Those who are working outside the home should not return for their garments. Here Jesus describes the horrible nature of the event and the intensity of the abomination; it will be so sudden that there will not be enough time for material things. It also teaches that the focus should be on survival rather than on one's possessions; life is more valuable and more important than worldly goods.

17 But woe to them that are with child, and to them that give suck in those days! 18 And pray ye that your flight be not in the winter.

Describing further the horrific nature of the signs of the end times and how difficult it will be, Jesus calls to mind the condition of the most vulnerable in the society: pregnant women and nursing mothers—the weakest of all people in times of emergency. The word "woe" (Gk. *ouai*, **oo-AH-ee**) is an "exclamation of grief." Here Jesus expresses sadness and concern for this group of people because of the degree of difficulty they would experience. It is a heart-wrenching sight to see people—especially pregnant and nursing mothers—running for their dear lives during wars or other types of disasters. This writer had a personal experience and witnessed the awfulness of military conflict and the plight of the most vulnerable during the Nigerian-Biafran War of 1967–1970. Although Jesus mentioned pregnant women and nursing mothers, they represent anyone, including the weak, the aged, and the feeble that are forced to flee for their very lives under very difficult circumstances.

Since the exact time of these events is unknown (v. 32), Jesus urges the faithful to intercede with prayer that "your flight be not in the winter"—a season when the weather is most hostile. For those in cold regions, "winter" represents the time when the weather is frigid and blizzards can occur. It makes any journey very difficult and uncomfortable.

19 For in those days shall be affliction, such as was not from the beginning of the creation which God created unto this time, neither shall be.

The certainty of the event is made apparent by the phrase "For in those days" (v. 19). The tone here sounds like the voice of one who is certain and confident of what he is saying. And, of course, He is! Although Jesus was living in human form during His earthly life, His divine attributes, such as His omniscience (all-knowing ability), were never withdrawn, though they were only on display at certain times. He describes that period as a time of great "affliction"—distress to the point that has never been experienced since the beginning of creation—a time never to be equaled. The word translated "affliction" is the Greek *thlipsis* (**THLIP-sis**), which means "anguish, burden, persecution, tribulation, trouble." Many scholars, because of the intensity of the suffering, generally refer to it as "the Great Tribulation" (Daniel 12:1; Revelation 6–18).

20 And except that the Lord had shortened those days, no flesh should be saved: but for the elect's sake, whom he hath chosen, he hath shortened the days.

There are a variety of interpretations to the statement in verse 20, "And except that the Lord had shortened those days, no flesh should be saved." Some hold the view that the statement means that the affliction and suffering will be so severe that, if allowed to continue, there will be no survivors—everyone will be destroyed. Some others hold the view that it means that the previously determined time will be cut short, such as the seven days (Daniel 9:27) or the 42 months (Revelation 11:2; 13). But for the elect's sake, the chosen ones, Jesus affirms, the Lord has shortened the day. Here is a demonstration of God's mercy! For the sake of His chosen ones and on the basis of His love and compassion, Jesus says that the period of the Tribulation has been shortened. Had it not been shortened, no soul would be able to survive.

21 And then if any man shall say to you, Lo, here is Christ; or, lo, he is there; believe him not:

Jesus says that the second coming of the Messiah will be marked by certain occurrences. He maintains that the period of "the Great Tribulation," or affliction, and indeed the Second Coming will be marked by religious counterfeits. Jesus warns about the confusion that will be created by false rumors about the appearance of Christ. People will spread rumors that they have seen the Lord or that He has appeared in certain places, but He cautions the elect not to believe them.

22 For false Christs and false prophets shall rise, and shall show signs and wonders, to seduce, if it were possible, even the elect. 23 But take ye heed: behold, I have foretold you all things

Furthermore, Jesus cautions that different people will spring up claiming to be the Christ, and many false prophets will also rise and will perform signs and different miraculous things. These miraculous feats will look so authentic that "even the elect," might be carried away and would be deceived if it were not for God preparing them (see Matthew 24:24; 2 Thessalonians 2:8–12; Revelation 13; 16:13–16; 19:20). The only reason God's elect will escape the deception is that Christ has forewarned them. Four times in this chapter (Mark 13:5, 9, 23, 33), Jesus warns His disciples to be careful—"take heed" and be watchful.

24 But in those days, after that tribulation, the sun shall be darkened, and the moon shall not give her light, 25 And the stars of heaven shall fall, and the powers that are in heaven shall be shaken.

Having answered the immediate question about the destruction of the temple and the Great Tribulation, Jesus now turns to the signs that will usher in His coming again. The phrase "in those days" refers to the period immediately following the Tribulation. The affliction and tribulation just described will be followed by events that are expressed as cosmic alterations. Here Jesus is quoting from the prophecy of Isaiah 13:10 and 34:4, where the prophet describes the suspension of cosmic entities which he associates with the coming Day of the Lord (see also Joel 2:10; 3:15).

The language here is also a subject of debate. Whether these phrases refer to actual alterations in the universe or to events so disorienting and cataclysmic that only strong metaphors suffice, the central point is that Christ's return will clearly change the course of history forever. These cosmic changes will include the suspension of light from the sun and the moon; the displacement of stars from their normal positions; and the shaking of atmospheric powers. The phrase "the powers that are in heaven" (Mark 13:25) tends to refer to satanic hosts or forces that now rule the atmosphere (Ephesians 2:1–3;

6:12). As recorded in Revelation (12:7–12), these forces will be cast down to earth for three and one-half years beforehand. Isaiah predicts that they shall be defeated at the end of this age (24:21–22; 34:4).

26 And then shall they see the Son of man coming in the clouds with great power and glory. 27 And then shall he send his angels, and shall gather together his elect from the four winds, from the uttermost part of the earth to the uttermost part of heaven.

After these signs and occurrences, then comes "the Son of man" in the clouds with great power and glory. His coming will not be in secret; there will be no confusion, doubt or denial about His appearance. Everyone will see Him! The phrase "Son of man coming in the clouds with great power and glory" means that Jesus will return as the eternal Ruler of His kingdom; He will have dominion over His creation; all inhabitants of the earth will worship Him as King (Daniel 7:13–14). As His disciples gathered at the Mount of Olives and watch Him ascend into heaven, two angels in white garments will say to them, "Men of Galilee,...why do you stand looking into the sky? This same Jesus, who has been taken from you into heaven, will come back in the same way as you have seen watched him go into heaven" (Acts 1:11, NIV; see also Mark 8:38; Daniel 7:13; 2 Thessalonians 1:6–10).

The coming of the Son of man will be a tremendous event for all believers; it will result in the great gathering of the faithful—the chosen ones from all corners of the world—"from the farthest ends of the earth and heaven" (Mark 13:27, NLT). As revealed in Revelation 5:9 and 7:9, this will be a multitude from every ethnic group, language, and nation. What a consolation!

Say It Correctly

Maccabeus. mak'-uh-BEE-uhs.
Nebuchanezzar. neb'-uh-kuhd-NEZ-uhr,
ne'-byuh-kuhd-NE-zuhr.
Thessalonica. thes'-uh-luh-NI -kuh,
thes'-uh-loh-NI-kah.
Thessalonians. thes'-uh-LOH-nee-uhnz.
Zeus. ZOOS.

Daily Bible Readings

M: Terror for the Proud and Lofty
Isaiah 2:5–12

T: Peril in Distressing Times
2 Timothy 3:1–9

W: The Day of Judgment
2 Peter 3:3–10

T: What You Ought to Be
2 Peter 3:11–18

F: Beware!
Mark 13:1–13

S: Be Watchful!
Mark 13:28–37

S: Coming of the Son of Man
Mark 13:14–27

Notes

_____

_____

_____

_____

_____

Lesson 1, December 5

Baltes, A. J., ed., Biblespeech.com. http://www.biblespeech.com (accessed September 23, 2009).

Henry, Matthew. "Isaiah Chapter 40." *Matthew Henry's Commentary on the Whole Bible, Volume IV (Isaiah to Malachi).* Christian Classics Ethereal Library. http://www.ccel.org/ccel/henry/mhc4.Is.xli.html (accessed May 19, 2009).

Isaiah, Chapter 39. Today's Parallel Bible: New Living Translation. Grand Rapids, MI: Zondervan, 2000. 1643.

Kiel, Carl Frederick and F. Delitzsch. "Isaiah." *Commentary on the Old Testament.* Grand Rapids, MI: Eerdmans Publishing, 1988. 162–63.

Merriam-Webster Online Dictionary. Merriam-Webster, Inc. http://www.merriam-webster.com (accessed December 12, 2009).

Unger, Merrill F. "Animal Kingdom: Eagle." *The New Unger's Bible Dictionary.* R. K. Harrison, ed. Chicago, IL: Moody Press, 1988. 70, 120.
——Ibid. "Astronomy." 120–21.
——Ibid. "Captivity: Captivity of Judah." 211.
——Ibid. "Isaiah." 628–29.
——Ibid."Manasseh." 811.
——Ibid. "Road." 1083–84.

Lesson 2, December 12

Baltes, A. J., ed., Biblespeech.com. http://www.biblespeech.com (accessed December 12, 2009).

"Box-tree." "Cedar." "Cypress." "Fir." "Myrtle." "Oil Tree." "Pine." "Shittah-tree." *WebBible* 5. ChristianAnswers.net, s.v. http://christiananswers.net/dictionary (accessed July 2009).

Enns, Paul P. *The Moody Handbook of Theology.* Chicago, IL: Moody Press, 1989. 110.

Henry, Matthew. "Isaiah Chapter 41." *Matthew Henry's Commentary on the Whole Bible, Volume IV (Isaiah to Malachi).* http://www.ccel.org/ccel/henry/mhc4.Is.xlii.html (accessed May 19, 2009).

Kiel, Carl Frederick and F. Delitzsch. "Isaiah." *Commentary on the Old Testament.* Grand Rapids, MI: Eerdmans Publishing, 1988. 162–63.

Life Application Study Bible. Wheaton, IL: Tyndale House, 1996. 1097.

Merriam-Webster Online Dictionary. Merriam-Webster, Inc. http://www.merriam-webster.com (accessed December 12, 2009).

Strong, James. *The New Strong's Exhaustive Concordance of the Bible.* Nashville, TN: Thomas Nelson Publishers, 1990.

Unger, Merrill F. "Vegetable Kingdom: Acacia, Cedar, Fir, Myrtle, Olive." *The New Unger's Bible Dictionary.* R. K. Harrison, ed. Chicago, IL: Moody Press, 1988. 269–70, 1326, 1329–31, 1335, 1337.

Vine, W. E. *Vine's Complete Expository Dictionary.* M. F. Unger and William White, Jr., eds. Nashville, TN: Thomas Nelson Publishers, 1996. 34, 199–200.

Lesson 3, December 19

Baltes, A. J., ed., Biblespeech.com. http://www.biblespeech.com (accessed December 12, 2009).

Kiel, Carl Frederick and F. Delitzsch. "Isaiah." *Commentary on the Old Testament.* Grand Rapids, MI: Eerdmans Publishing, 1988. 162–63.

Life Application Bible. Wheaton, IL: Tyndale House, 1991. 1184, 1188–89.

Merriam-Webster Online Dictionary. Merriam-Webster, Inc. http://www.merriam-webster.com (accessed December 12, 2009).

New Interpreter's Bible Commentary. Nashville, TN: Abingdon Press, 2001. 142–44.

Strong, James. *New Exhaustive Strong's Numbers and Concordance with Expanded Greek-Hebrew Dictionary.* Seattle, WA: Biblesoft, and International Bible Translators, 1994. 2003.

Lesson 4, December 26

"Isaiah 43." Scripture4All Foundation. http://www.scripture4all.org (accessed June 28, 2009).

Kiel, Carl Frederick and F. Delitzsch. "Isaiah." *Commentary on the Old Testament.* Grand Rapids, MI: Eerdmans Publishing, 1988. 162–63.

Merriam-Webster Online Dictionary. Merriam-Webster, Inc. http://www.merriam-webster.com (accessed December 12, 2009).

New Interpreter's Bible Commentary, The. Vol. VI: Introduction to Prophetic Literature. Nashville, TN: Abingdon Press, 2001. 372–82.

Strong, James. *New Exhaustive Strong's Numbers and Concordance with Expanded Greek-Hebrew Dictionary.* Seattle, WA: Biblesoft, and International Bible Translators, 1994. 2003.

Tyndale Bible Dictionary. Wheaton, IL: Tyndale House, 2001. 405.

Lesson 5, January 2

Baltes, A. J., ed., Biblespeech.com. http://www.biblespeech.com (accessed December 12, 2009).

Brown, Francis. *The New Brown-Driver-Briggs-Gesenius Hebrew and English Lexicon, Christian.* Peabody, MA: Hendrickson, 1979.

Denton, R. C. "Redeem, Redeemer, Redemption." *The Interpreter's Dictionary of the Bible R–Z.* Nashville, TN: Abingdon Press, 1962. 21–22.

Holy Bible (New International Version), The. Grand Rapids, MI: Zondervan, 1990.

Holy Bible (New Living Translation), The. Wheaton, IL: Tyndale House, 1996.

Layman's Bible Dictionary, The. Uhrichsville, OH: Barbour Publishers, 2000. 92, 163, 173, 302.

Life Application Bible. Wheaton, IL: Tyndale House, 1991. 1244–45.

Mendelsohn, I. "Divination." *The Interpreter's Dictionary of the Bible A–D.* Nashville, TN: Abingdon Press, 1962. 856–58.

Merriam-Webster Online Dictionary. Merriam-Webster, Inc. http://www.merriam-webster.com (accessed December 12, 2009).

Milton, John P. *Preaching from Isaiah.* Minneapolis, MN: Augsburg Publishing House, 1953. 98–100.

Strong, James. *New Exhaustive Strong's Numbers and Concordance with Expanded Greek-Hebrew Dictionary.* Seattle, WA: Biblesoft, and International Bible Translators, 1994. 2003.

Westerman, Claus. *Isaiah 40–66: A Commentary.* Philadelphia, PA: Westminster Press, 1969. 139, 157.

Lesson 6, January 9

Brown, Francis. *The New Brown-Driver-Briggs-Gesenius Hebrew and English Lexicon, Christian.* Peabody, MA: Hendrickson Publishers, Inc., 1979.

Halley, Henry H. *Halley's Bible Handbook.* Grand Rapids, MI: Zondervan, 1965. 302.

Hanson, Paul D. *Isaiah 40–66. Interpretation: A Commentary for Teaching and Preaching.* Louisville, KY: John Knox Press, 1995. 107–12.

Holman Bible Dictionary. Nashville, TN: Broadman & Holman Publishers, 1991. Database NavPress Software.

Holy Bible (New International Version), The. Grand Rapids, MI: Zondervan Bible Publishers, 1990.

Holy Bible (New Living Translation), The. Wheaton, IL: Tyndale House Publishers, 1996.

Merriam-Webster Online Dictionary. Merriam-Webster, Inc. http://www.merriam-webster.com (accessed December 12, 2009).

North, Christopher R. *Isaiah 40–55: Introduction and Commentary.* London: SCM Press Ltd., 1959. 92–94.

"Preacher's Outline, Sermon Bible and Commentary." *Holman Bible Dictionary.* Nashville, TN: Broadman & Holman Publishers, NavPress Software, 1991.

Strong, James. *New Exhaustive Strong's Numbers and Concordance with Expanded Greek-Hebrew Dictionary.* Seattle, WA: Biblesoft, and International Bible Translators, 1994. 2003.

Westerman, Claus. *Isaiah 40–66: A Commentary.* Philadelphia, PA: Westminster Press, 1969. 171–76.

Lesson 7, January 16

Baltes, A. J., ed., Biblespeech.com. http://www.biblespeech.com (accessed December 12, 2009).

Brown, Francis. *The New Brown-Driver-Briggs-Gesenius Hebrew and English Lexicon, Christian.* Peabody, MA: Hendrickson Publishers, Inc., 1979.

Halley, Henry H. *Halley's Bible Handbook.* Grand Rapids, MI: Zondervan, 1965. 303.

Hamlin, E. John. *A Guide to Isaiah 40–66: TEF Study Guide 16.* London: SPCK, 1979. 111.

Hanson, Paul D. *Isaiah 40–66 Interpretation, A Commentary for Teaching and Preaching.* Louisville, KY: John Knox Press, 1995. 124–25.

Holman Bible Dictionary. Nashville, TN: Broadman & Holman Publishers, 1991. Database NavPress Software.

Holy Bible (New International Version), The. Grand Rapids, MI: Zondervan, 1990.

Holy Bible (New Living Translation), The. Wheaton, IL: Tyndale House, 1996.

Lockyer Sr., Herbert, ed. *Nelson's New Illustrated Bible Dictionary.* Nashville, TN: Thomas Nelson. 1995. 254–55

Merriam-Webster Online Dictionary. Merriam-Webster, Inc. http://www.merriam-webster.com (accessed December 12, 2009).

North, Christopher R. *Isaiah 40–55: Introduction and Commentary.* London: SCM Press Ltd., 1959. 92–94.

Westerman, Claus. *Isaiah 40–66: A Commentary.* Philadelphia, PA: Westminster Press, 1969. 201–5.

Lesson 8, January 23

Baltes, A. J., ed., Biblespeech.com. http://www.biblespeech.com (accessed December 12, 2009).

Brown, Francis. *The New Brown-Driver-Briggs-Gesenius Hebrew and English Lexicon, Christian.* Peabody, MA: Hendrickson Publishers, Inc., 1979.

Clifford, Richard J. "Isaiah, Book of (Second Isaiah)." *Anchor Bible Dictionary,* Vol. 3. David Noel Freedman, ed. New York, NY: Doubleday, 1992. 492–93.

Clifford, Richard J. "Isaiah 40–66." *Harper's Bible Commentary.* James L. Mays, ed. San Francisco, CA: Harper & Row, 1988. 580–81.

Hamlin, E. John. *A Guide to Isaiah 40–66: TEF Study Guide 16.* London: SPCK, 1979. 118–22.

Hanson, Paul D. *Isaiah 40–66 Interpretation: A Commentary for Teaching and Preaching.* Louisville, KY: John Knox Press, 1995. 126–30.

Holy Bible (New International Version), The. Grand Rapids, MI: Zondervan, 1990.

Holy Bible (New Living Translation), The. Wheaton, IL: Tyndale House, 1996.

Hoppe, Leslie J. "Israel, History of (Monarchic Period)." *Anchor Bible Dictionary,* Vol. 3. David Noel Freedman, ed. New York, NY: Doubleday, 1992. 565–66.

MacRae, Allen A. "The Servant of the Lord." In *Holman Bible Dictionary for Windows.* Nashville, TN: Holman Bible Publishers, 1994.

Merriam-Webster Online Dictionary. Merriam-Webster, Inc. http://www.merriam-webster.com (accessed December 12, 2009).

North, Christopher R. *Isaiah 40–55: Introduction and Commentary.* London: SCM Press, Ltd., 1959. 108–10.

Roberts, J. J. M. "Isaiah." *The HarperCollins Study Bible.* Wayne A. Meeks, ed. New York, NY: HarperCollins, 1993. 1083.

Walters, Stanley D. "Jacob Narrative." *Anchor Bible Dictionary*, Vol. 3. David Noel Freedman, ed. New York, NY: Doubleday, 1992. 599.

Westerman, Claus. *Isaiah 40–66: A Commentary*. Philadelphia: Westminster Press, 1969. 206–12.

Yates, Kyle M. *Preaching from the Prophets*. Nashville, TN: Broadman Press, 1942. 99–100.

Lesson 9, January 30

Ackerman, Susan. "Isaiah." *The New Interpreter's Study Bible New Revised Standard Version with the Apocrypha*. Walter J. Harrelson, ed. Nashville, TN: Abingdon Press, 2003. 1011, 1031.

Baltes, A. J., ed., Biblespeech.com. http://www.biblespeech.com (accessed December 12, 2009).

Carroll, Robert P. "Isaiah, Book of (Second Isaiah)." *Anchor Bible Dictionary*, Vol. 3. David Noel Freedman, ed. New York, NY: Doubleday, 1992. 569–76.

Croatto, J. Severino. "Isaiah 40–55." *Global Bible Commentary*. Daniel Patte, ed. Nashville, TN: Abingdon Press, 2004. 198–99.

Keil and Delitzsch. *Commentary on the Old Testament: New Updated Edition*, electronic database *Barne's Notes*. (accessed August 9, 2009).

Merriam-Webster Online Dictionary. Merriam-Webster, Inc. http://www.merriam-webster.com (accessed December 12, 2009).

Strong, James. *Biblesoft's New Exhaustive Strong's Numbers and Concordance with Expanded Greek-Hebrew Dictionary*. Seattle, WA: Biblesoft, and International Bible Translators, 1994, 2003. http://www.biblesoft.com (accessed May 4, 2009).

Lesson 10, February 6

Baltes, A. J., ed., Biblespeech.com. http://www.biblespeech.com (accessed December 12, 2009).

Clarke, Adam. *Adam Clarke's Commentary. Biblesoft's New Exhaustive Strong's Numbers and Concordance with Expanded Greek-Hebrew Dictionary*. Seattle, WA: Biblesoft, and International Bible Translators, 1994, 2003. http://www.biblesoft.com (accessed May 28, 2009).

Donahue, John R. "Mark 8:22–10:52." *Harper's Bible Commentary*. James L. Mays, ed., San Francisco, CA: Harper & Row, 1988. 994–95.

Donfried, Karl P. "Peter." *Anchor Bible Dictionary*, Vol. 5. David Noel Freedman, ed. New York, NY: Doubleday, 1992. 251, 254–55.

ESV Study Bible, (English Standard Version), The. Wheaton, IL: Crossway Bibles, 2008.

Hollenbach, Paul W. "John the Baptist." *Anchor Bible Dictionary*, Vol. 3. David Noel Freedman, ed. New York, NY: Doubleday, 1992. 887–99.

Johnson, Siegfried S. "Elijah." *Anchor Bible Dictionary*, Vol. 2. David Noel Freedman, ed. New York, NY: Doubleday, 1992. 463–66.

Kutsko, John. "Caesarea Philippi." *Anchor Bible Dictionary*, Vol. 1. David Noel Freedman, ed. New York, NY: Doubleday, 1992. 803.

Marcus, Joel. "Uncommon Sense." *Christian Century*. August 30–September 6, 2000. 860.

Strong, James. *New Exhaustive Strong's Numbers and Concordance with Expanded Greek-Hebrew Dictionary*. Seattle, WA: Biblesoft, and International Bible Translators, 1994. 2003.

Thurman, Howard. *Jesus and the Disinherited*. Foreword by Vincent Harding. Boston, MA: Beacon Press, 1996.

Tolbert, Mary Ann. "Mark." *The New Interpreter's Study Bible New Revised Standard Version with the Apocrypha*. Walter J. Harrelson, ed. Nashville, TN: Abingdon Press, 2003. 1824–25.

Lesson 11, February 13

Adeyemo, Tokunboh, gen. ed. *Africa Bible Commentary*. Nairobi, Kenya: WordAlive, 2006.

Baltes, A. J., ed., Biblespeech.com. http://www.biblespeech.com (accessed December 12, 2009).

Barnes' Notes. Electronic Database. Seattle, WA: Biblesoft, and International Bible Translators, 1997, 2003. http://www.biblesoft.com (accessed May 10, 2009).

Gibbons, James E. "Peter, James, and John." *Editorial Byways*. Mt. Airy, NC: http://www.jgibbons.8m.com (accessed June 14, 2009).

Henry, Matthew. *Matthew Henry's Commentary on the Bible*. Peabody, MA: Hendrickson Publishers, Inc., 1997. 186–87.

Merriam-Webster Online Dictionary. Merriam-Webster, Inc. http://www.merriam-webster.com (accessed December 12, 2009).

Smith, William. *Smith's Bible Dictionary*. Peabody, MA: Hendrickson Publishers, Inc., 1990. 242.

Strong, James. *Biblesoft's New Exhaustive Strong's Numbers and Concordance with Expanded Greek-Hebrew Dictionary*. Seattle, WA: Biblesoft, and International Bible Translators, 1997, 2003. http://www.biblesoft.com (accessed May 10, 2009).

Lesson 12, February 20

Adeyemo, Tokunboh, gen. ed. *Africa Bible Commentary*. Nairobi, Kenya: WordAlive, 2006.

Baltes, A. J., ed., Biblespeech.com. http://www.biblespeech.com (accessed December 12, 2009).

Biblesoft's New Exhaustive Strong's Numbers and Concordance with Expanded Greek-Hebrew Dictionary. Biblesoft, Inc. and International Bible Translators, Inc., 1994, 2003. http://www.biblesoft.com (accessed June 20, 2009).

"Does the Bible Record the Death of the Apostles? How Did Each of the Apostles Die?" http://www.gotquestions.org/apostles-die.html (accessed June 26, 2009).

ESV Study Bible, (English Standard Version), The. Wheaton, IL: Crossway Bibles, 2008.

Henry, Matthew. *Matthew Henry's Commentary on the Bible*. Peabody, MA: Hendrickson Publishers, Inc., 1997. 191–92.

NIV Study Bible: New International Version, The. Grand Rapids, MI: Zondervan, 2008.

Smith, Henry. *Smith's Bible Dictionary*. Peabody, MA: Hendrickson Publishers, Inc., 1990. 266, 315.

Strong, James. *New Exhaustive Strong's Numbers and Concordance with Expanded Greek-Hebrew Dictionary*. Seattle, WA: Biblesoft, and International Bible Translators, 1994. 2003.

Unaegbu, Alajemba. *Attitudes for Living: Commentary on Paul's Epistle to the Philippians, An African Perspective*. Baltimore, MD: PublishAmerica, 2006.

Lesson 13; February 27

Adeyemo, Tokunboh, gen. ed. *Africa Bible Commentary*. Nairobi, Kenya: WordAlive, 2006.

Baltes, A. J., ed., Biblespeech.com. http://www.biblespeech.com (accessed December 12, 2009).

Biblesoft's New Exhaustive Strong's Numbers and Concordance with Expanded Greek-Hebrew Dictionary. Biblesoft and International Bible Translators, 1994, 2003.

Dake's Annotated Reference Bible. Lawrenceville, GA: Dake Bible Sales, 1963.

*ESV Study Bible, (*English Standard Version*), The*. Wheaton, IL: Crossway Bibles, 2008.

Henry, Matthew. *Matthew Henry's Commentary on the Bible*. Peabody, MA: Hendrickson Publishers, Inc., 1997. 198–99.

http://www.biblesoft.com (accessed June 21, 2009).

Merriam-Webster Online Dictionary. Merriam-Webster, Inc. http://www.merriam-webster.com (accessed December 12, 2009).

NIV Study Bible: New International Version, The. Grand Rapids, MI: Zondervan, 2008.

Smith, Henry. *Smith's Bible Dictionary*. Peabody, MA: Hendrickson Publishers, Inc., 1990. 135–36.

Strong, James. *New Exhaustive Strong's Numbers and Concordance with Expanded Greek-Hebrew Dictionary*. Seattle, WA: Biblesoft, and International Bible Translators, 1994. 2003.

We Worship God

This quarter's study offers a New Testament survey of worship in the early church. Hymns, prayers, apocalyptic visions, and letters of instruction reveal the spiritual culture and practice of the first Christians and provide contemporary believers with a biblical model of worship.

UNIT 1 • A GUIDE FOR WORSHIP LEADERS

The four lessons in this unit are largely a consideration of the instructions given to Timothy regarding spiritual leadership in the church. (1 Timothy 3:16).

Lesson 1: March 6, 2011
Instructions About Worship
1 Timothy 2:1–6; 3:14–16
The first concern in this passage is for a quiet and peaceable life with dignity. The verses include everyone, even kings and officials.

Lesson 2: March 13, 2011
Qualifications of Worship Leaders
1 Timothy 3:1–13
In this passage, Paul gives a designation of the offices of bishop and deacon, as well as a list of qualifications that show the high degree of development and maturation of the early church.

Lesson 3: March 20, 2011
Prepare for Leadership
1 Timothy 4:6–16
Paul makes clear the need for Timothy to set an example of correct Christian living.

Lesson 4: March 27, 2011
Worship Inspires Service
1 Timothy 5:1–8, 17–22
Paul explains the relationship between and among the generations in the church family. His admonition for care of widows by their families echoes Exodus 20:12 (the fifth commandment). He affirms the elders and speaks of the double honor that may come from respect for their age and their effectiveness as leaders. Paul indicates that the elders and widows should live lives that are pure and godly.

UNIT 2 • ANCIENT WORDS OF PRAISE

This unit takes the learners through the final weeks of Lent and into the Easter season. Each week's lesson is selected from a different book of the New Testament, but all share the common theme of praising Jesus Christ.

Lesson 5: April 3, 2011
Remembering Jesus Christ
2 Timothy 2:8–15
At times under Roman rule, Christians were viewed as criminals. Therefore, in this passage, Paul reminds Timothy of Jesus' resurrection and Davidic descent in order to give him courage to endure in difficult times.

Lesson 6: April 10, 2011
Praise Builds Us Up
Jude 17–25

This lesson gives assurance for living out our faith daily in Jesus Christ and discloses how praise builds up the Body of Christ.

Lesson 7: April 17, 2011
Hosanna!
Mark 11:1–11

Jesus' entry into Jerusalem for the Passover celebration marked the beginning of His final days. In Jewish tradition, the Mount of Olives (v. 1) was associated with the coming of the Messiah. Jesus' riding on a colt fulfills the prophecy in Zechariah 9:9. People placed garments and leafy branches on the ground (v. 8) much as they did during royal processions (2 Kings 9:13).

Lesson 8: April 24, 2011
Christ Is Risen!
Matthew 28:1–17

When the women went "to see" (v. 1) the tomb (Mark 16), they came to bring spices to anoint the body of Jesus. An angel told them that Jesus was alive.

Lesson 9: May 1, 2011
The Christ Hymn
Philippians 2:1–11

Philippi was a Roman colony. The proclamation by Philippian believers of Jesus as Lord would be viewed as a political challenge. Paul envisioned a community of believers who adopted Jesus as the model for personal relationships, and he presented Christ as a perfect example to emulate.

UNIT 3 • JOHN'S VISION OF WORSHIP

These four passages from Revelation contain some of the New Testament's most doxological (or praise) texts. They are wonderful texts of worship and praise that inspire hope in God's new heaven and new earth.

Lesson 10: May 8, 2011
Heavenly Worship
Revelation 4:1–2, 6b–11

In this passage, the vision of the throne, the One seated on it, and the living creatures who sing "Holy, holy, holy" recalls the vision God gave to Isaiah (Isaiah 6) and Ezekiel (Ezekiel 1:10).

Lesson 11: May 15, 2011
Thankful Worship
Revelation 7:9–17

John's vision included an unlimited international group gathered before the throne. Those in white robes generally symbolize the baptized, who are clothed in righteousness. The people in white robes carry palm branches, which are symbols of victory and thanksgiving.

Lesson 12: May 22, 2011
All Things New
Revelation 21:1–8

Dwelling in perfect peace and union with God is the reward of those who persevere in struggle and retain their faith against the odds. The ultimate fulfillment of God's promise in Christ is depicted in this vision of the Holy City, the New Jerusalem.

Lesson 13: May 29, 2011
Tree of Life
Revelation 22:1–9

The water of life and the tree of life are highly important in signifying the sacredness of existence. Through it all, God is the focal point of this worshipful setting.

Come, Let Us Worship and Adore Him!

And I saw a new heaven and a new earth:
for the first heaven and the first earth
were passed away;
and there was no more sea.

And I John saw the holy city,
new Jerusalem,
coming down from God out of heaven,
prepared as a bride adorned for her husband.

And I heard a great voice out of heaven saying,
Behold, the tabernacle of God is with men,
and he will dwell with them,
and they shall be his people,
and God himself shall be with them,
and be their God.

And God shall wipe away all tears from their eyes;
and there shall be no more death,
neither sorrow,
nor crying,
neither shall there be any more pain:
for the former things are passed away.

And he that sat upon the throne said,
Behold, I make all things new.
And he said unto me,
Write:
for these words are true and faithful
(Revelation 21:1–5).

COME, LET US
WORSHIP AND ADORE
THE LORD, OUR GOD!

Why Do We Attend Church?

by Aja M. Carr

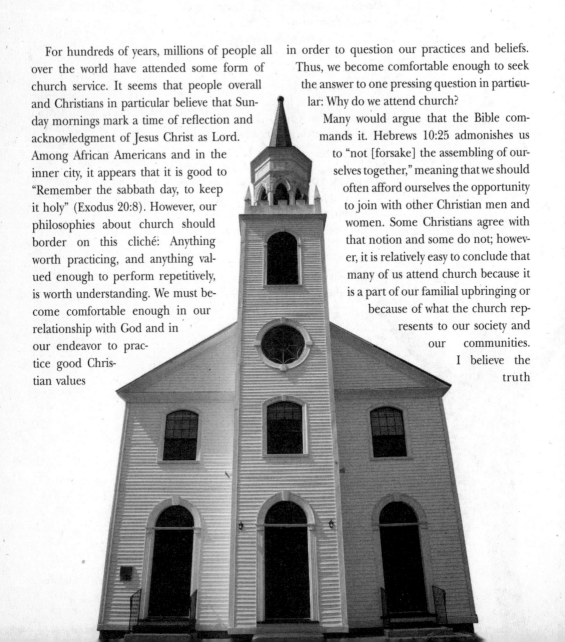

For hundreds of years, millions of people all over the world have attended some form of church service. It seems that people overall and Christians in particular believe that Sunday mornings mark a time of reflection and acknowledgment of Jesus Christ as Lord. Among African Americans and in the inner city, it appears that it is good to "Remember the sabbath day, to keep it holy" (Exodus 20:8). However, our philosophies about church should border on this cliché: Anything worth practicing, and anything valued enough to perform repetitively, is worth understanding. We must become comfortable enough in our relationship with God and in our endeavor to practice good Christian values in order to question our practices and beliefs. Thus, we become comfortable enough to seek the answer to one pressing question in particular: Why do we attend church?

Many would argue that the Bible commands it. Hebrews 10:25 admonishes us to "not [forsake] the assembling of ourselves together," meaning that we should often afford ourselves the opportunity to join with other Christian men and women. Some Christians agree with that notion and some do not; however, it is relatively easy to conclude that many of us attend church because it is a part of our familial upbringing or because of what the church represents to our society and our communities. I believe the truth about our theology as churchgoers is deeply rooted in our upbringing. It is apart of our familial matrix. We attend church because our parents attended or because our families have been members of a particular church for years. It represents a place where we all come together in fellowship and worship. One could survey any given church and interview countless parishioners capable of testifying about the positive experiences afforded to their families because of their commitment to attending service. Ultimately we can, throughout history, point to the church as a place that has allowed all of God's children to be a family. Even during slavery, the church represented the one place where the slave family might be allowed to go together. Slaves attended the church of their masters, and as long as the family worked on the same plantation, they could almost be assured that Sundays represented a small space in time where they could be with their families and be encouraged through some scriptural interpretation.

Marvin McMickle writes, "What better way is there to view the ministry of churches in inner-city areas than as agents that both prolong life and help to avoid decay in communities where almost every other business and institution has abandoned the area? In some respects, churches are among the very few institutions that have remained in the inner city. A drive through any of America's inner-city communities will reveal that barbershops and beauty salons, bars (and liquor stores), and a wide assortment of small businesses and churches of various sizes occupy almost every corner, amid a sea of vacant lots and abandoned buildings. This flight from the inner cities has resulted in the loss of a tax base, the rapid decline in the size of the middle-class remaining in the cities. Almost everything that inner city residents need in order to have a meaningful life is located outside of their community, ranging from medical care to adequate shopping facilities to employment beyond minimum wage jobs at fast-food restaurants" (57–58).

The city of Chicago, for instance, is home to several megachurches. Still, these churches are primarily located in the inner city in predominately African American neighborhoods. Churches like the Salem Baptist Church of Chicago, which boasts some 15,000+ members, sits in the heart of the Roseland community (largely African American and partially Latino). The Apostolic Church of God, pastored by Dr. Byron Brazier, and the Trinity United Church of Christ, pastored by Rev. Otis Moss III, are both situated on the South Side of the inner city and are predominantly African American.

The African American church is the only inner city community presence that has not uprooted itself from the community. While the quality of life for many of the parishioners *has* increased—allowing them to relocate to suburban areas—the church *has not* relocated. I believe many African Americans continue to attend churches in our community for that reason. The church has always been there as a part of the community, and it is viewed as an entity that will remain. It is a prototype of the nature of Christ in the community; its presence will remain steadfast and unmovable.

As we have changed and grown, so have our churches. The emergence of the African American middle-class brought with it the emergence of the African American megachurch. Many scholars committed to the study of church growth and trends would argue that the birth of the megamall brought with it an influx of megachurches. However, I would argue that the expansion of the African American middle-class and their ability to participate as valuable consumers in society (meaning that we could now shop at the megamalls) also gave us the affluence to support and become a part of larger church ministries. This supports the claim that some of us continue to attend church because its complexion has changed to represent the color of society as a whole. And every time society "upgrades," we have watched the church "upgrade," creating social constructs in the church. We subscribed to cable television because it was new and exciting; it offered us more channels and more programs. Likewise, the church began to embrace the insurgence of cable markets. Now, we see church services broadcasted on cable television. The African American church has aligned itself with the culture of our society and we continue to attend because we can relate to that.

The argument about the theology of churchgoers exists: We attend church because it has conformed itself to a changing society, but we also attend church to be rescued emotionally from that very same society. Moreover, the argument exists regarding the role of the church. The church has been a steadfast and unchanging part of our community, but the economic incline of the parishioners and the rise of mega-entities have caused the church to change, and we can relate to the fluctuation. Because these arguments are easily debated, they do not carry as much weight as this argument: We attend church because of our love for Jesus Christ.

Countless theologians have harvested mounds of information regarding church membership, trends in church growth, and the theology of churchgoers, but none can easily refute the idea that many Christians simply love the Lord which is why they attend church services. Church represents the one place in society where we can worship and praise God in our own way and with few inhibitions. While we might acknowledge the role of our families in our relationship with God, and might identify with the consistent and conversely changing roles of the church, it is beyond debate that Jesus is the number one reason that Christians attend church.

Source:
McMickle, Marvin. *Preaching to the African American Middle Class*. Valley Forger, PA: Judson Press, 1989. 57–58.

Aja M. Carr is the Editor of the Young Adult publications at UMI. She holds a Bachelor of Arts degree in history from the University of Illinois at Urbana-Champaign and a Master's in Theological Studies from the Garrett Evangelical Theological Seminary.

We Worship You, O Lord!

by Whitney M. DuPreé

When I was 14, I had the opportunity to visit Israel with my church. Even before the plane landed, I knew everything we would see. The tour guide would take us to see Bethlehem, the city where our Lord and Savior was born. We would be baptized in the Jordan River and visit the tomb of Lazarus. We would take a boat ride in the Dead Sea and look upon the Garden of Gethsemane. We would follow the path Jesus took as He carried the Cross on His back, which is called the Via Dolorosa, and we would look at what is believed to be the tomb where He was laid but not bound.

I was looking forward to seeing the places I had read about in Sunday School come to life. And even though I knew God to be omnipresent (all-present or present everywhere), I felt there would be a special aura in the birthplace of Christianity. I knew I would experience true worship and peace in Israel. I was eager to be immersed in what I thought would be a spiritually relaxing trip.

While my trip to the Holy Land was emotionally moving, enlightening, and fun, it certainly wasn't spiritually relaxing. The trip challenged me to question not my beliefs, but my practices and actions. My experience in Israel showed me the importance of truly revering God in all I do.

When I looked upon the Garden of Gethsemane, I was somber. I thought about the enormous pressure that weighed on Jesus' shoulders and His desire to only please His Father. I could not help but stand quietly and honor Him. I stood in awe at the entrance of Lazarus' tomb wondering how a man wrapped in cloth could maneuver through a structure that I, free of binding burial garments, could barely do. I walked the Via Dolorosa, tired and sore with only a book bag on my back, not the heavy wooden Cross our Savior bore. I couldn't imagine the physical pain Jesus must have suffered during that journey, and yet, He continued on. I was moved by the great sacrifice Jesus made and was in awe of God at each of the sacred sites. Later, I learned that this was not enough.

It is well known that Israel is home to three of the world's most popular religions: Christianity, Judaism, and Islam. All three claim the Holy Land, and all three are very apparent throughout the land. Every day we would visit a Christian landmark, and we would also see a mosque or a temple. The streets were full of Christians, Jews, and Muslims in their traditional religious garbs going about their everyday lives. Initially, my young radical American mind was offended at the sight of seeing so many non-Christians in such a scared land. The juxtaposition of cultures confused me. I was unable to grasp what I considered disrespect in the Holy Land. I couldn't understand why they didn't believe, even though they walked and lived in the places I could only read about. I could not comprehend why people with so much archeological evidence would refuse to worship Jesus.

However, this foolish spiritual arrogance came to an abrupt end when I toured the Old City of Jerusalem and I came to realize how much I needed to learn about true worship. The Old City is divided into four quarters: the Jewish Quarter, the Armenian Quarter, the Muslim Quarter, and the Christian Quarter. There are no segregation laws, and it is easy to pass from one quarter to another without considering one's ethnicity or religious beliefs. In fact, most of the Via Dolorosa lies throughout the Muslim Quarter. The Old City reminded me of the markets and bazaars one would see in old Middle Eastern movies. As the group walked through the Old City, merchants were constantly trying to entice us and everyone else who was passing by. I saw people haggling over postcards, jewelry, clothes, and even meat. The streets were made of cobblestone, and it was extremely hot. The air was thick with the stench of human odors, and the high walls made it difficult to feel a breeze.

Suddenly, I heard bells ringing and crowds flooded the marketplace. I was pressed against a wall as crowds and crowds of people rushed passed me. They were all headed in the same direction.

As I frantically searched for my church group, I saw a mother rushing through the marketplace with her daughter and young son following closely behind her. Somehow the daughter and son became separated from their mother, and the son began to cry. The mother turned her head to see that her children had fallen back in the crowd. The young son reached toward her, and she did what any devout Muslim trying to get to prayer would do—she kept running toward the mosque. I was shocked and outraged. Why would that mother leave her children! I looked at the daughter and saw her pick up her little brother and run right along with the crowd to prayer. I was amazed.

In less than three minutes, the overcrowded and nearly suffocating marketplace was completely empty. Carts had been abandoned. Shops had been left unattended and open. Everyone was in prayer. Our Jewish tour guide told us this was a regular occurrence, five times a day. He said dedicated Muslims abandoned all tasks so they wouldn't be late to pray and worship. Minutes later, the marketplace was noisy and bustling with activity, but I would never forget what had occurred moments before.

Once a week, Christians across America make their way to praise and worship services. Oftentimes, they pass several churches before arriving at the worship center of their choice. While it can be assumed that few are excited about showing up to church late, tardiness isn't a major concern. If we scan church parking lots, we see congregants casually strutting toward the church, no sense of urgency in the air. Stores are not left unmanned and unlocked simply because a worship service is taking place. If a mother and father rushed ahead of their young teen, chances are that teen would want to hang outside the church instead of following his or her parents into the service. We comfort ourselves by saying we can worship our God any time and any place, but do we have spiritual discipline? We pride ourselves on having a merciful and gracious God, but do we take advantage of our Lord and show a lack of respect in the process?

My trip to the Holy Land showed me what a true yearning to worship looked like, and it encouraged me to be critical of my own life and priorities.

Whitney M. DuPreé is the Market Research Analyst at Urban Ministries, Inc. After graduating from high school as salutatorian in 2004, she went on to receive a Bachelor of Engineering in civil engineering from Vanderbilt University in 2008. She believes strongly in uplifting the community, and she expresses this through her membership in Alpha Kappa Alpha Sorority Inc., the Jackie Robinson Foundation, the NAACP, and her continued support of her alma mater.

Richard Smallwood

As a renowned gospel singer, pianist, and composer, Richard Smallwood is known the world over for his distinct blend of classical and traditional sounds. His expertise in his field has influenced gospel music for generations.

Smallwood expressed interest in music at a young age. At only 5 years old he played the piano by ear, and he formed his first gospel group at 11 years old. Smallwood was also a scholar of music. He graduated magna cum laude with a degree in both piano and vocal performance from Howard University, one of the premiere historically Black colleges and universities. During his time at Howard, Smallwood formed the university's first gospel group, *The Celestials*. The group met with tremendous success and even traveled to Switzerland for the Montreux Jazz Festival. Smallwood's leadership and travels continued when he founded Howard's first gospel choir, the Richard Smallwood Singers, which became the first gospel group to sing in the Soviet Union.

Smallwood set the stage at a young age for a career with no boundaries. He began his highly anticipated recording career in the seventies with the album entitled *The Richard Smallwood Singers*. This first album stayed on Billboard's gospel chart for 87 weeks. He received his first Grammy for his follow up album, *Psalms*. Some of his most famous songs include "Total Praise" and "Center of My Joy," which debuted on Smallwood's second Grammy-winning album, *Textures*. Smallwood went on to receive countless awards, including another Grammy and a Dove Award.

Smallwood's honors have extended beyond traditional accolades. The Smithsonian Institution honors him as a gospel innovator and songwriter. His hometown of Washington, DC, also created the Richard Smallwood Day. Richard Smallwood has had the opportunity to lead worship at the Kennedy Center and even the White House. He has also toured with the musical theatre production *Sing, Mahalia, Sing* and had a guest appearance on *Ryan's Hope*, an ABC television show. Richard Smallwood continues to be an ambassador of worship and influences the entire world with his anointed ministry.

Sources:
http://www.richardsmallwood.com/bio.htm
http://www.peoplesinauguralgala.com/smallwood.php

Teaching Tips

March 6
Bible Study Guide 1

1. Words You Should Know

A. Supplications (1 Timothy 2:1) *deesis* (Gk.)—Seeking, asking God.

B. Intercessions (v. 1) *enteuxis* (Gk.)—Petitions to God on behalf of others.

2. Teacher Preparation

Unifying Principle—The Search for Meaning. Citing an ancient hymn, 1 Timothy affirms that Christ is the measure of all truth about God.

A. Pray for your students and ask God to meet their spiritual needs.

B. Study and reflect on the entire text and its surrounding sections. Prepare to lead a discussion on: (1) "When it comes to God, what is 'true' worship?" and (2) "Why should we intercede for those who have authority over us?"

3. Open the Lesson

A. Open with prayer, including the Aim for Change.

B. Write the above questions about true worship of God, our spiritual search, and interceding for those who have authority over us on the board. Discuss.

C. Tie the In Focus story into Paul's teachings on true worship and the true mission of the church.

4. Present the Scripture

A. Have volunteers read the Focal Verses.

B. Now use The People, Places, and Times; Background; Search the Scriptures; At-A-Glance outline; In Depth; and More Light on the Text to clarify the verses.

5. Explore the Meaning

A. Lead a discussion of the Discuss the Meaning, Lesson in Our Society, and Make It Happen sections.

B. Have volunteers connect these sections to the Aim for Change and the Keep in Mind verse.

6. Next Steps for Application

A. Have students write in the Follow the Spirit and Remember Your Thoughts sections what true worship of a holy God is.

B. Challenge them to meditate on what they have written during the week and pray that God will help them to worship Him with enthusiasm.

C. Close with prayer.

Worship Guide

For the Superintendent or Teacher
Theme: Instructions About Worship
Theme Song: "Let's Just Praise the Lord"
Devotional Reading: Hebrews 8:6–12
Prayer

Instructions About Worship

Bible Background • 1 TIMOTHY 2:1–6; 3:14–16
Printed Text • 1 TIMOTHY 2:1–6; 3:14–16 | Devotional Reading • HEBREWS 8:6–12

————————— Aim for Change —————————

By the end of the lesson, we will: EXPLAIN how to worship Almighty God; FEEL the need to worship Almighty God; and WORSHIP God with enthusiasm.

—————————  In Focus —————————

A few years ago, some members of a certain congregation exerted much pressure on their pastor to use his pulpit and influence during an election to get worshipers to vote in a certain way. However, the pastor refused to compromise or capitulate. Instead, he insisted that worshiping God entails giving one's total and sole allegiance to Christ, which is not to be considered identical to supporting a political party. About one-fifth of the congregation left the church within a few weeks' time and refused to continue their worship there.

While some make the error of too easily linking political agendas with fidelity to Christ, many people want to define worship to Christ as merely participating in a Sunday service or simply manifesting some intellectual adherence to particular doctrinal truths. Yet we must realize that worship to God is holistic. In other words, it encompasses every area of our lives. Our lives must reflect Christlike attitudes in our daily living and relationships.

In 1 Timothy, Paul is encouraging his close friend Timothy to refute the teachings of false teachers and instruct the people concerning proper doctrine, leadership, and worship.

————————— Keep in Mind —————————

"For there is one God, and one mediator between God and men, the man Christ Jesus" (1 Timothy 2:5).

"For there is one God, and one mediator between God and men, the man Christ Jesus" (1 Timothy 2:5).

303

Focal Verses

KJV 1 Timothy 2:1 I exhort therefore, that, first of all, supplications, prayers, intercessions, and giving of thanks, be made for all men;

2 For kings, and for all that are in authority; that we may lead a quiet and peaceable life in all godliness and honesty.

3 For this is good and acceptable in the sight of God our Saviour;

4 Who will have all men to be saved, and to come unto the knowledge of the truth.

5 For there is one God, and one mediator between God and men, the man Christ Jesus;

6 Who gave himself a ransom for all, to be testified in due time.

3:14 These things write I unto thee, hoping to come unto thee shortly:

15 But if I tarry long, that thou mayest know how thou oughtest to behave thyself in the house of God, which is the church of the living God, the pillar and ground of the truth.

16 And without controversy great is the mystery of godliness: God was manifest in the flesh, justified in the Spirit, seen of angels, preached unto the Gentiles, believed on in the world, received up into glory.

NLT 1 Timothy 2:1 I urge you, first of all, to pray for all people. Ask God to help them; intercede on their behalf, and give thanks for them.

2 Pray this way for kings and all who are in authority so that we can live peaceful and quiet lives marked by godliness and dignity.

3 This is good and pleases God our Savior,

4 who wants everyone to be saved and to understand the truth.

5 For there is only one God and one Mediator who can reconcile God and humanity—the man Christ Jesus.

6 He gave his life to purchase freedom for everyone. This is the message God gave to the world at just the right time.

3:14 I am writing these things to you now, even though I hope to be with you soon,

15 so that if I am delayed, you will know how people must conduct themselves in the household of God. This is the church of the living God, which is the pillar and foundation of the truth.

16 Without question, this is the great mystery of our faith: Christ was revealed in a human body and vindicated by the Spirit. He was seen by angels and announced to the nations. He was believed in throughout the world and taken to heaven in glory.

The People, Places, and Times

Timothy. Timothy was a native of Lystra, born of a mixed marriage. His father was a Greek and his mother a Jew (Acts 16:1). He was taught the Jewish Scriptures from his earliest childhood by his mother Eunice and his grandmother Lois (2 Timothy 1:5; 3:15). He was a convert of Paul's early ministry (c. A.D. 46), a young disciple chosen by Paul as a companion during his second missionary journey. Timothy became very close to Paul to the extent that Paul writes in Philippians 2:20, "I have no one like him" (NRSV). In 1 Corinthians 4:17, Paul describes him as "my beloved son, and faithful in the Lord." Moreover, Paul entrusted Timothy to minister in his stead, calling the church to sound doctrine, proper worship, and Christ-honoring relationships.

Background

First Timothy is not an exhaustive manual for understanding leadership qualifications or a proper order of worship. Nonetheless, Paul deals with many of these issues in this particular correspondence as he contrasts proper leadership qualifications and character with that of the elders who were false teachers. As Paul traveled to Macedonia, he instructed Timothy to remain in Ephesus in order to confront the problem of false teachers in the church (1 Timothy 1:3). In light of Acts 20:30, where Luke says, "Of your own selves shall men arise, speaking perverse things," it is quite likely that the false teachers were, in fact, Ephesian elders with whom Timothy had to contend.

At-A-Glance

1. We Pray for Everyone (1 Timothy 2:1–4)

2. Jesus Gave His Life for Everyone (vv. 5–6)

3. The Church as a People of Truth (3:14–16)

In Depth

1. We Pray for Everyone (1 Timothy 2:1–4)

Paul does not only connect his present discussion with what he has previously said, but also goes on to suggest the course of action to be taken by the use of the word "therefore" (v. 1). It is clear from 1 Timothy 1:3 that the situation in the Ephesian church was precarious. There were those (apparently elders) who were wayward in their teaching and influence, leading others astray. Paul commissioned young Timothy to set things in order in his stead. In so doing, he must first address the issue of prayer.

Realizing the problems that some leaders in the church were causing, Paul instructs Timothy (and the Ephesian church indirectly) that prayer must be made for *all* persons, especially those in positions of influence and authority. The importance of prayer is underscored. Paul's broader context is Christians' public worship. Paul's instruction to Timothy about prayer has two components. First, Timothy (and by implication all Christians today) must not limit prayers to his own life, concerns, family, or situations. Most Christians find it easy to pray for their families, friends, and loved ones. Although such prayers are necessary and important, it should not end there. We should also pray for our *enemies* and for those with whom we have conflict or disagreement. We should pray for those who annoy us and for those who oppose us.

Second, by Paul instructing that prayers be made for "kings" and "all that are in authority" (v. 2), he connects the position of leadership with the need for divine guidance. Too frequently, one hears of persons in leadership falling into terrible situations of immorality or endorsing a systemic injustice that benefits the wealthy and marginalizes the poor. People in positions of influence can make or break a community, state, or country. Such decisions, day-to-day pressures, and vision are in dire need of the gracious leading of God. Therefore, we pray for those who are in authority. No matter what their political party, family history, level of education, or favorite sports team, we sincerely ask God to direct leaders in a way that affects peace, justice, and equality for all persons.

2. Jesus Gave His Life for Everyone (vv. 5–6)

As a means of further explicating God's love for all humanity, Paul draws upon what appears to be an early creed of the church. There is one God (v. 5). The Jewish people were staunchly monotheistic ("mono" means "one," "theistic" means "believer in God"). Twice daily, Jewish persons would repeat what is known as the *shema`* (their creed) as found in Deuteronomy 6:4ff. However, at the heart of the Jewish insistence in "one God" is more than simply the nature of God's being. It is a matter of one's allegiance. Is our allegiance to the many false gods of our culture? Or are we pledging our lives, by faith, to the one true God?

Paul goes on to explain that there is also only one mediator between God and humankind. This prohibits believers from worshiping other persons, for example Caesar or kings. Even in our day, there tends to be infatuation with popular sports figures, politicians, entertainers, and some preachers. This sometimes goes to the point of hero worship. Paul would denounce such a thing and encourages Timothy and others to remember that there is one God and only one mediator between God and humankind, "the man Christ Jesus" (1 Timothy 2:5). No matter how admirable someone may be, no one other than Jesus Christ is an embodiment of God.

Further, in stating that there is only one mediator, Jesus Christ, Paul contends that humanity stands in need of being restored to a proper relationship with God. Apart from Christ, there is no way for such restoration.

3. The Church as a People of Truth (3:14–16)

Evidently, Paul desired to visit Timothy and the church at Ephesus. But in case this was not possible, he wrote the previous exhortations (1 Timothy 1–3). Due to the false teachers, the Ephesian congregation was being led astray from the proper response to God and His gracious salvation. Thus, Paul has addressed "how thou oughtest to behave thyself in the house of God" (3:15). This is not simply an allusion to a physical church building, made of wood, brick, metal, or mortar. Paul is speaking of Christians as being the "household of God" (NRSV), wherein proper, healthy doctrine should be manifest in the transformed lives of sisters and brothers in Christ.

In Paul's day, there were many religions that were couched in various "mysteries." Such mysteries were oftentimes considered privy to a select few. However, Paul uses (as he often does) the language of the day in order to illuminate a Gospel truth. The "mystery of godliness" (v. 16) is not something hidden to many and revealed to a few. The mystery of "godliness" (this term stands for the Christian faith) is a truth gone public in the person and work of Jesus Christ.

Search the Scriptures

1. For whom are we to intercede (1 Timothy 2:1)?

2. Who is the mediator between God and humankind (v. 5)?

Discuss the Meaning

1. In light of what Paul explains in chapter two, that God wants everyone to be saved, how should we handle situations where we have a hard time forgiving or liking someone? What if it is someone you do not know personally, such as a politician, movie star, or someone who ran into your car?

2. Why is it important to learn how to behave in the house of God? To what does "the house of God" refer, and why would a person's behavior be different within or without the house of God? Should it be so? Explain your viewpoint.

Lesson in Our Society

In the church, it is often easy to segment our lives, even unintentionally, into a secular place and a sacred place. The tendency is to keep politics, work, finances, or other things separate from "church" things. However, true worship is giving every aspect of our lives to God. This includes our prayers and thanksgivings for all people in our nation, place of work, bank, restaurant, and the list goes on.

Make It Happen

Part of worship is praying for others and thanking God for all persons. These actions aren't merely for those who are easy to love.

We should be praying and thanking God for everyone in our lives. Throughout this week, pray and thank God for someone who is difficult for you to love or respect.

Follow the Spirit

What God wants me to do:

_____

_____

_____

_____

Remember Your Thoughts

Special insights I have learned:

_____

_____

_____

_____

More Light on the Text

1 Timothy 2:1–6; 3:14–16

2:1 I exhort therefore, that, first of all, supplications, prayers, intercessions, and giving of thanks, be made for all men; 2 For kings, and for all that are in authority; that we may lead a quiet and peaceable life in all godliness and honesty.

The word "therefore," which begins verse 1, does not only refer to what precedes, but also serves as a transition to something new that the writer is about to say. Given the problem of heresies in the church, the apostle Paul considered it appropriate to offer some specific instructions on how to combat the challenge. Significantly, Paul starts with an admonition about prayer. For Paul, prayer is not an option. Rather, it is an absolute necessity. So he encourages the believers to pray. The verb "exhort" (Greek *parakaleo*, **par-ak-al-EH-o**) may be translated "urge," "appeal," or "beseech." It indicates the urgency of the admonition. The phrase "first of all" does not suggest something that is at the top of a "to-do list." Instead, it denotes something of primary importance.

In the Greek New Testament, there are various nouns used for prayer. Four of them occur in this verse. First is the Greek word *deeseis* (**DEH-ay-sis**), which means literally "requests," but is translated here as "supplications." It was a regular term for a petition to a superior, and it carries the idea of desire or need. Effective prayer must be accompanied by a sense of need and a deep desire (cf. Luke 18:1–10; James 5:16). Second, there is the Greek word *proseuche* (**pros-yoo-KHAY**). It is the most general word for prayer. It is translated as "prayers," and it always signifies praying to God both in private or in public. Third, there is *enteuxis* (**ENT-yoo-ksis**), a Greek word that is found only here and in 4:5, and is rightly translated as "intercession." The fundamental idea of the word was "boldness of access to God's presence." The fourth Greek word used here is *eucharistia* (**yoo-khar-is-TEE-ah**), from which the word "eucharist" is derived. It simply means "giving of thanks" (KJV), something that should be a part of all praying.

Paul urges believers to engage in prayers on behalf of everyone. We are to engage in all kinds of prayers for all kinds of people (v. 1). To pray for "everyone" does not suggest that we must mention each person by name, but rather that our prayers should include all groups of human beings. Prayer must be non-discriminatory. We should pray for all humanity, regardless of race, nationality, or social standing. Without doubt, if we must pray for all people, we must believe that God loves them without distinction and that Christ died for them all. We must pray especially "for kings and all those in authority." In Paul's day, the Greek term *basileus* (**bas-il-YOOCE**) or "king" was applied to the emperor of Rome as well as to lesser rulers. *Huperocho* (**hoop-er-EKH-o**) is a Greek word that refers to persons in place of prominence or to prominent officials. The Roman emperor at the time the epistle was written was Nero—the man who later put Paul to death. The point is that we should pray for our present rulers, regardless of their political persuasions. Prayer for "all those in authority" in various levels of government ought to be part of public worship.

The last part of verse 2 reveals both the content and purpose of prayer—that we may live peaceful and quiet lives in all godliness and honesty. We as Christians must pray that our leaders will have the knowledge and wisdom needed to guide them in their duties.

3 For this is good and acceptable in the sight of God our Saviour; 4 Who will have all men to be saved, and to come unto the knowledge of the truth.

Paul now states the reason that praying for all people is important: it is good and pleasing to God. The Greek word *kalos* (**kal-OCE**), translated here as "good," can also mean "excellent." The antecedent of "this" is the reference to prayer for all people in verse 1. Paul stated that God is pleased to see believers earnestly concerned for the salvation of all humankind and not simply of an elite group. The knowledge that such prayer pleases God provides great incentive to pray. Paul described God as "our Savior" because he was dealing with the concept of salvation in the verses that follow.

Verse 4 provides the basis for the statement in the previous verse that prayer for all people is good and pleasing to God. God desires that all be saved. Hence, intercession for all humanity is pleasing to Him. One must not confuse God's desire or "will" (v. 4, KJV; Gk. *thelō*, **THEL-o**) for all humanity with universalism. Christ died for all humanity, but the benefits of His death must be personally appropriated. The Gospel of Christ should be proclaimed to all, and it is the duty of all who know it to proclaim it far and wide. When it is made known, it is the duty of those who hear it to acknowledge and receive it.

5 For there is one God, and one mediator between God and men, the man Christ Jesus; 6 Who gave himself a ransom for all, to be testified in due time.

Verse 5 is one of the most important verses in the New Testament. It is a bold declaration that "there is one God." Just as it was important in the polytheistic world of the first century, it is important in today's pluralistic society. But Paul goes further. He affirms the uniqueness of Jesus as the only mediator between God and humanity. The statement echoes the words of Jesus: "I am the Way, the Truth and the Life. No man comes to God except by me" (John 14:6)

The Greek word for "mediator" (*mesites*, **mes-EE-tace**) occurs only once in the Septuagint (the Greek translation of the Old Testament, commonly referred to as the LXX). There, Job expressed his frustration that God was not a man with whom he could converse. In despair he concluded, "Neither is there any daysman [*mesites*] betwixt us, that might lay his hand upon us both" (Job 9:33). The basic meaning of *mesites* is a "go-between," that is, a person who intervenes between two people, in order to make or restore peace and friendship, to form a

compact, or for ratifying a covenant. Christ is the answer to this cry for help. God's mercy and grace are available to all humankind, but there is only one mediator by and through whom they could be appropriated, one way by which forgiveness may be obtained. The phrase "for all" occurs for the third time in this paragraph (2:1, 4), and it is Paul's emphatic insistence on the universal sufficiency of the atonement, limited only by human rejection.

As the Mediator, Christ removed the separation caused by sin and reconciled humankind with God. As the God-Man, Christ is uniquely qualified to serve as a go-between who can bring sinful people into God's family.

3:14 These things write I unto thee, hoping to come unto thee shortly: 15 But if I tarry long, that thou mayest know how thou oughtest to behave thyself in the house of God, which is the church of the living God, the pillar and ground of the truth.

The apostle Paul wrote with the intent of visiting Timothy in Ephesus. However, anticipating a possible delay, he proceeded to give instructions to Timothy on how people were to conduct themselves in the "household of God." The translation of the Greek word *oikos* (**OY-kos**) as "household" in NLT instead of "house" in KJV is more accurate and preferred by some contemporary scholars. Readers have often taken the word as a reference to church building, but the focus is on the local congregation, God's family, rather than the building. The imagery of the "household of God" reinforces the relationship of believers as brothers and sisters.

The word "behave" unfortunately suggests to the ordinary reader the idea of personal deportment. Paul was not describing behavior suitable for the church building, but the type of conduct that befits a person who belongs to God's family.

16 And without controversy great is the mystery of godliness: God was manifest in the flesh, justified in the Spirit, seen of angels, preached unto the Gentiles, believed on in the world, received up into glory.

The phrase "without controversy" (KJV), or "beyond all question" as some modern translations have it, suggest that Paul is writing about something on which there is common consent among believers. It is the Greek word *homologoumenos* (**hom-ol-og-ow-MEN-nos**), which means "confessedly." It occurs only here in the New Testament, and it may be translated "by common agreement," "without controversy," or "by common profession." It expresses the unanimous convictions of Christians and introduces an aspect that had the unanimous consent of Christians—"the mystery of godliness." The term "mystery" also appears in 3:9 and is translated "deep truths." It refers to truth that is now revealed. The mystery of the Christian religion to which Paul pointed refers to God's redemptive plan that had been kept secret but was now revealed. Paul was extolling God's powerful actions that form the basis of the gospel and the transforming results that derive from accepting it.

Say It Correctly

Antioch. AN-tee-ok.
Eucharist. ʹyū-k(ə-)rəst.
Hymenaeus. hi-ʹmuh-NEE-uhs.
Iconium. i-KOH-nee-uhm.
Lycaonian. Lik-uh-OH-nee-uhn, lik'ay-OH-nee-uhn.
Lystra. LIS-truh.
Shema. SHEE-muh, SHEE-mah.
Tertullian. tuhr-ʹTUHL-ee-uhn.

Daily Bible Readings

M: The Ministry of the Mediator
Hebrews 8:6–12

T: Worship and Thanksgiving
Psalm 95:1–7

W: Prayer and Supplication
Ephesians 6:18–24

T: The Spirit's Intercession
Romans 8:22–27

F: Instructions on Prayer
Luke 11:1–13

S: The Goal of Instruction
1 Timothy 1:1–7

S: The Great Mystery
1 Timothy 2:1–6; 3:14–16

Teaching Tips

March 13
Bible Study Guide 2

1. Words You Should Know

A. True (1 Timothy 3:1) *pistos* (Gk.)—Trusty, faithful, can be relied on.

B. Blameless (v. 2) *anegkletos* (Gk.)—Not open to censure, irreproachable.

C. Novice (v. 6) *neophutos* (Gk.)—A new convert; one who has recently become a Christian.

2. Teacher Preparation

Unifying Principle—Choosing a Good Leader. This passage suggests that spiritual maturity is an important factor when choosing leaders.

A. Pray for your students and ask God to meet their spiritual needs.

B. Study and reflect on the entire text and its surrounding sections.

C. As you study, note the qualifications of a bishop and a deacon and prepare to list them on the board.

3. Open the Lesson

A. Open with prayer, including the Aim for Change.

B. Have a volunteer read the In Focus story.

C. Discuss Derrick's dilemma and Sean's concern about character transformation in those who minister.

4. Present the Scripture

A. Have volunteers read the Focal Verses.

B. Write on the board the words "bishop" and "deacon."

C. List the attributes discussed in today's Scripture text as your students read the Focal Verses.

D. Use The People, Places, and Times; Background; Search the Scriptures; At-A-Glance outline; In Depth; and More Light on the Text to clarify the verses.

5. Explore the Meaning

A. Have three volunteers lead a discussion of the Discuss the Meaning, Lesson in Our Society, and Make It Happen sections.

B. Have three more volunteers connect these sections to the Aim for Change and the Keep in Mind verse.

6. Next Steps for Application

A. Summarize the qualification of a "deacon" and "bishop" in God's church.

B. Close with prayer.

Worship Guide

For the Superintendent or Teacher
Theme: Qualifications of Worship Leaders
Theme Song: "Lead Me, Savior"
Devotional Reading: 1 Peter 5:1–5
Prayer

Qualifications of Worship Leaders

Bible Background • 1 TIMOTHY 3:1–13
Printed Text • 1 TIMOTHY 3:1–13 | Devotional Reading • 1 PETER 5:1–5

Aim for Change

By the end of the lesson, we will: LIST the qualifications and responsibilities of spiritual leaders as set forth in 1 Timothy 3; REFLECT on these qualities in our own leadership roles in the church; and PRAY that God will help all of His leaders to obey His commands.

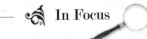 In Focus

Derrick recently transferred to a Christian university. Just prior to his transfer, he had surrendered his life to Jesus Christ and sensed the call of God to preach the Gospel. In the middle of his second semester at the new school, he became dissatisfied with the corporate model of ministry that many of his friends were chasing. It seemed that many of his peers saw Jesus as a CEO of a multi-million-dollar company, rather than the Chief Shepherd. After a few months, this image of leadership began to wear on him. Finally, Derrick came to the point of spiritual exhaustion and was ready to give up on ministry. That is, until he met Sean, a local pastor who was more concerned about character transformation than about the ABCs of ministry—"attendance, buildings, and cash."

Rather than focusing solely on the administrative side of ministry, Sean helped Derrick see how God desires to shape our character as leaders. In this way, one must also be careful to focus on Christlike virtues that portray an exemplary Christian life.

While 1 Timothy 3 does not offer an exhaustive manual for leadership, we do know that at the heart of Christian leadership is character transformation.

Keep in Mind

"Holding the mystery of the faith in a pure conscience" (1 Timothy 3:9).

Focal Verses

KJV **1 Timothy 3:1** This is a true saying, if a man desire the office of a bishop, he desireth a good work.

2 A bishop then must be blameless, the husband of one wife, vigilant, sober, of good behaviour, given to hospitality, apt to teach;

3 Not given to wine, no striker, not greedy of filthy lucre; but patient, not a brawler, not covetous;

4 One that ruleth well his own house, having his children in subjection with all gravity;

5 (For if a man know not how to rule his own house, how shall he take care of the church of God?)

6 Not a novice, lest being lifted up with pride he fall into the condemnation of the devil.

7 Moreover he must have a good report of them which are without; lest he fall into reproach and the snare of the devil.

8 Likewise must the deacons be grave, not doubletongued, not given to much wine, not greedy of filthy lucre;

9 Holding the mystery of the faith in a pure conscience.

10 And let these also first be proved; then let them use the office of a deacon, being found blameless.

11 Even so must their wives be grave, not slanderers, sober, faithful in all things.

12 Let the deacons be the husbands of one wife, ruling their children and their own houses well.

13 For they that have used the office of a deacon well purchase to themselves a good degree, and great boldness in the faith which is in Christ Jesus.

NLT **1 Timothy 3:1** This is a trustworthy saying: "If someone aspires to be an elder, he desires an honorable position."

2 So an elder must be a man whose life is above reproach. He must be faithful to his wife. He must exercise self-control, live wisely, and have a good reputation. He must enjoy having guests in his home, and he must be able to teach.

3 He must not be a heavy drinker or be violent. He must be gentle, not quarrelsome, and not love money.

4 He must manage his own family well, having children who respect and obey him.

5 For if a man cannot manage his own household, how can he take care of God's church?

6 An elder must not be a new believer, because he might become proud, and the devil will cause him to fall.

7 Also, people outside the church must speak well of him so that he will not be disgraced and fall into the devil's trap.

8 In the same way, deacons must be well respected and have integrity. They must not be heavy drinkers or dishonest with money.

9 They must be committed to the mystery of the faith now revealed and must live with a clear conscience.

10 Before they are appointed as deacons, let them be closely examined. If they pass the test, then let them serve as deacons.

11 In the same way, their wives must be respected and must not slander others. They must exercise self-control and be faithful in everything they do.

12 A deacon must be faithful to his wife, and he must manage his children and household well.

13 Those who do well as deacons will be rewarded with respect from others and will have increased confidence in their faith in Christ Jesus.

The People, Places, and Times

Bishop. Our religious culture has given us different ideas of what a bishop is. In some denominations, the position of a bishop is the apex of Christian ministry; in other denominations, any ordained minister is designated as a "bishop." Some of these latter bishops are not even pastors over churches. But the word "bishop" in New Testament Greek, *episkopos*, literally means "an overseer." A bishop is someone with *oversight* in the church; this persion is a leader. A bishop in any of the Pauline churches had the responsibility of oversight in the believing community (cf. Acts 20:28; Philippians 1:1; 1 Peter 5:1–2). Further more, Titus 1:5–7 as well as Acts 20:17–28 suggest that the term "bishop/overseer" may be used interchangeably with "elder," although elders who were bishops/overseers had the responsibility of teaching (cf. 1 Timothy 3:2; 5:17; Titus 1:9). According to Titus 1:9, the main responsibilities of bishops were to preach with "sound doctrine" and correct those who contradicted such.

Deacons. The person who fulfilled the role of deacon in the Pauline churches had a very similar description as that of the bishops. Noteworthy is the fact that Paul did not list "apt to teach" as a qualification for a deacon (1 Timothy 3:2). Also, it appears from 1 Timothy 3:11 that women were quite likely serving as deacons ("their" is not in the Greek text, and the word translated "wives" can be translated "women," as in NRSV). While we do not know for certain how else deacons were distinguished from bishops, they nonetheless served in an important capacity of leadership in the early church. In Methodist churches, this role is referred to as "steward."

Background

As one reads the qualifications for bishops and deacons as set forth by Paul in 1 Timothy 3:1–13, it is necessary to keep the historical situation in mind. Paul has instructed Timothy to "charge some that they teach no other doctrine" (1 Timothy 1:3). Apparently, there were elders within the Ephesian church who were leading others astray in matters of faith and practice (cf. Acts 20:28; 1 Timothy 1:3–7; 4:1–5; 6:3–5). Thus, Paul strategically discusses what the qualifications are of those exercising leadership in the church. The qualities that he mentions are intended to contrast with the false teachers who had arisen among the Ephesians.

At-A-Glance

1. Qualifications of a Bishop/Overseer
(1 Timothy 3:1–7)

2. Qualifications of a Deacon
(vv. 8–13)

In Depth

1. Qualifications of a Bishop/Overseer (1 Timothy 3:1–7)

Having instructed the Christians about the importance and scope of public prayer, Paul now takes up the matter of church organization. This organization of the church is not exhaustive. Instead, there seems to be some flexibility on *structure* and an emphasis on the *character* of leaders. Since there were those within the church who presented a false image of proper church leadership, Paul proceeds to discuss character qualifications of a bishop/overseer. The passage is not a manual for bishops per se, but one in which Paul addresses concrete issues that related to that particular congregation. The first qualification that Paul addresses strikes at the heart of the major character-related problem of false teachers. A bishop/overseer "must be blameless" (3:2).

At issue is the way that the false teachers were bringing disrepute upon the church. It was not a matter of maintaining a religious mask so as not to show weakness or problems. The trouble was that the actions of these teachers were, at the core, un-Christlike and not even up to par with a worldly expectation of leadership. Thus, Paul attempts to recharge the position of bishop/overseer with a healthy image of displaying the character of Christ. Beyond simply a skillful person, the position requires someone who exemplifies an honorable life spent for the kingdom of God.

Paul then goes on to list several character traits that must mark the life of the bishop. A bishop/overseer must be "the husband of one wife" (3:2). Put in other words, a bishop/overseer's fidelity to his spouse brings honor to the marriage covenant, an emphasis that came during a time that deemed such commitment as uncommon.

The bishop/overseer was not to be controlled by outside pressures of culture or inward desires that led him contrary to the ways of Christ. Verse 2 goes on to stress other necessary traits for a bishop: someone should be clear-minded ("vigilant"), self-controlled ("sober"), and respectable ("of good behaviour"). In this way, there was an evident focus as to one's witness in leading others. These qualities were actually prized in the worldly system of Paul's day. How much more should someone who is a Christian leader exemplify such traits?

Further, one who aspires to be a bishop/overseer should be "given to hospitality." Of course, such concern for others would seem to be obvious for Christian leaders. However, the false teachers in the Ephesian church were not looking out for the best interests of others (cf. 2 Timothy 3:6; Titus 1:11). So, Paul highlights that a welcoming attitude toward others, where we make room for them in our lives, is a must. A bishop/overseer should epitomize Christlike hospitality.

It is in this context of God-honoring virtues that a bishop/overseer is to be a good teacher. This is where a noticeable difference has existed between the role of deacons and that of bishops/overseers. Deacons are not described as needing to be "apt to teach," while it is a qualification of a bishop/overseer. Again, Paul implicitly criticizes the false teachers who misrepresent the Gospel, whether in content or behavior. A bishop/overseer needs to be able to instruct others in the true Gospel, as well as to defend the truth in the face of naysayers.

2. Qualifications of a Deacon (vv. 8–13)

Similarly to his treatment of bishops/overseers, in this section of the passage Paul addresses necessary virtues that must characterize those who function as deacons in church leadership. In so doing, he highlights qualifications concerning the character and conduct of those who embrace this ministry. One of the most obvious differences between deacons and bishops/overseers is the requirement of being "apt to teach." Apparently, deacons were responsible for more of a "hands-on" type of ministry, while bishops/overseers specifically handled matters of instruction.

Paul noted some similarities between deacons and bishops/overseers. Deacons were to live respectable lives. They were to be trustworthy in what they said; they were to avoid drinking wine and avoid a love of money. Such standards parallel those of the bishops/overseers. Once more, this list of virtues is by no means exhaustive. It contrasts the false teachers who rejected their consciences, shipwrecked their faith, and perverted the Gospel (cf. 1 Timothy 1:5–6, 19–20).

Paul goes on to say that deacons must be "holding the mystery of the faith in a pure conscience" (1 Timothy 3:9). Put another way, the revealed truth of God's salvation through Jesus Christ is to be graciously lived out in our lives by faith.

Thus, those who served as deacons were to "be proved" concerning the ministry (v. 10). Rather than some type of formalized testing, this quite likely referenced a communal validation of one's ministry. Such validation offers a means of accountability among the leadership of a local assembly. This is one of the struggles in the contemporary church when fellowships rely solely upon classroom settings or educational degrees to verify a person's readiness to lead. Their ministry must be proven in the context of the faith community.

Furthermore, verse 11 addresses women; they are either "wives" of the male deacons (KJV) or "women" deacons (NRSV) in their own right. Either way, the women have an important role to play in the church. However, it seems quite likely that Paul is alluding to women who were serving as deacons. (The word "deaconesses" had not yet been coined; cf. Romans 16:1.) Their qualifications were cognate with those of male deacons. The women were to "be grave, not slanderers, sober, faithful in all things" (1 Timothy 3:11).

After discussing the women in verse 11, Paul returns to his previous list regarding deacons: "Let the deacons be the husbands of one wife, ruling their children and their own houses well" (v. 12). As with the bishops/overseers, the faithfulness and leadership played out in one's family serves as a gauge by which to measure one's effectiveness in church leadership. If one does not manage his or her household well, then how might he or she lead the church in the right direction?

Search the Scriptures

1. Why is it important that a bishop know how to manage his own household (v. 4)?

2. Why must a bishop not be a recent convert (v. 6)?

Discuss the Meaning

Compare and contrast the qualities of a bishop and those of a deacon given by Paul. Compare these qualities to the leaders in your church, or to yourself if you are a leader. Do we consistently desire these qualities in the leaders in our churches? Why or why not?

Lesson in Our Society

Just as in our society, the church must choose leaders, whether they are deacons, elders, Sunday School teachers, youth workers, etc. This Scripture passage gives some high standards for choosing such leaders, one of which includes spiritual maturity. In a society where a person's image is so prized, it is sometimes difficult to determine whether a person has the qualities listed by Paul.

Make It Happen

It is part of our responsibility as Christians to choose good leadership. Take time this week to pray for God to give us wisdom in choosing leaders. Also, pray for those people who are currently our leaders, that God will strengthen them to hear and obey the voice of the Holy Spirit.

Follow the Spirit

What God wants me to do:

_____

_____

_____

_____

Remember Your Thoughts

Special insights I have learned:

_____

_____

_____

_____

More Light on the Text

1 Timothy 3:1–13

1 This is a true saying, if a man desire the office of a bishop, he desireth a good work.

Paul states his second trustworthy saying ("true saying," KJV). He describes the aspiration to the position of an overseer as a desire for "good" or noble work. Paul's discussions emphasized qualifications for office and not duties. Aside from a reference that the overseer must be "able to teach" (v. 2, NLT), Paul did not mention the function of the overseer. Some of the duties of the leaders are evident from the qualifications Paul asked. Paul focused on describing someone who directed the affairs of the church (1 Timothy 5:17). This was a noble, important task; Paul commended it as desirable. Paul's objective was to stress that church leaders must have the highest qualifications. In Greek, the word is *episkopos* (**ep-IS-kop-os**) translated as "bishop," which literally means "overseer," while the noun *episkope* (**ep-is-kop-AY**) means "office of overseer" (cf. KJV, "the office of a bishop"). The word is used in this sense in Acts 1:20.

2 A bishop then must be blameless, the husband of one wife, vigilant, sober, of good behaviour, given to hospitality, apt to teach;

Starting from verse 2, Paul lists the specific qualifications of the overseer. The overseer must be "blameless." The Greek word

anegkletos (**an-ENG-klay-tos**) used only here and in 5:7 and 6:14 means "to be above reproach," "beyond criticism," or "unimpeachable." It depicts an observable conduct. The leader's conduct must withstand assaults and criticisms from opponents inside or outside the church (v. 7). Paul proceeds to give a concrete explanation and details six positive attributes. First, the overseer must be the husband of one wife. The idea here is not merely monogamy but faithfulness to one's spouse. Implicit in this qualification is the fact that a minister's private life has great consequences for the congregation.

Second, the overseer must be "vigilant." The Greek word *nephaleos* (**nay-FAL-eh-os**) means "sober," "sober-minded," and "clear-headed." It occurs again in v. 11 and in Titus 2:2. In classical Greek, the word meant "not mixed with wine," denoting abstinence from alcohol, but here it has a wider, metaphorical sense. To be "temperate" shows that the church leader has to be free from rash actions. The word describes self-control with regard to use of intoxicants, but it can also be used to describe a mental self-control that rules out all forms of excess. Vigilance is the opposite of drunkenness or fuzzy thinking.

The third attribute is "sobriety." The Greek word *sophronos* (**so-FRON-oce**), used here as well as in Titus 1:8; 2:2, 5, means to be "of sound mind." So it carried the sense of "self-controlled" or "sober-minded." Fourth, the overseer must be of good behavior (Gk. *kosmios*, **KOS-mee-os**), implying a respectable, well-ordered, observable, and "modest" demeanor that emanates from an inner self-control. It describes a person whose life is well ordered and well arranged. He is "dignified." This quality is seen in a leader's outward behavior—his dress, his manners, his speech, and the way he relates to the opposite sex. It describes how he keeps his home and how he handles the various affairs of life.

317

The fifth qualification is "given to hospitality" or simply "hospitable." The Greek word *philoxenos* (**fil-OX-en-os**) literally means "loving strangers." Hospitality was an important Christian virtue in that day, often because of the needs of traveling Christian messengers. In those days, there were no motels or five-star hotels where traveling Christians could safely spend the night. Therefore, when Christians traveled and arrived in certain towns, they had to stay with other Christians who opened their homes to them.

The sixth quality is "ability to teach." The pastor is not only wise, but he is able and ready to communicate his wisdom to others. His delight must be to instruct the ignorant and correct those who err from the truth.

3 Not given to wine, no striker, not greedy of filthy lucre; but patient, not a brawler, not covetous;

The overseer's qualities are stated both negatively and positively. Negatively, an overseer must not be "given to wine" (Gk. *paroinos*, **PAR-oy-nos**). This word suggests rowdy or violent behavior that results from drunkenness. It is a sad commentary on the culture of that day that such a warning would have to be given concerning church overseers. It is much needed today as well.

The overseer must be no striker. This means one who is not quarrelsome, but who is peaceable and gentle. A leader must be able to get along with others and respect differing opinions. A leader must not be contentious. Rather, he or she must be forbearing, considerate, and magnanimous.

The leader must not be a greedy person or a "lover of money." This is the literal translation of the Greek word *aischrokerdes* (**ahee-skhrok-er-DACE**), used only here and in Hebrew 13:5. The love of money (cf. 1 Timothy 6:10) is one of the greatest dangers confronting every Christian worker in any generation.

4 One that ruleth well his own house, having his children in subjection with all gravity;
5 (For if a man know not how to rule his own house, how shall he take care of the church of God?)

The attention now shifts to the family of the overseer. The overseer of the church must be one who can "manage his own family well." His children must be obedient and respectful. For the father to see that his children are in subjection does not demand or imply excessive force or sternness. The addition "with all gravity" (KJV) or "with all dignity" (NIV, NRSV) either defines the demeanor expected of the overseer's children or the attitude with which the father is to bring his children into obedience. To rule or manage carries the idea of governing, leading, and giving direction to the family. The overseer's fitness to lead the church is measured in his ability to maintain the obedience of his own children.

In verse 5, Paul makes the logical point (in the form of a rhetorical question) that if one cannot rule, that is manage his own house, then he could not be expected to take proper care of God's church. The point is that the church leader must be an example in controlling his family and that the experience the leader gained in the home would develop sensitive compassion for his role in the church.

6 Not a novice, lest being lifted up with pride he fall into the condemnation of the devil.

The overseer must not be a novice, or literally "a recent convert." The Greek word is *neophutos* (**neh-OF-oo-tos**), from which the word "neophyte" is derived, an adjective that literally means "newly planted." Paul spells out the reason for the prohibition in the rest of the verse, which is the danger that such a person might become conceited or be filled with pride. This, in turn, will lead to condemnation.

7 Moreover he must have a good report of them which are without; lest he fall into reproach and the snare of the devil.

The last requirement of an overseer is to "have a good report" among outsiders— literally "a good testimony" (Gk. *martureo*, **mar-too-REH-O**). This is an appeal that the church leader should have a good name and standing in the wider community. The mention of the leader's name should not cause derision among the opponents of the Gospel. The behavior of the leader should provide an example of integrity and commitment to the Gospel he professes. If an overseer did not have a good testimony among outsiders, he would fall into reproach. Along with the overseer, the congregation itself could be derided. When a leader in the church has a bad reputation in the community, it often brings irreparable damage to the local congregation and indeed to the entire cause of Christ. A church leader must have a good reputation so that he will not fall into the snare of the devil (2 Timothy 2:26).

8 Likewise must the deacons be grave, not doubletongued, not given to much wine, not greedy of filthy lucre;

The qualifications demanded of the deacons are similar to those required of the overseers. The term "deacon" (Gk. *diakonos*, **dee-AK-on-os**) refers literally to someone who serves. It is used in the New Testament to refer to a church office only in two passages (here and in Philippians 1:1). It is used in Romans 16:1 in reference to Phoebe (translated as "servant"), but it is debatable wheth-

er the reference was to a church office or to Phoebe's function as a servant. Paul's use of the same word in reference to himself (see "servant" in Colossians 1:23) is a reference to his function and not to his office.

The deacon must be "grave" (KJV), or literally "worthy of respect." This is the Greek word *semnos* (**sem-NOS**, cf. 1 Timothy 2:2; 3:4), and it suggests that deacons are to be serious-minded persons with characters that merit respect. The term combines such ideas as dignity, earnestness of purpose, and winsome attractiveness.

Next, the deacon must not be "doubletongued." The Greek adjective *dilogos* (**DIL-og-os**), only here in the New Testament, has the idea of saying something twice, with the bad connotation of saying one thing to one person and something else to another. Bunyan characteristically writes in *Pilgrim's Progress* of "the parson of our parish, Mr. Two-Tongues." As a frequent visitor in homes, the deacon must be consistent in what he reports to others. The translation of *dilogos* as "sincere" (NIV) obscures the fact that the word has the meaning of *not* double-tongued and refers primarily to controlling one's speech. The prohibition against indulging "in much wine" is the same as the demand of 3:3 for the overseer. In the same manner as the overseer, the deacon is to avoid the temptations of materialism by "not pursuing dishonest gain."

9 Holding the mystery of the faith in a pure conscience.

Although the next requirement is applicable to all believers, it is particularly important that Christian leaders prove themselves to be unconnected with false teachers. The Greek word *musterion* (**moos-TAY-ree-on**) was used for a secret that was unknown to the masses but disclosed to the initiated. In the

New Testament, it signifies the secret of salvation through Jesus Christ, which is revealed by the Holy Spirit to all who will believe. The "mystery of faith" is the content of faith, the sound teaching whose content is well known to the believers. It is the revelation of salvation in Christ, as proclaimed by Paul. The deacon must hold on to the mystery in a "pure conscience." In other words, sound behavior must accompany a profession of faith. The deacon's adherence to the faith is to be unquestioned, and his conduct is to be appropriate to the faith he professes.

10 And let these also first be proved; then let them use the office of a deacon, being found blameless.

This verse indicates that before a person assumes the role of a deacon in the local congregation his demeanor must be tested by the community. Such persons must be first "proved" (Gk. *dokimion,* **dok-IM-ee-on**). To be proved means to be "tested, judged," or "scrutinized." It refers to the screening of a candidate for an office. Paul did not specifically mention a process of testing for the office of overseer. However, Paul's description of the qualifications sought in the overseer implies such an action. After the experience of testing, those who had "nothing against them" served as deacons. The Greek word translated "blameless," or literally "nothing against them" (*anegkletos,* **an-ENG-klay-tos**), is a synonym for "above reproach" of verse 2 and signifies someone against whom no specific charge of wrongdoing can be laid. The candidate's reputation both inside and outside the church must pass the test. Paul's requirements assure that the deacon would not normally be a recent convert. Following this demand would prevent the premature acceptance of unworthy men (1 Timothy 5:22).

11 Even so must their wives be grave, not slanderers, sober, faithful in all things.

The Greek word *gune* (**goo-NAY**), translated here as "wives," is also used for women in general. Since this single word is found here for "their wives," there are three possible interpretations as to which group Paul is talking about. First, the NIV and KJV assume that "these women" were the wives of the deacons. The main argument against this is that the word for "their" is missing in the Greek. Second, it may be argued that Paul is speaking of women in general. Third, the word may refer to "the women who are deacons" or "deaconesses" such as, arguably, Phoebe (Romans 16:1). This option, which is adopted here, fits best with the context. The "even so," "likewise," or "in the same manner" (Greek *hosautos,* **ho-SOW-toce**) of 1 Timothy 3:8 appears to begin the enumeration of requirements for an office by reference to the previous requirements of 3:1–7.

12 Let the deacons be the husbands of one wife, ruling their children and their own houses well.

Paul returns to the specific qualifications of male deacons. He says that the deacon, like the overseer (v. 2), must be the husband of one wife. He must also "manage his children and his household well" (cf. v. 4). They must exhibit skilful management in the household.

13 For they that have used the office of a deacon well purchase to themselves a good degree, and great boldness in the faith which is in Christ Jesus.

Paul concludes the list of requirements for deacons by stating the rewards of those who serve well. They gain "a good degree." The Greek noun *bathmos* (**bath-MOS**), only here in the New Testament, literally means "a step," and so metaphorically "threshold," "standing." Some suggest it means great respect in the eyes of the church. Others relate it to good standing in God's sight. Probably the best interpretation is a combination of the two.

Second, the deacons will have great boldness in the faith which is in Christ Jesus. They also develop sufficient confidence. Faithful service will not only deepen the deacon's faith but also further strengthen his or her relationship with the Lord.

Say It Correctly

Lucre. lü-k r.
Novice. nä-v s.

Daily Bible Readings

M: Tending the Flock of God
1 Peter 5:1–5

T: Leading God's People Astray
Isaiah 9:13–17

W: Leaders as God's Stewards
Titus 1:5–9

T: Imitate Your Leaders' Faith
Hebrews 13:1–7

F: Obey Your Leaders
Hebrews 13:17–25

S: Good Stewards of God's Grace
1 Peter 4:7–11

S: Qualifications for Leaders
1 Timothy 3:1–13

Teaching Tips

1. Words You Should Know

A. Minister (1 Timothy 4:6) *diakonos* (Gk.)—Servant.

B. Labour (v. 10) *kopiao* (Gk.)—To toil to the point of exhaustion or weariness.

2. Teacher Preparation

Unifying Principle—Fitness for Leadership. Paul encourages Timothy to give himself to God's work without neglecting his personal spiritual quest.

A. Pray and ask God to give clarity to the lesson.

B. Prayerfully study the entire lesson.

C. Reflect on why there is a need for trained spiritual leaders in the church.

D. Research some Web sites where students might get quality Christian education training. Prepare to share your findings.

3. Open the Lesson

A. Open with prayer, including the Aim for Change.

B. After prayer, ask, "Why do leaders in the church need to prepare for leadership?" Discuss.

C. Ask, "What are some of the problems that Christians can encounter while living out their faith when they have **not** received accurate teaching of God's inerrant Word?"

D. Discuss and then expound salient points in today's In Focus story.

4. Present the Scriptures

A. Have volunteers read the Focal Verses.

B. Now use The People, Places, and Times; Background; Search the Scriptures; At-A-Glance outline; In Depth; and More Light on the Text to clarify the verses.

5. Explore the Meaning

A. Lead a discussion of the Discuss the Meaning, Lesson in Our Society, and Make It Happen sections.

B. Have volunteers connect these sections to the Aim for Change and the Keep in Mind verse.

6. Next Steps for Application

A. Share your list of Web sites where students might get quality Christian education training, including leadership training. Discuss.

B. Close with prayer.

Worship Guide

For the Superintendent or Teacher
Theme: Prepare for Leadership
Theme Song: "I Am on the Battlefield for
My Lord"
Devotional Reading: Philippians 3:17–4:1
Prayer

Prepare for Leadership

MAR 20th

Bible Background • 1 TIMOTHY 4:6–16
Printed Text • 1 TIMOTHY 4:6–16 | Devotional Reading • PHILIPPIANS 3:17–4:1

—————— Aim for Change ——————

By the end of the lesson, we will: EXPLAIN why spiritual leaders need training and preparation for Christian service; REFLECT on the gifts for ministry that God has given us; and PRAY that God will empower us to use our gifts with excellence.

—————— In Focus ——————

As I stood before the casket, hand on the shoulder of the sobbing mother, those around us began to walk to the back of the funeral home. Through streaming, agonized, and swollen eyes, she strained to ask me, "Why did God do this?" Her broken, frail voice grew stronger as her exhaustion was masked by anger. I prayed silently, asking God for the best way to show His love. How can one see the Lord as the source of such heartache and disaster?

Over the next few months I discovered one of the reasons for the grieving mother's question. During a counseling session with her, she told me that she was taught from a very young age that God makes everything happen, good and bad. She thought of God as sovereign, but without any sense of God's loving mercy and greater providential purposes. From that framework, she sought to understand why her teenage daughter was snatched from her very arms.

The teaching ministry of the church carries with it great responsibility. The apostle Paul knew this as he sought to confront teachers in Ephesus, who were teaching a false message and leading the congregation toward the shipwreck of their faith.

—————— Keep in Mind ——————

"Take heed unto thyself, and unto the doctrine; continue in them: for in doing this thou shalt both save thyself, and them that hear thee"
(1 Timothy 4:16).

"Take heed unto thyself, and unto the doctrine; continue in them: for in doing this thou shalt both save thyself, and them that hear thee"

Focal Verses

KJV 1 **Timothy 4:6** If thou put the brethren in remembrance of these things, thou shalt be a good minister of Jesus Christ, nourished up in the words of faith and of good doctrine, whereunto thou hast attained.

7 But refuse profane and old wives' fables, and exercise thyself rather unto godliness.

8 For bodily exercise profiteth little: but godliness is profitable unto all things, having promise of the life that now is, and of that which is to come.

9 This is a faithful saying and worthy of all acceptation.

10 For therefore we both labour and suffer reproach, because we trust in the living God, who is the Saviour of all men, specially of those that believe.

11 These things command and teach.

12 Let no man despise thy youth; but be thou an example of the believers, in word, in conversation, in charity, in spirit, in faith, in purity.

13 Till I come, give attendance to reading, to exhortation, to doctrine.

14 Neglect not the gift that is in thee, which was given thee by prophecy, with the laying on of the hands of the presbytery.

15 Meditate upon these things; give thyself wholly to them; that thy profiting may appear to all.

16 Take heed unto thyself, and unto the doctrine; continue in them: for in doing this thou shalt both save thyself, and them that hear thee.

NLT 1 **Timothy 4:6** If you explain these things to the brothers and sisters, Timothy, you will be a worthy servant of Christ Jesus, one who is nourished by the message of faith and the good teaching you have followed.

7 Do not waste time arguing over godless ideas and old wives' tales. Instead, train yourself to be godly.

8 "Physical training is good, but training for godliness is much better, promising benefits in this life and in the life to come."

9 This is a trustworthy saying and everyone should accept it.

10 This is why we work hard and continue to struggle, for our hope is in the living God, who is the Savior of all people and particularly of all believers.

11 Teach these things and insist that everyone learn them.

12 Don't let anyone think less of you because you are young. Be an example to all believers in what you say, in the way you live, in your love, your faith, and your purity.

13 Until I get there, focus on reading the Scriptures to the church, encouraging the believers, and teaching them.

14 Do not neglect the spiritual gift you received through the prophecy spoken over you when the elders of the church laid their hands on you.

15 Give your complete attention to these matters. Throw yourself into your tasks so that everyone will see your progress.

16 Keep a close watch on how you live and on your teaching. Stay true to what is right for the sake of your own salvation and the salvation of those who hear you.

The People, Places, and Times

Laying on of hands. During Paul's day, this referred to an occasion of commissioning by a group of elders. The act of "laying on of hands" was seen as a time where authority and spiritual power were transferred. This was especially common when a person was consecrated for a particular ministry.

Training. Whether it relates to physical exercise or another area of human endeavor, training implies intentionality, deliberateness, goals, and effort. If believers are to live godly lives as demanded by God, these aspects are crucial. We cannot be careless or adopt cavalier attitudes in our Christian lives and expect to grow or become all that God intends us to be.

Background

Certain false teachers who are proving toxic to the health of the church have crept into the congregation at Ephesus. So Paul commissions his close companion, Timothy, to set things in order as Paul makes his way to Macedonia (1 Timothy 1:3). The apostle writes to Timothy as a means of both encouragement and instruction for the church. It is clear that Paul's words are carefully selected in light of the current situation of wayward elders whose influence could prove fatal for the church.

Up until this point in the letter, Paul has focused mainly on issues in the congregation concerning worship and specific leadership qualifications. In chapter four, he turns to matters of Timothy's personal life and ministry. Yet again, in addressing Timothy personally, Paul skillfully rebukes the elders in Ephesus who are not setting the example that young Timothy is called to set.

At-A-Glance

1. Train Yourself in Godliness!
   (1 Timothy 4:6–10)

2. Set an Example for Believers
   (vv. 11–16)

In Depth

1. Train Yourself in Godliness! (1 Timothy 4:6–10)

Paul highlights the dynamic nature of walking with God and growing (being "nourished up") in one's relationship with God and others (v. 6). There is simply no substitute for the daily nourishment that believers need from God. It is far too common in the church world to view salvation as merely a static, positional reality without corresponding life experiences. We must carefully watch over our lives and see whether we are growing in the Lord or declining in faith.

The apostle Paul realizes the importance of believing the right things as well as living one's life in accordance with such belief. Thus, he underscores Timothy's need to be "nourished" in the Gospel. At issue is more than simply accepting Jesus or receiving Jesus in his heart. Timothy was to live with a Gospel-centered trajectory. The faith that began him on this journey with God is also necessary for Timothy to continue becoming the man that God intends him to be. It is quite dangerous to grow complacent in relation to following Jesus. Our priority must be on God's Word, not on the words of humans. Paul cautioned Timothy to keep focused on the Word, not on things that come from humankind. We must put the greatest effort into learning from God's Word.

Paul also instructs Timothy to have nothing to do with "profane and old wives' fables" (v. 7). Timothy must shun the influence of unholy

326

teaching, having nothing to do with worldly tales and superstitions. This exhortation is a direct rebuttal of the false teachers of Ephesus (cf. 1 Timothy 1:4). Unlike these false teachers, Timothy is to focus on "good [healthy] doctrine" (4:6). The same exhortation holds true today. There is a temptation in the church to become enamored with the next "new" or "hidden" insight from the Scriptures. It is important to learn all of the deep truths revealed in the "old, old story." Salvation is more than the proverbial "get out of hell free card." To be saved is to become a follower of Jesus. Our character is being changed to be more like that of Christ. Spiritual discussions or religious myths that detract from the salvation provided through Jesus Christ are not worth trusting.

Therefore, one must train in godliness. Implicit in Paul's injunction is the fact that living out one's faith is not simply an arbitrary task. One needs to be intentional about growing in his or her relationship with God. Moreover, ministers must instruct others in how they are to live a disciplined, faithful life devoted to God. In verse 8, Paul quotes what seems to be a popular (and trustworthy) saying of his day: "but godliness is profitable unto all things, having promise of the life that now is, and of that which is to come." Here is the crux of the matter. If physical exercise can profit us in this life only, then wouldn't it be wise to train in spiritual matters that benefit both now and later?

2. Set an Example for Believers (vv. 11–16)

As a means of counteracting the negative influence of false teachers, Paul reminds Timothy of the means of turning things around. It happens with sound teaching. Put another way, Timothy's life and message works to correct the skewed picture of leadership and salvation that the Ephesian

false teachers were spreading. Thus, by all means, Timothy was instructed to teach the truth.

This reminds us of the important role that teaching has in the church today. While some may view "doctrine" as a bad word, the fact remains that healthy doctrine is crucial for the life of the church. Furthermore, one's age or position is in no way a guarantee of right belief or action. Timothy, without a doubt a young man, was told by Paul to serve as an "example...in word, in conversation, in charity, in spirit, in faith, [and] in purity" to the entire faith community (v. 12).

Until Paul arrived, Timothy was to "give attendance to reading, to exhortation, to doctrine" (v. 13). This is not simply a protocol for public meeting times in the church. These were the tools by which Timothy would contend with false teachings as well as continue his personal formation. In the hectic schedules of the day, it is challenging to make time for such things. It seems as though ministers often wear so many hats that it becomes easy to forget the importance of reading and teaching the Scriptures. Believers, nonetheless, must prioritize daily Scripture reading. It is important to read, hear, pray, and teach the Scriptures.

Timothy was gifted to teach. Consequently, Paul encourages him to allow the gift of teaching and preaching to operate in his life for the health of the faith community. By way of reminder, Paul refers to the gift imparted by the Holy Spirit that resides in Timothy's life (v. 14). This reference would serve to encourage Timothy while further validating his authority in the church. After all, what good is it to be gifted for ministry and not operate in such gifting for the betterment of the community of faith?

Paul desired Timothy to be a blazing example of what it meant to read and teach the Scriptures properly.

Search the Scriptures

1. What does Paul tell Timothy to train himself in (1 Timothy 4:7)?

2. What is the purpose of our struggling and toiling in ministry (v. 10)?

Discuss the Meaning

In many churches and in the lives of many Christians, there is little room for discipleship. Learning about God and the right way to live takes time and sacrifice. However, Paul instructs Timothy to focus on reading, exhorting, and teaching the Word of God. What is the danger in a church where teaching or discipleship are not priorities? How can we rearrange our lives to make learning about God a priority in our homes?

Lesson in Our Society

In a world that is so busy, it seems there is always noise and confusion. However, we see in this passage that Paul exhorts Timothy to pay attention to himself. Any leaders must have some time where they can reflect upon their lives. We must all evaluate where we stand with God, how our process of learning more about Him is going, and so on.

Make It Happen

God has given all of us gifts to use for His service. Throughout this week, prayerfully reflect on the gifts God has given you and how you could use them to minister to other people. If you have children, pray about ways that you could help your children begin to develop their gifts and use them in ministry.

Follow the Spirit

What God wants me to do:

_____

_____

_____

_____

Remember Your Thoughts

Special insights I have learned:

_____

_____

_____

_____

More Light on the Text

1 Timothy 4:6–16

6 If thou put the brethren in remembrance of these things, thou shalt be a good minister of Jesus Christ, nourished up in the words of faith and of good doctrine, whereunto thou hast attained.

Paul wrote that Timothy was to "put the brethren in remembrance" (1 Timothy 4:6), or literally, lay these things before the community. "These things" (Gk. *tauta*, **TOW-tah**) refer to the instructions that Paul has given so far to Timothy. If Timothy does so, he would prove himself not only to be a loyal and faithful disciple of Paul, but more importantly a good "minister" (Gk. *diakonos*, **dee-AK-on-os**, "servant," probably carrying here the modern technical connotation of "minister"). To be "a good minister of Christ Jesus" should be the aim of every pastor today.

In the Greek, Paul describes the members of the community as *adelphos* (**ad-el-FOS**), meaning "brothers and sisters," an important kinship and familial language suggesting a warm and friendly relationship. We must always bear in mind that believers are a family.

As Timothy endeavors to do his work as God's minister, he is continually nourished up in the words of faith and good doctrine. The form of the Greek word *gumnasia* (**goom-nas-EE-ah**), meaning "trained" or "nurtured," suggests a continual process. Timothy was to continue relying on words of faith and good doctrine that he had been taught.

7 But refuse profane and old wives' fables, and exercise thyself rather unto godliness. 8 For bodily exercise profiteth little: but godliness is profitable unto all things, having promise of the life that now is, and of that which is to come.

Paul alluded to the teachings of the false teachers as "profane and old wives" fables, or literally "godless and old wives" myths. Instead of being engaged in such things, Paul admonishes Timothy to "exercise himself unto godliness," which means to train himself to be godly. The Greek word for "train" (KJV, "exercise") is *gumnaze*, from which we get the word "gymnastics." It implies the need for the kind of discipline that is demanded from an athlete. "Physical training" (KJV, "bodily exercise") also clearly refers to athletic discipline. In order to highlight the importance of godliness, Paul contrasts it with physical training. The latter, Paul says, though of some value, is little and lasts only a short time. The KJV translation of the Greek *oligos* (**ol-EE-gos**), as "little" does injustice to the sense of the word and is somewhat derogatory, is often understood as being of no value. Paul's point is that although bodily exercises or gymnastics are "beneficial" (Gk. *ophelimos*, **o-fel-EH-mos**, "useful, profitable"), the benefits are little when compared with spiritual exercise, which has value for eternity.

9 This is a faithful saying and worthy of all acceptation. 10 For therefore we both labour and suffer reproach, because we trust in the living God, who is the Saviour of all men, specially of those that believe.

Again we find one of the "faithful" or "trustworthy" sayings. Commentators generally agree that this verse refers to the preceding about godliness in verse 8. Verse 10 refers back to the second part of verse 8, with Paul resuming the train of thought once more. Because godliness is such a crucial virtue, those who accept the saying about it must labor and struggle. People of God must labor and strive for godliness. "Labor" and "strive" (rather than "suffer reproach" in KJV) are both strong terms. "Labor" (Gk. *kopiao*, **kop-ee-AH-o**) means to toil to the point of exhaustion or weariness. It is more than mere work. "Strive" (Gk. *agonizomai*, **ag-o-NID-zom-ahee**), from which the English word "agonize" is derived, means "to struggle" or to exert oneself. Taken together, the two words speak of Paul's incredible effort and exertions in the proclamation of the Gospel.

11 These things command and teach. 12 Let no man despise thy youth; but be thou an example of the believers, in word, in conversation, in charity, in spirit, in faith, in purity.

Timothy was possibly a shy, timid young man. His timidity could have hindered a bold proclamation of the Gospel. "Command" and "teach" are both in the present tense of continuous action. Timothy is to keep on doing these two things. He is to exercise his authority as pastor. Paul wants Timothy to speak with authority. As a teacher, Timothy was to urge his listeners to obedience. Paul advised Timothy to conduct himself so that no one would look down condescendingly on his youthfulness. The Greek word for "youth" (KJV) is *neotes* (**neh-OT-ace**), which is used of grown-up military age, extending to the 40th year. Timothy was to be "an example." The Greek word *tupos* (**TOO-pos**) meant "a figure, image" and then ethically "an example, pattern." Timothy was to present the proper image of a Christian, and he was to be a pattern for other believers to follow.

Paul lists specific areas in which Timothy was to serve as an example. These are all vital parts of Christian living. Carelessness in any one of these areas can spell failure and even disaster. Timothy was to be an example in "word" (Gk. *logos*, **LOG-os**), literally "in speech." The next area is "conduct" (Gk. *anastrophe*, **an-as-trof-AY**), which means "manner of living" (not "conversation," as in the King James Version). This is followed by "love" and "faith," both of which sum up the Christian life. The list ends with "purity" or "holiness" (Gk. *hagneia*, **hag-NI-ah**), a word which occurs only here and in chapter 5 verse 2. This includes, but is not limited to, sexual conduct (cf. 5:2). Timothy should be free from anything that would contaminate himself or his ministry. Holiness should affect one's relationship with others. As the list suggests, effective ministry and godliness are two sides of the same coin; they are inseparable.

13 Till I come, give attendance to reading, to exhortation, to doctrine.

Paul intended to visit Timothy, but pending his arrival, he commands Timothy to "give attendance" or to devote himself "to the public reading of Scripture" (NIV, ESV, etc.). "Reading" (Gk. *anagnosis*, **an-AG-no-sis**) is a technical term for reading of the Scriptures in the assembly of believers (cf. Acts 13:15; 2 Corinthians 3:14). Timothy was also to devote himself to "exhortation"

or admonition (Gk. *paraklesis*, **par-AK-lay-sis**). "Exhortation" means giving someone motivation to change his or her behavior. It can imply either rebuke or encouragement. The third important function of Timothy is "teaching." The people need instruction in Christian living, and the pastor should give it to them. Significantly, Paul cites the reading of the Scriptures before Timothy's responsibility of teaching. In doing so, Paul implies that the Scriptures must be the foundation on which Timothy was to base his activities of teaching and proclamation.

14 Neglect not the gift that is in thee, which was given thee by prophecy, with the laying on of the hands of the presbytery.

This verse begins the conclusion of Paul's lengthy charge to Timothy in which he seeks to inspire his enthusiasm. Verses 14–16 explain what is at stake in Timothy's faithful and effective fulfillment of his ministry. First, Timothy must not neglect his spiritual "gift" (Gk. *charisma*, **KHAR-is-mah**). The Greek verb *ameleo* (**am-el-EH-o**), "neglect," is not used elsewhere by Paul. It literally means to be careless about something. The verse associates Timothy's reception of the gift with the laying on of hands by the presbytery. Paul's point in mentioning this incident was not to insist that Timothy had been ordained as an elder, but to remind him and the Ephesian congregation that Timothy had spiritual gifts that had been confirmed by the prophetic message. The affirmation Timothy received through "laying on of the hands" allowed him the freedom to minister with greater effectiveness among the Ephesians.

15 Meditate upon these things; give thyself wholly to them; that thy profiting may appear to all.

Timothy is to nurture his gifts and to "meditate" upon all that Paul has said. The

Greek verb *meletao* (**mel-et-AH-o**) means "to take care," "think about," "to practice," "to cultivate," or "to take pains with." Effective ministry demands diligence. This word translates the Greek *en toutois isthi* (**en too-tois is–thi**) to literally mean to "be in these things." The NASB puts the phrase "give thyself wholly to them" into "Be absorbed in them." Timothy is to become so closely acquainted with these injunctions that they become second nature to him. This was so that everybody might see Timothy's "profiting." The Greek word *prokope* (**prok-op-AY**) is used only here and in Philippians 1:12, 25, and it is better translated as "progress." Timothy was to make progress in his own spiritual life and in his effectiveness in the ministry.

16 Take heed unto thyself, and unto the doctrine; continue in them: for in doing this thou shalt both save thyself, and them that hear thee.

Paul is well aware that the danger of neglecting one's own salvation is greater in the Christian minister than in others. So Paul instructs Timothy to take heed to his life and doctrine. He is to keep a strict eye on himself. The Greek imperative *epecho* (**ep-EKH-o**) means "to hold upon," "to give heed to," "to give attention to," or "to fix attention upon." Timothy, and every pastor or Christian worker, must examine constantly the two great areas of concern—one's life and one's teaching. The Greek word *didaskalia* (**did-as-kal-EE-ah**) may refer to either Timothy's teaching ability or to what is taught. The latter is more appropriate here. Failing to give heed to these two important areas would mean peril for both Timothy and for those in his congregation. Timothy must first watch himself, not only his outward life but also his inner thoughts and feelings. No matter how correct a person may be in his or her doctrine or how effective he or she may be in his or her teaching, if there is a flaw in his or her inner or outer life, it will ruin him or her. This is where many ministers have failed tragically. While he or she is watching over others, the pastor must keep an eye on him- or herself.

Say It Correctly

Ephesians. Eh-FEE-zhuhnz.
Ephesus. EH-fuh-suhs.

Daily Bible Readings

M: Stand Firm in the Lord
Philippians 3:17–4:1

T: Trustworthy Service
Luke 19:12–23

W: Single-minded in Purpose
1 Chronicles 29:18–25

T: God's Words in Your Heart
Deuteronomy 11:13–21

F: Taught and Led by God
Psalm 25:1–10

S: Pursue Love
1 Corinthians 13:1–14:1

S: Guidance for Faithful Leaders
1 Timothy 4:6–16

Teaching Tips

1. Words You Should Know

A. Rebuke (1 Timothy 5:1, 20) *epiplesso* (Gk.)—To strike upon; to chastise with words.

B. Elder (vv. 1, 17, 19) *presbuteros* (Gk.)—An elderly man or elderly woman; a senior.

2. Teacher Preparation

Unifying Principle—All in the Family. The writer of 1 Timothy says to serve the widows who need help and the elders who have earned honor.

A. Pray for your students and ask God to help them to reach out to widows and elders in need.

B. Study and reflect on the entire text and its surrounding sections.

3. Opening the Lesson

A. Help your class to list ways that they can reach out and serve widows and elders in your communities and church.

B. Have a volunteer retell the In Focus story.

C. In light of today's theme, discuss how Debbie and her church met Annie's needs through Christian service.

4. Present the Scriptures

A. Have volunteers read the Focal Verses.

B. Divide the class into three groups, and have the groups select a spokesperson for each group.

C. Have them draw three salient points from The People, Places, and Times; Background; At-A-Glance outline; In Depth; Search the Scriptures; and More Light on the Text to clarify the Focal Verses. Discuss.

5. Explore the Meaning

A. Lead a discussion of the Discuss the Meaning section.

B. Summarize the Lesson in Our Society and Make It Happen sections.

6. Next Steps for Application

A. Have students write at least two ways in the Follow the Spirit and Remember Your Thoughts sections on how they will help widows and elders in their communities.

B. Challenge them to pray about their lists and then implement them during the week.

C. Close with prayer.

Worship Guide

For the Superintendent or Teacher
Theme: Worship Inspires Service
Theme Song: "This Little Light of Mine"
Devotional Reading: John 12:20–26
Prayer

Worship Inspires Service

Bible Background • 1 TIMOTHY 5:1–22
Printed Text • 1 TIMOTHY 5:1–8, 17–22 | Devotional Reading • JOHN 12:20–26

—————— Aim for Change ——————

By the end of the lesson, we will: EXPLAIN what 1 Timothy says about honoring widows and elders; REFLECT on how honoring widows and elders honors God; and DETERMINE ways to honor those in our faith community who have faithfully served God.

————— In Focus —————

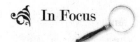

Debbie has been following Christ for a many years now. She has had the privilege of raising her two girls in the fear and admonition of the Lord. Taking great pride in her ministry as a mother and wife, Debbie prayed about how else she could share the love of Christ to those in her community. The answer came when she met Annie.

Annie was almost 80 years of age with no supportive family living around her. She lived in abject poverty and barely had enough food to survive. Debbie's heart was broken when she discovered Annie's living situation. There were so many churches in the area that it was mind-boggling that Annie was not being taken care of. Debbie talked with her husband about getting their church to help meet Annie's needs. After a few phone calls and several visits, Annie's pantry was stocked with fresh groceries and necessary medicines. And Annie's pantry is regularly stocked to this day.

So often, the church misses key opportunities to minister to the widows of the community. However, they and others in need should be our priority. In this lesson, we will explore Paul's admonition to Timothy about how widows in need and fruitful elders were to be treated by the faith family.

————— Keep in Mind —————

"But if any provide not for his own, and specially for those of his own house, he hath denied the faith, and is worse than an infidel"
(1 Timothy 5:8).

"But if any provide not for his own, and specially for those of his own house, he hath denied the faith, and is worse than an infidel" (1 Timothy 5:8).

Focal Verses

KJV **1 Timothy 5:1** Rebuke not an elder, but intreat him as a father; and the younger men as brethren;

2 The elder women as mothers; the younger as sisters, with all purity.

3 Honour widows that are widows indeed.

4 But if any widow have children or nephews, let them learn first to shew piety at home, and to requite their parents: for that is good and acceptable before God.

5 Now she that is a widow indeed, and desolate, trusteth in God, and continueth in supplications and prayers night and day.

6 But she that liveth in pleasure is dead while she liveth.

7 And these things give in charge, that they may be blameless.

8 But if any provide not for his own, and specially for those of his own house, he hath denied the faith, and is worse than an infidel.

5:17 Let the elders that rule well be counted worthy of double honour, especially they who labour in the word and doctrine.

18 For the scripture saith, thou shalt not muzzle the ox that treadeth out the corn. And, The labourer is worthy of his reward.

19 Against an elder receive not an accusation, but before two or three witnesses.

20 Them that sin rebuke before all, that others also may fear.

21 I charge thee before God, and the Lord Jesus Christ, and the elect angels, that thou observe these things without preferring one before another, doing nothing by partiality.

22 Lay hands suddenly on no man, neither be partaker of other men's sins: keep thyself pure.

NLT **1 Timothy 5:1** Never speak harshly to an older man, but appeal to him respectfully as you would to your own father. Talk to younger men as you would to your own brothers.

2 Treat older women as you would your mother, and treat younger women with all purity as you would your own sisters.

3 Take care of any widow who has no one else to care for her.

4 But if she has children or grandchildren, their first responsibility is to show godliness at home and repay their parents by taking care of them. This is something that pleases God.

5 Now a true widow, a woman who is truly alone in this world, has placed her hope in God. She prays night and day, asking God for his help.

6 But the widow who lives only for pleasure is spiritually dead even while she lives.

7 Give these instructions to the church so that no one will be open to criticism.

8 But those who won't care for their relatives, especially those in their own household, have denied the true faith. Such people are worse than unbelievers.

5:17 Elders who do their work well should be respected and paid well, especially those who work hard at both preaching and teaching.

18 For the Scripture says, "You must not muzzle an ox to keep it from eating as it treads out the grain." And in another place, "Those who work deserve their pay!"

19 Do not listen against an elder unless it is confirmed by two or three witnesses.

20 Those who sin should be reprimanded in front of the whole church; this will serve as a strong warning to others.

21 I solemnly command you in the presence of God and Christ Jesus and the holy angels to obey these instructions without taking sides or showing favoritism to anyone.

22 Never be in a hurry about appointing a church leader. Do not share in the sins of others. Keep yourself pure.

The People, Places, and Times

Widows. There were widows in the Ephesian congregation who were young and could remarry. There were also widows with family members who could support them financially. Paul's concern was that the church should not be burdened to support these groups of widows. However, there were also widows who had no means of support and yet were faithful in service to God and others. Paul admonished the church of Ephesus to support such women. In this way, the church's resources would go as far as possible in helping people who had no one else to rely upon.

Background

Since Paul had to travel to Macedonia, he instructed Timothy to exert apostolic authority in both teaching and lifestyle to the Ephesian church (cf. 1 Timothy 1:3–7). Dealing with false teachers who were setting the wrong example and teaching false doctrines, Timothy bore a great responsibility. Considering his age, the task could be somewhat daunting. Paul instructs Timothy not to allow people to despise his youthfulness, for he was to serve as an "example...in word, in conversation, in charity, in spirit, in faith, [and] in purity" to the entire congregation—including his seniors (1 Timothy 4:11–16). Now, in chapter five, Paul addresses differing relationships in the family of faith. As members of the community, people had to be careful how they dealt with one another. Thus, Paul offers instructions.

At-A-Glance

1. How to Treat Family
(1 Timothy 5:1–2)

2. How to Treat Widows (vv. 3–8)

3. How to Treat Elders (vv. 17–22)

In Depth

1. How to Treat Family (1 Timothy 5:1–2)

The diversity of the church should be celebrated. People from various backgrounds, jobs, cultures, and countries, comprise the Body of Christ. Yet Paul understands that in the context of such an extended family, there are likely to be miscommunications and tensions. He instructs Timothy on how to deal with persons who are older or younger than he is. When dealing with older men and women, Timothy is to treat them as parents. This underscores the familial nature of the church and shows why it is important that leaders not lead with iron fists. When speaking to one's father or mother, there should be a respectful approach and no speaking down to them.

Furthermore, when addressing younger persons, Timothy is to treat them as siblings. Again, this is not a demeaning or bullying manner. This instructs us to be caring and gentle in dealing with younger men and women. Importantly, Paul adds the phrase "with all purity." This offers a subtle yet firm qualifier for dealing with members of the opposite sex. Paul obviously realizes the dangers of inappropriate motives or behavior and leaves no room for them in leadership.

2. How to Treat Widows (vv. 3–8)

The church should assist those who have no one to help them meet their basic needs. By doing so, the church is "Jesus with skin on" to people from whom society usually turns away. It is especially so for the widows, who should receive care and financial aid from the church. Paul lists some qualifications to consider when offering such assistance.

First, if a widow had children or grandchildren who were believers, then they should provide for her. To not do so was considered unacceptable to the point of deviating from the faith! Families of widows should not expect the church to provide monetary assistance for the widow. It is the family's duty to provide for their mother or grandmother, who, it must be remembered, had no means of provision on her own in Paul and Timothy's society.

Second, if a widow does not have family members to help meet basic needs, then she still must meet the qualification of having served (and still be serving) the church (cf. 1 Timothy 5:10). Such service merits the support of the faith community. In this way, Paul circumvents those who may be tempted not to serve in the family of faith while awaiting financial support later in life upon the death of a spouse. The point is to serve within the faith family in whatever way possible. One should not aspire to coast on the hard work of others. In other words, all people have an opportunity for Christian service.

3. How to Treat Elders (vv. 17–22)

After discussing the necessary care to give to widows in need, Paul shifts his attention to the treatment of elders. Some consider this a third distinct group in the company of bishops/overseers and deacons. Others consider "elders" to be an umbrella term which connects both bishops/overseers and deacons. Still others see bishops/overseers as used interchangeably, for the most part, with "elders," with the understanding that bishops/overseers were the "teaching elders."

Whoever these persons were, we must not miss Paul's point—Paul desired those elders who "rule well [to] be counted worthy of double honour" (v. 17). Considering the Scriptures Paul references, one from Moses (Deuteronomy 25:4) and another from Jesus (Luke 10:7), the elders who minister faithfully and effectively deserve to be taken care of monetarily (cf. 1 Corinthians 9:9, 14). This is especially true, Paul states, for those who work in the area of preaching and teaching (1 Timothy 5:17). This does not mean that such elders were to make a great deal more money than others. It simply exhorts the church to support those who labor in preaching and teaching the Gospel.

Many ministers today are often perceived as money-hungry. However, the church cannot allow the bad teaching of a select few to hinder our fulfillment of Paul's instruction. Those who do well in teaching and preaching in the church should not have to worry how their needs will be met. If at all possible, such elders should be well compensated. Paul uses this exhortation to move to a more pressing matter—that of wayward (sinning) elders.

If there is a single accusation with no witnesses against an elder, then Timothy is to see it for what it most likely is—unsubstantiated. However, if there are two or three witnesses who attest that an elder is practicing sin, then the situation must be handled seriously and publicly (vv. 19–20). This is because of the public nature of the elders' ministry. Also, it is to dissuade other elders from teaching and living in a way that would bring disrepute upon Christ and His church.

Such discipline must be carried out without showing favoritism. Wayward elders are to be weighed on the scales of their faithfulness and integrity, or in this case, the lack thereof. Upon removing the false teachers, Timothy is told to choose carefully who will replace them (v. 22). No matter how close a friend Timothy is with someone or how brightly one may shine for a moment, the ministry of an elder is too important for him to endorse persons in a flippant manner. Otherwise, the church runs the risk of appointing someone who is unprepared for the responsibilities or lacks the necessary character.

Search the Scriptures

1. How should we speak to older men and younger men (1 Timothy 5:1)?

2. According to Paul, who is a "widow indeed" (v. 5)?

Discuss the Meaning

Paul strictly warns Timothy to do nothing on the basis of partiality. However, are there times when you have been tempted to make decisions in your church based upon favoritism? What is the danger in giving preferential treatment to some people in a congregation? How can a leader avoid this without offending his or her personal friends?

Lesson in Our Society

This passage of Scripture contains information on honoring widows and elders not merely with words, but with actions (that is, providing for widows who have no relatives). In a society where there is little value placed upon the elderly, Paul's instruction for honoring them may seem uncomfortable to some.

Make It Happen

Throughout this week, pray that God will show you ways to honor the leaders and elders in your church and community. Spend some time thanking God for the contributions these people have made to your church community and reflecting on what you can learn from these people about ministry.

Follow the Spirit

What God wants me to do:

_____

_____

_____

_____

Remember Your Thoughts

Special insights I have learned:

_____

_____

_____

_____

More Light on the Text

1 Timothy 5:1-8, 17-22

1 Rebuke not an elder, but intreat him as a father; and the younger men as brethren; 2 The elder women as mothers; the younger as sisters, with all purity.

Paul starts with the instruction "rebuke not an elder." The Greek word for "rebuke," *epiplesso* (**ep-ee-PLACE-so**), used only here in the New Testament, means "to strike upon," "to strike at," or "to scold sharply." Older men are to be treated with gentleness and kindness. "Elder" (Gk. *presbuteros*, **pres-BOO-ter-os**) is better translated here as "older man." It does not describe the church office of an elder, but it simply refers to a man who is older. This interpretation is more accurate for two reasons. First, it is parallel to *presbuteras* (**pres-BOO-ter-as**), "older women" in verse 2. Second, Paul's main focus in this section is not on church leadership; rather, it is about how Timothy is to relate with people of different ages and gender. "Exhort" and "intreat" (KJV) are both correct translations of the Greek *parakaleo* (**par-ak-al-EH-o**), which also means "encourage." Grammatically, the word is applicable to all the age groups in vv. 1–2. In line with the social custom of that day and other biblical injunctions (cf. Leviticus 19:32; Lamentations 5:12), Paul's admonition to Timothy to encourage older men as fathers and older women as mothers means to treat them with respect, dignity, and honor. It entails gentle persuasion rather than browbeating. What a lesson for our world today, where there is not much respect for age.

The "younger men" (Gk. *neotes*, **neh-OT-ace**) are not necessarily younger than Timothy but about his age (see "youth," 4:12). They are to be treated as brothers. The "younger women" (Gk. *neoteras*, **neh-OT-eh-ras**) are to be treated as sisters. However, Paul adds a note of caution, "with all purity," by using the Greek word *hagneia* (**hag-NI-ah**), which he previously used in 4:12. As noted in that Scripture, the word means "holiness" and carries the nuance of "sexual chastity." In sum, Timothy should treat all church members as family—fathers, mothers, brothers, and sisters. His approach should not be one of domination but one of encouragement, including respect and honor. Especially when it comes to Timothy's ministry with younger women, he is to be careful, both for the sake of his personal well-being and for the sake of the ministerial example he is to set.

3 Honour widows that are widows indeed.

Widows are to be honored, that is, properly recognized. The Greek word *timao* (**tim-AH-o**) carries with it not only the idea of respect but material support. Several passages in the Old Testament underscore the importance of taking care of widows (see, for example, Exodus 22:22; Deuteronomy 10:18; Psalm 68:5; 94:6; 146:9). A similar concern is present in the New Testament (Luke 2:37; Acts 6:1–6; 9:36, 39, 41; James 1:27). Paul's concern in this verse is that Timothy and his congregation take care of "widows indeed," namely widows who are truly in need, but not be burdened with those who could provide for themselves.

4 But if any widow have children or nephews, let them learn first to shew piety at home, and to requite their parents: for that is good and acceptable before God.

Paul now turns his attention to widows who have children and grandchildren. The word "nephew" in the KJV is better understood as "grandchildren." Hence, Paul enjoins children and grandchildren, who have the means, to take responsibility for caring for their widowed, aged parents and grandparents (Gk. *progonos*, **PROG-on-os**). By putting their faith into practice as they care for their parents and grandparents, they demonstrate Christian piety. This is shown especially through the word "requite"—literally "to give" (Gk. *antapodidomi*, **an-tap-od-EE-do-mee**) or "repaying," which occurs only here in the New Testament. First, such help is a sign of true piety or godliness. To care for aged parents or other relatives is an evidence of the same godliness that Paul later commends in 4:7. Paul also saw the giving of care to one's parents and grandparents as a "repayment" (Gk. *apodidomi*, **ap-od-EED-o-mee**) for the earlier care that children had received. Finally, Paul states that care for older widows is pleasing to God.

5 Now she that is a widow indeed, and desolate, trusteth in God, and continueth in supplications and prayers night and day.

Paul then lists the characteristics of a "true" Christian widow. First, she is "desolate," or literally "left entirely alone" (Gk. *eremos*, **ER-ay-mos**). She is probably childless. Second, she is a woman who puts her hope in God. She has no one to take care of her; she relies on God alone. As an African proverb says, "It is only God who wards off the flies that hound a horse without a tail." Such is the plight of a real widow. She has no earthly hopes. There are no relatives to support her, and she has no source of material support or encouragement. Hence she had learned to depend on God alone. Third, she "continueth in supplications and prayers night and day." One is reminded of the widow Anna, 84 years old, who "never left the temple, but worshiped night and day, fasting and praying" (Luke 2:37).

6 But she that liveth in pleasure is dead while she liveth.

In contrast to the godly widows described above are those who live in pleasure or self-indulgence. The phrase "liveth for pleasure" translates the Greek word *spatalao* (**spat-al-AH-o**). It is rarely used in the New Testament, occurring elsewhere only in James 5:5 in James's condemnation of the self-indulgent rich person whose wealth is the result of cheating his workers. The phrase is also used to describe Sodom: "Nevertheless this is the transgression of Sodom, your sister: pride. She and her daughters were living for pleasure in satiety of bread and in abundance of wine" (Ezekiel 16:49). Its basic meaning is to live luxuriously or self-indulgently. Paul says that although these widows are alive, they in fact have died and continue in that state.

7 And these things give in charge, that they may be blameless.

Paul issues a strong command to Timothy to insist on the things he has just said. *Tauta parangelia* (**TOW-tah par-ang-gel-EE-ah**) can be translated from the Greek as "command these things." They are not optional instructions. This is so the people of God may be "irreproachable" (Greek *anepileptos*, **an-ep-EEL-ape-tos**), which literally means "blameless." Paul continues to express his concern for integrity of the body. The holiness of the church is non-negotiable.

8 But if any provide not for his own, and specially for those of his own house, he hath denied the faith, and is worse than an infidel.

Again, Paul speaks strongly on the issue of caring for the needy widows. He reprimands those who fail to "provide for" their own relatives, especially those of their immediate family. Paul says such people have denied the faith and are worse than unbelievers. It is such an inexcusable and egregious failure that is contrary to a claim of piety that any church could make. The connection between church and family are noticeable. The Gospel does not relieve us of our family obligations. It is indeed shameful when Christians do not live up to the standards of unbelievers in the matter of caring for their own—or in any other matter.

5:17 Let the elders that rule well be counted worthy of double honour, especially they who labour in the word and doctrine.

Beginning from this verse Paul turns to another area of concern—officials of their church and their remuneration. The elders are described as those that rule the church. The Greek word *proisthemi* (**pro-IS-tay-mee**) means "to stand first," "to maintain," or "to rule." It refers to directing the affairs of the church or providing leadership. As such, the word excludes any suggestion of aggressive, dictatorial style of leadership. Paul has previously used the same word in 1 Timothy 3:4, 12, to describe the firm but gentle activities of a father. There it connotes management. Those who rule well are to be accorded "double honour" (5:17). According to Thayer and Smith, the Greek word for "double," (*diplous*, **dip-LOOCE**) which Paul uses here means, "twofold" rather than "double." Gordon Fee is probably correct here in suggesting that the Greek word *diple* (**dip-le-e**) is better translated as "two-fold" (Fee, 89). When Paul speaks of "double honour," he has in mind both respect and remuneration. Those who give leadership to spiritual affairs should at least expect financial support from the church (cf. 2 Corinthians 11:8–9; Galatians 6:6). Special honor is to be given to "those who labour in the word and doctrine," which literally means "those laboring to teach God's Word and Christian beliefs."

18 For the scripture saith, thou shalt not muzzle the ox that treadeth out the corn. And, The labourer is worthy of his reward.

Paul now quotes the Old Testament (Deuteronomy 25:4) to support what he has just said about the financial support for elders. His citation of this particular passage (as he does in 1 Corinthians 9:9) justifies the assertion made in the previous verse that financial remuneration was at least a part of the "honour" to which he referred. In its Old Testament context, refusing to muzzle the ox was allowing it an occasional bite to eat as it moved about the threshing floor. For Paul, the principle expressed in the command is broader than a mere statement about care for animals. Specifically, Paul quoted the verse

to justify his case for the proper treatment for the pastor—if God could show concern for the laboring ox, the congregation needed to show proper concern for its leader.

19 Against an elder receive not an accusation, but before two or three witnesses. 20 Them that sin rebuke before all, that others also may fear.

Paul turns to another matter of serious importance relating to the discipline of elders. False accusations always have devastating and disruptive effects. In order to protect people from false accusations, the Law of Moses required the testimony of two or three persons to corroborate an accusation (Deuteronomy 17:6; 19:15). So in line with the Old Testament, Paul warns Timothy not to entertain an accusation against an elder unless it is brought by two or three witnesses (cf. 2 Corinthians 13:1). Paul was not advocating or pleading special treatment for the elders. Rather, he wanted to protect them from groundless accusations. Once the truthfulness of an accusation was established, discipline was to be exercised in form of public rebuke. Its intent was to promote a fear of sin among the leadership and the entire church.

21 I charge thee before God, and the Lord Jesus Christ, and the elect angels, that thou observe these things without preferring one before another, doing nothing by partiality.

Paul now gives a solemn "charge" (Gk. *diamarturomai*, **dee-am-ar-TOO-rom-ahee**) to Timothy to keep the instructions he has given "without preferring one before another," or without "partiality" (Greek *prokrima*, **PROK-ree-mah**), meaning without "prejudging" or "prejudice," used only here in the New Testament. It is normal and natural to develop favorites among people with whom we work. But effective and godly leadership demands that we work just as supportively with those we may not like as well. Timothy must not allow his personal prejudices to tip the scales of justice.

22 Lay hands suddenly on no man, neither be partaker of other men's sins: keep thyself pure.

Although there is no consensus of opinion on what the "lay[ing] hands" in this verse means, it is nevertheless agreed that Paul's warning to Timothy relates to the danger of making hasty appointments to Christian offices. Paul hinted that one who participates in such an appointment shares in the sinful results that can easily follow.

Paul also appealed for personal purity in Timothy. If Timothy faithfully followed Paul's exhortation, it would assure that he would find leaders of stable commitment for positions in the church. Paul's awareness of the sins of others may have led him to remind Timothy of the importance of keeping his own life in order.

Say It Correctly

Deuteronomy. doo'-tuh-RON-uh-mee.
Ephesians. eh-FEE-zhuhnz.
Ezekiel. i-zē-kyəl, -kē-əl.
Macedonia. mas'-uh-DOH-nee-uh.

Daily Bible Readings

M: Chosen to Serve
Acts 6:1–6

T: Served by the Master
Luke 12:35–40

W: Support for Parents
Mark 7:9–13

T: Honoring Elders
Leviticus 19:31–37

F: A Widow's Gift
Mark 12:41–44

S: Assisting Widows
1 Timothy 5:9–16

S: Duties Toward Believers
1 Timothy 5:1–8, 17–22

Teaching Tips

1. Words You Should Know

A. Gospel (2 Timothy 2:8) *euaggelion* (Gk.)—Preaching and teaching of the kingdom of God.

B. Evil Doer (v. 9) *kakourgos* (Gk.)—A wrongdoer, criminal, troublemaker.

C. Eternal (v. 10) *aionios* (Gk.)—Everlasting.

2. Teacher Preparation

Unifying Principle—Communicating Personal Beliefs. The experience of worship moves Christians to a deeper understanding of what they believe.

A. Pray for your students and ask God to meet their spiritual needs.

B. Study the entire text and its surrounding sections.

C. Be prepared to share your church's mission statement or beliefs with your class.

D. Link the discussion to the In Focus story.

3. Open the Lesson

A. Open with prayer, including the Aim for Change.

B. Write on the board, "Why is it important in our day to know what we believe?" Discuss.

C. Share your church's mission statement and your own personal testimony of faith.

4. Present the Scriptures

A. Have volunteers read the Focal Verses.

B. Use The People, Places, and Times; Background; Search the Scriptures; At-A-Glance outline; In Depth; and More Light on the Text to clarify the verses.

C. Explain that we should know what we believe in Christ and should be able to articulate it with others.

5. Explore the Meaning

A. Lead a discussion of the Discuss the Meaning, Lesson in Our Society, and Make It Happen sections.

B. Have volunteers connect these sections to the Aim for Change and the Keep in Mind verse.

6. Next Steps for Application

A. Summarize key points from the lesson—the take-away elements.

B. Close with prayer.

Worship Guide

For the Superintendent or Teacher
Theme: Remembering Jesus Christ
Theme Song: "Only Believe"
Devotional Reading: Titus 3:1–7
Prayer

Remembering Jesus Christ

Bible Background • 2 TIMOTHY 2:8–15
Printed Text • 2 TIMOTHY 2:8–15 | Devotional Reading • TITUS 3:1–7

—————————— Aim for Change ——————————

By the end of the lesson, we will: ARTICULATE our Christian beliefs and values as reflected in 2 Timothy 2; REFLECT on the reasons why we should articulate our beliefs and values; and DEVELOP a strategy to share the Gospel with others.

———————— In Focus ————————

David was a Christian who was not ashamed of the Gospel of Jesus Christ. He believed wholeheartedly in God and in God's Word and sought to live for Christ. One day, he encountered John, who studied world religions. They began to talk about current events, and David posed this question to John. "If you were to die today, what do you think would happen to your soul?"

John replied, "Nothing would happen to my soul—that's it—it is the end!"

David quoted some Scriptures to him, but he began to get frustrated because John referred to Christianity as folklore.

Finally, David discerned that John's issues went deeper than the surface he presented. David knew that as a child, John had suffered some awful wounds at the hands of a hypocritical clergyman and, as a result, John decided there must be a better way to God than Christianity. David was a strong apologist (defender of the Word of God), but he knew that it would not serve the kingdom of God well for him to continue debating with John. John's mind was already made up.

We as Christians must be firm in what we believe and must be ready and able to articulate our beliefs in a convincing manner.

———————— Keep in Mind ————————

"Study to show thyself approved unto God, a workman that needeth not to be ashamed, rightly dividing the word of truth" (2 Timothy 2:15).

"Study to show thyself approved unto God, a workman that needeth not to
be ashamed, rightly dividing the word of truth" (2 Timothy 2:15).

Focal Verses

KJV **2 Timothy 2:8** Remember that Jesus Christ of the seed of David was raised from the dead according to my gospel:

9 Wherein I suffer trouble, as an evil doer, even unto bonds; but the word of God is not bound.

10 Therefore I endure all things for the elect's sakes, that they may also obtain the salvation which is in Christ Jesus with eternal glory.

11 It is a faithful saying: For if we be dead with him, we shall also live with him:

12 If we suffer, we shall also reign with him: if we deny him, he also will deny us:

13 If we believe not, yet he abideth faithful: he cannot deny himself.

14 Of these things put them in remembrance, charging them before the Lord that they strive not about words to no profit, but to the subverting of the hearers.

15 Study to show thyself approved unto God, a workman that needeth not to be ashamed, rightly dividing the word of truth.

NLT **2 Timothy 2:8** Always remember that Jesus Christ, a descendant of King David, was raised from the dead. This is the Good News I preach.

9 And because I preach this Good News, I am suffering and have been chained like a criminal. But the word of God cannot be chained.

10 So I am willing to endure anything if it will bring salvation and eternal glory in Christ Jesus to those God has chosen.

11 This is a trustworthy saying: If we die with him, we will also live with him.

12 If we endure hardship, we will reign with him. If we deny him, he will deny us.

13 If we are unfaithful, he remains faithful, for he cannot deny who he is.

14 Remind everyone about these things, and command them in God's presence to stop fighting over words. Such arguments are useless, and they can ruin those who hear them.

15 Work hard so you can present yourself to God and receive his approval. Be a good worker, one who does not need to be ashamed and who correctly explains the word of truth.

The People, Places, and Times

Early Christians. Due to their strong faith in Jesus Christ as the Messiah, believers in the early church were persecuted. They were perceived as suspicious criminals. Gentile rulers in the Roman Empire, as well as aristocrats, believed in multiple gods. They worshiped at the throne of their own intellect and developed their own philosophies. They did not want anything to upset the status quo. In addition, Jews who did not believe in the resurrection of Jesus also brought opposition to early Christians. The persecution came to a head under Nero's rule. He used Christians as scapegoats when Rome was set ablaze in A.D. 64. Historians believe that Nero started the fire in a fit of rage and put the blame on Christians. Many Christians were brutally persecuted and murdered under his reign until A.D. 68. The apostle Paul suffered, too; he was imprisoned and later beheaded in A.D. 66.

Background

Paul, imprisoned for what was believed to be his final time, was locked up on a more serious charge than his first arrest. Treated as a common criminal, Paul instructed Timothy, "Be not thou therefore ashamed of the testimony of our Lord, nor of me as his prisoner: but be thou a partaker of the afflictions of the gospel" (2 Timothy 1:8). Timothy was a much younger man than Paul, who was a senior by now. Timothy was often timid because of his age, especially when it came to leading those older than he was. In this light, Paul encouraged Timothy in his letters to be strong, to endure hard times, to avoid getting sidetracked, and to boldly instruct those who followed him. Also, Paul sought to warn Timothy about wickedness and admonish him to represent the Gospel of Jesus Christ well. This second letter to Timothy, written about A.D. 66, was very

personal for Paul as he passes the torch. He reminds Timothy of Timothy's heritage (2 Timothy 1:5) and charges him to use the gifts that God has given him at the laying on of Paul's hands when Timothy was first called into the ministry (v. 6). Paul speaks candidly to Timothy as a father in the ministry, who is soon leaving his son and wants to give him as much of God's wisdom as he can before his departure. Paul takes this occasion to reinforce key messages, to encourage Timothy warmly and to say goodbye.

At-A-Glance

1. A Reminder of Whom We Serve (2 Timothy 2:8–10)

2. A Reminder of the True Rewards of Serving (vv. 11–13)

3. A Reminder to Know What We Believe (vv. 14–15)

In Depth

1. A Reminder of Whom We Serve (2 Timothy 2:8–10)

Paul reminds Timothy not only to be strong in the grace that is in Christ Jesus (2 Timothy 2:1), but to remember who Christ is as the heir to the throne of God, as promised to David (cf. 2 Samuel 7:12–13, 16; Psalm 89:3–4; Luke 1:31–33). He reminds Timothy of who we as believers serve. In other words, he reminds him of the Good News, the Gospel of Jesus Christ. This Gospel is God's atonement for our sins and ministry of reconciliation between God and humankind "for it is the power of God unto salvation to everyone that believeth; to the Jew first, and also to the Greek" (Romans 1:16). Paul, in baring his soul to his son in the ministry, admits that while he is suffering as a common criminal ("an evil doer"), the Word of God is not bound but continues to reach the lost (2 Timothy 2:9).

2. A Reminder of the True Reward of Serving (vv. 11–13)

Paul has presented Timothy with the realities of Christian fellowship, such as the truth of Jesus Christ and who He is as our salvation, the persecution current and future, and those who would deny Christ and join in with other malefactors. Then Paul reminds him of the true reward that lies ahead for those who endure to the end. He recalls for Timothy the tenets of the faith as revealed to him by Christ. Jesus Himself said, "There is no man that hath left house, or brethren, or sisters, or father, or mother, or wife, or children, or lands, for my sake, and the gospel's, But he shall receive an hundredfold now in this time, houses, and brethren, and sisters, and mothers, and children, and lands, with persecutions; and in the world to come eternal life" (Mark 10:29–30). God Himself will reward His good and faithful servants with the eternal life that He secured for them through the blood of Jesus Christ.

The apostle Paul assures Timothy that as new creatures in Christ, we shall experience the highs and lows of life all with God's intent to fashion us into His image—molding and making us into His character. The writer of Hebrews says, "Though he were a Son, yet learned he obedience by the things which he suffered" (Hebrews 5:8) If we are resurrected with Christ in order to live and reign with Him, we, too, must die to self and will suffer persecution as we carry our own crosses. We, too, should learn obedience to God by the things which we suffer. This, however, does not negate the reward that we will receive when all is said and done on this earth (Romans 5:5–8).

3. A Reminder to Know What We Believe (vv. 14–15)

Timothy is charged with not only reading what has been said in this letter to him, but to "put them in remembrance" by urging those who are led by him to do so out of the fear or reverence of God (2 Timothy 2:14). Timothy is to admonish believers not to spend time getting involved in verbal challenges with those who subvert the truth of God in Christ, for it only gives them an unwarranted audience.

At this time, Timothy was facing opposition from false teachers who looked for people to follow and esteem them as great and who often distorted the truth (v. 18). Paul writes to Timothy, "Study to show thyself approved unto God" (v. 15), or as he said on another occasion, "Walk worthy of the vocation wherewith ye are called" (Ephesians 4:1). Because Paul knows that Timothy was called out by God from his youth for the Gospel, and that he laid hands on Timothy to commission him to carry out his duties in the kingdom of God, he now exhorts him to stand firm in what he believes and to make understanding the Word a priority.

This text teaches us that it does not benefit God or us as Christians to argue with unbelievers just for the sake of debates that may be meaningless. Later on in this letter, Paul reaffirms, "All Scripture is given by inspiration of God, and is profitable for doctrine, for reproof, for correction, for instruction in righteousness" (2 Timothy 3:16). We should know God's Word and rightly divide the Word of truth so that we can grow in the wisdom and knowledge of God and walk in His Word. But we should not engage in heated arguments just to prove how much we know; this is detrimental to God's kingdom-building initiative.

Search the Scriptures

1. Why was it important for Paul to remind Timothy and others about the ancestry and kingship of Jesus Christ (2 Timothy 2:8)?

2. What does Paul mean when he said the Gospel is "not bound" (v. 9)?

Discuss the Meaning

1. Why is it important to know what we believe?

2. What role does worship play in expressing our faith?

Lesson in Our Society

There is a lot of strange doctrine, and many prominent people are viewed as influencers in shaping public opinion. However, no matter the star power, if what they propagate conflicts with the Word of God, we must be ready to refute arguments and stand up for what we believe. Worship is central to expressing what we believe, and it does not take place only in church. Worship is a lifestyle rooted in abiding belief in living by the Word of God.

Make It Happen

Are you spending enough time in prayer, praise, and worship? Determine this week to spend extra time in the Word of God. If you have not done so already, carve out a place in your home for quiet time with the Lord. Ask God to reveal His will for your life and show you how you can better serve and represent Him in your everyday life.

Follow the Spirit

What God wants me to do:

_____

_____

_____

_____

Remember Your Thoughts

Special insights I have learned:

_____

_____

_____

_____

More Light on the Text

2 Timothy 2:8–15

8 Remember that Jesus Christ of the seed of David was raised from the dead according to my gospel:

Christ is the ultimate example of perseverance leading to success. He is the example to always remember. The continued remembrance of Christ's resurrection has practical consequences in proportion as it is understood in its fullness. The power available to Timothy is founded on mighty facts about Christ: He was really raised from the dead, and He descended from David. These facts are vital for Christian proclamation and for Christian life.

Christ was raised from the dead. The Greek verb *egeiro* (**eg-I-ro**), "to raise," is in the perfect tense (an action already accomplished, but its results are still present) marking a permanent condition. It means that Christ is now up from the grave and will never die again. He is alive permanently. The resurrection of Christ is the most important

Christian truth. It contains the guarantee of all other aspects of the work of Christ. It is the final proof of Christ's deity and of the fact that God has accepted His sacrifice for the sin of humanity (Romans 1:3–4; 4:25). It is the pledge of the future resurrection of believers, for Christ is the first fruits of those who have fallen asleep (1 Corinthians 15:20). It is a call to live in newness of life (Romans 6:4, 11; Colossians 3:1).

Christ's Davidic lineage points to the fact that He was human and the Messiah indeed (cf. Acts 2:29–35; Romans 1:3–4). Truly, He became human, was qualified to be the Messiah, and really did suffer. Timothy must always keep these facts in mind, because just as a disciple is like his master, he will suffer, too. However, suffering is followed by resurrection. "According to my gospel" means the Gospel that Paul preached (cf. Romans 2:16; 16:25). The truth about the humanity and resurrection of Christ was emphasized in the Gospel preached by Paul.

9 Wherein I suffer trouble, as an evil doer, even unto bonds; but the word of God is not bound.

The verse reveals Paul as an imitator of Christ and an example to Timothy and the believers (cf. v. 3). If Paul can endure, Timothy can and we can. The Greek construction *en hoi* (**en hoi**), "on account of which," indicates the Gospel as the domain of Paul's sufferings. It is Paul's work "in the gospel" that has caused him to be mistreated by the Roman authorities. The Greek word *kakourgos* (**kak-OOR-gos**, "evildoer") suggests that Paul was being treated as a common criminal (cf. Luke 23:32, 39). *Kakourgos* here describes those crucified with Jesus; it is the only other use of the word in the New Testament. The apostle Paul had been in prison and had been treated like a criminal because of the Gospel on many

occasions (Acts 9:25; 2 Corinthians 11:33; cf. Luke 23:32–39; Philippians 2:8;).

In contrast to Paul's own condition is the absolute freedom of the Word of God. The persecution of preachers may slow down the progress of the Gospel, but it cannot prevent the Word of God from spreading. The Word does not lie in chains like the man who had spent days in preaching it. It is living and active (Hebrews 4:12). It is still with us, and it still needs preachers (Romans 10:14–17). God raises up people to preach it (Acts 4:20; 1 Corinthians 9:16).

10 Therefore I endure all things for the elect's sakes, that they may also obtain the salvation which is in Christ Jesus with eternal glory.

Paul, then, gives a reason that he can "endure" (Gk. *hupomeno*, **hoop-om-EN-o**, meaning "to take patiently"). It is for the sake of the "elect" (Gk. *eklektos*, **ek-lek-TOS**), or "the chosen." The "elect's sake" here seems to mean those who are chosen but do not yet believe. They have to hear the Word of God to believe. It can also refer to those who had been and were being saved through the apostle's ministry. Paul had spent many years spreading the Gospel. He had seen many people receive the Word and be saved (Acts 16:31). Thus, the churches of Macedonia were his "crown" and his "joy" (Philippians 4:1; 1 Thessalonians 2:19). The expression in 2 Timothy 2:10 "with eternal glory" refers to the consummation of salvation. Paul in his writings often links glory with salvation (Romans 5:1–2; 8:21–25; 2 Thessalonians 2:13–14). Salvation may be enjoyed in part in this life. It will be consummated in eternal glory (2 Corinthians 4:16–18; 5:1–10).

11 It is a faithful saying: For if we be dead with him, we shall also live with him: 12 If we suffer, we shall also reign with him: if we deny him, he also will deny us: 13 If we believe not, yet he abideth faithful: he cannot deny himself.

Paul here introduces a quote with an expression very familiar in the pastoral epistles (cf. 1 Timothy 1:15; 3:1; 4:9; Titus 3:8). It attests that the saying is "faithful." The saying is presented in four statements with a double facet: the first two are expressed in a positive manner (vv. 11–12a) and the last two are characterized by a negative (vv. 12b-13). In view of the use of the Greek verb tense *sunapothnesko* (**soon-ap-oth-NACE-ko**, "to die together with"), the phrase "If we be dead with him" is referring to a past event, an experience of identification with Christ such as baptism (see Romans 6:1–8). The Greek word for "suffer" (Greek *hupomeno*, **hoop-om-EN-o**) means "to persevere" (see verse 10). "We shall also reign with him" expresses an identification of the believer with Christ.

The experience of identification with Christ forms the basis of Christian living (Colossians 3:3). Christ suffered, but one day He will reign (1 Corinthians 15:25). In the same way, the believers, who are suffering now, will reign one day with Him (Revelation 3:21). We may go through hardship in the present, but there are great things to look forward to (cf. 2 Corinthians 4:16–5:10). Having risen to a new life, we are called to patiently endure. The result of endurance is blessings (Romans 8:17; James 1:12; 5:11). Jesus Himself endured and is now seated at the right hand of the throne of God (Hebrews 12:2).

The statement in 2 Timothy 2:12, "If we deny him, he also will deny us," refers to a possibility of apostasy (cf. Matthew 10:33; 1 Timothy 4:1; Hebrews 10:38–39; 2 John 9). Regardless of one's stance on the issue of eternal security, we all have observed those who have identified with Christ, at least for a time, but later denied Christ. If we are faithless, He remains faithful. Even if we are lacking in loyalty, He remains trustworthy (cf. Romans 3:3–4). He is loyal to His promises (1 Corinthians 1:8; Hebrews 10:23; 11:11; cf. Psalm 89:28). Christ's faithfulness to His own promises gives the believer his or her greatest security. God cannot lie; thus, He will do what He says He will do (Numbers 23:19; 1 Samuel 15:29; Malachi 3:6; Titus 1:2; Hebrews 6:18). It is unthinkable that any incident could affect God's faithfulness because He cannot contradict Himself. He cannot be false to His own nature. Our powerlessness cannot affect Him in His nature.

14 Of these things put them in remembrance, charging them before the Lord that they strive not about words to no profit, but to the subverting of the hearers.

The tense of "put...in remembrance" (Gk. *hupomimnesko*, **hoop-om-im-NACE-ko**) means "call to mind" or "remember" and is the imperative present indicating regularity. Paul exhorted or urged Timothy to remind people of "these things" regularly. Paul gives specific instructions to guide Timothy in his inevitable encounters with false teachers. He must first maintain the right doctrine. Everyone is to be reminded regularly of the apostles' teachings. Therefore, the deposit of the Christian truth is to be guarded (2 Timothy 1:12–14; 2:2; see Jude 3).

The Greek word for "charge" is *diamarturomai* (**dee-am-ar-TOO-rom-ahee**), which means "to testify" or "to confirm a thing by testimony." Timothy had to instruct the converts to avoid strife over mere words. They should not engage in word battles. It does no good. It can actually be harmful. The Greek word *katastrophe* (**kat-as-trof-AY**) means "subversion" or "ruin" and literally "turning upside down." Verbal strife can upset the faith of many. It is the antithesis of edification or building up. We should always ask if the subject under discussion is worth a fight and if it is for building up or tearing down God's kingdom (cf. 2 Corinthians 10:8; 13:10).

15 Study to show thyself approved unto God, a workman that needeth not to be ashamed, rightly dividing the word of truth.

The meaning of "study" (Gk. *spoudazo*, **spoo-DAD-zo**) means "to hasten," "to be eager," or "to do one's utmost" (cf. Matthew 20:1, 8). Timothy must persistently live in a way "approved" (Gk. *dokimos*, **DOK-ee-mos**) meaning "accepted after testing" by God. Timothy must maintain the standard at all times. He is always under God's eye. The most effective way to refute error is to live out the truth (see the book of James). Therefore, Timothy must be a teacher, who without shame, can submit his work for God's approval (cf. Mathew 25:14–30). He must remain in the truth so that all deviations will be evident. "Rightly dividing the word of truth" means doing a correct analysis of the Word of God. Therefore, we cannot give a correct analysis if we do not know the Word and the God-intended meaning of the Word.

Daily Bible Readings

M: Raised from the Dead
Acts 3:11–16

T: Descended from David
Romans 1:1–7

W: Our Savior
Titus 3:1–7

T: Remembering Jesus' Sacrifice
Matthew 26:17–30

F: Proclaiming the Lord's Death
1 Corinthians 11:23–33

S: Now Is the Day of Salvation
2 Corinthians 6:1–10

S: Salvation in Christ Jesus
2 Timothy 2:8–15

Say It Correctly

Colossians. kuh-LOSH-uhnz,
also -shee-uhnz.
Ephesians. ih-FEE-zhuhnz.
Macedonia. mas'-uh-DOH-nee-uh.

Teaching Tips

April 10
Bible Study Guide 6

1. Words You Should Know

A. Mockers (Jude 18) *empaiktes* (Gk.)—Scoffers; false teachers.

B. Compassion (v. 22) *eleeo* (Gk.)—Pity, mercy.

C. Faultless (v. 24) *amomos* (Gk.)—Blameless.

2. Teacher Preparation

Unifying Principle—Assurance for Daily Living. Jude's benediction expresses complete confidence in God's ability to sustain us.

A. Pray that your students will have someone in their lives to build them up in their faith when they need it the most.

B. Study the entire text and its surrounding sections.

C. Prepare to introduce the words in the Words You Should Know section.

3. Open the Lesson

A. Open with prayer, including the Aim for Change.

B. Have one volunteer role-play an "encourager" and the other "the encouraged."

C. Ask the "encourager" what words he or she would use to build up his or her classmate's faith in the Lord.

D. Summarize the In Focus story and discuss the problems that Kevin had on his job and with family and friends.

E. Ask, "Was Kevin really being sanctimonious or overbearing because of his faith?" Discuss.

F. Ask, "What could Kevin do to share his faith and not push everyone away?" Discuss.

4. Present the Scriptures

A. Have volunteers summarize the Focal Verses.

B. Use The People, Places, and Times; Background; Search the Scriptures; At-A-Glance outline; In Depth; and More Light on the Text to clarify the verses.

5. Explore the Meaning

A. Lead a discussion of the Discuss the Meaning, Lesson in Our Society, and Make It Happen sections.

B. Connect these sections to the Aim for Change and the Keep in Mind verse.

6. Next Steps for Application

A. Ask, "How can we build ourselves up in this most holy faith, according to the Scriptures?" Summarize the lesson.

B. Close with prayer.

APR
10th

Worship Guide

For the Superintendent or Teacher
Theme: Praise Builds Us Up
Theme Song: "I Need You to Survive!"
Devotional Reading: 2 Corinthians 4:1–12
Prayer

Praise Builds Us Up

Bible Background • JUDE 17–25
Printed Text • JUDE 17–25 | Devotional Reading • 2 CORINTHIANS 4:1–12

—————— Aim for Change ——————

By the end of the lesson, we will: TELL how God is able to sustain and keep us in our Christian life; BE assured that God is able to sustain and keep us; and THANK God that He does sustain and keep us.

—————  In Focus —————

Kevin was having a rough time. He was catching flack at work, from extended family, and among his friends. After allowing his faith to grow lax, he reaffirmed his commitment to Christ, and now it seemed that the moment he gained momentum in his walk, trouble hit. His friend Darnell kept telling him he had become a drag. His siblings thought he was being sanctimonious at family gatherings when he did not want to participate in the revelry. His coworkers shunned him in the lunchroom, fearing they would get another sermon. Kevin felt as though he had hit an all-time low.

His wife Kimberly stepped in to encourage him. "Honey, you know, I was praying for you today," she said. "You should memorize: 'Cast your burden on the LORD and he will sustain you; he will never permit the righteous to be moved' (Psalm 55:22, NRSV)."

Kevin took the verse with him where ever he went. When he needed encouragement, he recalled that Scripture and began to praise God because God would do what His Word promised.

As we walk this Christian journey, our faith will be tested. Today's lesson is a reminder about the power of God and how we are to remain in faith through the expression of praise unto Him.

————— Keep in Mind —————

"Now unto him that is able to keep you from falling, and to present you faultless before the presence of his glory with exceeding joy, To the only wise God our Saviour, be glory and majesty, dominion and power, both now and ever. Amen" (Jude 24–25).

"Now unto him that is able to keep you from falling, and to present you faultless before the presence of his glory with exceeding joy, To the only wise God our Saviour, be glory and majesty, dominion and power, both now and ever. Amen" (Jude 24–25).

Focal Verses

KJV **Jude 17** But, beloved, remember ye the words which were spoken before of the apostles of our Lord Jesus Christ;

18 How that they told you there should be mockers in the last time, who should walk after their own ungodly lusts.

19 These be they who separate themselves, sensual, having not the Spirit.

20 But ye, beloved, building up yourselves on your most holy faith, praying in the Holy Ghost,

21 Keep yourselves in the love of God, looking for the mercy of our Lord Jesus Christ unto eternal life.

22 And of some have compassion, making a difference:

23 And others save with fear, pulling them out of the fire; hating even the garment spotted by the flesh.

24 Now unto him that is able to keep you from falling, and to present you faultless before the presence of his glory with exceeding joy,

25 To the only wise God our Saviour, be glory and majesty, dominion and power, both now and ever. Amen.

NLT **Jude 17** But you, my dear friends, must remember what the apostles of our Lord Jesus Christ said.

18 They told you that in the last times there would be scoffers whose purpose in life is to satisfy their ungodly desires.

19 These people are the ones who are creating divisions among you. They follow their natural instincts because they do not have God's Spirit in them.

20 But you, dear friends, must build each other up in your most holy faith, pray in the power of the Holy Spirit,

21 and await the mercy of our Lord Jesus Christ, who will bring you eternal life. In this way, you will keep yourselves safe in God's love.

22 And you must show mercy to those whose faith is wavering.

23 Rescue others by snatching them from the flames of judgment. Show mercy to still others, but do so with great caution, hating the sins that contaminate their lives.

24 Now all glory to God, who is able to keep you from falling away and will bring you with great joy into his glorious presence without a single fault.

25 All glory to him who alone is God, our Savior through Jesus Christ our Lord. All glory, majesty, power, and authority are his before all time, and in the present, and beyond all time! Amen.

The People, Places, and Times

Jude. He was the half-brother of Jesus and was also known as Judas (not Judas Iscariot, who betrayed Jesus). Jude was referenced in Matthew 13:55 and Mark 6:3 as a point of familiarity to the community that raised questions about Jesus being "the Christ" (the Anointed One), the promised Messiah. Along with his brothers, Jude was not persuaded initially about Jesus' deity. He sought VIP treatment, and he tried to cajole Jesus to show off to provide evidence (Matthew 12:46–50; Mark 3:31–35; Luke 8:19–21; John 7:1–10). However, Jude and his other brothers were among those sequestered in the upper room awaiting the arrival of the promised Holy Spirit as instructed by Jesus (Acts 1:14). Interestingly, in opening his letter, Jude does not refer to himself at all as the half-brother of Jesus; he names himself, "The servant of Jesus Christ, and brother of James."

False Teachers. Jude's letter addressed a time when there were a lot of strange doctrines and heretical teachers who led people astray from the faith. This apostasy was similar to what Paul addressed in Acts 20:29–31; 1 Timothy 4:1–2; 2 Timothy 3:1–9, 13; 4:3; and the tone and manner of Peter's message in 2 Peter 2:1–22. False teachers were dangerous because they had tasted of the heavenly gift, turned away from it, and misconstrued the truth for their own willful purposes.

Background

Scholars vary on the exact date Jude wrote his epistle (letter); it is believed that his letter was written anywhere from A.D. 50 to A.D. 80. This book of the Bible is believed to have been written after Peter's death but before the destruction of Jerusalem, and then later circulated. It is also generally believed that

Jude's letter was not targeted to a particular church, but meant as a general epistle to warn saints about false teachers who were misleading those who were not rooted in the church. Although Jude strongly chides those would-be infiltrators of the truth, the purpose of his letter was also to encourage those who would read it to recall the words of the Lord Jesus Christ. Jude exhorts them to stand strong in the face of opposition.

At-A-Glance

1. A Warning for Believers (Jude 17–19)

2. A True Foundation for Believers (vv. 20–23)

3. A Benediction of Praise to God for Believers (vv. 24–25)

In Depth

1. A Warning for Believers (Jude 17–19)

In Jude 1–16, readers are earnestly warned to be on the lookout and contend or fight for the faith which was delivered to and received by them (v. 3), a major theme of this epistle. Recalling how in times past those who lived irreverently and with no restraint were dealt with, the writer lovingly calls attention to the predictions of the apostles of our Lord Jesus Christ that these times would come (Acts 20:29–31; 1 Timothy 4:1–2; 2 Timothy 3:1–9). Jude further extends this love by giving believers a sense of belonging to the family of God through the lordship of Jesus Christ (v. 17). The warning for believers is that these mockers of the truth caused confusion and division among the saints in the end time. These false teachers were "devoid of the Spirit" (v. 19, NRSV), indulgent in their own ungodly lust, and troublesome for the church of Jesus Christ.

2. A True Foundation for Believers (vv. 20–23)

The foundation for believers is the love of God as displayed through His plan of salvation—the finished work of Jesus Christ on Calvary's Cross and His imminent return. Faith in Jesus Christ alone is able to keep believers during this time of great apostasy and the heat of affliction. Jude admonishes each individual who should read or hear this letter to get a firm footing on what they believe about Jesus, knowing that their labor will not be in vain (cf. 1 Corinthians 15:58). He places special emphasis on sacredness of their faith by calling it their "most holy faith" (Jude 20). He further implores them to give the utmost attention to building this faith by praying in the Holy Ghost as Paul instructs in Romans 8:26 and Ephesians 6:18. The Holy Spirit comforts, consoles, and keeps believers strong in the love of God.

As believers maintain focus on the love and mercies of God, they are to look to God with hope of the promised life to come with the Lord Jesus Christ, which is to sustain them in troubled times. These believers are also called upon to reassure and build up those who are wavering in the faith and help them to stand strong (see also Romans 15:1–2). They are told to strive to save others, who are wavering, by putting the fear of God in them in the hopes of bringing them back to their spiritual senses. As well, they are to hate and reprove the very appearance of evil in the flesh as they keep themselves unspotted from the world (Ephesians 5:11–13, Jude 23).

3. A Benediction of Praise to God for Believers (vv. 24–25)

Paul's use of the phrase "now unto Him" (cf. Romans 16:25; Ephesians 3:20) denotes the absolute power of God, through Jesus Christ, to provide stability for believers. Jude similarly provides a strong conclusion to his letter to believers by pronouncing a blessing upon Christians in the early church. He commends them to the One who is able to keep, preserve, and sustain them from the harm of falling short or falling away (Jude 24). He further states that because of the remission of sins at His expense, Jesus is able to present them faultless and without blame in the presence of God's glory (Colossians 1:22–23). The writer ascribes to God the Father and our Savior all the glory, majesty, sovereignty, and authority due to Him forever. This praise and adulation foretells the future that is to come for the saints of God, reflected in John's revelation (Revelation 7:11–12; 19:6–8). This is the foundation of the hope we have as believers which enables us to "not be weary in well doing, for in due season we shall reap if we faint not" (Galatians 6:9).

Search the Scriptures

1. What does Jude instruct readers to remember (Jude 17–18)?

2. What did Jude call on believers to do (vv. 21–23)?

Discuss the Meaning

1. Why is it important to know what you believe?

2. How can you be sure in your faith and grounded in what you believe?

Lesson in Our Society

The Word of God gives us instruction for daily living about how to overcome obstacles and stand strong in the face of opposition. As it was at the time the book of Jude was written, the Word of God is questioned and misinterpreted today to suit the fancy of the carnal mind. As well, in the spirit of political correctness, our country has fallen away from the rudiments of the guiding principles which make us a blessed nation by failing to honor and revere God's authority and rulership. The Word of God calls Christians to uphold the standard of holiness and to win back those who are lost by walking in God's love and mercy.

Make It Happen

Think about how you can ascribe to God the glory, honor, and power due Him in your everyday life. Determine to live a life that is free from selfish ambition and interest, and inquire of God what He would have you do for His kingdom. Seek to strengthen your relationship with God through prayer and praise. As you place the will of the Lord above all else, worship will be simple as He will begin to show you great and marvelous things.

Follow the Spirit

What God wants me to do:

_____

_____

_____

_____

Remember Your Thoughts

Special insights I have learned:

_____

_____

_____

_____

More Light on the Text
Jude 17–25

17 But, beloved, remember ye the words which were spoken before of the apostles of our Lord Jesus Christ;

In this verse, the conjunction "but" opposes the recommended attitude to the behavior of the heretics denounced in verse 16. Jude urges the readers to "call to mind" the things announced by the apostles about the "mockers." It is important for believers to cultivate the habit of going back to the Word or the apostolic teaching.

18 How that they told you there should be mockers in the last time, who should walk after their own ungodly lusts.

In the use of the imperfect tense (which represents an action as continued, repeated, or habitual), the word "told" (Gk. *lego*, **LEG-o**) stresses the repeated nature of the apostolic warnings. (See warnings like Paul's in Acts 20:29–30; 1 Timothy 4:1–3; 2 Timothy 3:1, and Peter's in 2 Peter 2:1–3; 3:3–4.) Jude is referring to a specific subject in the apostolic teaching: the prophecies about the "last time" or "end time." The Greek word *asebeo* (**as-eb-EH-o**) means "impiety" or "ungodly," and it can translate as "desires for lusts" or "evil things." The false teachers' desires are ungodly.

The expression "in the last time" is equivalent to "in the last days" (see 2 Timothy 3:1; James 5:3; 2 Peter 3:3). The existence of the mockers is thus a proof that the last days are near (see Matthew 24:24; 2 Thessalonians 2:3–4, 9; 2 Timothy 4:1). In the New Testament, the period of the last days is both future (2 Timothy 3:1) and present (1 Peter 1:20; Hebrews 1:2). It is partly realized through the coming of Jesus and partly awaiting consummation. The prediction about the things to come includes present fulfillment and prolongation into a future date which cannot be set.

19 These be they who separate themselves, sensual, having not the Spirit.

Jude uses contemptuously the word *houtos* (**HOO-tos**), which means "these." He sets it in contrast with "but you, beloved" in verse 20 (see vv. 12, 16, and 17). Then he goes on to describe the impious. They are called "they who separate themselves," meaning that they create division or make a distinction between themselves and other people. They see themselves as superior. They are arrogant and controlled by their own natural desires (Romans 16:17; Galatians 5:20). They claim to be spiritual, but they do not have the Spirit. The Greek *psuchikos* (**psoo-khee-KOS**) means "sensual" or "natural," and it is the antithesis of *pneumatikos* (**pnyoo-mat-ik-OCE**), meaning "spiritual" (cf. 1 Corinthians 2:13–15; 15:44–46). The description of the impious people confirms that in them the apostolic predictions are fulfilled.

20 But ye, beloved, building up yourselves on your most holy faith, praying in the Holy Ghost, 21 Keep yourselves in the love of God, looking for the mercy of our Lord Jesus Christ unto eternal life.

These two verses constitute one long phrase. The main verb of the phrase is "keep" (Gk. *tereo*, **tay-REH-o**). It is in the imperative voice. It is surrounded by participles, two in front ("building" and "praying") and one after ("looking"). Thus, the main point of the exhortation is the relationship of the believer with the love of God (Gk. *agape theos*, **ag-AH-pay THEH-os**). Here, the readers are urged to stay within the sphere of God's love. It was God's love which drew them to Himself (see v. 1). They must abide in that love. We abide in His love by keeping His commands (John 15:9–10).

For the second time, Jude calls the readers "beloved" (Gk. *agapetos*, **ag-ap-ay-TOS**), and on each occasion it is in contrast to the false teachers (see v. 17). With this expression, he shows a genuine deep affection for the readers. He gives them instruction on Christian life. If it is followed, the instruction he gives will preserve them from contamination by the heretics.

The readers are instructed to build themselves up in the apostolic teaching (cf. Acts 2:42; 20:32). The use of the present participle "building up" (Gk. *epoikodomeo*, **ep-oy-kod-om-EH-o**) suggests that the edification is not limited to being inserted in the construction. It needs the will to remain and do the given task. Building up is a continual process. Believers must study the Scriptures continually if they are to grow in the faith and abide in God's love (cf. Hebrews 5:12; 2 Timothy 2:15). The "most holy faith" is a reference to the Scriptures, the Christian revelation handed down by the apostles (as in verse 3; 2 Timothy 3:16–17).

22 And of some have compassion, making a difference: 23 And others save with fear, pulling them out of the fire; hating even the garment spotted by the flesh.

Two groups of people are mentioned here. The first group is those whose faith is wavering (Gk. d*iakrino*, **dee-ak-REE-no**, meaning "be of two minds," "doubt," or "waver"). The readers must show compassion to them. Showing compassion is not a passive attitude. True love tries the impossible: to pull the undecided out of the fire of judgment that is waiting the lost. Compare Amos 4:11 and Zechariah 3:2; fire is the figure of judgment in Matthew 13:42, 50; 18:8; Revelation 19:20. Many different ways must be found to persuade them. The expression in Jude 23, "pulling them out of fire," denotes urgency.

The second group includes the heretics. They are not at a hesitation stage; they are being pulled away by the stream of apostasy. The readers must exercise great care while getting alongside them, lest they themselves become "spotted" (Gk. *spiloo*, **spee-LO-o**), which means "defiled" or "polluted" (cf. 2 Corinthians 7:1). They are to love the sinners and hate their sin (cf. Matthew 18:17; 1 Corinthians 5:11; Titus 3:10; 1 John 2:10–11).

24 Now unto him that is able to keep you from falling, and to present you faultless before the presence of his glory with exceeding joy,

Jude ends his exhortation with heartfelt adoration to the One who is able to keep the believers from falling. We have here the announcement of the great victory and the great assurance of the redeemed. God has the "power" (Gk. *dunamai*, **DOO-nam-ahee**), which means to "be able." The phrase "to keep from falling" (Gk. *aptaistos*, **ap-TAH-ee-stos**) means "stop from stumbling" (cf. 1 Peter 1:5); it has the same root as the verb "fall" in 2 Peter 1:10. Believers are not left without help. God can guard them so that they do not stumble. He will make them stand before His glory. We will stand "faultless" (Gk. *amomos*, **AM-o-mos**, see also Ephesians 1:4; 5:27; cf. 1 Peter 1:19) and "in jubilation" (Gk. *agalliasis*, **ag-al-LEE-as-is**) because we are in Christ.

25 To the only wise God our Saviour, be glory and majesty, dominion and power, both now and ever. Amen.

Doxologies (words of honor, praises) are usually addressed to God in order to give Him "glory" (Gk. *doxa*, **DOX-ah**), which refers to "the brilliance of God's being," which is what He reveals of His perfection. The word "majesty" (Gk. *megalosune*, **meg-al-**o-SOO-nay), "dominion" (Gk. *kratos*, **KRAT-os**), and "might" (Gk. *exousia*, **ex-oo-SEE-ah**) are aspects of His glory. To God alone belongs the glory! He is the only God.

Say It Correctly

Iscariot. is-KAR-ee-uht, is-KAIR-ee-uht.
Judas. JOO-duhs.
Jude. JOOD.

Daily Bible Readings

M: Treasure in Clay Jars
2 Corinthians 4:1–12

T: Praise from the Restored
Jeremiah 31:2–9

W: Live for the Glory of God
1 Corinthians 10:23–31

T: A Message That Builds Up
Acts 20:28–35

F: Protection from Evil
John 17:6–19

S: The Good and the Right Way
1 Samuel 12:19–25

S: Build Yourselves Up in Faith
Jude 17–25

Teaching Tips

1. Words You Should Know

A. Bethphage (Mark 11:1) *Bethphage* (Gk.)—"The name of a hamlet [village] between Jericho and Jerusalem."

B. Hosanna (vv. 9–10) *hosanna* (Gk.)—A crying out or shout whose intent is encouragement, favor, or great promise; literally means "please save (the person shouting)."

2. Teacher Preparation

Unifying Principle—Lavishing Praise. Mark's gospel says that the people shouted "Hosanna" to Jesus because they believed He was bringing the reign of God.

A. Pray that your students will understand the meaning of this lesson and its connection with the death, burial, and resurrection of our Lord and Savior, Jesus Christ.

B. Study the entire text and its surrounding sections.

C. Bring a palm branch to class and be prepared to discuss why we celebrate Palm Sunday.

3. Open the Lesson

A. Open with prayer, including the Aim for Change.

B. Display your palm branch and present your material on why we celebrate Palm Sunday.

C. Summarize and tie in the In Focus story.

4. Present the Scriptures

A. Have volunteers read the Focal Verses.

B. Use The People, Places, and Times; Background; Search the Scriptures; At-A-Glance outline; In Depth; and More Light on the Text to clarify the verses.

C. Ask a volunteer to explain what Jesus' triumphal entry into Jerusalem means to him or her and to the people who heaped lavish praises on Him.

5. Explore the Meaning

A. Have volunteers summarize the Discuss the Meaning, Lesson in Our Society, and Make It Happen sections.

B. Connect these sections to the Aim for Change and the Keep in Mind verse.

C. Lead a discussion of the Search the Scriptures questions.

6. Next Steps for Application

A. Summarize today's lesson.

B. Close with prayer.

Worship Guide

For the Superintendent or Teacher
Theme: Hosanna!
Theme Song: "Hosanna, Blessed Be the Rock!"
Devotional Reading: 1 Chronicles 16:8–15
Prayer

Hosanna!

Bible Background • MARK 11:1–11
Printed Text • MARK 11:1–11 | Devotional Reading • 1 CHRONICLES 16:8–15

—————— Aim for Change ——————

By the end of the lesson, we will: RECOUNT the story of Jesus' triumphal entry into Jerusalem; REFLECT on the meaning of Jesus' triumphal entry into Jerusalem; and DEVELOP a prayer in praise of Jesus' triumphal entry.

——————  In Focus ——————

Reggie was always a star. He was an athlete and a scholar throughout his high school and college years. Reggie was also a top draft pick for a leading national football league team in the first round, and he was excited about his future. He had just signed a major deal with his new team and was primed to be a franchise player. With his mother and fiancée in the audience, he accepted his new team jersey as the press took pictures and asked questions. As he left the press conference, fans cheered for him. People were screaming his name; fans were trying to get his attention, maybe even an autograph or a picture with him. Reggie thought, *I have really arrived; all of my dreams are coming true!*

Athletes, entertainers, political figures, and the like are esteemed by the public for their abilities and achievements. However, only what we do for Christ will last, and only God is worthy of such lavish praise and adulation. In today's lesson, we will take a look at Jesus' triumphant return to Jerusalem as people believed He would set up an earthly kingdom and deliver them from their enemies.

—————— Keep in Mind ——————

"Hosanna; Blessed is he that cometh in the name of the Lord"
(from Mark 11:9).

"Hosanna; Blessed is he that cometh in the name of the Lord" (from Mark 11:9).

Focal Verses

KJV **Mark 11:1** And when they came nigh to Jerusalem, unto Bethphage and Bethany, at the mount of Olives, he sendeth forth two of his disciples,

2 And saith unto them, Go your way into the village over against you: and as soon as ye be entered into it, ye shall find a colt tied, whereon never man sat; loose him, and bring him.

3 And if any man say unto you, Why do ye this? say ye that the Lord hath need of him; and straightway he will send him hither.

4 And they went their way, and found the colt tied by the door without in a place where two ways met; and they loose him.

5 And certain of them that stood there said unto them, What do ye, loosing the colt?

6 And they said unto them even as Jesus had commanded: and they let them go.

7 And they brought the colt to Jesus, and cast their garments on him; and he sat upon him.

8 And many spread their garments in the way: and others cut down branches off the trees, and strawed them in the way.

9 And they that went before, and they that followed, cried, saying, Hosanna; Blessed is he that cometh in the name of the Lord:

10 Blessed be the kingdom of our father David, that cometh in the name of the Lord: Hosanna in the highest.

11 And Jesus entered into Jerusalem, and into the temple: and when he had looked round about upon all things, and now the eventide was come, he went out unto Bethany with the twelve.

NLT **Mark 11:1** As Jesus and his disciples approached Jerusalem, they came to the towns of Bethphage and Bethany on the Mount of Olives. Jesus sent two of them on ahead.

2 "Go into that village over there," he told them. "As soon as you enter it, you will see a young donkey tied there that no one has ever ridden. Untie it and bring it here.

3 If anyone asks, 'What are you doing?' just say, 'The Lord needs it and will return it soon.'"

4 The two disciples left and found the colt standing in the street, tied outside the front door.

5 As they were untying it, some bystanders demanded, "What are you doing, untying that colt?"

6 They said what Jesus had told them to say, and they were permitted to take it.

7 Then they brought the colt to Jesus and threw their garments over it, and he sat on it.

8 Many in the crowd spread their garments on the road ahead of him, and others spread leafy branches they had cut in the fields.

9 Jesus was in the center of the procession, and the people all around him were shouting, "Praise God! Blessings on the one who comes in the name of the LORD!

10 Blessings on the coming Kingdom of our ancestor David! Praise God in the highest heaven!"

11 So Jesus came to Jerusalem and went into the Temple. After looking around carefully at everything, he left because it was late in the afternoon. Then he returned to Bethany with the twelve disciples.

The People, Places, and Times

Passover. According to Jewish tradition, the festival of Passover lasts for seven or eight days and commemorates God's sparing Jewish lives while they were in brutal servitude to the Egyptians. The name of the holiday comes from the fact that God "passed over" the houses of the Jews when he was slaying the firstborn of Egypt. In Hebrew, it is known as *Pesach* (meaning "passing over" or "protection"). The significance of Jesus coming into Jerusalem at the time of Passover marks His own coming sacrifice at the Cross as the "Passover Lamb" who would take away the sins of the world in the days to come. The first day of Passover observes the escape of the Jews from the 10th plague, while the remaining seven days mark their liberation from slavery and exodus from Egypt. The Jewish people hold a feast called the Seder on the first night of Passover.

Mount of Olives. It is located east of Jerusalem and stands between Jerusalem and Bethany. Jesus preached from the Mount of Olives and would retreat alone to it at the end of the day, as was His custom (Luke 22:39). This was also the place where He wept over Jerusalem. Not far off, at the bottom of the Mount of Olives, is the Garden of Gethsemane where Jesus prayed with great anguish in His final hours before His betrayal. The first mention of the Mount of Olives in Scripture was when David escaped there on the run from his son Absalom (2 Samuel 15:30). As David's descendant and prophesied heir to his throne, it was quite befitting that Jesus would spend His final hours as David did. As David wept over the events that occurred with his son, the Lord Jesus, after a triumphant entry into Jerusalem, retreated to the Mount of Olives to weep over the holy city (Luke 19:28–44).

Background

Jesus is near the end of His earthly journey. In the previous passage, Mark 10:32–34, for the third time Jesus warns His disciples of what was to come as they go into Jerusalem. The Lord foretells that He will be falsely accused, delivered to the chief priest and scribes, and ultimately condemned to death. Jesus lets His disciples know that although He will be beaten, mocked, and killed, He will rise again on the third day.

Even as Jesus tells the disciples of the horrors to come, James and John request to have special positions and sit at Jesus' right hand and left hand when He comes into His kingdom (Mark 10:34–45). Jesus chides them by letting them know that they do not know what they are really asking for, and anyway, the only one who has the authority to give that placement is God the Father. Around the time of Passover, Jesus continues en route to Jerusalem with His disciples; He also has a great number of people following Him to Jerusalem. He stops through Jericho and has an encounter with blind Bartimaeus, whom He later healed and who immediately followed Jesus, too. According to Luke's account, as Jesus neared the holy city, He knew the people were looking for the kingdom of God to come. Like John and James, in their minds His coming meant immediate political power, restoration, and freedom from Roman rule. Jesus tells them the parable of the 10 talents with a warning He warns those who do not want Him to rule over them that they would be destroyed in His presence (Luke 19:11–27).

At-A-Glance

1. Preparation Fit for a King (Mark 11:1–6)

2. Praise Fit for a King (vv. 7–11)

In Depth

1. Preparation Fit for a King (Mark 11:1–6)

With His disciples, Jesus set out toward the Holy City of Jerusalem to celebrate Passover. This celebration marks the remembrance of God's great act of deliverance of His people from Egyptian slavery with His mighty hand. The blood of an unblemished lamb was placed on the doorpost of every Israelite, and the death angel passed over them. The Egyptians endured God's final plague for Pharaoh's defiance.

Jesus sent two of His disciples ahead and gave them specific instructions to obtain a colt that was tied up and had never been ridden. Just as Jesus was without blemish or sin, it was fitting that the animal He rode upon also would be untouched. Jesus told the disciples to untie and bring it to Him. When asked what they were doing, they were to say, "The Lord needs it" (Mark 11:3, NLT). Everything occurred just as Jesus said it would, and the disciples obtained the colt on His behalf. Zechariah prophesied that the King would come with great rejoicing, riding on a donkey (Zechariah 9:9). This prophecy was fulfilled; Jesus was able to command attention and to get what He needed because He is Lord.

Those who follow Jesus must humbly submit to His authority. We must pave the way for the coming King with hearts that are yielded to His Lordship and is expressed through prayer, praise, and worship.

2. Praise Fit for a King (vv. 7–11)

As they brought the colt to Jesus, the disciples placed the cloaks on it as a sign of royalty, and the people began to put their cloaks down on the road. Others cut down palm branches and spread them down on the ground to mark the entrance of the King. Palm branches were used at the Feast of Tabernacles or Festival of Booths. These festivals recognized the time Israeli ancestors, under Joshua's leadership, dwelt in booths (temporary shelters) formed from the branches of trees; the celebrations commemorated their temporary habitations during the journey through the wilderness. For seven days during the Festival of Booths, there was great celebration and then a time of solemn focus on the Law (see Nehemiah 8:12–18).

Palm branches are fruitful and have the ability to flourish in spite of the hottest heat. Yet they can grow tall, and their foliage is able to stay green even in arid places. The Jews use palm branches as tokens of victory and peace, which the coming King would bring to His people. As Jesus entered Jerusalem, a crowd went before Him crying out, "Hosanna," which is an exclamation of adoration that means "please save us."

As they cried out to Jesus, they also shouted, "Blessed is he that cometh in the name of the Lord" (Mark 11:9). This phrase was prophesied and sung in Psalm 118:25–26. The psalm depicts praise for a great King who is bringing salvation and who will avenge the enemies of God and His people by bringing great deliverance and restoration of order. We, too, wait for this great day of deliverance from the troubles of this world. Jesus is that King and is worthy of every bit of praise that is due to His name. We will appear in the great congregation in heaven, at His throne with white robes and palm branches, to declare His Kingship, as noted in Scripture

(Revelation 7:9–10). Every tribe and every nation will declare, "Salvation to our God which sitteth upon the throne, and unto the Lamb" (Revelation 7:10).

Search the Scriptures

1. Before reaching Jerusalem, what did Jesus send the disciples in search of (Mark 11:1–2)?

2. What did Jesus tell them to do if they were stopped (v. 3)?

Discuss the Meaning

1. What can we learn from our lesson today about how to lavish praise on the Lord Jesus?

2. Like the palm tree, even in tough times, how can you maintain an attitude of gratitude through prayer and praise?

3. How do you anticipate the Lord's triumphant return at His second coming?

Lesson in Our Society

Everyone today is seeking their 15 minutes of fame, and technology has made it possible for anyone who is willing to get noticed. More importantly, our world worships daily at the altar of celebrity through the media. Consequently, voyeurism in our society is born from people coveting praise and adulation. People spend more time swooning over fleshy carnal things than they spend praising the mighty King who gave His life to save ours. There is nothing wrong with fame in the right perspective; there are many people who use their celebrity to bring attention to worthy causes. But we as believers must keep fame and fortune in their rightful places by giving all glory and credit to the One who makes it possible. God rewards those who diligently seek Him, but we must never forget the Giver of the gift.

Make It Happen

Every day is a day of thanksgiving! Therefore, it should be a way of life and not an afterthought for Christians to lavish praise on our worthy King. Since the Lord inhabits the praises of His people, we can have unbroken fellowship with Him by blessing Him at all times and keeping His praises continually in our mouths.

Follow the Spirit

What God wants me to do:

_____

_____

_____

_____

Remember Your Thoughts

Special insights I have learned:

_____

_____

_____

_____

More Light on the Text

Mark 11:1–11

1 And when they came nigh to Jerusalem, unto Bethphage and Bethany, at the mount of Olives, he sendeth forth two of his disciples,

Jesus and His disciples "came nigh" to Jerusalem (Gk. *eggizo*, **eng-ID-zo**), which means "approached." The naming of Bethphage and Bethany was to define the logistics. Jesus sent two of His disciples ahead into the village. This could have been either Bethany or Bethphage. The Greek verb used for "sendeth" is *apostello* (**ap-os-TEL-lo**), which means "to send on a commission to do something."

2 And saith unto them, Go your way into the village over against you: and as soon as ye be entered into it, ye shall find a colt tied, whereon never man sat; loose him, and bring him.

Jesus directed the disciples to go and get a colt which had never been ridden, for it would be for a sacred use (cf. Numbers 19:2; Deuteronomy 21:3; 1 Samuel 6:7). They were to bring the animal back to Him. Anything that is used in service to the King of kings and Lord of lords is sacred and should be treated as such. Therefore, even the place we assemble to worship our God (our church building) should be considered a sacred place, and in this light, we must be careful that no sin enters there. We must treat it as a holy place. It must not be defiled by anything that is not pleasing in a holy God's sight; His house is a house of prayer.

Far more importantly, when our lives are dedicated to God, He makes us holy as new creations in Christ (2 Corinthians 5:17). We are His temple, and since He removes our sins and uses us in His service, our lives are sacred to Him. Therefore, our conduct should represent Christ.

3 And if any man say unto you, Why do ye this? say ye that the Lord hath need of him; and straightway he will send him hither.

Jesus anticipated a possible difficulty which might arise when the disciples took the animal. Therefore, He instructed them to say to the owner that the Lord had need of the colt and would return it "straightway" (Gk. *eutheos*, **yoo-THEH-oce**), which means "without delay" (cf. 1:10), after He had used it.

4 And they went their way, and found the colt tied by the door without in a place where two ways met; and they loose him. 5 And certain of them that stood there said unto them, What do ye, loosing the colt? 6 And they said unto them even as Jesus had commanded: and they let them go.

It happened as Jesus said it would. The disciples found the animal exactly as Jesus said; the animal was outside the house and fastened by the door "in a place where two ways met" (Gk. *amphodon*, **AM-fod-on**), which literally means "a road which leads round, or a street with houses on both sides." The bystanders (according to Luke's gospel, "the owners") asked the disciples what they were doing there. The reason they were satisfied with the disciples' answer can possibly be explained by the fact that Jesus was well known in the neighborhood (cf. John 11). They knew that He could be trusted. Therefore, the owners of the colt "let them go" (Gk. *aphiemi*, **af-EE-ay-mee**), which means they gave permission to the disciples to untie the animal and take it to Jesus.

7 And they brought the colt to Jesus, and cast their garments on him; and he sat upon him. 8 And many spread their garments in the way: and others cut down branches off the trees, and strawed them in the way.

The disciples put their spare clothes on the animal, and as Jesus rode into Jerusalem, they threw clothing and branches on the road for Him to ride over (see John 12:13; cf. 2 Kings 9:12–13). These were gestures in honor of the King.

9 And they that went before, and they that followed, cried, saying, Hosanna; Blessed is he that cometh in the name of the Lord: 10 Blessed be the kingdom of our father

David, that cometh in the name of the Lord: Hosanna in the highest.

The people were crying out "Hosanna" which strictly means "please save," invoking God's saving action. Through liturgical use, "Hosanna" was dissociated from its original meaning and was used as a shout of acclamation. It came to have the sense of "praise Yahweh" (Psalm 118:17–27). The word "blessed" (Gk. *eulogeo,* **yoo-log-EH-o**) means "to eulogize," "to speak well of," or "to praise." Thus, they shouted out their convictions that Jesus was coming in the name of God, He was bringing the kingdom of God (cf. Mark 1:15; 2 Samuel 7:16; Amos 9:11–12), and He was the promised Son of David.

By these acts, Jesus was declared the King of Israel, the fulfillment of the Old Testament prophecies (Zechariah 9:9). Jesus purposely made a public entry into Jerusalem. He came to Jerusalem to die, and He desired that all of Jerusalem should know it. He was about to suffer at the hands of sinful men; the great sacrifice for sin is about to be offered up. He therefore prepared it so that His death was eminently a public death; He died before many witnesses.

11 And Jesus entered into Jerusalem, and into the temple: and when he had looked round about upon all things, and now the eventide was come, he went out unto Bethany with the twelve.

Jesus entered Jerusalem and came to the temple. He stayed there looking around at what was happening in the temple area. He stayed in the "temple" area (Gk. *hieron,* **hee-er-ON,** cf. Mark 11:15, 27), and He did not go into the "sanctuary" (Gk. *naos,* **nah-OS,** cf. Mark 14:58; 15:29, 38). The Greek prefix *peri-* in *periblepo* (**per-ee-BLEP-o**) means "around" in the sense of a circle. Thus Jesus did a comprehensive inspection, probably to determine whether the purpose God

intended was being fulfilled. Instead, the temple was being used commercially by people who owned or ran small businesses. They found it more convenient to use the temple as a means for selling their goods.

Say It Correctly

Bethany. BETH-uh-nee.
Bethlehem. BETH-lih-hem('),
also BETH-lee-uhm.
Bethphage. BETH-fuh-jee.
Hosanna. hoh-ZAN-uh, -ZAHN.
Pesach. PAY-sahkh.
Pharaoh. FAIR-oh, FAR-oh.
Zechariah. zak'-uh-RI-uh.

Daily Bible Readings

M: Call on God to Save
Psalm 55:16–22

T: O Lord, Save Us
2 Kings 19:14–19

W: At the Right Hand of the Needy
Psalm 109:21–31

T: The Lord Rescues
Psalm 22:1–8

F: Sing Praises to the Lord
1 Chronicles 16:8–18

S: Children Shout, "Hosanna!"
Matthew 21:12–17

S: Welcome the King
Mark 11:1–11

Teaching Tips

1. Words You Should Know

A. Sepulchre (Matthew 28:1, 8) *taphos* (Gk.)—Tomb, burial, grave.

B. Doubted (v. 17) *distazo* (Gk.)—Was uncertain, hesitated.

2. Teacher Preparation

Unifying Principle—Eternal Remembrance. When the angel reported that Jesus had risen from the dead, those who heard the news worshiped.

A. Pray for your students and ask Him to bring clarity to the lesson.

B. Prayerfully study the entire lesson.

C. Reflect on the fact that Jesus' resurrection is foundational to our Christian faith. If He had not risen, there would be no atonement for our sins.

D. Reflect on the fact that because Jesus arose from the dead He won victory over sin, death, and hell. Be prepared to share these points with the class.

E. Secure a CD of the song "Rise Again" by Dallas Holm.

3. Open the Lesson

A. As students enter the class, have the song "Rise Again" playing.

B. Then open with prayer, including the Aim for Change.

C. Ask, "What does Jesus' resurrection mean to you?"

D. Allow students to answer the question.

E. Assign roles and have volunteers dramatically read the In Focus story.

4. Present the Scriptures

A. Have volunteers read the Focal Verses.

B. Using the At-A-Glance outline, In Depth, More Light on the Text, and Lesson in Our Society sections and Matthew 28:19–20, explore the Focal Verses.

C. Discuss the Search the Scriptures questions.

5. Explore the Meaning

A. Lead a discussion of the Discuss the Meaning and Make It Happen sections.

B. Have volunteers connect these sections to the Aim for Change and the Keep in Mind verse.

6. Next Steps for Application

A. Summarize the lesson.

B. Close with prayer.

APR
24th

Worship Guide

For the Superintendent or Teacher
Theme: Christ Is Risen!
Theme Song: "Up from the Grave He Arose"
Devotional Reading: 1 Corinthians 15:1–8
Prayer

Christ Is Risen!

Bible Background • MATTHEW 28:1–17
Printed Text • MATTHEW 28:1–17 | Devotional Reading • 1 CORINTHIANS15:1–8

——————— Aim for Change ———————

By the end of the lesson, we will: TELL the story of Jesus' resurrection; APPRECIATE the Resurrection as the ultimate display of God's love for us; and PRAISE and worship the Risen Christ.

——————— In Focus ———————

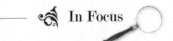

"Can you believe this?" said Maria. "Look at the headline on this news magazine: 'Did Jesus Really Rise from the Dead?'"

"What does it say?" asked John.

"The writers interview a lot of scholars and historians. Apparently, they've discovered that the Resurrection was a myth the early Christians invented."

"Is that so?" said John. "And how did they figure that out?"

"Something about ancient documents or something."

"They do an article like that every year. Controversy is a good way to sell magazines, even if it's made up."

"You don't think it's true?" asked Maria. "There are some really educated scholars quoted in here."

"Anybody can come up with a story that sounds convincing if they use big words," said John, "but the question is, what really happened? The Bible has the only good explanation."

The story of the Resurrection creates interest and controversy even today. While some people scoff at what the Bible says, and others find it hard to believe, the idea that Jesus rose from the dead still provides hope, encouragement, and transformation. He also provides eternal life.

——————— Keep in Mind ———————

"And as they went to tell his disciples, behold, Jesus met them, saying, All hail. And they came and held him by the feet, and worshipped him" (Matthew 28:9).

"And as they went to tell his disciples, behold, Jesus met them, saying, All hail. And they came and held him by the feet, and worshipped him" (Matthew 28:9).

Focal Verses

KJV **Matthew 28:1** In the end of the sabbath, as it began to dawn toward the first day of the week, came Mary Magdalene and the other Mary to see the sepulchre.

2 And, behold, there was a great earthquake: for the angel of the Lord descended from heaven, and came and rolled back the stone from the door, and sat upon it.

3 His countenance was like lightning, and his raiment white as snow:

4 And for fear of him the keepers did shake, and became as dead men.

5 And the angel answered and said unto the women, Fear not ye: for I know that ye seek Jesus, which was crucified.

6 He is not here: for he is risen, as he said. Come, see the place where the Lord lay.

7 And go quickly, and tell his disciples that he is risen from the dead; and, behold, he goeth before you into Galilee; there shall ye see him: lo, I have told you.

8 And they departed quickly from the sepulchre with fear and great joy; and did run to bring his disciples word.

9 And as they went to tell his disciples, behold, Jesus met them, saying, All hail. And they came and held him by the feet, and worshipped him.

10 Then said Jesus unto them, Be not afraid: go tell my brethren that they go into Galilee, and there shall they see me.

11 Now when they were going, behold, some of the watch came into the city, and shewed unto the chief priests all the things that were done.

12 And when they were assembled with the elders, and had taken counsel, they gave large money unto the soldiers,

NLT **Matthew 28:1** Early on Sunday morning, as the new day was dawning, Mary Magdalene and the other Mary went out to visit the tomb.

2 Suddenly there was a great earthquake! For an angel of the Lord came down from heaven, rolled aside the stone, and sat on it.

3 His face shone like lightning, and his clothing was as white as snow.

4 The guards shook with fear when they saw him, and they fell into a dead faint.

5 Then the angel spoke to the women. "Don't be afraid!" he said. "I know you are looking for Jesus, who was crucified.

6 He isn't here! He is risen from the dead, just as he said would happen. Come, see where his body was lying.

7 And now, go quickly and tell his disciples that he has risen from the dead, and he is going ahead of you to Galilee. You will see him there, Remember what I have told you."

8 The women ran quickly from the tomb. They were very frightened but also filled with great joy, and they rushed to give the disciples the angel's message.

9 And as they went, Jesus met them and greeted them. And they ran to him, grasped his feet, and worshiped him.

10 Then Jesus said to them, "Don't be afraid! Go tell my brothers to leave for Galilee, and they will see me there."

11 As the women were on their way, some of the guards went into the city and told the leading priests what had happened.

12 A meeting with the elders was called, and they decided to give the soldiers a large bribe.

KJV cont.

13 Saying, Say ye, His disciples came by night, and stole him away while we slept.

14 And if this come to the governor's ears, we will persuade him, and secure you.

15 So they took the money, and did as they were taught: and this saying is commonly reported among the Jews until this day.

16 Then the eleven disciples went away into Galilee, into a mountain where Jesus had appointed them.

17 And when they saw him, they worshipped him: but some doubted.

NLT cont.

13 They told the soldiers, "You must say, 'Jesus' disciples came during the night while we were sleeping, and they stole his body.'

14 If the governor hears about it, we'll stand up for you so you won't get in trouble."

15 So the guards accepted the bribe and said what they were told to say. Their story spread widely among the Jews, and they still tell it today.

16 Then the eleven disciples left for Galilee, going to the mountain where Jesus had told them to go.

17 When they saw him, they worshiped him—but some of them doubted!

The People, Places, and Times

Pharisees. The Pharisees were a group of orthodox Jews who prided themselves on strict faithfulness to the Law of Moses. Jesus' emphasis on the grace of God and the hypocrisy of self-righteousness had led to many clashes between them, and the leaders of the Pharisees were complicit in Jesus' arrest and execution.

Mary Magdalene. Mary of Magdala was one of Jesus' closest followers. According to the Gospels, He had cast seven demons out of her (Mark 16:9; Luke 8:2). She was faithful to Jesus, even watching at the foot of the Cross while He died (Matthew 27:55–56).

Background

Jesus was dead. He had been publicly executed and then buried in an underground tomb, blocked off by a large stone. However, Jesus had predicted that He would rise from the dead on the third day, so the religious leaders of the Pharisees obtained a guard to prevent any unforeseen events. For added security, a Roman seal was placed on the tomb (Matthew 27:64, 66). This probably involved attaching a cord to the stone and

to the tomb, affixing a wax seal to both ends to prevent any tampering. Of course, Jesus' disciples were disheartened and scattered, and Jesus Himself was dead, so there was not much for the Pharisees to worry about...or was there?

At-A-Glance

1. The Guards' Response to the Resurrection (Matthew 28:1–4)

2. The Women's Response to the Resurrection (vv. 5–10)

3. The Priests' Response to the Resurrection (vv. 11–15)

4. The Disciples' Response to the Resurrection (vv. 16–17)

In Depth

1. The Guards' Response to the Resurrection (Matthew 28:1–4)

When we think of the Resurrection, we likely recall a modern-day celebration involving bright new outfits, Easter lilies, candy, baby animals, and upbeat praise songs. It's a time to be happy that Jesus is alive, right? Maybe so, but not if our happiness distracts us from the story of the Resurrection itself. If we look past the centuries of religious traditions, we might find a different emotional mood.

The story begins in a graveyard. It's still mostly dark in the early morning. A small team of soldiers has been sitting alone in the cemetery all night, guarding a tomb against grave robbers. When you're by yourself in a cemetery at night, surrounded by crypts and corpses, the last thing you want is to hear an unexplained noise or to see an unexpected movement. All was quiet for a while—then there was a sudden, violent earthquake. A supernatural being that looked "like lightning" (v. 3) materialized in midair, floated downward, grabbed the enormous gravestone, shoved it out of the way, and sat on it. And he stayed there.

Quite understandably, the guards didn't feel happiness or joy when they saw this. These professional soldiers were paralyzed with terror: "The guards shook for fear of him and became like dead men" (v. 4, NASB). This doesn't seem like a little children's happy Sunday School story; the guards at least might have classified it as a horror story! Whatever the genre, the point of the narrative is that a dead man came back to life and got out of His grave. It's certainly appropriate to have a sense of awe and even fear when considering this event that redefines everything we know about God, life, and death.

Still, while the soldiers' fear may help give perspective to this remarkable story, it misses some key parts of the real significance of what took place. Their fear of the unknown and the supernatural kept them from investigating any further. Ultimately, this led to an outright refusal to accept the truth and made them willing to circulate a story they knew to be false. The fear of the Lord may be the beginning of wisdom (see Proverbs 9:10), but it does no good if we don't go past the beginning.

2. The Women's Response to the Resurrection (vv. 5–10)

Mary Magdalene and "the other Mary" (v. 1) had also come to the graveyard to visit Jesus' tomb and pay their respects. Like the soldiers, they were frightened at the brilliant appearance of the angel sitting on the tombstone, and it probably didn't help matters to see that the soldiers had fainted in terror.

But the women had other things on their mind; they were "looking for Jesus" (v. 5, NLT). The angel addressed them directly. He told them to stop being afraid and mentioned that he knew they were looking for Jesus. Then he dropped the bombshell: "He is not here: for he is risen, as he said" (v. 6).

This stunning news was supported by three pieces of evidence. First, it happened "just as he said" (v. 6). Jesus had foretold His resurrection many times before (see Matthew 16:21; 17:23; 20:19). If that wasn't enough—it is a hard prediction to swallow, after all—there was the empty tomb: "Come, see the place where the Lord lay" (v. 6). And, even if that wasn't enough, they were soon to meet the risen Christ face to face: "...he is going ahead of you to Galilee. You will see him there" (v. 7, NLT).

The angel gave the women an assignment: "And now, go quickly and tell his disciples that he is risen from the dead" (v. 7). The combination of "go" and "tell," of course, foreshadows the upcoming Great Commission (Matthew 28:18–20), making these women the first "missionaries" to tell the good news of the Resurrection.

The women responded three ways at once. They were still fearful, but their fear was combined with "great joy" and a ready willingness to obey the angel's directions (v. 8). In this mingling of *fear, joy, and obedience,* they met Jesus. Jesus greeted them, and they worshiped Him (v. 9).

3. The Priests' Response to the Resurrection (vv. 11–15)

Not everyone was joyful to hear the news of the empty tomb. The religious leaders in Jerusalem had bitterly opposed Jesus during His life and plotted to bring about His death (Matthew 12:14; 26:4). When some of the soldiers made it back to them with the report of the goings-on in the graveyard, the priests' response was about as opposite from the women's worship as possible. They called a meeting of the religious elders to decide what to do. Then they brought the soldiers back in and bribed them with "large money" (v. 12).

Their plan was to circulate an alternate explanation for the empty tomb. They paid the soldiers to tell the story like this: "His disciples came by night, and stole him away while we slept" (v. 13). As lies go, that's a very unconvincing one. It doesn't even bother to deny that the tomb is empty. The explanation quickly falls apart on a closer look. If the guards had been sleeping, how could they possibly have seen that it was the disciples who stole the body? Furthermore, sleeping on the job was a capital offense for soldiers, which explains why the priests offered to placate the governor if he heard the news (v. 14).

Why would anyone want to believe such a silly story? The only other explanation was that Jesus was risen just as He said. That had implications which would be very uncomfortable for the religious leaders. For some people, it seems better to believe in a self-invented, transparently obvious lie than to face the truth!

4. The Disciples' Response to the Resurrection (vv. 16–17)

Jesus' disciples followed the women's message and went to the mountain in Galilee where He had promised they would meet Him. The momentous meeting is described succinctly: "And when they saw him, *they worshipped him: but some doubted*" (v. 17, emphasis added).

Doubt seems like an odd response to introduce at this moment; haven't they been presented with irrefutable evidence that Jesus had risen? Even in the face of such evidence, however, the events and their implications can be hard to understand. It takes time for people to reconsider everything they previously believed about God, life, and death.

Fortunately, this kind of doubt is entirely compatible with worship. It is not doubt but rejection of Jesus that gets in the way of faith. Although some of the disciples had their doubts about what this all meant, that did not stop them from responding in worship to Jesus. Jesus does not require us to understand everything but simply to respond to Him. What is your response to the news that Jesus is risen?

Search the Scriptures

1. What response did the angel create in the people who saw him (Matthew 28:4–5)?

2. What three pieces of evidence did the angel offer that Jesus was risen (vv. 6–7)?

Discuss the Meaning

1. Why were some of the disciples doubtful? What causes people to doubt the Resurrection? Do you have doubts?

2. What is your response to the news that Jesus is risen? Why?

Lesson in Our Society

Sometimes we can take the Resurrection for granted as part of our Easter celebrations but fail to connect it to our daily Christian experience. Read 1 Corinthians 15. In what ways does the Bible say that the resurrection of Jesus is foundational to our faith? How does belief in the Resurrection give us hope, newness of life, and reason to trust in Jesus' promises?

Make It Happen

The angel commissioned the women at the tomb to go and tell the disciples the news of the Resurrection. Later, Jesus Himself commissioned all His disciples to go and tell the news to the whole world. Find someone who needs some encouragement and share with them how your response to the Resurrection has helped you find hope and faith in Jesus.

Follow the Spirit

What God wants me to do:

_____

_____

_____

_____

Remember Your Thoughts

Special insights I have learned:

_____

_____

_____

_____

More Light on the Text

Matthew 28:1–17

1 In the end of the sabbath, as it began to dawn toward the first day of the week, came Mary Magdalene and the other Mary to see the sepulchre.

The New Testament does not give us a description of the resurrection of Jesus. What we have here in Matthew are two consequences (or proof) of the resurrection: the empty tomb (vv. 1–15) and the meeting of Jesus with His disciples (vv. 16–20). Matthew describes the impact of the Resurrection on the disciples—fear and joy, doubt and certitude, dumbfounded and revived.

The expression "in the end of the Sabbath" (Gk. *opse sabbaton*, **op-SEH SAB-bat-on**) should be rendered "after the Sabbath," probably early on Sunday morning as suggested both by the Greek verb *epiphosko* (**ep-ee-FOCE-ko**), translated "dawn," and the Greek preposition *opse*, meaning "after."

Mary Magdalene and the other Mary (Matthew 26:56) came as soon as possible after the Sabbath rest to finish the anointing of the body of Jesus (according to Mark 16:1; Luke 23:56). Matthew was more interested in the unexpected experience which awaited the women than the reason for their visit to the tomb. They were the only ones to get up early before sunrise to take care of Jesus (Luke 8:1–3). They received the honor of being the first to see their Lord resurrected and to proclaim it to others (Matthew 28:9).

2 And, behold, there was a great earthquake: for the angel of the Lord descended from heaven, and came and rolled back the stone from the door, and sat upon it.

The "great earthquake" may have been only local, as its main purpose seems to have been to scare the guards (cf. 27:51). In the Old Testament, earthquakes are an expression symbolizing the power of God (Judges 5:4; Psalm 114:7–8), particularly His power in judging (Joel 3:16; Nahum 1:5–6).

The angel of the Lord appeared for the first time since the beginning of Matthew's gospel (chapters 1–2). He rolled away the stone from the door of the tomb. The stone was rolled away not to let Jesus out but to let the women in. They were invited to see for themselves that Jesus' body was gone (see v. 6).

3 His countenance was like lightning, and his raiment white as snow: 4 And for fear of him the keepers did shake, and became as dead men.

The description of the angel of the Lord echoes Daniel 10:6. The apparition of the angel so terrified the guards posted at the tomb that they were rendered unconscious. The women were also in fear (see Matthew 28:5, 8; cf. Daniel 10:7–9; Revelation 1:17). According to Mark's gospel, the women were speechless (Mark 16:5). One can understand the fear of the women in the light of the circumstances that surrounded the death of their Master.

The scene is an image of what will happen on the advent of the King of glory. It will be terror for some (Matthew 24:30) and joy for others (Luke 21:25–28; 1 Peter 1:6–9).

5 And the angel answered and said unto the women, Fear not ye: for I know that ye seek Jesus, which was crucified. 6 He is not here: for he is risen, as he said. Come, see the place where the Lord lay. 7 And go quickly, and tell his disciples that he is risen from the dead; and, behold, he goeth before you into Galilee; there shall ye see him: lo, I have told you.

Verses 5, 6, and 7 ignore the presence of the guards. The angel spoke to the women only. The reaction of the believing women is set in sharp contrast with the reaction of the pagan soldiers. The angel reassured them that there was no need for them to be afraid.

The words of the angel echo throughout the Scriptures (see Matthew 28:10; Luke 2:10). They were meant to cheer the hearts of Christians in every age in the expectation of the Resurrection. They remind us that true Christians have no cause for alarm, whatever may happen in the world. God does not want His servants to dwell in fear. It is the people who do not seek Jesus who should fear (Psalm 34:5–7).

The crucified Jesus, who the angel knew to be the object of their search, had in fact been raised. If they looked inside the tomb, they would see that His body was not there. His resurrection happened as He had told them it would (Matthew 16:21; 17:23; 20:19).

8 And they departed quickly from the sepulchre with fear and great joy; and did run to bring his disciples word.

The fear of the women did not disappear completely, but it was replaced with a "great joy" because of the reality of the Resurrection. This mixed emotion is the natural consequence of the things they just witnessed. They ran to tell the disciples.

9 And as they went to tell his disciples, behold, Jesus met them, saying, All hail. And they came and held him by the feet, and worshipped him.

"All hail" (Gk. *chairo*, **KHAH-ee-ro**) is literally "rejoice." It is an ordinary greeting familiar to the women (see Matthew 27:29). These are the first words that the resurrected Jesus says to the women who had been thrown into great sorrow by His death. The women react to Jesus' greetings by holding Him by the feet. By this action they are showing their submission to Jesus, as practiced in their culture when a subject rendered obeisance to a sovereign prince. They prostrate themselves in adoration.

10 Then said Jesus unto them, Be not afraid: go tell my brethren that they go into Galilee, and there shall they see me.

Jesus uses for the first time the word "brethren" (Gk. *adelphos*, **ad-el-FOS**) to refer to His disciples (see John 20:17). In Matthew 12:50, the word "brethren" is more general and symbolic (see Matthew 25:40). The more familiar term used by Jesus before is "friend" (John 15:15). If we think of their recent infidelity and cowardliness shown at the time of Jesus' suffering, to call the disciples brethren is surprising. By calling them "brethren," Jesus is not showing them His love only; He is also underlining their privileged position as sharers with Him of His inheritance (Romans 8:17).

11 Now when they were going, behold, some of the watch came into the city, and shewed unto the chief priests all the things that were done. 12 And when they were assembled with the elders, and had taken counsel, they gave large money unto the soldiers,

The soldiers, although terrified by the earthquake, the angel, and the stone-rolling, had enough strength to go and report what had happened. It is interesting to notice that the enemies of Jesus had knowledge of the Resurrection even before the apostles from the guards they had posted in front of the tomb. Being incapable of refuting the evidence and not willing to accept it, they tried to suppress it by illegal means. Their decision was not taken lightly. All the elders (the Sanhedrin) were involved. This shows how far people are willing to go when they do not want to face the truth.

The betrayal of Judas cost them only 30 silver coins (Matthew 26:15). The effort to cover up their crime is going to cost them even much more (Matthew 23:13): "they gave large [amounts of] money unto the soldiers." The guards received enough money to bribe them to invent a lie.

13 Saying, Say ye, His disciples came by night, and stole him away while we slept. 14 And if this come to the governor's ears, we will persuade him, and secure you. 15 So they took the money, and did as they were taught: and this saying is commonly reported among the Jews until this day.

The penalty for a guard or soldier sleeping on duty was death (Acts 12:19). The elders probably hoped to corrupt Pilate also with money (Ecclesiastes 10:19). He probably could care less about the corpse of a Jew.

16 Then the eleven disciples went away into Galilee, into a mountain where Jesus had appointed them.

Matthew has the habit of shortening his story by including only people and events that seem to be essential to the theme he is presenting. Here, he mentions only the 11 disciples. It is possible that the women (28:7) were present as well as the more than 500 people mentioned in 1 Corinthians 15:6. The mountain may be the same as the mountain of the Beatitudes in Matthew 5:1. It is quite an appropriate location for meeting a crowd (1 Corinthians 15:6).

17 And when they saw him, they worshipped him: but some doubted.

Some of the disciples doubted (John 20:24–29). The doubt manifested by some of the disciples authenticates the story of Matthew. Doubt is sometimes the indication of honesty of heart. Doubt becomes sin when it questions the faithfulness of the Lord or when it reveals a lack of trust in Him (Romans 14:22–23). The doubt of some of the disciples did not prevent Jesus from using them to transform the world as His ambassadors. The Greek word for "doubted" (*distazo*, **dis-TAD-zo**) does not imply a fixed unbelief, but an uncertainty, a hesitation (Romans 14:26–28, 31). Jesus many times reproached the disciples for their unbelief (Matthew 6:30; 8:26; 14:31).

Say It Correctly

Ecclesiastes. eh-klee-sih-AS-teez.
Magdalene. MAG-duh-leen.
Pontius Pilate. pän-chəs, 'pən-chəs 'pī-lət.
Sanhedrin. SAN-heh-drihn, SAN-ih-drihn.
Sepulchre. SEP-uhl-kuhr.

Daily Bible Readings

M: Good News of First Importance
1 Corinthians 15:1–8

T: The Plot to Kill Jesus
Matthew 26:1–5

W: The Judgment Against Jesus
Matthew 27:15–26

T: The Crucifixion of Jesus
Matthew 27:32–44

F: Witnesses to Jesus' Death
Matthew 27:45–56

S: Witnesses to Jesus' Burial
Matthew 27:57–61

S: Witnesses to Jesus' Resurrection
Matthew 28:1–17

Teaching Tips

1. Words You Should Know

A. Consolation (Philippians 2:1) *paraklesis* (Gk.)—Comfort, encouragement.

B. Esteem (v. 3) *hegeomai* (Gk.)—To consider one as having authority over another.

C. Glory (v. 11) *doxa* (Gk.)—Honor, praise, and worship.

2. Teacher Preparation

Unifying Principle—Emulating Others. We imitate Christ Jesus as a pattern for living and worship because of His life and sacrifice on our behalf.

A. Pray that God will help you to bring clarity to the lesson.

B. Prayerfully study the entire lesson.

C. Reflect on the unity or lack thereof in the Body of Christ. Be prepared to discuss.

3. Open the Lesson

A. Open with prayer, including the Aim for Change.

B. Ask, "What causes disunity in the Body of Christ?"

C. Allow volunteers to answer the question. Discuss.

D. Assign roles and have volunteers dramatically read the In Focus story. Discuss.

E. Ask, "When there is disunity in the Body of Christ, does the world really know the church by believers' love for one another? Why? Why not?" Discuss.

4. Present the Scriptures

A. Have volunteers read the Focal Verses.

B. Using the At-A-Glance outline, In Depth, More Light on the Text, and Lesson in Our Society sections and Philippians 2, explore the Focal Verses.

C. Discuss the Search the Scriptures questions.

5. Explore the Meaning

A. Lead a discussion of the Discuss the Meaning and Make It Happen sections.

B. Have volunteers connect these sections to the Aim for Change and the Keep in Mind verse.

6. Next Steps for Application

A. Summarize the lesson.

B. Close with prayer.

Worship Guide

For the Superintendent or Teacher
Theme: The Christ Hymn
Theme Song: "May the Work I've Done
Speak for Me"
Devotional Reading: 1 Peter 2:18–25
Prayer

The Christ Hymn

Bible Background • PHILIPPIANS 2:1–11
Printed Text • PHILIPPIANS 2:1–11 | Devotional Reading • 1 PETER 2:18–25

Aim for Change

By the end of the lesson, we will: EXPLAIN why Jesus is worthy of our honor; REFLECT on the need to honor and praise Jesus for what He has done; and IDENTIFY a way to honor and praise Jesus with our lives.

In Focus

Pastor Michael had heard some people in his church complaining about the new musicians who wanted to change the service to a more contemporary style. But he hadn't realized how upset people had become until an after-church meeting got out of control. A discussion on music became more and more heated as people from the two factions argued with each other.

"What are you people doing to our church's music?"

"We want to do something that's more relevant to people today. Is that a problem?"

"I've been playing the organ here for 25 years; you can't just walk in and change it!"

"If we want our church to grow, then we have to use music that's with it. We can't keep doing what we've always done."

"So then it has to be exactly what you want?"

Horrified, Pastor Michael stood up and dismissed the meeting. Afterward, he escaped into his study, near tears. "Lord, what have I been doing wrong?" he prayed. "Why is there so much division in my own church? What have we all been missing?"

Even among Christians, selfishness can lead to conflict and disunity. It's easy to be blind to our own selfish attitudes. The alternative is to look away from ourselves to the sacrificial life of Jesus.

MAY 1st

Keep in Mind

"Let this mind be in you, which was also in Christ Jesus" (Philippians 2:5).

"Let this mind be in you, which was also in Christ Jesus"
(Philippians 2:5).

Focal Verses

KJV **Philippians 2:1** If there be therefore any consolation in Christ, if any comfort of love, if any fellowship of the Spirit, if any bowels and mercies,

2 Fulfil ye my joy, that ye be likeminded, having the same love, being of one accord, of one mind.

3 Let nothing be done through strife or vainglory; but in lowliness of mind let each esteem other better than themselves.

4 Look not every man on his own things, but every man also on the things of others.

5 Let this mind be in you, which was also in Christ Jesus:

6 Who, being in the form of God, thought it not robbery to be equal with God:

7 But made himself of no reputation, and took upon him the form of a servant, and was made in the likeness of men:

8 And being found in fashion as a man, he humbled himself, and became obedient unto death, even the death of the cross.

9 Wherefore God also hath highly exalted him, and given him a name which is above every name:

10 That at the name of Jesus every knee should bow, of things in heaven, and things in earth, and things under the earth;

11 And that every tongue should confess that Jesus Christ is Lord, to the glory of God the Father.

NLT **Philippians 2:1** Is there any encouragement from belonging to Christ? Any comfort from his love? Any fellowship together in the Spirit? Are your hearts tender and compassionate?

2 Then make me truly happy by agreeing wholeheartedly with each other, loving one another, and working together with one mind and purpose.

3 Don't be selfish; don't try to impress others. Be humble, thinking of others as better than yourselves.

4 Don't look out only for your own interests, but take an interest in others, too.

5 You must have the same attitude that Christ Jesus had.

6 Though he was God, he did not think of equality with God as something to cling to.

7 Instead, he gave up his divine privileges; he took the humble position of a slave and was born as a human being. When he appeared in human form,

8 he humbled himself in obedience to God and died a criminal's death on a cross.

9 Therefore, God elevated him to the place of highest honor and gave him the name above all other names,

10 that at the name of Jesus every knee should bow, in heaven and on earth and under the earth,

11 and every tongue confess that Jesus Christ is Lord, to the glory of God the Father.

The People, Places, and Times

Philippi. Located in Macedonia near the Mediterranean Sea, Philippi was a prosperous center of commerce due to its placement on the Via Egnatia (a major trade route), its strategic location between Europe and Asia, and its nearby gold and silver mines. It was named for Philip II of Macedon, the father of Alexander the Great, who made significant improvements to the city in 462 B.C. In the second century B.C., Philippi became a Roman colony, with Roman soldiers and citizens placed there to establish Roman culture throughout the region. It is described in Acts as "the chief city of that part of Macedonia" (Acts 16:12).

Paul. Apostle Paul's spiritual biography is found in the book of Acts. After seeing a vision of Jesus, Paul was converted from an anti-Christian zealot to a Christian missionary. He is largely responsible for igniting the spread of the Gospel around the world, as well as for writing letters that make up much of our New Testament. On his third missionary journey, Paul was directed by the Holy Spirit to the city of Philippi, where he preached with Silas and was eventually thrown into prison. In spite of (or perhaps because of) this persecution, several converts established a healthy church in Philippi (see Acts 16).

Background

Paul wrote to the Philippian church while he was chained in a prison cell for the crime of preaching the Gospel (Philippians 1:12–14). The Philippian believers heard of his hardship and sent him a generous financial gift (4:15–18). Paul's response is more than a simple acknowledgment of thanks; it is a delighted testimony to the joy he found in the Lord in the midst of his suffering. Paul commends the Philippian believers for their "partnership in the Gospel" (1:5), he and encourages them to stand firm in their faith in Jesus during their own hardships (1:27–30).

At-A-Glance

1. The Principles of a Sacrificed Life
(Philippians 2:1–5)

2. The Example of a Sacrificed Life
(vv. 6–8)

3. The Reward of a Sacrificed Life
(vv. 9–11)

In Depth

1. The Principles of a Sacrificed Life (Philippians 2:1–5)

Like Paul, the Christians at Philippi faced opposition, harassment, imprisonment, and even death for simply believing in Jesus. This intense stress on a group of people might cause personal conflicts and division. Paul appeals to the believers' experience of Jesus: encouragement in Christ, the consolation of love, the fellowship of the spirit, affection, and compassion (Philippians 2:1, NASB). These four things that we have in Christ, Paul indicates, should lead to positive results in the way we treat others: "Being of the same mind, maintaining the same love, united in spirit, intent on one purpose" (v. 2, NASB). The implication is clear: the way Christ loves you should be the way you love others.

The exhortation toward like-mindedness and "being of one accord" (v. 2) is not a demand for conformity. Rather, it demonstrates what will happen when different people are transformed by the same Christ. True unity comes not from external pressure but from inward spiritual agreement. We find this agreement when we look to Jesus Christ (v. 5).

The "one mind" or purpose we are called to share is to love each other with the same kind of love that Jesus has. In verse 4, Paul offers parallel sentences of advice: don't be selfish or conceited, but be humble and regard others as more important than yourself. Don't just look out for your own interests, but also for the interests of others.

Paul does not ask us to make our own effort to imitate the example of Christ. That would be a worthy goal but impossible to achieve. Rather, as Jesus spiritually indwells us, the same mind or attitude that is in Him will come to be in us. This attitude enables us to live sacrificially as Jesus did.

2. The Example of a Sacrificed Life (vv. 6–8)

Reflecting on the sacrificial attitude of Jesus, Paul recounts Jesus' life in a beautiful lyric poem. Because of the unique poetic structure and vocabulary of this passage (beginning in verse 6), many scholars believe that Paul was likely quoting an early Christian hymn or statement of faith, possibly one that the Philippian church used in their worship as well. (The Roman official, Pliny the Younger, observed in the second century that at a meeting of Christians, the worshipers "sang a hymn to Christ as to a god.") This "Christ Hymn" testifies to the great sacrifice Jesus made out of His own humility.

As the hymn begins, it states that Jesus existed "in the form of God"—that is, everything God was, Jesus was. Scripture directly identifies Jesus with all the attributes of God: He is described as the Creator (Colossians 1:16), the Almighty (Philippians 3:20–21), the Judge (2 Corinthians 5:10), and the Eternal One (Colossians 1:17),

among many other titles and actions that clearly belong to God alone. Jesus Himself is recorded as claiming eternal pre-existence (John 8:58), omnipresence (Matthew 18:20), the ability to forgive sins against God (Mark 2:7–10), and even the equal right to receive honor with God the Father (John 5:23).

Jesus' total equality with God, however, was not something He held onto selfishly. Rather, He willingly "emptied Himself" (Gk. *kenosis*, Philippians 2:7). There is some debate among theologians about what exactly Jesus put aside from Himself, but the process was clearly one of great humility and selflessness. Neglecting the form of God and equality with God, Jesus took the form of a servant and the likeness of a human. He went from infinite power and glory to a low place in a humble society of oppressed and weak people.

As though that was not enough humility, Jesus went even further. He was totally obedient to the will of His Father even when it resulted in rejection, persecution, and ultimately death—an execution by torture reserved for murderers and rebels.

By His death, Jesus was able to take the penalty of our sins and bring about the redemption of all who trust in Him. Jesus could have remained in heaven with all the glory, peace, and power that came from equality with God. But He willingly chose to sacrifice all this to live a limited, oppressed human life on earth, and then even to sacrifice His earthly life, simply out of obedience to the Father and His love for humanity (John 3:16–17; Romans 5:8). What marvelous humility and love!

3. The Reward of a Sacrificed Life (vv. 9–11)

Jesus' death was not a defeat but a victory. Because of Jesus' sacrificial life and love, God

387

raised Him from the dead and exalted Him to the highest place of honor in the universe (v. 9). The exalted name of Jesus will inspire every knee to bow and every tongue to say that Jesus Christ is Lord. Everything Jesus put aside He received back and more. God says through the prophet Isaiah that every knee will bow and every tongue will swear to God alone (Isaiah 45:23). So to say this of Jesus is to say that Jesus is fully and completely equal with God.

Jesus spoke of His death with the analogy of a grain of wheat: "I tell you the truth, unless a kernel of wheat falls to the ground and dies, it remains only a single seed. But if it dies, it produces many seeds. The man who loves his life will lose it, while the man who hates his life in this world will keep it for eternal life. Whoever serves me must follow me; and where I am, my servant also will be. My Father will honor the one who serves me" (John 12:24–26, NIV).

If a grain of wheat were to jealously hold onto its identity as a single seed, nothing would ever become of it. But by falling into the ground and becoming something other than a grain, it is able to grow up into a plant that produces many more seeds that can benefit many more people. In the same way, Jesus says, hanging on to your life as your own will cause you to miss its real purpose and the benefit you could have for others. If we are serious about following Jesus, we will be as willing to sacrifice our privileges and comforts as He was.

Search the Scriptures

1. What character qualities does Paul exhort believers to have in themselves (Philippians 2:1–4)?

2. What actions did the "mind of Christ" lead Christ to take (vv. 6–8)?

Discuss the Meaning

This passage is one of many places in Scripture where Jesus is stated to be fully equal to God. What other Scriptures can you think of that also make this point? (Consult a Bible reference book if you're not sure.) Since Jesus is God, how does the description of Jesus' character in this passage affect our view of God?

Lesson in Our Society

As much as we would like our churches, communities, and families to be peaceful all the time, selfishness and strife can get in the way. How does Jesus undo strife and self-importance in our church and our communities?

Make It Happen

Think of a person or situation in your life that gives you difficulty. Is there someone you don't get along with? Where do you see discord, conflict, or lack of unity? With that in mind, write a personalized version of this passage of Scripture, inserting your name in place of the general statements. (Example: "Let this mind be in [your name], which was also in Christ Jesus.") What specific changes does this suggest for your attitude or actions? Pray that Jesus will fill you with His attitude in these areas so that your life can honor and praise Him.

Follow the Spirit

What God wants me to do:

_____

_____

_____

_____

Remember Your Thoughts

Special insights I have learned:

_____

_____

_____

_____

More Light on the Text

Philippians 2:1–11

1 If there be therefore any consolation in Christ, if any comfort of love, if any fellowship of the Spirit, if any bowels and mercies,

The Greek for "consolation" is *paraklesis* (**par-AK-lay-sis**), which means "comfort," but it can also mean "exhortation." Paul is pointing us to Christ as our example. Jesus exhorts us and consoles us through His example in His sufferings. We read in Hebrews 4:14–16 that Jesus went through the same trials, temptations, and sufferings that we experience, so He is able to help us, and He provides the example of how to face the difficulties in our lives.

In addition to consolation in Christ, we have the comfort of the love of God, the Father. Third, we have fellowship together in the Spirit, the third Person of the Trinity. When we receive Jesus Christ as our Savior, we have a fellowship with one another through the Spirit that goes beyond even the bond of blood relatives.

This causes the deep tenderness and care for each other that the words "bowels and mercies" express. "Bowels" is a translation from the Greek word *splagchnon* (**SPLANGKH-non**), which literally means the spleen or intestines, but figuratively means pity, sympathy, or tenderness. We think of love and tenderness as coming from the heart, but the Greeks thought of them as coming from the bowels or intestines. These emotions do not come from any organ of our body, so neither "heart" nor "bowels" is literal. In this verse, Paul is inviting the Philippians and all believers to base our conduct toward each other on our relationship with God and the example of Jesus Christ.

2 Fulfil ye my joy, that ye be likeminded, having the same love, being of one accord, of one mind.

When Paul got to the last chapter of his letter to the Philippians (4:2–3), he mentioned Euodia and Syntyche, who were not getting along. These two women were great church workers but had come to some disagreement. This was in direct opposition to Paul's great concern that Christians would work together in harmony. Unfortunately, Christians through the ages have fought each other, causing churches to split, causing people to stop speaking to each other, and in general creating a bad witness to the world. This is the sort of thing that grieves the heart of a godly pastor; and so Paul, with his pastor's heart, says that he will be full of joy when the Philippians are in one accord.

In this verse, Paul is urging the Philippians (and us) to have the same disposition or attitude of mind. The Greek word for "mind" is *phroneo* (**fron-EH-o**), which conveys the idea of being mentally interested. "Likeminded" and "of one mind" from the end of this verse are translations of the same Greek word. In other words, we should be always thinking in a way that promotes unity of the Body.

The phrase "the same love" points back to the comfort of God's love mentioned in verse 1 of this chapter. We should be echoing God's love toward us to one another.

3 Let nothing be done through strife or vainglory; but in lowliness of mind let each esteem other better than themselves.

"Strife" means antagonism or quarreling. "Vainglory" is unwarranted pride in oneself. These two words give us a picture of someone who is out to bring glory and honor to him- or herself, no matter how many toes he or she steps on. "Lowliness of mind" is just the opposite. In Greco-Roman society, just as today, humility was not seen as a virtue. The phrase "lowliness of mind" is the Greek word *tapeinophrosune* (**tap-i-nof-ros-OO-nay**). Witherington says it means "base-minded," "shabby," or "no account" (63). It meant to have the mentality of a slave. No wonder pagans of that day thought of Christianity as a slave religion.

However, the Bible elevates humility (see Proverbs 3:34; 11:2; 15:33; Job 5:11). The Greek word for "esteem" is *hegeomai* (**hayg-EH-om-ahee**), and it implies authority over another. In the Greco-Roman society, where there were very distinct social classes, this was truly revolutionary. The Christian slave-owner was to think of his born-again slave as having authority over him. In fact, the slave could be a church elder and the slave-owner would be under his spiritual authority. In the Roman Empire, where slaves out-numbered slave-owners, some have thought that this revolutionary idea contributed to the downfall of the empire. Every Christian is to be submissive to every other Christian (Ephesians 5:21). We are to consider others better than ourselves and be their servants.

4 Look not every man on his own things, but every man also on the things of others.

We naturally look out for ourselves first, but it is only through the Holy Spirit that we are able to look after our brothers and sisters' needs and concerns. When the Bible speaks of humility, it is not the false modesty with which one replies to a compliment with "Oh, this old rag!" This just makes the one who compliments feel their judgment is being questioned. Nor is biblical modesty that which calls attention to oneself. When you are talking to the truly humble brother or sister, this person is so concerned about you that you hardly see them.

5 Let this mind be in you, which was also in Christ Jesus:

Now Paul directs us to the true example of humility—Jesus. Our mindset and thought patterns should be the same as His. We tend to think that if we can say the right words and do the right things, then we are all right, but this verse makes it clear that even our thoughts should be the same as our Lord's. Not only our actions should be humble, but our inner attitudes as well. The Greek word for "mind" is the same as that used in verse 2.

6 Who, being in the form of God, thought it not robbery to be equal with God:

Verses 6–11 are an early Christian hymn full of rich theology, especially concerning Christ. In this first verse of the hymn we see Jesus not striving to be God because He already is God. "Being" in the Greek is *huparcho* (**hoop-AR-kho**). Barclay writes, "It describes that which a man is in his very essence and which cannot be changed. It describes that part of a man which, in any circumstances, remains the same. So Paul begins by saying that Jesus was essentially and unalterably God" (35).

In English we only have one word for "form," but Greek has two. In this sentence, Paul uses *morphe* (**mor-FAY**), which figuratively means "shape," but actually means "the same in nature." If he had used the word *schema* (**SKHAY-mah**) instead, we would have had an entirely different meaning. *Morphe* is the unchanging essential nature. The *schema* (the actions, manner, bearing) of a thing may change, but the *morphe* does not. Jesus in His very essence is God. When you take something that belongs to you, it is not robbery. So when Jesus Christ accepted worship as God (John 5:18; 9:38; 10:30–33), when He claimed to be "I am" (John 8:58–59), and when He forgave sins (Mark 2:5–11), which is something only God can do, He was acknowledging His deity. He accepts equality with God because He is God.

7 But made himself of no reputation, and took upon him the form of a servant, and was made in the likeness of men:

Jesus acknowledged that He was God, yet He came to earth as a man—born in a stable, stepson of a carpenter. He was the Creator of the universe, but He began His adulthood hammering boards together to support His mother, His stepbrothers, and His stepsisters after Joseph died.

"Made himself of no reputation" means He literally "emptied" Himself (Gk. *kenoo*, **ken-O-o**). When Jesus came to earth and became a man, He did not become any less God in His essential being, but He emptied Himself of the independent expression of His deity. He accepted the human limitations of time, space, and knowledge. He could have drawn upon His powers as God, but instead He became dependent upon His Father and the Holy Spirit. He became dependent upon prayer, just as we humans are. But He remained in His essential being still fully God.

To become a man was more degrading to Jesus than we could possibly imagine, but He also became one of the lowest of men. The Greek that the KJV translates as "servant" is actually a slave (*doulos*, **DOO-los**)! Again we see the word "form," which refers to His essential being. He was not just play-acting as a man. He actually became a man. In these verses, we see the great truth of the incarnation. Jesus was fully God, remained fully God, and at the same time became fully human. He truly felt pain, hunger, tiredness, and all the other physical feelings that we as human beings feel and experience.

But Jesus became a servant or a slave in a much deeper sense than membership in socio-economic class. Jesus came to earth to serve. Jesus tells us that the purpose of His coming was to serve and to give His life for us (Mark 10:45). He could have demanded to be treated as a king, but He came to serve us.

8 And being found in fashion as a man, he humbled himself, and became obedient unto death, even the death of the cross.

The Greek word translated "fashion" is *schema,* which implies that this was not the original nature of our Lord. Jesus became a man when He came to earth. To become a man was extremely humbling to our Lord, but He did this as part of the divine plan of salvation.

Nothing could be more human than to die a human death. When we think about the Son of God, the Creator and Sustainer of the universe, dying, it truly boggles the mind. How could He die? No wonder the sky became as dark as night in the middle of the day! No wonder the dead were seen walking about the streets of Jerusalem! But only by becoming a human being could Jesus die on the Cross and take the punishment for our sins. Only a human death could pay for our sins, so Jesus obeyed His Father and became a man. Yet only the Son of God could live a perfect, sinless life that was essential to His dying for us and not for Himself.

The death He died was the most degrading. Jesus did not desire to exalt Himself. He renounced His glory for our sakes. The Jews knew that death on a cross was a curse, because we read in Deuteronomy 21:23 that anyone who is hanged on a tree is cursed of God. For the Romans, it was such an awful death that no Roman citizen could be hung on a cross; only a slave or the most awful criminal could be crucified. But in the most extreme act of humility, Jesus died on the Cross for us.

9 Wherefore God also hath highly exalted him, and given him a name which is above every name:

But the Cross is not the end of the story, nor is it the end of this beautiful hymn. The Philippian believers who received this letter, were suffering for our Lord, and it surely encouraged them to hear that the name they were being persecuted for would one day be exalted. *Huperupsoo* (**hoop-er-oop-SO-o**) is the Greek word for "exalted," and it means to raise to the highest degree possible. Jesus humbled Himself as low as anyone could lower himself, but God the Father will raise Him higher than anyone has ever been raised or ever could be raised.

What is the name that is above every name? The next verse seems to tell us that it is Jesus. In Matthew 1:21, the angel told Joseph to name the child Jesus, for He would save His people from their sins. Jesus comes from the Hebrew name *Yhowshuwa* (**yeh-ho-SHOO-ah**) or *Yhowshua*, and it means "the Lord (Yahweh) saves." So this is the name that Jesus was given at His earthly birth (the beginning of His humiliation) and it tells us His purpose in coming—He came to save us.

10 That at the name of Jesus every knee should bow, of things in heaven, and things in earth, and things under the earth;

In our culture, a name is usually chosen just because a parent likes the sound, but in many cultures, the meaning of the name is most important and is thought to describe the essence of the person or represents the person. The Scripture says that everyone who calls upon the name of the Lord will be saved (Acts 2:21). But this is not just a superstitious type of name calling. Jesus warns that not everyone who says, "Lord, Lord," will enter the kingdom of heaven, not even those who have done miracles in His name (Matthew 7:21–23). No, calling upon His name means receiving Jesus as one's Savior from sin and Lord of one's life.

Bowing at the name of Jesus is more than a physical act; it is the heart attitude of worship and obedience to our Lord and Savior Jesus Christ for all that His name represents. Those who have decided to follow Jesus are already bowing before Him.

11 And that every tongue should confess that Jesus Christ is Lord, to the glory of God the Father.

The earliest Christians understood that "Lord" was how Jews referred to God (Yahweh) without daring to say His most holy name aloud. And Paul tells us that in calling Jesus "Lord," God is glorified. God has called Jesus "God." As Christians, we call Jesus our Lord and our God. Peter referred to Jesus as "our God and Savior Jesus Christ" (2 Peter 1:1, NIV).

The word translated "confess" is *exomologeo* (**ex-om-ol-og-EH-o**), which means to acknowledge or to fully agree. This is not just saying the words. "Glory" is *doxa* (**DOX-ah**), which means honor, praise, and worship. So everyone will acknowledge that Jesus deserves all honor as part of the almighty three-in-one God. Sad to say, this does not mean that everyone will be saved at this time. But those who did not receive Jesus as Lord and Savior while here on earth will realize what a mistake they have made, and at that time it will be too late to rectify it. Jesus died a cruel death on the Cross to make salvation possible for them, and they rejected Him.

As we conclude this wonderful hymn, let us keep in mind that Christ is not only our God, but He is also our wonderful example of what it means to be truly humble. He served us, so we must serve one another.

Say It Correctly

Euodia. yoo-O-dee-uh.
Isaiah. i -ZAY-uh, -yuh.
Macedonia. mas'uh-DOH-nee-uh;
mas'uh-DOH-nee-uhn.
Philippi. fi-l-p, f-li-p.
Philippian. f-li-p-nz.
Syntyche. SIN-tih-kee.

Daily Bible Readings

M: Follow in Christ's Steps
1 Peter 2:18–25

T: Good Lives Shown in Works
James 3:13–18

W: Being Worthy of Jesus
Matthew 10:34–39

T: Lives Worthy of Your Calling
Ephesians 4:1–6

F: Lives Worthy of the Lord
Colossians 1:9–18

S: Lives Worthy of the Gospel
Philippians 1:27–30

S: Living the Mind of Christ
Philippians 2:1–11

Notes

_____

_____

_____

_____

_____

Teaching Tips

May 8
Bible Study Guide 10

1. Words You Should Know

A. Holy (Revelation 4:8) *hagios* (Gk.)—Sacred: pure, morally blameless, consecrated.

B. Worthy (v. 11) *axios* (Gk.)—God supremely deserves to receive the glory, honor, and power that is given to Him.

2. Teacher Preparation

Unifying Principle—Communicating Through Symbols. For John, the symbolism in the book of Revelation, patterned after Hebrew Scriptures, points to worship and praise of God.

A. Pray and ask God to give lesson clarity.

B. Prayerfully study the entire lesson.

C. Study the tenets of apocalyptic literature in the Background section of this lesson and be prepared to discuss.

D. Research on the Internet or in a Bible dictionary the word "symbol" or "symbolism," and be prepared to explain how the Bible uses symbolism in the book of Revelation.

E. Prepare to read the song "Holy, Holy, Holy" dramatically to your class or have a volunteer do so.

3. Open the Lesson

A. Open with prayer, including the Aim for Change.

B. Present your information on apocalyptic literature and "symbols" or "symbolism."

C. Dramatically read the song "Holy, Holy, Holy" to the class or have a volunteer do so.

D. Tie in the In Focus story.

4. Present the Scriptures

A. Have volunteers read the Focal Verses.

B. Now use The People, Places, and Times; Background; Search the Scriptures; At-A-Glance outline; In Depth; and More Light on the Text to clarify the verses.

5. Explore the Meaning

A. Lead a discussion of the Discuss the Meaning, Lesson in Our Society, and Make It Happen sections.

B. Connect these sections to the Aim for Change and the Keep in Mind verse.

6. Next Steps for Application

A. Challenge your students to worship and praise God for who He is.

B. Close with prayer.

Worship Guide

For the Superintendent or Teacher
Theme: Heavenly Worship
Theme Song: "Holy, Holy, Holy"
Devotional Reading: Psalm 11
Prayer

Heavenly Worship

Bible Background • REVELATION 4
Printed Text • REVELATION 4:1–2, 6b–11 | Devotional Reading • PSALM 11

─────────── **Aim for Change** ───────────

By the end of the lesson, we will: EXPLAIN how the symbolism in Revelation points to worship and praise of God; REFLECT upon the meaning of the symbolism in today's lesson; and WORSHIP God for who He is and for what He does.

───────────  In Focus ───────────

Browsing through an art gallery, Sheri turned a corner and found herself wandering through a display of paintings by a local artist. The paintings were boldly colored, sometimes dark, sometimes flashy, but always of unusual images. One showed bizarre sea creatures in photo-realistic detail; it was hard to believe such creatures could be real. Another showed a still life of a bowl of fruit; only after you had looked at it for a while did you see that it was also the shape of a man's face.

Sheri found the paintings strangely beautiful and stared at them intently. Then she noticed a man standing off to one side of the gallery, watching her with a smile. "Do you like it?" he said.

"I think so," said Sheri. "They're really beautiful, but I'm not entirely sure what they're supposed to mean."

"I'll tell you this much: everything I put into them is a bit of my own life story."

Works of art show off not only an artist's technical skill but also his or her interests and personalities. In the book of Revelation, God reveals Himself as the Creator and Lord of the universe. God's marvelous works and His holy character give us reason to praise Him.

MAY 8th

─────────── **Keep in Mind** ───────────

"And immediately I was in the spirit: and, behold, a throne was set in heaven, and one sat on the throne" (Revelation 4:2).

"And immediately I was in the spirit: and, behold, a throne was set in heaven, and one sat on the throne" (Revelation 4:2).

Focal Verses

KJV **Revelation 4:1** After this I looked, and, behold, a door was opened in heaven: and the first voice which I heard was as it were of a trumpet talking with me; which said, Come up hither, and I will shew thee things which must be hereafter.

2 And immediately I was in the spirit: and, behold, a throne was set in heaven, and one sat on the throne.

4:6b In the midst of the throne, and round about the throne, were four beasts full of eyes before and behind.

7 And the first beast was like a lion, and the second beast like a calf, and the third beast had a face as a man, and the fourth beast was like a flying eagle.

8 And the four beasts had each of them six wings about him; and they were full of eyes within: and they rest not day and night, saying, Holy, holy, holy, LORD God Almighty, which was, and is, and is to come.

9 And when those beasts give glory and honour and thanks to him that sat on the throne, who liveth for ever and ever,

10 The four and twenty elders fall down before him that sat on the throne, and worship him that liveth for ever and ever, and cast their crowns before the throne, saying,

11 Thou art worthy, O Lord, to receive glory and honour and power: for thou hast created all things, and for thy pleasure they are and were created.

NLT **Revelation 4:1** Then as I looked, I saw a door standing open in heaven, and the same voice I had heard before spoke to me like a trumpet blast. The voice said, "Come up here, and I will show you what must happen after this."

2 And instantly I was in the Spirit, and I saw a throne in heaven and someone sitting on it.

4:6b In the center and around the throne were four living beings, each covered with eyes, front and back.

7 The first of these living beings was like a lion; the second was like an ox; the third had a human face; and the fourth was like an eagle in flight.

8 Each of these living beings had six wings, and their wings were covered all over with eyes, inside and out. Day after day and night after night they keep on saying, "Holy, holy, holy is the Lord God, the Almighty—the one who always was, who is, and who is still to come."

9 Whenever the living beings give glory and honor and thanks to the one sitting on the throne (the one who lives forever and ever),

10 the twenty-four elders fall down and worship the one sitting on the throne (the one who lives forever and ever). And they lay their crowns before the throne and say,

11 "You are worthy, O Lord our God, to receive glory and honor and power. For you created all things, and they exist because you created what you pleased."

The People, Places, and Times

John. The author of Revelation introduces himself as "John" (Revelation 1:1–2). Church tradition and scholarship generally agree that this John is the same as the author of the fourth Gospel and the three New Testament epistles bearing his name. John was a fisherman who became one of the first disciples called by Jesus (Matthew 4:21–22), one of the Twelve chosen to be apostles (Luke 6:13–16) and an elder in the early church (2 John 1). By all accounts, he was an exceptionally close friend to Jesus (Luke 8:51; John 21:20, 24). His writing is characterized by thoughtfulness, simplicity, and a deep insight into the heart of Jesus' message.

Patmos. According to John, the book of Revelation was written on "the island of Patmos" (1:9). This small island in the Aegean Sea (off the coast of modern-day Turkey) was used as a Roman penal colony. Like other persecuted believers, John was probably exiled to Patmos as punishment for preaching the Gospel.

Background

At the time Revelation was written, Christians in general were suffering persecution for their faith in Christ, including imprisonment and even death (1:9; 2:10, 13; 6:9). Though many Roman emperors persecuted Christians (most notably Nero in A.D. 64), this particular wave of persecution probably took place under the reign of Emperor Domitian (A.D. 81–96). The book of Revelation is filled with encouraging words and imagery for persecuted or suffering believers.

The book begins with John's vision of the exalted Jesus, who dictates a series of short prophetic letters that encourage the suffering churches of Asia Minor to repent and remain strong in their faith (chapters 1–3). However, the writing style rapidly changes to a genre known as *apocalypse*, from the Greek word for "unveiling." Apocalyptic literature depicts a vision or revelation from God, usually with fantastic imagery and mysterious symbols. Old Testament prophets such as Ezekiel, Zechariah, and Daniel also wrote in the apocalyptic genre. While their symbolism may be hard for us to understand fully, the underlying message of the vision in Revelation always points back to hope in God and the supremacy, glory, and eternal victory of Jesus Christ.

At-A-Glance

1. John's Vision of the Heavenly Throne: Symbols of God's Nature (Revelation 4:1–2, 6b-8a)

2. The Heavenly Creatures Worship God for Who He Is (vv. 8b-9)

3. The Elders Worship God for What He Does (vv. 10–11)

In Depth

1. John's Vision of the Heavenly Throne: Symbols of God's Nature (Revelation 4:1–2, 6b-8a)

John's account begins with the sight of an open door in the sky and the sound of a voice inviting him to visit heaven and see a glimpse of the future. Before he even has a chance to respond, he is immersed in a spiritual vision of the throne room of God. At the center of the vision is a throne with "one" sitting upon it (v. 2). The symbolism of the throne, at least, is obvious. As the place where kings hold court, a throne shows the king's authority, sovereignty, power, and majesty. As the King of kings and Ruler of the universe, God deserves our respect, worship, and awe.

The imagery becomes less predictable as the throne is described in terms of precious stones, rainbows, thunder, and lightning—things that are beautiful, inspire awe, and show God's creative work in nature (vv. 3, 5). A "sea of glass" surrounds the throne (v. 6).

"Twenty-four elders" are seated around the throne of God in 24 thrones of their own, dressed in white with gold crowns (v. 4). Some interpreters believe that these elders may be the 12 apostles and the 12 patriarchs of Israel, who are alluded to elsewhere in the vision (Revelation 21:12, 14). However, as is typical in apocalyptic literature, they aren't definitely identified here.

The 24 elders in verse 4 are upstaged by a sight that is nothing short of bizarre: four "beasts" (KJV) or "living beings" (NLT) in the inner ring around the throne (v. 6b). One is in the form of a lion, one like a calf, one like a man, and one like a flying eagle. There the normality ceases. Each has six wings and is covered with eyes on every side of its body.

John was not the first prophet to mention such creatures. Isaiah and Ezekiel also had visions of heavenly beings that were somewhat similar, though with tantalizing differences. Isaiah's vision includes six-winged "seraphim" that fly around the throne of God, though he does not give a further description of their shape or form (Isaiah 6:2). Ezekiel also saw flying angelic creatures around God's throne. In his case, each creature had two wings and four faces—the faces of a man, a lion, an ox, and an eagle (Ezekiel 1:1–10).

2. The Heavenly Creatures Worship God for Who He Is (vv. 8b–9)

The four creatures in John's vision may look outlandish, but they have a unique occupation. Day and night, without any rest, they continually sing a song of worship to God. As portrayed in the Scriptures, worship is not an activity that we are required to perform at certain times such as Sunday mornings. It is a way of life that should fill every moment. In the Old Testament, a team of musicians was assigned to worship before the ark of God in rotating shifts (1 Chronicles 16; 25), and in the New Testament, believers are enjoined to "Rejoice evermore. Pray without ceasing" (1 Thessalonians 5:16–17). This doesn't mean that we always have to be on our knees or singing a song, but that our attention should be constantly fixed on God and constantly responding to thoughts of Him.

The heavenly creatures embody this idea with their unending song: "Holy, holy, holy, Lord God Almighty, which was, and is, and is to come" (Revelation 4:8). These words focus entirely on God's nature and character. Holiness is the only one of God's character qualities to be given a threefold repetition in Scripture, a poetic flourish that gives a word the strongest possible emphasis. The other occurrence is in Isaiah's vision of God's throne, where the six-winged seraphim also sing "Holy, holy, holy" (Isaiah 6:3). God's holiness—His perfect goodness and His total separation from evil—identifies Him better than anything else.

God is also described as "Almighty." There is no possible being with greater power than God, and God has unlimited power to do anything He desires. "Is there any thing too hard for me?" God asks rhetorically (Jeremiah 32:27), and Scripture concurs: God "is able to do exceeding abundantly above all that we ask or think" (Ephesians 3:20).

Finally, God is eternal: "which was, and is, and is to come" (Revelation 4:8). God's existence does not depend on our time frame; He "liveth forever and ever" (Revelation 4:9). He is Lord of the past, the present, and the future. As Genesis shows, He existed before He created the world, and as Revelation shows, He will continue to exist after our world ends. He is not limited by anything—even time itself—that seems permanent to us.

Thinking about who God is leads us to worship Him. Just as we naturally feel awe when we see a mountain or naturally laugh when we hear a good joke, so worship is the natural response to a glimpse of what God is really like. Worship here consists simply of describing God's character. God's position as the almighty, infinite Creator calls for our reverence and awe.

3. The Elders Worship God for What He Does (vv. 10–11)

The 24 elders are moved by the song of the heavenly beings. They prostrate themselves in worship before God and throw down their crowns in front of His throne (v. 10). Bowing with one's face to the ground is a sign of deep humility, while a crown is a symbol of honor, victory, or authority. The elders recognize that even their exalted state is nothing before the awesome majesty of God. Any serious reflection on the greatness of God must end in a genuine sense of deep humility.

The elders add counterpoint to the chorus of praise with a song of their own: "Thou art worthy, O Lord, to receive glory and honour and power: for thou hast created all things, and for thy pleasure they are and were created" (v. 11).

Like the four living creatures, the elders begin with a declarative statement about God's nature: God is worthy. "Worthy" is another term of value. If we say that something is worthy, we mean that it deserves a certain response. Something is due to it; it's only right that it should receive it. The psalmist expressed it well: "Give unto the LORD *the glory due unto his name*, worship the LORD in the beauty of holiness" (Psalm 29:2, emphasis added). God is worthy to receive glory, honor, and power. Every good quality has its origin in Him and comes back to Him.

The elders worship God for who He is, but also for what He does. Like a creative artist who enjoys his or her work, God created because He wanted to. Artists take pleasure, care, and delight in their creative work, and they enjoy it when they can make a project simply to please themselves. All good artists reflect aspects of themselves in their work. In the same way, God's creation reflects His glory, majesty, creativity, and His personal connection and involvement in what He has made.

When we worship God for what He does, we acknowledge not only His character and His power, but that He is personally involved in our world. God's work reflects His character and shows that it translates into action.

Because of who He is and what He has done, God is worthy of worship from every created being. The heavenly beings of every order bow and sing praises to God, and we as redeemed humans join in their chorus of worship.

Search the Scriptures

1. How does John describe the four living creatures (Revelation 4:6–7)?

2. What characteristics of God are identified in the words that the living creatures and elders sing (vv. 8–11)?

Discuss the Meaning

1. John intended the book of Revelation to encourage persecuted believers. How can this heavenly perspective encourage you when you are going through a hard time?

2. How does your understanding of God move you to worship Him?

Lesson in Our Society

If we're used to going to church a lot, it's easy for us to mistakenly think of "worship" as a routine activity of mindlessly singing songs or just showing up once or twice a week. What should we do differently? How does this realization help us to pray for our pastors, worship leaders, and church musicians? How can we use our times of corporate worship to redirect our attention to God?

Make It Happen

Try creating an original work of art based on what you have read about God in the Scriptures. Paint a picture, compose a song, make a sculpture, write a poem, or do whatever takes your fancy. It doesn't have to be professional, just sincere. Describe some of God's characteristics, something God has done for you, and a symbol or metaphor that illustrates this. Use your own God-given creativity to worship God. If you like, share it with some friends or people in your church so they can use it to worship God as well.

Follow the Spirit

What God wants me to do:

_____

_____

_____

_____

Remember Your Thoughts

Special insights I have learned:

_____

_____

_____

_____

More Light on the Text

Revelation 4:1–2, 6b–11

1 After this I looked, and, behold, a door was opened in heaven: and the first voice which I heard was as it were of a trumpet talking with me; which said, Come up hither, and I will shew thee things which must be hereafter.

The ultimate mind-boggling fact about heaven is that the saints are in God's presence. John gives us a recap of his heavenly visit; although he most definitively is honored to receive a heavenly call to the throne, he avoids any hint of personal privilege. John had received an invitation he was not worthy of and could not refuse.

The opening phrase literally means "after these things, I looked and behold." The word *idou* (**id-OO**) translated "behold" is a Greek word used to emphasize what follows. In this context what follows is a door in heaven and a voice that sounded like a trumpet. It was as if John was saying, "Now that the church

401

knows what God thinks about some of its priorities on earth [see Revelation 2–3], God wants to declare what heaven's priority is." One thing is for sure: heaven had John's attention. When a heavenly trumpet is sounded, it is time to listen (Revelation 1:10; Exodus 19:16), for God is about to speak. And speak He did. God commanded John to come up to heaven, for he would be shown great things that had yet to come.

John himself did not ascend to heaven; rather he was taken in the spirit. When the revelation began, John says he was "in the spirit" (Revelation 1:10). Unbridled communion with God is always a working of the Spirit (Galatians 5:5, 16–25).

2 And immediately I was in the spirit: and, behold, a throne was set in heaven, and one sat on the throne.

As John was prepared to be in God's presence, suddenly he saw a throne set in heaven and the One who sat on the throne. This is the focus of this section. Attempts could be made to elaborate on earthly thrones to provide examples of what it means to sit in the place of absolute authority and power. However, Jesus declared that heaven is God's throne (Matthew 5:34).

If heaven is God's throne and John saw a throne set in heaven, then heaven is filled with the presence of God. The word "set" (Gk. *keimai*, **KI-mahee**) implies more than that which occupies time and space; in this passage it means something that has predestined continuity and purpose. A passage in Luke explains the significance of this word in relation to Jesus. Simeon, a man full of the Holy Spirit, says to Mary and Joseph, "Behold, this child is set for the fall and rising again of many in Israel; and for a sign which shall be spoken against" (Luke 2:34). The throne is about an eternal plan

that sees its fulfillment in an eternal Person, in whom all power, rule, and authority reside.

The second part of Revelation 4:2 literally means "I [John] observed [or envisioned] the One sitting on the throne." The Greek word for "sitting" originates from the Hebrew word *yashab* (**yaw-SHAB**), which means to inhabit a permanent dwelling place.

The relationship between the throne and the One sitting on the throne are eternal in nature and affirm the will of God. When God's throne and the One sitting on the throne are the subject, all thoughts must be directed at who He is, what He has done, and why we have been granted the privilege to be in His presence.

6b In the midst of the throne, and round about the throne, were four beasts full of eyes before and behind.

We think of cherubs as chubby-cheeked baby angels, not the beasts that are described in these verses. The Greek for "beast" is *zoon* (**DZO-on**), which is better translated as "a living thing" or "an animal." Ezekiel 1:6, 10, 22, 26 describe similar creatures, except that each of the creatures in Ezekiel had four different faces—the faces of a man, a lion, an ox, and a calf. In Ezekiel 10:20, the prophet tells us that these creatures are *cherubim* (cherubs). The Hebrew word *k@ruwb* (**ker-OOB**) with the English ending *-im* is the plural form. These creatures are always found around the throne of God and constantly engaged in praising and worshiping God.

7 And the first beast was like a lion, and the second beast like a calf, and the third beast had a face as a man, and the fourth beast was like a flying eagle.

Bible scholars have spent much time analyzing and looking for symbolism in the descriptions of the four beasts. These flying creatures of adoration spend all their time in the presence of God, so it seems likely that they reflect certain aspects of Him, especially of the Son of God. The lion is the king of the beasts, known for its power and authority. So this cherub reflects the leadership and royal power of our Lord. The calf is the animal of sacrifice; this cherub reminds us that Jesus Christ came to give His life giving His blood for us. The cherub with the appearance of a man can represent the incarnation of Jesus, His lowering of Himself to come in human form. And some have thought that the eagle represents the Holy Spirit who hovers over us.

Almost from the earliest days of Christianity, Bible scholars have tried to match the four beasts with the four Gospels, and St. Augustine of North Africa proposed the most widely accepted identifications. Matthew is best represented by the lion because he portrays Jesus as the Lion of Judah, the King of the Jews. Mark is represented by the cherub with the face of the man because he focuses on the human life of our Lord. Luke is best represented by the calf because he presents Jesus as the sacrifice for all men and women everywhere. John represents the eagle because the eagle flies so high that it is said to look into the face of the sun, and the thoughts in the Gospel of John are the deepest and highest of the four Gospels.

8 And the four beasts had each of them six wings about him; and they were full of eyes within: and they rest not day and night, saying, Holy, holy, holy, LORD God Almighty, which was, and is, and is to come.

These beasts or creatures have been described as having the highest intelligence of all beings as represented by their many eyes (Phillips, 86). They employ their intellects, their hearts, and their wills toward one activity: to constantly worship God. Although

we may rest in sleep, rest on the Sabbath, and rest in death, these living creatures never rest, but are constantly praising God. There is never any time among God's creation that He is not being praised.

These cherubim have six wings, just as the seraphim of Isaiah 6:2 do. Isaiah wrote that the seraphim used two wings to cover their faces, two to cover their feet, and two for flying. In other words, four of the wings are used to show their reverence and humility in the presence of God.

This doxology, the song of praise of the cherubim, praises God for three aspects. First, it praises God for His holiness. The Greek word for "holy" in this passage is *hagios* (**HAG-ee-os**), which means sacred—physically sacred, pure, morally blameless, ceremonially clean, consecrated. The basic idea of holiness is difference. God is completely separate and different from human beings and any other created beings. That is why we are moved to adore Him. If He were simply bigger and grander than us, we would not be moved to worship Him. He is totally other. "The very mystery of God moves us to awed admiration in his presence and to amazed love that that greatness should stoop so low for us men [and women] and for our salvation" (Barclay, 162).

The second aspect of the doxology of the cherubim is praising God for His omnipotence. Omnipotence is the all-powerfulness of God. God is the Almighty. When John wrote the book of Revelation, most of the then-known world was under the rule of the Roman Empire. History books sometimes call this era the *Pax Romana* (Roman peace). This was because any opposition was ruthlessly stamped out. Under the Roman Empire many of the early Christians were martyred. It was surely comforting to these early believers to know that the One standing behind them was the Almighty. As believers, we, too, may feel helpless against our situations, but we can know that for sure God will triumph in the end. God will keep us safe both in life and in death.

The third aspect of the cherubim's song of worship was praising God for His eternality; He is the God who was, who is, and who is to come. Although as believers we can look forward to eternity with Him, we cannot look back on our own eternity. Only God has always existed. And while we look at things from a timeline in which our memories of the past became vague with age and tomorrow is almost completely unknown, God is always existent. In addition to knowing everything from the very beginning, He can see tomorrow just as clearly as He sees today. He endures unchanging, while all around the empires we create are falling apart.

9 And when those beasts give glory and honour and thanks to him that sat on the throne, who liveth forever and ever, 10 The four and twenty elders fall down before him that sat on the throne, and worship him that liveth forever and ever, and cast their crowns before the throne, saying, 11 Thou art worthy, O Lord, to receive glory and honour and power: for thou hast created all things, and for thy pleasure they are and were created.

As the elders testified to the worship of "the living creatures," they could do nothing but fall down before Him, give back the crowns they had been given, and declare His praises. This was no inadvertent falling; the elders cast themselves down. The Greek word for "fall down" is *pipto* (**PIP-to**). It does not matter where the praise is coming from or who is giving it; when God is praised, the proper response is for everyone else in the room to fall down and worship. They worship Him because He is "worthy" (*axios*, **AX-ee-os**).

God supremely deserves to receive the glory, honor, and power that is given to Him.

Through John, the Spirit of the Lord says to the church that the redeemed are to offer continual, unbridled praise to God because (1) all things were created by Him and (2) all things were created for His pleasure. God has one design for us, which is to glorify Him.

Say It Correctly

Aegean. ih-JEE-uhn.
Apocalypse. uh-POK-uh-lips'.
Cherubs. CHER-uhb.
Domitian. duh-MISH-uhn,
  duh-MISH-ee-uhn.
Irenaeus. i-'ruh-NEE-uhs.
Seraphim. SER-uh-fim.

Daily Bible Readings

M: In the Holy Temple
Psalm 11

T: Holy, Holy, Holy
Isaiah 6:1–5

W: The Lord God Almighty
Exodus 6:2–8

T: The King of Glory
Psalm 24

F: King Forever and Ever
Psalm 10:12–26

S: Worship the Lord
Psalm 96

S: You Are Worthy, O Lord
Revelation 4:1–2, 6b–11

Teaching Tips

1. Words You Should Know

A. Number (Revelation 7:9) *arithmosai* (Gk.)—An amount, fixed or indefinite; source of the English word "arithmetic."

B. Blessing (v. 12) *eulogia* (Gk.)—Speaking well of, commending in eloquent language, and praising our living God.

2. Teacher Preparation

Unifying Principle—Where We Look in Times of Trouble. John depicted a large group of excited worshipers who had come through a difficult ordeal. This serves as a model for how we, too, in the midst of trouble must look to God.

A. Pray and ask God to meet the needs of your students through this lesson.

B. Prayerfully study the entire lesson.

C. Reflect on a time in your own life when in the time of trouble, you truly focused on God and His faithfulness.

D. Meditate on Revelation 7:17, "God shall wipe away all tears from their [the saved] eyes."

E. Bring a praise CD to class.

3. Open the Lesson

A. As your praise CD is playing softly, open with prayer.

B. Ask, "In your time of trouble, whom do you focus on? Whom do you turn to?" Discuss.

C. Discuss the dilemmas that Patricia faced in the In Focus story.

D. Then turn up your praise CD and allow your class to listen to the words and worship.

4. Present the Scriptures

A. Have volunteers read the Focal Verses.

B. Use The People, Places, and Times; Background; Search the Scriptures; At-A-Glance outline; In Depth; and More Light on the Text to clarify the verses.

5. Explore the Meaning

A. Lead a discussion of the Discuss the Meaning, Lesson in Our Society, and Make It Happen sections.

B. Connect these sections to the Aim for Change and the Keep in Mind verse.

6. Next Steps for Application

A. Challenge your students to thank God that His kingdom will come.

B. Close with prayer.

MAY 15th

Worship Guide

For the Superintendent or Teacher
Theme: Thankful Worship
Theme Song: "Thank You, Lord"
Devotional Reading: Psalm 23
Prayer

Thankful Worship

Bible Background • REVELATION 7:9–17
Printed Text • REVELATION 7:9–17 | Devotional Reading • PSALM 23

—————— Aim for Change ——————

By the end of the lesson, we will: EXPLAIN why we can look to God in times of trouble; REFLECT on how God has been a very present help in times of trouble; and WORSHIP God for His faithfulness in times of trouble.

——————  In Focus ——————

"I hate you, Mom," 17-year-old Curtis shouted as he slammed the door behind him. Patricia sank down in a kitchen chair, too weary to engage in another battle with her headstrong teenager. Her head was throbbing, and her heart was aching. First, her husband had lost his job. Then, her mother was diagnosed with cancer. And now, her son was rebelling against everything he had been taught.

Whom could she call? Where could she go? Standing up to pace around the kitchen, Patricia began to think back over the last few years of her life. She had been through many difficult times before. She closed her eyes and took a deep breath. God had been with her, helping her through all of those times. Patricia's heart lifted as she remembered God's faithfulness. She could trust Him to do what He said He would do.

How do we find the faith to trust God in difficult times? When we remember God's track record of grace and mercy, our faith is strengthened, giving us the courage to trust Him again. In times of trouble, we can count on God to keep His promises.

—————— Keep in Mind ——————

"And cried with a loud voice, saying, Salvation to our God which sitteth upon the throne, and unto the Lamb" (Revelation 7:10).

"And cried with a loud voice, saying, Salvation to our God which sitteth upon the throne, and unto the Lamb" (Revelation 7:10).

Focal Verses

KJV **Revelation 7:9** After this I beheld, and, lo, a great multitude, which no man could number, of all nations, and kindreds, and people, and tongues, stood before the throne, and before the Lamb, clothed with white robes, and palms in their hands;

10 And cried with a loud voice, saying, Salvation to our God which sitteth upon the throne, and unto the Lamb.

11 And all the angels stood round about the throne, and about the elders and the four beasts, and fell before the throne on their faces, and worshipped God,

12 Saying, Amen: Blessing, and glory, and wisdom, and thanksgiving, and honour, and power, and might, be unto our God for ever and ever. Amen.

13 And one of the elders answered, saying unto me, What are these which are arrayed in white robes? and whence came they?

14 And I said unto him, Sir, thou knowest. And he said to me, These are they which came out of great tribulation, and have washed their robes, and made them white in the blood of the Lamb.

15 Therefore are they before the throne of God, and serve him day and night in his temple: and he that sitteth on the throne shall dwell among them.

16 They shall hunger no more, neither thirst any more; neither shall the sun light on them, nor any heat.

17 For the Lamb which is in the midst of the throne shall feed them, and shall lead them unto living fountains of waters: and God shall wipe away all tears from their eyes.

NLT **Revelation 7:9** After this I saw a vast crowd, too great to count, from every nation and tribe and people and language, standing in front of the throne and before the Lamb. They were clothed in white robes and held palm branches in their hands.

10 And they were shouting with a mighty shout, "Salvation comes from our God who sits on the throne and from the Lamb!"

11 And all the angels were standing around the throne and around the elders and the four living beings. And they fell before the throne with their faces to the ground and worshiped God.

12 They sang, "Amen! Blessing and glory and wisdom and thanksgiving and honor and power and strength belong to our God forever and ever! Amen."

13 Then one of the twenty-four elders asked me, "Who are these who are clothed in white? Where did they come from?"

14 And I said to him, "Sir, you are the one who knows." Then he said to me, "These are the ones who died in the great tribulation. They have washed their robes in the blood of the Lamb and made them white."

15 That is why they stand in front of God's throne and serve him day and night in his Temple. And he who sits on the throne will give them shelter.

16 They will never again be hungry or thirsty; they will never be scorched by the heat of the sun.

17 For the Lamb on the throne will be their Shepherd. He will lead them to springs of life-giving water. And God will wipe every tear from their eyes."

The People, Places, and Times

Authorship. The author of Revelation identifies himself as "John" (1:4). Most of the early church scholars identified this "John" as the apostle John, son of Zebedee and brother of James. John, the writer of Revelation, was exiled to the island of Patmos as a consequence for spreading the Word of God and testifying to the existence and ministry of Jesus Christ. It was during this time of exile that he received the vision from God, the "revelation," which he faithfully recorded according to Jesus' instruction and for future generations (1:11).

The Great Multitude. John's vision included an unlimited international group gathered before the throne. Those in white robes generally symbolize the baptized that are clothed in righteousness, and they are identified in Revelation 7:14 as those who "came out of great tribulation." There is some debate about what exactly is meant by "great tribulation," but most Bible scholars agree that the "great multitude" can generally be considered as martyrs of the faith.

White Robes. In ancient times, white garments were reserved for special occasions such as weddings and religious ceremonies. This probably came about as a matter of practicality—dusty streets and manual labor would have mandated sturdy, functional clothing.

Worshipers often wore white robes to the many celebrations at the Tabernacle and later at the Temple (see 2 Samuel 6:14 and Isaiah 61:2–3). The phrase "white robes [clothes]" appears 16 times in the New Testament, nine of those times in the book of Revelation. All New Testament references to white robes, including those in Revelation, refer to Jesus' transfiguration, resurrection, or ascension, or to the resurrected righteous believers in heaven. In Revelation 7:9, the "great multitude" are standing before the throne of God, wearing white robes and waving palm branches.

Palm Branches. In the Old Testament, palm branches were waved or shaken in conjunction with singing hymns and psalms, usually to celebrate a victory, but also during the reading of certain portions of Scripture. Palm branches were also used in much the same way during the ceremonial feast days at the Tabernacle. In Revelation, we see the multitude waving palm branches, joyously praising God for the incomparable victory of salvation from sin.

Living Water. The multitude will enjoy eternal blessings, including "living fountains of water" (7:17). "Living" water is water that is not stagnant; it is flowing from some source such as a spring or a river. It is constantly being renewed.

Spiritually speaking, Jesus is the source of "living water" to those who are believers. He is the source of life, holiness, godliness, and righteousness for His people. When it is the right time, this living water will flow through the world, cleansing it (see Isaiah 35:5–10; Zechariah 14:20–21) until God's glory will once again fill the earth (see Psalm 57; 108:5; Isaiah 6:3). Jesus, the Lamb of God, will lead His people to experience this glorious renewal (Revelation 7:17).

Background

In Revelation 5, John saw God holding a scroll that was sealed with seven seals. Jesus, "the Lion of the tribe of Judah" was the only one in heaven who was worthy to open the seals (5:5). Each time Jesus opened one of the seals, a corresponding judgment was visited upon the earth. Revelation 7 opens with four angels holding back the wind, signaling an interlude between the opening of the sixth and seventh seals. The events of our text today concerning the "great multitude" (7:9) take place during this lull.

At-A-Glance

1. The Great Multitude (Revelation 7:9–10)

2. The Great Choir (vv. 11–12)

3. The Great Promises (vv. 13–17)

In Depth

1. The Great Multitude (Revelation 7:9–10)

John the Revelator, exiled on the island of Patmos, was given an amazing vision which is recorded in the book of Revelation. In his vision up to this point, John has had a deeply spiritual, but a surely terrifying and amazing experience. Now, there is a moment when he no doubt draws a deep breath and concentrates on the scene before him: a "great multitude" of people—so many that no one could count them (v. 9). They are of all different races, different ages, different cultures, different languages, perhaps even different time periods of history. Nevertheless, all of these people have much in common with one another. All are wearing the white robes of the redeemed. All are waving the palm branches of the victorious. All are singing and worshiping, crying out their victory chant: "Salvation to our God, who sitteth upon the throne, and to the Lamb" (v. 10).

All have come through some sort of great tribulation in order to ultimately stand and worship at the throne of their King. They made it through! All had faced suffering of some sort: perhaps betrayal, hunger, abandonment, pain, sorrow, or death. But they remained faithful in the midst of their struggles, realizing that the ultimate victory was worth the temporary discomfort.

We, too, face these same trials in our own lives as believers. Satan has waged a war against every person who chooses to follow Jesus Christ as Lord. We may not face an executioner's sword, but we will be tested and tried as we live out our lives of service to God. How can we, like the "great multitude," remain faithful, focusing on God even in the midst of trouble? How can we possibly worship God in the middle of a difficult, pain-filled situation?

Deuteronomy 7:9 (NIV) says, "Know therefore that the LORD your God is God; he is the faithful God, keeping his covenant of love to a thousand generations of those who love him and keep his commands." The key is this: God is always faithful to His own. When we are faced with an untenable situation, we must look back to what God has already done on our behalf. When we start to meditate on God's faithfulness, we will begin to feel our faith rise to meet the challenge of the day.

2. The Great Choir (vv. 11–12)

Joining in the praises of the great multitude are the rest of God's heavenly inhabitants—the angels, elders, and the "four living creatures" (Revelation 7:11). The *NIV Study Bible* describes these four living creatures as "an exalted order of angelic beings whose task is to guard the heavenly throne and lead in worship and adoration of God...nothing escapes their attention" (1930).

These heavenly beings are constantly around the throne, worshiping and singing praise to God. In response to the worship of the great multitude, this heavenly choir leads the inhabitants of the throne room in a doxology, consisting of seven specific attributes and beginning and ending with an "amen" (v. 12). According to some scholars, this seven-fold list represents "complete" or "perfect" praise (*NIV Study Bible*, 1933).

3. The Great Promises (vv. 13–17)

During the great praise celebration around the throne, one of the elders turned to John and asked him if he knew who the people in the white robes were. John replied that he did not. The elder then explained that these were the people, God's redeemed, who had overcome. They had been cleansed by the blood of the Lamb, all of their sins washed away. They had remained faithful through great tribulation and trials (vv. 13–14). Because of this, they would now receive eternal rewards.

Standing in the very presence of God Almighty is the first of these blessings. Believers, who so faithfully served Him, will now be able to dwell in His presence for all eternity, never to leave. What a glorious hope that is to us who are still living here on earth! Right now as we struggle through life's difficulties. We say with the psalmist, "My soul yearns, even faints, for the courts of the LORD; my heart and flesh cry out for the living God" (Psalm 84:2, NIV). But take heart! There will come a day when we will no longer groan and long for His presence. We will live and serve in His courts forever.

Because there can be no lack in God's presence, we will never again have any need. God will "spread his tent" over us (Revelation 7:15, NIV). In other words, He will protect us, shield us, and fellowship with us. Never again will we suffer homelessness (v. 15) because we will live with God! He will reveal Himself as Jehovah Jireh, our Provider. Never again will we be physically or spiritually hungry or thirsty (v. 16).

And Jesus, the Lamb of God, will be our Shepherd. He will lead us to those springs of living water—His very life, flowing through us. And there will be no more suffering or pain (v. 17). God will wipe away every tear from our eyes. What joy! What reward! Our God loves us with an everlasting love! And because God always keeps His promises, we have the courage to be faithful to a faithful God.

Search the Scriptures

1. John saw a "great multitude" standing before the throne. What was the multitude doing (Revelation 7:9–10)?

2. Who else was standing around the throne besides the multitude (v. 11)?

Discuss the Meaning

1. The great multitude was enthusiastically worshiping God around the throne after coming through great trials and tribulation. How can their example help us to live the life to which God has called each one of us?

2. The angels, elders and creatures sang a doxology, ascribing praise to God in seven different ways. What are some specific aspects of God's nature for which Christians should praise Him? Why should we do this?

Lesson in Our Society

Many people in our world today are concerned about the future. They wonder and worry about the economy, the environment, world peace, and their own families and friends. Christians are not excluded from the troubles and trials of this fallen, flawed world in which we live. But we have what the rest of the world does not— we have hope. Because of God's record of faithfulness in His Word, and to us personally, we have hope to face life's uncertainties.

Make It Happen

Remembering what God has done in your life is an effective faith-building exercise. Keeping a journal will aid you in remembering and rejoicing in God's faithfulness to you personally.

Follow the Spirit

What God wants me to do:

_____

_____

_____

_____

Remember Your Thoughts

Special insights I have learned:

_____

_____

_____

_____

More Light on the Text

Revelation 7:9–17

9 After this I beheld, and, lo, a great multitude, which no man could number, of all nations, and kindreds, and people, and tongues, stood before the throne, and before the Lamb, clothed with white robes, and palms in their hands;

The expressions "after this" and "after these things" are familiar time markers moving us forward in the book of Revelation, either in the order of events or in the order of John's visions about the events (see 1:19; 4:1; 7:1, 9; 18:1; 19:1).

John has just seen a group of 144,000 (a number made famous by its frequent misuse on the part of Jehovah's Witnesses). Now "after this," John sees a crowd beyond calculation. The Greek word for "number" is *arithmos* (**ar-ith-MOS**) from which we get the word "arithmetic." These are believing individuals from "all nations, and kindreds, and people, and tongues."

Having "palms in their hands" reminds us of the festive celebration at Jesus' triumphal entry during the last week of His earthly life (John 12:13). Palm branches had been used regularly at the Jews' annual Feast of Tabernacles (also called the Feast of Booths; see Leviticus 23:40).

10 And cried with a loud voice, saying, Salvation to our God which sitteth upon the throne, and unto the Lamb.

"Salvation to our God" may mean that salvation belongs to God. God is the only source of rescue from the ultimate ruin and judgment to come. Therefore, salvation "is the gift of God" (Ephesians 2:8). Have you reached out and received God's gift of salvation with gratitude?

11 And all the angels stood round about the throne, and about the elders and the four beasts, and fell before the throne on their faces, and worshipped God,

Picture a series of circles around the heavenly throne. The outer ring is composed of all the angels. Nearer are the 24 elders and the four living creatures—the cherubim, each with a face of a different creature and each with six wings completely covered with eyes (see last week's lesson). The inside circle is composed of the throng dressed in white (we shall see in verse 16 who they are). Each group gives praise to God. Now the angels fall prostrate before God and worship Him, but first let's examine who the elders are.

We are first introduced to the 24 elders in Revelation 4:4. In this verse we see that they are dressed in white, wearing crowns, and sitting on thrones. In verse 4:10, they cast their crowns before the throne of God. We also read that they continually worship and praise God (Revelation 5:11, 14; 11:16; 14:3; 19:4); they bring to God the prayers of the saints (5:8); they encourage John when the vision causes him to cry; and then in verse 13 of today's passage, one of them helps John understand the vision.

The Greek for "elders" is *presbuteros* (**pres-BOO-ter-os**), which means older or senior persons and can also mean representatives. So who are these elders? Many have thought that they represent the 12 tribes of Israel plus the 12 apostles. This is thought to show the unity of the Old Testament believers with the believers of the New Testament era (Vincent, 478; Barclay, Vol. 1, 154). Remember that in Matthew 19:27–29, the apostles were promised 12 thrones for following the Lord.

Others have seen in them an illusion to the 24 representative priestly leaders (there were too many priests for all to serve) first mentioned in 1 Chronicles 24:1–19. One of the foremost duties of the priests was to offer up to God the prayers of the people as Revelation 5:8 describes the 24 elders doing. So the 24 elders may represent the heavenly ideal of worship, of which our earthly worship is just a pale copy (Barclay, Vol. 1, 154.).

Barclay further posits that the 24 elders symbolize all the faithful people of God. Their white robes are the robes which are promised to the faithful in Revelation 3:4, and their crowns are those which believers who are faithful unto death are to receive (Revelation 2:10). But others have said that we really cannot tell if the elders are meant to be symbolic at all. They may simply be heavenly beings devoted to the continual worship of God (Michaels, 92).

12 Saying, Amen: Blessing, and glory, and wisdom, and thanksgiving, and honour, and power, and might, be unto our God for ever and ever. Amen.

Now the angels are fallen prostrate before God, saying "amen" to the previous praise of the multitude and then giving their own words of praise, every word of which is meaningful. First they ascribe blessing to God. The Greek for "blessing" is *eulogia* (**yoo-log-EE-ah**), which is the same root as for "eulogy," the words of praise we offer the dead at a funeral. The Greek word includes the sense of speaking well of, commending in eloquent language, and praising our living God. We should be always blessing God because He both created us and redeemed us.

Next, the angels ascribe "glory" to God. God is our Father. Because of Jesus Christ, we can come before Him, but we should never forget His majesty. Adoration and glory rightly belong to our God.

The angels also ascribe "wisdom" to God. The Greek word is *sophia* (**sof-EE-ah**), but this is wisdom in the spiritual sense as well as in the sense of knowledge. All truth and all knowledge come from God.

Then the angels offer thanksgiving to God. David said, "Bless the LORD, O my soul, and forget not all his benefits" (Psalm 103:2). We also should be continually thanking God for all the wonderful things He is doing and has done for us.

Fifth, the angels ascribe "honour" to God. God is God and He is to be worshiped. In our prayers, we may forget and focus on the things we want from God, instead of worshiping Him with our entire being and offering up ourselves in worship to Him.

Then the angels ascribe "power" to God. God's hand is never shortened so that it cannot save us (Isaiah 59:1). In the end, everything will be worked out according to His will. Amazingly, He uses His power to save us.

Finally, the angels ascribe "might" to God. Another word for might is "strength." We often find we do not have the strength in ourselves to do the things we wish to do for our God, but the secret is in drawing upon His strength. As we look at the angels' words of continuous praise, we can meditate upon these words and offer them up to God as well.

13 And one of the elders answered, saying unto me, What are these which are arrayed in white robes? and whence came they?

At this juncture, one of the 24 elders speaks up for only the second time in the book of Revelation (see Revelation 4:4, 10; see also 5:5). In the Old Testament, individuals ask similar questions (compare Daniel 7:16 and Zechariah 4:1–6).

14 And I said unto him, Sir, thou knowest. And he said to me, These are they which came out of great tribulation, and have washed their robes, and made them white in the blood of the Lamb.

The Bible uses the term "tribulation" in two ways: (1) to refer to the general trials throughout all the ages (Acts 14:22; Romans 5:3; Revelation 1:12) and (2) to refer to the specific time of tribulation prior to end-time events. Examples of the second usage include Daniel 12:1: "There shall be a time of trouble [or tribulation], such as never was since there was a nation [in existence] even to that same [future] time." Hundreds of years later, Jesus also foretells, "For there shall be a great tribulation, such as was not since the beginning of the world [up] to this time" (Matthew 24:21). This multitude could be comprised of those who have experienced tribulation in both senses.

The phrase "made them white" is translated from the Greek verb *leukaino* (**lyoo-KAH-eeno**) and is related to the Greek adjective *leukos* (**lyoo-KOS**) in verse 13. This is the word from which we derive our word "leukemia," a disease that results from an overload of white cells in the blood system. However, this "whitening" or cleansing is like none other on earth, for these people have washed their robes in the blood of the Lamb. This is why we sing, "What can wash away my sins? Nothing but the blood of Jesus."

15 Therefore are they before the throne of God, and serve him day and night in his temple: and he that sitteth on the throne shall dwell among them.

The last three verses are often read or quoted at funerals because they beautifully depict the current condition of those who are now with the Lord. The afterlife is not a do-nothing time of leisure and laziness. His people "serve him day and night" (v. 15). Of course, there in that perfect environment we won't have any tiredness, drudgery, poor pay, or lack of motivation, for His sinless servants "serve" Him willingly and joyfully. We will be engaged in wonderful work without any weariness. While our deceased loved ones who belong to God currently enjoy His presence, after the final resurrection we will worship God in this way with our new bodies. No tired muscles or minds then! Revelation 22:4 echoes this truth.

God is pictured throughout Revelation as the One who sits upon or occupies the Throne. God will (literally) "dwell" among us. The Greek verb *skenosei* (**skay-NO-say**) means "will tabernacle" (related to the Old Testament "tabernacle" or tent structure where the Israelites worshiped). Similarly, John 1:14 says, "The Word [Jesus] dwelt among us" (literally "tabernacled" in Greek, which means "to make His abode with us").

16 They shall hunger no more, neither thirst any more; neither shall the sun light on them, nor any heat.

In contrast to the problems faced by many desert-dwelling people (such as the Israelites of long ago), there will be no hunger, thirst, or heat. In those times and places, an oasis could mean the difference between life and death. Remember how Hagar and Ishmael (after being kicked out of their home base) wandered in the desert until their water ran out (Genesis 16:14–19)? Today, many of us are often strapped with bills that chase us from payday to payday. None of that there! No needs unsupplied. No stress or frustration. No more doing without.

17 For the Lamb which is in the midst of the throne shall feed them, and shall lead them unto living fountains of waters: and God shall wipe away all tears from their eyes.

The book of Revelation gives many paradoxical pictures that surprise and baffle us. For example, we see the Lion who is a Lamb (Revelation 5:5–6) who is the light (21:23). Revelation 7:17 reveals another one of these amazing pictures: the Lamb who is our Shepherd (NLT). Jesus said, "I am the good shepherd: the good shepherd giveth his life for the sheep" (John 10:11).

The last benefit in Revelation 7:17 is that "God shall wipe away all tears from their eyes." When drive-by shootings, abandoned newborns, gambled-away money, and hungry children cause us to cry, we have the promise of God that one day He will take His giant eraser and all that will be gone (see also Revelation 22:4). In response to

this wonderful truth, His people can only shout, "Hallelujah!" Yes, eventually we will live happily ever after.

Say It Correctly

Cherubim. CHER-uh-bim', CHER-yuh-bim'.
Patmos. PAT-muhs.
Zebedee. ZEB-uh-dee, ZEB-ih-dee.
Zechariah. zek'-uh-RI -uh, zek'-uh-RI-ah.

Daily Bible Readings

M: The Lord Is My Shepherd
Psalm 23

T: God, the True Shepherd
Ezekiel 34:11–16

W: The Good Shepherd
John 10:11–16

T: The Shepherd's Compassion
Matthew 9:35–38

F: The Shepherd's Judgment
Matthew 25:31–40

S: The Shepherd's Steadfast Love
Psalm 107:1–9

S: The Lamb as the Shepherd
Revelation 7:9–17

Teaching Tips

May 22
Bible Study Guide 12

1. Words You Should Know

A. Dwell (Revelation 21:3) *skenoo* (Gk.)—God localizes and centralizes His presence with His people.

B. Fearful (v. 8) *deilos* (Gk.)—Timid, also implies faithless.

2. Teacher Preparation

Unifying Principle—New Beginnings. The Revelation of John tells us that God, who is the beginning and the end, will make all things new. This is the promise of God for those who receive salvation through Jesus Christ.

A. Pray and ask God to bless your students with hope from this lesson.

B. Prayerfully study the entire lesson.

C. Reflect on some of the changes that you would like to see made in our world (what you would like God to erase).

D. Secure the CD *All Your Promises Are True*—Shannon Wexelberg/arranger.

3. Open the Lesson

A. As the class enters, softly play the CD *All Your Promises Are True.*

B. Open with prayer, including the Aim for Change.

C. Play the CD and listen to the words.

D. Ask, "What are some bad things happening in our world?" List answers on board and discuss. Then erase the answers.

E. Explain that in the new heaven and new earth, God will make all things new.

4. Present the Scriptures

A. Have volunteers read the Focal Verses.

B. Use The People, Places, and Times; Background; Search the Scriptures; At-A-Glance outline; In Depth; and More Light on the Text to clarify the verses.

5. Explore the Meaning

A. Lead a discussion of the Discuss the Meaning, Lesson in Our Society, and Make It Happen sections.

B. Connect these sections to the Aim for Change and the Keep in Mind verse.

6. Next Steps for Application

A. Challenge your students to worship and praise God for keeping all of His promises.

B. Close with prayer.

Worship Guide

For the Superintendent or Teacher
Theme: All Things New
Theme Song: "O, I Want to See Him"
Devotional Reading: Isaiah 43:15–21
Prayer

All Things New

Bible Background • REVELATION 21
Printed Text • REVELATION 21:1–8 | Devotional Reading • ISAIAH 43:15–21

Aim for Change

By the end of the lesson, we will: EXPLAIN how God has promised believers to make all things new; REFLECT on the new heaven and new earth; and THANK God that all of His promises are true.

In Focus

Robert's phone rang, and he buried his head in the hard hospital pillow. He didn't want to talk to anyone. He was too ashamed and too broken. He thought over the past few decades of his life. What had gone wrong?

His life had started out so promising—marrying his high school sweetheart, graduating from one of the country's best universities, landing his dream job. But then, the addictions took control of his life. Drugs, alcoholism, gambling, adultery—he had done them all. He sighed deeply. Now he was alone. He was just an old, broken, bitter man. If only he had never taken that first drink. If only he had never bet that first dollar. If only he had never cheated on Shari...if only...if only...

He let the tears come, rolling down his cheeks. "God, what I wouldn't give for a second chance," he prayed. "I've made such a mess of my own life. If You're really there, please help me. Help me!"

Now, Robert looks back on that day as the time when he really began to live. God heard his prayer and sent someone who shared the Gospel with him. God gave him the new beginning he had prayed for so desperately. God has restored Robert's family, and he thanks God every day. Robert now lives with the assurance that he will one day dwell with God for all eternity.

Many people would like to have a new beginning. What is it like to begin anew? How can Robert's testimony demonstrate the hope of a new beginning to others?

Keep in Mind

MAY 22nd

"And he that sat upon the throne said, Behold, I make all things new. And he said unto me, Write: for these words are true and faithful" (Revelation 21:5).

"And he that sat upon the throne said, Behold, I make all things new. And he said unto me, Write: for these words are true and faithful" (Revelation 21:5).

Focal Verses

KJV **Revelation 21:1** And I saw a new heaven and a new earth: for the first heaven and the first earth were passed away; and there was no more sea.

2 And I John saw the holy city, new Jerusalem, coming down from God out of heaven, prepared as a bride adorned for her husband.

3 And I heard a great voice out of heaven saying, Behold, the tabernacle of God is with men, and he will dwell with them, and they shall be his people, and God himself shall be with them, and be their God.

4 And God shall wipe away all tears from their eyes; and there shall be no more death, neither sorrow, nor crying, neither shall there be any more pain: for the former things are passed away.

5 And he that sat upon the throne said, Behold, I make all things new. And he said unto me, Write: for these words are true and faithful.

6 And he said unto me, It is done. I am Alpha and Omega, the beginning and the end. I will give unto him that is athirst of the fountain of the water of life freely.

7 He that overcometh shall inherit all things; and I will be his God, and he shall be my son.

8 But the fearful, and unbelieving, and the abominable, and murderers, and whoremongers, and sorcerers, and idolaters, and all liars, shall have their part in the lake which burneth with fire and brimstone: which is the second death.

NLT **Revelation 21:1** Then I saw a new heaven and a new earth, for the old heaven and the old earth had disappeared. And the sea was also gone.

2 And I saw the holy city, the new Jerusalem, coming down from God out of heaven like a bride beautifully dressed for her husband.

3 I heard a loud shout from the throne, saying, "Look, God's home is now among his people! He will live with them, and they will be his people. God himself will be with them.

4 He will wipe every tear from their eyes, and there will be no more death or sorrow or crying or pain. All these things are gone forever."

5 And the one sitting on the throne said, "Look, I am making everything new!" And then he said to me, "Write this down, for what I tell you is trustworthy and true."

6 And he also said, "It is finished! I am the Alpha and the Omega—the Beginning and the End. To all who are thirsty I will give freely from the springs of the water of life.

7 All who are victorious will inherit all these blessings, and I will be their God, and they will be my children.

8 But cowards, unbelievers, the corrupt, murders, the immoral, those who practice witchcraft, idol worshipers, and all liars—their fate is in the fiery lake of burning sulfur. This is the second death."

The People, Places, and Times

New Jerusalem. The Israelites of old, along with all of God's people down through the ages, longed for the coming time when we will live in complete, eternal peace. The New Jerusalem spoken of in Revelation 21:1–2 was predicted in Isaiah 65:17; 66:22. When speaking of a city, we are speaking of not only the physical infrastructure, but also the people who dwell in that city. In this sense, the new Holy City of Jerusalem is symbolic of the church as the redeemed Bride of Christ.

Devout Jews prayed regularly for the restoration of Jerusalem. Eventually, the idea of "New Jerusalem" came to symbolize hope for the Jewish nation. This new city would be a place built by God, where the righteous would dwell with Him in perfect peace forever.

Alpha and Omega. Alpha and omega are, respectively, the first and last letters in the Greek alphabet. By referring to Himself as "the Alpha and Omega," God the Father is making it clear that He is the source of everything. He is the Beginning and the End; He is sovereign, reigning over every aspect of His creation. In Revelation 21:6, Jesus calls Himself "the Alpha and Omega."

Lake of Fire. The "fiery lake of burning sulfur" (Revelation 21:8, NIV) that John refers to is what has become known to us today as "hell." In biblical times, there was an actual pagan worship site called "gehenna," located in a deep valley south of Jerusalem. Cultic practices, including human sacrifice to the god Molech, were conducted at this site. This site eventually "became a sort of perpetually burning city dump and later a figure for the place of final punishment" (*NIV Study Bible*, 1446).

Background

The book of Revelation records four visions of John. The first vision, recorded in 1:12–3:22, is of Jesus and His message to the seven churches. The second vision (4:1–13:18) depicts Jesus Christ at the Throne of God, the opening of the seven seals, and the seven trumpet blasts. The third vision (14:1–16:21) describes Christ on Mount Zion. Our lesson today opens with the beginning of the fourth vision, in which we will learn about the ultimate fulfillment of God's promise in Christ—the Holy City, the New Jerusalem.

At-A-Glance

1. The Presentation (Revelation 21:1–2)

2. The Proclamation (vv. 3–4)

3. The Promises (vv. 5–8)

In Depth

1. The Presentation (Revelation 21:1–2)

Genesis 1 gives us the account of the creation of the world. God divided the light from the darkness and the land from the seas. He created fish, birds, plants, animals and then He created humans. In Revelation 21, God reveals His creativity by first presenting the church, the Body of Christ, as the "Bride." He then goes on to describe the place where the Bride will dwell—a new heaven and new earth. The old world, with all of its problems, will have passed away.

The new heaven and the new earth will be a fitting place for the Bride, the redeemed of the Lord, to dwell. The prophet Joel describes the new city: "In that day the mountains will drip new wine, and the hills will flow with milk; all the ravines of Judah will run with water. A fountain will flow out of the LORD's house and will water the valley of acacias" (Joel 3:18, NIV). This sounds like a description of the Garden of Eden, painting a picture of abundance and beauty for those who made it through the trials and tribulations of the old world.

Those who are believers have received new life. We have been charged to walk in newness of life through the power of the Holy Spirit. We are to put aside our old ways of thinking, speaking, and living in order to fulfill God's plan for us. We must live with the goal of showing others the way to the new city of God.

2. The Proclamation (vv. 3–4)

In the Garden of Eden, God came down and physically fellowshipped with Adam and Eve. They walked with Him and conversed with Him on a regular basis. But sin destroyed this fellowship. Now in verse 3, after presenting the New Jerusalem, God joyfully proclaims His intention to dwell with His people in the new city. Verses 3 and 4 are a sort of chant summarizing the blessings that the Holy City's inhabitants will enjoy. Verse 3 restates Ezekiel 37:27, where God promises to one day dwell with His people in the fullest sense of the word.

Here on the earth our sense of God's presence is often dimmed, interrupted, or obscured. God dwells with us through the Holy Spirit, and we perceive Him by faith. But in the Holy City, we will live in the full measure of God's physical presence. We will no longer accept His presence by faith alone. We will truly be with Him! What a glorious thought! When we are struggling through life here on earth, we can rejoice in the hope that one day we will live with our loving Creator, never to be parted from Him again.

In Scripture, the idea of God dwelling with His people and being their God is covenant language. God is saying that we will be His people in the fullest sense of the word. While on earth, we enjoy some of the blessings of being children of God: salvation, peace, joy, wisdom, and others. But when the New Jerusalem arrives, we will fully be His people and He will be our God, and we will dwell together. The sense here is of a prospective bride and groom who have been longing to consummate their marriage, to belong exclusively to one another, to have the right and the opportunity to live in each other's presence forever. God is exulting over His plan that has finally brought His redeemed, His beloved, to His side, never to be parted from her again.

Perfect peace and joy result from God's eternal presence with His people. In God's perfect presence, there will be no more sorrow, no more pain, and no more suffering for all eternity. Verse 4 echoes Revelation 7:17; both verses promise that God Himself will tenderly care for His people, as a bridegroom cares for his bride. He will dry our tears and comfort us with the fact that the old has passed away. All is new. Never again will we experience the trials and tribulations of the old world.

3. The Promises (vv. 5–8)

God, seated on His throne, directs John to write down His words to reiterate that He meant what He said. God says, "I am making everything new!" (v. 5, NIV). He means it! And He is doing it now! The present tense of the verb "to be" assures us that God is even now working on our behalf, transforming us into the image of His dear Son (2 Corinthians 3:18) and readying us for the day when we will be completely new. We can rest assured that "he who began a good work in us will carry it on to completion until the day of Christ Jesus" (Philippians 1:6, NIV).

God pronounces that His own words are "true and faithful" (Revelation 21:5), and then adds, "It is done" (v. 6). God always finishes what He has begun. In the same sense that Jesus spoke the words "It is finished" (John

19:30) as He drew His last breaths on the Cross, God is announcing that His plan is accomplished. Our sovereign God, the Alpha and the Omega, is the beginning and end of all things (Revelation 21:6). He began everything by His will, and He will bring His plan to fruition according to His will and for His glory.

This coming age, when we will see God's promises once and for all, is portrayed in Scripture as flowing with abundant water (Isaiah 35:1–2; Ezekiel 47:1–12). For Middle Eastern people living in the desert, water was often a scarce and valuable commodity. This promise of plenteous water therefore symbolized life and prosperity. God promises that His people will be able to drink freely "from the spring of the water of life" (Revelation 21:6, NIV).

Many people today do not lack physical water with which to quench their thirst, but they do lack what they need to quench their spiritual thirst. God created every human being to have a desire for his or her Creator. As believers, we are compelled to hold out the promise of living water to unbelievers, as Jesus did with the woman at the well (John 4:10). But even though we serve and love God here on earth, our thirst to know Him and to dwell in His presence is never fully quenched. Only when we reach that New City will our thirst for God be replaced with His eternal presence.

Only those who overcome, who fight the good fight of faith, will be able to enter the Holy City. But for those who do, the rewards are immense. We will belong to God as His children for all eternity (Revelation 21:7). We are His heirs, entitled to all of the benefits of a son or daughter.

Those who rejected God in this world will experience a "second death" (v. 8). The first death is, of course, physical death here on earth. The second death is an eternal dying—a perpetual burning in hell, the lake of fire. Instead of dwelling with God, these people will be eternally separated from Him.

Search the Scriptures

1. What physical aspect of the New Jerusalem will be different from today's world (Revelation 21:1)?

2. To what was the Holy City compared (v. 2)?

Discuss the Meaning

1. What is the significance of the symbolism of New Jerusalem appearing as a bride?

2. Why did God want John to write down His words?

Lesson in Our Society

What would it be like to be able to begin anew? People today are always longing for a fresh start—a new diet, a new job, a new house, a new school, a new marriage, etc. Some will take drastic measures to try to change their lives for the better.

As Christians, we know that God offers the ultimate new beginning, which is salvation through Jesus Christ.

Make It Happen

Remember that God's promises are sure. You can count on Him to keep every promise. As you live your life of faithfulness before God, you can be assured that He will complete what He started in you.

Others need to know this assurance as well. But people need to know they are sinners before they can recognize their thirst for what it is: a need for relationship with God. This week, pray for your unsaved loved ones and acquaintances. Pray that God will reveal to them their need for salvation. Pray that God will give you opportunities and wisdom to share the Good News of a true new beginning.

Follow the Spirit

What God wants me to do:

_____

_____

_____

_____

Remember Your Thoughts

Special insights I have learned:

_____

_____

_____

_____

More Light on the Text

Revelation 21:1–8

1 And I saw a new heaven and a new earth: for the first heaven and the first earth were passed away; and there was no more sea.

Revelation 21 and 22 present us with the Bible's longest and best portrait of what people commonly call "heaven," although we notice that "a new heaven and a new earth" comes "down from God out of heaven" (21:1–2). Isaiah 65:17 also predicted "new heavens and a new earth."

Second Peter 3:10 also reveals a cosmic changeover or a total transformation. It describes a time when the current "heavens [or atmosphere] shall pass away" and "the earth...shall be burned up." Second Peter 3:12 amplifies: "the [present] heavens being on fire shall be dissolved." We see a different angle in Romans 8:21 (NIV): "Creation itself will be liberated from its bondage to decay and brought into the glorious freedom of the children of God." The strong language in 2 Peter indicates the magnitude of this renewal, while Romans indicates the continuity with the original creation even as it finally becomes what God always intended. Therefore, Christians await "new heavens and a new earth" (2 Peter 3:13).

2 And I John saw the holy city, new Jerusalem, coming down from God out of heaven, prepared as a bride adorned for her husband.

"The holy city, new Jerusalem" is also referred to in Galatians 4:26 and Hebrews 12:22. Hebrews 12:22 refers to the "city of the living God," and verse 23 refers to the "general assembly and church." Similar word pictures occur in Revelation 21:2: "the holy city" and the church as Christ's "bride" (compare 2 Corinthians 11:2; Ephesians 5:25–27; Revelation 19:7–8). Just as the groom wants to be with the bride, so Christ wants His church to be with Him.

The word "adorned" (v. 2) in Greek is *kosmeo* (**kos-MEH-o**). This verb comes from the noun *kosmos* (**KOS-mos**), which is the Greek word for "the ordered world" and also means "ornament." From this Greek word, we get our word "cosmetics."

3 And I heard a great voice out of heaven saying, Behold, the tabernacle of God is with men, and he will dwell with them, and they shall be his people, and God himself shall be with them, and be their God.

In Old Testament times, God localized and centralized His presence with His people at the tabernacle (Leviticus 26:11–13; Ezekiel 37:27). In New Testament times, God came in the form of a man, and He "dwelt among us" (John 1:14). The word "dwell" occurs in both in Revelation 7:15 and 21:3. In Greek, "dwell" is *skenoo* (pronounced **skay-NO-o**).

4 And God shall wipe away all tears from their eyes; and there shall be no more death, neither sorrow, nor crying, neither shall

there be any more pain: for the former things are passed away. **5 And he that sat upon the throne said, Behold, I make all things new. And he said unto me, Write: for these words are true and faithful.**

God speaks directly at the beginning (1:8) and at the end (21:5) of the book of Revelation. Each of those who receives Christ in this life is already "a new creation" (2 Corinthians 5:17, NIV), but we live in a sinful world (Romans 8:19–22) until the time that it will become new.

6 And he said unto me, It is done. I am Alpha and Omega, the beginning and the end. I will give unto him that is athirst of the fountain of the water of life freely.

Just as Jesus said "It is finished" when His work which provided our salvation was complete (John 19:30), so also God will announce "It is done" at the end of human history (Revelation 21:6). Here, Christ is called the "Alpha and Omega." Alpha and omega are the first and last letters of the Greek alphabet. The author explains this first phrase by adding that Jesus is "the beginning and the end."

The One who once offered a woman at a well "living water" (John 4:10) and said that "living water" could spring up inside of His people (John 7:37–38; cf. Zechariah 14:8) promises in Revelation to give unto those who thirst of "the fountain of the water of life freely." This is similar to the invitation given in Isaiah 55:1.

7 He that overcometh shall inherit all things; and I will be his God, and he shall be my son.

In Greek, the word for "overcometh" is *nikao* (**nik-AH-o**). It is also found in 1 John 5:4–5, as well as throughout Revelation 2 and 3. A Christian is intended to be a world-conqueror, to hold fast to the belief that faith in Christ conquers temptations and persecutions.

Not only does God "make all things new" (21:5), but the Christian overcomer "shall inherit all things" (21:7). First Corinthians 3:21 announces to the Christian that "All things are yours."

8 But the fearful, and unbelieving, and the abominable, and murderers, and whoremongers, and sorcerers, and idolaters, and all liars, shall have their part in the lake which burneth with fire and brimstone: which is the second death.

This last very sobering verse tells us that not all will be overcomers. Not all are true followers of Jesus; those who are not will face eternal judgment. The Greek for "fearful" is *deilos* (**di-LOS**), which means "timid" or "cowardly," but also implies faithless. If we consider the context of persecution under Rome, it helps us see that John was thinking of those who were too afraid to stand for Christ. During the time of trial, they were ashamed to say whose they were and whom they served. This word is not talking about the feeling of fear. Many exhibit true courage when they persevere in doing right even when they are very much afraid. What is condemned is letting fear keep us from standing up for our Lord.

Unbelievers are found in many places, even in the church. These are those who have not put their trust in Jesus Christ as their Savior. Verses like this one compel us to tell others how to be saved. Hell is real. If we truly care about others, if we truly believe the truth of God's Word, we must share the Gospel, even with the dire warnings.

The "abominable" are those who have allowed themselves to be saturated with the sinfulness of this world. Decadent ways of living were common in the days of the Roman Empire in which John lived, and who can deny the decadence of our world today? It's so easy to be polluted by the things that flash across our computer screens, by the celebrated lives of rap stars, by news, gossip, and entertainment offered night and day by mass media, and so on. We must make a concerted effort to keep our thoughts, our values, our words, and our actions clean before God.

Then we come to "murderers" (v. 8). John may have been thinking of those who persecuted Christians unto their deaths, but before we clear ourselves, we should remember that Jesus said, "Anyone who says, 'You fool!' will be in danger of the fire of hell" (Matthew 5:22, NIV). We may congratulate ourselves because we never use the word "murderer" to describe ourselves, but think of the times we may have muttered, "You idiot!" under our breaths to the driver who just cut us off in traffic. Isn't this just the same?

"Whoremongers" (Revelation 21:8) are fornicators, those who have sexual relations outside of marriage. In our culture, it is very common for unmarried couples to live together, but it is definitely against God's Word. The next to be thrown into the lake of fire are the "sorcerers, idolaters." This describes the worship of anything other than the one true God, and most often some aspect of God's creation, from other human beings to superstitions to various material objects. Although we may not be in a context with idol worship as in Bible days, making material goods come before God is very common. This is a case in which we need to examine our hearts to see where our priorities are. The last in the list are the "liars." Included in this title are those who are insincere, those who lie by their silence, or those who practice any other kind of untruth. But this is probably especially directed at those who claim to follow Christ but actually do not.

As we examine this list and ourselves, chances are that most of us know that we are guilty of some of these sins. If so, we need to repent and ask for God's forgiveness as well as for God's power through the Holy Spirit to make a more thorough progress in the path of sanctification. The point of this text is not that we earn salvation by works, but it does point out our responsibility for obedience and perseverance in the Christian life. God's Word gives us assurance that Christ's work saves us, but we are always commanded to live as those who are actively following Christ. If we do so, we can live in confident assurance that we will not be cast into the lake of fire at the last judgment.

Say It Correctly

Gehenna. gih-HIN-uh.
Molech. MOH-lek.

Daily Bible Readings

M: God Will Do a New Thing
Isaiah 43:15–21

T: A New Commandment
John 13:31–35

W: A New Covenant
Luke 22:14–23

T: A New Way of Life
Ephesians 4:17–24

F: A New Jerusalem
Revelation 21:9–14

S: A New Light
Revelation 21:22–27

S: A New Heaven and New Earth
Revelation 21:1–8

Teaching Tips

1. Words You Should Know

A. Pure (Revelation 22:1) *katharos* (Gk.)—Sincere, genuine, blameless, unstained.

B. Curse (v. 3) *katanathema* (Gk.)—Sin which pollutes our world today.

C. Reign (v. 5) *basileuo* (Gk.)—Refers to the rule of the Messiah.

2. Teacher Preparation

Unifying Principle—Appreciating Abundance. The Revelation to John made it clear that there is no more appropriate response to what God has done than to worship God.

A. Pray and ask God to give lesson clarity.

B. Prayerfully study the entire lesson.

C. Reflect on how our lives are blessed by God with abundance and be prepared to share with the class.

D. Reflect on the life to come—the "Tree of Life." Prepare to discuss.

3. Open the Lesson

A. Open with prayer, including the Aim for Change.

B. Ask, "Can you identify ways God has blessed our lives with abundance?" Discuss.

C. Contrast Cynthia's and Jennifer's lives in the In Focus story, stressing their blessings.

4. Present the Scriptures

A. Have volunteers read the Focal Verses.

B. Have the class count off from 1–3 and then form three groups.

C. After they choose spokespeople, assign The People, Places, and Times to the first group, Background to the second, and Search the Scriptures to the third, and have them present their findings to the whole class.

D. Explain the Focal Verses using the At-A-Glance outline, In Depth, and More Light on the Text.

5. Explore the Meaning

A. Lead a discussion of the Discuss the Meaning, Lesson in Our Society, and Make It Happen sections.

B. Have volunteers connect these sections to the Aim for Change and the Keep in Mind verse.

6. Next Steps for Application

A. Challenge your students to thank God for His abundant blessings.

B. Close with prayer.

Worship Guide

For the Superintendent or Teacher
Theme: Tree of Life
Theme Song: "Thank You, Lord"
Devotional Reading: Ephesians 3:14–21
Prayer

Tree of Life

Bible Background • REVELATION 22
Printed Text • REVELATION 22:1–9 | **Devotional Reading • EPHESIANS 3:14–21**

Aim for Change

By the end of the lesson, we will: IDENTIFY ways God has blessed our lives with abundance; APPRECIATE the abundance that God has provided in our lives; and CREATE a prayer in praise of God as Jehovah Jireh (our Provider).

In Focus

Cynthia woke up to the sunlight pouring through her bedroom window. She smiled at her still-sleeping husband, Frank. She was looking forward to the surprise she had in store for him. After four long years, Frank was finally graduating from medical school. He already had a lucrative job offer, and they had just signed a contract on a new home. The children would even be able to attend the Christian school! The whole family was coming over tonight for a surprise graduation party. Even Frank's elderly parents were able to come and celebrate this moment with their son.

However, Jennifer sighed as she peered into her refrigerator. Not many groceries left to last until next week's paycheck. And the car payment was due in a couple of days. She really hoped Bob got that sales job for which he was applying. They could sure use the money! But God would see them through—He always did.

Today's lesson speaks of the abundance that God offers to those who are called by His name— He has prepared a place for them. But in the meantime, we would do well to recognize the abundance in our lives in the here and now. Compared to Cynthia, does Jennifer still have abundance?

Keep in Mind

"In the midst of the street of it, and on either side of the river, was there the tree of life, which bare twelve manner of fruits, and yielded her fruit every month: and the leaves of the tree were for the healing of the nations" (Revelation 22:2).

MAY 29th

"In the midst of the street of it, and on either side of the river, was there the tree of life, which bare twelve manner of fruits, and yielded her fruit every month; and the leaves of the tree were for the healing of the nations"

Focal Verses

KJV **Revelation 22:1** And he shewed me a pure river of water of life, clear as crystal, proceeding out of the throne of God and of the Lamb.

2 In the midst of the street of it, and on either side of the river, was there the tree of life, which bare twelve manner of fruits, and yielded her fruit every month: and the leaves of the tree were for the healing of the nations.

3 And there shall be no more curse: but the throne of God and of the Lamb shall be in it; and his servants shall serve him:

4 And they shall see his face; and his name shall be in their foreheads.

5 And there shall be no night there; and they need no candle, neither light of the sun; for the Lord God giveth them light: and they shall reign for ever and ever.

6 And he said unto me, These sayings are faithful and true: and the Lord God of the holy prophets sent his angel to shew unto his servants the things which must shortly be done.

7 Behold, I come quickly: blessed is he that keepeth the sayings of the prophecy of this book.

8 And I John saw these things, and heard them. And when I had heard and seen, I fell down to worship before the feet of the angel which shewed me these things.

9 Then saith he unto me, See thou do it not: for I am thy fellowservant, and of thy brethren the prophets, and of them which keep the sayings of this book: worship God.

NLT **Revelation 22:1** Then the angel showed me a river with the water of life, clear as crystal, flowing from the throne of God and of the Lamb.

2 It flowed down the center of the main street. On each side of the river grew a tree of life, bearing twelve crops of fruit, with a fresh crop each month. The leaves were used for medicine to heal the nations.

3 No longer will there be a curse upon anything. For the throne of God and of the Lamb will be there, and his servants will worship him.

4 And they will see his face, and his name will be written on their foreheads.

5 And there will be no night there—no need for lamps or sun—for the Lord God will shine on them. And they will reign forever and ever.

6 Then the angel said to me, "Everything you have heard and seen is trustworthy and true. The Lord God, who inspires his prophets, has sent his angel to tell his servants what will happen soon."

7 "Look, I am coming soon! Blessed are those who obey the words of prophecy written in this book."

8 I, John, am the one who heard and saw all these things. And when I heard and saw them, I fell down to worship at the feet of the angel who showed them to me.

9 But he said, "No, don't worship me. I am a servant of God, just like you and your brothers the prophets, as well as all who obey what is written in this book. Worship only God!"

The People, Places, and Times

Tree of Life. The tree of life was depicted in Genesis as being at the center of the Garden of Eden. After Adam and Eve sinned, humanity was not allowed access to the tree (Genesis 3). The term "tree of life" in Revelation 22 is used collectively to include a number of trees growing alongside the crystal river in the New Jerusalem.

The Celestial River. Alternate names for the celestial river (Revelation 22:1) are "water of life" or "crystal sea." This river, the water of life, flows from the throne of God, and then it joins with three other channels that will come together to form one river in the New Jerusalem. According to Arrington and Stronstad, "the last time four rivers intersected on earth was in Eden, where a river flowed out of Eden to water the garden, and there it divided and became four rivers" (*Full Life Bible Commentary*, 1624). These four rivers are named in the Bible as the Pishon, the Gihon, the Tigris, and the Euphrates (Genesis 2:11–14).

Background

Revelation 22 further describes the features of the Holy City, continuing the description from Revelation 21 and ending with a promise from Jesus Christ: "I am coming soon" (v. 20, NIV). It is interesting to note that John's visions recorded in the book of Revelation are not completely new ideas, but rather, the visions serve to fulfill and confirm prophecies of old. Jewish readers would have instantly understood the references to these prophecies found in the Old Testament books of Ezekiel, Daniel, Isaiah, Zechariah, and others. The book of Revelation was written to encourage all of the believers down through the ages to live out their faith boldly and energetically, remembering that ultimately we will receive our reward if we are faithful to the end.

At-A-Glance

1. The City of Abundance (Revelation 22:1–5)

2. The King Is Coming (vv. 6–9)

In Depth

1. The City of Abundance (Revelation 22:1–5)

John's angel-guided tour of the New Jerusalem is continued from Revelation 21 as the angel showed John the "pure river of water of life, clear as crystal" (22:1). In the desert-parched lands of the Middle East, having enough or more than enough water was the ultimate blessing. God's people of old were dependent upon Him to provide the water needed for their very sustenance. Water was a precious commodity, needed for people, livestock, crops, and even ceremonial cleansing. Unless God provided enough water, the people were destitute.

In the Holy City, the celestial river flows out from God's throne, bringing abundant life to all in the city. This living water represented the precious and generous outpouring of God's provision for His beloved people—physical life, health, peace, salvation. All is provided for in the streams of living water. Ezekiel 47:1–12 tells us that the river expands as it flows, eventually becoming a wide, rushing river too vast to cross, containing all kinds of fish and water-dwelling creatures. This incredible river flows down the middle of the City, bringing life-giving moisture to the trees of life lining its banks.

The trees of life have a unique feature: instead of bearing one crop per year, as we are used to here on earth, these trees bear a new crop every month! "Their leaves will not wither, nor will their fruit fail. Every month they will bear, because the water from the sanctuary flows to them" (Ezekiel 47:12, NIV). The living water of the river is an extension of God's healing and nurturing power. He is the Sustainer of life itself! He causes the trees of life to bear fruit that will provide food for the hungry and healing for the sick—all we need, we find in Him (Revelation 22:2)!

Not only will the inhabitants of the New Jerusalem enjoy the abundant, healing fruit of the trees of life, we will no longer live under the curse of sin (v. 3). Hallelujah! No more will we need to don the full armor of God, because Jesus, the Conqueror, will have vanquished our enemy once and for all! The curse of sin that entered the world through the first Adam has been reversed by the second Adam, our Lord and Savior, Jesus Christ. We will have rest from the fight; we will live in complete peace, unlike anything we can know on this earth.

In the Holy City, God will provide everything—even light! Verse 5 tells us that there will be no more night, nor will we need lamps or even the sun, because He is the light. As we live on this earth, we often speak of God figuratively as the "light." But in New Jerusalem, we will live in the actual, physical light of God's presence. We will reign forever with Jesus, secure in His life-giving, tangible presence.

2. The King Is Coming (vv. 6–9)

Verse 6 marks the beginning of the conclusion of the book of Revelation. The angel affirms to John that the visions he had seen and the words he had heard were "faithful and true" and, therefore, were trustworthy. The angel also called God the "Lord God of the holy prophets"

and reminded John that God was not only making new promises, He was also fulfilling the promises He had made throughout the ages. Our God is the God of the past, present, and future! God sent the angel to show God's servants—everyone living in the Holy City—that which would soon take place.

Jesus Himself promises in verse 7 that He is "coming soon" (NIV). This is a promise to cling to! When life gets difficult, remember that Jesus is coming for His bride, the church. He will not leave us hopeless and abandoned. He *is* coming back—that's a promise we can count on! While we are waiting for Him, however, we need to keep the faith. Jesus is coming back only for those who are His followers, only those who obey His words. Jesus promises, "Blessed is he that keepeth the sayings of the prophecy of this book" (v. 7). This "beatitude" is to be taken very seriously. In the following verses of Revelation 22, God issues a stern warning to those who would try to detract from, add to, or otherwise change the revelations which He gave John. The consequences for disobeying this command are severe (vv. 18–19).

Conversely, the rewards for obeying God's Word are innumerable—both now and in the Holy City. Surely one of the greatest blessings of all will be to dwell in His presence, looking upon His face for all eternity. Being surrounded by tens of thousands of the redeemed, all worshiping God in unison, will be a time unparalleled by any experience in our lives here on earth.

When John had heard and seen all of these visions, he was overcome. He fell down at the feet of the angel and began to worship (v. 8). The angel rebuked John (v. 9), reminding him that angels are created beings, just like humans. Only God is worthy to be worshiped.

In light of the book of Revelation, how should we live our lives? We should patiently wait for Jesus' return. We should not grow weary in doing well. We should eagerly anticipate the time when we will live in the Holy City. But in the meantime, we would do well to recognize the abundance in our lives in the here and now. God's Word says that Jesus has come to give us life, and more than just life—abundant life (John 10:10).

Abundant life here on earth is not about material possessions. God does often bless His people materially, but our greatest blessings are intangible—peace, joy, healing, forgiveness, salvation. The list is infinite. The Revelation to John made it clear that there is no more appropriate response to what God has done than to worship God.

Search the Scriptures

1. What was notable about the River of Life (Revelation 22:1–2)?

2. What was the purpose of the trees of life that were growing along the banks of the River of Life (v. 2)?

Discuss the Meaning

1. What significance does the tree of life hold for believers, both now and in the future?

2. Why is it important that God will put His name on our foreheads?

Lesson in Our Society

Our society is awash in materialism. Everywhere we look, we see people crying out for more—more money, more food, more toys, more education. People are never satisfied with enough. Even believers sometimes get caught up in wanting more things.

God loves His children, and He often blesses us materially. However, He is more concerned about our spiritual condition than He is about our economic status. It is His will that every single human being receive the gift of salvation.

Make It Happen

What are some of the blessings God has graciously given to you? Pray that God would give you insight to see your life and your circumstances through His eyes. Worship Him for His blessings in your life.

Follow the Spirit

What God wants me to do:

_____

_____

_____

_____

Remember Your Thoughts

Special insights I have learned:

_____

_____

_____

_____

More Light on the Text

Revelation 22:1–9

1 And he shewed me a pure river of water of life, clear as crystal, proceeding out of the throne of God and of the Lamb.

The context of the last chapter of the last book of Scripture brings to a close human history. Like ultimate bookends of humankind's inimitable story, our beginning and our end are contrasted and compared by authors Moses and John. In Genesis, the serpent tempts the first Adam, he falls, and Paradise is lost. In Revelation, the serpent is destroyed, the second Adam is victorious, and Paradise is regained and fulfilled. The significant elements of the garden Paradise were two people, the tree of life, and a river that watered the garden (Genesis 2:9–10). In the New Jerusalem, the fountain of life flows from the throne of God (Revelation 22:1–2; 4:6), and lining both sides of the river are many trees of life (22:14) that are not only freely accessible but ever fruitful for the enjoyment and healing of many nations (Psalm 46:4, Revelation 22:2). In Eden, one tree was forbidden; in the Holy City, nothing is forbidden.

2 In the midst of the street of it, and on either side of the river, was there the tree of life, which bare twelve manner of fruits, and yielded her fruit every month: and the leaves of the tree were for the healing of the nations.

The picture here is that of Main Street in New Jerusalem (see v. 2, NLT), which becomes a river of life. Ezekiel pictured many fruit trees (Ezekiel 47:12), but here we have just one kind of fruit tree—the tree of life. After the Fall, the fruit from the tree of life was forbidden. This was God's gracious provision. After Adam and Eve had eaten the fruit of the tree of the knowledge of good and evil, they became infected with sin; human nature became tainted. If they had been allowed to eat of the tree of life, they would have been condemned to live forever in such a state. But in the heavenly Jerusalem, there will be no more sin. Not only will our sins be forgiven, but the presence of sin of any kind will be gone forever. Now it's time to eat the fruit of the tree of everlasting life.

What a wonderful tree this is! It has a variety of kinds of fruit, it continues giving fruit all 12 months of the year, and the leaves heal the nations. The river of life reminds us of the Holy Spirit, and so does this tree. Just as the tree has a variety of fruit, so we read of the variety of fruit that the Holy Spirit gives to believers (Galatians 5:22–23). And perhaps the picture of fruit for all 12 months of the year symbolizes how God gives us special gifts and grace for each season of life, from youth to old age (Barclay, 222). The healing in the leaves which applies to all nations reminds us that the Holy Spirit gives His gifts to people from every tribe and nation.

3 And there shall be no more curse: but the throne of God and of the Lamb shall be in it; and his servants shall serve him:

The Greek for "curse" is *katanathema* (**kat-an-ATH-em-ah**). The root of this word is *anathema* (**an-ATH-em-ah**), which is the same in English, and it means "accursed." In God's holy city, there will be none of the sin which pollutes our world today; there will be nothing that will cause us to stumble in our Christian walk. We will finally be able to serve our Lord God with nothing to block us from a purity of life. This is an undoing of the curse that was put upon all humankind and the entire earth in Genesis 3:14–19.

Once more, we are reminded of the fact that God the Father and Jesus the Lamb are in the throne. When we think of a throne, we think "on," not "in." "Throne" does not always refer to an elaborate seat upon which a king or queen sits. It can refer to a position of dominion or authority (*Oxford Universal Dictionary*). Because God is in the throne, He is in His position of sovereign power over all, and we as His subjects are in the position of serving Him in continual worship.

4 And they shall see his face; and his name shall be in their foreheads.

Paul said, "For now we see through a glass, darkly; but then face to face: now I know in part; but then shall I know even as also I am known" (1 Corinthians 13:12). We also read the promise of Jesus in the Beatitudes, "Blessed are the pure in heart: for they shall see God" (Matthew 5:8). Think about this— even Moses was told that he could not look upon God's face because anyone who looked upon Him would die (Exodus 33:20, 23). But in Christ we will be able to look upon the Lord God Almighty. And when we look upon Him, we will finally be worshiping Him as He deserves.

We do not know what sort of divine mark will appear on our foreheads, but we know that God has already written our names on the palms of His hands (Isaiah 49:16). We can only imagine. Perhaps He has symbolically engraved a heart around our names and a cross will be engraved upon our foreheads.

5 And there shall be no night there; and they need no candle, neither light of the sun; for the Lord God giveth them light: and they shall reign for ever and ever.

When Paul saw the Lord Jesus on the road to Damascus, he saw a light that outshone the noonday sun and was so bright it blinded him (Acts 9:1–18). Even when we read John's description of the Lord God in the book of Revelation, it is always a bright, shining light so intense we wonder how he could bear to look. It is only by the blood of the Lamb that we will be able to look upon God's face. We will never need a candle or lamp of any kind because God's glory will light up all of heaven and earth.

6 And he said unto me, These sayings are faithful and true: and the Lord God of the holy prophets sent his angel to shew unto his servants the things which must shortly be done.

This is the third time the angel used the words "faithful and true," which also are applied directly to Christ (Revelation 3:14; 19:11). As Christ is faithful and true, so His words sent via prophets or angels are faithful and true.

The same "truth assurances" could be said for both the book of Revelation and the entirety of God's Word. The apparent redundancy here must indicate the special importance to the church of these particular words—even while underscoring that God always has, in the same trustworthy manner, revealed the future through His prophets. *The Living Bible* paraphrases this clause as "who tells his prophets what the future holds," explaining why the prophets of the past are linked to the current vision given to John.

7 Behold, I come quickly: blessed is he that keepeth the sayings of the prophecy of this book.

After reinforcing this element of surprise, the angel encourages believers but subtly implies that those who *don't* "keep the true sayings in this book" *won't* be "blessed" at Jesus' sudden appearance. In this Revelation beatitude, believers will be blessed, more likely ecstatic, as our time of vindication and the completion of our redemption will have come at long last. In stark contrast, one can imagine an almost deafening, collective "Oh, no!" coming from the entire unsaved world, as it simultaneously realizes both its folly not to have believed and its imminent, certain judgment.

It is important that each succeeding generation anticipate, prepare, watch, and be ready for Jesus' return. For those unfamiliar with the term, the Greek word *parousia* (**par-oo-SEE-ah**) means Christ's second coming (Matthew 24:3; 1 Thessalonians 2:19). Rather than just looking for a distant event, each generation in a sense has been running along the edge of the cliff, from the time of the apostles until now. Our sense of time must surrender to God's.

8 And I John saw these things, and heard them. And when I had heard and seen, I fell down to worship before the feet of the angel which shewed me these things. 9 Then saith he unto me, See thou do it not: for I am thy fellow servant, and of thy brethren the prophets, and of them which keep the sayings of this book: worship God.

For the second time, John tries to worship the angel, and again he is immediately rebuked. It is a natural human tendency to want to express gratitude and love to the bearer of good news. But to supersede gratitude and begin to worship any created being is sinning against God who alone is to be worshiped (Exodus 20:3; Deuteronomy 5:6; 6:13).

Say It Correctly

Euphrates. yoo-FRAY-teez.
Gihon. GI-hon.
Tigris. TI-gris.
Zechariah. zek'-uh-RI-uh

Daily Bible Readings

M: Bowing Before the Father
Ephesians 3:14–21

T: A Glimpse of God's Glory
Exodus 33:17–23

W: The Throne of God
Psalm 47:5–9

T: Living Water
John 4:7–15

F: The Tree of Life
Revelation 2:1–7

S: I Am Coming Soon
Revelation 22:10–21

S: Worship God!
Revelation 22:1–9

Notes

_____

_____

_____

_____

_____

Lesson 1, March 6

Baltes, A. J., ed. BibleSpeech.com. http://www.biblespeech.com (accessed September 11, 2009).

Brown, Raymond E. *An Introduction to the New Testament*. New York, NY: Doubleday, 1997.

Fee, Gordon D. *1 and 2 Timothy, Titus*. Peabody, MA: Hendrickson Publishers Inc., 2002. 7–10, 61–66, 78–95.

Merriam-Webster Online Dictionary. Merriam-Webster, Inc. http://www.merriam-webster.com (accessed September 11, 2009).

Mounce, William D. *Pastoral Epistles. Word Biblical Commentary*, Vol. 46. Nashville, TN: Thomas Nelson, 2000. 152–212.

Neill, Stephen and Tom Wright. *The Interpretation of the New Testament*. Oxford, England: Oxford University Press, 1988. 17–21, 27–41.

Quimby, Chester Warren. *Paul for Everyone*. New York, NY: Macmillan, 1946. 17–21, 27–41.

Strong, James. *New Exhaustive Strong's Numbers and Concordance with Expanded Greek-Hebrew Dictionary*. Seattle, WA: Biblesoft, and International Bible Translators, 1994. 2003.

"Tertullian." Christian History Institute. http://www.chitorch.org/index.php/eras/early-church/tertullian/ (accessed January 6, 2010).

Lesson 2, March 13

Bunyan, John. *Pilgrim's Progress*. Christian Classics Ethereal Library. http://www.ccel.org/ccel/bunyan/pilgrim.html (accessed January 7, 2010).

Collins, Raymond F. "Bishop." *The New Interpreter's Dictionary of the Bible*, Vol. 1. Katherine Doob Sakenfeld, gen. ed. Nashville, TN: Abingdon Press, 2006. 471–73.

Fee, Gordon D. *1 and 2 Timothy, Titus*. Peabody, MA: Hendrickson Publishers, Inc., 2002. 20–23, 78–90.

Merriam-Webster Online Dictionary. Merriam-Webster, Inc. http://www.merriam-webster.com (accessed October 23, 2009).

Mounce, William D. *Pastoral Epistles (Word Biblical Commentary*, Vol. 46). Nashville, TN: Thomas Nelson, 2000. 152–212.

Neill, Stephen and Tom Wright. *The Interpretation of the New Testament*. Oxford, England: Oxford University Press, 1988. 27–37.

Quimby, Chester Warren. *Paul for Everyone*. New York, NY: Macmillan, 1946. 27–37.

Strong, James. *New Exhaustive Strong's Numbers and Concordance with Expanded Greek-Hebrew Dictionary*. Seattle, WA: Biblesoft, and International Bible Translators, 1994. 2003.

Lesson 3, March 20

Baltes, A. J., ed. BibleSpeech.com. http://www.biblespeech.com (accessed October 20, 2009).

Bassler, Jouette M. *1 Timothy, 2 Timothy, Titus*. Nashville, TN: Abingdon, 1996.

Drury, Clare. "The Pastoral Epistles." *The Oxford Bible Commentary*. John Barton and John Muddiman, eds. New York, NY: Oxford University Press, 2001. 1226.

Fee, Gordon D. *1 and 2 Timothy, Titus*. Peabody, MA: Hendrickson Publishers, Inc., 2002. 102–09.

Merriam-Webster Online Dictionary. Merriam-Webster, Inc. http://www.merriam-webster.com (accessed October 20, 2009).

Mounce, William D. *Pastoral Epistles (Word Biblical Commentary*, Vol. 46). Nashville, TN: Thomas Nelson, 2000. 299–300.

Neill, Stephen and Tom Wright. *The Interpretation of the New Testament*. Oxford, England: Oxford University Press, 1988. 45–53.

Quimby, Chester Warren. *Paul for Everyone*. New York, NY: Macmillan, 1946. 45–53.

Sanders, Oswald. *Spiritual Leadership*. 2nd revised ed. Chicago, IL: Moody Press, 1994.

Strong, James. *New Exhaustive Strong's Numbers and Concordance with Expanded Greek-Hebrew Dictionary*. Seattle, WA: Biblesoft, and International Bible Translators, 1994. 2003.

Lesson 4, March 27

Baltes, A. J., ed., BibleSpeech.com. http://www.biblespeech.com (accessed October 15, 2009).

Clarke, Adam. *Clarke's Commentary: Matthew–Revelation*. Nashville, TN: Abingdon, 1977.

Fee, Gordon D. *1 and 2 Timothy, Titus*. Peabody, MA: Hendrickson Publishers, Inc., 2002. 89, 114–18, 127–32.

Gorman, Michael J. *Apostle of the Crucified Lord: A Theological Introduction to Paul & His Letters*. Grand Rapids, MI: Eerdmans, 2004. 563–65.

Merriam-Webster Online Dictionary. Merriam-Webster, Inc. http://www.merriam-webster.com (accessed October 15, 2009).

Mounce, William D. *Pastoral Epistles (Word Biblical Commentary*, Vol. 46). Nashville, TN: Thomas Nelson, 2000. 299–300.

Strong, James. *New Exhaustive Strong's Numbers and Concordance with Expanded Greek-Hebrew Dictionary*. Seattle, WA: Biblesoft, and International Bible Translators, 1994. 2003.

Thayer and Smith. "Greek Lexicon Entry for Diplous." *KJV New Testament Greek Lexicon*. Bible Study Tools.com. http://www.biblestudytools.com/lexicons/greek/kjv/diplous.html (accessed January 7, 2010).

Lesson 5, April 3

Baltes, A. J., ed. Bible Speech.com. http://www.biblespeech.com (accessed September 2, 2009).

Bauer, Walter. *A Greek-English Lexicon of the New Testament and Other Early Christian Literature*. Chicago, IL: University of Chicago Press, 1979.

Easton, Matthew G. "Paul." Christian Answers.net. http://www.christiananswers.net/dictionary/paul.html (accessed July 1, 2009).

Hanson, A. T. *The Pastoral Epistles (The New Century Bible Commentary)*. Grand Rapids, MI: Eerdmans, 1982.

Rochedieu, Charles. *Les Trésors du Nouveau Testament*. Saint-Légier, Switzerland: Éditions Emmaüs, 1979.

"Treasures of Rome: Saint Paul Outside the Walls." Earlychristians.org. http://www.earlychristians.org/treasures_rome/saint_paul_outside_walls.html (accessed July 1, 2009).

Strong, James. *New Exhaustive Strong's Numbers and Concordance with Expanded Greek-Hebrew Dictionary.* Seattle, WA: Biblesoft, and International Bible Translators, 1994. 2003.

Zodhiates, Spiros, exec. ed. *Hebrew Greek Key Word Study Bible* (King James Version). Second ed. Chattanooga, TN: AMG Publishers, 1991. 1494, 1502–04.

Lesson 6, April 10

Baltes, A. J. ed. BibleSpeech.com. http://www.biblespeech.com (accessed September 3, 2009).

Bauer, Walter. *A Greek-English Lexicon of the New Testament and Other Early Christian Literature.* Chicago, IL: University of Chicago Press, 1979.

Benetreau, Samuel. *La Deuxième Epître de Pierre et l'Epître de Jude.* Vaux-sur-Seine, France: Edifac, 1994.

Knight, George. *Know Your Bible: All 66 Books Explained and Applied.* Uhrichville, OH: Barbour Publishing, 2008. 93.

Rochedieu, Charles. *Les Trésors du Nouveau Testament.* Saint-Légier, Switzerland: Éditions Emmaüs, 1972.

Sidebottom, E. M. "James, Jude, 2 Peter." *The New Century Bible Commentary.* Grand Rapids, MI: Eerdmans, 1982.

Strong, James. *New Exhaustive Strong's Numbers and Concordance with Expanded Greek-Hebrew Dictionary.* Seattle, WA: Biblesoft, and International Bible Translators, 1994. 2003.

Zodhiates, Spiros, ed. *Hebrew Greek Key Word Study Bible* (King James Version). Second ed. Chattanooga, TN: AMG Publishers, 1991. 1556.

Lesson 7, April 17

Anderson, Hugh. "The Gospel of Mark." *The New Century Bible Commentary.* Grand Rapids, MI: Eerdmans, 1981.

Baltes, A. J., ed. Bible Speech.com. http://www.biblespeech.com (accessed September 11, 2009).

Bauer, Walter. *A Greek-English Lexicon of the New Testament and Other Early Christian Literature.* Chicago, IL: University of Chicago Press, 1979.

Johnson, Ashley S. *Condensed Biblical Encyclopedia.* http://www.biblestudytools.com/encyclopedias/condensed-biblical-encyclopedia/ (accessed July 10, 2009).

"History of Passover." Theholidayspot.com. http://www.theholidayspot.com/passover/history_of_passover.htm (accessed July 10, 2009).

Lane, William L. *"The Gospel According to Mark." The New International Commentary on the New Testament.* Grand Rapids, MI: Eerdmans, 1974.

Life Application Study Bible. Wheaton, IL: Tyndale House, 1996. 1508–9.

Easton, Matthew G. "Mount of Olives." Christiananswers.net. http://www.christiananswers.net/dictionary/olivesmountof.html (accessed July 10, 2009).

Smith, William. "Palm Tree." *Smith's Bible Dictionary. 1901.* http://www.biblestudytools.com/Dictionaries/SmithsBibleDictionary/smt.cgi?number=T3309 (accessed July 10, 2009).

Rochedieu, Charles. *Les Trésors du Nouveau Testament.* Saint-Légier, Switzerland: Éditions Emmaüs, 1979.

Strong, James. *New Exhaustive Strong's Numbers and Concordance with Expanded Greek-Hebrew Dictionary.* Seattle, WA: Biblesoft, and International Bible Translators, 1994. 2003.

Zodhiates, Spiros, ed. *Key Word Study Bible: Greek Dictionary of the New Testament* (KJV). Chattanooga TN.: AMG Publishers, 1991. 79.

Lesson 8, April 24

Baltes, A. J., ed. Biblespeech.com. http://www.biblespeech.com (accessed October 21, 2009).

Bauer, Walter. *A Greek-English Lexicon of the New Testament and Other Early Christian Literature.* Chicago, IL: University of Chicago Press, 1979.

France, Richard T. *L'Evangile de Mattieu Commentaire Evangélique de la Bible),* Vol. 2. Vaux-sur-Seine, France: Edifac, 2000.

Hill, David. "The Gospel of Matthew." *The New Century Bible Commentary.* Grand Rapids, MI: Eerdmans, 1981.

Life Application Bible (New International Version). Wheaton, IL: Tyndale House, 1991. 1719.

Merriam-Webster Online Dictionary. Merriam-Webster, Inc. http://www.merriam-webster.com (accessed October 21, 2009).

NIV Archaeological Study Bible: An Illustrated Walk through Biblical History and Culture. Grand Rapids, MI: Zondervan, 2006.

Rochedieu, Charles. *Les Trésors du Nouveau Testament.* Saint-Légier, Switzerland: Editions Emmaüs, 1972.

Strong, James. *New Exhaustive Strong's Numbers and Concordance with Expanded Greek-Hebrew Dictionary.* Seattle, WA: Biblesoft, and International Bible Translators, 1994. 2003.

Wright, Nicholas T. *The Resurrection of the Son of God (Christian Origins and the Question of God).* Minneapolis, MN: Augsburg Fortress Publishers, 2003.

Lesson 9, May 1

Baltes, A. J., ed. BibleSpeech.com. http://www.biblespeech.com (accessed October 22, 2009).

Barclay, William. *The Daily Study Bible: The Letters to the Philippians, Colossians, and Thessalonians.* Philadelphia, PA: Westminster Press, 1975. 31–40.

Easton, M. G. *Easton's Bible Dictionary.* Oak Harbor, WA: Logos Research Systems, 1996, c1897.

Fee, Gordon D. *Paul's Letter to the Philippians.* Grand Rapids, MI: Eerdmans, 1995. 174–230.

Lightfoot, Joseph Barber. *Saint Paul's Epistle to the Philippians.* Grand Rapids, MI: Zondervan, 1953. 107–15.

Merriam-Webster Online Dictionary. Merriam-Webster, Inc. http://www.merriam-webster.com (accessed October 22, 2009).

NIV Archaeological Study Bible: An Illustrated Walk through Biblical History and Culture. Grand Rapids, MI: Zondervan, 2006.

Strong, James. *New Exhaustive Strong's Numbers and Concordance with Expanded Greek-Hebrew Dictionary.* Seattle, WA: Biblesoft, and International Bible Translators, 1994. 2003.

Strong, James. *Strong's Exhaustive Concordance of the Bible.* Nashville: Thomas Nelson Publishers, 1990.

Torrey, R. A. "Christ Is God." *Torrey's New Topical Textbook.* Christian Classics Ethereal Library.http://www.ccel.org/ccel/torrey/ttt.html?term=Christ is God (accessed July 23, 2009).

Vincent, Marvin R. *Word Studies in the New Testament, Vol. III: The Epistles of Paul.* Grand Rapids, MI: Eerdmans, 1957. 428–37.

Witherington III, Ben. *Friendship and Finances in Philippi: The Letter of Paul to the Philippians.* Valley Forge, PA: Trinity Press International, 1994. 56–70.

Zondervan Handbook to the Bible. revised ed. Grand Rapids, MI: Zondervan, 2005.

Lesson 10, May 8

Baltes, A. J., ed. BibleSpeech.com. http://www.biblespeech.com (accessed October 23, 2009).

Barclay, William. *The Daily Study Bible: The Revelation of John,* Vol. 1. Philadelphia, PA: Westminster Press, 1976. 149–64.

Cox, Steven L. "Angel." *Holman Illustrated Bible Dictionary.* Trent C. Butler, gen. ed. Nashville, TN: Holman Bible Publishers, 2003. 66–67.

Merriam-Webster Online Dictionary. Merriam-Webster, Inc. http://www.merriam-webster.com (accessed October 23, 2009).

NIV Archaeological Study Bible: An Illustrated Walk through Biblical History and Culture. Grand Rapids, MI: Zondervan, 2006. 2043-49.

Philips, John. *Exploring Revelation.* Neptune, NJ: Loizeaux Brothers, 1991. 84–86.

Strong, James. *Strong's Exhaustive Concordance of the Bible.* Nashville, TN: Thomas Nelson Publishers, 1990.

Strong, James. *New Exhaustive Strong's Numbers and Concordance with Expanded Greek-Hebrew Dictionary.* Seattle, WA: Biblesoft, and International Bible Translators, 1994. 2003.

Zondervan Handbook to the Bible. Revised ed. Grand Rapids, MI: Zondervan, 2005.

Lesson 11, May 15

Arrington, French L. and Roger Stronstad, eds. *Full Life Bible Commentary to the New Testament.* Grand Rapids, MI: Zondervan, 1999. 1575–81.

Baltes, A. J., ed. BibleSpeech.com. http://www.biblespeech.com (accessed December 5, 2009).

Barclay, William. *The Daily Study Bible: The Revelation of John,* Vol. 1. Philadelphia, PA: Westminster Press, 1976. 152–54.

———. *The Daily Study Bible: The Revelation of John,* Vol. 2. Philadelphia, PA: Westminster Press, 1976. 25–39.

Merriam-Webster Online Dictionary. Merriam-Webster, Inc. http://www.merriam-webster.com (accessed December 5, 2009).

NIV Study Bible, Tenth Anniversary Edition. Grand Rapids, MI: Zondervan, 1995. 1930, 1933.

Philips, John. *Exploring Revelation.* Neptune, NJ: Loizeaux Brothers, 1991. 111–14.

Strong, James. *Strong's Exhaustive Concordance of the Bible.* Nashville, TN: Thomas Nelson Publishers, 1990.

Strong, James. *New Exhaustive Strong's Numbers and Concordance with Expanded Greek-Hebrew Dictionary.* Seattle, WA: Biblesoft, and International Bible Translators, 1994. 2003.

Lesson 12, May 22

Arrington, French L. and Roger Stronstad, eds. *Full Life Bible Commentary to the New Testament.* Grand Rapids, MI: Zondervan, 1999. 1546–48, 1620–21.

Baltes, A. J., ed., BibleSpeech.com. http://www.biblespeech.com (accessed October 12, 2009).

Barclay, William. *The Daily Study Bible: The Revelation of John,* Vol. 2. Philadelphia, PA: Westminster Press, 1960. 263–64.

Henry, Matthew. *Matthew Henry's Commentary in One Volume.* Grand Rapids, MI: Zondervan, 1961. 1984.

Keener, Craig S. *The IVP Bible Background Commentary: New Testament.* Downers Grove, IL: InterVarsity Press, 1993. 815–16.

Merriam-Webster Online Dictionary. Merriam-Webster, Inc. http://www.merriam-webster.com (accessed October 12, 2009).

Michaels, J. Ramsey. *Revelation, The IVP New Testament Commentary Series.* Grant R. Osborne, series ed. Downers Grove, IL: InterVarsity Press, 1997. 239–40.

NIV Study Bible, Tenth Anniversary Edition. Grand Rapids, MI: Zondervan, 1995. 1446, 1947.

Gill, John. "Revelation Chapter 21." *John Gill's Exposition of the Bible.* http://www.biblestudytools.com/commentaries/gills-exposition-of-the-bible/revelation-21/ (accessed June 14, 2009).

Philips, John. *Exploring Revelation.* Neptune, NJ: Loizeaux Brothers, 1991. 250.

Strong, James. *Strong's Exhaustive Concordance of the Bible.* Nashville, TN: Thomas Nelson Publishers, 1990.

Strong, James. *New Exhaustive Strong's Numbers and Concordance with Expanded Greek-Hebrew Dictionary.* Seattle, WA: Biblesoft, and International Bible Translators, 1994. 2003.

Lesson 13, May 29

Arrington, French L., and Roger Stronstad, eds. *Full Life Bible Commentary to the New Testament.* Grand Rapids, MI: Zondervan, 1999. 1624–25.

Baltes, A. J., ed. BibleSpeech.com. http://www.biblespeech.com (accessed October, 14, 2009).

Barclay, William. *The Daily Study Bible: The Revelation of John,* Vol. 2. Philadelphia, PA: Westminster Press, 1976. 220–24.

Keener, Craig S. *The IVP Bible Background Commentary: New Testament.* Downers Grove, IL: InterVarsity Press, 1993. 819–20.

Merriam-Webster Online Dictionary. Merriam-Webster, Inc. http://www.merriam-webster.com (accessed October 14, 2009).

Michaels, J. Ramsey. *Revelation. The IVP New Testament Commentary Series.* Grant R. Osborne, series ed. Downers Grove, IL: InterVarsity Press, 1997. 246–49.

NIV Study Bible, Tenth Anniversary Edition. Grand Rapids, MI: Zondervan, 1995. 925, 1444.

Oxford Universal Dictionary, The. Revised and edited by William Little. London: Oxford University Press, 1961.

Philips, John. *Exploring Revelation.* Neptune, NJ: Loizeaux Brothers, 1991. 256–58.

Ross, Hugh. *The Genesis Question.* Colorado Springs, CO: Navpress, 2001. 78–79.

Strong, James. *Strong's Exhaustive Concordance of the Bible.* Nashville, TN: Thomas Nelson Publishers, 1990.

Strong, James. *New Exhaustive Strong's Numbers and Concordance with Expanded Greek-Hebrew Dictionary.* Seattle, WA: Biblesoft, and International Bible Translators, 1994. 2003.

God Instructs the People of God

The study focuses on our relationship with God as a community of faith. The Old Testament books of Joshua, Judges, and Ruth form the backdrop for a study of what it means to live out the love of God in community.

UNIT 1 • GOD'S PEOPLE LEARN FROM PROSPERITY

These lessons examine Israel's early life as they prepare to enter the Promised Land. Selected texts from the book of Joshua highlight God's blessing in response to obedience and God's anger in response to disobedience.

Lesson 1: June 5, 2011
God's Promises Fulfilled
Joshua 1:1b-6; 11:16–19, 21–23
Following the death of Moses, Israel prepared to enter the Promised Land under Joshua's command.

Lesson 2: June 12, 2011
God Has Expectations
Joshua 1:7–16
As Israel prepared to enter the Promised Land, we learn that three tribes were suppose to fight alongside the others. However, after they helped their brothers subdue the land and defeat the inhabitants, they could return to live on the land east of the Jordan.

Lesson 3: June 19, 2011
God Protects
Joshua 2:3–9, 15–16, 22–24
The conquest of the Promised Land involved complete trust in carrying out God's plans. The news of God's victories preceded the arrival of the Israelite spies into Jericho. Rahab deceived the King of Jericho by covering for the Israelite spies.

Lesson 4: June 26, 2011
God Is Victorious
Joshua 6:2–3, 4b, 12–20b
At God's command, Joshua and the children of Israel marched around Jericho for seven days. On the final day as Israel conquered the city, God miraculously caused the walls to collapse.

UNIT 2 • LISTENING FOR GOD IN CHANGING TIMES

These five lessons study the book of Judges and give a glimpse of Israel's life after they enter the Promised Land. They examine the repeated cycle of disobedience, oppression, repentance, and renewed faithfulness.

Lesson 5: July 3, 2011
God Reacts to Disobedience
Joshua 7:1, 10–12, 22–26
Sanctification is an important biblical concept. God sometimes gives very specific instructions in the Bible regarding how to accomplish a given task. When Achan disobeyed God's command and kept the "devoted things," which were the unclean things that were supposed

to be destroyed, his sin caused Israel to fail in battle.

Lesson 6: July 10, 2011
Listen to God's Judges
Judges 2:11–19

This passage is an introduction to the book of Judges, which explains Israel's recurring cycles of national apostasy.

Lesson 7: July 17, 2011
Use God's Strength
Judges 3:15–25, 29–30

Eglon, the King of Moab, oppressed Israel for 18 years with a burdensome tax of money or produce. God raised up Ehud, of the tribe of Benjamin, as the judge or military leader.

Lesson 8: July 24, 2011
Let God Rule
Judges 7:2–4, 13–15; 8:22–25

The children of Israel were being oppressed by the Midianites, a nomadic tribe traditionally related to Israel (Genesis 25:1–6). Gideon became the judge of Israel and was instructed to limit the size of his army.

Lesson 9: July 31, 2011
Return to Obedience
Judges 10:10–18

Despite God's repeated deliverance, Israel fell again into idolatry. They responded to oppression by confessing their sin against God.

UNIT 3 • A CASE STUDY IN COMMUNITY

These four lessons all relate to the story of Ruth and her eventual marriage to Boaz. This marriage continues the Davidic line. This is the line through which Jesus Christ, the Messiah, will come.

Lesson 10: August 7, 2011
Walk in God's Path
Judges 13:1–8, 24–25

After an angel informs Manoah's wife that she will give birth, Manoah prays for knowledge regarding how to raise their child. When Samson was born, the Spirit of the Lord became evident in his young life.

Lesson 11: August 14, 2011
Choosing a Community
Ruth 1:8–18

Confronted with famine and the death of her husband and two sons, Naomi felt that she had nothing to share with her daughters-in-law except adversity. Naomi realized that for Ruth, Orpah, and herself, becoming widows meant the loss of security and identity. She implored her daughters-in-law to return to their families in Moab while she returns to Judah. Ruth refused to go home, but made a passionate plea to remain with Naomi, her people, and her God.

Lesson 12: August 21, 2011
Empowering the Needy
Ruth 2:8–18

In the time of the judges, widows were vulnerable and subject to being ignored, taken advantage of, and often forced into poverty. Boaz followed God's Law by allowing Ruth to glean in His field (Leviticus 19:9–10 and Deuteronomy 24:19–22).

Lesson 13: August 28, 2011
Respecting Community Standards
Ruth 4:1–10

Boaz sought to redeem the land of Naomi's husband and son and to secure the hand of Ruth in marriage. Naomi's family line continued through her grandson Obed to King David (Ruth 4:22).

Foundations of Jewish Belief

by Rabbi Yechiel Eckstein

Torah (Teachings)

While traditional Jews and conservative Christians may share much in common on the fundamental question of the divinity and inerrancy of Scripture (at least, the Old Testament or Hebrew Bible portion of it), there are, of course, key differences as well. Today I propose to explore one of the foundational aspects of the Jewish faith—Torah—through the unique perspective of a rabbi.

To speak of the Jew and his faith is to focus on the quintessential dimension of that faith, Torah. The term "Torah" (Heb. *'imrah*, **im-RAW**), has a variety of connotations. Etymologically, it means "teachings," not "law," as it is so often mistranslated. In its broadest sense, "Torah" means "correct" or "properly Jewish," as in "leading a Torah way of life." More narrowly, it refers to all Jewish religious writings, including the Hebrew Scriptures, Talmud, responsa literature (Jewish scholars' authoritative replies to inquiries regarding Jewish law), rabbinic commentaries, and others. The term is most generally used, however, in reference to the Bible or written scriptures that Jews refer to as the Tanakh (**tah-NAKH**) and Christians refer to as the Hebrew Bible or Old Testament. In its narrowest sense, the term "Torah" refers to the five books of Moses, or Pentateuch.

The traditional view of the Torah is that it is the embodiment of God's Word par excellence, the sine qua non (absolute essentials) of our knowledge of God and of the divine will for humankind. Although given to the people of Israel at a particular juncture in history, it is, nevertheless, eternally valid and authoritative. Everything there is to know about life, claim the rabbis, can be derived from the Torah. (The term "the rabbis" is used throughout this piece in reference to the collective body of rabbis through the centuries, but particularly those in the Talmudic Period—200–500 C.E. Christians use A.D. and Jews use C.E. for "Common Era"). As the psalmist declared, "The law [Torah] of the Lord is perfect, reviving the soul" (Psalm 19:7, NIV). Without the Torah humankind has precious little knowledge of God and the divine intent, nor of the means by which He might link up with them.

The Torah is considered divine in the sense that every word and letter—even the designs or "crowns" on top of the letters as they appear written in the parchment scrolls—are believed to have been revealed by God. The rabbis regarded the concept of torah mishamayim (**MEE'show-MIE-eem**) or "torah from heaven" (i.e., its divinity), as one of the most central of all Jewish affirmations. The Torah is written on parchment and tied together in a scroll. It is the holiest ritual object in Judaism in that it contains both the name and message of God. The Torah is to be treated with utmost reverence and respect, not lightly or frivolously. It may not be desecrated or defiled. Indeed, there are numerous laws pertaining to the sanctity with which we are to treat the Torah. Scrolls that are old or torn, for example, may not be discarded but must be buried in the earth like human beings. If a Torah scroll accidentally falls, a fast day is decreed for all those who saw it drop. If a printed Torah text drops, we kiss it as a sign of our respect. The meticulous care involved in writing a Torah scroll, letter by letter (writing a scroll takes, on the average, one full year), and it is another reflection of its sacredness in the eyes of Jews.

How did God reveal His Word through the Torah? Did He "dictate" it verbatim to Moses on Sinai? Was Moses "inspired" to write it down? Was it all written by humans and then sanctioned retroactively by God? These and many other explanations are proffered as to how God actually communicated His will to humankind. In whatever way traditionalists understand the mechanics of the Sinai theophany, however, they all regard the Torah as we have it today as the primary source of our knowledge of God's Word to humankind, and, indeed, of God Himself.

God is not a physical being that mortal humans can ever come to fully know, nor can we expect to completely comprehend His immutable (unchanging) ways. Even Moses, the greatest of all prophets who talked with God "face to face" (Exodus 33:11), was allowed to "see" only God's "back" (Exodus 33:20, 23). But if the Torah is, in a very real sense, God's Word, we can come as close as humanly possible to "knowing" God Himself by studying its content. By immersing ourselves in the sacred act of Torah study, we can come to better understand both the content and source of that divine Word. For this reason Jewish education, and particularly Talmud Torah, or "study of the Torah," is one of the most important mitzvot (**MTS-vōt**), "religious duties," in all of Judaism. The Talmud states that good deeds such as honoring parents, acting kindly toward strangers, visiting the sick, attending the dead, devotion in prayer, and bringing peace among people are all important, but that "the study of Torah excels them all. It is the Jew's loftiest spiritual pursuit."

Traditional Judaism affirms that the Torah is not only God's revealed Word to humankind, but it also has been passed on to us from generation to generation without error. This doctrine of inerrancy underlies the traditional Jewish hermeneutic (interpretation of Scripture) which derives laws and theological concepts from each word (and, at times, from each letter) in the Torah. The validity of this exegetical method rests upon the belief that every word in the Torah as we have it today is divine, without error, and, consequently, imparted to humans for an express purpose. (The possibility of error is, indeed, reduced since Torah scribes must be pious individuals who work slowly and meticulously in the arduous task of transcribing each letter of the Torah onto the scroll parchment. If a scribe makes even the slightest mistake in writing the name of God, for example, he must undergo ritual acts of purification.)

The Torah constitutes the primary component of the Jewish "written tradition," which also includes the Neviim (**nuh-vee-EEM** or **nuh-VEE-im**, prophets) and Ketuvim (**kuh-too-VEEM** or **kuh-TOO-vim**; writings comprising the Scrolls of Esther, Psalms, Song of Songs, Ecclesiastes, Job, Ruth, Lamentations, and Proverbs, as well as the Books of Daniel, Ezra, Nehemiah, and 1and 2 Chronicles). This written tradition, more widely known by its acronym, Tanakh (T for Torah, N for Neviim, K for Ketuvim), came to a close roughly after 586 B.C.E., with the destruction of the first temple and end of the prophetic period (Ezra and Nehemiah are considered the last prophets). It was not canonized, however, until after the first century C.E. Christians generally refer to the Tanakh, or written tradition, as the Old Testament, although many, in deference to Jewish sensitivities, have come to use the term Hebrew Bible since Old Testament implies the existence of a New Testament, something that Jews deny.

The Jewish hermeneutical treatment of the Torah is fundamentally different from that of the rest of the Tanakh (Bible). For while all other holy writ in the Tanakh (i.e., the prophets and writings) are sacred and divine, none carries the same authoritative force as the Torah, wherein every word is regarded as divine and inerrant and, consequently, is to be interpreted by humans. In the case of the rest of Scripture, only the concepts are sacred and divine. Laws cannot be derived exegetically from every word or letter.

While the Jewish view of the inerrancy of the Torah suggests that its every word is from God, portions, such as the Genesis account of the Garden of Eden, can legitimately be interpreted allegorically rather than literally. In contrast, a conservative Christian view of inerrancy might not suggest that each and every word and letter of the Torah is to be interpreted exegetically (much like the Jewish view of the rest of Scripture), although it would be inclined to claim that they are to be understood literally. In Judaism, the Torah, which is inerrant, is interpreted through the eyes of the rabbis and oral tradition, which at times treat certain portions allegorically, though always as the embodiment of the Word of God.

Unlike other faiths that are founded upon the revelatory experiences of an individual, Judaism was born out of a divine revelation to an entire people. The very concluding phrase in the Torah, "in the sight of all Israel" (Deuteronomy 34:12), points to the centrality of this concept within Judaism. By addressing the people of Israel collectively and directly, God sought to teach them that Moses was His trusted servant and that all that he would speak and write in God's name would equally be His Word (see Exodus 19:9). In other words, Moses' position of authority as transcriber of the Word of God was vindicated by God having revealed Himself to the community of Israel and publicly endorsing Moses as such.

It is the Torah that brings solace, inner strength, and spiritual fulfillment to the Jew during times of joy, security, and prosperity, as well as during periods of wandering, suffering, and ad-

versity. It is the Torah that guides the Jew's path, shapes his or her character, and links him or her with ultimacy. The Torah is the lens through which the Jew perceives life and reality; it is that which unites him or her indissolubly with his or her fellow Jew. The Torah is the very lifeblood of the Jewish people.

Adapted from *How Firm a Foundation: A Gift of Jewish Wisdom for Christians and Jews* by Rabbi Yechiel Eckstein, Brewster, MA: Paraclete Press, 1997, 3–11. Adapted with permission of the copyright holder, Rabbi Yechiel Eckstein.

Sources:

Eckstein, Yechiel. How Firm a Foundation: A Gift of Jewish Wisdom for Christians and Jews. Brewster, MA: Paraclete Press, 1997. 3–11.

Jacobs, Joseph and Ludwig Blau. "Torah." Jewish Encyclopedia.com. Kopelman Foundation. http://www.jewishencyclopedia.com/view.jsp?artid=265&letter=T&search=Torah#993 (accessed December 27, 2009).

"Ketuvim." Dictionary.com. http://dictionary.reference.com/browse/ketuvim (accessed December 27, 2009).

"Mitzvah." Answers.com. http://www.answers.com/topic/mitzvah (accessed December 27, 2009).

"Neviim." Dictionary.com. http://dictionary.reference.com/browse/neviim (accessed December 27, 2009).

Old Testament Hebrew Lexicon. Bible Gateway.com http://www.biblegateway.com/lexicons/hebrew (accessed December 26, 2009).

"Responsa." Webster's Encyclopedic Unabridged Dictionary of the English Language. New York, NY: Gramercy Books, 1994. 1222.

"Tanakh." Answers.com. http://www.answers.com/topic/tanakh (accessed December 27, 2009).

Rabbi Yechiel Eckstein *has devoted more than 25 years to building bridges of understanding between Christians and Jews and broad support for the State of Israel. He received Orthodox Rabbinic ordination from Yeshiva University in New York and master's degrees from Yeshiva University and Columbia University. In 1983, Rabbi Eckstein established The International Fellowship of Christians and Jews (www.ifcj.org) to help Christians and Jews work together on projects promoting the safety and security of Jews in Israel and around the world. In recent years, The Fellowship has provided more than $100 million to help Jews immigrate to Israel from countries around the world, fight poverty in Israel, and help poor, elderly Jews and orphans in the former Soviet Union.*

TLC: Therapeutic Lifestyle for Christians

by Clyde Oden, M.D.

Many African Americans are in poor health due to preventable, or at least manageable, reasons. The problem is that we have chosen toxic lifestyles over therapeutic lifestyles. We are living to die, rather than living to live. The goal of this essay is not to bemoan our difficulties but to point out options available to us today if we choose to follow a TLC: Therapeutic Lifestyle for Christians.

In a radio address on February 21, 1998, President Bill Clinton committed the United States of America to an ambitious goal of eliminating the disparities in health status experienced by racial and ethnic minority populations by the year 2010. The United States Department of Health and Human Services (DHHS) selected six focus areas in which racial and ethnic minorities experience significant disparities in health access and outcomes.

As reported by the DHHS, a snapshot of African Americans in the six focus areas reveals the following:

1. Infant Mortality—African American babies are dying at birth and within the first 28 days of birth at a rate of 2½ times that of White babies.

2. Heart Disease—Coronary heart disease (CHD) kills more Americans than nearly all other diseases combined.

3. Cancers—Cancer is the second leading cause of death, but for African Americans the incidents of many forms of cancer is much higher than that of nearly every other ethnic group living in America.

4. Diabetes—According to the National Diabetes Information Clearinghouse report issued on September 20, 1998, diabetes is a very serious problem in the African American community. This report reveals the following:

• In 1998, of 35 million African Americans, about 1.5 million have been diagnosed with diabetes. This is almost four times the number known to have diabetes in 1968.

• About 730,000 African Americans have diabetes but do not know they have the disease. Identifying undiagnosed cases and providing additional clinical care and treatment for diabetes is a major challenge for the health care community.

• For every six White Americans who have diabetes, 10 African Americans have diabetes.

• Diabetes is particularly common among middle-aged and older adults and among African American women. Among African Americans age 50 years or older, 19% of men and 28% of women have diabetes.

• African Americans with diabetes are more likely to develop complications from the disease and to experience greater disability than White Americans with diabetes.

• Death rates for people with diabetes are 27% higher for Blacks than Whites.

5. Immunizations—In a report issued on April 17, 2000, Donna Shalala, secretary for the Department of Health and Human Services, reported that while 83% of White children (19 to 35 months old) have received the most commonly recommended series of vaccinations by age 2, only 74% of Black children and 77% of Hispanic children are fully vaccinated. For adults, the African Americans' rate was nearly half the targeted goal for those 65 years and older.

6. HIV Infections/AIDS—According to United States Government Centers of Disease Control, HIV and AIDS is a particularly serious problem among African Americans. Representing only an estimated 12% of the total U.S. population, African Americans make up almost 37% of all AIDS cases reported in this country.

When we look at these statistics for African Americans, we begin to understand the analogy of the "pool at Bethesda." If Jesus were walking near the pool at Bethesda today, He would find this group of African Americans lying around the pool looking for a miracle, and I believe that He would look deep in our souls and ask the question: "Do you want to be well?" In response, we must answer and take action. Jesus commanded the invalid man who had been at the pool for 38 years to get up and do something positive about his life—or as the Scripture reports in John 5:8, "Then Jesus said to him, 'Get up! Pick up your mat and walk.'"

Briefly, here are the steps that are involved in obeying Jesus' command today:

1. Know your current health status. Get a regular comprehensive health check-up to establish a baseline which everything can be compared as you monitor your health in subsequent years. The disgraceful status of health insurance coverage in this nation is that nearly 20% of all African Americans do not have any form of health insurance. However, there are 80% who do have coverage. Find out what is going on with your body—ignorance is a sin! (See 1 Corinthians 6:19.)

2. Follow the instructions given to you by your health professional. If you don't agree with him or her, find another qualified health professional and follow that person's instructions. Whatever you do, don't substitute their opinion with that of your hair dresser, barber, baker, local shopping mall clerk, health food store employee, or any other person who tells you what you want to hear.

Take your medications, follow the regiment given to you, and if you have problems or questions, ask your doctor.

3. Start living a healthy life by avoiding harmful and sinful habits, behaviors, and choices. For example, Jesus would never authorize His followers to smoke cigarettes, cigars, pipes, marijuana, crack cocaine, heroine, or any substance that needs to be lit and sucked into your lungs. We were created to breathe clean air.

Similarly, the sin of sex outside of marriage is destroying our families and our lives. The consequences of this behavior are also evident in the statistics. A majority of our infants are born in unmarried families. We have some of the highest rates of sexually transmitted diseases of any people in the United States. The portion of African American women being infected by the HIV virus is greater than any other ethnic group in this country. These are just a few of the results of having sex outside of marriage or having sex with people who have multiple sexual partners. There are no acceptable explanations for polluting our bodies with harmful chemicals or destroying our health through poor lifestyle choices. Doing so is a sin before God! (See James 4:17.)

4. Change to a lifestyle of therapeutic eating habits. We are killing ourselves in the kitchens, in our dining rooms, and in those convenient fast food places in our neighborhoods. We eat too much animal fat, too many fried foods, too few vegetables, too few fruits, and too much snack food. One of our gifts as a people is that we've developed the skill to make fatty meat taste good. We call it barbecue. The problem is that we no longer eat this food sparingly and in moderation. Barbecue is okay to eat four times a year or at holiday gatherings. But it is deadly when we are eating it every week.

Our diet, along with our failure to monitor our health, keep our blood pressure low, and check our cholesterol levels, produces a toxic lifestyle. Jesus asked the question: "Do you want to be well?" We, as a people, must eat properly in order to be well. We must eat to live, and not to die.

Soul food is good in moderation, but it is vitally important that we significantly reduce our intake of fatty meats, cheeses, dairy products, and eggs and increase our daily intake of vegetables, fruits, water, and grains.

5. Exercise to live longer. African Americans have been blessed with wonderful bodies. Our physiques, our shapes, and our musculature are the envy of the world. But if we don't use it, we lose it; and the fact of the matter is, many of our people are overweight and out of shape. As a result, we are "lying around the pool of Bethesda" with our stomachs larger than our chests. These are all physical indications that we are not exercising enough. Exercise can be simple and inexpensive. All that is needed is a 20–30 minute walk in the neighborhood. Encourage others to take action. Walk in pairs or in groups of three or four. Walk with your children, especially those who are also overweight. Our toxic lifestyles keep us in front of the TV or lying on the couch all day. If we want to be well, we will get up and exercise.

6. Take control of our neighborhoods and communities. Instead of waiting for a miracle, we must understand that we have been given the power to change the world, starting with our own houses and neighborhoods. It is unhealthy to sit around and complain about what "they aren't doing" to make your community safer, cleaner, or a better place in which to live. We must use the empowerment that is available through the Holy Spirit to let our lights shine in the communities in which we live. Don't stand (or lie) passively by and think the politicians are going to do it for you and your family. We must speak out, act out, and get out and make a difference in our community.

7. Pray and meditate in order to achieve healthy living. There are some things that your doctor and your health professionals cannot do for you. Prayer is powerful, yet personal. You have to spend time with God; it is unhealthy and downright antithetical to Christian living not to have a healthy relationship with the Lord. A personal relationship with God and communication in prayer allows one with health problems to talk with God about them. Healing begins with revelation from God.

8. Finally, one additional factor is essential in TLC: regular expressive praise and worship. Too many Christians are in poor health today because they fail to take advantage of the therapeutic environment found in the worship experience. This is something that cannot be achieved by listening to the radio or watching television. In order to get the full therapeutic value of praise and worship, you have to be there. Not only must one be present, but there must also be some involvement by the individual. It is healthy every now and then to give out a shout for the Lord.

The Lord is calling His people to live healthier lives. Yes, everyone in this country should have available, accessible, affordable, and high quality health care. Yes, there should be qualified health professionals in every neighborhood, town, and city in this nation. Yes, America's health care system can be much improved. But there is no excuse for the disparities in health now experienced by African Americans. Our health is governed more by the choices we make, rather than the resources that are currently unavailable to us. As Christians, we can make a difference in the health status of African Americans. We can begin to make the difference by adopting a TLC—Therapeutic Lifestyle for Christians.

Clyde W. Oden Jr., M.D., is the Senior Pastor of Bryant Temple African Methodist Episcopal Church in Southern California, which has a membership of more than 700 people. He served as President and Chief Executive Officer of Watts Health Systems and the Watts Health Foundation, Inc. He is Chairperson of the Working Committee, which serves the Statewide HIV/AIDS Church Outreach Advisory Board; a member of the Board of Directors and Treasurer of Community Build, Inc.; Vice Chairman of the African American Summit on Violence Prevention, Inc.; and a member of the Board of Directors of Freedom from Hunger, Inc.

Redemption

by Harold Dean Trulear, Ph.D.

1787 was an important year in American history. In 1787, the United States adopted its constitution, a document significantly, seriously, and regularly called the most important document of political freedom in human history. Delaware became the first state in the newly named United States of America. Silicon was discovered. It was a significant year.

1787 also marked the beginning of the Free African Society in Philadelphia, a mutual aid organization where Blacks gathered for community affairs, insurance and banking, health care, and education. African Americans also recall 1787 as the year that the United States Federal Government enacted a compromise between slaveholding and non-slaveholding states to account for enslaved Africans in the regular federal census—the now infamous "three fifths compromise" determining that for the purposes of the census, Blacks were "three-fifths" of a human being. The only reason the South wanted enslaved Africans counted at all was that representation in congress depended on census numbers.

By the way, did you know that in the current practice of the United States Census Bureau, prisoners are counted as part of the census for the communities that host the prisons in which they live? A significant amount of public money is distributed according to census data, which means that the majority or all White communities that host prisons receive public dollars for community projects based on their being the communities in which African American prisoners are held. In both cases, Blacks are counted but not as citizens.

1787 also marks the birth of an incredible African American woman—Sally Thomas—who represents the best in the human realm of what the lessons of our quarter have to teach us about the character and will of God concerning redemption.

Sally Thomas was born in 1787 in Albemarle County, Virginia. She was a fair-skinned, enslaved African American who was led to her pursuit by wealthy White slave owners because of purposes in violation of biblical principles. Eventually she had three children by two White slave owners, neither of whom ever acknowledged paternity. Sally Thomas determined that her life's goal would be the freedom of her three sons. In that regard, she mirrored the holy intention of God.

The freedom of God's people dominates our lessons for this quarter. The life of Sally Thomas shows us how God commits Himself to our freedom—even as she did for the freedom of her sons. She sacrificed, worked hard to earn enough money to purchase the freedom of one, aid in the escape of a second, and arrange for a job that led to the freedom of the third. There was nothing more important to Sally Thomas than the freedom of her children. So, too, does God value the freedom of His children.

God commits to the freedom and redemption of His people out of His love and faithfulness. He expressed His commitment to Israel through the Exodus. He raised up prophets and priests, kings and judges for His people, even in the midst of their unfaithfulness. He expressed His ultimate love in sending Jesus for us "while we were yet sinners." Gardner C. Taylor was right when he told young preachers training his charge, "The Bible has only one major theme: God is getting back what belonged to Him in the first place."

Redemption is paying the price to buy something back. Sally Thomas paid the price for her sons' redemption through work, money, and sound connections with the business world. God paid the price for our redemption by sending His Son Jesus into the world to die for our sins. The resurrection of Jesus gives hope to all who trust Him as Savior. The apostle Paul says that without the hope of the resurrection "we are the most miserable" of all people. Peter says that the Christian has been "born again into a living hope" by the Resurrection. Truly, the resurrection of Jesus brings us hope. It is the hope of redemption.

Just as enslaved Africans were objects of redemption in the ante-bellum period of the United States, a new cohort of persons in our society are candidates for redemption in today's society. Over 2 million men and women live their lives behind the bars of our state and federal prisons, and countless more languish in county and city jails. The United States incarcerates its citizens at a higher rate than any nation on the earth. And the disproportionate numbers of those prisoners who are African American should give call for pause and prayer, preaching and prophesying in our congregations. According to the Pew Center, in 2008 one in every 100 Americans was incarcerated. For African American males between the ages of 25 and 34, the numbers were one in nine. Our young men need redemption.[1]

In addition, the overwhelming majority of inmates eventually returned to society. In 2008, the number approached 700,000.[2] And this number did not include those returning from county and city jails. For men and women returning from incarceration, redemption means more than just the personal regeneration occurring when a person gives his or her life to Christ. Redemption includes being reconciled with God and humanity, and those leaving the prisons and jails of our country struggle to be reconciled with family and friends, community and society.

Many of our congregations have prison ministry programs. They do good work in providing worship services, Bible studies, and some counseling and working in conjunction with jail and prison chaplains. Yet so much more is needed. We need the work of full redemption.

When redemption comes to a person, it does more than change them internally. It changes his or her relationship to the community and world, as well as his or her relationship to God. God redeems His people to make them a people and a community of the redeemed who become agents of reconciliation in the world. A prisoner may give his or her life to Christ, but they also need support in reforming and revitalizing the relationships with others. And sometimes they need support to begin new relationships where there once were either bad relationships or no relationships at all.

A group of religious leaders met in Baltimore in 2006 at the Annie E. Casey Foundation to discuss ways in which congregations could be a part of the redemption of prisoners, especially those about to return from incarceration. They pointed to relationships as the key concept in assisting people returning from incarceration. As several of them met over the next year, they were joined by leadership from the Progressive National Baptist Convention, which formed a Social Justice and Prison Ministry Commission. That Commission worked with representatives of the Foundation and other key Christian leaders to produce a model for relationally based prison ministry and prisoner reentry called Healing Communities.[3]

In the Healing Communities model, each congregation identifies families in their own church who have an incarcerated loved one—a father, mother, son, daughter, etc. The congregation then begins to minister to the family and the inmate just as they would if that inmate were hospitalized. They provide prayerful counsel and support, visitation to the prison, and assistance with financial matters when appropriate. One group of congregations began using their church vans to provide rides for families on visiting days. Another developed financial support for families with phone bills (a collect call from a state prison can cost as much as two dollars and fifty cents per minute). Yet another church, recognizing how important it is to keep families in touch during incarceration, set up a video conferencing program with a prison seven hours away so that inmates could have real time video visits with loved ones.

These congregations grew in their ability to be communities of redemption. They became more sensitive to the difficult transition from incarceration back into society by ministering to inmates and their families during the period of incarceration and by becoming welcoming congregations upon the return of the inmate. They even moved away from using the term "ex-offender," preferring the term "returning citizen." One pastor, who had served significant prison time prior to his entering the ministry, told a group of churches that were beginning this ministry, "How would you like to be forever known by a title describing the worst moments of your life?"

This same pastor freely shares his having been incarcerated as a way of helping congregations overcome the stigma of incarceration. Many members of our churches have families living with a sense of shame that their family member is incarcerated. But as we look at so many people who have made the successful transition home and share their stories and hopes, we can reduce the stigma and shame and provide real support for all persons affected by crime and incarceration. Some pastors are even preaching sermons about prisoner reentry, citing Peter's ambivalent reception upon return from prison in Acts 12, the return of the Jews from Babylonian captivity in Isaiah 49, and John coming home from exile with a fresh revelation from heaven.

All of us must be held accountable for our actions. For some, it means the consequences of incarceration. But if we are willing to be changed—to be redeemed—then congregations must stand ready to be communities of redemption, no matter how far someone may have fallen. We should be prayerfully open to God's heart for the redemption of the prisoner and his or her family. After all, our Redeemer paid the price for us while a prisoner Himself.

Footnotes:
[1] Info taken from "One in 100 Behind Bars in America," Pew Center for the States, 2008.

[2] See www.reentry.gov, a website of the Department of Justice, Office of Justice Programs.

[3] See the Annie E. Casey Foundation website www.aecf.org, keywords "Healing Communities" to download the handbook "What Shall We Then Do?" prepared by the Foundation and the Progressive National Baptist Convention.

Harold Dean Trulear, Ph.D., is an Associate Professor of Applied Theology at Howard University in Washington, DC, and the president of GLOBE Community Ministries in Philadelphia, Pennsylvania.

Mary Burnett Talbert

Mary Burnett Talbert was never ordinary. In 1886, at 20 years old, she was the only African American woman in her graduating class at Oberlin College. Following college, Burnett left her hometown of Oberlin and worked as the assistant principal of Union High School in Little Rock, Arkansas. At this time, 1887, she held the highest position of any African American woman in the state. Later, she was a national and international voice for the oppressed. She was also a powerful speaker on anti-lynching and women's suffrage. In 1915 she spoke at "Votes for Women: A Symposium by Leading Thinkers of Colored Women" in Washington, DC.

In 1905, after marrying William Talbert and moving to his home in Buffalo, New York, Talbert helped found the Niagara Movement, led by W.E.B. Du Bois. The Niagara Movement was developed to fight for desegregation and suffrage. Talbert was also heavily involved in women's clubs that placed leaders, as a voice, in the community. Talbert created platforms for women's issues and worked with her church, Michigan Avenue Baptist Church, on abolition. In 1910, Talbert co-founded the first chapters of the NAACP in Texas, Louisiana, and Buffalo. Talbert also founded the Christian Culture Congress, which bridged the gap between the church and Black leaders in the community.

Talbert was not only a community leader, but also a humanitarian. During World War I, she served as a YMCA secretary and Red Cross nurse in France. She also taught classes to African American soldiers who were not educated. Her international experience extended to a tour of 11 European nations, lecturing on the conditions of African Americans in the United States. She was also responsible for selecting female nominees for positions in the League of Nations, the forerunner of the United Nations. In 1920, Talbert's international successes led to her election as the first African American delegate to the International Council of Women at their fifth congress in Norway.

Mary Burnett Talbert died in 1923. Her honors continued posthumously in 2005, when Talbert was inducted into the National Women's Hall of Fame in Seneca Falls, New York.

Sources:

"Mary Burnett Talbert." Answers.com. http://www.answers.com/topic/mary-burnett-talbert (accessed July 15, 2009).

"Mary Morris Burnett Talbert." http://womenshistory.about.com/library/etext/bl_mary_burnett_talbert_1902_essay.htm (accessed July 15, 2009).

Williams, Lillian S. "Mary Morris Burnett Talbert." In *Black Women in America: An Historical Encyclopedia*, Vol. 2. Darlene Clark Hine, Elsa Barkley Brown, and Rosalyn Terborg-Penn, eds. Bloomington, IN: Indiana University Press, 1993. 1137–39.

Teaching Tips

1. Words You Should Know

A. Minister (Joshua 1:1b) *sharath* (Heb.)—Person who serves, waits upon, and attends to.

B. Cut off (11:21) *karath* (Heb.)—Totally uprooted and exterminated.

2. Teacher Preparation

Unifying Principle—A Job Well Done. God makes promises that may seem to be unfulfilled, but we can be confident that God stands behind them and will fulfill every promise.

A. Pray for your class that God will bring clarity to this lesson.

B. Read the Daily Bible Readings, the entire text, and the surrounding sections for today's lesson.

C. Reflect on some broken promises in your own personal life and how they affected your life. Be prepared to share how God is a promise keeper—a covenant keeper.

3. Open the Lesson

A. Open with prayer, including the Aim for Change.

B. Ask, "How does it feel to have someone break a promise to you?" Discuss.

C. Summarize the In Focus story and discuss Mary and John's broken promises to each other and to God.

4. Present the Scriptures

A. Have volunteers read the Focal Verses.

B. Now use The People, Places, and Times; Background; Search the Scriptures; At-A-Glance outline; In Depth; and More Light on the Text to clarify the verses.

5. Explore the Meaning

A. Have volunteers summarize the Discuss the Meaning, Lesson in Our Society, and Make It Happen sections.

B. Connect these sections to the Aim for Change and the Keep in Mind verse.

6. Next Steps for Application

A. Summarize the lesson.

B. Praise and thank God because all of His promises are true.

C. Close with prayer.

Worship Guide

For the Superintendent or Teacher
Theme: God's Promises Fulfilled
Theme Song: "He's an On Time God"
Devotional Reading: Acts 26:1–7
Prayer

God's Promises Fulfilled

Bible Background • JOSHUA 1:1–6; 11–12
Printed Text • JOSHUA 1:1b–6; 11:16–19, 21–23 | Devotional Reading • ACTS 26:1–7

Aim for Change

By the end of the lesson, we will: IDENTIFY scriptural support that God keeps His promises; FEEL blessed that God stands behind His promises; and PRAISE God that His promises are true.

 **In Focus**

Mary and John were madly in love. They had gone through marital counseling, and their pastor had explained in detail each promise they would pledge to each other in their wedding vows. The couple assured the pastor that they fully understood the promises they were making and were prepared to honor them for a lifetime. Finally, their wedding day arrived. As all the invited guests looked on, in the presence of God, John and Mary announced their intention to love, honor, cherish, and to remain physically, emotionally, and mentally faithful to each other in any circumstance and under all conditions as long as they both lived.

For the first few years, everything was fine. However, after a while, the little things John once found cute about Mary began to grate on his nerves. His complaints to her soon became put-downs and later hurtful verbal abuse. During pastoral counseling, John realized that through his verbal abuse he had broken his promise to love, honor, and cherish Mary.

Broken promises are a fact of human life. In today's lesson, we will see how Joshua's absolute faith in the faithfulness of God to honor His promises led to the conquest of the Holy Land.

Keep in Mind

"As the LORD commanded Moses his servant, so did Moses command Joshua, and so did Joshua; he left nothing undone of all that the LORD commanded Moses"
(Joshua 11:15).

"As the LORD commanded Moses his servant, so did Moses command Joshua, and so did Joshua; he left nothing undone of all that the LORD commanded Moses" (Joshua 11:15).

Focal Verses

KJV Joshua 1:1b That the LORD spake unto Joshua the son of Nun, Moses' minister, saying,

2 Moses my servant is dead; now therefore arise, go over this Jordan, thou, and all this people, unto the land which I do give to them, even to the children of Israel.

3 Every place that the sole of your foot shall tread upon, that have I given unto you, as I said unto Moses.

4 From the wilderness and this Lebanon even unto the great river, the river Euphrates, all the land of the Hittites, and unto the great sea toward the going down of the sun, shall be your coast.

5 There shall not any man be able to stand before thee all the days of thy life: as I was with Moses, so I will be with thee: I will not fail thee, nor forsake thee.

6 Be strong and of a good courage: for unto this people shalt thou divide for an inheritance the land, which I sware unto their fathers to give them.

11:16 So Joshua took all that land, the hills, and all the south country, and all the land of Goshen, and the valley, and the plain, and the mountain of Israel, and the valley of the same;

17 Even from the mount Halak, that goeth up to Seir, even unto Baalgad in the valley of Lebanon under mount Hermon: and all their kings he took, and smote them, and slew them.

18 Joshua made war a long time with all those kings.

19 There was not a city that made peace with the children of Israel, save the Hivites the inhabitants of Gibeon: all other they took in battle.

NLT Joshua 1:1b The LORD spoke to Joshua son of Nun, Moses' assistant. He said,

2 "Moses my servant is dead. Therefore, the time has come for you to lead these people, the Israelites, across the Jordan River into the land I am giving them.

3 I promise you what I promised Moses: 'Wherever you set foot you will be on land I have given you—

4 from the Negev wilderness in the south to the Lebanon mountains in the north, from the Euphrates River in the east to the Mediterranean Sea in the west, including all the land of the Hittites.'

5 No one will be able to stand against you as long as you live. For I will be with you as I was with Moses. I will not fail you or abandon you.

6 Be strong and courageous, for you are the one who will lead these people to possess all the land I swore to their ancestors I would give them."

11:16 So Joshua conquered the entire region—the hill country, the entire Negev, the whole area around the town of Goshen, the western foothills, the Jordan Valley, the mountains of Israel, and the Galilean foothills.

17 The Israelite territory now extended all the way from Mount Halak, which leads up to Seir in the south, as far north as Baal-gad at the foot of Mount Hermon in the valley of Lebanon. Joshua killed all the kings of those territories,

18 waging for a long time to accomplish this.

19 No one in this region made peace with the Israelites except the Hivites of Gibeon. All the others were defeated.

KJV cont.

11:21 And at that time came Joshua, and cut off the Anakims from the mountains, from Hebron, from Debir, from Anab, and from all the mountains of Judah, and from all the mountains of Israel: Joshua destroyed them utterly with their cities.

22 There was none of the Anakims left in the land of the children of Israel: only in Gaza, in Gath, and in Ashdod, there remained.

23 So Joshua took the whole land, according to all that the LORD said unto Moses; and Joshua gave it for an inheritance unto Israel according to their divisions by their tribes. And the land rested from war.

NLT cont.

11:21 During this period Joshua destroyed all the descendants of Anak, who lived in the hill country of Hebron, Debir, Anab, and the entire hill country of Judah and Israel. He killed them all and completely destroyed their towns.

22 None of the descendants of Anak were left in all the land of Israel, though some still remained in Gaza, Gath, and Ashdod.

23 So Joshua took control of the entire land, just as the LORD had instructed Moses. He gave it to the people of Israel as their special possession, dividing the land among the tribes. So the land finally had rest from war.

The People, Places, and Times

The Promised Land. Around 2000 B.C., the Lord called Abraham from Ur of the Chaldeans, showed him the land of Canaan, and said, "I will give this land to your descendants" (Genesis 12:7, NLT). Later, He told Abraham, "You can be sure that your descendants will be strangers in a foreign land where they will be oppressed as slaves for 400 years. But I will punish the nation that enslaves them, and in the end they will come away with great wealth. (As for you, you will die in peace and be buried at a ripe old age.) After four generations your descendants will return here to this land" (15:13–16a, NLT).

God sent Moses, the great deliverer, to lead the people out of Egyptian bondage into a land "flowing with milk and honey." After the death of Moses, God commanded Joshua to take all the territory specified by Moses, "from the Negev wilderness in the south to the Lebanon mountains in the north, from the Euphrates River in the east to the Mediterranean sea in the west, including all the land of the Hittites" (Joshua 1:4, NLT).

We don't know the exact boundaries of the Promised Land. God revealed to Abraham that his descendants would receive the land of Canaan, but He originally promised them a much greater area than that. When Abraham and his nephew Lot separated, God told Abraham, "'Look as far as you can see in every direction—north and south, east and west. I am giving all this land, as far as you can see, to you and your descendants as a permanent possession'" (Genesis 13:14–15, NLT).

Background

When the Lord told Moses that he would see the Promised Land but die before entering it, Moses' first thoughts were not about himself. Instead, he thought about the welfare of the people he would leave behind. He was concerned that the LORD's people would be "like sheep without a shepherd" (Numbers 27:17, NLT). Moses asked God to choose a successor who would lead the Israelites both in the battles to come and in their obedience to God's commands. God chose Joshua, whom Moses had appointed as leader of the army and who had served as Moses' close personal assistant since the time the Israelites were still at Mount Sinai (Exodus 17:8–13; 24:12–13).

The Lord instructed Moses to lay his hand on Joshua and present him to Eleazar, the high priest, in front of the entire Israelite community and then commission him to lead the people. He was also to transfer some of his current authority to Joshua so that the people would learn to obey him (Numbers 27:22–23).

Later, after leading the Israelites to the plain of Moab, directly east of the Jordan River, Moses, who was about 120 years old, realized that the time of his death was nearing. He called the congregation together and reaffirmed that it would be Joshua and not he who would lead them across the Jordan River to take possession of the land God had promised them.

At-A-Glance

1. The Promises Made (Joshua 1:1b–6)

2. The Promises Fulfilled (11:16–19, 21–23)

In Depth

1. The Promises Made (Joshua 1:1b–6)

"Now after the death of Moses the servant of the LORD it came to pass, that the LORD spake unto Joshua the son of Nun" (Joshua 1:1). The opening words of the book of Joshua describe a period of transition. It marks not only a change in leadership, but a change in purpose. The people would change from Moses to Joshua and also from wanderers to warriors. This change would not only be difficult for the fledging nation, but also for Joshua. The death of Moses was a heavy blow to the Israelites. He was the one who had led them out of the oppressive

Egyptian bondage. When the Israelites were thirsty, God used Moses to cause water to flow from a stone. When the Israelites were hungry, God answered Moses' prayers and sent quail and bread from heaven. For almost 40 years, Moses had served as the Israelite's leader and legislator. He alone spoke face-to-face with God on their behalf. But now he was dead!

Israel was still encamped on the plains of Moab, directly east of the Jordan River, at the very edge of the Promised Land. For 30 days they mourned Moses, their beloved leader, but now it was time to inherit the land God had promised to Abraham and their forefathers hundreds of years earlier (Genesis 15:7–21). Joshua, the new leader of the Israelites, had been commissioned by Moses before his death (Numbers 27:22–23), and he was now being ordained by God.

The Lord commanded Joshua to prepare himself and the people to cross the Jordan River and take possession of the land. He makes three promises to His new leader: (1) A promise of land, "'Wherever you set foot, you will be on land I have given you'" (Joshua 1:3, NLT); (2) A promise of victory, "No one will be able to stand against you as long as you live" (from 1:5, NLT); and (3) A promise of presence, "For I will be with you as I was with Moses. I will not fail you or abandon you" (1:5b, NLT).

A promise of land: "'Wherever you set foot, you will be on land I have given you'" (Joshua 1:3, NLT). Joshua was going to experience the fulfillment of the promise God made to Abraham and repeated to his sons Isaac and Jacob. He would lead the people into the land that had been promised to Moses. The Israelites would occupy the land from the great river to the great sea. The area described is roughly the same area God promised to Abraham (Genesis 15:18–20).

A promise of victory: "No one will be able to stand against you as long as you live" (1:5a, NLT). God promised Joshua victory over anybody and everybody who came against him. This promise was not limited to the taking of the Promised Land, but was extended for as long as Joshua lived. However, this promise came with a warning. The people who lived in the land were protected by powerful armies and fortified cities. The battles would be hard fought. As it was in Canaan, the Christian life is a life of conflict with enemies who must be confronted and overcome. Although the outcome of our battle is assured, we must be prepared for conflict if we are to claim the kingdom's earthly promise of righteousness, peace, and joy in the Holy Spirit (Romans 14:17, NLT).

A promise of presence: "For I will be with you as I was with Moses. I will not fail you or abandon you" (from Joshua 1:5, NLT). These words call our attention to one of the great truths of the Bible. Israel would get into the land of promise the *same way* they got out of the land of bondage. They trusted in the power of the Lord to free them and the presence of the Lord to guide them. Likewise, Christians enter into the life of Christ the *same way* we were delivered from the wrath of God, by trusting in the power of the blood to free us from sin and the presence of the Lord to lead us and guide us through our lives.

2. The Promises Fulfilled (11:16–19, 21–23)

After Joshua's victories over the city-states of Jericho and Ai, word spread throughout the hill country and down the entire coast of the Mediterranean Sea. The kings in the southern region of the Promised Land joined together to defend themselves against the Israelite invaders. However, the people of Gibeon rejected the military coalition and tricked the Israelites into signing a peace treaty with them (Joshua 9:1–26). When the other five kings of the coalition heard about the treaty, they were enraged and gathered their armies to attack Gibeon. The Gibeonites immediately sent word to Joshua to come to their aid.

Just as He had at Jericho (6:1–5) and again at Ai (8:1–3), God assured Joshua that He would deliver the opposing armies into his hands and that their victory was guaranteed (10:8). At God's word, Joshua assembled the Israelite army and marched all night from their camp at Gilgal to Gibeon. Joshua led a surprise attack on the coalition forces. Just as God had promised, the Israelites routed the much larger army and went on to subdue all the remaining cities in the southern area of the Promised Land.

Joshua then led the Israelites to capture the royal cities in the area. They took the spoils for themselves, including the livestock, and they killed all the people. In doing this, they obeyed God's command to them through Moses, leaving nothing undone. This was the end of the major battles Israel needed to fight. They had overcome the greatest armies from the greatest cities. They followed their initial conquests by a long period of war against the surrounding cities and their kings. Then finally after a long and exhausting campaign, "Joshua took control of the entire land, just as the LORD had instructed Moses. He gave it to the people of Israel as their special possession dividing the land among the tribes. So the land finally had rest from war" (v. 23, NLT).

Search the Scriptures

1. What event occasioned the Lord to speak to Joshua (Joshua 1:2)?

2. How much of the land on the other side of the Jordan did God promise to Joshua and the Israelites (v. 3)?

Discuss the Meaning

If the kingdom of God is promised to believers and the manifestation of the kingdom within believers is righteousness (goodness), peace, and joy, why are so many Christians miserable and troubled?

Lesson in Our Society

One of the biggest problems facing Black people in urban settings is increasing gun violence and disregard for human life. Based on God's promise to Solomon in 2 Chronicles 7:14, how can the Black church as a spiritual community confront and defeat this enemy that dehumanizes, demoralizes, and destroys our children?

Make It Happen

Many people that we know are facing insurmountable problems that have robbed them of their peace and joy. When Joshua was confronted with these circumstances, he first looked to God and then went to war. Over the next week, identify someone who is on the verge of being overcome by the circumstances they are facing. Ask God what you can do to help them and sit silently, allowing God to speak to your heart. Then get up and go to war, doing exactly what He put in your heart to do. You may not be able to win the war, but you may help win a battle.

Follow the Spirit

What God wants me to do:

_____

_____

_____

_____

Remember Your Thoughts

Special insights I have learned:

_____

_____

_____

_____

More Light on the Text

Joshua 1:1b–6; 11:16–19, 21–23

1:1b That the LORD spake unto Joshua the son of Nun, Moses' minister, saying,

In Joshua 1:1, NLT, Moses is described as "the LORD's servant." The Hebrew word for "servant" is `ebed (**EH-bed**). It helps to view this title in the Middle Eastern context in which it was applied. This is the picture of the relationship of a slave toward his sovereign, in which the slave approaches his master in humble submission and complete obedience as an inferior to the superior. God is the Most High, the Ruler of all worlds, the Lord of hosts. All of us should be humbly prostrating ourselves before Him. The title of servant is applied to Moses often (see Deuteronomy 34:5; 1 Kings 8:56; 2 Kings 18:12; Psalm 105:26).

The KJV describes Joshua as the "minister" of Moses. The Hebrew word for "minister" is *sharath* (**shaw-RATH**), and it means "one who serves, waits upon, and attends to as an inferior serving or worshiping a superior." Note that this word differs from the word used to describe Moses. The word for minister as applied to Joshua is more like adjutant, or chief aide.

2 Moses my servant is dead; now therefore arise, go over this Jordan, thou, and all this people, unto the land which I do give to them, even to the children of Israel.

Sometimes the smallest words can say the most. When we read the word "do," which in Hebrew is `asah (aw-SAW) and means "accomplish, bestow, perform, or fulfill," we see what God is doing. This verb describes something that is happening in the present. The promise to give Abraham this land was hundreds of years before, and now the Children of Israel are at the actual moment of receiving the land which God promised to them. They are standing on the banks of the Jordan River and can look across at the Promised Land.

The Hebrew word for "give" is nathan (naw-THAWN). It can mean "grant, deliver, put, let, hand over, assign, designate, allot, or make." God as the giver of the land was an important concept for the people to understand. Although the land was treated as an inheritance which was to be passed on through the generations, in reality it was a trust given from God.

3 Every place that the sole of your foot shall tread upon, that have I given unto you, as I said unto Moses.

We read in Deuteronomy 11:24 the exact same promise given to Moses, but now this is a promise that will soon be fulfilled based upon what the people do. Unfortunately, the people did not obey; they did not take possession of the land. As a result, much of the land remained inhabited by various Canaanite people. This became a snare to the Israelites as they intermarried with the Canaanites and began worshiping their gods.

There is a twofold aspect to the promise given to Joshua. God promises the land, but the people must take it for themselves. They must fight in accord with God's instructions, but to receive the Promised Land is not a passive thing. So it is with God's promises to us—we must aggressively take those things He has promised us. In Joshua 1:3 the Hebrew word for "every" is kol (kole), and it means "the whole, all, every part" or "every place." If we sit back passively and do not pursue the spiritual blessings God has promised us, we will not come into possession of them.

4 From the wilderness and this Lebanon even unto the great river, the river Euphrates, all the land of the Hittites, and unto the great sea toward the going down of the sun, shall be your coast.

As the chosen people looked across the Jordan River, they might barely have seen the mountains of Lebanon in the distance. It must have been an awesome sight to God's people, who had been wandering around in the wilderness. But new sights were yet promised to them. No doubt Father Abraham had seen the great Euphrates River because he came from Ur of the Chaldees, a city on the Euphrates River. But this wandering band, whose parents had just come out of slavery in Egypt, had never seen this river.

5 There shall not any man be able to stand before thee all the days of thy life: as I was with Moses, so I will be with thee: I will not fail thee, nor forsake thee.

Imagine being the leader chosen to follow Moses. Moses had led the Israelites out of slavery and was the conduit for the 10 plagues. He was the institutor of the Law. He led the Children of Israel through the wilderness. All of this was very difficult, and sometimes even Moses faltered. Now Joshua had the job of leading the people in one battle after the next. We can imagine that he was nearly petrified with fear, but three times (vv. 6–7, 9) God urged him to have courage.

So, in verse 5, God made some great promises to Joshua. Just as God was with Moses, so would He be with Joshua, too. God promised in almost the same words to Moses that no one would be able to stand against him (Deuteronomy 7:24).

6 Be strong and of a good courage: for unto this people shalt thou divide for an inheritance the land, which I sware unto their fathers to give them.

The Hebrew word for "strong" is *chazaq* (**khaw-ZAWK**). The word for "courage" is *'amats* (**aw-MATS**). Both words have similar meanings. God, through Moses, had given Joshua this very same instruction in Deuteronomy 31:6–7, 23. Each time Joshua is given this command, it is based upon a promise from God. In this case, courage is for the task of dividing up the Promised Land among God's chosen people, and the promise is that God has promised them this land. Later, in Joshua 1:18, God's people exhorted Joshua to be strong, and in 10:25 Joshua turned around and exhorted the people to be strong.

Nachal (**naw-KHAL**) is the Hebrew word for "inheritance." This is the central concept in the book of Joshua, which revolves around the Israelites taking possession of the land which God had promised them.

11:16 So Joshua took all that land, the hills, and all the south country, and all the land of Goshen, and the valley, and the plain, and the mountain of Israel, and the valley of the same;

How exciting to jump over to chapter 11 and see the results of Joshua's courage and obedience to the Lord! For all practical purposes, the Israelites have conquered the land, although not to the extent described in 1:4. Verse 16 of chapter 11 mentions the regions conquered, and verse 17 gives us the borders.

17 Even from the mount Halak, that goeth up to Seir, even unto Baalgad in the valley of Lebanon under mount Hermon: and all their kings he took, and smote them, and slew them.

Mount Halak, which represents the southern boundary of Israel, is a desert peak south of Kadesh Barnea. This mountain pointed to Seir, which is in Edom, the land that the descendants of Esau settled. This is a wild, rocky area southeast of the Dead Sea. Baal-gad (note the connection to the name of the idol Baal) is a Canaanite city to the north in the region of Lebanon. This verse tells us that it lies at the foot of Mount Hermon. This verse tells us that Joshua took the kings and killed them. Chapter 12 lists the kings whom he slew—an incredible number.

18 Joshua made war a long time with all those kings.

If we didn't have this verse, we might have thought that Joshua's battle to conquer the Promised Land was swift, but this verse tells us that it was "a long time"—literally many days. In 14:10 we read that Caleb said it was 45 years since he had spied out the land. When we subtract the 38 to 40 years which the Israelites spent wandering in the wilderness, we come up with five to seven years. This is a long time for battle, as long as the American Revolutionary War or the Vietnam War.

19 There was not a city that made peace with the children of Israel, save the Hivites the inhabitants of Gibeon: all other they took in battle.

As foolish as this might look to us, all the cities of Canaan fought against Israel, even though there was ample evidence that God was on the side of the Hebrew people. Only Rahab put her trust in the Lord God. Only the Gibeonites made a treaty with Israel. Although this week's Scripture passage

461

omits 11:20, looking at this verse gives us some necessary theological background for this. The danger in living a life completely opposed to God is that eventually God will harden the heart, and the nation or individual living in such a manner will find that God has hardened their hearts.

11:21 And at that time came Joshua, and cut off the Anakims from the mountains, from Hebron, from Debir, from Anab, and from all the mountains of Judah, and from all the mountains of Israel: Joshua destroyed them utterly with their cities.

The Anakim were the giants that scared the 10 spies when they checked out the land before the wilderness wanderings (Numbers 13:22, 28, 32–33). We read in Deuteronomy 1:28 that these people were taller than the Hebrew people and their cities were great with towering walls. The completeness with which Joshua and the people exterminated the Anakim is revealed in the Hebrew language twice in just this one verse. The Hebrew for "cut off" is *karath* (**kaw-RATH**), and it means "totally uprooted and exterminated." Later in this same verse we read that Joshua "destroyed them (the Anakim) utterly"—he "completely destroyed their towns" (v. 21, NLT). The Hebrew for "destroyed" is *charam* (**khaw-RAM**), and it means "exterminated or annihilated completely." The Anakim had an awesome reputation and were very intimidating to the Israelites, so it was necessary to show that God was able to totally eliminate them.

22 There was none of the Anakims left in the land of the children of Israel: only in Gaza, in Gath, and in Ashdod, there remained. 23 So Joshua took the whole land, according to all that the LORD said unto Moses; and Joshua gave it for an inheritance unto Israel

according to their divisions by their tribes. And the land rested from war.

This verse summarizes the battles of chapters 9 through 11 and looks forward to the division of the land in chapters 13 through 19. It emphasizes that the battles were to accomplish what the Lord directed Moses to do and passed on to Joshua. Joshua took the land as fulfillment of the promises of the Lord. Peace from the battles was necessary for an orderly division of the land.

Say It Correctly

Anakims. AN-uh-kims.
Chaldees. KAL-dees'.
Debir. DEE-buhr.
Eleazar. El'ee-AY-zuhr.
Negev. NEG-ev.
Seir. SEE-uhr.

Daily Bible Readings

M: Hope in God's Promises
Acts 26:1–7

T: God's Promises to Israel
Romans 9:1–5

W: Children of the Promise
Romans 9:6–12

T: Children of the Living God
Romans 9:22–26

F: Since We Have These Promises
2 Corinthians 6:14–7:1

S: Abound in Hope
Romans 15:7–13

S: God's Promises to Moses Fulfilled
Joshua 1:1b–6; 11:16–19, 21–23

Teaching Tips

June 12
Bible Study Guide 2

1. Words You Should Know

A. Strong (Joshua 1:7) *chazaq* (Heb.)—To be valiant, established, firm, or mighty.

B. Courageous (v. 7) *'amats* (Heb.)— Brave, bold, solid, firm.

2. Teacher Preparation

Unifying Principle—Living by the Rules. The Bible teaches that prosperity and success are contingent on obeying God.

A. Pray for lesson clarity.

B. Prepare to give a testimony of disobedient to God and the consequences.

3. Open the Lesson

A. Open with prayer, using the Aim for Change.

B. Share your testimony.

C. Summarize the In Focus story, and explain the importance of obedience in the Cherokee Indian youth's rite of passage.

D. Compare and contrast the story with the obedience God expects from us.

4. Present the Scriptures

A. Have volunteers read the Focal Verses.

B. Now use The People, Places, and Times; Background; Search the Scriptures; At-A-Glance outline; In Depth; and More Light on the Text to clarify the verses.

5. Explore the Meaning

A. Summarize the Discuss the Meaning, Lesson in Our Society, and Make It Happen sections.

B. Connect these sections to the Aim for Change and the Keep in Mind verse.

6. Next Steps for Application

A. Challenge your students to ask God to help them to obey Him.

B. Close with prayer.

Worship Guide

For the Superintendent or Teacher
Theme: God Has Expectations
Theme Song: "I Surrender All"
Devotional Reading: Deuteronomy 5:22–33
Prayer

463

God Has Expectations

Bible Background • JOSHUA 1
Printed Text • JOSHUA 1:7–16 | Devotional Reading • DEUTERONOMY 5:22–33

―――――――― **Aim for Change** ――――――――

By the end of the lesson, we will: EXPLAIN why God expects us to obey His commands; FEEL a desire to obey God; and IDENTIFY ways to obey God.

―――――――――  **In Focus** ―――――――――

Have you heard of the legend of the Cherokee Indian youth's rite of passage? His father leaves him alone in a forest blindfolded. He is told to sit on a tree stump the whole night and not remove the blindfold until the rays of the morning sun shine through it. He is forbidden to cry out or seek help from anyone. Once he survives the night, he is a man. Because each kid must come into manhood on his own, he cannot tell the other boys of this experience.

The boy is naturally terrified. He can hear all kinds of noises. Wild beasts must surely be all around him. Maybe even some human might do him harm. The wind blows the grass and shakes the tree stump, but the boy sits stoically, never removing the blindfold.

Finally, after a horrific night, the sun appears and the boy removes his blindfold. To his surprise and delight, he discovers his father sitting on the stump next to him. The proud father has been there the entire night, watching over and protecting his son from harm.

In today's lesson, God commands Joshua to be strong and courageous in the face of fear and discouragement, and to overcome his fear and discouragement with the knowledge of God's abiding presence.

―――――――――― **Keep in Mind** ――――――――――

"Only be thou strong and very courageous, that thou mayest observe to do according to all the law, which Moses my servant commanded thee: turn not from it to the right hand or to the left, that thou mayest prosper whithersoever thou goest" (Joshua 1:7).

Focal Verses

KJV Joshua 1:7 Only be thou strong and very courageous, that thou mayest observe to do according to all the law, which Moses my servant commanded thee: turn not from it to the right hand or to the left, that thou mayest prosper whithersoever thou goest.

8 This book of the law shall not depart out of thy mouth; but thou shalt meditate therein day and night, that thou mayest observe to do according to all that is written therein: for then thou shalt make thy way prosperous, and then thou shalt have good success.

9 Have not I commanded thee? Be strong and of a good courage; be not afraid, neither be thou dismayed: for the LORD thy God is with thee whithersoever thou goest.

10 Then Joshua commanded the officers of the people, saying,

11 Pass through the host, and command the people, saying, Prepare you victuals; for within three days ye shall pass over this Jordan, to go in to possess the land, which the LORD your God giveth you to possess it.

12 And to the Reubenites, and to the Gadites, and to half the tribe of Manasseh, spake Joshua, saying,

13 Remember the word which Moses the servant of the LORD commanded you, saying, The LORD your God hath given you rest, and hath given you this land.

14 Your wives, your little ones, and your cattle, shall remain in the land which Moses gave you on this side Jordan; but ye shall pass before your brethren armed, all the mighty men of valour, and help them;

15 Until the LORD have given your brethren rest, as he hath given you, and they also have possessed the land which the LORD your God giveth them: then ye shall return

NLT Joshua 1:7 "Be strong and very courageous. Be careful to obey all the instructions Moses gave you. Do not deviate from them, turning either to the right or to the left. Then you will be successful in everything you do.

8 Study this Book of Instruction continually. Meditate on it day and night so you will be sure to obey everything written in it. Only then will you prosper and succeed in all you do.

9 This is my command—be strong and courageous! Do not be afraid or discouraged. For the LORD your God is with you wherever you go."

10 Joshua then commanded the officers of Israel,

11 "Go through the camp and tell the people to get their provisions ready. In three days you will cross the Jordan River and take possession of the land the LORD your God is giving you."

12 The Joshua called together the tribes of Reuben, Gad, and the half-tribe of Manasseh. He told them,

13 "Remember what Moses, the servant of the LORD, commanded you: 'The LORD your God is giving you a place of rest. He has given you this land.'

14 Your wives, children, and livestock may remain here in the land Moses assigned to you on the east side of the Jordan River. But your strong warriors, fully armed, must lead the other tribes across the Jordan to help them conquer their territory. Stay with them

15 until the LORD gives them rest, as he has given you rest, until they, too, possess the land the LORD your God is giving them. Only then may you return and settle here on the east side of the Jordan River in the land

KJV cont.

unto the land of your possession, and enjoy it, which Moses the LORD's servant gave you on this side Jordan toward the sunrising.

16 And they answered Joshua, saying, All that thou commandest us we will do, and whithersoever thou sendest us, we will go.

NLT cont.

that Moses, the servant of the LORD, assigned to you."

16 They answered Joshua, "We will do whatever you command us, and we will go wherever you send us."

The People, Places, and Times

Canaan. In Hebrew this word is *K@na`an* (ken-AH-an). It was also called the Promised Land. Today, it is called Israel.

Joshua. Joshua had been the understudy (apprentice) of Moses for more than 40 years. Now that Moses was dead, God chose Joshua to be Moses' successor to lead the Israelites into the Promised Land (Canaan). Due to his obedience to the one true God, Joshua was not only a brilliant military leader, but a strong spiritual influence on the often disobedient, stiff-necked, rebellious Israelites who God called him to lead.

Joshua and Caleb. Out of nearly two million people who left Egypt, they were the only two to enter the Promised Land. They were blessed to do so because they trusted and believed God's promises rather than what they saw with their own eyes. The others died in the wilderness because of their disobedience. Joshua and Caleb gave the minority scouting report recorded in Numbers 13:30–14:9, which showed they were indeed men of faith and courage.

Background

Before settling in the land on the east side of the Jordan River, two great and climactic battles had yet to be fought. Moses sent emissaries to Sihon, the king of the Amorites, and requested peaceful passage through his territory. As far as the Israelites were concerned, the Promised Land was on the west side of the Jordan and they had no quarrel with the Amorites. Sihon refused the Israelites' request and instead mustered his army and attacked the Israelites. In a pitched battle, the Israelites defeated the mighty Amorite army, "put him (Sihon) to the sword," and captured all the Amorite cities (Numbers 21:24, NIV).

After defeating the Amorites, Moses sent his forces against Og, the king of Bashan. At the battle of Edrei the Israelites slaughtered the enemy force and took possession of their land. Then the Israelites camped in their captured territory on the east side of the Jordan River at the entrance to the Promised Land (Numbers 21:21–22:1).

Sometime later the tribes of Reuben and Gad sent their leaders to Moses and Eleazar the high priest with a controversial request. Both these tribes had large herds of livestock, and they saw that the land had excellent grazing pastures. They requested that they be allowed to settle in the land east of the Jordan and not be forced to cross the river with the rest of the Israelites. Moses immediately flashed back to the first time the Israelites had camped east of the Jordan and the people had refused to cross over (14:1–44). The great deliverer denied their request and promised that God would destroy all the Israelites if these two tribes deserted them.

The tribal leaders convinced Moses that they had no intention of deserting their brethren. If Moses would allow their families and livestock to stay behind in fortified cities, then the Reubenites and the Gadites would not only cross—go with them—but they would lead the charge across the river and fight with them until all the land was taken. Moses relented and gave them the land they requested. Later, half the tribe of Manasseh decided to join their brethren and settle east of the Jordan (Numbers 32:1–32).

In today's lesson, Joshua, the new leader of the Israelites, reminds the three tribes of their promise to Moses and charges them to honor their word.

At-A-Glance

1. God Commands Joshua (Joshua 1:7–9)

2. Joshua Commands the People (vv. 10–16)

In Depth

1. God Commands Joshua (Joshua 1:7–9)

Can you imagine what it must have been like to step into the sandals of Moses? God had used Moses as His instrument to deliver the Israelites from Egyptian bondage. Moses had communed face-to-face with God on His holy mountain, had prayed down manna from heaven to feed them, and had brought water from a rock to quench their thirst. Under the leadership of Moses, the Israelites defeated every army that had come against them. Now the great deliverer was dead, and Joshua was ordered to step into his place and lead these 2.5 million people into the Promised Land. Even the strongest of people would wilt at the thought of this great responsibility, so God ordered Joshua to be strong and courageous. God expects His people to be leaders by example. The apostle Paul told Timothy, "Keep a clear mind in every situation. Don't be afraid of suffering

for the Lord. Work at telling others the Good News and fully carry out the ministry God has given you" (2 Timothy 4:5, NLT). This kind of godly leadership requires strength and courage that will stand up under pressure.

God's second command to Joshua, "Be thou strong and very courageous" (Joshua 1:7), was given to ensure that Joshua would prosper and be successful in every area of his life. God was not simply interested in Joshua the leader; His concern was for Joshua the man.

Before his death, Moses had committed the Book of the Law to writing. To be successful and prosperous, Joshua had to be more than a casual reader of the Scripture. He had to ingest it and make it a vital part of his character. To accomplish this, he would have to meditate on it day and night, and allow it to dictate the actions and decisions of his life. He was not to deviate from the Law because of his own understanding of a situation, the moral values of his society, or the pressure to conform to the cultural norms of others. Joshua had been set apart, and this meant that he had to submit himself to a higher standard of obedience just as he had submitted himself to his higher calling. God's command to Joshua is applicable to all believers who have been called by Christ. Our success in life is directly related to our obedience to God.

God's final command to Joshua to be strong and courageous (Joshua 1:9) was a command to overcome fear and discouragement. Fear is probably the greatest obstacle to success. Three hundred sixty-five times the Scripture commands us to "fear not," once for every day of the year. Joshua had a number of reasons to be fearful. By replacing Moses, would the people accept him as leader? Did he have the ability to lead these people? Would he be able to overcome all the kings and their armies in the land he was entering?

God also knew that there would be difficult times ahead for the new leader of His people. Even though Joshua had been called and commissioned by God, that did not mean that the road to success and victory would be easy and that pitfalls and failures would not come up. Our Lord Jesus cautioned believers who would come to Him, "But don't begin until you count the cost" (Luke 14:28, NLT).

2. Joshua Commands the People (vv. 10–16)

After receiving his orders from God, Joshua immediately springs into action. There is an old maxim that says "strike while the iron is hot." The longer we delay in following God's direction, the more reluctant we become to comply with His requirements. Procrastination can lead to hardening against God's will and to outright disobedience. Whenever God speaks to our hearts, we must respond like the psalmist who wrote, "I will hurry, without delay, to obey your commands" (Psalm 119:60, NLT).

Joshua calls a meeting of the leaders and commands them to go through the camp and tell the people to gather their supplies and prepare themselves. His confidence in God is demonstrated in the orders he gives. "'In three days you *will* cross the Jordan River and take possession of the land the LORD your God is giving you'" (Joshua 1:11, NLT, emphasis added). After 40 years of wandering, they had come at last to the Promised Land, only to find the river overflowing its banks (3:15). The normal course of action would be to wait for the waters to recede, but Joshua was operating on God's schedule. They faced an insurmountable obstacle, but instead of concentrating on the difficulty, Joshua focuses on God's Word. Too often we undermine our focus on the Lord and His power by thinking about all the negatives, about what might happen if we move forward.

Next he directs his attention to the tribes of Reuben, Gad, and the half-tribe of Manasseh. The Word of the Lord was the authority for Joshua's challenge to these tribes. Joshua was not asking a favor to himself. The appeal and authority came from the facts of the Word of God. Servants of God must learn to lean on the power of the Word to motivate and minister to others and to accomplish God's purposes. He reminds them, "'The LORD your God is giving you a place of rest. He has given you this land'" (from 1:13, NLT), followed by the words, "until the LORD gives them rest, as he has given you rest, and until they, too, possess the land the LORD your God is giving them" (v. 15, NLT). Joshua was reminding them of their obligation to their brethren and placing an additional obligation on them based on gratitude for what God had already done for them.

Search the Scriptures

1. What command did God repeat several times for Joshua to follow (Joshua 1:6–7, 9)?

2. What were the two things Joshua had to do relating to Scripture if he was to prosper and live a successful life (v. 8) ?

Discuss the Meaning

When God commissioned Joshua, He told him three times to be strong and courageous.

1. Do you think this command is meant only for Christian leaders or does living faithful Christian lives require strength and courage by all believers?

2. How can believers draw strength from God's promise to never leave us or forsake us?

Lesson in Our Society

Many people, including believers, are controlled by their passions. Our uncontrolled desires are often the cause of a majority of our problems and illnesses. People with anger problems have a hard time maintaining meaningful relationships, eating disorders can be the cause of diseases like hypertension and diabetes, and so on. Does God give believers the power to overcome the desires of their flesh? If so, why do we so often fall victim to the passions within us?

Make It Happen

When God called you out of darkness, He also called you into service. It may seem amazing to you, but God has expectations for you. What gifts, talents, and skills has God blessed you with? How can you use the gifts, talents, and skills to benefit your community and your church? God and our people are looking to bless our communities through the use of others within the community. Can He use you?

Follow the Spirit

What God wants me to do:

_____

_____

_____

_____

Remember Your Thoughts

Special insights I have learned:

_____

_____

_____

_____

More Light on the Text
Joshua 1:7–16

7 Only be thou strong and very courageous, that thou mayest observe to do according to all the law, which Moses my servant commanded thee: turn not from it to the right hand or to the left, that thou mayest prosper withersoever thou goest.

This verse starts out almost the same as the preceding verse which commanded Joshua, "Be strong and of a good courage." In verse 7 the word "very" is added, which in Hebrew is *m@`od* (**meh-ODE**). It adds intensity to the word "courageous" and highlights the seriousness of the command to obey God's Law.

The Hebrew word for "the law" is *towrah* (**to-RAH**). The Torah is generally recognized by Jews as the first five books of Moses— Genesis, Exodus, Leviticus, Numbers, and Deuteronomy. These five books were probably the only Scripture available to Joshua.

The key to Joshua's success is not his military genius or his leadership ability, but the key is in his obedience to the Lord. He is not to deviate from Scripture, even a tiny bit to the right or left. The end result of following the Lord is that Joshua will prosper wherever he goes. The Hebrew word for "prosper" is *sakal* (**saw-KAL**). We may think of prosperity in terms of financial wealth, but this word is not used in Scripture that way but rather points to wise choices. When our lives are completely focused on God and we are truly obedient to all that the Bible teaches, we will make the right decisions.

8 This book of the law shall not depart out of thy mouth; but thou shalt meditate therein day and night, that thou mayest observe to do according to all that is written therein: for then thou shalt make thy way prosperous, and then thou shalt have good success.

The Hebrew word for "meditate" is *hagah* (**daw-GAW**), which literally means "to mutter" or "to murmur." Our contemporary concept of meditation may be skewed by eastern mysticism, which views meditation as emptying one's mind or perhaps thinking on a single word or a single picture. Biblical meditation is just the opposite. It is filling our minds with God's Word. Those in biblical times meditated aloud. Imagine reciting Scripture aloud and answering in spoken prayer. It might sound like a private conversation between the believer and the Almighty God as the Word is spoken aloud and the one meditating responds orally. Perhaps we should try this method at times when we find our minds wandering instead of focusing on God's Word.

The Eastern concept of meditation can be a dangerous one. We read in Matthew 12:43–45 that when an evil spirit is cast out, if there remains a vacuum, the evil spirit will return with seven additional evil spirits. This reminds us of the old adage that an empty mind is the devil's playground. Our objective should not be to empty our minds but to fill them with God's Word.

The previous verse used the word "prosper," and this verse contains the word "success." Again "health and wealth" preachers have misinterpreted the word. "Success" in Hebrew is *yarash* (**yaw-RASH**), meaning "to take possession of" or "to inherit." This word as well as "prosper" have nothing to do with individual financial wealth. It refers to succeeding in proper endeavors. Thus, success is granted by God and not by human achievement. What God counts as success is often quite different from what this world counts as success.

9 Have not I commanded thee? Be strong and of a good courage; be not afraid, neither be thou dismayed: for the LORD thy God is with thee whithersoever thou goest.

Once again Joshua is commanded to be strong and courageous, but this time the thought is enhanced by the negative—do not be afraid or dismayed. To be "afraid" in Hebrew is `arats (**aw-RATS**), which gives us the picture of shaking or trembling. The Hebrew word for "dismayed" is *chathath* (**khaw-THATH**). It also gives a mental image, but this image is of falling down in great terror. God's command to be strong and courageous is backed up with the wonderful promise that God was going to be with Joshua wherever he went. As long as Joshua obeyed God's Word, he was assured of the Lord's presence, and this promise is for us, too. We are in the center of God's will; He is always with us.

10 Then Joshua commanded the officers of the people, saying,

The officers of the people were administrative officers appointed by Moses and not by military officers. They were respected leaders in Israel with spiritual qualifications (Numbers 11:16–17; Deuteronomy 1:15–16) and with responsibility for teaching God's Law as well as judging the people. A key word in this first chapter of Joshua is "command," which in Hebrew is *tsavah* (**tsaw-VAW**), This word is found in verses 7, 9, 10, 11, 13, 16, and 18, and it can be translated as "give a charge to." Most of the time this word is used for God's commands to His people, but sometimes it also has the sense of God's delegated authority for giving commands. In this case we see Joshua who is given the order from the Lord, and then he passes it on to the leaders who pass it on to the people. In verses 16 and 18 the people respond by promising to obey God's commands that were passed down to them. Here is where Joshua demonstrated his leadership strength in delegating God's orders.

11 Pass through the host, and command the people, saying, Prepare you victuals; for within three days ye shall pass over this Jordan, to go in to possess the land, which the LORD your God giveth you to possess it.

So far, all of the instructions that the Lord gave Joshua were non-military, and this verse continues in this direction. In God's sight, possession of the Promised Land was a done deal, so the overall strategy had nothing to do with military preparedness. Instead the people were to get food ready for the next few days before they entered the Promised Land. Manna probably ceased when they left the wilderness and entered the land of Edom.

We read the word "possess" twice in verse 11. The Hebrew is *yarash* (**yaw-RASH**), and the original meaning was "to inherit" but includes the sense of appropriating through military force. So to possess the land was not simply a passive act but involved action by the people. Receiving blessings from the Lord is rarely a passive act. Even those who followed our Lord Jesus had to seek Him out for themselves. Jesus shared much spiritual truth in the form of parables. Those who really wanted the truth sought Him out for the explanations, such as Nicodemus did in coming to Him at night (John 3:1–21) and certainly as His apostles and other disciples did.

12 And to the Reubenites, and to the Gadites, and to half the tribe of Manasseh, spake Joshua, saying,

Before the Israelites had crossed the Jordan, these two and a half tribes (known as the Transjordan tribes) had staked a claim to property on the east side of the Jordan. In Numbers 32, we read that they had asked Moses for permission to settle there because the land was good for pasturing their animals. (See Numbers 32:1, which tells us that the Reubenites and the Gadites had a great multitude of cattle.) Moses granted this to them on the condition that they would help the rest of the Israelites to conquer the Promised Land on the west side of the Jordan River. Moses reminded the people of their promise in Deuteronomy 3:16–20, which Joshua quotes almost verbatim in the verses that follow here.

13 Remember the word which Moses the servant of the LORD commanded you, saying, The LORD your God hath given you rest, and hath given you this land.

The Hebrew word for "rest" is *nuwach* (**NOO-akh**), which means "to settle down" or "to remain confident." We see this word again in Joshua 1:15. Rest in the context of the first chapter of Joshua is specifically rest from war. The biblical theme of rest starts in Genesis 2:2 where we read that God rested after the six days of creation and continues throughout the Bible with special emphasis upon a spiritual rest in Hebrews 4:1–11. The tribes of Reuben, Gad, and the partial tribe of Manasseh were in a unique position. They already had their land and already had rest from war, but they were not going to really rest until all of Israel could settle down as one nation.

14 Your wives, your little ones, and your cattle, shall remain in the land which Moses gave you on this side Jordan; but ye shall pass before your brethren armed, all the mighty men of valour, and help them;

The men of the east Jordan tribes were to lead the remainder of the Israelites in battle. They were "armed"—in Hebrew, *chamush* (**khaw-MOOSH**). They were also "mighty men of valour"—in Hebrew, *chayil* (**KHAH-**

yil), which means they were the military elite. These men had already driven out the inhabitants of the land east of Jordan, had finished their own battles, and already had rested in their own tribal areas. Now they were going to be the leaders in the battle for the Promised Land on the west side of the Jordan River. This verse is almost identical to Deuteronomy 3:19, except here the word "land" is used instead of the word "towns" in Deuteronomy 3:19 (NLT). This change emphasizes God's gift of "the land" to His people.

15 Until the LORD have given your brethren rest, as he hath given you, and they also have possessed the land which the LORD your God giveth them: then ye shall return unto the land of your possession, and enjoy it, which Moses the LORD's servant gave you on this side Jordan toward the sunrising.

The emphases of this verse are on rest and possession of the land. Joshua's rest is a rest from military endeavors in the Promised Land. Isaiah 28:12 tells us that God desires for His people to have rest, but Israel repeatedly rejected it. We read in Matthew 11:28 that wonderful invitation from Jesus to us, "Come unto me, all ye that labour and are heavy laden, and I will give you rest." How often we find ourselves too busy to enjoy His rest! It is in just those times that we need it most.

16 And they answered Joshua, saying, All that thou commandest us we will do, and whithersoever thou sendest us, we will go.

Scholars differ on whether this response is from all the Israelites or just the Reubenites, Gadites, and the half-tribe of Manasseh, but this enthusiastic response from the people must have been very encouraging to Joshua. They were probably quite sincere in this response. But it reminds us of the response of their fathers just before Moses gave them

the Ten Commandments: "All that the LORD hath spoken we will do" (Exodus 19:8). And yet by the time Moses came down from Mount Sinai with the tablets of stone, the people were already building a golden calf to worship (Exodus 32). Israel's history was full of such instances. But lest we get too smug, we need to examine ourselves to see if we have obeyed all the commands of our God.

Say It Correctly

Bashan. BAY-shuhn.
Manasseh. ma-NAS-uh, muh-NAS-uh.

Daily Bible Readings

M: God's Commandments Given
Deuteronomy 5:28–33

T: Listen and Learn
Deuteronomy 31:7–13

W: Treasure God's Word
Psalm 119:9–16

T: Walk in God's Ways
1 Kings 2:1–4

F: As Long as He Sought God
2 Chronicles 26:1–5

S: Teach Me, O Lord
Psalm 119:33–40

S: The Key to Success
Joshua 1:7–16

Teaching Tips

1. Words You Should Know

A. Search (Joshua 2:3) *chaphar* (Heb.)—To hunt for, also implies to pry into or to spy.

B. Flax (v. 6) *pishteh* (Heb.)—The plant from which linen fabric is made.

C. Fords (v. 7) *ma`abar* (Heb.)—Places for crossing a river.

2. Teacher Preparation

Unifying Principle—Knowing Whom to Trust. God used Rahab to protect the spies from harm when she hid them from the soldiers that the king of Jericho had sent to find them.

A. Pray for lesson clarity.

B. As you study and meditate on this lesson, reflect on how you have been able to depend on God for protection in dire situations. Prepare to share.

3. Open the Lesson

A. Open with prayer, including the Aim for Change.

B. After prayer, introduce today's subject of the lesson and have your students read the Aim for Change and Keep in Mind verse in unison. Discuss.

C. Share your testimony of God's protection in your life.

D. Allow volunteers to also share their testimonies.

E. Then have a volunteer summarize the In Focus story. Discuss.

F. Compare and contrast this story with how we as believers should trust in God to protect us at all times, even to give us eternal life as He promised.

4. Present the Scriptures

A. Have volunteers read the Focal Verses.

B. Now use The People, Places, and Times; Search the Scriptures; At-A-Glance outline; In Depth; and More Light on the Text to clarify the verses.

C. Assign one of the students to read the Background material and explain how Satan uses worldly enticements to cause believers to turn away from God and suffer the consequences of sin.

5. Explore the Meaning

A. Have volunteers summarize the Discuss the Meaning, Lesson in Our Society, and Make It Happen sections.

B. Connect these sections to the Aim for Change and the Keep in Mind verse.

6. Next Steps for Application

A. Ask volunteers to summarize what they learned from this lesson.

B. Challenge them to pray and ask God to help them to praise Him for His faithfulness.

C. Close with prayer.

Worship Guide

For the Superintendent or Teacher
Theme: God Protects
Song: "O to Be Kept by Jesus"
Devotional Reading: James 2:18–25
Prayer

God Protects

Bible Background • JOSHUA 2
Printed Text • Joshua 2:3–9, 15–16, 22–24 | Devotional Reading • James 2:18–25

―――――――――― **Aim for Change** ――――――――――

By the end of the lesson, we will: CITE proof that God protects us and we can trust in Him; APPRECIATE God's protection; and EXPRESS praises to God for His protection and faithfulness.

―――――――――― 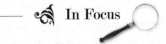 **In Focus** ――――――――――

A sick man turned to his doctor as he was preparing to leave the examination room and said, "Doctor, I am afraid to die. Tell me what lies on the other side."

Very quietly, the doctor said, "I don't know."

"You don't know? You, a Christian man, do not know what is on the other side?" The doctor was holding the handle of the door. On the other side came a sound of scratching and whining, and as the doctor opened the door, a dog sprang into the room and leaped on him with an eager show of gladness. Turning to the patient, the doctor said, "Did you notice my dog? He's never been in this room before. He didn't know what was inside. He knew nothing except that his master was here, and when the door opened, he sprang in without fear. I know little of what is on the other side of death, but I do know one thing—I know my Master is there, and that is enough."

Scripture confirms what is appointed to us once we die, and that is the judgment. The determining factor at judgment will be where you placed your trust in life.

In today's lesson, two spies sent out by Joshua put their trust in God, and He leads them to successfully complete their mission.

―――――――――― **Keep in Mind** ――――――――――

"And they said unto Joshua, Truly the LORD hath delivered into our hands all the land; for even all the inhabitants of the country do faint because of us" (Joshua 2:24).

"And they said unto Joshua, Truly the LORD hath delivered into our hands all the land; for even all the inhabitants of the country do faint because of us" (Joshua 2:24).

Focal Verses

KJV **Joshua 2:3** And the king of Jericho sent unto Rahab, saying, Bring forth the men that are come to thee, which are entered into thine house: for they be come to search out all the country.

4 And the woman took the two men, and hid them, and said thus, There came men unto me, but I wist not whence they were:

5 And it came to pass about the time of shutting of the gate, when it was dark, that the men went out: whither the men went I wot not: pursue after them quickly; for ye shall overtake them.

6 But she had brought them up to the roof of the house, and hid them with the stalks of flax, which she had laid in order upon the roof.

7 And the men pursued after them the way to Jordan unto the fords: and as soon as they which pursued after them were gone out, they shut the gate.

8 And before they were laid down, she came up unto them upon the roof;

9 And she said unto the men, I know that the LORD hath given you the land, and that your terror is fallen upon us, and that all the inhabitants of the land faint because of you.

2:15 Then she let them down by a cord through the window: for her house was upon the town wall, and she dwelt upon the wall.

16 And she said unto them, Get you to the mountain, lest the pursuers meet you; and hide yourselves there three days, until the pursuers be returned: and afterward may ye go your way.

2:22 And they went, and came unto the mountain, and abode there three days, until the pursuers were returned: and the pursuers sought them throughout all the way, but found them not.

NLT **Joshua 2:3** So the king of Jericho sent orders to Rahab: "Bring out the men who have come into your house, for they have come here to spy out the whole land."

4 Rahab had hidden the two men, but she replied, "Yes, the men were here earlier, but I didn't know where they were from.

5 They left the town at dusk, as the gates were about to close. I don't know where they went. If you hurry, you can probably catch up with them."

6 (Actually, she had taken them up to the roof and hidden them beneath bundles of flax she had laid out.)

7 So the king's men went looking for the spies along the road leading to the shallow crossings of the Jordan River. And as soon as the king's men had left, the gate of Jericho was shut.

8 Before the spies went to sleep that night, Rahab went up on the roof to talk with them.

9 "I know the LORD had given you this land," she told them. "We are all afraid of you. Everyone in the land is living in terror."

2:15 Then, since Rahab's house was built into the town wall, she let them down by a rope through the window.

16 "Escape to the hill country," she told them. "Hide there for three days from the men searching for you. Then, when they have returned, you can go on your way."

2:22 The spies went up into the hill country and stayed there three days. The men who were chasing them searched everywhere along the road, but they finally returned without success.

KJV cont.

23 So the two men returned, and descended from the mountain, and passed over, and came to Joshua the son of Nun, and told him all things that befell them:

24 And they said unto Joshua, Truly the LORD hath delivered into our hands all the land; for even all the inhabitants of the country do faint because of us.

NLT cont.

23 Then the spies came down from the hill country, crossed the Jordan River, and reported to Joshua all that had happened to them.

24 "The LORD had given us the whole land," they said, "for all the people in the land are terrified of us."

The People, Places, and Times

The Immorality of Canaanite Religions. The Bible firmly states that the Canaanites' religion and lifestyle were immoral. The Canaanites destroyed themselves by their sinful living. This is what God means when He tells Abraham, "But in the fourth generation they (Abraham's descendants) shall come hither again: for the iniquity of the Amorites (Canaanites) is not yet full" (Genesis 15:16). God will not give the land to His people too soon. God will wait until evil has run its course.

God warned His people through Moses, "Thou shalt not bow down to their gods, nor serve them, nor do after their works: but thou shalt utterly overthrow them, and quite break down their images....Thou shalt make no covenant with them, nor with their gods. They shall not dwell in thy land, lest they make thee sin against me: for if thou serve their gods, it will surely be a snare unto thee" (Exodus 23:24, 32–33).

The Bible and the Canaanite texts at Ugarit use the Hebrew words *qadesh* (**kaw-DASHE**) and *qedesha* which mean "holy one"—the first masculine, the second feminine. These "holy ones" were homosexual and female priests and priestesses who acted as prostitutes.

We find strong Hebrew reaction against this type of cultic prostitution in passages such as Leviticus 19:29 where it says, "Do not prostitute thy daughter, to cause her to be a whore." One of Josiah's reforms was "he brake down the houses of the sodomites" (2 Kings 23:7).

The immorality of Jericho was so bad that God's word to His people was: "And the city (Jericho) shall be accursed, even it, and all that are therein, to the LORD...And they utterly destroyed all that was in the city, both man and woman, young and old, and ox, and sheep, and ass, with the edge of the sword" (from Joshua 6:17, 21).

Background

When the king of Moab saw how Israelites had defeated the superior forces of both Sihon, king of the Amorites, and Og, king of Bashan, he realized that these Israelites would never be defeated by military might alone. Instead of assembling his army and attacking Balak, the king of the Moabites recruited a prophet from Mesopotamia named Balaam to curse Israel. He thought the well-known prophet would be able to bring evil upon the Israelites by influencing the will of the gods. However, instead of cursing the Israelites, God caused Balaam to bless them (Numbers 22–24). Although the prophet failed in his mission to curse the Israelites, he advised Balaam of another means to possibly defeat the Israelites (see Numbers 31:16).

"While the Israelites were camped at Acacia Grove, some of the men defiled themselves by having sexual relations with the local Moabite women. These women invited them to attend sacrifices to their gods, so the Israelites feasted with them and worshiped the gods of Moab. In this way, Israel joined in the worship of Baal of Peor, causing the LORD's anger to blaze against his people" (Numbers 25:1–3, NLT). Balaam understood the only way to defeat God's people was to cause them to turn away from their God.

The Lord commanded Moses to apprehend the ringleaders of the apostasy and execute them in broad daylight so all the people could witness their punishment. One of the men was so bold that he paraded a Midianite woman before Moses and all the people and took her into his tent to have sex with her. His actions so enraged Phinehas, the son of Eleazar, the high priest, that he took a spear and rushed into the man's tent and drove the spear through him and the woman at once.

The killing of this man and the leaders of the apostasy appeased God's anger, and He ended the plague against the people, but not before 24,000 of them had perished. The 24,000 who died from the plague were the last of the generation who revolted against God and Moses the last time they were at the entrance to the Promised Land (see Numbers 14:29–30; cf. 26:64–65).

Two years after these incidents, the Israelites were stilled camped at Shittim, the Acacia Grove. They were under the leadership of Joshua, preparing to go in and take their inheritance. Isn't it just like God to use a pagan prostitute to accomplish His will?

At-A-Glance

In Depth

1. God Protects the Spies (Joshua 2:3–9, 15–16)

Before launching an attack, a good leader will always try to gather as much information about his or her enemy as possible. However, Joshua remembered what had happened when Moses publicly sent the 12 spies on a mission to gather information on the opposition they faced. The men brought back a report that struck fear into the hearts of the people and caused them to revolt against Moses and God. This commander was taking no chances. He secretly sent out two spies to check out the enemy, with particular emphasis on Jericho, and report back to him.

Somehow the two men made their way across the Jordan River and traveled the eight miles over land to Jericho without being spotted by any lookouts. They made their way to an inn being run by a prostitute named Rahab (a "harlot" or in Hebrew zanah, **zaw-NAH,** see Joshua 2:1) and stayed there. God's divine protection is not only in the fact that the two men managed to cross the Jordan River and reach the city undetected, but also in the house they chose. The entire city must have been on alert for strangers coming to spy out the city. However, God directed the Israelite spies at that time to one person in all of Jericho whom He had chosen for divine appointment. Scripture simply describes her as "Rahab the prostitute." In pagan Canaan, prostitutes who served in the worship of Baal-Peor were highly honored and respected in the community (see Numbers 25:1–2). It was not unusual for strangers and foreigners to go to Rahab's house, or hotel, and so the spies would not appear suspicious there. Others who passed through the house would provide the spies with information on the situation in Jericho.

Somehow the spies were spotted either before they made it to Rahab's house or maybe their questions in the house caused suspicion. At any rate, the news was reported back to the king of Jericho. When the king heard the news of the two spies in the city, he immediately dispatched a contingent to Rahab's house to capture them. The king's men arrived at Rahab's house and ordered her, "'Bring out the men who have come into your house, for they have come here to spy out the whole land'" (Joshua 2:3, NLT). Somehow Rahab had been alerted to the coming of the king's men and had hidden the two spies. She met the king's men at the door and deceived them into thinking that the spies had gone. She first acknowledged that the men had indeed arrived there earlier, but she denied knowing who they were. Then she lied to the king's men: "'I don't know where they went. If you hurry, you can probably catch up with them'" (v. 5, NLT).

Many have argued whether Rahab's lying was justified, but the argument misses the point. Rahab was a pagan. She was acting according to her own convictions, not the Law. God knew when He directed the men to the house of a pagan prostitute that she would resort to sin to achieve her ends. The means did not justify the end, but when she later turned to God (v. 11), her lying as well as her pagan prostitution were forgiven.

2. The Spies Encourage Joshua (vv. 22–24)

After confessing her trust in the one true God, Rahab demanded a promise from the spies: "'Now swear to me by the LORD that you will be kind to me and my family since I have helped you. Give me a guarantee that when Jericho is conquered, you will let me live, along with my father and mother, my brothers and sisters, and all their families'" (Joshua 2:12–13, NLT). The two spies agreed to her terms, and later on she helped them

to escape. The walls of Jericho were said to be more than 10 feet high and 12 feet thick; this allowed for houses such as Rahab's to be built into the wall themselves. Using a rope, the two spies lowered themselves down through her window to the ground outside the city. Rahab instructed them to go into the hills and wait three days before making their way back across the Jordan River. The spies instructed Rahab that when they returned with the Israelite army, she was to tie a scarlet cord in the window that they had just climbed down from. This cord would serve to identify Rahab's house to the attacking Israelites and cause them to spare all within (v. 18). The scarlet cord reminds us of the lamb's blood above the doorpost in Egypt which caused the "death angel" to pass by the houses of the Israelites (Exodus 12:1–23); the cord also looks forward to the redemptive work of Jesus that saves us all (Mark 14:12–16; John 1:29; Hebrews 11:26–28).

The spies then departed and went to the mountains and waited as Rahab had instructed. Meanwhile the king's men continued to diligently search for them but to no avail. After the three days had passed, the spies descended from the mountains and made their way back across the Jordan River and gave their report to Joshua: "'The LORD has given us the whole land,' they said, 'for all the people in the land are terrified of us'" (Joshua 2:24, NLT).

Joshua's trust in God was rewarded with a glowing report from the spies. The new leader did not have to worry about the armies they would face and the hardships they would endure.

Search the Scriptures

1. How did Rahab respond to the king's order to bring out the two men who had entered her house (Joshua 2:4–5)?

2. What promise did Rahab extract from the two men for hiding them and helping them escape (vv. 12–13)?

Discuss the Meaning

When the king's men arrived at Rahab's house to apprehend the two spies, Rahab lied to them and told them the spies had gone. Was she justified in lying to protect God's people? Can lying ever be justified to God or is it always sinful?

Lesson in Our Society

Before gaining salvation knowledge of the Lord, Rahab earned her living as a prostitute. Yet this woman married a man who was an ancestor of King David and is listed in the bloodline of Christ (Matthew 1:5–6). Both James and the writer of Hebrews commend her for her faith (Hebrews 11:31; James 2:25). How does Rahab's story relate to the undesirable people in our community? Is it possible that God has a special mission for some gangbanger, drug addict, or prostitute in our communities?

Make It Happen

Rahab demonstrated her faith in God by doing a great kindness to two strangers she had never met. This week, pray and ask God to direct you to some stranger who needs a bit of kindness. And then show your love and faith in God by extending that kindness.

Follow the Spirit

What God wants me to do:

_____

_____

_____

_____

Remember Your Thoughts

Special insights I have learned:

_____

_____

_____

_____

More Light on the Text
Joshua 2:3–9, 15–16, 22–24

3 And the king of Jericho sent unto Rahab, saying, Bring forth the men that are come to thee, which are entered into thine house: for they be come to search out all the country.

The Hebrew word for "king" is *melek* (**MEH-lek**). A large, heavily fortified city like Jericho was like a small kingdom, and it had its own king. This was true of other similar cities in Canaan. We are not told the name of the king of Jericho, but we discover that the king quickly found out about the spies' "secret" mission (see verse 1). He knew that Joshua had sent two spies, and he knew exactly where they had gone. So the spies were failures as covert agents, but God used this reconnaissance mission as an encouragement to His people.

Verse 2 tells us that the spies went to the house of Rahab the prostitute. Her home was an inn, the place for many to pass through. Though a few commentators have thought that the spies went here for sexual purposes, the inn of the prostitute was a natural place for spies to get information, since many people were in and out of there and much news and gossip were sure to be shared. When we look at Joshua 7:24–25 and see how severely God punished the sin of greed in Achan, we are sure that God would not be blessing the mission of the spies if they had so blatantly disobeyed God and not kept themselves pure.

Joshua 2:1 seems to imply that the spies were being sent to spy out the entire land, and the king of Jericho thought so, too. But Joshua's previous direction to the people to gather food for only three days (1:11) would seem to indicate that the spy mission was expected to be brief—only to check out the city of Jericho.

The Hebrew word for "search" is *chaphar* (**khaw-FAR**), and it also implies "to pry into" or "to spy." Thus we see that the mission of the spies was known to the enemies at the highest levels. Rahab's hiding of the spies was definitely treason, so she was, in effect, renouncing her Canaanite citizenship and casting herself with the Israelites and their God.

4 And the woman took the two men, and hid them, and said thus, There came men unto me, but I wist not whence they were:

"Wist" is an old-fashioned word for "know" and in Hebrew is *yada*ʿ (**yaw-DAH**). This indicates the beginning of Rahab's deceit. Though Scripture does not comment on the morality of her lies, Scripture has always taught that honesty is always God's Law. However, Rahab, as a prostitute and a Canaanite, may not have even realized that this lie was wrong. Biblical scholars have long debated over this issue: Is it ever right to lie to protect human life?

5 And it came to pass about the time of shutting of the gate, when it was dark, that the men went out: whither the men went I wot not: pursue after them quickly; for ye shall overtake them.

When the light of the day turned into darkness, the gate (or gates in some cases) of ancient cities were closed for safety's sake. Rahab's deceit continued, but her suggestion

that the posse hurry after the spies assured that they were not lingering to make a more thorough search of her home. Although the text does not mention it, surely God was protecting Rahab and the men in this instance. It is surely true in our own lives that we are unaware of the many times God is protecting us.

6 But she had brought them up to the roof of the house, and hid them with the stalks of flax, which she had laid in order upon the roof.

"Flax," which in Hebrew is *pishteh* (**pish-TEH**), is the plant from which linen fabric is made. Egyptians cultivated flax before the Exodus and the Canaanites were cultivating it when the Israelites arrived. The process involved pulling and drying the stalks and was often a household task. The stalks were deseeded, soaked, and then redried. The fiber was coarse and short and could be woven into cloth. The seeds could also be used to make linseed oil. So this picture of Rahab hiding the men under the flax as it dried would be a picture of life in that era.

7 And the men pursued after them the way to Jordan unto the fords: and as soon as they which pursued after them were gone out, they shut the gate.

This was the logical direction for the pursuers to go—toward the Jordan River, since the Israelites were encamped on the other side of the river. Rahab had acted dumb and said she did not know where the spies had gone, but she had suggested that the king's men take off after the two men quickly. This was a smart move because this got them out of her house quickly before the Canaanites had time to look through it more carefully. As soon as the pursuers left, the city gate was shut. This gives us a picture of a very heavily guarded city. Rahab knew it would not be smart to take the spies out through the city gate anyways.

The Hebrew for "fords" is *ma`abar* (**mah-ab-AWR**) and means "places for crossing a river." We read in Joshua 3:15 that this was the harvest season, and at this time the Jordan River was overflowing its banks, making it very dangerous to cross it. At this point, the spies were completely dependent upon Rahab for their safety. The gates were shut, and she alone could provide another way out of Jericho.

8 And before they were laid down, she came up unto them upon the roof;

The word "roof" in Hebrew is *gag* (**gawg**). As in the Middle East of the era, roofs were flat. On warm evenings, people would often sleep on the roof, but the spies had not yet gone to sleep.

9 And she said unto the men, I know that the LORD hath given you the land, and that your terror is fallen upon us, and that all the inhabitants of the land faint because of you.

This verse provides the military intelligence that the spies needed. Although Jericho and many other Canaanite cities were heavily fortified, the people were demoralized concerning their ability to fight against God's people. It was already prophesied (Exodus 15:15) that the hearts of the inhabitants of the land would melt for fear. However, it was only Rahab who allowed this frightening situation to draw her to side with the LORD God. The Hebrew word for "know," *yada`* (**yaw-DAH**), is the same as for "wist" in verse 4. Before, she lied and said she did not know. Now she begins her declaration with "I know" as she describes how she has come to put her trust in the God of the Israelites.

This verse is just the beginning of Rahab's great statement of faith. Whenever the Old Testament spells LORD in all capital letters, it indicates the personal name of God: *Yhovah* (**yeh-ho-VAW**). God revealed Himself to Moses by this name (Exodus 3:15). When God speaks of Himself, He says, I AM. When we speak of Him, we say, HE IS. This name indicates His eternal existence. He was, He is, and He will be.

In Joshua 2:10 and 11, Rahab recounted in accurate detail how the Lord parted the Red Sea for the Israelites (Exodus 14) and how He empowered His people to overcome the Amorites and their kings, Sihon and Og (Numbers 21:21–35). Then Rahab gave this amazing testimony, "The LORD your God, he is God in heaven above, and in earth beneath" (Joshua 2:11). Rahab was a Canaanite, and the Canaanites had many gods. They believed that the most powerful god was Baal and secondly, his consort Asherah. But when Rahab made her statement of faith, she was declaring that there is only one God and Yahweh (LORD) is His name.

2:15 Then she let them down by a cord through the window: for her house was upon the town wall, and she dwelt upon the wall. 16 And she said unto them, Get you to the mountain, lest the pursuers meet you; and hide yourselves there three days, until the pursuers be returned: and afterward may ye go your way.

Rahab continued to show concern for the safety of the spies as she directed them to hide in the hills to the west of Jericho. The Hebrew for "mountain" is *har* (**har**), which can mean mountain or a range of hills. The hills referred to here were the Qarantal Hills, which were west of Jericho and were filled with many caves and grottos in which the spies could hide. This was the opposite direction from going back toward the Israelites on the other side of the Jordan

River. Rahab had already seen to it that the posse went east toward the Jordan. So she directed the two men to stay in the hills for three days, at which time the posse pursuing them would have given up the search.

2:22 And they went, and came unto the mountain, and abode there three days, until the pursuers were returned: and the pursuers sought them throughout all the way, but found them not.

The two spies were not found by their pursuers, but this again is surely a case of God's unseen hand protecting His people. This verse tells us that the spies stayed at the mountain three days. This is reckoned according to the measurement of time that the Jews of Jesus' day still used. This means at least one portion of each of three days.

23 So the two men returned, and descended from the mountain, and passed over, and came to Joshua the son of Nun, and told him all things that befell them:

As mentioned earlier, the Jordan River was in flood stage and crossing over it was extremely dangerous. The two spies were probably very strong swimmers, but we are sure that God was taking care of them all the way. We can imagine the spies sitting down with Joshua and telling him the whole long story of hiding under the flax with trembling hearts, following Rahab's advice, and so on.

24 And they said unto Joshua, Truly the LORD hath delivered into our hands all the land; for even all the inhabitants of the country do faint because of us.

The report of the spies in this verse is almost an exact quotation of Rahab's witness to the spies in verse 9. The book of Joshua presents the Israelite hero—Joshua—but in this chapter we see a Canaanite heroine. She encouraged the chosen people in the task of conquering the Promised Land, and she reminds us of God's promise to Abraham that in his descendants all families of the earth would be blessed (Genesis 12:3).

Say It Correctly

Bashan. 'bā-shən.
Eleazar. ehl-ih-EE-zar.
Shittim. SHIH-tim.

Daily Bible Readings

M: The Promises of God
2 Corinthians 1:16–20

T: God's Promises Kept
Joshua 21:43–22:6

W: Rahab's Confession of God
Joshua 2:10–14

T: Rahab's Pact with the Spies
Joshua 2:17–21

F: Rahab's Help Rewarded
Joshua 6:22–25

S: Rahab and Her Works
James 2:18–25

S: Rahab's Protection of the Spies
Joshua 2:3–9, 15–16, 22–24

Teaching Tips

1. Words You Should Know

A. Rereward (Joshua 6:13) *'acaph* (Heb.)—A military term for the rear guard troops.

B. Accursed (v. 17) *cherem* (Heb.)— Something that is dedicated or devoted to destruction.

2. Teacher Preparation

Unifying Principle—The Thrill of Victory. The Bible teaches that God used the destruction of Jericho for the benefit of God's people.

A. Pray for your students and that God will bring clarity to this lesson.

B. Study and meditate on the entire text.

C. Prepare a Power Point or bring news clippings of historical incidents that you and others have prayed much about.

3. Open the Lesson

A. After prayer, introduce today's subject of the lesson.

B. Have your students read the Aim for Change and Keep in Mind verse in unison. Discuss.

C. Share your presentation.

D. Then ask, "Has God delivered you from anything?"

E. Allow volunteers to share their personal testimonies.

F. Now have a volunteer summarize the In Focus story. Discuss.

G. Then ask, "Why is it so hard to wait on God and follow His directions?" Discuss.

4. Present the Scriptures

A. Have volunteers read the Focal Verses.

B. Now use The People, Places, and Times; Background; Search the Scriptures; At-A-Glance outline; In Depth; and More Light on the Text to clarify the verses.

5. Explore the Meaning

A. Have volunteers summarize the Discuss the Meaning, Lesson in Our Society, and Make It Happen sections.

B. Connect these sections to the Aim for Change and the Keep in Mind verse.

6. Next Steps for Application

A. Summarize the lesson.

B. Close with prayer and praise God for the victory He's won in their lives and for who He is.

Worship Guide

For the Superintendent or Teacher
Theme: God Is Victorious
Song: "Victory Is Mine"
Devotional Reading: Psalm 98:1–6
Prayer

God Is Victorious

Bible Background • JOSHUA 5:13–6:27
Printed Text • JOSHUA 6:2–3, 4b, 12–20b | Devotional Reading • PSALM 98:1–6

———————— Aim for Change ————————

By the end of the lesson, we will: TELL how God brings victory to our lives; FEEL confident in obeying God's instructions; and RECALL some of the past victories that God won for us and praise Him.

———————— In Focus ————————

Phil is in a predicament. He knows he must make a decision, but he is having difficulty. Phil's family and friends all have suggestions about what he should do, and all the suggestions seem logical. The problem is Phil believes that God is directing him toward a certain decision, but he feels that it does not make sense.

Phil then remembers another time he had to make a decision. Although that situation did not in any way resemble this one, the similarity was that God granted a solution that did not seem logical in Phil's eyes or in the eyes of his family and friends. Phil's choice was difficult in the past, but in the end, he followed God's direction. Phil's friends and family immediately mocked him, but his decision quickly proved to provide the most amazing outcome. This memory helped Phil with his current predicament, and like the Israelites at the wall of Jericho, Phil chose to do exactly what God asked of him.

Why is it sometimes difficult to follow God's direction? Even when God has proven Himself repeatedly, we often want to do our own thing. What can we do to make it easier to follow God's plan in the future?

———————— Keep in Mind ————————

"And it came to pass at the seventh time, when the priests blew with the trumpets, Joshua said unto the people, Shout; for the LORD hath given you the city" (Joshua 6:16).

"And it came to pass at the seventh time, when the priests blew with the trumpets, Joshua said unto the people, Shout; for the LORD hath given you the city" (Joshua 6:16).

Focal Verses

KJV **Joshua 6:2** And the LORD said unto Joshua, See, I have given into thine hand Jericho, and the king thereof, and the mighty men of valour.

3 And ye shall compass the city, all ye men of war, and go round about the city once. Thus shalt thou do six days.

4b And the seventh day ye shall compass the city seven times, and the priests shall blow with the trumpets.

6:12 And Joshua rose early in the morning, and the priests took up the ark of the LORD.

13 And seven priests bearing seven trumpets of rams' horns before the ark of the LORD went on continually, and blew with the trumpets: and the armed men went before them; but the rereward came after the ark of the LORD, the priests going on, and blowing with the trumpets.

14 And the second day they compassed the city once, and returned into the camp: so they did six days.

15 And it came to pass on the seventh day, that they rose early about the dawning of the day, and compassed the city after the same manner seven times: only on that day they compassed the city seven times.

16 And it came to pass at the seventh time, when the priests blew with the trumpets, Joshua said unto the people, Shout; for the LORD hath given you the city.

17 And the city shall be accursed, even it, and all that are therein, to the LORD: only Rahab the harlot shall live, she and all that are with her in the house, because she hid the messengers that we sent.

18 And ye, in any wise keep yourselves from the accursed thing, lest ye make yourselves accursed, when ye take of the accursed thing, and make the camp of Israel a curse, and trouble it.

19 But all the silver, and gold, and vessels of brass and iron, are consecrated unto the LORD: they shall come into the treasury of the LORD.

20b And the people shouted with a great shout, that the wall fell down flat, so that the people went up into the city, every man straight before him, and they took the city.

NLT **Joshua 6:2** But the LORD said to Joshua, "I have given you Jericho, its king, and all its strong warriors.

3 You and your fighting men should march around the town once a day for six days.

4b On the seventh day you are to march around the town seven times, with the priests blowing the horns.

6:12 Joshua got up early the next morning, and the priests again carried the Ark of the LORD.

13 The seven priests with the rams' horns marched in front of the Ark of the LORD, blowing their horns. Again the armed men marched both in front of the priests with the horns and behind the Ark of the LORD. All this time the priests were blowing their horns.

14 On the second day they again marched around the town once and returned to the camp. They followed this pattern for six days.

15 On the seventh day the Israelites got up at dawn and marched around the town as they had done before. But this time they went around the town seven times.

16 The seventh time around, as the priests sounded the long blast on their horns, Joshua commanded the people, "Shout! For the LORD has given you the town!

17 Jericho and everything in it must be completely destroyed as an offering to the LORD. Only Rahab the prostitute and the others in her house will be spared, for she protected our spies.

18 Do not take any of the things set apart for destruction, or you yourselves will be completely destroyed, and you will bring trouble on the camp of Israel.

19 Everything made from silver, gold, bronze, or iron is sacred to the LORD and must be brought into his treasury."

20b They shouted as loud as they could. Suddenly, the walls of Jericho collapsed, and the Israelites charged straight into the town and captured it.

The People, Places, and Times

Jericho. It is one of the oldest known fortified cities in the ancient world and could very well be the oldest city on the earth. It is thought that the name "Jericho" sounds like the Hebrew word for "moon"—*y@riychow* (**yer-ee-KHO**). This led many to believe that it could have been the central place of moon worship. It is also believed that the destruction of Jericho was commanded by God in Deuteronomy 20:16–17 because of its paganism.

Dates. The Exodus and the victory over Jericho are interrelated; that much the Bible tells us. However, there is confusion about whether the Exodus took place around 1446 B.C. (fifteenth century) or 1220 B.C. (thirteenth century), which both fall into what historians call the Late Bronze Age (1550–1200 B.C). Most of the archeological research supports the battle at Jericho happening around 1250 B.C. This would have meant that the Exodus took place under Pharaoh Rameses II. However, a good case is also made for 1406 B.C., when Amunhotep II was pharaoh. The exact time remains questionable today because at this time biblical text referred to any pharaoh only as "Pharaoh" and never by his individual name.

The Israelites. Known as God's chosen people, the Israelites are held in a special covenant with God. However, 40 years prior to the period of Joshua's leadership, at the time of the Exodus, Israel disappointed God by fearing humans—the Canaanites—and believing in their own abilities as opposed to having faith in Him. Because of this, God declared that nobody from that generation would enter the Promised Land—except for Joshua and Caleb. But because God is a promise keeper, He kept the covenant He made with Abraham about providing a permanent place for his heirs (Genesis 15:13, 16, 18; 17:8).

Joshua. Early in life, Joshua was known as Hosea, which means "salvation." However, Joshua had the honor of being renamed by Moses, and he received his more common name, which means "the Lord saves (or the Lord gives victory)." The Greek form of Joshua is *Iesous* (**ee-ay-SOOCE**), which of course became Jesus, the most beloved name. Joshua was a man of honor, a man who trusted God. He was also known as the "new Moses" (Joshua 1:1–9). He was the man who was to lead the Israelites into the Promised Land. He was given this honor because he was one of two spies out of 12 who returned with a positive message for Moses after spying on the land that God had promised (Numbers 13:30). Because Joshua trusted in the Lord instead of fearing the Canaanites, God granted him and Caleb their generation's sole opportunity to enter the Promised Land. Joshua remained faithful to God as he was chosen to take over Moses' work and bring the Israelites into the Promised Land.

Background

Today's lesson begins shortly after the end of the 40 years that the Israelites wandered in the desert. Because the Israelites did not trust God at the time of the Exodus and rebelled against Him, He did not allow them into the land that was promised to them. Instead, He made sure that all of that generation died out—all but Joshua and Caleb.

Moses was part of the generation that was unable to enter the Promised Land. Instead, Joshua inherited his duties. Joshua lived through Egypt's rule and experienced the miracles that God conducted to lead the Israelites out of bondage, including the parting of the Red Sea. Since the Israelites needed a leader, God commissioned Joshua, His chosen servant, because He knew Joshua would follow His instructions as he had in the past.

At-A-Glance

1. A Promise to the Israelites (Joshua 6:2)

2. Instructions to the Israelites
(vv. 3–4b)

3. The Choice of the Israelites
(vv. 12–20b)

In Depth

1. A Promise to the Israelites (Joshua 6:2)

God promised the Israelites a land in which they could settle. The last of the old generation had passed, and it was time for the promise to be fulfilled. God showed them that He had delivered the land and its inhabitants to them. However, God gave them a task that must be completed. They had to work for their gift and follow God's direction.

Because God is almighty, He easily could have destroyed the city on His own and given His people the land, but instead they had to work for it. And the work was not easy, or necessarily practical. However, success was guaranteed if they followed His direction, just as He promised.

2. Instructions to the Israelites (vv. 3–4b)

After reiterating His promise, God told the Israelites what must be done. He gave them specific directions to follow which would guarantee their entry into the Promised Land. Again, God could have delivered the city to the Israelites immediately, but they were to follow a set of specific instructions perfectly for a week.

The Israelites were to circle Jericho, a fortified and seemingly impenetrable city, for seven days. The first six days required one circle around. The seventh day required seven circles, led by the seven priests blowing seven trumpets while carrying the Ark, signifying the Lord's presence. God's use of the number seven solidifies the sacred significance of the event. He used seven priests with seven trumpets, with the siege to take place in seven days, and the city was to be encircled seven times on that seventh day. This may have been done to signify the beginning of God's new order in the world, mirroring the seven-day creation of the world itself.

3. The Choice of the Israelites (vv. 12–20b)

The Israelites, led by Joshua, chose to follow the Lord's instructions exactly as He commanded. Not only did He give instructions about how to destroy the city, but He also provided instructions about what to do after the walls fell—to not take possession of anything. Perhaps the Israelite's decision to obey so readily stemmed from the history of their people. They were to enter the Promised Land unlike their fathers because of the past generation's failure to fully trust God. Although God's instructions were not familiar in warfare, it proved that He alone was responsible for the victory. Not only did the Israelites have a choice, but Rahab the prostitute had a choice. Rahab, who protected the spies and demonstrated her devotion to God, made a decision that allowed for her and her family to be spared (Joshua 2:1–24; 6:17).

Search the Scriptures

1. What did the Lord deliver to Joshua and the Israelites (Joshua 6:2)?

2. Why were Rahab and her family spared (v. 17)?

3. Why were the Israelites instructed to take nothing from the city (v. 18)?

Discuss the Meaning

1. Why were no other Canaanites spared from Jericho?

2. Why was it important that the Israelites take nothing from the city?

Lesson in Our Society

Our human brains always want to make sense of our world. However, our sense is never God's sense and we forget that. We forget that God is not human and that His perfection is the standard to bear in mind. He will not do things as we would do things, and we should follow Him. He has history, precedence, and authority on His side.

Remember we are children of a living God. His way is always *the* way. His timing is always *the* time. Instead of struggling to fit Him into your mold, mold yourself into His. Also, remember your own history. Has God delivered you from anything? How did He deliver you? What led you to put your trust in Him? Did you doubt His answer initially? What was the outcome?

Make It Happen

Pray that God will allow you to more readily trust Him. Pray that He will help your faith to grow. Remember that you may be a leader to others, so let them see that you allow God to be in control of your life. Your example may show them that even though what God is telling them may not make sense to them, it is the right way to go. Prepare to be an example in your action and in your words. Brainstorm different times that God directed you or provided you with deliverance and be ready to share it when a friend or an unbeliever has questions.

Follow the Spirit

What God wants me to do:

_____

_____

_____

_____

Remember Your Thoughts

Special insights I have learned:

_____

_____

_____

_____

More Light on the Text

Joshua 6:2–3, 4b, 12–20b

2 And the LORD said unto Joshua, See, I have given into thine hand Jericho, and the king thereof, and the mighty men of valour.

The verb form of "I have given" is the perfect tense; in other words, the battle has already been won. Joshua and the Israelites only needed to claim the victory. We never learn the name of the king of Jericho or any of his "mighty men of valour." Rahab is the only name of an inhabitant of Jericho that we ever learn. The king and his mighty men are the material defenses of Jericho, but the Israelites have the Lord God. This verse indicates that God has entrusted the leadership for this task to Joshua.

3 And ye shall compass the city, all ye men of war, and go round about the city once. Thus shalt thou do six days.

Archeologists tell us that ancient Jericho was about nine acres, so a walk around the entire city might only take 15 to 20 minutes.

However, it must have taken a long time for all the warriors to march around the city. If you live in a large city, think of rush hour. You may only have a short distance to travel, but because of all the other commuters, it will take a long time.

It must have been a little humiliating for the Israelites to march around the city day after day. The citizens of Jericho probably had very mixed feelings. At first they probably were shaking in their boots, wondering what the Israelite army was up to. Then as the days passed, they probably began to relax a little as they saw nothing happening.

4b And the seventh day ye shall compass the city seven times, and the priests shall blow with the trumpets.

The orders for winning the battle of Jericho sound much more like directions for a ceremony than a military strategy. The number seven is an important part of this narrative. There are four instances of seven in this verse alone and 14 mentions in the chapter. Seven represents perfection, totality, and completeness in Scripture. The sevens in this narrative represent the completeness of God's victory on behalf of Israel.

6:12 And Joshua rose early in the morning, and the priests took up the ark of the LORD.

Just as the day in which Joshua led the people in crossing over the Jordan River (Joshua 3:1), Joshua got up early in the morning. Both tasks were undertaken with Joshua leading and the priests carrying the Ark of the Covenant.

13 And seven priests bearing seven trumpets of rams' horns before the ark of the LORD went on continually, and blew with the trumpets: and the armed men went before them; but the rereward came after the ark of the LORD, the priests going on, and blowing with the trumpets.

Warriors, priests, and the Ark of the Covenant ("the ark of the LORD") make up the procession. Two different kinds of horns are mentioned here. The "rams' horns" in Hebrew is *yowbel* (**yo-BALE**). This type of horn was used as a signal to let the Israelites know when they were allowed to approach Mount Sinai. The "trumpets" mentioned in Joshua 6:13 are in Hebrew *showphar* (**sho-FAR**), another type of ram's horn. This type of horn is the most commonly mentioned one in the Old Testament, and it was often used for signaling in time of battle, as well as its use in religious ceremonies.

This verse tells us the order of the procession—first the armed guard, then the priests, and after them came the Ark. The word "rereward" in Hebrew is *'acaph* (**aw-SAF**) and is a military term for the rear guard troops, so at the end were more armed men. Following them were more priests blowing on trumpets.

14 And the second day they compassed the city once, and returned into the camp: so they did six days.

Each day the marchers returned to the camp at Gilgal (Joshua 5:10). Gilgal was the temporary camp for Joshua and the Israelites. In Joshua 9:6 and 10:6 we read that this was where they were still camped, both when the Gibeonites came and deceived them and when the Gibeonites requested their help.

15 And it came to pass on the seventh day, that they rose early about the dawning of the day, and compassed the city after the same manner seven times: only on that day they compassed the city seven times.

"It came to pass" in Hebrew is *hayah* (**haw-yaw**) and can be translated "and it happened." Look back at verse 12 where Joshua got up early in the morning; here all the warriors are getting up early. There will be lots to do on this day. The entire Israelite army will have to march around the city seven times. And when the walls fall down, the warriors will have a great military task.

The Hebrew word for "only" is *raq* (**rak**), and it emphasizes that this day is different.

16 And it came to pass at the seventh time, when the priests blew with the trumpets, Joshua said unto the people, Shout; for the LORD hath given you the city.

The word for "shout" in Hebrew is *ruwa`* (**roo-AH**), and it literally means "to burst the ear with sound." So when the priests blew with a long blast, the people were to shout with an ear-piercing sound. The reason for the shout was not to knock down the walls; the reason was to acknowledge God's accomplished destruction of Jericho.

17 And the city shall be accursed, even it, and all that are therein, to the LORD: only Rahab the harlot shall live, she and all that are with her in the house, because she hid the messengers that we sent.

Here, there is a pause in the instructions from Joshua—some very important things for the warriors and priests to obey. All the inhabitants of Jericho are to be killed. "Accursed" in Hebrew is *cherem* (**KHAY-rem**), and it means "something that is dedicated or devoted to destruction." God had His reasons for telling the Israelites to destroy the Canaanite people. In Deuteronomy 20:16–18,

NLT, He said, "In those towns that the LORD your God is giving you as a special possession, destroy every living thing. You must completely destroy the Hittites, Amorites, Canaanites, Perizzites, Hivites, and Jebusites, just as the LORD your God has commanded you. This will prevent the people of the land from teaching you to imitate their detestable customs in the worship of their gods, which would cause you to sin deeply against the LORD your God."

But there is one important exception—Rahab and her family are to be rescued. In Joshua 6:22, we read that Joshua assigned the two spies the task of escorting out Rahab and her entire family. Rahab has accepted the Lord God as her God and the nation of Israel as her people. She married an Israelite man and became one of the ancestors of our Savior (Matthew 1:5).

18 And ye, in any wise keep yourselves from the accursed thing, lest ye make yourselves accursed, when ye take of the accursed thing, and make the camp of Israel a curse, and trouble it.

Joshua clarifies the command regarding the things devoted to destruction by giving it in the negative, along with stating the consequences of disobedience. Keep away from such things, he is telling the Israelites, or you yourself will be accursed (headed for destruction) and will bring a curse on the chosen people.

19 But all the silver, and gold, and vessels of brass and iron, are consecrated unto the LORD: they shall come into the treasury of the LORD.

In this verse, we read of another way to devote things and that is to make them gifts to God. All the treasures of the city of Jericho are to be consecrated to the Lord. The

Hebrew word for "consecrated," *qodesh* (**KO-desh**), means "holy, set apart for God."

This is the first reference in the Bible to a treasury; the Hebrew word for "treasury" is *'owtsar* (**ow-TSAR**). We are not sure where this was located, but the logical guess is somewhere within the tabernacle.

20b And the people shouted with a great shout, that the wall fell down flat, so that the people went up into the city, every man straight before him, and they took the city.

Now Joshua has finished his parenthetical instructions to the Israelites, and we pick up where the story left off—as the Israelites are shouting and the walls of Jericho are falling down completely. Then the Israelites are following the final instruction for the battle—walk right into the city and overtake it.

Say It Correctly

Caleb. KAY-lehb.
Jericho. JER-uh-koh
Joshua. JAH-sh(uh-)wuh.
Hosea. hoh-ZEE-uh, not hoh-ZAY-uh, HOH-zay.

Daily Bible Readings

M: The Victory of Our God
Psalm 98:1–6

T: A Victory to Anticipate
Isaiah 25:6–10

W: Victory Through Christ
1 Corinthians 15:50–57

T: The Victory of Faith
1 John 5:1–5

F: A Petition for Victory
Psalm 20

S: Assurance Before the Battle
Joshua 5:10–15

S: God's Victory Over Jericho
Joshua 6:2–3, 4b, 12–20b

Notes

_____

_____

_____

_____

Teaching Tips

1. Words You Should Know

A. Covenant (Joshua 7:11) *bâriyth* (Heb.)—An alliance, pact, or agreement.

B. Messengers (v. 22) *mal'ak* (Heb.)—Representatives.

2. Teacher Preparation

Unifying Principle—The Agony of Defeat. The Bible teaches that the consequence of disobeying God is severe punishment.

A. Pray for lesson clarity.

B. Study and meditate on the complete lesson.

C. Reflect on "sin"—disobeying God's commands and real situations where there have been generational curses (such as alcoholism, drug abuse, spousal abuse, child abuse, etc.).

D. Read Genesis 3 and prepare to discuss how Adam and Eve's disobedience to God in the Garden of Eden opened the door for all kinds of sin to come into God's perfect world (such as murder, hatred, lies, theft, etc.).

3. Open the Lesson

A. Open with prayer, including the Aim for Change.

B. Then ask your students to reflect on a situation where generations suffered because of the sins of forefathers and foremothers. Discuss.

C. Explain that the penalty for sin is death (eternal separation from a Holy [set apart from sin] God).

D. Then summarize the In Focus story and discuss what led to Jason's fall at his place of employment.

4. Present the Bible Lesson

A Have volunteers read the Focal Verses.

B. Now use The People, Places, and Times; Background; Search the Scriptures; At-A-Glance outline; In Depth; and More Light on the Text to clarify the verses.

5. Explore the Meaning

A. Have volunteers summarize the Discuss the Meaning, Lesson in Our Society, and Make It Happen sections.

B. Connect these sections to the Aim for Change and the Keep in Mind verse.

6. Next Steps for Application

A. Summarize the lesson.

B. Close with prayer.

Worship Guide

For the Superintendent or Teacher
Theme: God Reacts to Disobedience
Theme Song: "Oh, to Be Kept by Jesus"
Devotional Reading: Romans 6:1–11
Prayer

God Reacts to Disobedience

Bible Background • JOSHUA 7:1–8:29
Printed Text • JOSHUA 7:1, 10–12, 22–26 | Devotional Reading • ROMANS 6:1–11

———————— Aim for Change ————————

By the end of the lesson, we will: EXPLAIN why disobeying God brings severe consequences; DESIRE to repent for personal sin; and ASK God to forgive us for our sin of disobedience.

JULY
3rd

————————  In Focus ————————

Jason was unhappy about the way things were going in his life. Only a few weeks ago, he was next in line for the big promotion and the big raise at work. Everybody in his office knew that he was favored to get them. However, things changed when Jason joined a fellow coworker in a certain financial "opportunity." Because he was part of a mega-company, Jason was sure that it would go unnoticed. His coworker had been taking part in this arrangement for a while now. It was not entirely illegal, and besides, Jason planned to only do it that one time.

But something went wrong. Jason's coworker was caught and subsequently terminated from his job. An investigation began. Jason's coworker was not naming any names, but it was only a matter of time before everything came back to Jason. Things were different in the office. It seemed as though people knew or at least suspected him. Even his boss was treating him differently. Jason wished he could have taken back that one decision. He knew that what he did was not God's will, but he had done it anyway. Now he was paying for it.

How is Jason's decision affecting him? Our behavior often results from our greed. What could or should have stopped Jason from making the decision that he made? Today's lesson focuses on how God reacts to disobedience—sin (transgressions of His Laws).

———————— Keep in Mind ————————

"But the children of Israel committed a trespass in the accursed thing: for Achan, the son of Carmi, the son of Zabdi, the son of Zerah, of the tribe of Judah, took of the accursed thing: and the anger of the LORD was kindled against the children of Israel" (Joshua 7:1).

Focal Verses

KJV **Joshua 7:1** But the children of Israel committed a trespass in the accursed thing: for Achan, the son of Carmi, the son of Zabdi, the son of Zerah, of the tribe of Judah, took of the accursed thing: and the anger of the LORD was kindled against the children of Israel.

7:10 And the LORD said unto Joshua, Get thee up; wherefore liest thou thus upon thy face?

11 Israel hath sinned, and they have also transgressed my covenant which I commanded them: for they have even taken of the accursed thing, and have also stolen, and dissembled also, and they have put it even among their own stuff.

12 Therefore the children of Israel could not stand before their enemies, but turned their backs before their enemies, because they were accursed: neither will I be with you any more, except ye destroy the accursed from among you.

7:22 So Joshua sent messengers, and they ran unto the tent; and, behold, it was hid in his tent, and the silver under it.

23 And they took them out of the midst of the tent, and brought them unto Joshua, and unto all the children of Israel, and laid them out before the LORD.

24 And Joshua, and all Israel with him, took Achan the son of Zerah, and the silver, and the garment, and the wedge of gold, and his sons, and his daughters, and his oxen, and his asses, and his sheep, and his tent, and all that he had: and they brought them unto the valley of Achor.

25 And Joshua said, Why hast thou troubled us? the LORD shall trouble thee this day. And all Israel stoned him with stones, and burned them with fire, after they had stoned them with stones.

NLT **Joshua 7:1** But Israel violated the instructions about the things set apart for the LORD. A man named Achan had stolen some of these dedicated things, so the LORD was very angry with the Israelites. Achan was the son of Carmi, a descendant of Zimri son of Zerah, of the tribe of Judah.

7:10 But the LORD said to Joshua, "Get up! Why are you lying on your face like this?

11 Israel has sinned and broken my covenant! They have stolen some of the things that I commanded must be set apart for me. And they have not only stolen them but have lied about it and hidden the things among their own belongings.

12 That is why the Israelites are running from their enemies in defeat. For now Israel itself has been set apart for destruction. I will not remain with you any longer unless you destroy the things among you that were set apart for destruction.

7:22 So Joshua sent some men to make a search. They ran to the tent and found the stolen goods hidden there, just as Achan had said, with the silver buried beneath the rest.

23 They took the things from the tent and brought them to Joshua and all the Israelites. Then they laid them on the ground in the presence of the LORD.

24 Then Joshua and all the Israelites took Achan, the silver, the robe, the bar of gold, his sons, daughters, cattle, donkeys, sheep, goats, tent, and everything he had, and they brought them to the valley of Achor.

25 Then Joshua said to Achan, "Why have you brought trouble on us? The LORD will now bring trouble on you." And all the Israelites stoned Achan and his family and burned their bodies.

KJV cont.

26 And they raised over him a great heap of stones unto this day. So the LORD turned from the fierceness of his anger. Wherefore the name of that place was called, The valley of Achor, unto this day.

NLT cont.

26 They piled a great heap of stones over Achan, which remains to this day. That is why the place has been called the Valley of Trouble ever since. So the LORD was no longer angry.

The People, Places, and Times

Achan. Of the tribe of Judah, Achan was the individual responsible for Israel's broken covenant. God gave the Israelites specific instructions after they defeated the people of Jericho. He told them not to take anything from the city into their possession. Everything that could be destroyed was to be destroyed, and all the silver, gold, bronze, and iron were to go into the treasury of the Lord (Joshua 6:18–19). This was commanded in order for all unclean things to be purged. However, Achan thought he could take what he wanted and escape punishment. Although he was an individual perpetrator, his actions affected the whole of Israel, as it is a covenant community. Because of his sin, the whole of Israel had sinned and was punished.

Israel. The Lord held a covenant with Israel. After they wandered in the desert for 40 years, God allowed them to finally enter the Promised Land. He gave specific instructions and expected them to be followed. Israel is considered a corporate unity in the covenant; therefore, one individual's decision will affect the entire nation. Achan's actions brought the Lord's anger upon the whole of Israel. Because Achan broke the covenant, the Israelites were made liable to destruction (7:12). Fresh off their first Canaanite victory, the Israelites were then defeated in Ai because there was sin in the camp or among them (vv. 4–5).

The Bible said the whole of Israel stoned Achan and his family (v. 25). This involvement of the entire community was necessary for the purification of the nation. It was also a way to ensure that no one individual had to be the only executioner.

The Valley of Achor. Here lies a monument of stones. "Achor" represents the Hebrew word `akowr (**aw-KORE**), similar to the Hebrew word `akar (**aw-KAR**), which means "to trouble, to disturb." The heap of stones served to remind the Israelites about what would happen if they failed to follow the instructions of the Lord. Achor is another form of Achan (see "Achar" in 1 Chronicles 2:7).

Background

At the start of today's lesson, Israel has broken the covenant that was made with the Lord. The nation has just experienced its first Canaanite victory at the battle of Jericho. Unfortunately, one person has disobeyed God's command to destroy all things and tried to hide the forbidden, stolen things; however, nothing can be hidden from God. Even though Joshua did not know of this betrayal, the fact that Israel's second attempt at defeating the Canaanites (at Ai) failed showed that there was a problem.

One man caused Israel's downfall. God shows that when He makes a covenant with a nation, each individual is responsible for the community. Achan's decision to break the covenant affected himself, his family, and Israel. God's anger did not dissipate until Achan and his family were killed and Israel was purged and purified.

At-A-Glance

1. A Nation's Trespasses (Joshua 7:1)

2. A Nation's Consequence (vv. 10–12)

3. A Nation's Purification (vv. 22–26)

In Depth

1. A Nation's Trespasses (Joshua 7:1)

Directly following the victory at Jericho, the people of Israel had trespassed against God. Although we may not think it is fair that one person's transgressions has a negative effect on an entire group of people, but that is how God's justice worked. He was in a covenant with the people; therefore, the fault of one man made the whole nation responsible.

Achan was a descendant of the tribe of Judah, a very fine pedigree, but his actions caused God's anger. God saw this as a betrayal, and His anger was directed against the Children of Israel.

2. A Nation's Consequence (vv. 10–12)

Joshua was confused. He was relishing the success at Jericho, the first Canaanite victory. He was confident that he would succeed in another battle; however, he was not aware that one of the Israelites broke the covenant with the Lord. When Joshua sent 3,000 men to Ai, they were defeated because the Lord did not endorse them. Joshua was baffled; God revealed Achan's betrayal to him and explained that one man's decision could have an adverse consequence on all the people. The only way to rectify it, God told Joshua, would be to eradicate the cursed from among them.

3. A Nation's Purification (vv. 22–26)

Once Joshua heard of Achan's transgressions, he sent messengers to his tent to see all that was taken. They found silver hidden under it. The solution to the problem was to gather Achan's entire family and all his belongings and destroy them. This was to ensure that the nation was purified, the evil was purged, and Israel was fit to remain in the covenant with the Lord. Therefore, Achan and his family were stoned and burned. Afterward, the people raised a monument over the body of Achan. It was left to remind the people of the consequences of a broken covenant.

Search the Scriptures

1. How did Israel trespass against God (Joshua 7:1–11)?

2. Describe what happened to Israel due to these trespasses (v. 12).

3. What did God say would happen if the Israelites failed to destroy the accursed (v. 12)?

Discuss the Meaning

1. Why would God punish an entire nation for the transgressions of one person?

2. Why was it necessary for the whole of Israel to take part in the punishment of Achan and his family?

Lesson in Our Society

In today's society, we tend to believe that we can pick and choose what we can and cannot do as God's children. We choose to follow God's will with a little modification of our own. God's plan is the best, and any detour off His path can have bigger ramifications than we can imagine.

Make It Happen

1. Pray that God will open your eyes to His will.

2. Ask Him to eliminate your ego so that you may see and choose His way.

3. Ask that He make His desires clear so that there is no question which way you should go.

Follow the Spirit

What God wants me to do:

_____

_____

_____

_____

Remember Your Thoughts

Special insights I have learned:

_____

_____

_____

_____

More Light on the Text

Joshua 7:1, 10–12, 22–26

1 But the children of Israel committed a trespass in the accursed the thing: for Achan the son of Carmi, the son of Zabdi, the son of Zerah, of the tribe of Judah, took of the accursed thing: and the anger of the Lord was kindled against the children of Israel.

In Joshua 6, the Lord had delivered Jericho into the hands of Israel. They marched around the city for six days, and on the seventh day the city's walls came tumbling down. Here in chapter seven, once again the Children of Israel have sinned against their God and have done evil in His sight. They committed "a trespass." The phrase "a trespass" in Hebrew is *ma`al* (**MAH-al**) and means "an unfaithful or treacherous act." Achan, an Israelite from the tribe of Judah, was guilty of stealing, and for this sin he lost his inheritance that would have been given to him freely in the Promised Land. He just needed to obey the Lord, but he did not.

Achan took things that did not belong to him and consequently found himself in a dreadful situation. His actions not only brought judgment upon himself, but his family as well—and even the whole nation of Israel. In addition, because of his sin not only did many men die, but Israel's army also succumbed in fear. When Joshua questioned God, God threatened to withdraw His presence because there was sin in the camp. Needless to say, God reacted to Achan's disobedience. In fact, all of this happened because there was no effort made by Achan to repent for breaking God's covenant with God's chosen people.

7:10 And the LORD said unto Joshua, get thee up; wherefore liest thou thus upon thy face?

Because of Achan's sin, God commanded that Joshua, His new chosen leader of the people, get up and deal with the matter. In fact, He essentially asked Joshua, "Why are you lying down, when Israel has broken my covenant?" The phrase "thou thus upon thy face" in Hebrew is *paniym* (**paw-NEEM**) and means "in the presence of, in the face of." Therefore, in the presence of a holy (set apart from sin) God, Israel has committed this sin. They transgressed against God's Laws. Also, a leader cannot turn away from or dismiss sin among God's people. He or she must deal with it and deal with it swiftly. Otherwise, the sin can infect the whole congregation.

11 Israel hath sinned, and they have also transgressed my covenant which I commanded them: for they have taken of the accursed thing, and have also stolen, and dissembled also, and they have put it even among their own stuff.

God not only accused them of sin in the camp, but He named the sin that Achan had committed; he had stolen. The phrase "hath sinned" in Hebrew is *chata'* (**khaw-TAW**), meaning "became guilty, deserving condemnation or punishment." Thus, God acknowledged that the Israelites had broken their covenant with Him. Even though Achan had stolen the things that God had commanded to be set apart for Himself, condemnation and judgment came upon the whole nation of Israel. We see this in families as well. The sins of the father or mother can destroy the whole family. The word "covenant" in Hebrew is *bâriyth* (**ber-EETH**) and means "an alliance, pact or agreement." Consequently, Israel at this point had fallen into the enemies' hands because once again they had disobeyed the Lord their God. Israel had stolen property that did not belong to them. The consequence of this sin was that they went into battle at Ai and lost. In reality Joshua, like Moses, found himself in a very difficult position trying to lead a people who had a tough time following the precepts of their God, who always kept His covenant with them.

12 Therefore the children of Israel could not stand before their enemies, but turned their backs before their enemies, because they were accursed: neither will I be with you any more, except ye destroy the accursed from among you.

Israel found herself in a defeated position with her enemy being in a superior position. They had brought a curse on themselves by not following what the Lord God Jehovah commanded them to do. *Cherem* (**KHAY-rem**) is the Hebrew word for "accursed," and it means "banned, utterly destroyed." Without God's presence with them, Israel was no match for her enemies; she was utterly destroyed. It is the same for all believers. We are no match for Satan on our own, and the sooner we recognize this fact, the better off we will be. Like the Israelites, we need the presence of Almighty God to win our physical and spiritual battles. Israel's God was not supporting them in their battle at Ai because someone among them (Achan) disobeyed by not giving the enemies' goods to the Lord's treasury. Instead, against God's commands, he took stolen silver and other valuables back to camp and hid them. Sin has a consequence, which is ultimately death. Often in life when we as believers don't follow God's edits, there are dire consequences which come to us in this life. We may try to blame our plight on God, but in reality we bring it upon ourselves. Therefore, even though God gives us a choice of whether to walk with Him or not, it is to our advantage to choose to walk with Him—to choose to obey Him. The sin of disobedience can cost us dearly. Even our innocent loved ones can suffer. Achan's sinful act was a personal sin for him, and it was corporate sin for his family and the nation.

When Achan brought the silver and other goods home to bring prosperity to his own family, why didn't someone question where he had gotten his riches? Why didn't a godly person in the family say, "Didn't God say for us not to take anything from the enemy camp except to give to the Lord's treasury? Why did you bring these things home?" Since there is nothing in the Bible to tell us otherwise, we can conclude that Achan did not get rebuked by anyone in his immediate family, and they all ended up paying a severe price for his act of disobedience. To make sure we hold our fellow believers accountable, we are called to be our brothers and sisters' keepers! From this lesson, we should be challenged to hold our own individual family members up to a godly standard.

7:22 So Joshua sent messengers, and they ran unto the tent: and behold, it was hid in his tent, and the silver under it.

Joshua sent "messengers" (Heb. *mal'ak*, **mal-AWK,** which means "representatives") to the tent of Achan to find the stolen goods that were the source of God's anger with His people. In order to once again enjoy God's presence, Joshua needed to rid the camp of the sin that was causing the problem. Purification was necessary. The Lord instructed Joshua to tell the people to be a holy (set apart from sin) people as He is! Israel was told to set themselves apart to do the work of the Lord. First Peter 2:9 (NIV) says that believers are "a chosen people, a royal priesthood, a holy nation." We are a people who belong to God, and therefore we were chosen to exemplify in our everyday living the excellent qualities of God. Because believers are a chosen people, we are held to a higher standard. Israel was a royal priesthood and was expected to be a holy nation; this is the reason the sin of Achan was taken so seriously by God. Any breach of God's commands should be taken seriously.

Since Joshua knew how important it was to be part of a holy nation, he found a way to deal with the sin of Achan. How often do we face the situation we are dealing with head on? As the leader of God's people, Joshua had to step up and deal with the sin that was causing the problem for Israel. This could not be swept under the rug or overlooked.

Time after time, Israel fell short of keeping God's commandments. Eventually after sending prophet after prophet, God sent His only Son to save humanity from sin. At the heart of this lesson is the issue of sin. Just as generation after generation has tried to cover up their sins and failed, Achan was in a similar situation. He tried to cover up his sinful act. He hid his treasures! But as we should all know, we cannot hide anything from an omniscient (all-knowing), omnipresent (all-present), and omnipotent (all-powerful God). He sees all, He knows all, and He deals with disobedience.

23 And they took them out of the midst of the tent, and brought them unto Joshua and unto all the children of Israel, and laid them out before the LORD.

The stolen goods were displayed before the Lord and for all the people to see the sin of Achan. It became a public matter for all of Israel to witness. It is always difficult to have your sin open before the public.

24 And Joshua, and all Israel with him, took Achan the son of Zerah, and the silver, and the garment, and the wedge of gold, and his sons, and his daughters, and his oxen, and his asses, and his sheep, and his tent, and all that he had: and they brought them unto the valley of Achor.

"Achor" in Hebrew (`Akowr, **aw-KORE**) means "the valley of trouble where Achan and his family were stoned." Note that even the animals were included in the punishment. Sin infiltrates; therefore, it must be completely destroyed. Joshua, who is probably best known for saying, "As for me and my house, we will serve the LORD" (Joshua 24:15), was the one who had to handle the mess Achan created for Israel. After years of watching Moses lead, Joshua was now striving to lead the people in obedience to their great God. Achan and everything he stole was now exposed, and Joshua as God's chosen leader led the way to address the sin that was in the camp of Israel.

Remember that Moses did not make it to the Promised Land because he also had a lapse in obedience when he got extremely frustrated with the people's disobedience. Joshua, being Moses' understudy, had an opportunity to learn plenty of leadership lessons—including the negative side of the job. He had to deal with this critical matter of sin, and he stepped up to address the problem that threatened to overwhelm Israel's progress. This passage shows us as believers that God is a loving God, but He is also a God that disciplines His people. He is also a God of wrath.

25 And Joshua said, Why hast thou trouble us? the LORD shall trouble thee this day. And all Israel stoned him with stones, and burned them with fire, after they had stoned them with stones.

The phrase "hast thou trouble" is `akar (**aw-KAR**) in Hebrew and means "to be disturbed, to be stirred up." Not many people want the reputation of being a troublemaker. But Achan earned this title as the person who brought the judgment of the Lord upon the people of Israel. Joshua called out the sin of Achan and told him he brought trouble upon himself for willfully disobeying what the Lord said not to do. It may seem incredibly cruel in our day to hear that Achan and his family were stoned to death and burned for his act of rebellion. Stoning was also a public notice to let all of Israel know that God would not tolerate sin.

26 And they raised over him a great heap of stones unto this day. So the LORD turned from the fierceness of his anger. Wherefore the name of that place was called, The valley of Achor, unto this day.

God is a God of order and a God of judgment. He also is a God of love. Most of the time people like to hear about the God of love, but not about the God of judgment.

Say It Correctly

Achan. AY-kan.
Ai. AY-i.
Omnipotent. om-NIP-uh-tuhnt, ahm-NIH-puh-tuhn.
Omnipresent. om'nuh-PREH-zuhnt, ahm'nih-PREHZ-uhnt.
Omniscient. om-NISH-uhnt, ahm-NIH-shuhnt.
Zabdi. ZAB-di.
Zerah. ZEE-rah, ZIHR-uh.

Daily Bible Readings

M: Victory Turned to Defeat
Joshua 7:2–9

T: The Reason for the Defeat
Joshua 7:12–15

W: The Sin Revealed
Joshua 7:16–21

T: The Wages of Sin
Romans 6:15–23

F: The Work of the Advocate
John 16:4b–11

S: Dead to Sin, Alive to God
Romans 6:1–11

S: The Outcome of Achan's Sin
Joshua 7:1, 10–12, 22–26

Teaching Tips

1. Words You Should Know
A. Evil (Judges 2:11, 15) *ra`* (Heb)—Bad, unpleasant, displeasing behavior.

B. Spoilers (v. 14) *shacah, shasah* (Heb.)—"Plunderers" or enemies.

C. Repented (v. 18) *nacham* (Heb.)—Was sorry or suffered grief.

2. Teacher Preparation
Unifying Principle—Help Is on the Way. In the period of the judges, the people ignored God when things were going well, but in times of trouble, they repented and cried out to God for help. God raised up a judge to provide the help they needed.

A. Pray for lesson clarity.

B. Study and meditate on the complete text.

C. Reflect on the Israelites' "continuous cycle of sin and the consequences."

D. Consider how the Israelites continuously broke their covenantal relationship with a covenant-keeping God.

3. Open the Lesson
A. Open with prayer, including the Aim for Change.

B. Ask, "What does it mean to be unfaithful?"

C. Discuss how God continuously showed love, mercy, and compassion for the Israelites and, in return, how they continuously disobeyed Him by being unfaithful.

D. Explain that the penalty for sin is death (eternal separation from a Holy God).

E. Summarize and tie in the In Focus story.

4. Present the Scriptures
A. Have volunteers read the Focal Verses.

B. Now use The People, Places, and Times; Background; Search the Scriptures; At-A-Glance outline; In Depth; and More Light on the Text to clarify the verses.

JULY 10th

5. Explore the Meaning
A. Summarize the Discuss the Meaning, Lesson in Our Society, and Make It Happen sections.

B. Connect these sections to the Aim for Change and the Keep in Mind verse.

6. Next Steps for Application
A. Challenge your students to ask God to help them to obey Him.

B. Close with prayer.

Worship Guide

For the Superintendent or Teacher
Theme: Listen to God's Judges
Theme Song: "I Will Trust in the Lord"
Devotional Reading: Psalm 78:1–8
Prayer

Listen to God's Judges

Bible Background • JUDGES 2; 21:25
Printed Text • JUDGES 2:11–19 | Devotional Reading • PSALM 78:1–8

Aim for Change

By the end of the lesson, we will: TELL why we need to listen to and obey God's commands; REFLECT on the impact of our obedience and disobedience in our relationship with God; and ASK God to help us to obey Him.

In Focus

Everyone at the office gambled, including those who announced their belief in God. Bets were taken for college games and professional games. James's coworkers regularly picked numbers to play the lottery, yet they did not understand why he refused to participate. The organizer of these activities cornered James, stating there was no harm in supporting his favorite sports team; besides, half of the money was going to the good cause of stocking the office refrigerator with snacks.

James thanked his coworker for his invitation to gamble and began to regularly donate money for the items he consumed from the office refrigerator. On some occasions he also brought in items that he had purchased to add to the office's snack supply. James did not judge what the other believers were doing. He simply established an example in the workplace for them to follow if they chose to.

James felt that he should not gamble but instead live out his faith in the workplace. He did not force his beliefs on others, but he lived out what he believed was right. Today's lesson tells us why we need to listen to and obey God's commands. We need to be the witnesses that He is calling for us to be to a lost and dying world.

Keep in Mind

"And yet they would not hearken unto their judges, but they went a whoring after other gods, and bowed themselves unto them" (from Judges 2:17).

"And yet they would not hearken unto their judges, but they went a whoring after other gods, and bowed themselves unto them" (from Judges 2:17).

Focal Verses

KJV **Judges 2:11** And the children of Israel did evil in the sight of the LORD, and served Baalim:

12 And they forsook the LORD God of their fathers, which brought them out of the land of Egypt, and followed other gods, of the gods of the people that were round about them, and bowed themselves unto them, and provoked the LORD to anger.

13 And they forsook the LORD, and served Baal and Ashtaroth.

14 And the anger of the LORD was hot against Israel, and he delivered them into the hands of spoilers that spoiled them, and he sold them into the hands of their enemies round about, so that they could not any longer stand before their enemies.

15 Whithersoever they went out, the hand of the LORD was against them for evil, as the LORD had said, and as the LORD had sworn unto them: and they were greatly distressed.

16 Nevertheless the LORD raised up judges, which delivered them out of the hand of those that spoiled them.

17 And yet they would not hearken unto their judges, but they went a whoring after other gods, and bowed themselves unto them: they turned quickly out of the way which their fathers walked in, obeying the commandments of the LORD; but they did not so.

18 And when the LORD raised them up judges, then the LORD was with the judge, and delivered them out of the hand of their enemies all the days of the judge: for it repented the LORD because of their groanings by reason of them that oppressed them and vexed them.

19 And it came to pass, when the judge was dead, that they returned, and corrupted themselves more than their fathers, in following other gods to serve them, and to bow down unto them; they ceased not from their own doings, nor from their stubborn way.

NLT **Judges 2:11** The Israelites did evil in the LORD's sight and served the images of Baal.

12 They abandoned the LORD, the God of their ancestors, who had brought them out of Egypt. They went after other gods, worshiping the gods of the people around them. And they angered the LORD.

13 They abandoned the LORD to serve Baal and the images of Ashtoreth.

14 This made the LORD burn with anger against Israel, so he handed them over to raiders who stole their possessions. He turned them over to their enemies all around, and they were no longer able to resist them.

15 Every time Israel went out to battle, the LORD fought against them, causing them to be defeated, just as he had warned. And the people were in great distress.

16 Then the LORD raised up judges to rescue the Israelites from their attackers.

17 Yet Israel did not listen to the judges but prostituted themselves by worshiping other gods. How quickly they turned away from the path of their ancestors, who had walked in obedience to the LORD's commands.

18 Whenever the LORD raised up a judge over Israel, he was with that judge and rescued the people from their enemies throughout the judge's lifetime. For the LORD took pity on his people, who were burdened by oppression and suffering.

19 But when the judge died, the people returned to their corrupt ways, behaving worse than those who had lived before them. They went after other gods, serving and worshiping them. And they refused to give up their evil practices and stubborn ways.

The People, Places, and Times

Bochim. The name (which means "weeping") of the place where the angel rebuked the Israelites for breaking their covenant with God (Judges 2:5, NLT).

Israelites. The name ascribed to the descendants of Jacob, the people of the Old Testament who were the people of God.

Baal. The deity of fertility, rain, and thunder, which the Israelites chose to worship instead of God.

Ashtoreth. The name of the goddess the Israelites chose to worship instead of God.

Judges. Leaders selected by God to deliver and guide the Israelites to remain obedient to the Word of God.

Background

The book of Judges begins with the success and failures of Israel's military campaigns in Canaan (the Promised Land). The new generation of Israelites, the generation that was in the land of Canaan after the death of Joshua, receives a sudden appearance from the angel of the LORD, who pronounces judgment on the new generation of chosen people for their disobedience and unfaithfulness. The Israelites' disobedience included not totally removing the Canaanites from the land. God noted their unfaithfulness to the Living God and their increasing propensity to worship other gods—their increasing propensity to be disobedient.

Evidence of God's anger is seen when God hands over the Israelites to their enemies. Yet God still shows His mercy and compassion toward His chosen people. He raises up judges to help win the battles against Israel's enemies and bring His chosen people back to a loving, covenant-keeping God.

At-A-Glance

1. The Israelites' Unfaithfulness to God (Judges 2:11–14)

2. God's Punishment of the Israelites and His Mercy (vv. 15–16)

3. The Israelites' Cycle of Sin and God's Continued Mercy (vv. 17–19)

In Depth

1. The Israelites' Unfaithfulness to God (Judges 2:11–14)

The Israelites continued a pattern of abandoning their faith in the one true God, the one who led them out of Egypt—the one who drowned Pharaoh's army in the Red Sea, the one who fought for their ancestors (Exodus 14:13–31), the one who made bitter waters sweet when they were thirsty (15:22–25), the one who fed their ancestors bread from heaven (manna) when they were hungry (16:4–14). They violated the first two of the Ten Commandments: "I am the LORD thy God, which have brought thee out of the land of Egypt, out of the house of bondage. Thou shalt have no other gods before me" (20:2–3). Instead, they chased after other gods; they worshiped the Canaanite gods, Baal and Ashtoreth. God deemed the Israelites' behavior as evil, and He deemed what they had done as abandonment of the one true God. Their disobedience of God's commandments stirred His anger against the people He had chosen to represent Him to the rest of the world.

To those who worshiped him, Baal was considered to be the god of storms and rains and thought to control vegetation and agriculture. On the other hand, Ashtoreth was believed to be the mother goddess of love, war, and fertility. She was also known as Astarter or Ishtar (1 Kings 11:5–8; *Life Application Study Bible*, 354). Not only did God's chosen people worship these idol gods, but even temple prostitution and child sacrifice were part of the worship of these Canaanite idols. God would not and did not tolerate the Israelites adding idols to their worship of Him. They could not possibly bow to an idol and still truly believe that He was the one true God. Therefore, His anger with the Israelites results in judgment on them. God gives the Israelites over to the "marauders" (their enemies, Judges 2:14). He delivers them into the power and hands of their enemies and removes His divine defense from around them.

2. God's Punishment of the Israelites and His Mercy (vv. 15–16)

Every time the Israelites went out to battle their enemies, they lost. God's arms of protection were no longer around them. In fact, before God's judgment against them when they went out to battle, it was the Lord Himself who fought against their enemies. Thus, the Israelites and their enemies were no match for an angry God. They were no match for the omnipotent (all-powerful) God. But the Israelites' disobedience demanded judgment, and God (the Righteous Judge) judged His chosen people. They had to suffer the consequences of their chosen actions. They had to pay their own sin-penalty.

3. The Israelites' Cycle of Sin and God's Continued Mercy (vv. 17–19)

Even though the Israelites break their covenantal relationship with God, He remains faithful to them. In spite of their disobedience to God's commands, He still loves them and shows them mercy and compassion. Because of this love, mercy,

and compassion, the Word tells us that He raises up judges who deliver the Israelites from their enemies. For a time, the judges return Israel to worshiping God. But over the long haul, God's chosen people do not listen to the judges and return to worshiping other gods. The Children of Israel continue in a cycle of sin: (1) rebelling against the one true God; (2) experiencing God's punishment which involves their enemies overrunning them; (3) crying out to God for deliverance after which He raises up a God-fearing judge to deliver the Israelites from their enemies; (4) remaining loyal to God until the appointed judge's death—they were loyal as long as they were near the appointed judge; (5) forgetting about their covenant with God after the judge's death; (6) again suffering punishment because God allows their enemies to overtake them; and (7) crying out yet again to God for deliverance. In essence, the Israelites allowed what appealed to their sensual nature and more short-range benefits to steal their affections for the one true God. They were drawn to worshiping gods who did not insist that the people be morally accountable for their behavior. In fact, not only were male and female prostitution allowed in idol worship, this was encouraged as a form of worship (*Life Application Study Bible*, 354).

Often, we want what we want and want nothing to stand in our way of getting it. This kind of thinking and action can cause death (eternal separation from a holy God). Following the one true God demands discipline and accountability. Following the one true God demands that we live holy lives and be holy as He is holy. Still, however, God feels compassion for the Israelites, hears their cries while they are oppressed, and provides judges who guide the Israelites back to worshiping the one true God. God's actions show that indeed He is a promise-keeping God. He is true to His Word.

Search the Scriptures

1. Why is it relevant to have faith in God (Judges 2:11–13)?

2. Does God really become angry? Does God really punish (vv. 14–15)?

3. Why is God's love and mercy important (v. 16)?

Discuss the Meaning

We should recognize and note that God does become angry with humankind for repeated offenses of disobedience. There is no debating that He is a God of love, mercy, and compassion, but He is also a God of wrath. The Israelites experienced God's anger firsthand when God delivered them into the hands of their enemies. This loss of favor or punishment lasted until the Israelites returned back to worshiping the one true God.

Lesson in Our Society

As with the Israelites, God has given us the opportunity to live responsibly before Him in a covenantal relationship. He allowed Adam and Eve to choose to obey Him, He did the same for the Israelites, and He does the same for us today. As we look around at the suffering in our world, much of it is due to the fact that too many have not chosen Jesus Christ as their Lord and Savior. Too many have not chosen to follow and obey Him and have instead chosen to go their own way. We must always remember that our way has led us down the path of sin and destruction.

Make It Happen

Pray for guidance to boldly proclaim the Good News of salvation to a world that often has deaf ears. We should tell people that the God we serve is the same God of yesterday,

today, and tomorrow. We should proclaim to our world that in spite of the hardships we are facing, God is still sovereign (He's in control of His universe and is never out of control of it). We should pledge to encourage people with God's unconditional love—a love that was there for us even when we did not return God's love.

Follow the Spirit

What God wants me to do:

_____

_____

_____

_____

Remember Your Thoughts

Special insights I have learned:

_____

_____

_____

_____

More Light on the Text

Judges 2:11–19

11 And the children of Israel did evil in the sight of the LORD, and served Baalim:

Joshua served the Lord faithfully and lived to be 110 years old. However, the next generation did not know the Lord. They "did evil in the sight of the LORD." The word "evil" in Hebrew is *ra`* (**rah**) and means "bad, unpleasant, displeasing" behavior. After Joshua and Moses, the Lord raised up judges to lead His chosen people—the Israelites. The judges were God's chosen leaders who were to deliver them from the hands of their enemies. The book of Judges shows what

509

happens when a nation falls into moral decay, and it also shows God's great mercy when His people repent and turn back to Him.

If the Israelites had obeyed God and only worshiped and feared (reverenced or respected) Him as their eternal God, they could have enjoyed a long life in the land that God has promised them (Canaan). However, Israel kept repeating their cycle which went from the blessings of God to the consequences of sin to deliverance and back again. Judges were needed because Israel had a problem of apostasy. They simply were not loyal to the one true God. They did not obey His commands.

12 And they forsook the LORD God of their fathers, which brought them out of the land of Egypt, and followed other gods, of the gods of the people that were round about them, and bowed themselves unto them, and provoked the LORD to anger.

God wanted Israel never to forget what He did when He delivered them from bondage (slavery) in Egypt. But they forsook the Lord and committed the sin of idolatry. The word "forsook" in Hebrew (`azab, **aw-ZAB**) means "left, abandoned, forsaken, neglected, apostatized." In essence, they deserted the Lord their God. Therefore, they needed "atonement" (Heb. *kaphar*, **kaw-FAR**), which means "propitiation" or "reconciliation" that would satisfy the demands of an offended, holy God because of their sin. Since the penalty for sin is death, the Israelites needed help in their dire situation.

In the Old Testament it is important to note that sacrifices never removed a person's sins. According to Hebrews 10:4, "It is impossible for the blood of bulls and goats to take away sin" (NIV). Their sins were covered but not removed. So because Israel once again forgot the One who had brought them out of the sin and suffering and slavery experienced in

Egypt, the Israelites' cycle of sin continued and ultimately they needed a *sinless* Savior to remove them. Israel seemed to forget regularly what God already did. Pharaoh had made life miserable for Israel, but a compassionate, merciful God heard their cry. He used Moses to deliver them from a life of slavery. He redeemed them from bondage, and He delivered them out with a mighty hand. Yet somehow the new generation, like their forefathers and foremothers, forgot how God used miracle after miracle to set them free.

If we do suffer from "spiritual amnesia" and forget what God has done, we have the opportunity to turn back to Him for forgiveness. The Word of God reminds us to confess our sins because He is faithful and just to forgive us of our sins and purify us from all unrighteousness (1 John 1:9). When we truly repent (have heartfelt sorrow for our sins and turn to God), He is able to get us back on the right track.

13 And they forsook the LORD, and served Baal and Ashtaroth.

Baal was the god worshiped by the Canaanites and Phoenicians. Baal literally means "lord." Ironically, Jesus is known as the King of kings and Lord of lords! The worship of Baal was so defiled that it involved prostitution and sometimes even child sacrifice. Ashtoreth (wife of Baal) was a goddess and represented many female deities. She was a physically beautiful goddess of war and fertility. The Babylonians worshiped her as "Ishtar," the Greeks as "Astarte" or "Aphrodite," and the Romans as "Venus." Worship of this goddess involved extremely lascivious behavior (1 Kings 14:24; 2 Kings 23:7). Unfortunately, as Israel forgot the saving acts of the Lord, the chosen people got caught up in their sinful ways and began to chase after these false gods. We often hear the phrase "there is nothing new under the sun." Sometimes we forget how long prostitution has been around. Here we are thousands of years later and it is still a major problem in society. It was a big problem for Israel as well. The words "worship" and "prostitution" should never be connected. One represents good and the other evil. How could Israel mix evil with the goodness of the Lord and the blessings of true worship? Israel's actions show that when people turn away from God, they can sink into shameful, debased acts under the guise of worship!

14 And the anger of the LORD was hot against Israel, and he delivered them into the hands of spoilers that spoiled them, and he sold them into the hands of their enemies round about, so that they could not any longer stand before their enemies.

The word "anger" in Hebrew 'aph (**af**), means "wrath." In essence, God was sick and tired of the Israelites' foolishness and disobedience, which provoked His wrath. So He "delivered" (Heb. nathan, **naw-THAWN**) them, meaning He "designated" or "appointed" or "assigned" them to be defeated by "spoilers" (Heb. shacah, shasah, **shaw-SAW**), "plunderers," or enemies. When a parent tells his or her child to stop doing something, the parent is normally doing it for the good of the child. When the Lord disciplines us He, too, does it for our good. We know we have come to know Him if we obey His commands. "And hereby we do know that we know him, if we keep his commandments. He that saith, I know him, and keepeth not his commandments, is a liar, and the truth is not in him. But whoso keepeth his word, in him verily is the love of God perfected: hereby know we that we are in him" (1 John 2:3–5).

Israel had a long history of falling away and not doing what God commanded them

to do. They were to remain loyal to God and love Him through their actions, but they did just the opposite.

15 Whithersoever they went out, the hand of the LORD was against them for evil, as the LORD had said, and as the LORD had sworn unto them: and they were greatly distressed.

We see illustrated in this verse that God's Word is true and is always truth. Wherever the Israelites went, God's hand was not with them but against them. Since they did not want to go with God, they found out what it was like to go against Him and for His hand to be against them. The old saying goes "when it rains it pours!" Because the Israelites rejected the righteousness of their God, it was really raining on Israel. Wherever they went, God's hand "was against them for evil." The fact that the chosen people continued to do what they wanted to do tells us that to some degree they were taking God for granted. Secondly, their continual turning away from the faith showed they had left their First Love—God! Whenever we do this, we invite the evil one into our lives. Needless to say, Israel was "greatly distressed" (Heb. yatsar, **yaw-TSAR**), meaning they were "vexed" and "besieged" because the hand of the Lord was against them for their evil acts. However, they had no one to blame for their sin but themselves. Holy (set apart from sin) God will not tolerate sin, including from His chosen people.

16 Nevertheless the LORD raised up judges, which delivered them out of the hand of those that spoiled them.

We see the merciful, compassionate, loving God, who kept His covenant with Israel in spite of their disobedience and breaking of their covenant with Him. Israel was given another opportunity to get her house in order. God "raised up" (Heb. quwm, **koom**), meaning "set up" or "brought on the scene" judges to deliver them from their enemies. This shows that indeed Sovereign God is in control of what happens to His people. When they were disobedient, He allowed their enemies ("spoilers," v. 14) to overtake them. Now, He assigned judges to deliver them from the hands of their enemies.

17 And yet they would not hearken unto their judges, but they went a whoring after other gods, and bowed themselves unto them: they turned quickly out of the way which their fathers walked in, obeying the commandments of the LORD; but they did not so.

It is amazing that Israel continued to go her own way—doing what she wanted to do—and kept on worshiping idol gods. Why were the Israelites so prone to go "a whoring" (Heb. *zanah*, **zaw-NAW**), meaning "committing adultery" and "behaving like harlots" with their sinful pursuit of belief in other gods? They were supposed to be faithful to the one true God. They were to give their complete allegiance to Him by loving Him with the totality of their beings. So why did they refuse to listen to the judges that God was using to help them find their way back to Him? In chasing other gods, in essence, the chosen people were saying that their God was not good enough or big enough to meet all their needs.

18 And when the LORD raised them up judges, then the LORD was with the judge, and delivered them out of the hand of their enemies all the days of the judge: for it repented the LORD because of their groanings by reason of them that oppressed them and vexed them.

As long as God's judges reigned over Israel, the people held to their covenant with Him, and He (the all-powerful God) delivered

them from their enemies. God's compassion, love, and mercy are so profound that He "repented" (Heb. *nacham,* **naw-KHAM**) for His people, meaning He "was sorry" or "suffered grief" that His chosen people were suffering at the hands of their enemies. Part of the Lord's grief was due to the Israelites' "groanings" (Heb. *nâ'aqah,* **neh-aw-KAW**), which they expressed in response to being "oppressed" (Heb. *lachats,* **law-KHATS**), meaning that which "afflicted" or "crushed" them. They were "vexed" (Heb. *dachaq,* **daw-KHAK**), meaning they were "oppressed" by their enemies. He heard their cries of despair and met their need. In other words, He delivered them; they could not deliver themselves. When we obey God's voice—His commands and edicts—God's presence and power are always with us. Just as He had used Moses and Joshua, the Lord used those judges to guide the Children of Israel in the right direction. What a blessing to have God directing us in the way that we should go—in the way that we should live!

19 And it came to pass, when the judge was dead, that they returned, and corrupted themselves more than their fathers, in following other gods to serve them, and to bow down unto them; they ceased not from their own doings, nor from their stubborn way.

Indeed, the story of Israel contains a great deal of tragedy. They constantly returned to their sinful ways—their disloyalty—and in following after idol gods the Israelites "corrupted" themselves, even more than their fathers and mothers had done. The word "corrupted" in Hebrew is *shachath* (**shaw-KHATH**) and means "marred, spoiled, injured, ruined, rotted." Sadly, this generation of Israelites was far worse than the generation before them. They, too, found a way to disobey God and do things that really made God angry. They did not cease from their stubborn ways. "Stubborn" in Hebrew is *qasheh* (**kaw-SHEH**) and means "hardhearted, cruel, obstinate, difficult, stiff-necked." Thus, the Israelites kept on sinning and ignited further the ire of God.

Israel's story is very sad because they turned their backs on a loving God. They did not totally surrender their whole beings to God, who loved them unconditionally—without reservation. The good news is we serve a God of a second chance—a God who remained with Israel through her waywardness—her rebelliousness. God will do the same thing for us if we repent of our sins and put our trust in Him.

Say It Correctly

Aphrodite. af'ruh-DI-tee.
Ashtoreth. ASH-tuh-reth, -reth.
Astarte. ə-'stär-tē.
Hapi. HAH-pee.
Ishtar. ISH-tahr.
Isis. I-sis.
Osirus. oh-SI-ruhs.

Daily Bible Readings

M: The Snare of Other Gods
Exodus 23:20–33

T: A Covenant to Obey God
Joshua 24:19–27

W: Better to Obey and Heed
1 Samuel 15:17–23

T: God's Wrath for the Disobedient
Ephesians 5:6–20

F: An Ignorant Generation
Judges 2:1–10

S: Teaching the Next Generation
Psalm 78:1–8

S: A Cycle of Stubborn Sin
Judges 2:11–19

Notes

_____

_____

_____

_____

_____

Teaching Tips

1. Words You Should Know

A. Left-handed (Judges 3:15) *'itter* (Heb.)—Impeded on the right hand.

B. Valour (v. 29) *chayil* (Heb.)—Strength or might.

C. Lusty (v. 29) *shamen* (Heb.)—Fat, rich, or robust, overindulgent.

2. Teacher Preparation

Unifying Principle—Help from Unexpected Sources. When the people cried to God for help, God answered by raising Ehud to save them from their oppressors.

A. Pray for lesson clarity.

B. Study the complete lesson.

C. Secure a CD or a written copy of the song "On Christ the Solid Rock I Stand" and prepare to use it during the class.

3. Open the Lesson

A. If you have a CD of the song "On Christ the Solid Rock I Stand," play it softly as your students enter the classroom.

B. Then open with prayer, including the Aim for Change.

C. Have your class listen to the words of the song. If you do not have a CD, have a volunteer dramatically read the words.

D. Ask, "What has God done for you lately? Has He been your strength in a time of trouble?" Share testimonies and discuss.

E. Summarize the In Focus story, and discuss Jamie's dilemma and how God was a very present help to her in her dire situation.

4. Present the Scriptures

A. Have volunteers read the Focal Verses.

B. Now use The People, Places, and Times; Background; Search the Scriptures; At-A-Glance outline; In Depth; and More Light on the Text to clarify the verses.

5. Explore the Meaning

A. Have volunteers summarize the Discuss the Meaning, Lesson in Our Society, and Make It Happen sections.

B. Connect these sections to the Aim for Change and the Keep in Mind verse.

6. Next Steps for Application

A. Ask volunteers to summarize what they learned from this lesson.

B. Close with prayer.

Worship Guide

For the Superintendent or Teacher
Theme: Use God's Strength
Theme Song: "Leaning on the Everlasting Arms"
Devotional Reading: Psalm 27:7–14
Prayer

Use God's Strength

Bible Background • JUDGES 3:7–31; 21:25
Printed Text • Judges 3:15–25, 29–30 | Devotional Reading • PSALM 27:7–14

—————— Aim for Change ——————

By the end of the lesson, we will: IDENTIFY the unexpected sources of help God provides; REFLECT on how God has helped us in times of trouble; and THANK God that we can use His strength in times of trouble.

—————— In Focus ——————

Jamie knew she was playing with fire, but she no longer felt the same excitement she did when she first got saved. She still read her Bible, prayed, and attended church, but the excitement was no longer there. One day Jamie felt that she should go to the homeless shelter to serve and help out. While at the shelter, Jamie encountered one of her former friends from her former life. Instead of Jamie glorifying God, she made the mistake of confiding in her former friend that the excitement of living for God was missing. The former friend invited Jamie to a party. Jamie went to the party and was not prepared to avoid the solicitation back into her former way of life. She pleaded with God; she cried out to God to remove her from that way of life.

God heard Jamie's pleas and Sis. Carroll led Jamie back to God and never judged or questioned why Jamie relapsed. She taught Jamie about the importance of an intimate relationship with God through prayer, daily Bible study, meditating on His Word, and walking in His Word.

Have you ever felt like Jamie about following God? Today's lesson is about how God raised up yet another judge to rescue His chosen people from their enemies and restore them back to Him.

—————— Keep in Mind ——————

"But when the children of Israel cried out unto the LORD, the LORD raised them up a deliverer, Ehud the son of Gera, a Benjamite, a man lefthanded: and by him the children of Israel sent a present unto Eglon the king of Moab" (Judges 3:15).

JULY 17th

Focal Verses

KJV **Judges 3:15** But when the children of Israel cried unto the LORD, the LORD raised them up a deliverer, Ehud the son of Gera, a Benjamite, a man lefthanded: and by him the children of Israel sent a present unto Eglon the king of Moab.

16 But Ehud made him a dagger which had two edges, of a cubit length; and he did gird it under his raiment upon his right thigh.

17 And he brought the present unto Eglon king of Moab: and Eglon was a very fat man.

18 And when he had made an end to offer the present, he sent away the people that bare the present.

19 But he himself turned again from the quarries that were by Gilgal, and said, I have a secret errand unto thee, O king: who said, Keep silence. And all that stood by him went out from him.

20 And Ehud came unto him; and he was sitting in a summer parlour, which he had for himself alone. And Ehud said, I have a message from God unto thee. And he arose out of his seat.

21 And Ehud put forth his left hand, and took the dagger from his right thigh, and thrust it into his belly:

22 And the haft also went in after the blade; and the fat closed upon the blade, so that he could not draw the dagger out of his belly; and the dirt came out.

23 Then Ehud went forth through the porch, and shut the doors of the parlour upon him, and locked them.

24 When he was gone out, his servants came; and when they saw that, behold, the doors of the parlour were locked, they said, Surely he covereth his feet in his summer chamber.

25 And they tarried till they were ashamed: and, behold, he opened not the

NLT **Judges 3:15** But when the people of Israel cried out to the LORD for help, the LORD again raised up a rescuer to save them. His name was Ehud son of Gera, a left-handed man of the tribe of Benjamin. The Israelites sent Ehud to deliver their tribute money to King Eglon of Moab.

16 So Ehud made a double-edged dagger that was about a foot long, and he strapped it to his right thigh, keeping it hidden under his clothing.

17 He brought the tribute money to Eglon, who was very fat.

18 After delivering the payment, Ehud started home with those who had helped carry the tribute.

19 But when Ehud reached the stone idols near Gilgal, he turned back. He came to Eglon and said, "I have a secret message for you." So the king commanded his servants, "Be quiet!" and he sent them all out of the room.

20 Ehud walked over to Eglon, who was sitting alone in a cool upstairs room. And Ehud said, "I have a message from God for you!" As King Eglon rose from his seat,

21 Ehud reached with his left hand, pulled out the dagger strapped to his right thigh, and plunged it into the king's belly.

22 The dagger went so deep that the handle disappeared beneath the king's fat. So Ehud did not pull out the dagger, and the king's bowels emptied.

23 Then Ehud closed and locked the doors of the room and escaped down the latrine.

24 After Ehud was gone, the king's servants returned and found the doors to the upstairs room locked. They thought he might be using the latrine in the room,

25 so they waited. But when the king didn't come out after a long delay, they became

KJV cont.

doors of the parlour; therefore they took a key, and opened them: and, behold, their lord was fallen down dead on the earth.

3:29 And they slew of Moab at that time about ten thousand men, all lusty, and all men of valour; and there escaped not a man.

30 So Moab was subdued that day under the hand of Israel. And the land had rest fourscore years.

NLT cont.

concerned and got a key. And when they opened the doors, they found their master dead on the floor.

3:29 They attacked the Moabites and killed about 10,000 of their strongest and most able-bodied warriors. Not one of them escaped.

30 So Moab was conquered by Israel that day, and there was peace in the land for eighty years.

The People, Places, and Times

Eglon. It is a Hebrew name (`Eglown,` **eg-LAWN**) which means "young bull." Eglon was the Moabite king who, along with the Ammonites and the Amalekites, defeated Israel and oppressed them for 18 years.

Moab. This region was located on a high plateau on the southeastern coast of the Dead Sea, approximately 3000 feet above sea level. Because they turned away from God, the Israelites served the Moabites for 18 years.

Ehud. The son of Gera of the tribe of Benjamin, Ehud was the judge God used to deliver Israel from the Moabite king, Eglon. He stabbed King Eglon with a long dagger.

Gera. He was from the tribe of Benjamin and was the father of Ehud.

Tribe of Benjamin. Members of this tribe, one of the 12 tribes of Israel, were known for their archery and slingshot skills. Many were also left-handed.

Background

After 18 years of doing "what was evil in the sight of the LORD" (including idol worship), Israel cries out to God and God responds by raising up Ehud from the tribe of Benjamin. Ehud follows Othniel in the line of judges that God raises up to bring the Israelites out of the oppression of other tribes. Ehud is left-handed and chosen by the Israelites to carry their tribute or tax assessment to the Moabite king, Eglon. As Ehud carries out his mission and escapes passing by the Moabite idols, the Israelites receive an exhortation from Ehud that the LORD has granted victory against their oppressors.

At-A-Glance

1. God Answered Israel's Pleas for Help (Judges 3:15)

2. God Used Ehud to Bring Israel Victory (vv. 16–25)

3. God Brought Deliverance and Peace to Israel (vv. 29–30)

In Depth

1. God Answered Israel's Pleas for Help (Judges 3:15)

After enduring oppression for 18 long years at the hands of the Moabites, who were Israel's enemies, God's chosen people cry out to God for help yet again. Their cycle of sin included: (1) worshiping idols; (2) being punished by a Holy (set apart from sin) God; (3) crying out for help from the same faithful God they had been unfaithful to; (4) being rescued by a judge raised up by the same faithful God who chose them as His people even though He knew they would be a hard-headed, stiff-necked bunch; (5) obeying God for a season—as long as the judge was over them; and (6) falling back into idolatry. They again go to their Source of strength—God Himself. They know that God is a promise keeper, and that God loves them and is merciful and compassionate toward them. They need God to be loving, merciful, and compassionate because they have been disloyal to Him and have been a covenant-breaking nation. Being true to God's Word, His response to their cries for help is to raise up a deliverer. As Israel's second judge, he uses direct action and is a frontline leader in the battle. His name is Ehud. He is to take the tax money (also called a tribute) that the Israelites are forced to pay to the king of Moab.

King Eglon of Moab conquered part of Israel and set up his throne in the city of Jericho, the same city God had used Joshua to conquer (Joshua 6). God gave King Eglon control over Israel; He delivered them into King Eglon's hands. This was Israel's judgment and punishment for disobedience. The Lord had already given the Israelites Jericho (see Joshua 6), but because of their sin God used their enemy, the Moabites, to retake it. Therefore, King Eglon chose to take Israel's tax monies (the annual payment to Eglon that Israel had to make as part of their subjection to the Moabites) at that city. However, after Ehud delivers Israel's tribute, he kills King Eglon and escapes into the hill country of Ephraim. There in the hill country, Ehud raises an army to cut off the Moabites trying to escape across the Jordan River (*Life Application Study Bible*, 356).

2. God Used Ehud to Bring Israel Victory (vv. 16–25)

Ehud has a plan. In fact, he takes radical and violent action to rid the Israelites of this menace to their freedom once and for all. Even though being left-handed in Ehud's day was considered to be a handicap, many from the tribe of Benjamin were left-handed. God uses this perceived weakness to bring victory. He uses the way Ehud is made and what Ehud had in order to win the battle through him.

The manufacturing of the dagger demonstrates that Ehud had plans other than to simply deliver the Israelites' tax money to King Eglon. The double-edged dagger symbolizes the double words Ehud would use to gain a second visit to the king. The fastening of the sword to Ehud's right thigh concealed the dagger, which permitted him to cross over with his left hand to draw the sword. King Eglon's bodyguards assumed Ehud was right-handed, an assumption that overlooked the concealed dagger. Locking the doors gave Ehud time to escape after he killed King Eglon.

3. God Brought Deliverance and Peace to Israel (vv. 29–30)

Ehud and his army attack the Moabites and kill about 10,000 of their strongest and bravest warriors. Not one of them escapes. So Israel conquers Moab. God gives the Moabites into the hands of the Israelites by arranging for the Israelites to lie in wait to ambush the Moabites, who are attempting to cross the Jordan River. After the successful defeat of the Moabites, the Israelites had 80 years of peace.

Make no mistake, it was the strength of the Lord that brought both victory and peace. It is also the strength of the Lord that will bring victory and peace into our lives. We must always remember that we are no match for Satan. We need God's strength to deal with our problems and to remain in faith as we deal with them. We need God's strength daily to walk with Him. We, too, must cultivate an intimate relationship with Him and appreciate that He is a God of love, mercy, and compassion. However, we should not forget that He is also a God of wrath. He means that we, too, should have no other god before Him.

Search the Scriptures

1. Does God really respond to our pleas for help (Judges 3:15)?

2. What was Ehud's strategy to win the battle (vv. 16–19)?

3. Who brought Israel victory and peace (vv. 29–30)?

Discuss the Meaning

God does respond to our pleas for help. Many believers can witness to this fact. The Bible contains various pleas for help, including: "Hear my voice when I call, O LORD; ...Do not hide your face from me, do not turn your servant away in anger; ... Do not reject me or forsake me" (Psalm 27:7, 9, NIV). Pleas to God are answered simply because of God's love and mercy for us.

Lesson in Our Society

As we look around at our world, we can see so much suffering, so much violence, and so much neglect. This is not just the case in our country; the world is crying out for a power bigger than you and me. We need God! We need Him right now and in the midst of our circumstances. Still, so many are looking to other gods for solutions. Just as God told Israel not to have any other gods before Him, He is still telling us today that He must be our only God—only He is the true and living God. We as a nation need to call on God to heal our land, but first we need to ask for forgiveness for writing Him out of our

daily lives. We must humble ourselves and pray. He will hear us! Only God's strength and power can solve the mess we have made of His world. We had better learn to tap into His omnipotent resources.

Make It Happen

Despite our disobedience and unfaithfulness, God still loves all of us. When we confess and cry out to God, He delivers, forgives, heals, and provides for us. He is our strength in times of trouble. He is our bridge over troubled waters. Cry out to Him today for your personal deliverance. Then pray for those around you and in foreign lands.

Follow the Spirit

What God wants me to do:

_____

_____

_____

_____

Remember Your Thoughts

Special insights I have learned:

_____

_____

_____

_____

More Light on the Text

Judges 3:15–25, 29–30

15 But when the children of Israel cried unto the LORD, the LORD raised them up a deliverer, Ehud the son of Gera, a Benjamite, a man lefthanded: and by him the children of Israel sent a present unto Eglon the king of Moab.

The story opens with the beginning of one of the few high points in the book of Judges, each of which comes as God's merciful response to the people's having "cried" out to God. "Cried" in verse 15 uses the same common Hebrew word (*za'aq*, **zaw-AK**) as did the Israelites in Egypt (cf. Exodus 2:23). This is a major Old Testament theme, reiterated throughout, which is eloquently expressed in the Psalms, both individually and collectively (see Psalm 18:6; 107:6, 13; 130:1–2), but nowhere more poignantly as in the overall bleak times of Judges. Indeed, the theme that disobedience brings judgement carries an almost intact lesson from 3,000 years ago, but genuine repentance brings mercy. Even though their plight is a consequence of their own rebellion (Judges 3:12), theirs is a heartfelt plea for divine justice (cf. Isaiah 2:4; 42:1–4). In this case, God's response was to raise up Ehud from the tribe of Benjamin in order to deliver them from the grip of the Moabites, who were led by King Eglon. It must be underlined that the only reason God allowed the Moabites (with help from the Ammonites and Amalekites; [Judges 3:13]) to dominate Israel in the first place was because of their sin. God, therefore, "raised up" the trial, and God also raised up the savior or "deliverer" (Heb. *yasha'*, **yaw-SHAH**), the same word applied to God Himself when He "saved" Israel from the Egyptians (Exodus 14:30) and a word used 20 times in Judges (also interpreted as "helped, rescued, defended, preserved," and "avenged").

The Moabites, who were descendants of Abraham's nephew, Lot (Genesis 19:36–37), crossed the Jordan and strategically occupied Jericho for their headquarters (also known as the "City of Palms," see Judges 1:16; 3:13, NIV), a major Canaanite city near an oasis in the Jordan Valley. They took Jericho from the tribe of Reuben. (See Joshua 6:26, in which

Joshua cursed the city, which apparently was prophetic for Eglon.) The area was adjacent to the territory of the Benjamites. For the next 18 years, Eglon oppressed the Israelites from his stronghold (Judges 3:14).

16 But Ehud made him a dagger which had two edges, of a cubit length; and he did gird it under his raiment upon his right thigh. 17 And he brought the present unto Eglon king of Moab: and Eglon was a very fat man. 18 And when he had made an end to offer the present, he sent away the people that bare the present. 19 But he himself turned again from the quarries that were by Gilgal, and said, I have a secret errand unto thee, O king: who said, Keep silence. And all that stood by him went out from him.

Some discussion has ensued among scholars regarding the interpreter's choice of the word "cubit," from the Hebrew *gōmed* (**GO-med**), which is used only here in the entire Old Testament. The Hebrew *'ammah* (**aw-MAW**), on the other hand, is used 245 times, and it is a much more common, normally translated word for "cubit"— roughly the length of an adult's forearm, or 18 inches. Keep in mind as well that a shekel (Heb. *sheqel*, **SHEH-kel**) was the Israelites' primary unit of measurement and that a pim (Heb. *peh*, **peh**) is one-third of a shekel. Thus Younger surmises a *gōmed* is two-thirds of a cubit (*'ammah*), or a 12-inch dagger (*Ibid*, 115). Ehud's plans are as thorough as they are risky. The dagger is long enough to kill, but it's short enough to conceal and double-edged to do the most damage. Undoing the control of the Moabites hinges entirely on the success of Ehud's plan—which must be executed flawlessly, within earshot of Eglon's guards. Anything could go wrong at any time.

The so-called "present" or "sacrifice" (Heb. *minchah*, **min-KHAW,** also translated "gift, meat offering, oblation," or "tribute")

most likely was the annual payment to Eglon that Israel had to make as part of their subjection to the Moabites. Interestingly, Eglon's name (Heb. `Eglown`, **eg-LAWN**) means "calf-like" and stems from the root word `agol` (**aw-GOLE**) meaning "round"—double entendres that no Israelite at the time would have missed. Younger's comments, "[W]hile pretending to bring tribute 'offering' to Eglon, it is actually Eglon, the 'fatted calf/bull,' who becomes the offering" (Ibid., 115–116), indicate that for the Israelites this is a case of pure poetic justice. Ehud's name (Heb. `Ehuwd`, **ay-HOOD**) has possible double entendres as well, which J. McCann says is related to the Hebrew word for "one" and "may connote something like 'loner'" and "thus, a characterization of the two main players could be the 'lone ranger' vs. the 'fat cat'" (2002, 43, 45).

20 And Ehud came unto him; and he was sitting in a summer parlour, which he had for himself alone. And Ehud said, I have a message from God unto thee. And he arose out of his seat. 21 And Ehud put forth his left hand, and took the dagger from his right thigh, and thrust it into his belly: 22 And the haft also went in after the blade; and the fat closed upon the blade, so that he could not draw the dagger out of his belly; and the dirt came out.

The ironies of the story continue as Eglon rises to receive the "message" from Ehud, which actually was a message of judgment and justice from God. Younger comments, "Eglon has become plump, defenseless, stupid game. Gullibly, he is taken in by the wily Ehud. Like a dumb animal, he is completely unaware of the danger" (Ibid., 117). It appears to be a classic "fat cat" syndrome, starting with the obvious meaning of Eglon's name, but continuing with the bad guy living large at the expense of the oppressed.

Like his two-edged sword and his name, Ehud's words have a double meaning that is anything but humorous. "Weapon and word work together to establish justice," says McCann (2002, 44). From Psalm 149:6–9 we read, "Let the high praises of God be in their mouth, and a twoedged sword in their hand; To execute vengeance upon the heathen, and punishments upon the people; To bind their kings with chains, and their nobles with fetters of iron; To execute upon them the judgment written: this honour have all his saints."

The "summer parlour" (Heb. `mâqerah` `aliyah`, **mek-ay-RAW al-ee-YAW**) in Judges 3:20 seems to have been an upper room of the palace that somehow was kept cooler, perhaps being open to let the breezes through. Here Ehud delivers the fatal "message" from God, which clearly took the king completely by surprise since he did not even cry out for help. Some have described the graphic detail as "the epic blow," which contributes to the "epic" quality of the book of Judges, since several such dramatic stories are recorded. Since he was unable to retrieve it, Ehud simply left the dagger inside Eglon and made his retreat. The "dirt" clearly was fecal matter (Heb. `parshâdon`, **par-shed-ONE**, another word used only here in the entire Old Testament) from a sliced abdomen, actually double-sliced by both edges of the sword, all part of the graphically stated narrative typical of the book.

23 Then Ehud went forth through the porch, and shut the doors of the parlour upon him, and locked them. 24 When he was gone out, his servants came; and when they saw that, behold, the doors of the parlour were locked, they said, Surely he covereth his feet in his summer chamber. 25 And they tarried till they were ashamed: and, behold, he opened not the doors of

the parlour; therefore they took a key, and opened them: and, behold, their lord was fallen down dead on the earth.

Further contributing to the extremely graphic description of events (which today might be rated R), Eglon's attendants were hesitant to enter through a locked door, presuming (perhaps by the strong odor) that the king "covereth his feet" (Heb. *cakak*, **saw-KAK**; NASB and NIV have "relieving himself"), a euphemism for using the bathroom (see also 1 Samuel 24:3). As all good attendants to a king will do, however, an unusually long wait outside a locked room overrode the king's potential embarrassment, and they finally unlocked the door, finding their assassinated king. It was their reluctance to enter that gave Ehud his window of escape, all part of a well-conceived plan. His route was toward "Seirah" (Judges 3:26), the region of the powerful Ephraimites, to the north, adjacent to the Benjamites' territory.

3:29 And they slew of Moab at that time about ten thousand men, all lusty, and all men of valour; and there escaped not a man. 30 So Moab was subdued that day under the hand of Israel. And the land had rest fourscore years.

The inevitable confusion surrounding the death of the Moab king created the perfect opportunity for Ehud to attack. The death of the king invigorated the oppressed Israelites, who properly interpreted it as a sign of God's intervention on their behalf, and they were inspired to fight. As Eglon was sacrificed, so too were his troops sacrificed. It must be noted, however, that the narrative does not condone political assassination, only that God permitted the events to transpire in order for Israel to benefit—in response to their prayers of repentance.

The passage states, perhaps in rounded numbers, that 10,000 men were killed, and

not a single Moabite escaped (3:29). As with other rounded numbers in the Old Testament, the point is clear that it was a resounding victory for the Israelites and a crushing defeat for the Moabites. The ensuing 80 years of peace are the longest of the entire book of Judges.

Say It Correctly

Amalekites. uh-MAL-uh-ki tz.
Ammonite. 'a-mə-ˌnīt.
Ephraimites. EE-fray-ihm-aits.
Gera. 'ger-ə.
Gilgal. GIL-gal.
Jephthah. JEF-thuh.
Moabite. 'mō-ə-ˌbīt.

Daily Bible Readings

M: The Lord Is My Stronghold
Psalm 27:1–6

T: Wait for the Lord
Psalm 27:7–14

W: A Cry for Help
Habakkuk 1:1–5

T: In God I Trust
Psalm 56:1–11

F: May the Lord Give Strength
Psalm 29

S: God Will Protect and Deliver
Isaiah 31:1–5

S: God Raises Up a Deliverer
Judges 3:15–25, 29–30

Teaching Tips

1. Words You Should Know

A. Interpretation (Judges 7:15) *sheber* (Heb.)—Discovery of the meaning of something, the shattering of something symbolic—it is like breaking a code.

B. Rule (8:22, 23) *mashal* (Heb.)—To have dominion, reign.

2. Teacher Preparation

Unifying Principle—Following Wise Leaders. The people should follow leaders who follow God.

A. Pray for lesson clarity.

B. After studying the entire text and the surrounding sections, reflect on the statement, "God's people should follow leaders who follow God."

C. Prepare to discuss.

3. Open the Lesson

A. Open with prayer, including the Aim for Change.

B. Ask, "What can happen when leaders do not follow God?" Discuss.

C. Tie in the In Focus story.

D. Discuss Gideon's character traits as a leader: weak, timid, and afraid. Then discuss the fact that God still used him and why He did so.

4. Present the Scriptures

A. Have volunteers read or summarize the Focal Verses.

B. Now use The People, Places, and Times; Background; Search the Scriptures; At-A-Glance outline; In Depth; and More Light on the Text to clarify the verses.

5. Explore the Meaning

A. Have volunteers summarize the Discuss the Meaning, Lesson in Our Society, and Make It Happen sections.

B. Connect these sections to the Aim for Change and the Keep in Mind verse.

6. Next Steps for Application

A. Challenge your students to pray over the leadership in the country and church.

B. Close with prayer.

JULY
24th

Worship Guide

For the Superintendent or Teacher
Theme: Let God Rule
Theme Song: "Where He Leads Me
I Will Follow"
Devotional Reading: 1 Samuel 2:1–10
Prayer

Let God Rule

Bible Background • JUDGES 6–8; 21:25
Printed Text • JUDGES 7:2–4, 13–15; 8:22–25 | Devotional Reading • 1 SAMUEL 2:1–10

—————— Aim for Change ——————

By the end of the lesson, we will: RECOUNT Gideon's attempts and mistakes in following God; FEEL confident that we can rely on God; and IDENTIFY areas where we need to let God rule our lives.

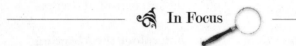

———— In Focus ————

After watching the effects of years of neglect by town officials toward the inner city, a group of prayer warriors met daily to pray for a new administration, beginning with the office of mayor. One of the prayer warriors was a local businessman who suggested that James consider running for mayor. After weeks of fasting and praying to God about his inadequacies, James accepted the bid for mayor and won by a landslide. After the inauguration, James continued meeting daily with the prayer warriors seeking guidance from God on managing city business.

As the city began to turn around, James exalted God and himself before the citizens. Crime rates dropped, school attendance improved, business developers moved into the inner cities, and unemployment rates decreased. With the success of the city, James aspired for higher political aspirations. As James began preparations for those aspirations, he discontinued the daily meetings with the prayer warriors, assembled a new staff, and began alliances with the former, dishonest leaders. Within six months James and these leaders were indicted and convicted of embezzling city funds.

Today's lesson reminds us that we should follow leaders who follow God.

—————— Keep in Mind ——————

"When Gideon heard the telling of the dream, and the interpretation thereof, that he worshipped, and returned into the host of Israel, and said, Arise; for the LORD hath delivered into your hand the host of Midian" (from Judges 7:15).

"When Gideon heard the telling of the dream, and the interpretation thereof, that he worshipped, and returned into the host of Israel, and said, Arise; for the LORD hath delivered into your hand the host of Midian" (from Judges 7:15).

Focal Verses

KJV **Judges 7:2** And the LORD said unto Gideon, The people that are with thee are too many for me to give the Midianites into their hands, lest Israel vaunt themselves against me, saying, Mine own hand hath saved me.

3 Now therefore go to, proclaim in the ears of the people, saying, Whosoever is fearful and afraid, let him return and depart early from mount Gilead. And there returned of the people twenty and two thousand; and there remained ten thousand.

4 And the LORD said unto Gideon, The people are yet too many; bring them down unto the water, and I will try them for thee there: and it shall be, that of whom I say unto thee, This shall go with thee, the same shall go with thee; and of whomsoever I say unto thee, This shall not go with thee, the same shall not go.

7:13 And when Gideon was come, behold, there was a man that told a dream unto his fellow, and said, Behold, I dreamed a dream, and, lo, a cake of barley bread tumbled into the host of Midian, and came unto a tent, and smote it that it fell, and overturned it, that the tent lay along.

14 And his fellow answered and said, This is nothing else save the sword of Gideon the son of Joash, a man of Israel: for into his hand hath God delivered Midian, and all the host.

15 And it was so, when Gideon heard the telling of the dream, and the interpretation thereof, that he worshipped, and returned into the host of Israel, and said, Arise; for the LORD hath delivered into your hand the host of Midian.

8:22 Then the men of Israel said unto Gideon, Rule thou over us, both thou, and thy son, and thy son's son also: for thou hast delivered us from the hand of Midian.

NLT **Judges 7:2** The LORD said to Gideon, "You have too many warriors with you. If I let all of you fight the Midianites, the Israelites will boast to me that they saved themselves by their own strength.

3 Therefore, tell the people, 'Whoever is timid or afraid may leave this mountain and go home.'" So 22,000 of them went home, leaving only 10,000 who were willing to fight.

4 But the LORD told Gideon, "There are still too many! Bring them down to the spring, and I will test them to determine who will go with you and who will not."

7:13 Gideon crept up just as a man was telling his companion about a dream. The man said, "I had this dream, and in my dream a loaf of barley bread came tumbling down into the Midianite camp. It hit a tent, turned it over, and knocked it flat!"

14 His companion answered, "Your dream can mean only one thing—God has given Gideon son of Joash, the Israelite, victory over Midian and all its allies!"

15 When Gideon heard the dream and its interpretation, he bowed down in worship before the LORD. Then he returned to the Israelite camp and shouted, "Get up! For the LORD has given you victory over the Midianite hordes!"

8:22 Then the Israelites said to Gideon, "Be our ruler! You and your son and your grandson will be our rulers, for you have rescued us from Midian."

KJV cont.

23 And Gideon said unto them, I will not rule over you, neither shall my son rule over you: the LORD shall rule over you.

24 And Gideon said unto them, I would desire a request of you, that ye would give me every man the earrings of his prey. (For they had golden earrings, because they were Ishmaelites.)

25 And they answered, We will willingly give them. And they spread a garment, and did cast therein every man the earrings of his prey.

NLT cont.

23 But Gideon replied, "I will not rule over you, nor will my son. The LORD will rule over you!

24 However, I have one request. Each of you can give me an earring from the plunder you collected from your fallen enemies." (The enemies, being Ishmaelites, all wore gold earrings.)

25 "Gladly!" they replied. They spread out a cloak, and each one threw in a gold earring he had gathered from the plunder.

The People, Places, and Times

Gideon. He was the youngest son of Joash, who was from the Abiezrite line of Manasseh. God called Gideon to serve as a judge during the seven years that Israel came under the dominion of Midian as punishment for their evil deeds.

Abiezrites. These descendants of Manasseh were a group of people given a district in the tribal territory of Manasseh, west of Jordan.

Joash. He was also an Abiezrite of the tribe of Manasseh. In addition, he was the father of Gideon. Biblical sources credit Joash as the owner of the Asherah and the altar to Baal that Gideon destroyed.

Midianites. Bible scholars suggest Midianites were both nomads and city dwellers. The territory in which they settled is identified as the eastern shore of the Gulf of Aqabah.

Background

One would think Israel finally would have learned her lesson, once and for all. But it wasn't long before she backslid yet again, and this time God permitted the thousands of nomadic Midianites (again with the help of the Amalekites) to raid the entire nation of crops and livestock for seven consecutive years (Judges 6:1–6), effectively bringing the

Israelites to their knees. As we saw in the previous lesson, God raised up the trial, and God raised up the deliverer. God inspired Gideon with the classic lines, "The LORD is with you...Go in the strength you have" (from 6:12, 14, NIV), after which Gideon asked for a sign, which resulted in a theophany (6:19–24). Just prior to this week's lesson, God told Gideon to tear down his father's altar to Baal (Heb. *Ba'al*, **BAH-al**) and build a new altar to the Lord, sacrificing a bull on it with wood from the Asherah pole. Asherah (Heb. *Asherah*, **ash-ay-RAW**) was the Babylonian-Canaanite goddess of fortune or happiness and consort of Baal, whose image was often affixed to a tree or wooden pole and set up near an altar (see also Deuteronomy 16:21; 1 Kings 16:33; 18:19; 2 Kings 17:16; 21:3). To put things in perspective, the Roman goddess Venus answered to Asherah, and Hercules answered to Baal.

When God calls someone to do His work, any connection with the world's idols must be destroyed. In reality, God is more concerned about Israel's idol worship than the oppression of the Midianites. God can overcome the Midianites more quickly than anyone can snap his or her fingers, but God was concerned about convincing Israel to worship Him alone and abandon the useless idols of the world. In a sense, it is remarkable that God continued to pursue Israel's faithfulness, even in the face of the chosen people's stubborn and recalcitrant unfaithfulness.

Tearing down their sacred idol and altar triggered the Midianites' wrath, who with the Amalekites gathered their armies (Judges 6:33–35)—which would have been their eighth major attack against Israel. In response to the assembling threat and Israel's cries, God anointed Gideon for the battle (6:34), who proceeded to set out his famous fleece, seeking reassurance of his impending victory against such a formidable enemy (6:36–40).

At-A-Glance

1. Victory Belongs to God (Judges 7:2–4)

2. Divine Assurance from God (vv. 13–15)

3. Gideon's New Boldness and Israel's Sin (8:22–25)

In Depth

1. Victory Belongs to God (Judges 7:2–4)

With Jerubbaal (Gideon) God chose a weak and unlikely leader to bring another victory to the Israelites. However, often God chooses ordinary people who will not be guilty of self-sufficiency, which is an enemy in itself because it causes us to believe that we can accomplish a goal under our own strength instead of the strength and power that comes from Almighty God.

To prevent the Israelites from boasting of their own strength in the victory that God was going to bring over the Midianites, God instructed Gideon (Israel's fifth judge) to downsize his army from 32,000 to 300. God even gave instructions on how the downsizing was to be carried out. Because

Gideon followed these instructions, God achieved victory through Gideon with just 300 men. Of course with an army this small, only God could have won. There was no way the Israelites could have defeated the Midianites under their own power and strength. Consequently, neither Gideon nor his 300 men could take the credit or the glory. Both belonged to Almighty God. It was God who caused the Midianite army to fall into panic, confusion, and disorder and then retreat. Neither Gideon nor his men had to even draw a sword to defeat Israel's enemy. The battle was God's, and He won the day. God showed Israel that it's not the strength of numbers that bring about the victory, but it's obedience and commitment to the one true God.

2. Divine Assurance from God (vv. 13–15)

Previously, Gideon required constant reassurance from God. Despite knowing that God would go with him and help him in battle, he was fearful and timid. In essence, Gideon saw that the Israelites had a big problem—the Midianites—and forgot that Israel had an even bigger God. Even after God commanded him to attack, God knew Gideon was still afraid and required a sign of reassurance. So God provided the sign by directing Gideon to sneak into the enemy camp, enabling Gideon to overhear the Midianites speak of their fear of him.

Empowered, Gideon did not let his fear and timidity stop him from doing what was right. Because he did not, he is a member of the Hall of Faith (Hebrews 11:32) and is noted for defeating the Midianite army. Even though he was slow to be convinced that he was the right man for the job, he did eventually act on his convictions. He was, therefore, rewarded for his obedience to his convictions—his obedience to God. When Gideon instructed his soldiers, "Arise; for the LORD hath delivered into your hand the host of Midian" (Judges 7:15), a subtle shift in Gideon's confidence has emerged. Before this victory, he was a judge called by God who needed constant reassurance. Now, he was an obedient servant of the Most High God.

3. Gideon's New Boldness and Israel's Sin (8:22–25)

Fresh from victory over the Midianites, the Israelites saw a new boldness and assertiveness in Gideon. So they asked him to become their ruler. However, Gideon recognized and stressed that God was to rule over them— they were God's chosen people. He never lost sight of how important God's rule and reign were for them as individuals and as a nation.

We, too, must recognize that our God is to be the One who rules and reigns over us as well. He is our King. He is the King of kings. He is our Lord. He is the Lord of lords. We must put Him first in our lives.

Even though Gideon refused Israel's request to rule over them and proclaimed that God would rule over them, his newly acquired independence resulted in his creating an idol from golden earrings. An *ephod* (**ay-FODE**) was a linen garment that the priests wore over their chests. This garment was considered holy (Exodus 28:6–35; 39:2–24; Leviticus 8:7–8). However, it was not to be worshiped. Only the one true God is to be worshiped. Even though Gideon probably had good intentions in creating the ephod, which would have been a visible remembrance commemorating the victory that God had brought them, the people made it an idol that they worshiped. Here again was another god before Almighty God. Whereas Gideon's motives might have been pure, the consequences were negative. We must worship the Creator and not the created. We must remember that God brings the victory in our lives.

Search the Scriptures

1. How was God instrumental in Israel's victory over the Midianites (Judges 7:13–15)?

2. Did Gideon believe he was in God's favor (v. 15)?

3. Did Gideon acknowledge God for his newly acquired boldness and independence (vv. 22–25)?

Discuss the Meaning

1. Why do we need to accept God's strength versus our own?

2. Do we initially accept God's changes in us? Explain.

3. Do we give God credit for the visible changes He makes in us? Why or why not?

Lesson in Our Society

Time after time we place unconditional trust in leaders. There have been numerous examples of politicians who were popular with their constituents and who started out doing an excellent job, only to lose the favor of their constituents because of being found guilty of an illegal or immoral act. As a society, we should continually pray that our leaders are seeking God's advice in their decision-making. As for those leaders who do not have a relationship with God, the body of Christ should pray for their salvation and ask God to use them as instruments for God's will.

Make It Happen

Pray for our leaders—the ones who have the rule over us. Also encourage and offer forgiveness to our leaders who have stumbled and fallen. We should also pray for God's help in stopping our habits of accepting immoral and illegal behavior.

Follow the Spirit

What God wants me to do:

_____

_____

_____

_____

Remember Your Thoughts

Special insights I have learned:

_____

_____

_____

_____

More Light on the Text

Judges 7:2–4, 13–15; 8:22–25

7:2 And the LORD said unto Gideon, The people that are with thee are too many for me to give the Midianites into their hands, lest Israel vaunt themselves against me, saying, Mine own hand hath saved me.

This verse is one of five occurrences of God's promise to use Gideon to save Israel (see also Judges 6:36; 7:7, 9, 14–15). "Although Gideon has much popular support and has a considerable fighting force at his disposal, he hesitates," observes Younger (2002, 187). Even though Gideon has been reassured by a double miracle involving his fleece (6:36–40), it was possible that at least some of his confidence lay in the size of the assembled armies of Israel. Despite a total of 32,000 men, however, he and his soldiers were outnumbered by the Midianites four to one (8:10), and surely he was quite surprised by God's instructions to reduce his forces. "[T]his horde [of Midianites] presents an almost insurmountable challenge to the undermanned Israelites," says Younger (2002, 185). It seems clear that God wanted to be sure Israel knew it was He who would deliver them, and in no way would it be the result of their own strength and resources. There was no way they could take credit for the upcoming victory, no way they could "vaunt" (Heb. *pa'ar*, **paw-AR**) themselves against God, or boast they won by their own "hand" (Heb. *yad*, **yawd**). In Ruth 7:2, the same word *yad* is used twice, once referring to the coming victory and once for the credit they might be tempted to take. The word indicates a state of being in control, and elsewhere in the book of Judges is used to refer to the "hand of the LORD" (2:15; 6:36–37).

3 Now therefore go to, proclaim in the ears of the people, saying, Whosoever is fearful and afraid, let him return and depart early from mount Gilead. And there returned of the people twenty and two thousand; and there remained ten thousand. 4 And the LORD said unto Gideon, The people are yet too many; bring them down unto the water, and I will try them for thee there: and it shall be, that of whom I say unto thee, This shall go with thee, the same shall go with thee; and of whomsoever I say unto thee, This shall not go with thee, the same shall not go.

The first reduction of troops—all who were "fearful" (Heb. *yare'*, **yaw-RAY**) or "afraid" (Heb. *charad*, **khaw-RAD**) were to remain at the spring of Harod (a derivative of *chared*), also known as the "Spring of Trembling" (Judges 7:1). Significantly, 22,000 left, more than two-thirds of Gideon's entire army (see Deuteronomy 20:1–8 for a parallel strategy of removing fearful or distracted soldiers). The second sorting would even more drastically decrease the army to a mere 300 men, based on how they drank water, presumably because the ones who were chosen stayed on their feet and thus remained more alert. But this particular test had nothing to do with the soldiers' ability, sufficiency, or level of courage, and had everything to do with God's sovereign ability and sufficiency, as Judges 7:2 clearly stated. As will become significant later in the story, when the 9,700 departed, they left their jars of provisions and their trumpets (v. 8).

7:13 And when Gideon was come, behold, there was a man that told a dream unto his fellow, and said, Behold, I dreamed a dream, and, lo, a cake of barley bread tumbled into the host of Midian, and came unto a tent, and smote it that it fell, and overturned it, that the tent lay along. 14 And his fellow answered and said, This is nothing else save the sword of Gideon the son of Joash, a man of Israel: for into his hand hath God delivered Midian, and all the host.

Gideon now had less than one percent of his original army, "a ridiculously small fighting force" says McCann (2002, 66–67), and understandably Gideon's faith again began to wane. At least there is no doubt whatsoever that they will take any credit away from God. Like Moses, Gideon had been unsure of his adequacy for the task from the beginning, and even after a personal visit by God, he had needed to put out a fleece for additional confidence (6:39–40). Now he needed reassurance again, since things just did not make sense from a human perspective. "Instead of growing more faithful," McCann notes, "he seems to be growing more faithless and more fearful" (Ibid.). Still, God cooperates with Gideon, about which Daniel Block observes, "The remarkable fact is that God responds to his tests. He is more anxious to deliver Israel than to quibble about this man's semi-pagan notions of deity" (1999, 273).

Judges 7:12 describes the intimidating and immeasurable number of the enemy's troops and their camels, using language from Abraham's promise (Genesis 22:17) of them numbering "as the sand by the sea side." This is a classic and timeless lesson of exercising faith and learning to trust. Our thoughts are not God's thoughts, nor are our ways God's ways (Isaiah 55:8–9). "When the outlook is bleak, try the up look," Warren Wiersbe once wisely advised (17). Precisely when we have come to the end of ourselves is when we finally begin to have genuine faith in God. And it is only when we truly trust in Him that we will experience genuine joy and peace (Romans 15:13; see also Psalm 115:11; Nahum 1:7; John 14:1).

At this point in the story, God directs Gideon to visit the enemy camp so he can overhear two of the enemy soldiers discussing a "dream" (Heb. *chalowm*, **khal-OME,** which can be either ordinary or prophetic) one of them had (Judges 7:9–11). Such a dream was taken more seriously in antiquity than today (see also Genesis 20:3; 31:11; 37:5; Numbers 12:6; 1 Samuel 28:6; Daniel 1:17).

15 And it was so, when Gideon heard the telling of the dream, and the interpretation thereof, that he worshipped, and returned into the host of Israel, and said, Arise; for the LORD hath delivered into your hand the host of Midian.

Gideon's response to the dream demonstrated his realization that both the dream and his overhearing the men talking about it were not coincidences. Amazingly, Gideon is more persuaded by hearing the enemy's nervous words than by God's direct promises of victory. Similarly today, it is easy to overlook some apparent coincidence when in reality God could be trying to speak to us through our circumstances. And sometimes we trust human agents more than

God Himself. While we should not begin to discern guidance in the arrangement of our coffee grounds (the prototypical Jesus image in a potato chip syndrome), we should both look and pray for God to guide us and confirm our major decisions as we serve and follow Him (see Psalm 31:3; Proverbs 3:5–6; Isaiah 49:10; 58:11). As Younger reminds us, "Gideon's propensity for signs and preoccupation with the tangible in religion matters" is a prevalent stumbling block among believers today (180).

While he could have dismissed the incident as a coincidence, Gideon eventually recognized God's sovereign hand and his natural reaction was heartfelt worship. With his own confidence in God restored, Gideon communicated the same to his troops. It is interesting that the Hebrew for "interpretation" (*sheber*, **SHEH-ber**) actually means "the shattering something symbolic"— in this case it is like breaking a code. The word "delivered" (Heb. *nathan*, **naw-THAWN**) was a bestowing or giving of the Midianites into Gideon's hand and was a lesser sense of the overall divine, sovereign "delivering" or "saving" act of God (Heb. *yasha`*, **yaw-SHAH**, cf. Judges 2:16, 18; 3:9, and numerous other uses), with or without the use of a human agent. Both terms occur side by side in 7:7, "I will save [*yasha`*] you, and deliver [*nathan*] the Midianites into thine hand."

8:22 Then the men of Israel said unto Gideon, Rule thou over us, both thou, and thy son, and thy son's son also: for thou hast delivered us from the hand of Midian. 23 And Gideon said unto them, I will not rule over you, neither shall my son rule over you: the LORD shall rule over you.

God won the battle for the Israelites, by using ordinary men. It did not take 32,000 to get the job done, and He showed this by reducing Gideon's army to 300. In fact,

Gideon's army watched as the Midianites fell into confusion, disorder, and panic (7:21). Gideon's army did not even have to draw a sword to defeat this adversary. God showed that He was in charge. After the victory, the men of Israel told Gideon that he, his son, and his grandson should be their rulers because he deserved this position for having rescued them from Midian.

In Judges 8:22–23 the word "rule" in Hebrew is *mashal* (**maw-SHAL**) and means "have dominion, reign." In essence, the Israelites desired to make Gideon their king. They forgot that God had rescued them and God was Israel's King. Their king was not to be a man, but Almighty God. However, Gideon had not forgotten. He stressed that the Lord was to rule over them. He had no desire to usurp the Lord's authority or position.

24 And Gideon said unto them, I would desire a request of you, that ye would give me every man the earrings of his prey. (For they had golden earrings, because they were Ishmaelites.) 25 And they answered, We will willingly give them. And they spread a garment, and did cast therein every man the earrings of his prey.

After so much insight as to who was Israel's true King, Gideon then made a major, detrimental choice. He asked that every man give him "earrings of his prey." The phrase "of his prey" in Hebrew is *shalal* (**shaw-LAWL**) and refers to "booty, spoil, plunder." This plunder was made of gold. Gideon wanted the treasures collected from their fallen enemies. Since these enemies were Ishmaelites, all of them wore gold earrings. The Israelites were glad to give Gideon what he requested, so they spread out a cloak and each of them threw a gold earring onto the cloak. They gave so much gold that the weight of the gold earrings was "forty-three pounds, not including the crescents and pendants, the royal clothing of the kings, or the chains around the necks of their camels" (Judges 8:26) (*Life Application Study Bible*, 368). All of this gold was used to make an ephod (a visible remembrance commemorating their victory against the Midianites), which the Israelites began to worship. Idol worship was again their downfall.

In spite of Gideon's faltering faith, he should not be judged too harshly. He did obey God's command to destroy the Baal altar and Asherah pole and to build a new altar to God. He followed God's words even though fear and doubt were in his heart—which is a good lesson for every believer at every level. When God tells us to cut the cords of our comfort zones with the world, to tear down our own idols and to build altars to Him in their place, we would do well to heed His words and let Him manage our fears and doubts after we have obeyed.

Daily Bible Readings

M: No Holy One Like the Lord
1 Samuel 2:1–10

T: Follow the Lord Only
Deuteronomy 13:1–5

W: Suffering Oppression
Judges 6:1–10

T: I Will Be with You
Judges 6:11–16

F: A First Act of Obedience
Judges 6:25–32

S: Seeking a Sign from God
Judges 6:36–40

S: The Lord Will Rule
Judges 7:2–4, 13–15; 8:22–25

Say It Correctly

Abiezrite. ab'ee-EHZ-rit, ay'bi-EZ-rit.
Aqabah. AK-uh-buh.
Asherah. ASH-uh-ruh, uh-SHIHR-uh,
uh-SHEER-uh.
Ephod. 'e-ˌfäd, 'ē-
Gideon. GID-ee-uhn.
Jerubbaal. jer'uh-BAY-uhl, -BAYL,
jer-uhb-BAYL.
Jephthah. JEF-thuh.
Joash. JOH-ash.
Manasseh. ma-NAS-uh, muh-NAS-uh.
Midianites. MID-ee-uh-nit'.
Othniel. OTH-nee-uhl, OTH-nee-el.

Teaching Tips

1. Words You Should Know

A. Cried (Judges 10:10, 12, 14) *za`aq* (Heb.)—Called out for mercy.

B. Grieved (v. 16) *qatsar* (Heb.)—Impatient, disgruntled.

2. Teacher Preparation

Unifying Principle—Improving Community. When the community standards of behavior are low, the community will suffer. The people must turn to God, realize their misdeeds, and repent in order to have any hope of rescue.

A. Begin with prayer and then study the entire lesson.

B. Think about some of the problems that your church community, city, and country have encountered because the community standards of behavior are low. Prepare to discuss.

3. Open the Lesson

A. Open with prayer, including the Aim for Change.

B. Have a volunteer summarize the In Focus story. Discuss.

C. Now discuss some of the problems that you and your students see in your communities and nation because the community standards are so low. (Make a list on the board.)

D. Highlight ways that we can improve our communities. Discuss.

4. Present the Scriptures

A. Have volunteers read the Focal Verses.

B. Now use The People, Places, and Times; Background; Search the Scriptures; At-A-Glance outline; In Depth; and More Light on the Text to clarify the verses.

5. Explore the Meaning

A. Lead a discussion of the Discuss the Meaning, Lesson in Our Society, and Make It Happen sections.

B. Have volunteers connect these sections to the Aim for Change and the Keep in Mind verse.

6. Next Steps for Application

A. Challenge your students to pray for their communities, nation, leaders, etc.

B. Close with prayer.

Worship Guide

For the Superintendent or Teacher
Theme: Return to Obedience
Theme Song: "I Want Jesus to Walk with Me"
Devotional Reading: 2 Corinthians 7:5–11
Prayer

Return to Obedience

Bible Background • JUDGES 10:6–11:33; 21:25
Printed Text • JUDGES 10:10–18 | Devotional Reading • 2 CORINTHIANS 7:5–11

—————— Aim for Change ——————

By the end of the lesson, we will: EXAMINE Israel's cycle of sin and the consequences; APPRECIATE that God allows us to suffer the consequences of our choices; and REPENT of bad choices and recommit to following the true God.

————— In Focus  —————

Marcus loved to play golf. Whenever the weather permitted, he went golfing with his buddies. At first this seemed like a healthy activity for Marcus. It got him out of the house and let him hang out with his friends. It allowed him to spend time relaxing outside.

But soon golf got in the way of Marcus' church life. It started when he signed up for a local golf tournament that was held on a Sunday morning. He told his wife, Carla, he would only miss church this one time. Carla didn't like the idea, but she let it slide, hoping it would only be a one-time thing.

Unfortunately, the one-time thing grew into a weekly thing. Marcus soon became irritated whenever Carla got on his case about not coming to church with her and the kids. He explained to her that he needed some "me time" once a week and that she just didn't understand.

JULY 31st

Carla asked Marcus why his "me time" had become so much more important than his "God time." Marcus sat quietly for a moment, contemplating his wife's comment. He enjoyed playing golf so much, but he realized that maybe his love of golf had become unhealthy for his spiritual life.

In today's lesson, we'll see how idols can hinder our walk with the Lord.

—————— Keep in Mind ——————

"And they put away the strange gods from among them, and served the LORD: and his soul was grieved for the misery of Israel" (Judges 10:16).

Focal Verses

KJV **Judges 10:10** And the children of Israel cried unto the LORD, saying, We have sinned against thee, both because we have forsaken our God, and also served Baalim.

11 And the LORD said unto the children of Israel, Did not I deliver you from the Egyptians, and from the Amorites, from the children of Ammon, and from the Philistines?

12 The Zidonians also, and the Amalekites, and the Maonites, did oppress you; and ye cried to me, and I delivered you out of their hand.

13 Yet ye have forsaken me, and served other gods: wherefore I will deliver you no more.

14 Go and cry unto the gods which ye have chosen; let them deliver you in the time of your tribulation.

15 And the children of Israel said unto the LORD, We have sinned: do thou unto us whatsoever seemeth good unto thee; deliver us only, we pray thee, this day.

16 And they put away the strange gods from among them, and served the LORD: and his soul was grieved for the misery of Israel.

17 Then the children of Ammon were gathered together, and encamped in Gilead. And the children of Israel assembled themselves together, and encamped in Mizpeh.

18 And the people and princes of Gilead said one to another, What man is he that will begin to fight against the children of Ammon? he shall be head over all the inhabitants of Gilead.

NLT **Judges 10:10** Finally, they cried out to the LORD for help, saying, "We have sinned against you because we have abandoned you as our God and have served the images of Baal."

11 The LORD replied, "Did I not rescue you from the Egyptians, the Amorites, the Ammonites, the Philistines,

12 the Sidonians, the Amalekites, and the Maonites? When they oppressed you, you cried out to me for help, and I rescued you.

13 Yet you have abandoned me and served other gods. So I will not rescue you anymore.

14 Go and cry out to the gods you have chosen! Let them rescue you in your hour of distress!"

15 But the Israelites pleaded with the LORD and said, "We have sinned. Punish us as you see fit, only rescue us today from our enemies."

16 Then the Israelites put aside their foreign gods and served the LORD. And he was grieved by their misery.

17 At that time the armies of Ammon had gathered for war and were camped in Gilead, and the people of Israel assembled and camped at Mizpah.

18 The leaders of Gilead said to each other, "Whoever attacks the Ammonites first will become ruler over all the people of Gilead."

The People, Places, and Times

Philistines. Originally these people were seafarers until they were defeated by the Egyptians. Then they settled along coastal areas at the southern part of Palestine, where they became the enemy of nearby Israel. The five main Philistine cities were Gaza, Ashdod, Ashkelon, Gath, and Ekron. The Philistines and the Israelites constantly fought over land.

On several occasions, God allowed the Israelites to be overtaken by the Philistines as punishment for their disobedience toward Him. Once a monarchy was established for Israel with Saul, they started to prevail over the Philistines, but it was not until King David came to power that they were able to conquer their enemy.

Background

Leading up to this passage, the Israelites had done "evil again in the sight of the LORD" (Judges 10:6). Instead of serving God, they were serving the false gods of Aram, Sidon, Moab, the Ammonites, and the Philistines. Even though the Lord had delivered the Israelites from enslavement and more, the Israelites were not faithful to Him.

Because of Israel's disobedience, God became angry and gave them over to the Philistines and the Ammonites. The Israelites were oppressed by these people for 18 years. Under this persecution, the Israelites realized their mistake and turned back to God.

At-A-Glance

1. Israel Cries Out to God (Judges 10:10)

2. God Rebukes Israel (vv. 11–14)

3. Israel Returns to Obedience (vv. 15–18)

In Depth

1. Israel Cries Out to God (Judges 10:10)

The Israelites were placed under the control of the Philistines. This was their punishment for participating in idol worship. Eighteen years later they would cry out to the Lord and confess their sins. During the interim, the Israelites faced persecution and many hardships. They were not a free nation, but a nation in bondage who needed a deliverer—the true Deliverer—God!

The fact that it took so long for the Israelites to confess their sin reveals the real nature of Israel's heart during this time. They were so stubborn, selfish, and foolish that they did not realize how much they needed God or how much He had done for them. Finally, they broke down and cried out to the Lord, confessing the error of their ways.

This passage, among the many others where Israel disobeyed God, shows how God waits for His people. He knew the Israelites would come around eventually. He does not give up on those He loves, even when they give up on Him.

2. God Rebukes Israel (vv. 11–14)

When God heard the cries of the Israelites, He did not respond with joy. He was angry with the Israelites and told them to go back to their false gods. Since they seemed to have chosen the false idols over God, God was implying that they had made their decision and were now stuck with it. We say in today's vernacular, "You made your bed, so lay in it!"

God was making a point. The Israelites had abandoned God for their false gods, but when things got difficult, they wanted God to bail them out. In essence, they wanted to use God. However, He wanted Israel to stop showing allegiance to both sides. He wanted them to realize that they were either with Him or against Him; there was no middle ground.

Over Israel's long history, God had experienced the cycle of rejection and acceptance from the Israelites on many occasions. He knew how they operated. When times were good, they ignored God and followed false gods. When times got difficult, they realized their false gods were no good, and they'd come running back to Him for help. This is not how God operates. The Israelites had a hard time realizing that being faithful to the Lord was a full-time commitment. It's all or nothing when it comes to the Lord. They wanted to pick and choose when to follow the Lord, and typically they only chose Him when times were bad. Even with their many trials, they still did not realize that God is a God for all seasons, both good and bad.

3. Israel Returns to Obedience (vv. 15–18)

It took a while, but Israel finally realized its sinfulness. The people confessed their sin to the Lord and got rid of their false idols. It is important to note that the Israelites not only confessed their sins, but for a time also changed their ways. This shows that they were truly remorseful when they needed God's deliverance—when they wanted to start fresh. They realized their sin, removed the sinful elements from their lives, and asked for forgiveness. Then the Lord rescued them from their misery.

Search the Scriptures

1. Why did the Israelites cry out to the Lord (Judges 10:10)?

2. What had the Lord previously done for the Israelites (vv. 11–12)?

3. How did the Israelites respond to God's anger (vv. 15–16)?

Discuss the Meaning

1. Why do you think the Israelites turned away from God after He had done so much for them? Why do we often turn away from God?

2. What was the result of the Israelites' sin? What does this tell us about disobedience to God?

Lesson in Our Society

Our culture is obsessed with the idols of wealth, fame, and power. Therefore, it should be no surprise that the number one television show in the country is called *American Idol.* Time and again, there are people who chase after these idols and become destroyed in the process. These worldly things cannot provide us with what the Lord can give us. This is why so many celebrities' lives end in destruction; they discover that fame, money, and success do not provide fulfillment.

Make It Happen

1. What are some idols that you have in your own life?

2. How do these idols hinder you in your walk with the Lord?

Follow the Spirit

What God wants me to do:

_____

_____

_____

_____

Remember Your Thoughts

Special insights I have learned:

_____

_____

_____

_____

More Light on the Text
Judges 10:10–18

10 And the children of Israel cried unto the LORD, saying, We have sinned against thee, both because we have forsaken our God, and also served Baalim.

Just as criminals can be repeat offenders, so too God's people can be repeat offenders and repeat repenters. In fact, throughout the book of Judges, Israel had been demonstrating a habit of committing "evil in the sight of the LORD" (see 2:11; 3:7; 4:1; 6:1, NIV), and they weren't finished yet, as chapter 13 will show. In addition, the list of other gods they served was growing—now it was not only Baal (and Asherah), but also the gods of Syria, Sidon, Moab, Ammon, and the Philistines (10:6). Consequently, God's dealings became increasingly harsher with each ongoing offense. For the first time, He allowed two nations, the Ammonites and Philistines, to take them into severe bondage for 18 years. (The Hebrew for "sold" in 10:7 is *makar*, **maw-KAR**, meaning human slavery, being given into slavery or handed over as slaves.) God also allowed these nations to approach the central territories of Israel for an even more total conquest.

Looking ahead, the Ammonites were routed, but the Philistines were not defeated, not even by Samson (13:5), in the book of Judges, which is a telling indication of God's increasing displeasure. As the chosen people had done so many times before, after their judgment became too much to bear, they again cried out to God (see 3:9, 15; 4:3; 6:7). The words "vexed" and "oppressed" (Heb. *ra`ats*, **raw-ATS**, and *ratsats*, **raw-TSATS**) in 10:8 are rhyming synonyms. "Vexed" means "shattered" or "dashed to pieces" (see Exodus 15:6 referring to God having "dashed in pieces" the Egyptians). "Oppressed" means "crushed" or "broken." *Ratsats* is the same

Hebrew word used for Abimelech's skull being "crushed" by a millstone in Lesson 8 (Judges 9:53; cf. Isaiah 42:3, NLT, "crush the weakest reed"). Under such severe dealings, the surprise is not that the Israelites "cried" (Heb. *za`aq*, **zaw-AK**), which means "called out" or "called out together" for mercy, but that they did not do so sooner.

11 And the LORD said unto the children of Israel, Did not I deliver you from the Egyptians, and from the Amorites, from the children of Ammon, and from the Philistines? 12 The Zidonians also, and the Amalekites, and the Maonites, did oppress you; and ye cried to me, and I delivered you out of their hand.

At this point, God had delivered Israel from a total of seven different oppressors, including the Egyptians (Exodus 14), Amorites (Joshua 2:10), Ammonites (with Moabites, Judges 3:13), Philistines (3:31), Zidonians (with the Canaanites, 4:1–3), Amalekites (twice, 3:13; 6:3), and Maonites (a name connected with numerous Arabian tribes named above; cf. 1 Chronicles 2:45; 4:41). In effect, Israel had become as corrupt and apostatized as they could be. In spite of the lengthy history of Israel's rebellion, God has consistently responded with mercy.

Another factor present in this situation is the matter of God apparently changing His mind after hearing His people's prayers (see also discussion on Judges 10:16). Exodus 32:14 reads, "And the LORD repented of the evil which he thought to do unto his people." We can note an elaboration on the use in Exodus 32 of the word "repented" (Heb. *nacham*, **NAKH-am**) in the NASB: "So the LORD changed His mind about the harm which He said He would do to His people." This change came about because of Moses' appeals on behalf of the heinously sinning nation, in spite of their recent miraculous deliverance from Egyptian slavery. The same word is used in Judges 2:18b, "It repented the LORD because of their groanings by reason of them that oppressed them and vexed them." It is revealing that the same Hebrew word is translated "comfort" in Isaiah 40:1, "Comfort ye, comfort ye my people, saith your God."

The book of Judges is a call to repentance. God's people can take hope and take heart in God's steadfast love (see Exodus 34:6–7; see also Lesson 11 for a detailed discussion of the Hebrew word *checed*, **KHEH-sed**). No one can expect to live a life of sin and evil, and then expect to have instant access to God's vending machine of sweet mercy and comforting forgiveness.

13 Yet ye have forsaken me, and served other gods: wherefore I will deliver you no more. 14 Go and cry unto the gods which ye have chosen; let them deliver you in the time of your tribulation.

God bailed out Israel over and over from her self-inflicted disasters—and here Israel has her hand out once again, not very much different from numerous similar circumstances where those in great distress call for merciful assistance. As we look on these situations in disgust, do we not all share, albeit in smaller ways, a similar lack of conscience and oblivion to consequences when we indulge in our own forms of corruption?

15 And the children of Israel said unto the LORD, We have sinned: do thou unto us whatsoever seemeth good unto thee; deliver us only, we pray thee, this day. 16 And they put away the strange gods from among them, and served the LORD: and his soul was grieved for the misery of Israel.

It is ironic that the Israelites told God to do what was right in His eyes, in response to

them doing evil in His eyes. What was right was exactly what He had done—to let them chafe under His punishment. What they were really asking was for Him to suspend what was right and to replace it with undeserved mercy—or in our New Testament language, unmerited favor, grace. While they did put away their idols, however temporarily, and apparently made a serious effort to return to God (they were genuinely miserable), what ultimately turned the tide of compassion, once again seemed to be their apparently incessant crying out to God.

Much scholarly effort has been extended to understand the nuances of Judges 10:16, in particular the word "grieved" (Heb. *qatsar*, **kaw-TSAR**), and also its use within the clause "grieved for the misery." McCann comments, "Actually, the ambiguity of the clause articulates, finally, God's suffering, consisting of God's ability and God's willingness to bear the burden of remaining faithfully in relationship with a persistently faithless people" (79). *Qatsar* is an agricultural term in Hebrew, meaning "to reap" or "to harvest" (as in cutting a crop short; cutting it close to the ground). It also means "short, impatient, vexed," which could suggest that God's quality of infinite patience was stretched, causing vexation or suffering, cutting Him to the quick. The Israelites' persistent wrongdoing consistently landed them in miserable situations. Proverbs 10:27 reads, "The fear of the Lord prolongeth days: but the years of the wicked shall be *shortened* [*qatsar*] (emphasis added)."

17 Then the children of Ammon were gathered together, and encamped in Gilead. And the children of Israel assembled themselves together, and encamped in Mizpeh.

Although God's answer was in the works, it probably seemed at the time as though the

Ammonites would have another victory. After all, God had told them He would not deliver them this time, and He was deafeningly silent for much of the story after that point. It is possible the Ammonites were gathering to replace the recently defeated Midianites in their previously profitable, fast-paced, and large-scale attacks to steal crops and livestock. In response, the Israelites gathered as well to defend their property and livelihood as best they could. The problem was that Israel lacked a leader, which would have resulted in a disorganized battle at best, with potentially disastrous results.

18 And the people and princes of Gilead said one to another, What man is he that will begin to fight against the children of Ammon? he shall be head over all the inhabitants of Gilead.

From their position of desperation, the people of Gilead were willing to make major concessions to avoid joining their comrades as fellow slaves to the Ammonites. While the selection of a leader is beyond the scope of this lesson's verses, the story is pertinent and a critical part of the context (see Judges 11). As it turned out, God's chosen deliverer was a warrior (cf. Gideon as a "mighty man of valour" in 6:12) named Jephthah the Gileadite, who earlier had been rejected and disinherited by his family because his mother was a prostitute (11:1–2). Jephthah had fled and basically became a soldier of fortune, gathering a small band of like-minded, renegade outlaws (11:3; cf. 9:4). David later proved that such a group of men could be shaped into an effective fighting force (1 Samuel 22:2). When the Gideanites called on Jephthah to deliver them, slyly offering to make him their "commander" in Judges 11:6 (Heb. *qatsiyn*, **kaw-TSEEN**), he rightfully rebuked their sudden interest compared to their earlier rejection, which understandably

had made him bitter. Ironically, Jephthah's complaint sounds like God's own complaint against Israel (10:14), coming to Him only as a last resort and in spite of earlier rejection.

Say It Correctly

Abimelech. uh-BIM-uh-lek.
Amalekite. uh-MAL-uh-kit.
Ammon. AM-uhn, AM-ahn'.
Ashkelon. ASH-kuh-lon.
Gilead. GIL-ee-uhd.
Jephthah. JEF-thuh.
Mizpeh. MIZ-puh.
Thebez. THEE-behz, THEE-biz.

Daily Bible Readings

M: Grief Leading to Repentance
2 Corinthians 7:5–11

T: The Path to Forgiveness
1 Kings 8:46–50

W: New Hearts and New Spirits
Ezekiel 18:25–32

T: Unless You Repent
Luke 13:1–9

F: God's Loving Reproof
Revelation 3:14–22

S: Proclaiming Repentance and Forgiveness
Luke 24:44–49

S: Repentance and Submission
Judges 10:10–18

Teaching Tips

1. Words You Should Know

A. Barren (Judges 13:2–3) `aqar (Heb.)— Sterile, childless.

B. Countenance (v. 6) mar'eh (Heb.)— Appearance.

2. Teacher Preparation

Unifying Principle—Preparing for Leadership. God instructed Manoah and his wife on how to raise their child to become a wise leader.

A. Prayerfully study the entire lesson.

B. Download some pictures from the Internet and research the biographical profiles of some famous leaders.

C. Be prepared to have your class help you list on the board some of the attributes that made your choices "good" leaders.

3. Open the Lesson

A. Open with prayer, including the Aim for Change.

B. After prayer, hand out your pictures to different students.

C. Have other volunteers read the biographies.

D. Then ask volunteers to help you list their "good" leadership qualities on the board. Discuss.

E. Discuss how God raises up "good" leaders to direct His people back to Him.

F. Then summarize the In Focus story and discuss Jasmine's dilemma in seeking leadership.

G. Finally, explain that the judges whom God raised up were military leaders who were to deliver the Israelites out of the hands of their enemies.

4. Present the Scriptures

A. Have volunteers read the Focal Verses.

B. Now use The People, Places, and Times; Background; Search the Scriptures; At-A-Glance outline; In Depth; and More Light on the Text to clarify the verses.

5. Explore the Meaning

A. Lead a discussion of the Discuss the Meaning, Lesson in Our Society, and Make It Happen sections.

B. Have volunteers connect these sections to the Aim for Change and the Keep in Mind verse.

6. Next Steps for Application

A. Challenge your students to meditate on this lesson during the week.

B. Close with prayer.

Worship Guide

For the Superintendent or Teacher
Theme: Walk in God's Path
Theme Song: "I'm on the Battlefield for My Lord"
Devotional Reading: Romans 2:1–8
Prayer

Walk in God's Path

Bible Background • JUDGES 13; 21:25
Printed Text • JUDGES 13:1–8, 24–25 | Devotional Reading • ROMANS 2:1–8

Aim for Change

By the end of the lesson, we will: RETELL the story of Samson's birth and how we must prepare for leadership; ACKNOWLEDGE the need for God's direction in preparation for quality leadership; and DETERMINE a strategy to walk on God's path.

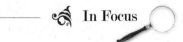

In Focus

Jasmine wanted to run for student body president at her small college. She had never run for a leadership position before, but she thought she would be good at it. She knew a lot of students were not happy with the current student body president, mainly because he did not seem to want to help the students. He held the position solely for the prestige. Jasmine actually wanted to make a difference at her school and would focus on the students' needs. She considered it to be a service-oriented role, instead of a role of power.

After lots of prayer, Jasmine decided to run for the leadership position, and she began to collect the required signatures. At first she was very excited and received lots of encouragement. Then after a few days, she began to doubt herself. She wasn't sure she'd be a good leader. She had very little experience, and she wasn't certain if she was good enough for the position.

AUG
7th

Throughout the Bible God has chosen people to be leaders who have not always been the most qualified, but that didn't mean they could not handle the job. In today's lesson, we learn that God equips His people with the abilities they need to serve His purposes.

Keep in Mind

"And the woman bare a son, and called his name Samson: and the child grew, and the LORD blessed him. And the Spirit of the LORD began to move him at times in the camp of Dan between Zorah and Eshtaol" (Judges 13:24–25).

Focal Verses

KJV **Judges 13:1** And the children of Israel did evil again in the sight of the LORD; and the LORD delivered them into the hand of the Philistines forty years.

2 And there was a certain man of Zorah, of the family of the Danites, whose name was Manoah; and his wife was barren, and bare not.

3 And the angel of the LORD appeared unto the woman, and said unto her, Behold now, thou art barren, and bearest not: but thou shalt conceive, and bear a son.

4 Now therefore beware, I pray thee, and drink not wine nor strong drink, and eat not any unclean thing:

5 For, lo, thou shalt conceive, and bear a son; and no razor shall come on his head: for the child shall be a Nazarite unto God from the womb: and he shall begin to deliver Israel out of the hand of the Philistines.

6 Then the woman came and told her husband, saying, A man of God came unto me, and his countenance was like the countenance of an angel of God, very terrible: but I asked him not whence he was, neither told he me his name:

7 But he said unto me, Behold, thou shalt conceive, and bear a son; and now drink no wine nor strong drink, neither eat any unclean thing: for the child shall be a Nazarite to God from the womb to the day of his death.

8 Then Manoah intreated the LORD, and said, O my Lord, let the man of God which thou didst send come again unto us, and teach us what we shall do unto the child that shall be born.

13:24 And the woman bare a son, and called his name Samson: and the child grew, and the LORD blessed him.

25 And the Spirit of the LORD began to move him at times in the camp of Dan between Zorah and Eshtaol.

NLT **Judges 13:1** Again the Israelites did evil in the LORD's sight, so the LORD handed them over to the Philistines, who oppressed them for forty years.

2 In those days a man named Manoah from the tribe of Dan lived in the town of Zorah. His wife was unable to become pregnant, and they had no children.

3 The angel of the LORD appeared to Manoah's wife and said, "Even though you have been unable to have children, you will soon become pregnant and give birth to a son.

4 So be careful; you must not drink wine or any other alcoholic drink nor eat any forbidden food.

5 You will become pregnant and give birth to a son, and his hair must never be cut. For he will be dedicated to God as a Nazirite from birth. He will begin to rescue Israel from the Philistines."

6 The woman ran and told her husband, "A man of God appeared to me! He looked like of God's angels, terrifying to see. I didn't ask where he was from, and he didn't tell me his name.

7 But he told me, 'You will become pregnant and give birth to a son. You must not drink wine or any other alcoholic drink nor eat any forbidden food. For your son will be dedicated to God as a Nazirite from the moment of his birth until the day of his death.'"

8 Then Manoah prayed to the LORD, saying, "Lord, please let the man of God come back to us again and give us more instructions about this son who is to be born."

13:24 When her son was born, she named him Samson. And the LORD blessed him as he grew up.

25 And the Spirit of the LORD began to stir him while he lived in Mahaneh-dan, which is located between the towns of Zorah and Eshtaol.

The People, Places, and Times

Samson. The name is derived from a Hebrew word meaning "sun" or "brightness." It is used in this story as either an expression of great joy over the birth of a child (which was originally thought to be impossible for Manoah's wife) or as a reference to the nearby town of Beth Shemesh, which means "house of the sun-god." Samson would grow up to be one of the judges of Israel and would be best known for his great strength.

Nazarites. The Bible mentions two different kinds of Nazarites: one kind was appointed by God while the others volunteered to be Nazarites for a certain period of time. Samson was appointed by God to be a Nazarite for life. Volunteer Nazarites or lifelong Nazarites had to follow certain regulations, which are found in Numbers 6. They could not eat any fruit of the vine. This included ripe, unripe, or dried fruit; and they could not have any intoxicating drinks. Also, Nazarites could not cut the hair on their heads, and they could not touch any dead bodies, including the bodies of family members.

Background

The title of this book, Judges, refers to the leaders of Israel during the period between when the elders outlived Joshua until the monarchy was established. The purpose of these judges was to lead and protect God's chosen people from raiders. Some consider Samuel to be the author of this book, but the author is actually unknown. The date when this book was written is also unknown, but it is believed to be during the monarchy because of the use of phrases such as "In those days Israel had no king" (Judges 18:1, NLT). This book depicts the life of Israel in the Promised Land after Joshua's death but before the monarchy. The accounts that take place include the fulfillment of some of God's promises, the chosen people's frequent apostasy, their urgent appeals to God during crises, and their continual disobedience. Overall, the fundamental issue in the book is Israel's faithfulness, or lack thereof, to God. The Israelites continually rejected God's Kingship and were continually punished for it.

At-A-Glance

1. God Punishes Israel for Disobeying Him (Judges 13:1)

2. God Prepares a Judge to Deliver Israel from Punishment (vv. 2–8)

3. God's Deliverer for Israel Is Samson (vv. 24–25)

In Depth

1. God Punishes Israel for Disobeying Him (Judges 13:1)

Israel's faithfulness to God was tested by the Philistines. The Israelites soon gave in to temptation and turned away from God. They began their cycle of sin: (1) disobeying God by worshiping idols; (2) being punished by God for disobedience; (3) crying out to God; (4) being delivered when God raised up judges; (5) turning back to God for a time; and (6) beginning the cycle all over again. In today's text, the Israelites adopted the idols and gods of the Philistines and abandoned the ways of the Lord. Judges 13:1 states, "And the children of Israel did evil *again* in the sight of the LORD; and the Lord delivered them into the hands of the Philistines forty years" (emphasis added). Note that it was the Lord who delivered them into the hands of their enemies to punish them. However, they brought this punishment on themselves. We should always be mindful that sin (disobedience) brings consequences.

For example, the Israelites were ruled by the Philistines for almost 40 years. During this time nothing is mentioned about Israel feeling remorse for their sins. It took the Israelites a long time to wise up to the fact that they needed the true and living God.

2. God Prepares a Judge to Deliver Israel from Punishment (vv. 2–8)

During this time of Israel's disobedience, a man named Manoah from the tribe of Dan lived with his wife in a town called Zorah. Manoah's wife's name was never mentioned. It is unclear how old she was, but we do know she was barren. This was particularly devastating for a family during this time because it meant there would be no heir (male child) to carry on the family name within the tribe. In this culture, a woman's worth was partially determined by her ability to produce children (especially a male child) for her husband. If she was unable to have children, it was considered to be a curse.

Although Manoah's wife was barren, she was visited by an angel of the Lord, who told her she would give birth to a son. This promise required some commitment on the part of Manoah and his wife. The Nazarite prohibitions were placed upon the woman and her child. She could not eat of the vine, drink any intoxicating beverages, cut her son's hair, and he could not touch any dead bodies (this was considered to be unclean).

After these requirements were made, the angel of the Lord described how important her son would be in Israel's history. Judges 13:5 explains that the child would be the one to start leading Israel out of the hands of the Philistines. This shows both that God is sovereign (in control of nations and events) and that God had not given up on Israel, even though they had turned away from God repeatedly. God still loved them and remained committed to them. He kept His end of the covenantal relationship with them, in spite of their disobedience.

Once the angel of the Lord left Manoah's wife, she went to tell her husband about the news. Manoah's immediate reaction was to pray to God and ask for guidance on how to properly raise the child (v. 8). This was obviously a time of great joy for the couple and also a time of great responsibility. Manoah showed his faith in God by seeking His counsel on how to care for the child that God had blessed them with. He had complete faith in the Lord. It is also important to note that God was in charge of delivering His people from bondage. They could not deliver themselves. We, too, must recognize that we may be responsible for getting ourselves into bondage, but more often than not, we need Almighty God to deliver us.

3. God's Deliverer for Israel Is Samson (vv. 24–25)

In due time Manoah's wife gave birth to a son, and they named him Samson. This great blessing was given to them by God, which was a great honor. God knew Manoah and his wife were the right couple to raise a future leader of Israel.

This story is another example of how God chooses ordinary people to accomplish extraordinary things. Samson needed a good, godly home in order to be a great leader. He needed parents to raise him in the fear and admonition of the Lord. He needed parents to teach him how to revere and obey God. Thus, God knew the hearts of Manoah and his wife and gave them the responsibility of raising Samson. Even during a time when God's people had rejected Him, God used them for His purpose and for their own good.

It is important that we draw from this lesson that we, too, are to raise our children in the fear (reverence) of Almighty God. We are to live our lives daily as testaments of how to walk and how not to walk with a holy (set apart from sin) God.

Search the Scriptures

1. Once again the Israelites disobeyed God. How did God punish them this time (Judges 13:1)?

2. Why was it significant that Manoah's wife was going to give birth to a child (vv. 2–3)?

3. What guidelines did the angel of the Lord give to Manoah's wife in regards to the baby (vv. 4–5)?

Discuss the Meaning

1. Are great leaders born or made? Consider the example of Samson and study the biographies of other godly leaders.

2. What happens to a community when it experiences poor leadership? Who suffers?

Lesson in Our Society

In our country today, people complain about corruption in politics, law enforcement, and corporations. It's easy to pick out the poor leaders, and it seems like the good ones are few and far between. What does it take for someone to be a good leader in these and other fields? What sort of training is required? It is important to remember that the world's idea of what makes a good leader may not mirror what God says.

Make It Happen

This week, spend some time studying some of the biblical leaders. Read their stories and decide what qualities were good and/or bad about their leadership styles. Make notes on the things you liked about their leadership skills and any particular flaws they had. Then aspire to be the best leader that you can be wherever God has placed you.

Follow the Spirit

What God wants me to do:

_____

_____

_____

_____

Remember Your Thoughts

Special insights I have learned:

_____

_____

_____

_____

More Light on the Text

Judges 13:1–8, 24–25

1 And the children of Israel did evil again in the sight of the LORD; and the LORD delivered them into the hand of the Philistines forty years.

Since the Israelites continued to do evil in the sight of God, they were punished by Him—they experienced His wrath, and God used the Philistines to carry out His punishment on His own people. Judges 13:1 tells us that the Israelites chose *sin* rather than *righteousness*—"did evil" (Heb. *ra`*, **rah**), which means "wickedness, wrong" in the sight of the omnipresent (all-present) holy (set apart from sin) Lord. He deemed that their actions were sinful; He "delivered" them (Heb. *nathan*, **naw-THAWN**), which means He "gave" them into the hands of their enemies for 40 years.

According to biblical scholars, the Philistines were a Gentile people of Cretan (Aegean) origin. They were also "an aggressive nation that occupied part of southwest Palestine from about 1200 to 600 B.C." (*Nelson's New Illustrated Bible Dictionary*, 986). The Philistines worshiped many gods, were deeply rooted in the pagan Canaanite culture which surrounded them and used soothsayers (astrologers, fortune-tellers, and clairvoyants).

In eleventh century B.C. when the Philistines began to attack the Israelites, these enemies possessed superior weapons of iron and were a very formidable adversary. Later, in battle during Samuel's time, they captured the Ark of the Covenant, which represented the presence of God with His people. Although the Ark was recovered later, the Philistines continued their conquering relationship with the Israelites (see 1 Samuel 10:5; *Nelson's New Illustrated Bible Dictionary*, 987). Yet, the Lord Himself used these people to punish the Israelites, His own children who were hardheaded, stiff-necked, and disobedient. For 40 long years, the Israelites were under the bondage of their foes.

2 And there was a certain man of Zorah, of the family of the Danites, whose name was Manoah; and his wife was barren, and bare not. 3 And the angel of the LORD appeared unto the woman, and said unto her, Behold now, thou art barren, and bearest not: but thou shalt conceive, and bear a son.

Just as the all-powerful, true, and living God was in charge in allowing the Philistines to take the Children of Israel into bondage, He was in charge in delivering them out. In looking at the cycle of sin that they carried out again and again, the Israelites now began to cry out to God for deliverance. God raised up their deliverer through a "barren" (Heb. *`aqar*, **aw-KAWR**), "sterile, childless, fruitless" woman. This is a clear case of God doing the impossible and that all things are possible through God. The man whose name

was Manoah lived in "Zorah" (Heb. *Tsor`ah*, **tsor-AW**), which was a town in Dan. The phrase in 13:2 "a certain man" should also remind us that God uses ordinary—often totally inadequate—people to do His work. Through these people, God can get all the glory and honor due Him for the outcomes He has caused.

Manoah was a descendant of Jacob (one of Jacob's 12 sons) and was from the tribe of Dan. The "angel" (Heb. *mal'ak*, **mal-AWK**), which means "messenger" of God brought Manoah and his wife good news of great joy. In spite of her barrenness, Manoah's wife was going to conceive and, not only that, she was going to bear Manoah a son—an heir to carry on his name and carry out the will of God.

God's plan to deliver the Israelites from Philistine bondage required Manoah and his wife to obey Him fully. Because of who Samson was to be to God and God's people—the role he was to play as the last judge, who would rule over the Israelites for 20 years—God issued three mandates. Manoah's wife must abstain from alcohol. Women can endanger the lives and health of their babies if the women drink alcohol while pregnant. Manoah's wife was also to eat no unclean thing, meaning she was to follow the strict dietary regulations regarding kosher food. And the couple was also to make sure that Samson's hair was not cut because he was going to be a "Nazarite" (Heb. *Naziyr, Nazir,* **naw-ZEER**), which means "consecrated or devoted one." These specifications were essential to set apart this child for service to God. "Samson's parents made the vow for him and even though a Nazirite vow was sometimes temporary, in Samson's case it was for life" (*Life Application Study Bible*, 377).

6 Then the woman came and told her husband, saying, A man of God came unto me, and his countenance was like

the countenance of an angel of God, very terrible: but I asked him not whence he was, neither told he me his name: 7 But he said unto me, Behold, thou shalt conceive, and bear a son; and now drink no wine nor strong drink, neither eat any unclean thing: for the child shall be a Nazarite to God from the womb to the day of his death.

Manoah's wife brought the good news to her husband and shared the details of what the messenger of God had told her. The word "countenance" in Hebrew is *mar'eh* (**mar-EH**) and means "appearance." She described the one she recognized as an angel as looking "terrible" (Heb. *yare'*, **yaw-RAY**), which means "inspiring fear." At first sight, the messenger probably appeared to be someone she should be afraid of. Indeed, she did not ask him where he came from and he did not give his name. The *Life Application Study Bible* (376) suggests, "In those days people believed that if they knew someone's name they knew his character and how to control him. By not giving his name, the angel was not allowing himself to be controlled by Manoah's wife. He was also saying that his name was a mystery beyond understanding too wonderful to imagine." Instead, the angel got straight to the point: He told her the good news that she would conceive and bear a son, how she was to carry him during her pregnancy, and that Samson "shall be a Nazarite to God" (13:7). In essence, this part of the passage tells us that God can call and anoint us (consecrate us) from the womb to do His will—call us before we are even born.

8 Then Manoah intreated the LORD, and said, O my Lord, let the man of God which thou didst send come again unto us, and teach us what we shall do unto the child that shall be born.

Manoah "intreated" (Heb. *'athar*, **aw-THAR**), which means "insisted, urged," or

"pleaded" by praying and asking the Lord to send "the man of God" (the angel) a second time to them. Manoah wanted to be sure about how he and his wife should parent Samson. It could have been also that this was such good news and so unexpected—so long hoped for, since they had probably tried to have a child for many years but to no avail—that Manoah did not want to do anything to hinder this blessing. He wanted to obey God to the letter. Manoah probably felt that having the messenger repeat God's instructions would insure that he and his wife made no mistakes in carrying them out.

13:24 And the woman bare a son, and called his name Samson: and the child grew, and the LORD blessed him.

There is a song that says, "All God's promises are true." This part of the text demonstrates that God fulfills His promises. Yes, His promises are indeed true! The woman who was barren for so many years gave birth to a son "and called his name Samson" (v. 24). In Hebrew, "Samson" is *Shimshown* (**shim-SHONE**) and means "like the sun." As long as Samson obeyed God, metaphorically he did shine like the sun in showing the glory of his God. Samson was also "blessed" (Heb. *barak*, **baw-RAK**), which means "saluted, adored"; Samson's blessings flowed from God. In other words, when Samson obeyed God and did God's will, Samson's life was blessed—it was to be saluted because the people could see the glory of God.

25 And the Spirit of the LORD began to move him at times in the camp of Dan between Zorah and Eshtaol.

God's Spirit denotes God's presence with His people. The word "Spirit" (Heb. *ruwach*, **ROO-akh**) means "wind, breath, mind, spirit," but here it refers to the presence and power of God at work in Samson. Ultimately, this is the third person of the Trinity carrying out the will of God. The one true God was preparing Samson to deliver God's people from the hands of their enemies. So God began to prepare him for his role as judge of Israel, where he would reign for 20 years. After 40 years, the Israelites were going to be set free from the Philistines' bondage and all that the Philistines could do is yield to the power of Almighty God. After the battle, they would know who the one true God is. This battle was not Samson's or the Israelites', but the Lord's.

Samson's tenure as judge was marked by moments of foolishness and tragedy. Even though Samson sinned terribly and often used poor judgment, God still accomplished much through him. Frail humanity cannot hinder the plans of Almighty God. Whatever our sovereign God decrees will certainly come to fruition. The bigger picture is that in spite of Samson's behavior—their appointed leader's disobedience—God wanted to free His chosen people from bondage and He did just that. The destiny of the Children of Israel and God's purpose for their lives were always in the hands of Sovereign God. In comparison, Samson was like the nation of Israel in that he was called by God to be a judge; the nation thrived as long as they obeyed God. Samson also thrived as long as he obeyed God. We, too, will thrive as long as we obey God and follow His inerrant Word.

From the book of Judges and this lesson, we should learn that a holy God hates sin and He punishes it as well. Sin has dire consequences. The ultimate penalty for sin is death, and God sets before us the way of life and the way of death (Jeremiah 21:8). At the other end of the spectrum is the fact that He also forgives sin; those that repent (turn from sin and turn to God) can be restored to a right relationship with Him.

Say It Correctly

Amorites. 'a-mə-ˌrīt.
Ashdod. 'ash-ˌdäd.
Ashkelon. ASH-kuh-lon.
Ekron. EK-ruhn, EK-ron.
Hittites. HIT-tit, HIT-it.
Hivites. HI-vit.
Jebusites. JEB-yoo-sit('),
-yuh-, -zit.
Manoah. muh-NOH-uh. ma-NOH-uh.
Nazarites. NAZ-uh-rit.
Philistines. 'fi-lə-ˌstēn; fə-'lis-tən, -ˌtēn;
'fi-lə-stən.

Daily Bible Readings

M: God's Righteous Judgment
Romans 2:1–8

T: Separated to the Lord
Numbers 6:1–8

W: The Holy and the Common
Leviticus 10:8–11

T: Keep the Commandments
Deuteronomy 5:6–10

F: Hold Fast to God
Deuteronomy 10:12–21

S: Wonders for God's Followers
Judges 13:15–23

S: God Prepares a Deliverer
Judges 13:1–8, 24–25

Teaching Tips

1. Words You Should Know

A. Go (Ruth 1:8, 11, 16, 18) *yalak* (Heb.)—To walk, depart, proceed, move, go away.

B. Return (vv. 8, 10, 15, 16) *shuwb* (Heb.)—To turn back, or go back.

2. Teacher Preparation

Unifying Principle—Choosing Community Wisely. Ruth chose to make her community with Naomi as an expression of her faith in the God of Israel.

A. Pray for lesson clarity.

B. Prayfully study the entire text and the surrounding sections.

C. Compare Ruth's circumstances with what happens in your own community.

3. Open the Lesson

A. Open with prayer, including the Aim for Change.

B. Ask your students to name the various communities that they are a part of. Discuss.

C. Have your students read the Aim for Change and Keep in Mind verse in unison.

D. Then summarize the In Focus story and discuss Valerie's need to connect with a faith community in her new home.

E. Compare and contrast Valerie's dilemma with that of Ruth and Naomi.

F. Explain Ruth's choice to leave her Moabite community to become a part of Naomi's community—even though it was a different region, culture, and religious group than her homeland.

4. Present the Scriptures

A. Have volunteers summarize the Focal Verses.

B. Now use The People, Places, and Times; Background; Search the Scriptures; At-A-Glance outline; In Depth; and More Light on the Text to clarify the verses.

5. Explore the Meaning

A. Have volunteers summarize the Discuss the Meaning, Lesson in Our Society, and Make It Happen sections.

B. Connect these sections to the Aim for Change and the Keep in Mind verse.

6. Next Steps for Application

A. Challenge your students to thank God for His provisions during the week.

B. Close with prayer.

Worship Guide

For the Superintendent or Teacher
Theme: Choosing a Community
Theme Song: "Blest Be the Tie That Binds"
Devotional Reading: Romans 10:5–13
Prayer

AUG 14th

Choosing a Community

Bible Background • RUTH 1:8–18
Printed Text • RUTH 1:8–18 | Devotional Reading • ROMANS 10:5–13

Aim for Change

By the end of the lesson, we will: RECALL the significance of Ruth making Naomi's community her own; REFLECT on how we choose or identify a faith community; and THANK God for our own faith community.

In Focus

Valerie and her twin son and daughter had been doing well, even after her divorce. She worked in Michigan at a car assembly plant for 25 years. Valerie had saved her money and invested in the stock market. However, she was laid off after her plant closed down. Valerie was not worried because she had invested her money and would use it to get by until she found another job. She called her financial advisor only to be told her stocks had lost most of their value.

She decided that her only option was to move to Florida. Her grandmother had left her a house there that was paid for in full along with a small convenience store. The house had stood empty because Valerie never had a desire to move down south. The store was rented and run by a cousin, and it generated a generous amount of money. Valerie knew it would not be easy relocating, but she intended to visit the church her grandmother attended to see if it suited her family's spiritual needs. Valerie knew she needed to connect with a community of faith.

In today's lesson, Ruth decides to remain with Naomi and go live with her in Judah. It meant she had to adjust to a new home, culture, and faith community.

Keep in Mind

"And Ruth said, Intreat me not to leave thee, or to return from following after thee: for whither thou goest, I will go; and where thou lodgest, I will lodge: thy people shall be my people, and thy God my God" (Ruth 1:16).

"And Ruth said, Intreat me not to leave thee, or to return from following after thee: for whither thou goest, I will go; and where thou lodgest, I will lodge; thy people shall be my people, and thy God my God" (Ruth 1:16).

Focal Verses

KJV **Ruth 1:8** And Naomi said unto her two daughters in law, Go, return each to her mother's house: the LORD deal kindly with you, as ye have dealt with the dead, and with me.

9 The LORD grant you that ye may find rest, each of you in the house of her husband. Then she kissed them; and they lifted up their voice, and wept.

10 And they said unto her, Surely we will return with thee unto thy people.

11 And Naomi said, Turn again, my daughters: why will ye go with me? are there yet any more sons in my womb, that they may be your husbands?

12 Turn again, my daughters, go your way; for I am too old to have an husband. If I should say, I have hope, if I should have an husband also to night, and should also bear sons;

13 Would ye tarry for them till they were grown? would ye stay for them from having husbands? nay, my daughters; for it grieveth me much for your sakes that the hand of the LORD is gone out against me.

14 And they lifted up their voice, and wept again: and Orpah kissed her mother in law; but Ruth clave unto her.

15 And she said, Behold, thy sister in law is gone back unto her people, and unto her gods: return thou after thy sister in law.

16 And Ruth said, Intreat me not to leave thee, or to return from following after thee: for whither thou goest, I will go; and where thou lodgest, I will lodge: thy people shall be my people, and thy God my God:

17 Where thou diest, will I die, and there will I be buried: the LORD do so to me, and more also, if ought but death part thee and me.

18 When she saw that she was stedfastly minded to go with her, then she left speaking unto her.

NLT **Ruth 1:8** But on the way, Naomi said to her two daughters-in-law, "Go back to your mothers' homes. And may the LORD reward you for your kindness to your husbands and to me.

9 May the LORD bless you with the security of another marriage." Then she kissed them good-bye, and they all broke down and wept.

10 "No," they said. "We want to go with you to your people."

11 But Naomi replied, "Why should you go on with me? Can I still give birth to other sons who could grow up to be your husbands?

12 No, my daughters, return to your parents' homes, for I am too old to marry again. And even if it were possible, and I were to get married tonight and bear sons, then what?

13 Would you wait for them to grow up and refuse to marry someone else? No, of course not, my daughters! Things are far more bitter for me than for you, because the LORD himself has raised his fist against me."

14 And again they wept together, and Orpah kissed her mother-in-law good-bye. But Ruth clung tightly to Naomi.

15 "Look," Naomi said to her, "your sister-in-law has gone back to her people and to her gods. You should do the same."

16 But Ruth replied, "Don't ask me to leave you and turn back. Wherever you go, I will go; wherever you live, I will live. Your people will be my people, and your God will be my God.

17 Wherever you die, I will die, and there I will be buried. May the LORD punish me severely if I allow anything but death to separate us!"

18 When Naomi saw that Ruth was determined to go with her, she said nothing more.

The People, Places, and Times

Moab. Moab was the son of Lot by an incestuous relationship with his eldest daughter (Genesis 19:36–37). His descendants were known as the Moabites and the land as Moab. As the account in Genesis suggests, "...the Israelites and the Moabites were Semites and kinsmen, and this is confirmed in a measure by the fact that the language of the Moabites is closely related to that of the Hebrews" (*Wycliffe*, 1143). Moab was a large plateau located east of the Dead Sea and spanned along part of the Arnon River. It had good land for grazing flocks of sheep and goats. Because of feuding over land and the fact that the religion and culture were very similar to that of the Canaanites, the Israelites and the Moabites harbored great hostility toward one another. The main road that ran through Moab was known as "the king's highway" which the Israelites were refused permission to cross after they left Egypt (Numbers 21:21–22, NIV). The Moabites even tried to get the prophet Balaam to place a curse on the Israelites because of their success (Numbers 22–24). In spite of their hostility toward one another, God would not allow the Israelites to harm the Moabites (Deuteronomy 2:9). However, the Moabites were excluded from being considered part of Israel (23:1–8).

Bethlehem-Judah. This city is five miles south of Jerusalem. Bethlehem translates to mean "house of bread." It is also known as the city of David. It was previously known as Bethlehem-Ephrathah. Therefore the people were called Ephrathites. David and his ancestors lived in Bethlehem (1 Samuel 16:1–5). The most important person in the Davidic line born there was Jesus. Its hyphenated name is to distinguish it from the town of the same first name in Zebulun.

Background

The author of Ruth is unknown. Some scholars believe the author was Samuel, but that cannot be proved because the mention of David suggests a later date (Ruth 4:17, 22). This book is closely tied with the book of Judges. The events in Ruth took place during the period of Judges (1375–1050 B.C.). In the Hebrew Bible, Ruth is one of the five Megilloth or Scrolls included in the "Writings," the third division of the Canon (Song of Solomon, Ruth, Lamentations, Ecclesiastes, Esther). The Jews read this book every year at the Feast of Weeks.

The climate during the time of the judges when the events of Ruth occurred can only be described as chaotic. Israel was facing moral decline, foreign attacks, and national chaos. Joshua helped the Israelites conquer major Canaanite cities and divided the land among the 12 tribes of Israel. But some Canaanites and other people remained. This caused serious problems. The Israelites were threatened with attacks from these people, who wanted the land back. Also, the Israelites married Canaanites and started worshiping their gods. Everyone was doing whatever he or she desired without concern for God's Laws. The Israelites ignored God and reaped the consequences of their sins (Judges 17:6; 21:25). One of the consequences of their spiritual depravity was a famine. This famine was so severe that it forced Naomi's husband, Elimelech (Heb. *Elimelech,* **el-eeMEH-lek**), whose name means "My God is King," to leave with his family and travel to Moab. They went to a pagan nation in order to survive (Ruth 1:1–2).

555

At-A-Glance

1. Time to Return (Ruth 1:8–9)

2. Time to Separate (vv. 10–13)

3. Time to Commit (vv. 14–18)

In Depth

1. Time to Return (Ruth 1:8–9)

The decision had been made. Naomi had to return to Bethlehem. Her husband, Elimelech, had passed away, had no relatives in Moab, and her sons had also died. She faced severe poverty and hardship as a widow. Her decision was thoroughly thought out. It is unknown how she heard that the famine in Israel had ended. However, Moab was only 15 miles from Bethlehem. Maybe other Israelites who passed by the area shared the news. Nevertheless, Naomi knew in her heart she had to go back to the place where God was providing for His people. After all, Bethlehem is translated to mean "house of bread." This was her home, her people, and the place where she could worship her God. Naomi had faith that her God would provide all she needed.

Naomi and her daughters-in-law, Orpah and Ruth, had traveled almost to the borders of Israel when she stopped to talk with them. It would be selfish for her to expect these Moabite women to go to a place whose culture and religion were strange to them. She had nothing to offer them. Moreover, they had no relatives in Israel. So Naomi urged Orpah and Ruth to return to Moab to their mothers' homes (v. 8).

Naomi asked the Lord to deal kindly with them, even as they had been toward their husbands and her (v. 8). Orpah and Ruth had been good wives. They treated her sons with love and respect while they were alive and after their deaths. Orpah and Ruth did not remarry but stayed with their mother-in-law to provide support for her. Naomi was grateful for their kindness and wanted God to bless them in a special way.

Naomi wanted the Lord to bless them each with another husband (v. 9). She was well aware of the perils of being a widow. It would be a hard life if they did not go back to their mothers' homes. It is not likely they would remarry in Israel due to the strained relationship with the Moabites as well as the restrictions based on God's Law. Naomi desired for them to stay in Moab and for the Lord to reward them with good remarriages. She also asked that God would help them "find rest" (v. 9). Naomi was implying she desired for them to have peace in their marriage and the provisions they needed.

2. Time to Separate (vv. 10–13)

Ruth and Orpah were so upset over their pending separation that they pleaded with Naomi to let them go with her to Israel (v. 10). Naomi once again told her "daughters" to return to their homeland. She had grown to love them as though they were her own children, but Naomi understood that returning to Bethlehem with her should not be an option. She questioned why they wanted to come with her. Naomi spoke about the possibility of conceiving more sons so they could become their husbands (v. 11). This was in reference to the custom called "levirate marriage" in which younger sons were required to marry the widow of his deceased brother (Deuteronomy 25:5–6; Matthew 22:24). It was done to protect the widow and preserve the family line.

Naomi once again told them to return home. She was up in age and could not bear any more children (Ruth 1:12). Naomi was a poor widow with no hope of a brighter future. If she could have children, it would not be fair to expect Orpah and Ruth to wait for them to come of age so they could marry them (v. 13).

3. Time to Commit (vv. 14–18)

They all wept again at the idea of their separation. This was a difficult moment. However, this was a turning point in their relationship. Orpah kissed her mother-in-law good-bye (Ruth 1:14). She had been convinced by Naomi's plea and decided to return to Moab. She wanted a better life, which could not be obtained by following Naomi. Orpah was concerned about her personal well-being. Orpah thought she would be better off in her own country. She knew the Israelites were hostile toward Moabites. She had suffered long enough as a widow. As Naomi pointed out to Ruth (v. 15), Orpah's commitment was to her people and the gods of the Moabites. These gods included Baal-peor and Chemosh (Numbers 21:29; 25:3). It is believed while married to Naomi's sons, Orpah and Ruth had embraced the God of Israel. But now, Orpah had decided to turn back to the false gods of her people.

In contrast, Ruth clung to Naomi, unwilling to separate from her. Orpah had started her journey back to Moab. Naomi tried to convince Ruth to go with Orpah (Ruth 1:15). She was not trying to persuade Ruth to go back to a belief in false gods, but to move toward what seemed to be a better future. The consequences of journeying to Israel would be great. Naomi did not want Ruth to regret her decision. She knew that Ruth's relationship with God would be tested if she decided to live in Israel with her.

Naomi's arguments did not convince Ruth to join Orpah. Ruth had resolved to go with her to Israel. She refused to let anything hinder her loyalty and love for her mother-in-law. Ruth knew it meant she could suffer affliction in Israel. This would be mild in comparison to the affliction Naomi may suffer as a widow. Ruth wanted to help support her.

Ruth's expression of love and loyalty in verses 16 and 17 truly reveal to us her inner character. She pled with Naomi not to make her go back to Moab. It would be devastating for her to leave. Ruth promised to go wherever Naomi went. She was promising to never leave her mother-in-law alone. Even if she traveled to Israel, Ruth would go with her. She also promised to stay wherever Naomi stayed. Since Naomi was a poor widow, she could possibly be homeless. Ruth also promised to become a part of the Israelite community. Ruth was willing to accept the people as well as comply with the laws, customs, and religion of Naomi's community. Naomi had been a good example for Ruth of the Israelite community. Most importantly, Ruth promised to accept Naomi's God as her God. This was an act of faith. Ruth decided to worship the true God. She was not going back to the false gods of the Moabites. Ruth wanted to serve the God of Israel. Ruth had made the most important commitment of her life, and her decision would change her life forever. It would also impact the world.

Ruth vowed to live and die with Naomi. She even wanted to be buried with Naomi. Her loyalty was beyond this life. She had desired to spend even her last resting place with Naomi. That is a love and bond only God could build between two people. Because she had placed her faith in Naomi's God, Ruth made an oath in the name of Israel's God to keep her promises.

Search the Scriptures

1. What was Naomi's prayer for her daughters-in-law (Ruth 1:8–9)?

2. Why did Naomi try to discourage Ruth and Orpah from traveling back with her to Judah (1:11–13)?

Discuss the Meaning

1. How do we choose which communities to belong to?

2. What racial, cultural, and religious barriers would Ruth have to deal with in Israel?

Lesson in Our Society

Ruth had to make a decision whether to return to Moab or go to Israel with Naomi. Ruth based her decision on what was best for Naomi. She felt as a widow, Naomi could not sustain herself in Israel. Ruth desired to help care for and support her mother-in-law; therefore, she decided to go to Israel. Ruth vowed to go wherever Naomi went, live with her, become part of the Israelite community, and accept Naomi's God as her own.

Today, we live and build relationships with others in multiple communities such as families, towns, work sites, and congregations. As we decide to identify with various groups, we should reflect on what motivates us to choose specific communities. Each community serves different purposes in our lives and benefits us in various ways. Our communities should be places that enable us to grow. This is a critical factor in determining whether to stay or join a different community.

Make It Happen

Our faith communities are integral parts of our lives. Within the faith community, we learn the Word and what God requires of us as His disciples. We learn to rejoice and weep with one another as the body of Christ. We share births, baptisms, graduations, Sunday School, communions, weddings, and funerals. Our faith community is the place we find comfort in the midst of life's storms. Today,

take the time to reflect on the blessings of being a part of your faith community. Pray and thank God for the fellowship, care, and support you receive.

Follow the Spirit

What God wants me to do:

_____

_____

_____

_____

_____

Remember Your Thoughts

Special insights I have learned:

_____

_____

_____

_____

More Light on the Text
Ruth 1:8–18

8 And Naomi said unto her two daughters in law, Go, return each to her mother's house: the LORD deal kindly with you, as ye have dealt with the dead, and with me. 9 The LORD grant you that ye may find rest, each of you in the house of her husband. Then she kissed them; and they lifted up their voice, and wept.

Due to famine and the death of their husbands, the world of Naomi, Orpah, and Ruth collapsed around them. Still, they displayed strength of character that is worth emulating. They showed love, faithfulness, selflessness, and concern for each other that should be named among all believers. Instead of a negative mother-in-law report about Naomi, the text portrays her as a godly woman, who in spite of her own suffering and loss is concerned about the well-being of her daughters-in-law, Orpah and Ruth. Life had dealt Naomi a devastating hand. Not only had her husband Elimelech died, but 10 years later, her two sons—Mahlon and Kilion—passed away as well (Ruth 1:1–5). Yet, Naomi was not so caught up in her own grief that she could not see the needs of her two daughters-in-law. In verses 8–9, the word "house" in Hebrew (*bayith,* **BAH-yith**) means "household" or "family." In the ancient world, there was almost nothing worse than being a widow, being without blood-related family, being without someone to provide or take care of you. This was the lot of Naomi, Orpah, and Ruth. Their husbands were all dead. Who would care for these women in their dire situation? They could be taken advantage of, ignored altogether, or swallowed up in poverty.

Because Orpah and Ruth had dealt kindly with her, Naomi also blessed them. She said, "The LORD deal kindly with you" (v. 8). The word "deal" in Hebrew is *`asah* (**aw-SAW**) and means "to attend to, to put in order" and "kindly" is *checed* (**KHEH-sed**), meaning "goodness, favor, and mercy." In other words, because Orpah and Ruth had shown goodness, favor, and mercy toward Naomi and her dead sons, she asked that God show them the same as they returned to their people. In addition, she wanted the Lord to bless them with "rest" (Heb. *mânowchah,* **maw-NO-akh**), meaning "quietness, a resting place, comfort." The phrase "may find" in Hebrew is *matsa'* (**maw-TSAW**), meaning "attain, cause to encounter." Naomi knew that with the loss she and her daughters-in-law had experienced, all three of them needed a place where they could rest, regroup from their sorrows, and receive nurturing and

care. She was confident that the three of them could find this when they returned home to their own people. After blessing them, all three of the women "wept" (Heb. *bakah,* **baw-KAW**) which means they "shed tears." Since they had already experienced great loss and now they could be separated from each other forever, they had much to cry about. The sadness of their predicament overwhelmed them.

10 And they said unto her, Surely we will return with thee unto thy people. 11 And Naomi said, Turn again, my daughters: why will ye go with me? are there yet any more sons in my womb, that they may be your husbands?

Naomi had the mindset for them to return to their own people; however, Orpah and Ruth had the mindset to go with Ruth to Judah—to return with Naomi to Naomi's people. They were at an impasse. Since Naomi had acted so selflessly toward them, Ruth and Orpah returned the kindness by acting selflessly toward her—they followed Naomi's example. Naomi sowed the seeds of love and kindness and reaped love and kindness in return. Since her daughters-in-law would not relinquish their desire to go with her, Naomi reminded them of her own sad situation.

12 Turn again, my daughters, go your way; for I am too old to have an husband. If I should say, I have hope, if I should have an husband also to night, and should also bear sons; 13 Would ye tarry for them till they were grown? would ye stay for them from having husbands? nay, my daughters; for it grieveth me much for your sakes that the hand of the LORD is gone out against me.

Again, Naomi pleaded with Ruth and Orpah to "turn again" (Heb. *shuwb,* **shoob**), meaning "go back" to their own people. In verse 12 she reminded them that she was "too old"—past child-bearing years to have sons for them to marry, and even if she did hope to remarry and bear sons, was it reasonable for them to "tarry" (Heb. *sabar*, **saw-BAR**) or "wait upon" the boys until they were grown up so the women could marry them? Naomi then answered her own questions, telling her "daughters" (Heb. *bath*, **bath**) "nay," which means "no." Naomi "grieveth" (Heb. *marar*, **maw-RAR**), meaning she "showed bitterness, was enraged" over her situation. She was bitter about what she perceived a sovereign God had done or allowed to be done to her. Here the word "hand" in Hebrew is *yad* (**yawd**) and means "strength, power." She believed that the strength and power of the Lord had gone against her in taking her husband and two sons.

Just as Naomi expressed her bitterness or outrage at God, many people today have similar feelings about their situations. Some blame God and have walked with Him no more because to them He caused or did not stop the wrongful circumstances that hurt them so deeply. What they do not realize is that God can take these valley experiences and work them to the good to help them mature in faith, be over-comers, and help others as well.

14 And they lifted up their voice, and wept again: and Orpah kissed her mother in law; but Ruth clave unto her.

Indeed this was a very trying time for the three women; their tears still were not spent. They all cried out and wept yet again. This time, though, Orpah took Naomi's advice and went back to her own people. She kissed Naomi before she departed. But Ruth "clave" (Heb. *dabaq*, **daw-BAK**), meaning she "clung to, stayed with" her mother-in-law. In other words, Ruth decided to remain by Naomi's side and go back to Judah, the Promised Land, with her. She would not let Naomi, old, tired, and bitter, go the journey alone. She would not leave her to fend for herself.

15 And she said, Behold, thy sister in law is gone back unto her people, and unto her gods: return thou after thy sister in law. 16 And Ruth said, Intreat me not to leave thee, or to return from following after thee: for whither thou goest, I will go; and where thou lodgest, I will lodge: thy people shall be my people, and thy God my God:

Naomi made a final appeal to Ruth. She reminded Ruth that Orpah had already gone back to her people and her gods. She asked Ruth to do as Orpah had done. However, Ruth asked Naomi not to make that request. The word "intreat" (Heb. *paga`*, **paw-GAH**) means "entreat, plead, reach out to." "Intreat" suggests that Ruth was urging Naomi to allow her to go with her to Judah. Here Ruth declared a quality of selflessness that has blessed so many down through the ages. She told her mother-in-law that she would go with her wherever she went; in verse 16 the word "lodgest" (Heb. *luwn*, *liyn*, **loon**) means "abide, dwell"—wherever Naomi abided or lived, that was where Ruth said that she would also dwell. In addition, Ruth affirmed that Naomi's people would be her people, and even more so, Naomi's God would be Ruth's God. In essence, Ruth—a Moabitess, whose people worshiped many gods—began to worship and affirm the one true God—the God of Abraham, Isaac, and Jacob and the God of God's chosen people, the Israelites. Ruth took a stand for God, and one significant outcome was her role in the lineage of our Lord and Savior, Jesus Christ. Ruth remarried; she and Boaz were the parents of Obed: "he is the father of Jesse, the father of David" (4:17). Although Ruth belonged to a race despised by God's chosen people, Almighty God blessed Ruth because of her faithfulness. In fact, she became the grandmother of King David and the direct ancestor of Jesus.

17 Where thou diest, will I die, and there will I be buried: the LORD do so to me, and more also, if ought but death part thee and me.

Ruth's selflessness and loyalty to her mother-in-law and Naomi's God went even further. She also affirmed that she would die and be buried wherever Naomi died and was buried. In fact, only death would part them. Ruth was determined—committed to live in the community her mother-in-law lived in. Nothing would deter that determination. Nothing would alter that commitment.

18 When she saw that she was stedfastly minded to go with her, then she left speaking unto her.

When Naomi saw Ruth was "stedfastly minded to go with her," she knew that there was nothing more to be said and she said nothing more. The phrase "stedfastly minded" in Hebrew is *'amats* (**aw-MATS**) and means "to be steadfast, strong, alert, courageous, brave, stout, bold, solid, hard." In other words, Ruth's mind was made up, and there was nothing more to be said.

Say It Correctly

Chemosh. KEE-mosh.
Chilion. KIL-ee-uhn.
Ecclesiastes. eh-klee-sih-AS-teez.
Elimelech. ee-LIHM-eh-lehk.
Ephrathah. EHF-ruh-thuh.
Lamentations. lam'en-TAY-shuhnz;
lam'en-TAY-shuhn.
Megilloth. mih-GIL-uh; mih-GIL-oth.
Moab. 'mō-ˌab.
Moabites. 'mō-ə-ˌbīt.
Orpah. OR-puh.
Zebulun. ZEB-yuh-luhn, ZEB-yoo-luhn.

Daily Bible Readings

M: The Lord of All
Romans 10:5–13

T: Bound Together in Christ
Romans 12:3–8

W: Seeking Unity in Community
Romans 14:1–9

T: Restoring Community
Genesis 50:15–21

F: Protecting Community
Exodus 1:8–21

S: Seeking Comfort in Community
Ruth 1:1–7

S: Choosing Community
Ruth 1:8–18

Teaching Tips

1. Words You Should Know
   A. Glean (Ruth 2:8, 15–18) *laqat* (Heb.)—To pick up, gather.
   B. Abide (v. 8) *dabaq* (Heb.)—To cling, stay close, follow closely.
   C. Grace (v. 10) *chen* (Heb.)—Denotes favor, beneficial treatment.

2. Teacher Preparation
   Unifying Principle—Depending on Community. The Bible illustrates the principle of sharing with the poor through the practice of gleaning.
   A. Prayerfully study the entire text.
   B. Think of one person you know who is in need within your family or church. Think about how you can help meet the need and then do so.

3. Open the Lesson
   A. Open with prayer, including the Aim for Change.
   B. Summarize the In Focus story and draw out the principles that your students can use in their own lives in helping those in need.
   C. Now ask the class to discuss the needs of those in their families, communities, and church and how they can meet some of those needs.

4. Present the Scriptures
   A. Have volunteers summarize the Focal Verses.

   B. Now use The People, Places, and Times; Background; Search the Scriptures; At-A-Glance outline; In Depth; and More Light on the Text to clarify the text.
   C. Highlight how Boaz had a heart of compassion to help Ruth and Naomi.

5. Explore the Meaning
   A. Discuss obstacles that may hinder us from offering help to the needy.
   B. After reading the Discuss the Meaning section, ask volunteers to recall an occasion when they offered help to someone and how the person responded.
   C. Lead a discussion of the Lesson in Our Society, Make It Happen, and Search the Scriptures sections.

6. Next Steps for Application
   A. Challenge your students to help someone in need during the week.
   B. Close with prayer.

Worship Guide

For the Superintendent or Teacher
Theme: Empowering the Needy
Theme Song: "My Father Is Rich in Houses and Lands"
Devotional Reading: Proverbs 22:1–9
Prayer

Empowering the Needy

Bible Background • RUTH 2–3; LEVITICUS 19:9–10
Printed Text • RUTH 2:8–18 | Devotional Reading • PROVERBS 22:1–9

———————————— Aim for Change ————————————

By the end of the lesson, we will: TELL how Boaz met Ruth and Naomi's need for survival; REFLECT on an appropriate response to a need of someone we know; and DETERMINE ways to help meet someone's need.

————————————  In Focus ————————————

After she lost her job in Michigan, Valerie and her children moved to Florida. She took control of the store her cousin was managing and renting from her. The community welcomed her, and she got to know the customers who came in regularly. There was Mr. Tull, for instance, the plumber who had fixed the water heater at the store during the past winter. Mr. and Mrs. Howard always stopped at the store on Wednesday nights after Bible study for ice cream.

There was one family that caught Valerie's attention every Friday. Mrs. Alexander and her three children always purchased one small bag of rice and two cans of beans. Valerie also noticed the children's clothes were worn-out and dirty. She asked her cousin where they lived. He told her Mrs. Alexander had lost her husband due to a heart attack in March. Since then, she had lost their home and was living with her children in a nearby motel. From that day on Valerie put extra food in the Alexanders' grocery bag every Friday.

Just as Valerie has a heart to help the needy, in today's lesson Boaz allows Ruth to glean in his field. It meant she was able to provide for herself and Naomi.

———————————— Keep in Mind ————————————

AUG 21st

"The LORD recompense thy work, and a full reward be given thee of the LORD God of Israel, under whose wings thou art come to trust" (Ruth 2:12).

"The LORD recompense thy work, and a full reward be given thee of the LORD God of Israel, under whose wings thou art come to trust" (Ruth 2:12).

Focal Verses

KJV **Ruth 2:8** Then said Boaz unto Ruth, Hearest thou not, my daughter? Go not to glean in another field, neither go from hence, but abide here fast by my maidens:

9 Let thine eyes be on the field that they do reap, and go thou after them: have I not charged the young men that they shall not touch thee? and when thou art athirst, go unto the vessels, and drink of that which the young men have drawn.

10 Then she fell on her face, and bowed herself to the ground, and said unto him, Why have I found grace in thine eyes, that thou shouldest take knowledge of me, seeing I am a stranger?

11 And Boaz answered and said unto her, It hath fully been shewed me, all that thou hast done unto thy mother in law since the death of thine husband: and how thou hast left thy father and thy mother, and the land of thy nativity, and art come unto a people which thou knewest not heretofore.

12 The LORD recompense thy work, and a full reward be given thee of the LORD God of Israel, under whose wings thou art come to trust.

13 Then she said, Let me find favour in thy sight, my lord; for that thou hast comforted me, and for that thou hast spoken friendly unto thine handmaid, though I be not like unto one of thine handmaidens.

14 And Boaz said unto her, At mealtime come thou hither, and eat of the bread, and dip thy morsel in the vinegar. And she sat beside the reapers: and he reached her parched corn, and she did eat, and was sufficed, and left.

15 And when she was risen up to glean, Boaz commanded his young men, saying,

NLT **Ruth 2:8** Boaz went over and said to Ruth, "Listen, my daughter. Stay right here with us when you gather grain; don't go to any other fields. Stay right behind the young women working in my field.

9 See which part of the field they are harvesting, and then follow them. I have warned the young men not to treat you roughly. And when you are thirsty, help yourself to the water they have drawn from the well."

10 Ruth fell at his feet and thanked him warmly. "What have I done to deserve such kindness?" she asked. "I am only a foreigner."

11 "Yes, I know," Boaz replied. "But I also know about everything you have done for your mother-in-law since the death of your husband. I have heard how you left your father and mother and your own land to live here among complete strangers.

12 May the LORD, the God of Israel, under whose wings you have come to take refuge, reward you fully for what you have done."

13 "I hope I continue to please you, sir," she replied. "You have comforted me by speaking so kindly to me, even though I am not one of your workers."

14 At mealtime Boaz called to her, "Come over here, and help yourself to some food. You can dip your bread in the sour wine." So she sat with his harvesters, and Boaz gave her some roasted grain to eat. She ate all she wanted and still had some left over.

15 When Ruth went back to work again, Boaz ordered his young men, "Let her gather grain right among the sheaves without stopping her.

KJV cont.

Let her glean even among the sheaves, and reproach her not:

16 And let fall also some of the handfuls of purpose for her, and leave them, that she may glean them, and rebuke her not.

17 So she gleaned in the field until even, and beat out that she had gleaned: and it was about an ephah of barley.

18 And she took it up, and went into the city: and her mother in law saw what she had gleaned: and she brought forth, and gave to her that she had reserved after she was sufficed.

NLT cont.

16 And pull out some heads of barley from the bundles and drop them on purpose for her. Let her pick them up, and don't give her a hard time!"

17 So Ruth gathered barley there all day, and when she beat out the grain that evening, it filled an entire basket.

18 She carried it back into town and showed it to her mother-in-law. Ruth also gave her the roasted grain that was left over from her meal.

The People, Places, and Times

Boaz. His name means "in him is strength" (Unger, 141). A wealthy landowner of Bethlehem, he was a caring farmer who had concern for his workers' welfare. Boaz was a relative of Elimelech, Naomi's husband. He felt responsible for taking care of his extended family. He was the kinsman-redeemer for Ruth and a symbol of Christ's role as our Redeemer.

Gleaning. During harvest time, farmers were required by Israelite law to help the poor, orphans, and strangers (Leviticus 19:9–10; 23:22; Deuteronomy 24:19–22). The workers were required to leave a remnant of the harvest for gleaning by the poor. They could not reap the field to the edge of the property, nor gather together the ears left on the field in the process of reaping. In the vineyard and olive groves, the fallen fruit was to be left. The poor, orphans, and strangers were permitted to gather leftover grain, grapes, and olives after the reapers had finished their work.

Background

Ruth's love and loyalty to her mother-in-law compelled her to stay with Naomi. Ruth vowed to remain with Naomi no matter where she lived, to accept the Israelite people as her own, and to worship the God of Israel. Ruth vowed only to let death separate her from Naomi (Ruth 1:16–17).

They journeyed to Bethlehem together. Upon their arrival, the women of the city were shocked to see Naomi. She told them to call her "Mara," which means "bitter" (1:20). She was expressing her heartfelt pain. Naomi felt the Lord had dealt with her harshly since she was now a poor widow. She had left Bethlehem with a husband and two sons only to return alone and poor. Sometimes we forget to look at the blessings we have in the midst of our pain. Naomi was not alone. Ruth was by her side. Also, spring harvest time had come. Naomi should have remembered about the law of gleaning.

Ruth, who wanted to care for her mother-in-law, asked for permission to go into the fields to glean grain (2:20). Naomi permitted her to go. Unknown to Ruth, she was gleaning in a field belonging to Boaz. He was a relative of Elimelech, Naomi's husband.

His salutation to the workers informs us that he was a godly man. Not all supervisors greet their workers by saying, "The LORD be with you" (2:4). Immediately he noticed Ruth and inquired about her identity. Boaz was told who Ruth was and how hard she worked gleaning in the fields. Her faithfulness was about to reap unexpected rewards.

At-A-Glance

1. Divine Favor (Ruth 2:8–13)

2. Divine Provisions (vv. 14–18)

In Depth

1. Divine Favor (Ruth 2:8–13)

Boaz was very kind to Ruth. He saw how she faithfully worked in the fields to provide for herself and Naomi (her mother-in-law). His initial conversation with Ruth expressed his compassion and concern for her. Boaz addressed her as "my daughter" (v. 8). This can be interpreted in two ways. Boaz was an older man and Ruth was a younger woman; maybe he was being respectful but affectionate in relation to the age difference. Or because Boaz was a relative of Elimelech and the foreman told him that Ruth had returned from Moab with Naomi, Boaz called her "daughter" to express his blood relation with the family. Either way, Boaz's words indicate that he wanted to make sure Ruth understood his motives were purely out of concern for her. Boaz asked that she not go glean in another field, which suggested he wanted to protect and take care of her (v. 9). He also told her to remain with his servant girls, who walked behind the men cutting the grain and bound the grain into sheaves. Ruth could then follow and glean what was left behind. Boaz also instructed the men not to touch her, and he told her to drink water whenever she got thirsty (v. 11).

Ruth was overwhelmed by his graciousness. She bowed down in humble gratitude before Boaz (v. 10). Ruth wanted to know why he was being so kind, especially since she was a foreigner. She was a Moabite and thus considered to be an enemy of Boaz and Naomi's people, the Israelites. Still, Boaz had heard about and witnessed Ruth's faithfulness (Ruth 2:11). Moreover, she had exhibited admirable qualities since she began working in his fields.

Boaz asked God to bless Ruth's life (v. 12), an indication of his godliness, his admiration for Ruth, and his hope for her future. It was clear that Ruth was willing to endure hardship for the sake of her mother-in-law. We must admit that none of us deserve blessings, but because of God's love and grace, we are often rewarded for our labors. He does not forget what we do on His behalf. "For God is not unrighteous to forget your work and labour of love, which ye have showed towards his name, in that ye have ministered to the saints, and do minister" (Hebrews 6:10). Because she embraced the God of Israel as her own and put her trust in Him, Ruth would receive both earthly and spiritual blessings. In spite of residing in a land of her people's enemies, Ruth felt secure under the care of the God of Israel (see Psalm 91:1–4).

2. Divine Provisions (vv. 14–18)

During mealtime, the workers went to a "shelter" where they also took a short break earlier in the workday (see Ruth 2:7, NIV). Although she might have been shunned since she was a Moabite, Boaz invited her to sit with his workers and eat bread dipped in vinegar (v. 14). This wine vinegar and bread (sometimes with olive oil as well) was and remains a typical dish in the Middle East. Boaz treated Ruth just like the others and also offered her some parched (today we might call this dehydrated or recently roasted) corn.

Ruth was given such a large amount of corn that she ate until full with some left over.

Note that Boaz went beyond the gleaning law in providing for Ruth's needs. As she returned to the fields to glean, he instructed the workers to pluck some stalks from their sheaves and leave them for Ruth (vv. 15–16). This was an extraordinary act of generosity and kindness. Boaz was a godly man and regarded Ruth's faithfulness worthy of special blessings.

Ruth carried her barley back to the city and took it to her mother-in-law (v. 18). Moreover, Ruth gave her the leftovers from her dinner which she had saved to give to Naomi. Naomi and Ruth had more than enough to eat. God takes care of His people. In the same way, we should help take care of each other, too. If we each give a little, everyone will have enough to live and thrive. "Whoever sows sparingly will also reap sparingly, and whoever sows generously will also reap generously" (2 Corinthians 9:6, NIV).

Search the Scriptures

1. What reason did Boaz give for showing favor toward Ruth (Ruth 2:11)?

2. How did Boaz order his workers to treat Ruth while she was in the fields (vv. 15–16)?

3. How did Ruth provide for Naomi's needs (vv. 17–18)?

Discuss the Meaning

1. How did Ruth take advantage of God's law of gleaning to help care for her mother-in-law?

2. What obstacles did Ruth have to overcome in finding provisions?

3. How can we learn to be more generous with those in need?

Lesson in Our Society

In recent years, the downturn in the economy has forced many people, who formerly had middle and upper class incomes, to seek out help from social service agencies. These agencies and food banks have seen the requests for assistance increase a hundredfold to two hundredfold. However, these organizations are forced to turn people away because corporate and private donations have dramatically decreased. The outcomes for many people have been an absence of food, proper housing, health care, childcare, and other basic necessities. As Christians, we see the need, but it can seem overwhelming. How does one person make an impact? If we, like Boaz, are generous with what God has given us, we can make a difference one person at a time.

Make It Happen

We see the needs of our family members, neighbors, coworkers, and church family. We each have the ability to do something to make a change in their lives. Pray and ask God who He desires for you to help. Set in motion a plan to meet someone's needs. If you require additional resources, pray and ask God to direct you to the person(s) who can help you. The person you help may just be someone God wants to lift up to make an impact in His kingdom.

Follow the Spirit

What God wants me to do:

_____

_____

_____

_____

Remember Your Thoughts

Special insights I have learned:

_____

_____

_____

_____

More Light on the Text

Ruth 2:8–18

8 Then said Boaz unto Ruth, Hearest thou not, my daughter? Go not to glean in another field, neither go from hence, but abide here fast by my maidens: 9 Let thine eyes be on the field that they do reap, and go thou after them: have I not charged the young men that they shall not touch thee? and when thou art athirst, go unto the vessels, and drink of that which the young men have drawn.

According to the biblical account, Boaz heard the inspiring story of how Ruth, an immigrant, had been faithful and gracious to Naomi, her mother-in-law, by leaving her family and other social ties behind in Moab. She had traveled to Bethlehem of Judah after what seemed to have been a hopeless family problem—after the death of Naomi's two children, Mahlon and Chilion, one of whom was Ruth's husband. It is evident that God's favor was upon the life of Ruth as the story progressed. Yet it is also important to state that the context of the first contact or conversation between Boaz and Ruth showed that the former had some prior knowledge about the faithfulness, sincerity, and goodness of the latter's life (see verse 11). Ruth's noble qualities had made a great impression on Boaz before he even met her. Boaz not only gave her permission to glean in his field, but he also provided an important working structure for her to succeed. First, Boaz identified with her in a special way. He

addressed her directly and used the word "daughter": "Then said Boaz unto Ruth, Hearest thou not, my daughter?" (2:8) He established a personal rapport, connection, and authentic relationship with her to help create avenues for effective channels of communication and trust.

First of all, as children of God, there is an important lesson to learn here, regarding building good relationships when we are faced with similar situations. Secondly, Boaz charged her with do's and don'ts regarding her initiative or approach when gleaning in the field. These were clear and precise instructions from an experienced field owner, Boaz, to a new or a novice person, Ruth, who needed some help and support in these areas. Boaz's instructions were in the form of restrictions, directions, and precautions about the proper attitude or steps she should take while at work.

10 Then she fell on her face, and bowed herself to the ground, and said unto him, Why have I found grace in thine eyes, that thou shouldest take knowledge of me, seeing I am a stranger? 11 And Boaz answered and said unto her, It hath fully been shewed me, all that thou hast done unto thy mother in law since the death of thine husband: and how thou hast left thy father and thy mother, and the land of thy nativity, and art come unto a people which thou knewest not heretofore.

It was clear that Ruth, in a vulnerable position, was utterly surprised at Boaz's generous gesture. In a posture of respect and humility, as was the known cultural-traditional practice of the ancient world, Ruth "fell on her face, and bowed herself to the ground" (Ruth 2:10). This form of expression indicated both social distance and sense of gratitude for Boaz's act of kindness and support. When we are in vulnerable or marginalized situations, it is important to let those who are helping or supporting us know that we are appreciative and grateful for their inspiring words or initiatives to redeem us from our perilous circumstances. The apostles Paul and Peter provided examples of this humility and thankfulness (Philippians 2:1–3; 4:10–13; 1 Peter 5:5–6). Ruth, a stranger, was very surprised by Boaz's generosity. So she asked, "Why have I found grace in thine eyes…?" (from Ruth 2:10). The word "why" in Hebrew is *madduwa`* (**mad-DOO-ah**). This word denotes someone who is fervently seeking information or instruction in order to understand or be educated about issues or events. In this sense, Ruth, who had initially portrayed deep appreciation, further sought to explore Boaz's motive or rationale for helping her.

12 The LORD recompense thy work, and a full reward be given thee of the LORD God of Israel, under whose wings thou art come to trust. 13 Then she said, Let me find favour in thy sight, my lord; for that thou hast comforted me, and for that thou hast spoken friendly unto thine handmaid, though I be not like unto one of thine handmaidens. 14 And Boaz said unto her, At mealtime come thou hither, and eat of the bread, and dip thy morsel in the vinegar. And she sat beside the reapers: and he reached her parched corn, and she did eat, and was sufficed, and left.

In verse 12, Boaz prayed and invoked Yahweh's intervention in the life of Ruth (and by extension on the life of Naomi). He acknowledged Almighty God as the sole source—Initiator and Finisher—of the blessings received in Ruth's endeavors because of her faithful sense of responsibility that guided her actions. Notice these phrases: "The LORD recompense thy work, and a full reward be given thee of the LORD God of Israel" (v. 12). By invoking the name of "the LORD"—Yahweh—in whom Ruth had come

to seek refuge and blessings, regardless of the fact that she came from Moab, he was essentially proclaiming Yahweh's covenant blessing upon her life. Boaz realized that any true and lasting rewards or blessings upon the Children of Israel come from only God— and only Him! On the one hand, Boaz, by his posture and words, was able to position himself as a mere instrument that God was using to bring about a holistic fulfillment of joy, goodness, and peace in the life of Ruth, a faithful and determined lady (2 Timothy 2:15–20; Hebrews 11:6; 12:2–3). On the other hand, Boaz demonstrated a sense of responsibility as a worthy instrument of God, who was able to create an appropriate environment to support Ruth's progress and well-being.

In Ruth 2:13, Ruth showed great humility and a deep sense of appreciation for Boaz's gracious efforts—which in essence was an initiative to accept Ruth into God's community of love and support.

15 And when she was risen up to glean, Boaz commanded his young men, saying, Let her glean even among the sheaves, and reproach her not: 16 And let fall also some of the handfuls of purpose for her, and leave them, that she may glean them, and rebuke her not. 17 So she gleaned in the field until even, and beat out that she had gleaned: and it was about an ephah of barley.

After the meal, Ruth returned to gleaning. In verse 15, the phrase "risen up" in Hebrew is *quwm* (**koom**) and as used in this text suggests a new beginning. The use of *quwm* here seems to suggest that after the special treat she received from her host, Ruth gained a new energy and motivation.

Boaz "commanded" (Heb. *tsavah*, **tsaw-VAW**) the young workers in his field to assist Ruth, and he gave instructions on how the workers should make sure she benefited from her gleaning. For instance, statements in verses 15–16, such as, "Let her glean even among the sheaves," "reproach her not," "let fall also some of the handfuls of purpose for her," "leave them, that she may glean them," and "rebuke her not," buttress the idea that Boaz meant to support her in every way possible. Boaz made sure that Ruth would be able to glean successfully; she would be able to gather abundantly without any possibility of danger.

However, it is equally critical to underscore the fact that Boaz intentionally *empowered* her to achieve her (and by extension Naomi's) goals and aspirations. Ruth wanted to make sure she and Naomi would have sustenance, a prominent concern for widows.

In verse 17, Scripture records that Ruth worked very hard. The Bible teaches us to refrain from being lazy or sluggish (see Proverbs 12:27; Romans 12:11). Rather, we must work extremely hard by being faithful, diligent, and focused as we trust God to open doors of blessing upon our families, churches, and communities. The results for Ruth, and therefore Naomi, were that Ruth's plate was full—she had abundance! The measurement given in Ruth 2:17 was "it was about an ephah of barley." *Ephah* (**ay-FAW**) was based on an Egyptian concept which connotes a basket's capacity—"basketful." What a favor and blessing for Ruth and Naomi!

18 And she took it up, and went into the city: and her mother in law saw what she had gleaned: and she brought forth, and gave to her that she had reserved after she was sufficed.

What did Ruth do with her blessings for the day? Of course, she took the barley home and she shared the food with her mother-in-law, Naomi. Ruth was a faithful and generous person who wanted to share the rewards of her labor with Naomi. She was empowered by Boaz to become successful, and this outcome meant survival and potential flourishing for her and Naomi. God wants to transform us and put us in strategic positions to transform the circumstances of others who are in need or vulnerable in our churches and communities.

Say It Correctly

Boaz. BOH-az.
Elimelech. ee-LIHM-eh-lehk.
Ephah. EE-fuh.
Orpah. OR-puh.

Daily Bible Readings

M: Sharing Bread with the Poor
Proverbs 22:1–9

T: Provision for the Poor
Leviticus 19:1–10

W: Generosity in the Kingdom
Matthew 20:1–15

T: Sharing Equally
1 Samuel 30:21–25

F: Ready to Share
1 Timothy 6:11–19

S: Taking Initiative
Ruth 2:1–7

S: A Kind Benefactor
Ruth 2:8–18

Teaching Tips

1. Words You Should Know

A. Kinsman (Ruth 4:1, 4, 6, 8) *ga'al* (Heb.)—To redeem (buy back, convert); do the part of next-of-kin.

B. Inheritance (vv. 5, 6, 10) *nachalah* (Heb.)—Possession, property, heritage.

2. Teacher Preparation

Unifying Principle—Caring for One Another. Boaz conducted his business according to the law and in front of the ruling elders so that he would have the support of the community.

A. Begin with prayer, asking God to bring lesson clarity.

B. Prayerfully study the entire lesson.

3. Open the Lesson

A. Open the class with prayer, using the Aim for Change.

B. Ask for a volunteer to summarize the In Focus story.

C. Discuss how Valerie's desire to help care for the needy caused a problem in her new community. How did Valerie resolve the conflict?

D. Now ask, "Has your desire to care for those in your family or community ever caused a conflict with others?" Let students share their experiences.

4. Present the Scriptures

A. Have volunteers summarize the Focal Verses.

B. Now use The People, Places, and Times; Background; Search the Scriptures; At-A-Glance outline; In Depth; and More Light on the Text to clarify the verses.

5. Explore the Meaning

A. Discuss the Discuss the Meaning, Lesson in Our Society, and Make It Happen sections.

B. Connect these sections to Aim for Change and the Keep in Mind verse.

C. Discuss how the desire to care for others can cause conflict in our communities if not done within the law.

6. Next Steps for Application

A. Challenge your students to pray for the needy and that their needs will be met.

B. Close with prayer.

Worship Guide

For the Superintendent or Teacher
Theme: Respecting Community Standards
Theme Song: "If I Can Help Somebody"
Devotional Reading: Philippians 1:3–11
Prayer

Respecting Community Standards

Bible Background • Ruth 4
Printed Text • RUTH 4:1–10   Devotional Reading • PHILIPPIANS 1:3–11

Aim for Change

By the end of the lesson, we will: RECOUNT how Boaz respected the standards of his community; REFLECT on the need to care for others in our communities; and DETERMINE to help care for others in our communities.

 In Focus

Valerie always liked helping others. Since she moved to Florida and took over the convenience store, Valerie was able to minister to others by giving them a listening ear, a kind word, or increasingly more free food. She started out only helping one widow and her children. However, the word spread that she took care of those in the community, and at least 15 people showed up every day for food. Valerie cooked food at home and took it to the store to share with those in need.

One day after her arrival, a man came into the store and wandered around for 30 minutes without buying anything. He kept watching Valerie as she gave out food to anyone who came seeking help. Finally, her cousin Howard got tired of the man staring at Valerie and confronted him. "Sir, is there a problem? You have been here over 30 minutes staring at my cousin."

"Well," the man said as he slowly walked over to the counter where Valerie was standing, "I have noticed you are feeding people cooked meals. Do you have a permit to do that?"

Valerie learned that she had to follow the rules of her new community, even when helping the poor. In today's lesson, Boaz wanted to redeem Naomi's husband and sons' land and secure Ruth's hand in marriage. He had to follow the kinsman-redeemer law and seek the approval of the elders first.

Keep in Mind

"Then said Boaz, What day thou buyest the field of the hand of Naomi, thou must buy it also of Ruth the Moabitess, the wife of the dead, to raise up the name of the dead upon his inheritance" (Ruth 4:5).

AUG 28th

"Then said Boaz, What day thou buyest the field of the hand of Naomi, thou must buy it also of Ruth the Moabitess, the wife of the dead, to raise up the name of the dead upon his inheritance" (Ruth 4:5).

Focal Verses

KJV **Ruth 4:1** Then went Boaz up to the gate, and sat him down there: and, behold, the kinsman of whom Boaz spake came by; unto whom he said, Ho, such a one! turn aside, sit down here. And he turned aside, and sat down.

2 And he took ten men of the elders of the city, and said, Sit ye down here. And they sat down.

3 And he said unto the kinsman, Naomi, that is come again out of the country of Moab, selleth a parcel of land, which was our brother Elimelech's:

4 And I thought to advertise thee, saying, Buy it before the inhabitants, and before the elders of my people. If thou wilt redeem it, redeem it: but if thou wilt not redeem it, then tell me, that I may know: for there is none to redeem it beside thee; and I am after thee. And he said, I will redeem it.

5 Then said Boaz, What day thou buyest the field of the hand of Naomi, thou must buy it also of Ruth the Moabitess, the wife of the dead, to raise up the name of the dead upon his inheritance.

6 And the kinsman said, I cannot redeem it for myself, lest I mar mine own inheritance: redeem thou my right to thyself; for I cannot redeem it.

7 Now this was the manner in former time in Israel concerning redeeming and concerning changing, for to confirm all things; a man plucked off his shoe, and gave it to his neighbour: and this was a testimony in Israel.

8 Therefore the kinsman said unto Boaz, Buy it for thee. So he drew off his shoe.

9 And Boaz said unto the elders, and unto all the people, Ye are witnesses this day, that I have bought all that was Elimelech's, and all that was Chilion's and Mahlon's, of the hand of Naomi.

NLT **Ruth 4:1** Boaz went to the town gate and took a seat there. Just then the family redeemer he had mentioned came by, so Boaz called out to him, "Come over here and sit down, friend. I want to talk to you."

2 Then Boaz called ten leaders from the town and asked them to sit as witnesses.

3 And Boaz said to the family redeemer, "You know Naomi, who came back from Moab. She is selling the land that belonged to our relative Elimelech.

4 I thought I should speak to you about it so that you can redeem it if you wish. If you want the land, then buy it here in the presence of these witnesses. But if you don't want it, let me know right away, because I am next in line to redeem it after you." The man replied, "All right, I'll redeem it."

5 Then Boaz told him, "Of course, your purchase of the land from Naomi also requires that you marry Ruth, the Moabite widow. That way she can have children who will carry on her husband's name and keep the land in the family."

6 "Then I can't redeem it," the family redeemer replied, "because this might endanger my own estate. You redeem the land; I cannot do it."

7 Now in those days it was the custom in Israel for anyone transferring a right of purchase to remove his sandal and hand it to the other party. This publicly validated the transaction.

8 So the other family redeemer drew off his sandal as he said to Boaz, "You buy the land."

9 Then Boaz said to the elders and to the crowd standing around, "You are witnesses that today I have bought from Naomi all the property of Elimelech, Kilion, and Mahlon.

KJV cont.

10 Moreover Ruth the Moabitess, the wife of Mahlon, have I purchased to be my wife, to raise up the name of the dead upon his inheritance, that the name of the dead be not cut off from among his brethren, and from the gate of his place: ye are witnesses this day.

NLT cont.

10 And with the land I have acquired Ruth, the Moabite widow of Mahlon, to be my wife. This way she can have a son to carry on the family name of her dead husband and to inherit the family property here in his hometown. You are all witnesses today."

The People, Places, and Times

Kinsman. During Bible times, "kinsman" described a person's nearest male relative. He had certain responsibilities according to the law. For example, the kinsman acted as an avenger. A wrong done to one member of a family was considered an offense against the entire group. Kinsmen were obligated to punish the wrongdoer. Also, the kinsman was obliged to act as redeemer and handle financial matters on family members' behalf. These responsibilities could include redeeming property that a relative might have sold due to poverty (Leviticus 25:25), ransoming (buying back) his kinsman who may have been sold into slavery (25:47), or acting as a go-between in case a person wanted to make restitution to a relative. The role of the kinsman-redeemer also included taking responsibility for the extended family. When a woman's husband died, the law provided she could marry a brother of her dead husband (25:48–49; Deuteronomy 25:5–10). If there were no brothers, the nearest relative to the deceased husband could become the kinsman-redeemer and marry the widow. If he chose not to, the next nearest relative could marry the widow. In order to provide for those widows who did not remarry, the "gleaning laws" were established (Leviticus 19:9–10).

Background

Boaz was very kind to Ruth; he provided protection for her while she worked in the fields. He went beyond what the "gleaning laws" required in that Boaz told his workers to pull wheat from the sheaves and leave this for Ruth to glean. Ruth worked from sunup to sundown gleaning in the fields to provide for herself and Naomi. One day's work yielded a week's worth of barley because of her effort and Boaz's kindness.

Naomi told Ruth that Boaz was a relative. She wanted Ruth to have a secure future so she put a plan in motion (Ruth 3:1–5). This plan depended on Boaz adhering to the Israelites' traditions and laws regarding a kinsman-redeemer. This was perhaps the only hope Ruth had of a new life among her mother-in-law's people.

At-A-Glance

1. Rejection of the Redemption
(Ruth 4:1–6)

2. Acceptance and Redemption
(vv. 7–10)

In Depth

1. Rejection of the Redemption (Ruth 4:1–6)

Boaz was a man of his word. He told Ruth he would resolve the issue of the kinsman-redeemer for her, and the next day he went and sat down at the city gate (4:1). The gate was a roofed building that served as the normal place for conducting business and legal transactions. Merchants set up their stalls every day near the gate to sell whatever the people needed. People continually passed through the gate, going in and out of the city, to buy items from the merchants or to work in the fields during harvest time. If Boaz wanted to find his relative, this was likely the place to do it. And no sooner had he sat down, then the person he was looking for came passing by. Boaz asked his relative to come sit down and used the term "friend" (v. 1). The other kinsman's name is never mentioned. However, his response to Boaz's invitation indicated that they were familiar with one another.

Boaz then gathered 10 elders to join them (v. 2). The elders were leading, influential men of the town who interpreted tradition-al Israelite laws and settled disputes. Typi-cally, two or three witnesses were present for normal business matters. However, several witnesses were required in judicial matters such as matrimony, divorce, or the transfer-ring of property (Jeremiah 32:11–12). Boaz needed their presence while he determined, as he told Ruth he would, who would serve as kinsman-redeemer for Elimelech's (Naomi's dead husband's) property, which included marriage to Ruth.

Boaz informed the unnamed kinsman that Naomi had returned from Moab and wanted to sell the land that belonged to her deceased husband (v. 3). Although we do not know the circumstances of the claim on this property, two possibilities do emerge. Naomi might have been so poor she needed to sell the land. Or Elimelech might have sold the land before they moved to Moab and now she wanted to redeem it according to the law (Leviticus 25:25).

The only closest male relatives to Naomi were the kinsman and Boaz. The kinsman was a closer relative than Boaz, and he had the first right to redeem the property (Ruth 3:12; 4:4). But since Ruth had expressed interest

in Boaz becoming her kinsman-redeemer, he brought the matter before the elders so there could be witnesses to the negotiations. At first, the kinsman said he wanted to redeem the property. But then Boaz also informed him that marriage to Ruth was included in the transaction (v. 5). Abruptly, the kinsman changed his mind and said he could not redeem the land if he had to marry Ruth as well, expressing concern about damaging his own inheritance (v. 6). It may have seemed like too much of a personal and financial burden.

2. Acceptance and Redemption (vv. 7–10)

The kinsman removed his shoe and gave it to Boaz (vv. 7–8). Among the Israelites, handing over your shoe symbolized the transfer of the owner's purchasing right. The kinsman's act was done in the presence of the 10 elders who acted as witnesses to confirm the transaction.

Boaz willingly took ownership of the land and the right to marry Ruth. He announced this to the elders and all who were present at the gate of the city. He had legally acquired from Naomi all that belonged to Elimelech and his two sons (v. 9). Boaz paid the value of the land to Naomi. Even though the widow of Chilion, Orpah, was still living, she had no claim on the land. She had returned to her homeland of Moab and consequently may have remarried or renounced all rights to an inheritance with the family of Elimelech. The eldest son of Naomi was Mahlon; therefore, he had full rights to his father's estate. The inheritance always went to the eldest son. Since Mahlon and his brother were dead, the estate was Naomi's.

Boaz also announced he had acquired the right to take Ruth, Moabitess and widow of Mahlon, to be his wife (v. 10). The marriage was a conditional aspect for whoever purchased the land. Since Ruth had turned from the false gods of the Moabites to trusting in the God of Israel (1:16; 2:12), Boaz could marry her and remain in good standing with the Israelite community. Boaz also was impressed by her loyalty, kindness, and generosity to others.

As Boaz pointed out in 4:10, the marriage had an additional, important result. Mahlon and his family's name would continue to be part of the land and the town. The city register would include his name. All the people and elders gathered that day were witnesses to all that was done.

Our knowledge of this family's connections to one another and their community increases in significance later on. Ruth and Boaz were married. She conceived a son whom they named "Obed," which meant "servant." Ruth and Boaz gave the world the grandfather of David, a descendant of our Kinsman-Redeemer, Jesus Christ (Matthew 1:5-6). Jesus Christ redeemed us by offering His life as a ransom for our sins. God loved and cared for us so much that He gave up His Son on our behalf.

Search the Scriptures

1. Why did Boaz go to the city gate (Ruth 4:1–3)?

2. What did Boaz tell the unnamed kinsman he had to do in addition to redeeming Elimelech's land (vv. 4–5)?

Discuss the Meaning

1. Why did Boaz request the elders of the community to be present?

2. How do following community practices and laws produce effective ministries?

3. How can our actions of caring for others affect society as a whole?

Lesson in Our Society

Christians often like to help other people. However, our actions must not be in conflict with a community's norms and standards. For example, missionaries often travel to faraway places such as Africa. In some African cultures, it is improper to talk with anyone in the community without first speaking with the tribal chief. If missionaries go into an area without knowing its customs and laws, they can cause more harm than good. It is necessary that we conduct ministry with sensitivity to the context of the specified community.

Similarly, community support is vital for the success of any ministry. For example, suppose you wanted to start ministering to HIV/AIDS-infected people. Since they live in particular settings, it is important to know if the surrounding community would support such an idea. An informational meeting with community leaders would be helpful and may result in some revamping of your approach and a more effective outcome. A vision for ministry is important, but we must also have wisdom to carry out that vision in a way best suited to a community.

Make It Happen

This week, think about how you can help care for others in your community or another one. Boaz took on the responsibility of redeeming the land of Elimelech and marrying Ruth. If he hadn't, Ruth and Naomi would have had no family inheritance nor anyone with whom they could carry on the family name. Take the initiative to make a difference in the lives of the poor, needy, widowed, orphaned, and others.

Follow the Spirit

What God wants me to do:

_____

_____

_____

_____

Remember Your Thoughts

Special insights I have learned:

_____

_____

_____

_____

More Light on the Text

Ruth 4:1–10

1 Then went Boaz up to the gate, and sat him down there: and, behold, the kinsman of whom Boaz spake came by; unto whom he said, Ho, such a one! turn aside, sit down here. And he turned aside, and sat down. 2 And he took ten men of the elders of the city, and said, Sit ye down here. And they sat down.

In Ruth 4:1 we are told, "Then went Boaz up to the gate, and sat him down there...." The gate area of most ancient cities or towns was a very important place to transact legal, social, and commercial business. It was also a place to locate people easily on their way to and from the fields, in route to the marketplace, or otherwise engaged in personal, social, and commercial activity (2 Kings 7:1; Jeremiah 17:19–20). In Boaz's day, the city gate was an excellent choice for the setting of his next steps.

A key component of how to achieve the purpose of being an authentic kinsman-redeemer in the Old Testament required that Boaz conduct the business according to the established laws or principles of the community. This must be carried out in front of the ruling elders of the community (v. 2). This approach was meant to solicit the cultural and legal support of the community as required by the traditions of the land. Therefore, Boaz took an important initiative, based on the community standards and processes, to locate and recruit the more qualified kinsman in order to set the ball rolling.

3 And he said unto the kinsman, Naomi, that is come again out of the country of Moab, selleth a parcel of land, which was our brother Elimelech's: 4 And I thought to advertise thee, saying, Buy it before the inhabitants, and before the elders of my people. If thou wilt redeem it, redeem it: but if thou wilt not redeem it, then tell me, that I may know, for there is none to redeem it beside thee; and I am after thee. And he said, I will redeem it.

Boaz proceeded to follow his community's established criteria for getting affairs of this kind properly resolved. The Israelites had a uniquely framed manner in which a kinsman redeemed his relative. The purpose was to sustain the family, and thus the nation's heritage, and thereby provide continuity for future generations.

In Ruth 4:4 Boaz used the word "redeem" (Heb. ga'al, gaw-AL) five times. In this context, "redeem" refers to "saving" or "buying back" family members' property or even relatives themselves from economic and social slavery (Leviticus 25:47–49). The use of "redeem" by Boaz and the Levitical background suggest that there were degrees of redeemer with respect to the person who was in a stronger position to become the kinsman-redeemer.

From the story in Ruth 4, it was clear that Boaz was a "secondary" kinsman-redeemer because as he said, "'I am next in line'" (4:4, NIV).

5 Then said Boaz, What day thou buyest the field of the hand of Naomi, thou must buy it also of Ruth the Moabitess, the wife of the dead, to raise up the name of the dead upon his inheritance. 6 And the kinsman said, I cannot redeem it for myself, lest I mar mine own inheritance, redeem thou my right to thyself; for I cannot redeem it. 7 Now this was the manner in former time in Israel concerning redeeming and concerning changing, for to confirm all things; a man plucked off his shoe, and gave it to his neighbour, and this was a testimony in Israel. 8 Therefore the kinsman said unto Boaz, Buy it for thee. So he drew off his shoe.

In order to emphasize the dual nature of the inheritance in question, Boaz pointed out that a piece of property belonging to Elimelech (now Naomi's) must be bought by the kinsman to keep the inheritance in the family and that the kinsman must marry Ruth in order to enable her to perform her role as mother-to-be of future heirs. Verse 6 features the closer kinsman's categorical refusal to be the kinsman-redeemer: "'You redeem it yourself. I cannot do it'" (NIV). He demonstrated his refusal and transfer of the role when he "plucked off his shoe, and gave it to his neighbour, and this was a testimony in Israel," which was a cultural and symbolic way of saying "no" in those days (v. 7). By these words and action, he waived his prior rights as ga'al and told Boaz to perform that responsibility.

9 And Boaz said unto the elders, and unto all the people, Ye are witnesses this day, that I have bought all that was Elimelech's, and all that was Chilion's and Mahlon's, of the hand of Naomi. 10 Moreover Ruth the Moabitess, the wife of Mahlon, have I purchased to be my wife, to raise up the name of the dead upon his inheritance, that the name of the dead be not cut off from among his brethren, and from the gate of his place: ye are witnesses this day.

Boaz took on the responsibility. He bought Elimelech's property (which Naomi inherited), and he went a step further, buying everything which belonged to Chilion and Mahlon, Naomi's deceased sons. Above all, Boaz "purchased" Ruth (Mahlon's widow) to be his wife. Notice that "purchased" in Hebrew is qanah (**kaw-NAW**), which means "obtained" or "acquired." However, this meaning refers to some deeply rooted scriptural ideas that connect originally with Adam and Eve: "I have gotten [qanah] a man from the LORD," Eve declared when she gave birth to Cain (Genesis 4:1).

The idea of taking seriously a blessing from God continues in another use of qanah, when the king of Sodom wants Abram to exchange material goods (plunder) for people and Abram tells the king, "'I have raised my hand to the LORD, God Most High, Creator of heaven and earth, and have taken [qanah] an oath'" (Genesis 14:22, NIV).

Closer in chronology to Boaz and Ruth was the worshiping that Moses led, in which he used qanah while singing about God. Deuteronomy 32 summarizes the history of Israel, including the chosen people's mistreatment of God's special care of them: "Do ye thus requite the LORD, O foolish people and unwise? is not he thy father that hath bought [qanah] thee? hath he not made thee, and established thee?" (32:6). In all four instances, "purchased" has to do with a God-given and blessed process by which, when we agree to do or be as God intends, we take on the steps whose results are as God wills them. Thus, Boaz did as he was supposed to do as a kinsman-redeemer; he did all he was supposed to do, which included taking Ruth in marriage. And by announcing his decision in public before the 10 elders especially, Boaz certified his willingness to accept the role and its responsibilities.

It is critical to note that in Ruth 4:10, Boaz for the first time identified Ruth as "Ruth the Moabitess." This indicates that Boaz was ready to accept and integrate "a foreigner"— who had decided to follow the God of Israel— into his people's traditions and community of faith. As salvation history progresses, we eventually see that the people of God extends beyond the biological inheritance of Israel to include Gentiles. The promise God made to Abraham is fulfilled as all the nations are blessed (Genesis 12:3; Acts 3:25). Revelation 5:9 and 7:9 give us a culminating vision of the people of God as those redeemed from every tribe, tongue, and nation. In the text for today, Boaz concluded, "…and from the gate of his place, ye are witnesses this day." He was highlighting the fact that there was proper and legal representation to "witness" a redeeming act—the saving of his relatives on behalf of future generations, in a manner that was consistent with the noble values of the community in which they lived.

While Boaz served as the kinsman-redeemer for Ruth and Naomi, his efforts also point to Jesus Christ, our ultimate Redeemer who brings us out of the bondage of sin (Ephesians 2:11–22). The story of Ruth and Naomi is not only a story about the hope that came to two widows; it is also a window into God's plan to accomplish our salvation.

Say It Correctly

Chilion. KIHL-ee-ahn.
Elimelech. ee-LIHM-eh-lehk.
Leviticus. lih-VIT-ih-kuhs.
Mahlon. MAH-lon, MAH-luhn.

Daily Bible Readings

M: Pray for the Faith Community
Philippians 1:3–11

T: The Blameless Walk
Psalm 15

W: Integrity of Heart
1 Kings 9:1–5

T: Walking in Integrity
Psalm 26:1–11

F: Integrity Provides Security
Proverbs 10:6–11

S: Persisting in Integrity
Job 2:1–9

S: Following Community Standards
Ruth 4:1–10

Lesson 1, June 5

Adeyemo, Tokunboh, ed., et al. *Africa Bible Commentary: A One-Volume Commentary Written by 70 African Scholars*. Nairobi, Kenya: Word Alive Publishers, 2006.

Auld, A. Graeme. *Joshua, Judges, and Ruth*. Philadelphia, PA: Westminster Press, 1984. 5–8, 74–78.

Baltes, A. J., ed. Biblespeech.com. http://biblespeech.com (accessed November 4, 2009).

Bible Study Tools.com. Old Testament Hebrew Lexicons. http://www.biblestudytools.com/lexicons/hebrew/kjv (accessed February 26, 2010).

Exell, Joseph S. *The Biblical Illustrator, Vol. 3: Joshua*. Grand Rapids, MI: Baker Book House, 1975. 22–32.

Gangel, Kenneth O. *Holman Old Testament Commentary, Vol. 4: Joshua*. Nashville, TN: Holman Reference, 2002. 7–16, 187–89.

Harris, J. Gordon, Cheryl A. Brown, and Michael S. Moore. *New International Biblical Commentary, Joshua, Judges, Ruth*. Peabody, MA: Hendrickson Publishers, Inc., 2000. 17–22, 71–73.

Hess, Richard S. *Tyndale Old Testament Commentaries, Vol. 6: Joshua*. Downers Grove, IL: InterVarsity Press, 1996. 73–81, 238–43.

Howard, David M., Jr. *The New American Commentary, Vol. 5: Joshua*. Nashville, TN: Broadman and Holman, 1998. 71–85, 271–76.

Ironside, H. A. *Joshua: An Ironside Expository Commentary*. Grand Rapids, MI: Kregel, 1950, reprinted 2008. 9–18, 105–10.

Keil, C. F. and F. Delitzsch. *Commentary on the Old Testament*, Vol. 2. Grand Rapids, MI: Eerdmans, 1980. 27–30.

Lange, John Peter. *Commentary on the Holy Scriptures: Critical, Doctrinal and Homiletical. Joshua–Ruth*. Translated by Philip Schaff. Grand Rapids, MI: Zondervan, 1976. 39–45, 106–10.

Packer, J. I., et al. *The Bible Almanac*. Nashville TN: Thomas Nelson, 1980. 382.

Spence, H. D. M. and Joseph S. Exell. *The Pulpit Commentary, Vol. 3: The Book of Joshua: 1–11*. Grand Rapids, MI: Eerdmans, 1975.

Strong, James. *New Exhaustive Strong's Numbers and Concordance with Expanded Greek-Hebrew Dictionary*. Seattle, WA: Biblesoft, and International Bible Translators, 1994. 2003.

Woudstra, Marten H. *The Book of Joshua*. Grand Rapids, MI: Eerdmans, 1981. 55–64, 193–99.

Lesson 2, June 12

Auld, A. Graeme. *Joshua, Judges, and Ruth*. Philadelphia, PA: Westminster Press, 1984. 8–15.

Baltes, A. J., ed. Biblespeech.com. http://biblespeech.com (accessed November 5, 2009).

Bible Study Tools.com. Old Testament Hebrew Lexicons. http://www.biblestudytools.com/lexicons/hebrew/kjv (accessed February 26, 2010).

Exell, Joseph S. *The Biblical Illustrator, Vol. 3: Joshua*. Grand Rapids, MI: Baker Book House, 1975. 22–32.

Gangel, Kenneth O. *Holman Old Testament Commentary, Vol. 4: Joshua*. Nashville, TN: Holman Reference, 2002. 13–26.

Harris, J. Gordon, Cheryl A. Brown, and Michael S. Moore. *New International Biblical Commentary, Joshua, Judges, Ruth*. Peabody, MA: Hendrickson Publishers, Inc., 2000. 71–73.

Hess, Richard S. *Tyndale Old Testament Commentaries, Vol. 6: Joshua*. Downers Grove, IL: InterVarsity Press, 1996. 78–86.

Howard, David M., Jr. *The New American Commentary, Vol. 5: Joshua*. Nashville, TN: Broadman and Holman, 1998. 85–94.

Ironside, H. A. *Joshua: An Ironside Expository Commentary*. Grand Rapids, MI: Kregel, 1950, reprinted 2008. 19–25.

Keil, C. F. and F. Delitzsch. *Commentary on the Old Testament*, Vol. 2. Grand Rapids, MI: Eerdmans, 1980. 27–30.

Lange, John Peter. *Commentary on the Holy Scriptures: Critical, Doctrinal and Homiletical. Joshua–Ruth*. Translated by Philip Schaff. Grand Rapids, MI: Zondervan, 1976. 42–45.

"Legend of the Cherokee Indian Youth's Rite of Passage." My Church.org. http://www.mychurch.org/blog/26610/Cherokee-Indian-youths-rite-of-passage.html (accessed March 1, 2010).

Life Application Study Bible (NLT). Wheaton, IL: Tyndale House, 1996. 308–9.

Spence, H. D. M. and Joseph S. Exell. *The Pulpit Commentary, Vol. 3: The Book of Joshua: 1–11*. Grand Rapids, MI: Eerdmans, 1975. 10–23.

Strong, James. *New Exhaustive Strong's Numbers and Concordance with Expanded Greek-Hebrew Dictionary*. Seattle, WA: Biblesoft, and International Bible Translators, 1994. 2003.

Woudstra, Marten H. *The Book of Joshua*. Grand Rapids, MI: Eerdmans, 1981. 62–66.

Lesson 3, June 19

Auld, A. Graeme. *Joshua, Judges, and Ruth*. Philadelphia, PA: Westminster Press, 1984. 15–22.

Baltes, A. J., ed. Biblespeech.com. http://biblespeech.com (accessed November 5, 2009).

Bible Study Tools.com. Old Testament Hebrew Lexicons. http://www.biblestudytools.com/lexicons/hebrew/kjv (accessed February 26, 2010).

Exell, Joseph S. *The Biblical Illustrator, Vol. 3: Joshua*. Grand Rapids, MI: Baker Book House, 1975. 32–39.

"Flax." *Holman Illustrated Bible Dictionary*. Butler, Trent C., gen. ed. Nashville, TN: Holman Bible Publishers, 1991. 497.

Gangel, Kenneth O. *Holman Old Testament Commentary, Vol. 4: Joshua*. Nashville, TN: Holman Reference, 2002. 27–42.

Harris, J. Gordon, Cheryl A. Brown, and Michael S. Moore. *New International Biblical Commentary, Joshua, Judges, Ruth*. Peabody, MA: Hendrickson Publishers, Inc., 2000. 71–73.

Hess, Richard S. *Tyndale Old Testament Commentaries, Vol. 6: Joshua*. Downers Grove, IL: InterVarsity Press, 1996. 88–107.

Howard, David M., Jr. *The New American Commentary, Vol. 5: Joshua.* Nashville, TN: Broadman and Holman, 1998. 99–117.

Ironside, H. A. *Joshua: An Ironside Expository Commentary.* Grand Rapids, MI: Kregel, 1950, reprinted 2008. 27–37.

Keil, C. F. and F. Delitzsch. *Commentary on the Old Testament,* Vol. 2. Grand Rapids, MI: Eerdmans, 1980. 27–30.

Lange, John Peter. *Commentary on the Holy Scriptures: Critical, Doctrinal and Homiletical. Joshua–Ruth.* Translated by Philip Schaff. Grand Rapids, MI: Zondervan, 1976. 45–52.

Life Application Study Bible (NLT). Wheaton, IL: Tyndale House, 1996.

Merriam-Webster Online Dictionary. Merriam-Webster, Inc. http://www.merriam-webster.com (accessed November 6, 2009).

Packer, J. I., Merrill C. Tenney, and William White Jr. *The Bible Almanac.* Nashville, TN: Thomas Nelson,1980. 143–44.

Spence, H. D. M. and Joseph S. Exell. *The Pulpit Commentary, Vol. 3: The Book of Joshua: 1–11.* Grand Rapids, MI: Eerdmans, 1975. 25–42.

Strong, James. *New Exhaustive Strong's Numbers and Concordance with Expanded Greek-Hebrew Dictionary.* Seattle, WA: Biblesoft, and International Bible Translators, 1994. 2003.

Woudstra, Marten H. *The Book of Joshua.* Grand Rapids, MI: Eerdmans, 1981. 66–76.

Lesson 4, June 26

Auld, A. Graeme. *Joshua, Judges, and Ruth.* Philadelphia, PA: Westminster Press, 1984. 36–42.

Baltes, A. J., ed. Biblespeech.com. http://biblespeech.com (accessed November 5, 2009).

Barker, Kenneth L., ed. *Zondervan NIV Study Bible.* Grand Rapids, MI: Zondervan, 2008. 287–89, 291, 297.

Beitzel, Barry J. *The Moody Atlas of Bible Lands.* Chicago, IL: Moody Press, 1985. 95.

Bible Study Tools.com. New Testament Greek Lexicons. http://www.biblestudytools.com/lexicons/greek/kjv (accessed February 26, 2010).

Bible Study Tools.com. Old Testament Hebrew Lexicons. http://www.biblestudytools.com/lexicons/hebrew/kjv (accessed February 26, 2010).

ESV Study Bible (English Standard Version). Wheaton, IL: Crossway Bibles, 2008. 287–89, 297, 389–96, 401–3.

Exell, Joseph S. *The Biblical Illustrator, Vol. 3: Joshua.* Grand Rapids, MI: Baker Book House, 1975. 116–34.

Gangel, Kenneth O. *Holman Old Testament Commentary, Vol. 4: Joshua.* Nashville, TN: Holman Reference, 2002. 97–112.

Harris, J. Gordon, Cheryl A. Brown, and Michael S. Moore. *New International Biblical Commentary: Joshua, Judges, Ruth.* Peabody, MA: Hendrickson Publishers, Inc., 2000. 47–50.

Hess, Richard S. *Tyndale Old Testament Commentaries, Vol. 6: Joshua.* Downers Grove, IL: InterVarsity Press, 1996. 141–46.

Howard, David M., Jr. *The New American Commentary, Vol. 5: Joshua.* Nashville, TN: Broadman and Holman, 1998. 167–75.

Ironside, H. A. *Joshua: An Ironside Expository Commentary.* Grand Rapids, MI: Kregel, 1950, reprinted 2008. 67–74.

Keil, C. F. and F. Delitzsch. *Commentary on the Old Testament, Vol. 2.* Grand Rapids, MI: Eerdmans, 1980. 27–30.

Lange, John Peter. *Commentary on the Holy Scriptures: Critical, Doctrinal and Homiletical. Joshua–Ruth.* Translated by Philip Schaff. Grand Rapids, MI: Zondervan, 1976. 69–75.

Merriam-Webster Online Dictionary. Merriam-Webster, Inc. http://www.merriam-webster.com (accessed January 15, 2010).

Spence, H. D. M. and Joseph S. Exell. *The Pulpit Commentary, Vol. 3: The Book of Joshua.* Grand Rapids, MI: Eerdmans, 1975. 97–100.

Strong, James. *New Exhaustive Strong's Numbers and Concordance with Expanded Greek-Hebrew Dictionary.* Seattle, WA: Biblesoft, and International Bible Translators, 1994. 2003.

Woudstra, Marten H. *The Book of Joshua.* Grand Rapids, MI: Eerdmans, 1981.109–14.

Lesson 5, July 3

Baltes, A. J., ed. Biblespeech.com. http://biblespeech.com (accessed October 26, 2009).

Barker, Kenneth L., ed. *Zondervan NIV Study Bible.* Grand Rapids, MI: Zondervan, 2008. 298–300.

Bible Study Tools.com. Old Testament Hebrew Lexicons. http://www.biblestudytools.com/lexicons/hebrew/kjv (accessed March 1, 2010).

ESV Study Bible (English Standard Version). Wheaton, IL: Crossway Bibles, 2008. 403–5.

Life Application Study Bible (NIV). Wheaton, IL: Tyndale House, 1991.

Merriam-Webster Online Dictionary. Merriam-Webster, Inc. http://www.merriam-webster.com (accessed October 26, 2009).

Scofield, C. I., ed. *Scofield Study Bible* (NIV). New York, NY: Oxford University Press, 1994–2009.

Strong, James. *New Exhaustive Strong's Numbers and Concordance with Expanded Greek-Hebrew Dictionary.* Seattle, WA: Biblesoft, and International Bible Translators, 1994. 2003.

Lesson 6, July 10

Baltes, A. J., ed. Biblespeech.com. http://biblespeech.com (accessed October 27, 2009).

Bible Study Tools.com. Old Testament Hebrew Lexicons. http://www.biblestudytools.com/lexicons/hebrew/kjv (accessed March 1, 2010).

Eerdmans Bible Dictionary. Grand Rapids, MI: Eerdmans, 1987.

Merriam-Webster Online Dictionary. Merriam-Webster, Inc. http://www.merriam-webster.com (accessed October 27, 2009).

New Interpreter's Bible, Volume II. Nashville, TN: Abingdon Press, 1998. 755–57.

Scofield, C. I., ed. *Scofield Study Bible* (New International Version). New York, NY: Oxford University Press, 2004.

Strong, J. *The Exhaustive Concordance of the Bible: Showing Every Word of the Test of the Common English Version of the Canonical Books, and Every Occurrence of Each Word in Regular Order.* 1996 (electronic ed.). Woodside Bible Fellowship: Ontario.

Strong, James. *New Exhaustive Strong's Numbers and Concordance with Expanded Greek-Hebrew Dictionary.* Seattle, WA: Biblesoft, and International Bible Translators, 1994. 2003.

Today's New International Version Study Bible. Colorado Springs, CO: International Bible Society, 2006.

Lesson 7, July 17

Baltes, A. J., ed. Biblespeech.com. http://biblespeech.com (accessed October 28, 2009).

Bible Study Tools.com. Old Testament Hebrew Lexicons. http://www.biblestudytools.com/lexicons/hebrew/kjv (accessed March 1, 2010).

Block, Daniel I. "Judges, Ruth." *The New American Commentary,* Vol. 6. Nashville, TN: Broadman and Holman, 1999.

Eerdmans Bible Dictionary. Grand Rapids, MI: Eerdmans, 1987.

Gaebelein, Frank E., ed. "Deuteronomy, Joshua, Judges, Ruth, 1 & 2 Samuel." *The Expositor's Bible Commentary,* Vol. 3. Grand Rapids, MI: Zondervan, 1991. 376, 379.

McCann, J. Clinton. "Judges." *Interpretation: A Bible Commentary for Teaching and Preaching.* Louisville, KY: John Knox Press, 2002. 43–45.

Merriam-Webster Online Dictionary. Merriam-Webster, Inc. http://www.merriam-webster.com (accessed October 28, 2009).

New Interpreters' Bible, Volume II. Nashville, TN: Abingdon Press, 1998. 770–72.

Strong, James. *New Exhaustive Strong's Numbers and Concordance with Expanded Greek-Hebrew Dictionary.* Seattle, WA: Biblesoft, and International Bible Translators, 1994. 2003.

Younger, K. Lawson, Jr. "Judges/Ruth." *NIV Application Commentary.* Grand Rapids, MI: Zondervan, 2002. 114–15, 117, 123.

Lesson 8, July 24

Baltes, A. J., ed. Biblespeech.com. http://biblespeech.com (accessed October 30, 2009).

Bible Study Tools.com. Old Testament Hebrew Lexicons. http://www.biblestudytools.com/lexicons/hebrew/kjv (accessed March 2, 2010).

Block, Daniel I. "Judges, Ruth." *The New American Commentary,* Vol. 6. Nashville, TN: Broadman and Holman, 1999. 273.

Eerdmans Bible Dictionary. Grand Rapids, MI: Eerdmans, 1987.

Gaebelein, Frank E., ed. "Deuteronomy, Joshua, Judges, Ruth, 1 & 2 Samuel." *The Expositor's Bible Commentary,* Vol. 3. Grand Rapids, MI: Zondervan, 1991.

McCann, J. Clinton. "Judges." *Interpretation: A Bible Commentary for Teaching and Preaching.* Louisville, KY: John Knox Press, 2002. 66–67.

Merriam-Webster Online Dictionary. Merriam-Webster, Inc. http://www.merriam-webster.com (accessed October 30, 2009).

New Interpreters' Bible, Volume II. Nashville, TN: Abingdon Press, 1998. 802–9.

Strong, James. *New Exhaustive Strong's Numbers and Concordance with Expanded Greek-Hebrew Dictionary.* Seattle, WA: Biblesoft, and International Bible Translators, 1994. 2003.

Wiersbe, Warren W. *The Bible Exposition Commentary: Old Testament: The Prophets,* Vol. 3. Colorado Springs, CO: Victor, 2003. 17.

Younger, K. Lawson, Jr. "Judges/Ruth." *NIV Application Commentary.* Grand Rapids, MI: Zondervan, 2002. 180–81, 183, 185, 187.

Lesson 9, July 31

Baltes, A. J., ed. Biblespeech.com. http://biblespeech.com (accessed November 2, 2009).

Barker, Kenneth L., ed. *Zondervan NIV Study Bible.* Grand Rapids, MI: Zondervan, 2002. 327–29, 347–48.

Bible Study Tools.com. Old Testament Hebrew Lexicons. http://www.biblestudytools.com/lexicons/hebrew/kjv (accessed March 2, 2010).

Block, Daniel I. "Judges, Ruth." *The New American Commentary,* Vol. 6. Nashville, TN: Broadman and Holman, 1999. 347–48.

Browning, W. R. F. "Philistines." *A Dictionary of the Bible.* 1997. Encyclopedia.com. http://www.encyclopedia.com/doc/1O94-Philistines.html (accessed June 29, 2009).

Gaebelein, Frank E., ed. "Deuteronomy, Joshua, Judges, Ruth, 1 & 2 Samuel." *The Expositor's Bible Commentary, Vol. 3.* Grand Rapids, MI: Zondervan, 1991. 448.

McCann, J. Clinton. "Judges." *Interpretation: A Bible Commentary for Teaching and Preaching.* Louisville, KY: John Knox Press, 2002. 25, 79.

Strong, James. *New Exhaustive Strong's Numbers and Concordance with Expanded Greek-Hebrew Dictionary.* Seattle, WA: Biblesoft, and International Bible Translators, 1994. 2003.

Lesson 10, August 7

Baltes, A. J., ed. Biblespeech.com. http://biblespeech.com (accessed August 19, 2009).

Barker, Kenneth L., ed. *Zondervan NIV Study Bible.* Grand Rapids, MI: Zondervan, 2002. 327.

Bible Study Tools.com. Old Testament Hebrew Lexicons. http://www.biblestudytools.com/lexicons/hebrew/kjv (accessed March 2, 2010).

Henry, Matthew. *Matthew Henry's Concise Commentary on the Whole Bible.* Nashville, TN: Thomas Nelson, 1997. 252–53.

Hoerber, Robert G., ed. *Concordia Self-Study Bible* (NIV). St. Louis, MO: Concordia Publishing House, 1992. 324–25.

Life Application Study Bible (NIV). Wheaton, IL: Tyndale House, 1996. 351, 376.

Merriam-Webster Online Dictionary. Merriam-Webster, Inc. http://www.merriam-webster.com (accessed August 19, 2009).

Packer, J. I., Merrill C. Tenney, and William White Jr., eds. *Illustrated Manners and Customs of the Bible.* Nashville, TN: Thomas Nelson, 2003.

"Philistine." *Wycliffe Bible Encyclopedia.* Charles F. Pfeiffer, Howard F. Vos, and John Rea, eds. Chicago, IL: Moody Press, 1975. 1332–35.

Strong, James. *New Exhaustive Strong's Numbers and Concordance with Expanded Greek-Hebrew Dictionary.* Seattle, WA: Biblesoft, and International Bible Translators, 1994. 2003.

Youngblood, Ronald F., ed. *Nelson's New Illustrated Bible Dictionary.* Nashville, TN: Thomas Nelson, 1995. 986–87.

Lesson 11, August 14

Baltes, A. J., ed. Biblespeech.com. http://biblespeech.com (accessed August 25, 2009).

Bible Study Tools.com. Old Testament Hebrew Lexicons. http://www.biblestudytools.com/lexicons/hebrew/kjv (accessed March 2, 2010).

Life Application Bible: New International Version. Wheaton: IL: Tyndale, 2005. 378–82.

Merriam-Webster Online Dictionary. Merriam-Webster, Inc. http://www.merriam-webster.com (accessed August 25, 2009).

"Moab, Moabite." *Wycliffe Bible Encyclopedia.* Charles F. Pfeiffer, Howard F. Vos, and John Rea, eds. Chicago, IL: Moody Press, 1975. 1143–45.

New International Version Study Bible, Tenth Anniversary Edition. Grand Rapids: MI: Zondervan, 1995. 360–63.

Pfeiffer, Charles F., Howard F. Vos, and John Rea, eds. *Wycliffe Bible Dictionary.* Peabody, MA: Hendrickson Publishers, Inc., 1998. 1143.

Strong, James. *New Exhaustive Strong's Numbers and Concordance with Expanded Greek-Hebrew Dictionary.* Seattle, WA: Biblesoft, and International Bible Translators, 1994. 2003.

Studylight.org. Online Commentaries, Study Tools, and Original Language Lexicons. http://www.studylight.org (accessed May 30, 2009).

Unger, Merrill F. *Unger's Bible Dictionary.* Chicago, IL: Moody Press, 1985. 139–41, 753–54.

Lesson 12, August 21

Baltes, A. J., ed. Biblespeech.com. http://biblespeech.com (accessed August 25, 2009)

Bible Study Tools.com. Old Testament Hebrew Lexicons. http://www.biblestudytools.com/lexicons/hebrew/kjv (accessed March 2, 2010).

Douglas, J. D., ed. *New Bible Dictionary: Second Edition.* Downers Grove, IL: InterVarsity Press, 1982. 145, 423.

Life Application Bible: New International Version. Wheaton, IL: Tyndale, 2005. 383–84.

New International Version Study Bible, Tenth Anniversary Edition. Grand Rapids, MI: Zondervan, 1995. 362–64.

Strong, James. *New Exhaustive Strong's Numbers and Concordance with Expanded Greek-Hebrew Dictionary.* Seattle, WA: Biblesoft, and International Bible Translators, 1994. 2003.

Studylight.org. Online Commentaries, Study Tools, and Original Language Lexicons. http://www.studylight.org (accessed June 10, 2009).

Unger, Merrill F. *The New Unger's Bible Handbook.* Chicago, IL: Moody Press, 1984. 141.

Lesson 13, August 28

Baltes, A. J., ed. Biblespeech.com. http://biblespeech.com (accessed November 3, 2009).

Bible Study Tools.com. Old Testament Hebrew Lexicons. http://www.biblestudytools.com/lexicons/hebrew/kjv (accessed March 2, 2010).

Hamlin, E. John. *Surely There Is a Future: A Commentary on the Book of Ruth.* Grand Rapids, MI: Eerdmans, 1996. 55–64.

LaCocque, André. *Ruth: A Continental Commentary.* Translated by K. C. Hanson. Minneapolis, MN: Fortress Press, 2004. 107–19.

Life Application Study Bible: New International Version. Wheaton, IL: Tyndale, 1991. 426–29.

Matthews, Victor. *The New Cambridge Bible Commentary: Judges and Ruth.* Cambridge, UK: Cambridge University Press, 2004. 237–43.

New International Version Study Bible, Tenth Anniversary Edition. Grand Rapids, MI: Zondervan, 1995. 366–67.

Sakenfield, Katharine Doob. *Ruth.* Louisville, KY: John Knox Press, 1989.

Strong, James. *New Exhaustive Strong's Numbers and Concordance with Expanded Greek-Hebrew Dictionary.* Seattle, WA: Biblesoft, and International Bible Translators, 1994. 2003.

Studylight.org. Online Commentaries, Study Tools, and Original Language Lexicons. http://www.studylight.org (accessed June 10, 2009).

Unger, Merrill F. *Unger's Bible Dictionary.* Chicago, IL: Moody Press, 1985. 142, 633–34.

A

Abomination: A foul and detestable thing.

Affliction: Anguish, burden, persecution, tribulation, or trouble.

Angels: God's messengers; they are not eternal or all-knowing, and are sometimes referred to as winged creatures known as "cherubim" and "seraphim."

Atonement: To "propitiate" (to satisfy the demands of an offended holy God) or "atone" (being reconciled to a holy God) because of sin.

Avenger: One who takes revenge, one who punishes.

B

Be Baptized: To dip repeatedly, to immerse, to submerge.

Blameless: Irreproachable, faultless, flawless.

Blessedness: Happiness, joy, prosperity. It is not based on circumstance, but is rooted in the deep abiding hope shared by all who have received salvation through Jesus Christ.

Bless the Lord: To simply speak well of Him.

Blood of the Lamb: The blood that Jesus shed on the Cross of Calvary when He suffered and died for humanity's sin.

Bowels: The place of emotions, distress, or love.

C

Called: Appointed or commissioned by God to fulfill a task.

Charge: Admonish, order, command.

Chosen: To be elected, be selected.

Christ: The Anointed One.

Commandments: God's mandates; the entire body of Laws issued by God to Moses for Israel.

Conduct: Manner of living.

Confess: To acknowledge or to fully agree.

Consider: To determine, make out.

Covenant: An agreement with God based on God's character, strength, and grace; an agreement and promise between God and humankind.

Crucifixion: Jesus suffered and died on the Cross.

D

Decalogue: The Ten Commandments; the words translated "Ten Commandments" literally mean "ten words."

Desolation: Making something deserted, uninhabited.

Disciples: Learners, pupils.

Dominion: Rule or reign.

Dwelling place: A location that is a person's refuge, home.

E

El: The Hebrew word for "god" or "mighty one."

Even from everlasting to everlasting: "Indefinite or unending future, eternity" (Strong).

Evil: To do "bad, unpleasant, displeasing" things.

Evil doer: A malefactor, wrongdoer, criminal, troublemaker.

Evil spirits: Messengers and ministers of the devil.

Exalt: To raise up; to raise to the highest degree possible.

Exhortation: Giving someone motivation to change his or her behavior. It can imply either rebuke or encouragement.

F

Faithfulness: Steadfastness, steadiness.

Fear of the Lord: Reverence or awe of who God is.

G

Gittith: A musical instrument resembling a Spanish guitar that, in ancient times, provided a musical tune or tempo during a ceremony or festival.

Glory: Splendor, unparalleled honor, dignity, or distinction; to honor, praise, and worship.

God called: To commission, appoint, endow.

God's Bride: The Church.

God's own hand: God's strength, power.

God's protection: Conveys the idea of staying in God's abode, staying constantly in His presence, getting completely acquainted or connected with Him, and resting permanently in Him.

Gospel: "The glad tidings of the kingdom of God soon to be set up, and later also of Jesus the Messiah, the founder of this kingdom" (Strong).

Graven image: An idol or likeness cut from stone, wood, or metal and then worshiped as a god.

Great Tribulation: A time of great suffering (Daniel 12:1, Revelation 6–18).

H

Hallowed: Consecrated, dedicated, or set apart.

Hear: Listen to, yield to, to be obedient.

Hearken: Pay attention to, give attention to.

Heart: The place, figuratively, where our

emotions and passions exist.

Heathen: Literally means "nations," and is used in the Old Testament to refer to the Gentiles, all those who are not a part of the people of God.

Holy: Anything consecrated and set aside for sacred use; the place made sacred because of God's presence; set apart from sin.

Honor: To revere, value.

Hosts: Those which go forth; armies.

I

Idolatry: The worship of anything other than God, our Creator.

Infidel: One who is unfaithful, unbelieving, not to be trusted.

Iniquities: Perversity, depravity, guilt.

In vain: A waste, a worthless thing, or simply emptiness.

J

Jesus' ascension: Forty days after Jesus' death, burial, and resurrection, He ascended or went back to heaven to sit at the right hand of the Father (Acts 1:9–11).

Jesus' transfiguration: While on the Mount of Olives with His closest disciples—Peter, James, and John—Jesus changed into another form. His face shone with the brightness like the sun and His raiment was white as snow (cf. Matthew 17:2; Mark 9:2; Luke 9:29).

Just: A word often rendered as "righteous"; that which is right and fair.

Justice: Righteousness in government.

K

Kingdom of Christ: It is the same as the "Kingdom of Heaven (Matthew 18:1–4); it is where Jesus reigns in "glory" (i.e., in "dignity or honor").

Know: To ascertain by seeing, have understanding, to acknowledge.

Knowledge: Discernment, understanding, wisdom.

L

Labor: To toil to the point of exhaustion or weariness.

Logos (LOG-os): The entire Word of God.

M

"Make a joyful noise": A command that literally means "shout."

Manna: Food from heaven.

Messiah: The Promised One; the Anointed One.

Minister: "A servant, an attendant, one who executes the commands of another" (Strong).

O

Omnipotent: All powerful.

Omnipresent: All present, present everywhere.

Omniscient: All knowing.

Ordained: Established and founded by God; founded, fixed, appointed, or established.

P

Parousia (par-oo-SEE-ah): Christ's Second Coming.

Path: Connotes an ongoing process of taking dynamic steps toward an expected end.

Peace: Denotes "wholeness, quietness, contentment, health, prosperity" (Strong); it is far more than an absence of conflict or problems, but that every part of life would be blessed.

Pentateuch: The Mosaic Law or Divine Law. The first five books of the Old Testament, as well as the Old Testament as a whole, reveal the entire set of legal and religious instructions which God gave, through Moses, for God's people. Terms that are synonymous for "Law" include commandments, ordinances, statutes, legal regulations, authoritative instructions, and teachings.

People(s): Most English versions translate "people" as "peoples." The New Living Translation goes even further: "Let the whole world bless our God."

Power: Boldness, might, strength, especially God's.

Prophets: They were filled with the Spirit of God and under the authority and command of God, pleaded God's cause and urged humanity to be saved.

Profit: To gain, benefit, avail.

Prosperous: To make progress, to succeed, especially in spiritual things. It often did not refer to personal profit. Rather it meant "to move forward or succeed" in one's efforts.

Proved: Examined, tested, and tried.

Psalm: A Hebrew title that means "praise."

Purity: "Sinless of life" (Strong).

R

Ransom: To redeem (buy back) from, to pay a price for a person. It is commonly used as a purchase price to free slaves.

Redeemed: Ransomed, purchaseed.

Refuge: Place of shelter; stronghold or fortress—a place to which we can run when the enemy threatens and be secure; a shelter from rain, storm, or danger.

Repent: To change (be transformed) or turn back from sin and turn to God in faith.

Righteous: To be declared "not guilty."

Righteousness: God's justness and rightness, which He works as a gift also in His people; refers to the right way to live as opposed to a lifestyle that treats others unfairly or unjustly.

S

Sabbath: In Hebrew, *shabbath* means "ceasing from work." A day set aside to worship God.

Sanctuary: A word which means "holy" when used as an adjective. The "holy place" of which David speaks is the tabernacle, the portable temple built under Moses' leadership after the Exodus from Egypt.

Salvation: Rescue, safety, deliverance.

Satan: An adversary or devil.

Savior: A defender, rescuer, deliverer.

Scribes: They were secretaries, recorders, men skilled in the law.

Secret place: A refuge, place of safety and a covering from all forms of destructive elements that seek to attack or destroy the children of God and to prevent us from experiencing the fullness of God's blessings, peace, and divine providence.

See: To behold, consider, discern, perceive.

Selah: This Hebrew expression (**SEH-lah**) is found almost exclusively in the book of Psalms. Some believe that Selah denotes a pause or a suspension in singing of the psalm or recitation, and the insertion of an instrumental musical interlude. The Greek Septuagint renders the word *dia'psalma*, meaning "a musical interlude." Still others think that the word *Selah* signaled a holding back of singing and allowed for silent meditation.

Septuagint: It means "seventy," and it is the ancient Greek translation of the Hebrew Old Testament by 70 Jewish scholars.

Servant: A slave, subject, worshiper.

Shalom: Means "peace."

Shekinah Glory: The awesome presence of the Lord; His honor, fame, and reputation.

Shofar (sho-FAR): Means "ram's horn," and was used in celebration as well as in signaling armies or large groups of people in civil assembly.

Soul: Refers to the immaterial part of the human being (what leaves the body when death occurs), or to the whole being—the self, one's life.

Stiffnecked: Obstinate and difficult.

Strengthen: To secure, make firm, make strong.

Strive: To struggle, to exert oneself.

Supplications: Seeking, asking, entreating, pleading, imploring, and petitioning God.

T

Tabernacles: Literally means "dwelling places," the name of the portable temple constructed by Moses and the people of Israel.

Teaching: Instruction in Christian living.

Tetragrammaton: Hebrew name for God (YHWH).

Torah: The Law, which means "instrument" or "direction"; the first five books of the Old Testament (Genesis, Exodus, Leviticus, Numbers, and Deuteronomy).

Transfigured: To change or transform.

Transgressions: Include sins, rebellion, breaking God's Law.

Tried: Smelted or refined, purified.

Trumpet: A ram's horn that was used in celebration as well as in signaling armies or large groups of people in civil assembly.

U

Understand: To consider, have wisdom.

W

Wisdom: "Prudence, an understanding of ethics" (Strong).

Woe: An exclamation of grief.

Worship: Bow down deeply, show obeisance and reverence.

Wrath: "Burning anger, rage" (Strong).

Y

Yahweh: Many scholars simply use the Hebrew spelling with consonants only, *YHWH*, which is God's name.

Source:

Strong, James. *New Exhaustive Strong's Numbers and Concordance with Expanded Greek-Hebrew Dictionary*. Seattle, WA: Biblesoft, and International Bible Translators, 1994. 2003.